CHINA

Titles in ABC-CLIO's *Asia in Focus* Series

China   Robert André LaFleur, Editor

Japan   Lucien Ellington, Editor

The Koreas   Mary E. Connor, Editor

CHINA

Robert André LaFleur, Editor

A B C  C L I O

Santa Barbara, California • Denver, Colorado • Oxford, England

Library of Congress Cataloging-in-Publication Data

China / Robert André LaFleur, editor.
    p. cm. — (Asia in focus)
  Includes bibliographical references and index.
  ISBN 978-1-59884-166-4 (hardcover : alk. paper) — ISBN 978-1-59884-167-1 (ebook)
  1. China—History. I. LaFleur, Robert André, 1959–
  DS706.C48724 2010
  951—dc22   2009034580

14 13 12 11 10   1 2 3 4 5

ISBN: 978-1-59884-166-4
E-ISBN: 978-1-59884-167-1

This book is also available on the World Wide Web as an eBook.
Visit www.abc-clio.com for details.

ABC-CLIO, LLC
130 Cremona Drive, P.O. Box 1911
Santa Barbara, California 93116-1911

This book is printed on acid-free paper ∞

Manufactured in the United States of America

Contents

3 POLITICS AND GOVERNMENT, 67

John A. Rapp

4 THE MODERN CHINESE ECONOMY, 103

Warren Bruce Palmer

The Chinese Economy Today, 134

5 SOCIETY, 163

Robert André LaFleur, Tamara Hamlish

Religion and Thought, 163

Literature, 250
Daniel Youd

Chinese Art, 270
Kenneth S. Ganza

Music in China, 284
Ann L. Silverberg

Food, 298
Robert André LaFleur, Tamara Hamlish

Leisure and Sports, 311
Robert André LaFleur, Tamara Hamlish, Kevin Latham

Popular Culture and Traditional Beliefs, 328
Robert André LaFleur, Kevin Latham, Tamara Hamlish

7 CONTEMPORARY ISSUES, 347

Anita M. Andrew

About the Editor
and the Contributors

Robert André LaFleur is professor of history and anthropology at Beloit College, where he chairs the Asian Studies program and teaches a wide variety of courses on East Asian history and culture. He received his Ph.D. from the University of Chicago's Committee on Social Thought, and taught at Lake Forest and Colby Colleges before coming to Beloit. He has held a number of research fellowships, most recently the Millicent C. McIntosh Fellowship from the Woodrow Wilson Foundation for his study of French sinologists in the early 20th century. His research focuses on the intersection of text and culture in Chinese life, and his published work has included studies of the Chinese Almanac and its role in popular religion, the exilic imagination in Northern Song dynasty (960–1127) China, the role of literary borrowing in Chinese historiography, and the five cosmological mountains of China.

Anita M. Andrew is an associate professor of history (China) at Northern Illinois University in DeKalb, Illinois. She was an adjunct faculty in the History Department at Beloit College from 1987 to 1994, and taught courses on Chinese history, comparative interdisciplinary courses on Asia, and Asian American history. She received her Ph.D. in history from the University of Minnesota, where she specialized in China's Ming dynasty (1368–1644). Her primary area of research is the autocratic ruling style of Zhu Yuanzhang, the founding emperor of the Ming dynasty. Her publications include *Assessing the Ming Founder: Historical Studies of Zhu Yuanzhang, 1981–1991* (editor, author of the "Editor's Introduction," and translator of two articles in a special issue of *Chinese Studies in History, 2000*) and *Autocracy and China's Rebel*

Founding Emperors: Comparing Chairman Mao and Ming Taizu (co-authored and edited with John Rapp: Rowman & Littlefield, 2000).

Kenneth S. Ganza received his doctorate in Asian art history from Indiana University and has taught at a number of American colleges and universities for nearly 25 years. He has a particular interest in Chinese landscape paintings in which artists commemorate travel experiences, and he has traveled extensively around China. He believes that Chinese art is much more accessible than many Westerners might believe.

Tamara Hamlish is a cultural anthropologist in the field of user-centered design, where she uses ethnographic research to provide insights into innovative product design and technologies. Her research focuses on consumer culture, especially the culture of museums, and visual arts. She served as an associate professor of anthropology and the Mouat Junior Professor of International Studies at Beloit College. Her research on women artists in China, contemporary Chinese art, and China's museums has appeared in volumes from Stanford University Press, Routledge, and the Shanghai Fine Arts Press, as well as in numerous journals. Tamara received her Ph.D. from the University of Chicago.

Warren Bruce Palmer is an associate professor in the Department of Economics and Management at Beloit College. Trained in the field of comparative economic systems, his research interests include the study of energy issues in the Chinese economy and the role of electric power in economic development. He teaches a variety of courses, including "The Chinese Economy and Economic Reform" and "Energy and Environmental Economics."

John A. Rapp is professor of political science at Beloit College and the founder and past chair of its Asian Studies program. He received his Ph.D. in political science from the University of Wisconsin-Madison and a Master of arts degree in East Asian studies from Indiana University. His scholarly work has included articles on the thought of Daoist anarchists in ancient and medieval China and Marxist dissidents in modern China, as well as recent work on China's Taiping Rebellion. He is coauthor of *Autocracy and China's Rebel Founding Emperors: Comparing Chairman Mao and Ming Taizu*. At Beloit, his courses have included "Chinese Politics," "Democracy in East Asia," "Chinese Dissent," "Communist and Post-Communist Systems," "Daoism," and "China: The Long Revolution." He has taught first-year seminars on China's Cultural Revolution, the Taiping Rebellion, and Tiananmen.

Shin Yong Robson is an adjunct associate professor in the Department of Modern Languages and Literatures at Beloit College. A native of Beijing, she received her Ph.D. in Chinese linguistics from the University of Wisconsin at Madison in 1993. Her published scholarly works address modern Chinese morphology, syntax, and semantics. Her research interests also include the history of Chinese writing and Chinese historical phonology. In addition to her scholarship in linguistics, she has published translations of modern literary works from Chinese to English. At Beloit

College, she teaches all levels of Chinese language studies, contemporary modes of translation, and Chinese calligraphy.

Ann L. Silverberg is professor of music (musicology/ethnomusicology) at Austin Peay State University in Clarksville, Tennessee, where she has taught music history, ethnomusicology, and introductory music courses for 15 years. Her wide-ranging research interests include Chinese music, American music, liturgical music, and women in music. She has traveled to China annually since 2004, and lived on the campus of Shenyang Conservatory (Shenyang City, Liaoning Province) in academic year 2007-2008, studying the *guzheng* (Chinese long zither), Chinese music, and Mandarin Chinese. Silverberg earned her Ph.D. in musicology at the University of Illinois (1992), after which she completed Master's degrees in library and information science (University of Illinois, 1993) and anthropology (Vanderbilt University, 1998). She also holds a Master of music degree in musicology from Indiana University Bloomington (1984) and a Bachelor of music degree in music education (with a minor in French) from Ithaca College (1981).

Daniel M. Youd is an associate professor of Chinese language and literature at Beloit College and chair of the Department of Modern Languages and Literatures. He received his Ph.D. in East Asian Studies from Princeton University. Both his teaching and research interests center on Ming and Qing dynasty vernacular fiction, comparative literature, and translation studies.

Introduction

PERSPECTIVES ON CHINA

On a cool afternoon in March 2009, I set out from the eastern city of Taian for an ascent of Mount Tai, a storied mountain that has appeared in Chinese writings for more than 2,500 years. The 10-kilometer (six-mile) climb up the mountain's winding path is punctuated by temples, teahouses, and arches. Hiking through the easily negotiated early section that weaves its way from the Dai Temple, through a great arch, and past several iconic sites tucked behind the city's streets, I came to a place where China's great sage, Confucius, was said to have looked down and remarked, "From here, even my home state of Lu seems small." Over the next three hours, I hiked—amidst throngs of people of all ages—from a few hundred feet above sea level to almost a mile, following a path similar to the one Confucius traveled over 2,500 years ago. Even in Confucius's time, the mountain was a cultural icon, if not a singular mountaineering feat. When he reached the summit, he is said to have looked down again and stated, "From the top of Mount Tai, the whole world ('all under heaven') looks small."

I often have similar sentiments when looking back at China's history and culture from the lofty vantage point of the early 21st century. Any single set of events seems small, indeed, when surveying the course of 3,000 years of written records, and 5,000 years of historical tradition. Examining the tumult during Confucius's time and attempting to understand his approach to government service and proper human conduct in an age he perceived as deeply flawed is not unlike trying to glimpse the Shandong countryside from a mountain temple on a blustery day. This analogy only begins to break down if we make the mistake of perceiving our 21st-century glimpses into the distance as a "peak." On the mountain top, there is nowhere else to go. In human history, we don't know what happens next, and we follow a continuing path with forks, intersections, and less trodden lanes.

This book is meant as an introduction to thinking about Chinese history and culture, as well as an approach to understanding China's role in our own complex world. The past decade alone has reflected profound changes in China's political, economic, and cultural influence on the world stage. At the turn of the last century, China had not yet been awarded the Olympic Games or the glittering opportunity of Expo 2010. As this book goes to press, China stands right between these two events—with the Olympics concluded and the finishing touches underway on Shanghai's facilities—in an influential position in a rapidly changing world.

For all its size and strength, China remains an enigma for many Westerners. With a language that is difficult to master, political institutions with roots in centuries-old practices, and social relationships deeply grounded in the cultivation of personal connections, China has long proven a formidable challenge for Western travelers. Even with China's present openness to foreign investment and travel, information is often difficult to find and even harder to interpret. What many students, travelers, and business people lack is the *context* for what they have learned from newspapers, travel, and the anecdotes of others. Between serious scholarly studies and the daily or weekly press lies a confusion of materials that is often extremely difficult for even the most devoted generalist to evaluate.

This book is intended to fill that middle ground between the academic study of China and the array of reports and volumes that one might find on any bookstore or library shelf. It is an introduction to China and the Chinese people for readers who are interested in a clear approach to the most important issues in China's history, politics, economy, society, and culture. It assumes no previous knowledge of China, but is written with the expectation that readers will be open to the challenges of learning about one of the world's greatest civilizations. The study of China is replete with such challenges—from language games that are difficult to decipher to historical references that outsiders strain to interpret—but deeper understanding is possible with the right tools and the right approach. China today is a vibrant society alive with change and connections to global issues that we all share. It is far too influential to ignore, and far too complex to marginalize by looking only at a narrow swath of contemporary issues. All of the contributors to this volume share a deep interest in the study of contemporary China, and all of us have spent significant amounts of time there over the years. All of the contributors also appreciate—as will be clear in each chapter—the rich connections that China, even in a changing present, has to a history that spans thousands of years.

EMPHASIS ON TEACHING

I have written this volume with the help of an array of contributors in and beyond the Asian Studies program at Beloit College. They have my gratitude for not only producing their individual chapters, but also for reading significant sections of the manuscript and making suggestions for revisions. I am just as indebted to Beloit College for its support of our teaching and writing on this project. I have used parts of this book in many of my classes, as have several of the contributors, and the feedback from students and colleagues has been invaluable.

In short, this is a general book on China written by experienced college teachers, each with a decade or more of experience in college classrooms. Our chapters have been written with the kind of understanding of beginning students that characterizes all of our introductory classes. We all know that beginning students (and readers of this volume) are capable of a great deal if they are taught correctly, with each theme building carefully upon the others until students attain a quite sophisticated understanding of the complex entity that is China. We have all seen the exhilarating changes in students' knowledge of Chinese history, politics, economics, society, and culture after only a single semester.

We have also found that it is much easier to create that kind of deep understanding for beginning students *in the classroom* than on the page. I asked contributors to create a sense of their introductory teaching styles as they wrote their chapters—to imagine that they were connecting with students through strategies similar to those employed during the academic semester. We have all found it to be a formidable challenge. In my own experience, translating my teaching of Chinese history into 20,000 words—or traditional Chinese beliefs into 5,000—constituted as challenging a writing project as any I have undertaken. In those sections, I have tried to convey the themes that I use in all of my teaching, but I have had to do so without the day-to-day interaction that I enjoy in the classroom. The contributors to this volume have voiced similar sentiments, but we have also found that writing these chapters has come to embody a special version of our classroom teaching experiences. Each of the chapters is meant to reflect the way that we convey ideas in the classroom, but to an audience that is much wider than any we are likely to find there. Our intent is that the book should mirror the freshness and pace of our own classes—to welcome those with little previous knowledge and leave them with a combination of analysis, stories, anecdotes, and useful information that will deepen their knowledge of this vast country.

Toward that end, I have asked each contributor to bear in mind two very clear examples of our audience. One is a high-school student writing a serious report on a country about which she knows little, and the other is an adult with no specific knowledge of China who is about to take a trip there for business or pleasure. College students may well end up reading parts of the book, but it is particularly addressed to general readers who may gain deeper skills after studying the book and beginning to pursue the references and suggested readings after each chapter. All of the contributors wrote with specific examples of that audience in mind. I, for example, envisioned my nephews and nieces in high school, along with several colleagues who will be traveling to China soon on business. None of them speaks or reads Chinese, and none will pursue the study of China at a professional level. They are among the intelligent readers who often get lost in the flurry of publications in today's book market.

CHAPTERS AND CONTRIBUTORS

I have written the opening two chapters (with Warren Palmer offering assistance at the beginning of the geography chapter) with the goal of introducing readers to China's rich history and vast landscapes. Throughout these chapters, I have tried to provide readers with a number of core themes that will help them to better understand the materials they will encounter in the rest of the book and gain a newfound appreciation for long-term changes in Chinese civilization. Chapter 3, "Chinese Politics and Government," was written by John Rapp, a professor of political science at Beloit College and the founder of the Asian Studies program. John has inspired me, as well as our students, with his knowledge of and enthusiasm for Chinese politics and issues of comparative studies. He is also the co-author (with Anita Andrew, another contributor) of a very fine book on two prominent Chinese leaders, the Ming founder Zhu Yuanzhang and Mao Zedong. Chapter 4, "The Chinese Economy," was written by Warren Palmer, an associate professor of economics and a former chair of the Asian Studies program. Warren also contributed mightily to other parts of the book, and wrote significant portions of the "Social Relationships and Etiquette" section of Chapter 6. I am deeply indebted to him.

Two large chapters follow: "Society" and "Culture." I have written the bulk of Chapter 5, "Society" (with sections contributed by Tamara Hamlish). I have tried to offer a sense of the connection between social relationships, kinship organization, gender, ethnicity, and thought in both China's history and its changing present. Tamara Hamlish, formerly an associate professor of anthropology at Beloit College, provides perspectives on Chinese society and culture derived from her own field studies, as well as personal experience that comes from a deep knowledge of the richly nuanced language and the practice of calligraphy. Chapter 6, "Culture," contains the widest range of contributions. The chapter begins with a section on language written by my colleague Shin Yong Robson, who used her experience teaching the Chinese language to give a fascinating overview of the rich diversity of spoken and written Chinese over several millennia. She is a trained linguist and a Chinese language professor with high standards and a good sense of humor. Her skills and ability to explain complex matters clearly are evident on each page of her section on Chinese language. I wrote the section on social relationships and etiquette with the help of Tamara Hamlish and Warren Palmer. The literature section is the work of associate professor of Chinese Daniel Youd. Daniel's scholarly work has focused on Ming and Qing fiction, but, as the chapter demonstrates, his knowledge of Chinese literature is extensive, and his ability to explain a great deal in a concise manner is matched by few people.

Chapter 6 continues with sections on Chinese art and music, written by two of my colleagues outside of Beloit College. Kenneth Ganza, formerly a professor of art history at Colby College, and I served as co-instructors of the "East Asian Civilization" course at Colby for four years, and I retain my admiration for his clear explanations and memorable anecdotes about Chinese material culture. Ann Silverberg, professor of music at Austin Peay University, has been a fellow seminar participant with me at the East-West Center, and has undertaken textual study and fieldwork dealing with

Chinese music, spending the 2007–2008 academic year in China focused on studying much of the material that can be found in her chapter. The chapter concludes with sections on "Food," "Leisure and Sports," and "Popular Culture." I am responsible for the bulk of that material, but contributions from Tamara Hamlish and Kevin Latham—author of *Pop Culture, China!*—are clearly noted. Finally, Anita Andrew, a professor of history at Northern Illinois University and a former professor at Beloit College, has written about the way that China often appears in our newspapers, magazines, and Internet materials, as well as the way that the Chinese media reports on both domestic and foreign issues. These are the often stark themes that confront readers when they encounter China in the press, and represent a fitting way to conclude a book that is meant to give readers a way to think intelligently about China in our changing world.

Many people besides the contributors have helped with the production of this book. I would first like to thank the editors at ABC-CLIO: Steven Danver, Lynn Jurgensen, Julie Dunbar, and Kim Kennedy White. They have guided the project through numerous challenges since I took it on in 2007, and I am indebted to them for their patience and good judgment. I want to thank Andrea Hugg of the Beloit College class of 2002 for coordinating the acquisition of materials from the Beloit College museums and archives for use in this book and its accompanying Web site. Paralleling what I have said about our Asian Studies program, it is the very rare college that offers research and teaching resources that are directly relevant to a book such as ours, right from our own collections. One of the reasons that I came to Beloit College a decade ago was because it possessed a fine college archival collection, two excellent museums, and a nationally recognized summer language institute. Fred Burwell, Bill Green, Nicolette Meister, Judy Newland, Joy Beckman, Marcus Eckhardt, and Patricia Zody have all been enormously helpful over the years in providing access to the collections, materials, and classes that have facilitated the writing process.

A number of people read portions of the manuscript, including all of the members of my Chinese history and culture class over the last several years. Jacob Peterson, Beloit College class of 2009, read the entire manuscript and provided excellent advice about the placement of prominent themes. Jasmine and Jordan Sundberg, as well as Rebecca and Catherine Bennett, read the manuscript with the eyes of young readers (ranging from high school to college) and intellectual energy beyond their years. Those who read parts of the manuscript are too numerous to name, but I deeply appreciate their help. Any mistakes or omissions that remain are the responsibility of the book's authors. All translations, unless otherwise marked, are our own.

Finally, I want to thank my students at Beloit College who, over the past decade, have taught me a great deal about writing and speaking to very intelligent nonspecialists. All of the contributors have been blessed by an enormous display of goodwill and patience from our students, and they have kept us going through the challenges of teaching about a civilization and a language as vast and complex as China's. We dedicate this volume to them all.

Geography

Robert André LaFleur
Warren Bruce Palmer

THE PHYSICAL SETTING AND CHINA'S POPULATION

To begin understanding China, let us start by comparing China to the United States. Both nations are among the world's largest countries, bigger than the Australian continent and slightly smaller than Europe. The surface area of the two is almost identical—only Russia and Canada cover greater areas. The northern tip of Heilongjiang province, the northernmost part of China, reaches beyond the latitude of Maine, but is further south than Alaska. Hainan Island, the southernmost part of China, is to the far south of Key West Florida and slightly south of Hawaii, Puerto Rico, or Mexico City. Still, much of China lies within the same northern latitudes as most of the United States, except that China has a much larger area in the far south. China is also slightly wider than the contiguous 48 states, although China's sparsely populated west has nothing like the coastal state population volume of Washington, Oregon, and California.

One of the greatest contrasts between the two nations is the size of their populations. China is the most populous nation on earth, with more than 1.3 billion people, whereas the United States has slightly more than 300 million people. To appreciate this population difference, imagine China with a billion fewer people, or the equivalent of just its 15-and-under population. It would still exceed the United States' population. Another way to think about the population difference is to imagine the United States as home to all of the people now living in North America, South America, and the European Union. The U.S. population would then match China's population—but only after adding another 100 million people. Now take 70 percent of those people (about 900 million) and place them east of the Mississippi River,

1

Map of China.

which would amount to the equivalent of more than five people for every one now living in that area. Then you have China Proper, the parts of the present-day People's Republic of China (PRC) with provincial status, excluding the provinces comprising Manchuria—that is, those parts that have constituted China for the past 2,000 years.

Both China and the United States are subdivided into smaller governmental units. China has 22 provinces (the PRC considers Taiwan a 23rd), four large cities with provincial status, and five autonomous regions. Many of China's provinces, like U.S. states, have areas and populations that are as large or larger than most nations. For example, the areas of Texas and Sichuan province are both over 50 percent larger than that of Germany. In terms of population, however, Sichuan and Germany have about the same number of people, between 80 and 90 million, whereas Texas is home to about 21 million people. China's largest political unit, Xinjiang, in the far west, has 20 percent more land area than Alaska, and is bigger than Spain, Italy, and France combined. The four cities with provincial status—Beijing, Chongqing, Shanghai, and Tianjin—have populations far greater than that of New York City, the largest

TABLE 1.1. Population by Region (2007) (Does not include Hong Kong SAR, Macao SAR, or Taiwan)

Region	Total Population (year-end) (10,000 persons)	Area (1,000 square miles)
National Total	132,129	
North		
Beijing	1,633	6.5
Tianjin	1,115	4.4
Hebei	6,943	72.6
Shanxi	3,393	60.3
Inner Mongolia	2,405	463.3
Northeast		
Liaoning	4,298	56.3
Jilin	2,730	53.3
Heilongjiang	3,824	182.8
East		
Shanghai	1,858	2.4
Jiangsu	7,625	39.6
Zhejiang	5,060	39.3
Anhui	6,118	53.9
Fujian	3,581	46.9
Jiangxi	4,368	64.4
Shandong	9,367	59.1
South-Central		
Henan	9,360	64.4
Hubei	5,699	72.4
Hunan	6,355	81.1
Guangdong	9,449	68.7
Guangxi	4,768	89
Hainan	845	13.1
Southwest		
Chongqing	2,816	31.8
Sichuan	8,127	218.8
Guizhou	3,762	68.1
Yunnan	4,514	151.4
Tibet	284	456.6
Northwest		
Shaanxi	3,748	79.2
Gansu	2,617	175.7
Qinghai	552	300.8
Ningxia	610	25.5
Xinjiang	2,095	631.4

Source: China Statistical Yearbook, China Statistical Information Network

Note: Data in the table are estimates from the 2007 National Sample Survey on Population Changes. Military personnel were included in the national total population, but were not included in the population by region.

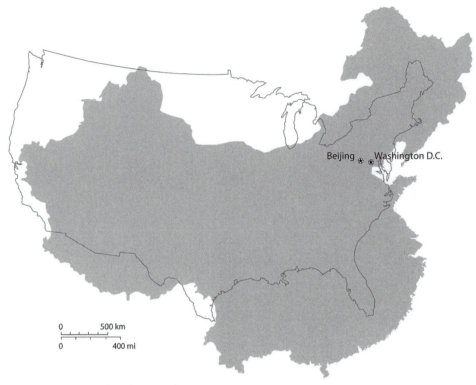

China superimposed on the United States.

city in the United States, and have land areas greater than that of smaller states, such as Rhode Island, Delaware, and Connecticut.

GEOGRAPHICAL REGIONS

Just as we conceptually divide the United States into geographical regions, China, too, can be usefully divided into regions. As in the United States, one of China's most important regional distinctions is between the north and south. We will return to this north-south distinction many times in this book. In China, the distinction is rooted in geography, climate, and history. From early times, distinct cultures have developed between north and south, and they have remained a lively topic of conversation for Chinese travelers for centuries. Regional differences are also of great interest to the Chinese because each region has its own customs, food, markets, and politics. Both China and the United States encompass a wide range of environments, from the frigid north to the sultry south, from high mountains to desert basins below sea level. However, of the two nations, China is more rugged and mountainous, with less arable land and far greater rainfall variability.

Unlike the United States, which has oceans to the east, west, and much of the south, China's climate is dominated by the vast bulk of Asia that surrounds it to the north, west, and southwest. The land to the west blocks all rain from that direction.

Yellow River in Huangnan prefecture, Qinghai province, China.
(Azenz/Dreamstime.com)

The Tibetan Plateau and the Himalayas on the southwest edge of the country block all moisture that would otherwise come from the Indian Ocean to the north of China. Major storm systems form primarily in the seas to the southeast and move northwest across the country, and rainfall is more plentiful in the south than in the north. China is also subject to the monsoon weather patterns caused by the Asian continent, so that precipitation is not spread evenly throughout the year as it is in much of the United States. Instead, monsoons produce the heaviest rains in the summer months. The amount of rainfall decreases and its variability increases as one travels from the southeast to the northwest. The western interior of China is a parched land with a very sparse population; most of it is ill-suited to agriculture because of its inadequate moisture and high elevation.

From east to west, China rises in a stair-step fashion to the Tibetan Plateau. Almost 70 percent of the country is higher than 3,200 feet above sea level, more than 40 percent is higher than 6,000 feet, and a large part of the Tibetan Plateau is higher than 16,000 feet above sea level. Even in the lower lying areas within 500 miles or so of the coast, China has a great deal of rugged terrain, especially in the southeastern provinces, such as Zhejiang, Jiangxi, Fujian, Hunan, Guangdong, and Guangxi. China's major rivers rise in Tibet and take an easterly course as they head to the sea, carving deep canyons as they descend the heights. Much of China's early history is closely connected with the geography of these rivers, and they remain vitally important in the 21st century as bearers of electrical power, trade, and natural resources.

The cradle of early Chinese civilization lies in northern China, in the vast drainage area of the Yellow River Valley. In fact, no other physical feature in early Chinese

---

RAINFALL, AGRICULTURE, SOCIETY, AND POLITICS

Until relatively recently, exceedingly wet or dry regions had tenuous connections to mainstream political and cultural life in China. The more arid northwest regions support a vastly different kind of economy than the lush southeast. The people who lived for generations in the arid regions beyond the Great Wall were never closely or continuously connected to the people and territories covered most often in Chinese civilization narratives, yet these nomadic peoples played an enormously important role in later history. The wetter regions of the far south also were not fully integrated into Chinese culture until the beginning of the Common Era—indeed, some have only been integrated within the past thousand years.

---

history played as prominent a role as the Yellow (or Huang) River, which supports agricultural civilization to this day. About 2,700 miles in length, the Yellow River has a vast flood plain from centuries of silt deposits. The silty loess sediments of the Yellow River would affect social and economic life unlike any other physical feature of the northern Chinese landscape. The river's frequent flooding created a continuing problem for Chinese rulers, who had to build dikes and clear sediments in order to keep the river on course. Indeed, the river has jumped its banks, broken its dikes, and changed course over the past 2,000 years, causing great devastation as it surged to the sea, giving the river its title of "China's Sorrow."

China's southern river, the Yangzi or Changjiang (often written as "Yangtze"), is less prone to flooding than the Yellow River. Even so, heavy rainfall on its vast watershed can quickly raise water levels to enormous heights. It, too, has caused frequent devastation throughout Chinese history. Today it is the home of the Three Gorges Dam, which is one of the most ambitious (some would say dangerous) experiments in water control in human history. The Yangzi River represents the geographical features of the south in other ways, as well. The Yangzi's vast networks of tributaries are reminiscent of what was called the "marshy southland" in early times. In fact, one of the most powerful differences between northern and southern China is the wetness of the lands in the Yangzi River valley and southward. This feature facilitates easy rice cultivation (grains such as wheat are far more prevalent in the north), fishing, and river trade.

China is also known for its vast and complex mountain ranges, many of which have figured in political history and, for that matter, in thousands of pages of poetry and prose written over three millennia. Most symbolic of all are what are called the "Five Cardinal Peaks," representing the range of early Chinese geography (they were concentrated in what today we could think of as central and northern China). These peaks denote each of the five directions that are integral to Chinese cosmological classification—north, west, south, east, and center. Mount Tai, in the east (in Shandong province), has been regarded for centuries as the foremost of the five sacred peaks, and has been a major destination for pilgrimages to this day. Aside from Mt. Heng (in Hunan province in the south), the mountains are tightly clustered in the

China's five cardinal peaks.

seat of Chinese civilization in the Yellow River drainage area. Mt. Song, the central mountain, is situated in Henan province between the cities of Luoyang and Zheng-zhou. The western mountain, Mt. Hua, is located near the ancient capital of Xi'an, and the northern mountain, Mt. Heng, is near Datong, which is a six-hour train trip from Beijing. Early kings were said to climb each of the cardinal peaks during the proper season (east being related to spring, south to summer, and so forth). By climbing the mountains and making sacrifices, the early kings were said to bring the seasons of the year into accordance with the human calendar, and make culture and nature cohere. They are geographical and cultural markers that have stood the test of Chinese history. To be sure, these mountains are small (between 1,200 and 2,200 meters, or 4,000–7,000 feet), but they are also pilgrimage locations quite unlike the major peaks of far-western China.

The major mountain ranges of central China and the near-west form great physical barriers that protected warring states, such as the Qin in the 3rd-century B.C.E., gave respite to rebel groups harassed by government troops (as in the case of the White Lotus rebels in the late 18th century), or even sheltered the Communist forces' Long March in the 1930s. The mountains of the far west are among the highest in the world, and—looking down as they do toward the coast many thousands of miles away—give the Chinese land mass its distinctive layered effect.

Finally, there is China's coastline, which comprises almost 9,000 miles of China's border. Until the 19th century, the coast did not represent a significant vulnerability to external threats. In fact, coastal defenses were something of an afterthought throughout Chinese history until the 19th century. To be sure, Japanese and other travelers arrived at Chinese ports, and coastal trade was present from early times. Still, China scarcely worried about its coastal borders until the British arrived with opium in the late 18th century, and expended minimal effort exploiting the possibilities beyond the coastal cities. Aside from a few missions initiated by the First Emperor of the Qin and a brief three decades of naval exploration that extended as far as Africa in the 15th century, life beyondthe sailing channels along China's coastline held little appeal to most prominent actors in Chinese history.

Rivers, mountains, coastlines, and other geographical features figure prominently in any narrative of China's past. It is important not to think of them as causes of historical change in and of themselves. Yet their very structural significance in terms of rainfall, flooding, mountainous respite, and coastal possibility figured greatly in the choices that historical figures made (or failed to make) in light of these enormous geographical features. They provided the physical backdrop and, often, the shelter or areas of strategic maneuver that would become a part of China's unfolding political and cultural history.

LAND, AGRICULTURE, AND THE LAOJIA

Even a cursory glance at a map of China shows the enormous influence of the Eurasian landmass on the country. To be sure, China has a sizable coastline, but from its earliest times, agriculture and a landed worldview have dominated political and social institutions throughout China. The origins of Chinese civilization in the Yellow River Valley are distinctly agricultural, and the early archaeological evidence shows a heavy reliance on fields and farming over more coastal pursuits, such as fishing and sea trade. Sheer numbers account for most of this effect: the population of the Chinese countryside dwarfed that of the coasts, and it was not until the 12th century that large coastal cities began to develop into powerful administrative and economic centers.

As early as the Western Zhou (c. 1050–722 B.C.E.), the political and social orders were framed by a profound connection to agriculture, place, and family in Chinese life. As many as 200 small states, each with a particular association with an agricultural micro-region, formed the early Chinese political system. While the political system would quickly fade as states became increasingly large in the first millennium before the Common Era, the link between families and micro-regions would be significantly longer lasting. As families intermarried and expanded, a sense of place would develop and extend into the 21st century. It is common for people in China and throughout

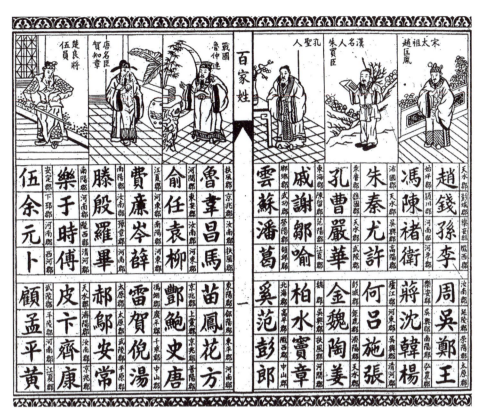

The Hundred Surnames. (*Rob LaFleur*)

the world to ask the location of a person's *laojia*. The term is sometimes translated as "hometown," but the Western connotation is too narrow: *laojia* does not refer so much to where any one individual comes from as to where his kin group originated. A literal translation of *laojia* gives us "old home," or "(your) venerable home." A useful extension might be "the original territory of (your) kin group."

For centuries, Chinese at home and abroad have asked each other for the location of their *laojia*. It is not a difficult question, and most people are able to answer with a precise location that he or she may never have seen, which would be a bit like asking a Western version of that question and having an Oklahoman answer "Norway." Traditional Chinese almanacs include a section known as "The Hundred Surnames," which includes the names and original locations of well over 500 families. The locations refer to the counties and administrative districts of historical eras, but almost everyone can give a present-day location, as well, even if she has never lived there.

A Chinese person's *laojia* answer is also almost always fuzzy. There is no great contradiction between a person's ability to note her family's origins and her difficulty in explaining her own, and her family's, residential locations. Throughout Chinese history, northern families have been displaced by famine, invasion, and even relocation. They took their possessions but left their land and their sense of family origin, remembering the territory of their fathers and mothers even as they bemoaned the fact that they were many thousands of *li* from the homeland.

My Deepest Sentiments
Lu You (1125–1210)

During these years, traveling ten-thousand *li* in search of merit
Fighting the barbarian cavalry at Liangzhou
The rivers and mountain passes disappear as if in a dream
And dust darkens my old fur uniform
Before the northern barbarians could be eliminated
My hair gray, my life in autumn
Tears matter not at all
How could I know that in this life,
My heart would reside at Mount Tian
Even as my body ages in the swampy southland.

(Zhang, *Songci yiwanshou*, 340)

It is not too great a stretch to say that such values dominated the political and diplomatic perspective of China, and that both power centers and elites were *grounded* in an agricultural and China-centered worldview. Indeed, travel abroad was prohibited during most periods of Chinese history before the 20th century, and Chinese nationals returning from abroad faced a range of consequences ranging from intense questioning to imprisonment. The standard assumption of Chinese foreign policy flowed from this enclosed, or centered, worldview. When powerful, China would be a center for other territories, whose diplomats would come to offer tribute. In times of great weakness, China would risk invasion by outside forces from the north or west. Even then, there was the assumption that China's cultural tradition would dominate that of the invader; rulers changed, but Chinese culture remained.

Although the precise historical situations were more complex than this model, the attitudes that grew from it carried enormous weight in almost all accounts—fictional or otherwise—of early Chinese travel. The earliest descriptions of long-distance travel or faraway locations possess an unmistakable architectural order, with the state at the center and increasing strangeness dominating as one goes farther into the unknown. The clear theme is that movement away from the center brought, at the very least, *difference*, and often difference of a sinister nature.

COMING TO CHINA: INVASION AND TRIBUTE

Between the extremes of greeting and antipathy lies a very important theme in Chinese civilization: the diplomatic worldview that said, in effect, "Come to our capital and our economic centers for we are the center of the world." During many periods of Chinese history, this was a somewhat hollow promise, but the Silk Road continued to fuel trade and cultural exchange through the centuries. During the heights of Chinese power—particularly during the Tang dynasty in the early 8th century and the Yuan dynasty in the early 14th century—the capitals of Chang'an and Beijing, respectively, were filled with diplomats, travelers, traders, and the elite of Chinese society. The diversity found at the far end of the Silk Road was welcomed during times of Chinese strength. It should not be forgotten, however, that Chinese officials perceived their cities as the destination for other travelers engaged in a vast tributary relationship. The capitals werenot perceived as mere outposts for travelers from afar or the beginning of the journey for Chinese travelers. The emphasis was emphatically *not* on leaving.

China was quite accustomed, however, to receiving the attention of visitors from afar, and Chinese civilization can be seen as a unifying magnet throughout East Asia, and as a significant force in Southeast Asia, as well. Japanese visits to the Tang court in the sixth, seventh, and eighth centuries—along with the enormous stores of texts and information that visitors brought back to Japan—played a fundamental role in shaping Japanese political structure and cultural life for centuries. Korean cultural borrowing from China had an even more dramatic influence on the Korean state, down to the social organization of family networks. It has often been noted that Koreans borrowed from the Confucian classics with such zeal that, during the Choson period lasting from the 14th century until the early 20th century, Koreans were more Confucian than the Chinese.

Tributary relationships with China were only one part of the story regarding immigration and emigration, however. From the earliest historical records, conflicts with northern groups are noted with particular attention. Even the vibrant and strong reign of Emperor Wu of the Han dynasty [r. 141–87 B.C.E.] was marked by conflict with the Xiongnu "barbarians," as the Chinese referred to most groups beyond their cultural and political reach. The first emigrants, from this perspective, were the women of the Han court who were married off to distant rulers in a diplomatic combination of alliance and appeasement. Just one from the many written lamentations on this theme will have to suffice here.

Lament of Hsi-chün
Hsi-chün (Xiqun), c. 100 B.C.E.

My people have married me
In a far corner of Earth:
Sent me away to a strange land,
To the king of the Wu-sun.
A tent is my house,
Of felt are my walls;
Raw flesh my food
With mare's milk to drink.
Always thinking of my own country,
My heart sad within.
Would I were a yellow stork
And could fly to my old home!

(Waley, 1918, 34–35)

The "old home" of which she writes recalls the *laojia* discussed above. The pathetic cry for the homeland has significant implications for understanding the role of gender in Chinese society. The tone of the lament, however, would play an even larger role in Chinese attitudes toward inner and outer realms when people left (for one reason or another) the area often described as "all under heaven."

It was not uncommon for expatriates to ask for eventual burial in their homeland—and specifically in the territory of their original kin group. This was true of those who were displaced during times of northern invasion across many periods of Chinese history.

It is useful to examine an example that constitutes the reverse of the *laojia* theme. Just one of the many pointed plaints about the tenacity of the "barbarians" can be found in a Han Dynasty poem attributed to an official named Li Ling. After his release from almost two decades of imprisonment by northern tribes, he was said to have chanted the following forlorn lines:

> I came ten thousand leagues
> Across sandy deserts
> In the service of my Prince,
> To break the Hun tribes,
> My way was blocked and barred,
> My arrows and swords broken.
> My armies had faded away,
> My reputation had gone.
> —
> My old mother is long dead.
> Although I want to requite my Prince
> How can I return?

(Waley, 1918, 34)

THEMES IN CHINESE GEOGRAPHY

Highways and the Rail System

China's infrastructure has played a significant role in its development over the past two centuries from its status as a regional power struggling against Western imperialism to that of a powerful player on the global stage. Beyond the major river systems and the trade routes, as well as the imperial highways of the Qing dynasty (1644–1911), lay the potential for the railways and public highways that cross China today. The modern railway system transports goods and travelers in all directions, and runs on a seven-day-a-week schedule that emphasizes productivity and reliability. Indeed, each municipality's railway station—from small towns to the multiple stations in Beijing, Shanghai (with a state-of-the-art train station that rivals many international airports), and other sites—is a center of trade, travel, and commerce.

Beijing cityscape. (Macmaniac/Dreamstime.com)

From extremely modest origins, China has also developed a sophisticated and ever-growing network of high-speed highways linking major cities on the north-south and east-west axes. The parallels to the American interstate highway system are striking, and their growth is proceeding at a speed that rivals that of the American model. Below the level of the expressway, which is limited to car and truck traffic, the most notable difference between the Chinese highway system and those in the United States, Europe, and Japan is the variability of the speeds undertaken by different streams of traffic. A well-paved, two-lane highway between regional centers may have car traffic moving at 60 miles per hour, utility vehicles at 30 miles per hour, and a smattering of motorbikes, bicycles, slow-moving vehicles, pedestrians, and animals. At first glance, such a scene resembles utter confusion, and drivers in China must be aware of a range of paces and speeds that drivers in other countries have often forgotten. If one's gaze is adjusted, one can see a thriving economy and enterprise on such crowded roads, as well. In fact, the crowded highways of today's China give an ever-so-slight hint of the teeming movement of goods and services in an earlier China, which persisted under far harsher conditions.

Local roads in China vary from the excellent and well-paved roads of prosperous communities to seriously compromised and pothole-filled dirt trails that call to mind carriage traffic of an earlier era. The most local of routes reflect a very ancient China that created connections, even in the earliest of times, to almost all of the communities in the empire. Many areas of China remain accessible only on small, local roads, and some villages (as readers may have seen on news reports after the 2008 Sichuan earthquake) have only small and barely accessible roads, even in good conditions.

The variation one sees in infrastructure, in short, is tremendous. Railway systems provide a consistent overlay throughout China, and connect most locations not rendered inaccessible by mountains. Highway construction is a great deal more uneven, and today's China is still dominated by roadways serving urban, coastal centers and a population that is heavily concentrated in the eastern half of the country.

Water and Land Resources

An aerial map of China shows a dearth of lakes and naturally enclosed water systems, other than rivers. Indeed, a close look at such a map is startling, especially when compared to the maps of North America, South America, Africa, or Europe. China has no truly large bodies of inland water, and depends on its river system and its ample coastline in ways that extend beyond those of most other countries. The geographical reality of sparse inland water has played a large role in the development of Chinese history. More so than in countries with ample lakes, Chinese history has developed along rivers and coastlines, with residents depending on them for fresh water sources, fish, and transportation. Due to the proximity of large percentages of the population to river systems, Chinese populations have always been particularly vulnerable to water disasters, and the millions of tons of silt produced by the Yellow River have affected even the most basic economic enterprises over the centuries.

China's dearth of water constitutes a serious problem as it enters the 21st century. Current estimates are that the Chinese land mass has less than a quarter of the world's per-capita average water. The combination of low water levels and burgeoning industry has been disastrous for China's environment and the health of its citizens. Based on even somewhat conservative Chinese government estimates, pollution represents a serious threat to a large percentage of the population, as industry dumps raw sewage into rivers and lakes while people living along them are offered little recourse. The pollution risks would still remain with greater water reserves, but the relatively small amounts available for consumption, combined with the unbridled growth of Chinese industry, has led to disasters, such as entire lakes turning green from sewage runoff and high rates of cancer and other illnesses along many of China's river systems.

Such situations present a significant challenge for a government that promotes rapid economic growth, even as it seeks to preserve social order. Local officials are caught in the middle, and are often the direct recipients of outrage from local citizens, who are unable to take their cases higher into a bureaucracy that (throughout Chinese history) has done everything that it could to keep politics and protests localized. It is difficult for observers to sympathize with local officials, but they, too, are caught in a nationwide net created by natural resources, infrastructure, a teeming economy, and a highly bureaucratized political system.

The Three Gorges Dam project was created to alleviate some of these pressures, and to provide power to a large portion of the country. As we shall see in Chapter 7, "Contemporary Issues," the dam project has had a checkered, if short, history. It is a hydroelectric dam crossing the Yangzi River in Hubei province. It constitutes the largest hydroelectric power station in the world, and is estimated to reach over

---

WATER CONTROL AND THE CHINESE STATE

One historian, examining Chinese dynastic historical records over 2 millennia, noted that flooding or drought accounted for almost 15 disasters a decade throughout Chinese history (Huang 1997). Water control has always been a challenge for China's rulers, and some of the earliest culture-hero stories in China center on the great rulers who quelled floods and managed the flow of rivers. The most revered of these was Great Yu, the third of three "sage kings." He was known for his water control and river engineering efforts, and set a precedent for later ages. In more recent times, labor teams organized by imperial governments would dredge the Yellow River as best they could, clean silt from the Grand Canal, and engineer the water flow on the Yangzi River.

20,000 megawatts of electrical capacity when it becomes fully operational after 2011. The construction of the dam caused mass relocations and the loss of cultural sites along the banks of the river. It will have indisputable potential as a power source if it works to capacity, and represents a dramatic attempt by China's leaders to harness the power of water—something rulers in China have been attempting for well over three millennia.

China's Climate

Any land mass as large of China's is likely to have significant climate variation. China is influenced by summer monsoons and warm moist air in the southwest, and in the north by high-pressure Siberian systems with cold, dry air and low-pressure systems coming in over the Bay of Bengal and the South China Sea. Northeastern China's summers are mild to hot and quite humid, while its winters are cold and dry. The northwest, protected by vast mountain ranges, experiences an arid climate year-round, with its wildly varying temperatures being dependent on elevation. The hottest temperatures ever recorded in China were in the Turpan Depression in Xinjiang Province, while the coldest average temperature was found (not surprisingly) on the summit of Mt. Everest in Tibet. The west is striking in its temperature variation, but the east is no different. The equation can be reversed, in effect, and one finds the coldest ever-reported temperature in Heilongjiang province in the far northeast of China and the hottest average temperature on Hainan Island in the far southeast.

The situation becomes even more interesting when we think about the way that heat and cold are experienced by the vast majority of the population. All four hot and cold locations mentioned in the paragraph above are in outlying areas with sparse populations. Statistics can be deceptive. In terms of popular perception, however, the hottest places in China are the "three furnaces" of Chongqing (Sichuan Province), Wuhan (Hubei Province), and Nanjing (Jiangsu Province). They are known for their intense summer heat and humidity, even though a climate map of July temperatures shows that heat intensity is spread quite evenly across northern, central, and southern China. A climate map of January temperatures is less surprising, with a fairly

Terrace farming in Guilin, China. Southern China can receive 100 to 200 inches of rain every year. (Polartern/Dreamstime.com)

even distribution of cold temperatures in the north and warmer temperatures in the south.

As we have already seen, the most dramatic climate map of China shows its rainfall distribution. From northwest to southeast, the yearly rainfall variation ranges from less than an inch to well over 100 inches in the entire lower third of the country (with averages extending well beyond 200 inches in many places). The differences are so dramatic that one-third of the country, the vast northwest, can only be farmed with the greatest of persistence and the lowest of expectations, another third, the heartland of Chinese civilization, near the Yellow River and to the northeast, with great challenges and uneven results, and another third, the vast southern region from Sichuan to Shanghai and down to Guangzhou and Fujian Province, with plentiful rainfall and fine agricultural conditions.

Today, the enormity of climate variation has a somewhat less drastic effect on the lives of people than it did before sophisticated transportation systems were developed. It is easier to transfer goods cross-country than it was in earlier times, but the stark fact remains that China is, in many ways, three distinctly different countries in terms of climate, the potential for agriculture, and the abundance of natural resources. The far west, or fully half of the country, is only tenuously related to the rapid changes taking place in northeast, central, and southeast China, and one of the great challenges of the 21st century will be how China manages its vast western frontier.

IMAGINATIVE GEOGRAPHY

Geography is not merely an objective set of facts or reference points. When we discuss geography, we often refer to land masses, populations, natural structures, climate, water use, and even political distinctions, such as provinces, counties, and municipalities. All of these factors are important, and that is why we have spent a good deal of time exploring the issues related to them with regard to China. In order to understand Chinese history and culture in a manner that encapsulates the thinking of many of its most brilliant minds over the centuries, however, it is necessary to shift the focus slightly and examine another set of geographical issues that have played an enormous role in the way that Chinese history and culture have unfolded.

We might think of imaginative geography as the ways in which people have perceived the world around them: its shapes, its boundaries, and the way that territories are related. We have already seen two examples of imaginative geography in China, and both are vitally alive to this day. The first can be seen with the five cardinal mountains. They retain a sense of qualitative direction that dates back several millennia in China. To be sure, all of the peaks "fit" the north-south-east-west-center schema, but a close look at the map above will show that they are hardly symmetrical. The point, as we shall see in the section on *yin-yang* and the five phases of Popular Culture, is that they form a pattern that represents a *total* world. It is not so much a matter of where they are in relation to a Global Positioning System (which did not exist, in any case, when the mountains were designated) as it is of how they, as five aspects of Chinese civilization, came to represent it all.

One way to think about this issue is to imagine the five mountains as individual entities; each one can be climbed, admired, and appreciated on its own, and that is exactly what early emperors were said to have done. Each was climbed in the proper season and, upon climbing the last one (Northern Mt. Heng) in the dead of winter, the year was said to be complete and the realm was brought back into order. Each mountain has its own distinctive quality, but the goal of traveling them was to bring time and space back into order—one, two, three, four, five . . . *totality*. There may be individual peaks, but the five mountains *are* the kingdom from this perspective.

Let us look at the matter of imaginative geography from another perspective, that of the early writers of history who imagined the area in which they lived to possess the greatest attributes that the physical world could provide. They saw their realm as being "all under heaven," and they meant that in a very particular way. Directly above, they saw the Pole Star of the Big Dipper. They imagined that its force shot straight down, like a pillar, to the central palace, from which the roadways were built to move north, south, east, and west, reaching the cardinal mountains (and beyond) with its virtue. The very centrality of the Pole Star and the palace lies at the heart of one of Confucius's most famous sayings, which, to the Chinese imagination, has always had a powerfully geographical flavor:

> Performing rule with virtue is, by analogy, like the Pole Star, which resides in its place while the multitudinous stars encircle it (Confucius, *Lunyu* 2.1).

Pilgrims climb the narrow path up Mount Hua, one of the sacred five peaks in China. (Zy.sky/Dreamstime.com)

The geography of China was thought to be fixed in place by the ruler, who was in turn responsible for making sure that order prevailed throughout the realm. As we can see from the quotation below, excerpted from the classic *Book of Documents*, virtue and goodness were thought to be centered in China, and the yearlong tour of the cardinal mountains was one of the ruler's responsibilities. The sage king Shun's tour of the realm can be seen as something of a map, but it is more than just that; it is a template for moral action set in a geographical context.

> In the second month of the year, [the sage emperor Shun] made a tour of inspection to the east as far as Mt. Tai, where he made a burnt offering to Heaven and sacrificed to the mountains and rivers. . . . He received the eastern nobles in an audience and put their calendar in order, standardized the musical notes and the measures of length and volume, as well as the five kinds of rituals. . . .
>
> After finishing his tour of inspection he returned to the capital. In the fifth month, he made a tour of inspection to the south, as far as the Southern Sacred Peak, to which he sacrificed in the same manner as he did at Mt. Tai. Likewise, in the eight month, he made a western tour of inspection as far as the Western Sacred Peak. In the eleventh month, he made a tour of inspection to the north, as far as the Northern Sacred Peak, where he sacrificed as he had in the west. Upon his return to the capital, he went to the Temple of the Ancestor and offered up an ox (to complete the cycle of the year and the realm) (Kong, *Wujing*: 348).

A further aspect of imaginative geography proceeds from the same foundation, and has the same idyllic overtones. There are many reasons why China has long considered itself to be the Middle Kingdom. As the text below illustrates, ancient Chinese perceptions of geography begin from the center and move outward, creating, in turn, an early imaginative ethnography, or study of peoples. To be sure, the geography is impossible; people cannot change in expanding zones of 500 *li* (a *li* is about a third of a mile). Yet here we have one of the earliest cultural documents in China asserting that goodness and proper culture lie in the center, and one begins to lose these attributes as one moves away from the influence of the center. Many religions and even secular governments throughout the world have played upon that theme in the 3,000 years since the text below—also from the *Book of Documents*—was written. It carries a quite simple, yet problematic, message: virtue is centered and those lying beyond are not fully "one of us." Despite its fanciful tones, this theme would be repeated throughout Chinese history, as Chinese governments realized, to their despair, that they had not understood the peoples who lived beyond the center—the Middle Kingdom.

> Throughout the Nine Provinces order was effected. . . . [The sage emperor Yu] . . . said, "Let me set the example of a reverent attention to my virtue, that none may act contrary to my conduct." The [central] five hundred *li* constituted the Imperial Domain. . . . Five hundred *li* beyond constituted the Domain of the Nobles, . . . Five hundred *li* farther beyond formed the Peace-Securing Domain, where they cultivated the lessons of learning and moral duties; in the other two hundred they showed the energies of war and defense.
>
> Five hundred *li* more remote still formed the Domain of Restraint. The first three hundred were occupied by the tribes of the Yi; the other two hundred by criminals undergoing the greater banishment. The most remote five hundred *li* constituted the Wild Domain. The first three hundred were occupied by the tribes of the *Man*; the other two hundred by criminals undergoing the greater banishment.
>
> On the east reaching to the sea, on the west extending to the Moving Sands, to the utmost limits of north and south—his fame and influence filled up all within the four seas. Yu presented the dark-colored symbol of his rank and announced the completion of his work (Waltham, 1971, 52 54).

In classifying the geography of the realm in the last paragraph, the great sage emperor Yu reunites north, south, east, and west with his central virtue and makes the kingdom whole. It is a place of goodness and correct behavior, as well as one (many hundreds of *li* away) of criminals, dangerous tribes, and people who have only imperfectly digested proper conduct. Even with its fanciful tone, it presents a model that will be quite useful in examining China's history, and its ever-changing relationship over 3,000 years between the peoples of the center and those on the periphery. North, south, east, and west are more than just directions in China's turbulent histories. They represent change and possibility (goods coming from afar), as well as stagnation and despair (such as China's utter failure to deal with Western aggression in the 19th century). China's imaginative geography is, indeed, a window onto its history, to which we now turn.

REFERENCES

Birrell, Anne. *Classic of Mountains and Seas*. London: Penguin Books, 2000.

Blunden, Caroline. *Cultural Atlas of China*. Rev. ed. New York: Checkmark Books, 1998.

Confucius. *Lunyu* [Analects]. Taipei: Qiming shuju, 1973.

Elvin, Mark. *The Retreat of the Elephants: An Environmental History of China*. New Haven, CT: Yale University Press, 2006.

Huang, Ray. *China: A Macrohistory*. Armonk, NY: M. E. Sharpe, 1997.

Kong, Linghe, ed. *Wujing zhushi [Annotated Five Classics]*. Jinan: Shandong Youyi Chubanshe, 2000.

Strassberg, Richard. *Inscribed Landscapes: Travel Writing from Imperial China*. Berkeley: University of California Press, 1994.

Waley, Arthur. *A Hundred and Seventy Chinese Poems*. London: Constable and Co., 1918.

Waltham, Clae. *The Shu Ching: Book of History*. Chicago: Henry Regnery Company, 1971.

Zhang Jucai. *Songci yiwanshou [Ten Thousand Song Lyrics]*. Beijing: Yanchu Chubanshe, 1996.

History

Robert André LaFleur

ARCHAEOLOGY

Many of the most exciting advances in our knowledge of Chinese history in the last 50 years have come from archaeological discoveries. Although a deep knowledge of traditional sources of Chinese history and culture will never be obsolete, since these sources have been a significant part of the cultural tradition for almost 3,000 years, there is no doubt that the most dramatic changes in our understanding of China are derived from archaeological sites. This is not only true of ancient history, either. Even for relatively recent periods, such as the Ming and Qing dynasties, archaeological evidence is reshaping the way that we perceive urban life, attitudes toward the deceased, and a plethora of assumptions that we have held about the practices of daily life. In fact, it is not an exaggeration to say that one cannot have a nuanced perspective on Chinese history and culture without understanding the significance of the archaeological finds of the past half-century.

These discoveries have transformed our knowledge of China's past. Beginning more than a century ago, farmers began digging up what they often referred to as "dragon bones" while tilling their fields. This led to the discovery that the writing on these bones (ox scapulae—shoulder blades—and tortoise shells) was an early form of Chinese script, and that the inscriptions were divinations made toward *tian*, or heaven. Over the past century, these early inscriptions have fostered a much deeper knowledge of government practice in the early periods than it would have been possible to acquire just decades ago. Even later discoveries, including tombs or sites dating to the first millennium B.C.E., show us whole tombs, such as that of the relatively insignificant Lady Dai, that are filled with items meant to accompany her in death. The yield there has provided so much information that

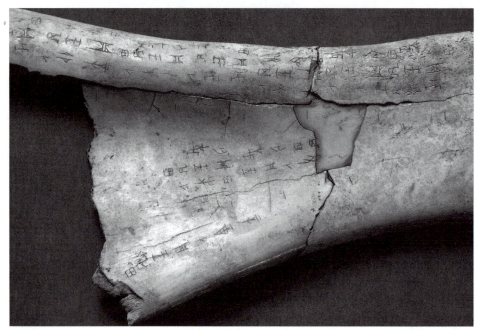

Shang Dynasty oracle bone, or "dragon bone," Luoyang, Henan, China. (Lowell Georgia/ Corbis)

one marvels at the possibilities for the tombs of figures with important stations in early China.

Even with all of the details that have bolstered our knowledge of China's past with archaeological discoveries, the fact remains that the previous three millennia have largely been informed by earlier anecdotes, myths, and legends. Whether or not we have found new etymological evidence about these stories, they were spoken of *as true* for more than 20 centuries. It is important to take that perspective seriously, even as we learn from fresh archaeological discoveries. In the remainder of this book, we will seek to achieve the balance sought by the sage himself, Confucius, who taught that contemporary events were best understood through the lens of older and even ancient ones.

FOUNDATION MYTHS AND EARLY HISTORY (TO c. 1100 B.C.E.)[1]

The myths of China's founding played an enormously important role in Chinese people's conceptions of their history. One creation story centers on Pangu, a figure that emerged from a cosmic egg to create the universe. His head became mountains, his flesh fields, and his bones rocks. His sweat was rain, and the insects, which finally found themselves on his body, were people. It is a story that has been retold in books on Chinese mythology in both East Asia and the West. This legend was, however, a late addition to a series of much earlier human culture stories that comprise the very foundation of early Chinese mythology.

Dancers perform during the Qingming Festival, or Tombs Sweeping Festival, at the Mausoleum of Huangdi (the Yellow Emperor), a legendary ancestor of the Chinese nation, in Huangling County of northwest China's Shaanxi Province, April 5, 2006. Every year, tens of thousands of Chinese gather to pay respects to the Yellow Emperor, who was said to have unified tribes along the Yellow River Valley 5,000 years ago. (AP/Wide World Photos)

Of the five legendary rulers, the first, Fuxi and Nüwa (a brother-sister pair), domesticated animals, built homesteads, taught people how to fish with nets, introduced fire, channeled rivers, created writing, and focused their mythical energies on the Yellow River. The second, Shen Nong, introduced agricultural techniques and medicine through herbs and other means. The third, Huangdi, the Yellow Emperor, quelled barbarian tribes, established a calendar, and created an infrastructure for plow carts and other vehicles. Huangdi also developed the subtle agricultural techniques that would remain at the heart of Chinese life into the 20th century. His wife, the first empress, practiced silk cultivation and initiated the tradition of women working with silk, which would stand as an ideal throughout imperial times. In these first three great mythical reigns, the idea of a Chinese state was created. It is the last two legendary rulers, however, who exemplify the core myths of Chinese civilization, and who have appeared prominently in Chinese political rhetoric for more than three millennia: Yao and Shun. The stories of these figures fall in the realm of mythology, but (although many texts disagree on the details of their rule) they also figure prominently in historical writings in China.

It is said that Yao was born after his mother observed a dragon of the auspicious color red. He devoted himself to the people, so the stories go, and even placed remonstrance drums and criticism tablets throughout the kingdom so that people with grievances could pound or write upon them and tell him of their troubles. Yao was completely devoted to his people and to ruling in a moral and righteous fashion that would solidify the growing state. When Yao grew old, he looked to his own sons for a successor, and was displeased. After asking his advisers to send him an upright person who could rule the empire with morality and skill, a commoner named Shun was brought to him. Through the force of his virtue, Shun had held together what we today might call a dysfunctional family as he persistently cared for his parents and siblings. Even as his stepmother sought to kill him, he remained a devoted son. Based on reasoning that would persist for thousands of years, he was the obvious choice, for surely one who knew how to manage a family was capable of managing the empire. In traditional political rhetoric, family management and imperial management were two sides of the same coin.

As Shun grew old, he realized that he had failed in only one respect; he had not lived long enough to quell the great floods that were overtaking China in the later years of his reign. He, too, looked beyond his own sons, as Yao had many years before, and found a virtuous, hard-working young man named Yu. Yu toiled to quell the floods and neglected the cries of his own family, never looking in on them, so focused was he on the problems of the empire. The tension between duty to family and to empire is part of this story, but its primary focus was a ruler who worked for the sake of his people above all else. Yu is the first ruler that we can call even remotely historical. He is known as the founder of the first dynasty, the Xia, for which we have only fragmented historical information. Together, Yao, Shun, and Yu are known for leading the "Three Dynasties" (*sandai*) and their rule has provided writers with longstanding images of strong leadership.

But Chinese history, at least as interpreted by readers and listeners over three millennia, is not only about the lofty good deeds of benevolent and talented leaders. There are also stories about the bad final rulers of dynasties, such as Jie and Zhou. Indeed, Chinese historical writing took on a distinct narrative pattern at an early stage: Dynasties were founded by able, hands-on, benevolent, and capable managers who would set the tone for decades, even centuries, of rule. Eventually, each dynasty would be undone by evil, lax, complacent rulers who were overthrown when they lost the Mandate of Heaven—the cosmic doctrine that anointed or dethroned rulers depending on their virtue and capabilities. We will discuss this theme in detail in the following section, but first let us consider the stories about two rulers who undid the achievements of their forefathers, and have gone down in Chinese history as the very embodiment of flawed and degenerate rulers.

Jie, at the end of the Xia dynasty (traditional dates: 18th century B.C.E.), and Zhou, at the end of the Shang dynasty (traditional dates: 11th century B.C.E.), gave themselves over to excesses and luxuries that shocked their subjects. Both are sometimes described as strong and even potentially heroic figures, but both turned their attention toward sensual and cruel pursuits. Jie had large parks built where he would conduct orgies, with his guests floating about in boats upon ponds of wine, dipping their cups to complete contentment. He also ordered the construction of meat trees from which his guests would carve off hunks of animal flesh. He was said to have an underground palace where even greater wickedness prevailed. He was

---

THE MANDATE OF HEAVEN

This concept, which dates back to at least the Zhou period, was used to legitimize ruling dynasties by noting the connection of rule to the will of heaven. Heaven was said to grace rulers who were able to bring order to "all under heaven" through the combined force of power and virtue. As a concept, the mandate was used to question government practices in times of confusion. The mandate was also employed by conquering armies, which often noted that governments in power had lost their connection to heaven's will. One illuminating case is that of the Manchu conquerors of the Ming dynasty in the 17th century, who claimed that the Ming rulers had squandered their mandate and proposed that they were the restorers of legitimate rule.

---

overthrown and imprisoned until his death, and a brilliant new leader founded the Shang dynasty.

More than six centuries later, Zhou was revealed to be as flawed as Jie. He, too, is described as strong and capable, yet unworthy of the kingship that he inherited. In imitation of Jie, he was said to have wild orgies on ponds of wine. His excesses also took the form of severe punishments, including making accused people walk over greased rods above hot coals. If they fell, they were pronounced guilty. He even shot passersby with arrows, it is said, in order to examine their still-warm organs. Zhou, too, was overthrown, and his severed head was exhibited on a post for all to see.

The exaggeration in these tales is clear enough, but they had a profound effect on political thought in Chinese history that should not be underestimated. The positive examples of Yao, Shun, and Yu combined with the negative examples of Jie and Zhou to provide a powerful template for later philosophers in the Chinese tradition. All a government official had to do to gain the attention of the sovereign was to mention the names of Yao, Shun, or Yu for a positive example, or of Jie or Zhou for a negative one. Even today, these names are synonymous with good government or utter depravity for Chinese readers. The lasting nature of these foundation myths is evident in one of China's greatest works of history, the *Comprehensive Mirror for Aid in Ruling*. In this passage, a government official criticizes the emperor he serves:

[Yang] Fu again sent up a critical memorial, saying: "Yao's abode was of modest thatch, yet the myriad states enjoyed peace. Yu's palace was simple, yet all under heaven happily labored. [For many years, rulers followed the precedent, and there was little extravagance]. Yet Jie built ornamented rooms and ivory halls; Zhou made the spacious Lu Terrace, by means of which he lost the nation. . . . Now among rulers who do not consider their subjects' strength and who follow desires of ear and eye—there has never been one who did not perish. Your majesty should take Yao, Shun, [and] Yu . . . as your standards. The examples of Jie, Zhou . . . should be taken as severe warnings (Sima Guang, 1956, 2307–2308).

Two millennia after these mythical figures were said to have lived, they were used as ways to persuade rulers to act with virtue and compassion. We will now look more closely at the author of the above passage and his approach to China's history.

CHARTING THE RISE AND FALL OF CHINA'S DYNASTIC TRADITION—SIMA GUANG'S PERSPECTIVE

Some of the most prominent themes in China's historical tradition, including in the extensive documentation of its official dynastic histories, are the mechanics of founding, ruling, and, ultimately, losing a dynasty. One of the greatest historians in China's long heritage of writing about the past was Sima Guang (1019–1086), who, in the later decades of the 11th century, compiled a book—*The Comprehensive Mirror for Aid in Ruling*—that is still influential in the present day. Bookstores throughout China still carry it, along with companion volumes focusing on particular stories or issues from the country's past. Sima Guang theorized that a pattern could be identified in the Chinese dynastic tradition, and he sensed that political actions did not take place in a temporal vacuum; how a ruler or minister of government behaved at different stages of dynastic growth, he argued, could profoundly influence the outcome of governmental affairs.

Dynastic Founding

In his preface to an 11th century treatise on historical theory, Sima Guang describes the different skills required of rulers at various stages of a dynastic cycle. Dynastic founders are distinguished by their ability to contend for power in lands that were far from settled. These figures needed to combine bravery and a unifying vision with the managerial skills required to shift the work of the battlefield to the capital. The complex combination of talents found in dynastic founders makes for quite interesting historical reading, on one hand, but also makes for fairly elusive material in terms of deriving lessons about rulers on the other hand. Throughout Chinese history (and in the pages of this book), one can observe the combination of brute force and skillful management of people and troops that attests to Sima's statement about dynastic founding: "If one does not possess knowledge, bravery, and talent . . . one cannot unify *all under heaven*." Still, the great problem for dynastic founders was that the decisions they made during the first several reigns of a dynasty had a powerful influence on later reigns—for good or ill. The power of precedence exerted itself on all dynasties, and only the best rulers knew how to adapt to it.

Dynastic Maintenance

Sima Guang writes about the different sets of talents held by rulers who *maintained* dynasties. Describing such rulers as possessing moderate talents, he adds that they are capable of leading, but must understand the role of political precedents if they are to be successful. He notes that their successes will bring lasting benefits to the dynasty, but that even minute mistakes can have long-term negative consequences.

Having taken shape with regard to official positions, heirs, and basic policies, the dynasty must be preserved, and it is the maintainer's responsibility to preserve it. Sima describes this as a kind of organizational repair job; the attentive maintainer will "patch what is worn and prop what is leaning."

It is easy to see that even with these two figures—the founder and the maintainer, who, from all perspectives, constitute positive pictures of relatively capable rule—the aging of the dynasty or imperial organization profoundly influences the kinds of actions that are required to uphold a thriving empire.

Dynastic Decay, Restoration, and Destruction

The final three talents that Sima Guang describes are linked closely to the aging and decline of a dynasty; the word for "talent" (*cai*) is neutral in Chinese, if not in English. The first is the ruler who begins the process of dynastic decay. Here, Sima Guang paints a picture of the first cracks in proper rule, describing such a personality as "accustomed to ease, negligence, and indolence, he confuses loyalty and evil." In a telling manner made all the more powerful by reading the examples of failure given above (those of Jie and Zhou), Sima describes this type of ruler as one who allows—usually through indifference—his ancestors' achievements to decline and erode until the dynasty is deeply imperiled.

The talents of the restoring ruler are very much in keeping with a deep-seated idea advanced in Chinese political theory from early times to the present day, namely that a declining dynasty is capable of being restored to vigor only if a perceptive ruler and capable ministers combine their talents in service to the dynasty. The restorer's abilities surpass those of his contemporaries, writes Sima Guang. Although raised in the imperial family, he understands the woes of the people. He is a hands-on manager of the officials who report to him. He honors the worthy and is quick to correct his own errors. Only this type of individual is able to return the state to the prime condition of his ancestors.

The final type of ruler that Sima Guang discusses is that of the dynastic destroyer—the individual who brings a downward spiral to its conclusion. Such an individual, writes Sima, is dull and incapable of change; he is unwilling or unable to follow rules or precedent. As opposed to rulers who allow slow decay, or even those who are able to steady a sinking ship of state, the flaws of dynastic destroyers are deeply evident to readers of Chinese history. Individuals of antiquity, such as Jie and Zhou, as well as several later rulers, remain memorable due to the very extremes of their excesses or incompetence.

Sima Guang, who fully embraced the rhetoric of dynastic decline, describes the destroyer as one who merely follows personal desire, ignoring the needs of the political order and the pleas of the people. The destroyer employs sycophants and dismisses those who speak out. Knowing no personal limits to his extravagance, he often pushes people beyond their limits, as well. Sima has no illusions about the fate of the dynasty in the hands of such individuals. If there is a strong enemy, it will destroy him; if there is no enemy, the people themselves will rise up: "If disaster does not appear from without, it will surely arise from within."

Sima Guang clearly has a similar picture in mind as he describes Han's fall in his commentary at the end of the *Comprehensive Mirror's* narrative on C.E. 219:

> From Xiaohe on down, imperial relatives arrogated power, favorites and syco-phants manipulated affairs, rewards and punishments were unregulated, bribery and corruption publicly transacted, virtuous and stupid lumped together, right and wrong turned upside down—this can be called disorder. . . . Unfortunately, the inherited excesses of decay and ruin were intensified by Huan and Ling's be-nighted cruelty; (they protected and nourished the perverse more than flesh and blood, and exterminated the loyal and kind more than brigands and rebels—increasing the *shi's* anger, accumulating rage within the four seas. Thereupon He Jin called men to arms and Dong Zhuo took advantage of discord; men such as Yuan Shao followed suit and created disorder, thereupon causing [imperial] carriages to wander aimlessly. Imperial temples, burial sites, and imperial houses were destroyed and overturned; the people muddied and blackened, the great mandate had fallen and broken, unable to be revived (Sima Guang, 1956: 2174).

This template, crafted by one of China's greatest historians as he looked back over almost 1,500 years, is a useful one for readers of the pages that follow. Chinese history does indeed contain a dizzying array of names, dates, and events. When read in rapid sequence, as a general book requires, it can seem that there is no structure at all. Sima Guang's categories of dynastic rulers will help the reader to understand a very useful traditional perspective on historical change in China. It is not the only one worthy of study, to be sure, but it has represented a time-honored tradition in Chinese historical writing. The founder, the maintainer, the ruler who allows decay to set in, the restorer, and, finally, the destroyer: these five historical types will give the careful reader a window into China's traditional views of its own history.

THE ZHOU DYNASTY (c. 1100–221 B.C.E.)[2]

The information that we have on Chinese history before the year 1000 B.C.E. is tenu-ous at best. We have growing archaeological evidence that suggests a developed calendar, sophisticated agricultural techniques, and a rich Bronze Age culture. By the time we reach the Zhou dynasty in the late second millennium, prior to the Common Era, we begin to see even more solid evidence of political culture, as well as social and economic life.

Early historical works, such as the *Book of History*, give vague accounts of a battle between Shang and Zhou forces, with a great victory occurring in 1122. Legend has it that only 50,000 Zhou troops defeated an army over 10 times that size, and that many Shang troops, unhappy with their degenerate ruler—the bad ruler Zhou mentioned above—joined the winning side. King Wu, the founding ruler responsible for the great victory, died only six years later, with the territory far from completely conquered. King Wu's brother, Tan, better known as the Duke of Zhou, is said to be the creator of the institutions that would lie at the center of the Zhou dynasty. He was fiercely criticized at the time because he served as a regent for young King Cheng, the

*Bronze spear from the Zhou Dynasty.
(Asian Art & Archaeology, Inc./Corbis)*

heir to the throne. Officials within his government attacked him for what they took to be usurpation, and rebelled. The texts tell us that the Duke of Zhou put down the rebellion, solidified the dynasty's rule, created a system of administration, organized life in the palace, and, after seven years, voluntarily gave up power in favor of Cheng, who was by then of age to rule. Having spent those years tutoring the young king on the methods of proper rule, he left the dynasty in capable hands.

This theme of regency is a persistent one in Chinese history. Confucius and other thinkers revered the Duke of Zhou as a leader who embodied the very ideal of regency—serving for a child, teaching the child, using his (or her, in later cases) talents to improve government, and leaving a better political situation in the hands of the heirs. The reality of regency in Chinese history was a good deal different, yet the example of the Duke of Zhou has persisted.

During the Zhou dynasty, China was never a fully integrated state. The eastern half of the territory—and this territory is far smaller than the China one will find on a map today, consisting mainly of the area surrounding the Yellow River—was held by royal family members who paid allegiance to the Zhou rulers. The western areas, which soon became small states, were never completely integrated into the system. In the first 500 years of Zhou rule, they loosely acknowledged the position of the Zhou king, but that acknowledgment quickly disappeared as the system weakened after 500 B.C.E. Both Chinese and Western historians have often referred to the Zhou as a feudal system. Although the term is a problematic one when referring to East Asian history, there was a connection between territorial lords and the retainers who served them. For the territorial lords, who were figuratively granted their territories by the

REGENCY

The very model for the ideal of regency in Chinese history, the Duke of Zhou was said to have ruled on behalf of little King Cheng, still a minor, until he came of age. The duke's motives were questioned and his rule contested, yet later texts praise him for his resolve in preserving the imperial order. As hazy as the documents might be as historical records, they speak to the ideal of governing on behalf of the dynasty until a legitimate heir can rule. Among the many regents in Chinese history who failed to restore the heirs to power and took power for themselves were Wang Mang (1st century C.E.), Empress Wu (7th–8th centuries C.E.), and the Empress Dowager, Cixi (19th–20th centuries C.E.).

Zhou, there was also the expectation that they accept the Zhou king and revere the ancestral spirits of the Zhou rulers.

These already tenuous ties between Zhou rule and the small territorial lords loosened in the centuries following the dynasty's founding. Over the course of seven centuries, warfare would reduce more than 100 small states to a handful of larger states by the third century B.C.E. Although the Zhou kings would continue to rule, as if by default, each territorial lord was the master of his own state. Diplomacy became an art that would endure throughout Chinese history. Works from the period note increasingly bloody conflicts between the so-called Warring States during the third and second centuries B.C.E. War was perpetuated because of territorial conflicts, but also in pursuit of a broader good; even the earliest historical writings speak of the ideal of a unified China.

THE QIN CENTRALIZATION (221–206 B.C.E.)

The unification of China under the power of the Qin state in 221 B.C.E. initiated 22 centuries of centralized imperial government over 8 major dynasties. Although the Zhou, even at its height, was never more than a loose alliance of powers under the nominal rule of the Zhou king, the Qin established the pattern for central rule in China. Indeed, central government under the rule of a single dynasty remained a powerful, though often distant, ideal, even during periods of division. Under the unifying force of the First Emperor, Qin armies defeated each of their rivals and initiated reforms that abolished the decentralized structure of the Zhou and extended the state's influence. The Qin reorganized the empire into 36 administrative divisions, which were in turn subdivided into counties, with all levels ultimately accountable to the central government—a system that persisted in its broad form throughout much of the imperial period.

The Qin also initiated a more central control through the standardization of scripts, weights, measures, and currency, and began the process of building thousands of miles of imperial highways and waterways to connect China's various regions,

A portion of a buried terracotta army, part of the mausoleum of Chinese Emperor Qinshi Huangdi. (Lihui/Dreamstime.com)

including work on northern fortifications that would, more than a millennium later, be part of the Great Wall. The process of standardization and centralization would play a role, both practically and symbolically, in later periods, as the Qin unification became the model of central government in Chinese history.

King Zheng succeeded to the throne in 247 B.C.E. and led the state to victories over each of the six other Warring States. He is known in history as Qinshi Huangdi, a flowery and imposing title meant to separate his new position from that of earlier kings. The name can be translated as "First Grand Emperor of Qin," and echoes a title previously reserved for the Yellow Emperor (Huangdi). By calling himself the First Emperor, he assumed an endless perpetuation of the Legalist machine that he and his advisers had created.

Because his rule was extremely harsh, and because he singled out for criticism and punishment scholars of the Confucian (*ru*) school—whose descendants would eventually write the histories of China—he is depicted as a cruel tyrant in traditional histories. By almost any standard, the First Emperor was a complex individual, and his dynasty ended abruptly after his death in 210 B.C.E. Yet his mark on Chinese history was indelible; his centralization of political power became the dominant pattern of later Chinese history and created a model for the state that persists to this day.

The centralization of the Qin state eliminated the decentralized nature of Zhou rule. The Qin abolished all of the old states and erected an entirely new administrative

Qin Dynasty coins. (Loveasmoke/Dreamstime.com)

and bureaucratic structure. Government centralization, however, also required the standardization of customs and institutions. The regionalism that flourished in the last centuries of the Zhou was characterized by diversity in such matters as weights and measures, coinage, scripts, and even axle widths (which were very important for the creation of a new infrastructure of dirt roads). The Qin government prescribed new universal standards in all of these areas and punished those who transgressed them.

The standardization of the vastly diverse schools of thought that distinguished early Chinese history was another challenge. The Qin prohibited the philosophical disputation that had marked the three preceding centuries, and launched attacks on those who (as did Confucius and Mencius centuries before) praised the past or criticized the present policy. Although the story is perhaps apocryphal, the burning of the books and the burying of the scholars is important in Chinese history, if only for the fact that it was spoken of as truth for two millennia. In 213 B.C.E., all previous writings were burned, with the exception of official Qin records and treatises on agriculture, medicine, and technical matters. Because many scholars—who developed their skills in the spirit of the diverse Zhou intellectual culture—could not accept the new policies, the First Emperor reportedly executed almost 500 of them and buried them together as a warning to future generations.

Finally, the Qin centralization was a time of great construction. Roads were built to connect every part of the empire with the new capital near modern-day Xi'an. Waterways were improved, and irrigation systems (using remarkably sophisticated technology) and canals were constructed. Such massive projects were possible largely because of the extremely harsh enforcement of Qin laws, which made hundreds of convicts into forced laborers.

One of the greatest mistakes made in studying the Qin is to focus only on the practical aspects of centralization. Although the First Emperor was a tough-minded ruler, he was also preoccupied with his own mortality. After surviving three assassination attempts, he became obsessed with notions of immortality and expended a great deal of effort seeking ways to lengthen his life and even to discover seemingly mythical islands, such as Penglai in the eastern seas, where immortal bird people were said to live.

After the First Emperor's death in 210 B.C.E.(while traveling in search of new elixirs), the Qin degenerated into a fight between factions of his lieutenants. It is somewhat ironic that the Qin order was largely undone by the severity of its own strictures—the very laws that had shaped Legalist philosophy but were administered, perhaps too strictly, by the managers of the Qin state. Another, perhaps apocryphal, story has been told for 22 centuries to describe Qin's fall: the spark that ignited the revolt was a commoner named Chen She who, having been put in charge of a group of laborers, was delayed by heavy rains. Under Qin law, the penalties for delay included death, with no consideration of extenuating circumstances. Chen is said to have persuaded his followers to rebel against the oppression rather than be put to death. Rebellions erupted throughout Qin, and by 206 B.C.E., the Qin order was destroyed.

THE HAN DYNASTY (206 B.C.E–C.E. 220)

The Han dynasty succeeded the Qin when Liu Bang, a commoner, reunited the empire in 202 B.C.E. after four years of fighting. Building upon the strengths of the Qin unification but carefully backing away from its excesses, Liu Bang and his successors oversaw 400 years of central rule. The Han dynasty cemented the institutional patterns that would define the Chinese state for the next two millennia.

Liu Bang, better known by his posthumous title of Han Gaozu ("lofty ancestor of Han"), was the first of two commoners in Chinese history to ascend the throne. For that reason, and because he retained, even as emperor, his forthright qualities— including speaking in what contemporaries described as crude, spontaneous language that shocked refined courtiers—he has always been one of the most celebrated Chinese emperors in the popular imagination. He was an astute ruler, though. Gaozu took the role of advisers in the governing process seriously and sought to heed their advice. In addition, in reaction to the Legalist excesses of the Qin and in accordance with the teachings of Mencius, Gaozu and his ministers softened the Qin message by asserting that the government was designed to help the populace.

One concession that he made was to grant most of the eastern half of the empire to his followers as a reward for their efforts in the great battles that occurred between 206 and 202 B.C.E. In some ways, this was a prudent decision that reflected the fact that Qin's level of integration was unrealistic, but it created the potential for long-term problems. The Han integration did indeed lighten the burdens on people, but the system showed considerable weakness after half a century. By then, the harsh memories of Qin's rule had faded over several generations, and Emperor Wu (r. 141– 87 B.C.E.), who ruled for a longer period than any emperor until the 17th century, saw the opportunity to more thoroughly solidify central rule than his predecessors.

Emperor Wu was paid a yearly tribute in horses by the Huns and the fierce tribes of the west after their defeat by the armies of the Han dynasty. Horses were highly prized by the Han dynasty because of the major role they played in battle. (Corel)

To begin, Emperor Wu centralized and extended imperial authority in domestic affairs, reappropriating the territories Gaozu had given his followers. He also dealt strongly with merchants who had taken advantage of the Han state's relaxed economic policies to control great fortunes, which were mostly untaxed, in iron, salt, liquor, and grain. Emperor Wu also created the ever-normal granary system in order to regulate the supply of grain through good years and bad.

Equally adept in foreign relations, Emperor Wu asserted Han strength over the northern and southern peoples who bordered the state. The greatest showdown was with the Xiongnu nomads to the north and west, who would continually threaten Han power in subsequent decades. The Han strategy included marriage alliances, diplomacy, and warfare. Although Emperor Wu was quite successful in his dealings with northern powers, the reality of outsiders in the Chinese historical picture would linger for 22 centuries, up to the present day. Chinese political history needs to be read as an ongoing, and often unfriendly, relationship with surrounding peoples who were at times strong enough to take control of China itself.

Emperor Wu's reign represented the height of Han power. Later rulers continued the general domestic and foreign policies instituted during his reign, yet few of his successors stood out. They do, however, reflect an important problem in Chinese rule: passing power from fathers to sons created the very real possibility that successors would be coddled as they grew up in the court, and unable to deal adequately with the problems of the larger world. The system benefited when a charismatic and powerful figure such as Emperor Wu emerged, but the pool for such talent was so narrow that mediocrity often became the norm.

At the beginning of the Common Era, factional infighting characterized court life, and there was economic turmoil in the countryside. Some advisers became convinced that the Han had lost the Mandate of Heaven, and prevailed upon an upright court official named Wang Mang to take over the regency for a child emperor. Wang was seen by many as a latter-day Duke of Zhou, whose rule was intended in every way to continue all that was good about the Han. He declared his own dynasty (Xin, "new"), and sought to reinstitute Zhou dynasty institutions and policies that, in his mind, marked a better era in Chinese history. He organized government with Zhou titles, changed the coinage system, and put into practice, as he saw it, a genuine form of Confucianism. In the year C.E. 9, Wang took the throne.

Wang's reign was a disaster of such staggering proportion that it is difficult to see why he and his ideas might have appealed to his contemporaries. Wang Mang remains an odd figure in Chinese history. Later historians reviled him as a usurper who destroyed Han's four centuries of rule. His reign was an attempt to simplify life and rule, and to return to a more innocent age. Nonetheless, his reforms ultimately antagonized all classes of society, and even nature seemed (in true cosmological Chinese fashion) to vent its displeasure. Changes in the weather patterns produced poor harvests. Drought ensued, and then the Yellow River flooded, eventually changing its course and killing thousands. Famine followed, and vagrants formed into bands of rebels, which included the prominent Red Eyebrows movement. In C.E. 23, rebels took the palace, murdering Wang Mang. The Han dynasty was restored to members of the Liu clan by C.E. 25, and the Wang interregnum became a cautionary divide between the Former Han and Later Han.

The restorers of the Han dynasty, Emperor Guangwu (r. C.E. 25–57) and his immediate successors, were strong rulers under whom the Han regained a considerable amount of the reputation, strength, and territory that it had held in the Former Han. The natural disasters and agricultural devastation that occurred under Wang's reign gradually abated and, during the first century of the Common Era, the population and economy rebounded. One of the most important themes in Chinese political thought is that of restoration, and the Later Han was a model for it. Following the Han precedent of domestic and international strength embodied by Emperor Wu, Guangwu and his followers reasserted military domination over the Xiongnu to the north, rebuilt roads, and eased the pressures on farmers. Amid the general optimism and excitement over state Confucianism, Guangwu created schools and academies for the moral and practical education of children.

In the first centuries of imperial rule, one can readily observe a pattern of unity and division that echoes the famous first lines of the epic Ming dynasty novel *The Romance of Three Kingdoms*: "All under heaven, long divided must unite; long united, must divide." Even within the history of a single dynasty, one can perceive patterns of founding, restoration, and decline. In the second century of the Common Era, that decline took root, eventually ending the four centuries of Han rule. The political deterioration began with a now familiar structural flaw in the ruling system: the succession of a minor to the throne. Palace intrigue and factional infighting colored the struggles for power, and this pattern of court politics persisted into the third century. Similarly, natural disasters (another constant in Chinese history) inspired peasant rebellions by the 170s and 180s, and Daoist-inspired cults, such as the Yellow Turbans and Five Pecks of Rice bands, wrought havoc in the countryside. Generals were called to support the Han and, even though they restored order by 190, the pattern of regional warlordism had been set. A Han emperor would remain on the throne for 30 more years, but real power had passed to a series of generals and territorial leaders.

General Dong Zhuo seized the capital, located near modern-day Luoyang, in 190, deposed the emperor, set up his chosen ruler, and murdered the empress dowager—the emperor's mother—imperial princes, and palace eunuchs. In this climate of intrigue and open warfare, Dong Zhuo was unable to maintain power; another general, Cao Cao, who styled himself as the protector of the empire, instead controlled the Han. Upon his death in 220, his son Cao Pi (r. 220–226) accepted the abdication of the Han emperor and established a new kingdom called Wei. After four centuries of rule that later ages saw as a model of imperial greatness, the Han came to a quiet end.

THE PERIOD OF DIVISION (220–589)

The late second-century rebellions and warlordism signaled the start of what would be four centuries of division—the longest period of time that the empire was to remain divided in subsequent Chinese history. Because of the rise and fall of kingdoms with little hope of anything beyond regional power, the period has traditionally been interpreted as something akin to a Middle Ages of Chinese history. It is vitally important to note, however, the tremendous social and cultural changes that occurred during this period, changes that would play a significant role in China for centuries.

Cao Cao and his successors were never able to reunite the empire. His most significant attempt occurred at the Battle of Red Cliffs in 208, where a combined force of his major rivals, Sun Quan and Liu Bei, defeated him. For the next 60 years, the kingdom was divided, as many texts of the time described it, "like three legs of a tripod" between these men and their states, Wei, Wu, and Shu Han. The period has been immortalized in the *Three Kingdoms* tales, and Chinese readers and listeners have known the major figures through that novel, as well as through popular drama and storytelling. Today, one can even find numerous comic books and video games highlighting the period and its personalities.

Despite Wei's struggles with the other kingdoms, a later family usurped the throne in 265 and changed the dynastic name to Jin. For a generation, China was united, but it was a tenuous consolidation at best, and the territory it controlled was much smaller than the Han dynasty at its height. By the beginning of the fourth century, factional infighting, assassination, and abdications characterized court politics, and the regional patterns of social and economic organization that had defined the Zhou almost 1,000 years earlier became entrenched. By the fourth century, in fact, what we now call China was very much a society dominated by large, landowning families, each with tenant farmers and, often, private armies.

The Xiongnu and other northern groups took advantage of the uncertainty and moved southward, killing the Jin emperor. By 316, the Jin's fragile unification was completely devastated, and for more than two centuries China was divided, north and south, into two very different social, economic, and political groups. Widening northern and southern cultural differences are among the most important and lasting effects of this period. Although southern groups made sporadic attempts to recover lost territories, they cast themselves, for the most part, as the preservers of the center of traditional civilization, even though that center had moved far southward into the marshy lands that had earlier been held by aboriginal groups. These aboriginal groups were slowly absorbed into the mainstream.

The period of division is one of the most challenging eras a student confronts in studying China. The political narrative is disjointed, and following it is so complex, with such meager results, that it is difficult to talk about anything beyond the most general of themes. Even so, the cultural heritage is remarkably rich. The era provided a setting in which Confucian, Daoist, and Buddhist thought would merge—although never without tension—throughout later Chinese history (this is covered in detail in the Religion and Thought chapter). The unified realms that would follow would be markedly influenced by the profound changes that China experienced during almost four centuries of political division.

THE SUI DYNASTY (581–617)

The centuries of reestablished unity under the Sui and Tang dynasties ushered in a re-integration of the vastly changed northern and southern territories. The Sui founder, Wendi (r. 581–604), was born into a part-nomad northern family. He had the difficult task of reuniting north and south through a centralized legal code and governmental institutions, as well as new roads and waterways—tasks that call to mind the Qin's short-lived centralization seven centuries earlier. An able administrator, Wendi combined a skillful blending of the Confucian, Daoist, and Buddhist traditions with superior military strength to subdue the southern states by the end of the 580s. Because for many decades there had been no great wars or rebellions of the kind that marked the later Han, both northern and southern China had prospered during the sixth century, even as their cultures grew further and further apart. Wendi's greatest success was to reconnect north and south, not only through a new infrastructure, but also by connecting scholars and thinkers who represented families that had become regionalized in the previous centuries of division.

Wendi rebuilt a rudimentary canal network to link the capital in Chang'an with the Yellow River, and he improved transportation and irrigation systems throughout the realm. This included the initiation of a project to link the Yellow and Yangzi Rivers by what would become known as the Grand Canal, which represented a new political connection between the regions. It also allowed the thriving wealth of the south to be shared more readily with the north through expanded trade networks. The Grand Canal, of course, also made the much faster readying of troops to the south possible, which helped to maintain order in a fragile political situation.

This stability collapsed under the rule of Wendi's son, Yangdi (r. 604–617), whose reign represents a classic example from Chinese historical writing of a two-generation good first ruler, bad last ruler pattern. Yangdi is remembered, along with

Detail from Portraits of Thirteen Emperors *showing Wendi, who reigned until 604.*
(Burstein Collection/Corbis)

the totalitarian excesses of the First Emperor and the debacle of Wang Mang's reign, as one of the worst rulers in Chinese history. He had many of the state-building and megalomaniacal qualities seen in the First Emperor. Yangdi built new roads and led troops on ambitious campaigns as far away as Korea and Vietnam, but was also obsessed with building lavish new palaces and taxing the people through corvée labor—unpaid labor on state-sponsored projects—and military service. In the traditional histories, he is also said to have led a life of licentiousness that rivaled even Jie and Zhou. Domestic revolts similar to those that occurred in the last years of Qin and Han sprang up throughout the empire.

A general named Li Yuan was ordered to quell the disturbances (following the now familiar pattern of relying on outside help to regain order once the center could not hold), and Yangdi fled to southern China. Li Yuan quickly broke ties with the Sui, set up an heir in Chang'an, and, after Yangdi's assassination by a courtier in 618, established his own dynasty, the Tang. It seems that the Sui dynasty, much like the Qin before it, was overwhelmed by the internal and external demands of reinventing central rule, and was unable to reign for more than two generations before giving way to a much more stable political order.

THE TANG DYNASTY (618–906)

The Tang dynasty, not unlike the Han before it, gained control of China during the confusion of the last years of a short-lived dynasty. The Tang founders inherited Sui's centralizing achievements, and quickly moved to solidify the state and display their military strength to the always problematic north. In both geographic expanse and cultural achievements, the Tang dynasty has traditionally been regarded among Chinese as the height of imperial China and a lasting model for later periods. From its capital in Chang'an, which became one of the richest and most cosmopolitan cities the world would see for many centuries, the Tang slowly solidified a bureaucratic structure that would persist throughout the imperial period and began to expand its military influence in all directions, including into Vietnam, Korea, and much of Central Asia.

The Tang imperial family represented the tensions that China had seen during the centuries of disunion. On one hand, the family claimed descent from a famous Han general, linking itself symbolically to that great dynasty and its ideals. On the other hand, the family had intermarried with alien nobility to such an extent that by that time it could be considered ethnically Chinese only in part. This kind of intermarriage and strategic descent claim characterized northern families during the period of disunion, as well as during the Sui and Tang eras.

The Tang dynasty took shape under the vigorous rule of Li Yuan's son, who is known to readers of history as Tang Taizong (r. 626–649). While he and his father were fighting on behalf of the Sui, northern China swarmed with dozens of rebellious movements. Taizong solidified the north by the year 624 and eventually accepted the abdication of his father in order to rule in his own right. Although the beginnings of his rule appear somewhat shady, there is no doubt that Taizong was enormously successful in building upon the centralizing drive of Sui. He practiced openness toward Buddhism and Daoism while reinstituting a strong government-sponsored Confucianism. His most famous work, an edict written for his successors, notes that fostering education, welcoming advice, and choosing able subordinates were the key elements of good rule.

The solidification of Tang rule continued unabated under Taizong's son, Gaozong (r. 649–683). He continued the military campaigns and development of key economic and legal institutions begun by his father and grandfather, but it is in his last years that one of the strangest periods of Chinese history began. He sent for a certain Lady Wu, one of his father's concubines, who had retired —following imperial regulations—after Taizong's death. The traditional histories state that Gaozong allowed her to conspire (and murder) her way to the position of empress and when Gaozong's health failed, to exercise power in his place, just as a regent would.

When Gaozong died in 683, Empress Wu kept her power by placing successive sons on the throne, finally taking power for herself in 690, the only woman in Chinese history to hold the title of emperor. She proclaimed a new dynasty with the Zhou name and ruled until 705, when she abdicated power in her eighties. Traditional historians have condemned Empress Wu as a ruthless usurper. Although it seems clear that she manipulated the institutions of government and staffed the palace with her favorites, it is hard to see how she let domestic or foreign affairs decline under her rule.

The Tang realized its height, as well as the seeds of its demise, during the reign of Emperor Xuanzong (r. 713–755). The early decades of his reign witnessed perhaps the greatest cultural displays that China had ever known, as well as capable and

The Flight of the Tang Emperor Minghuang to Shu. *Chinese painting in the Tang blue-and-green landscape style, depicting the Emperor Xuanzong, or Minghuang, the imperial concubine Yang Guifei, and the emperor's entourage when fleeing to Sichuan from the An Lushan Rebellion of 755. (Werner Forman/Corbis)*

efficient government machinery. The capital of Chang'an became a magnet for travelers on the Silk Road and beyond. It was a place of elegance and even decadence that can best be represented by the emperor's 100 trained horses, who danced, with teacups in their mouths and wearing vibrant yellow halters, to music played by court musicians. From dancing horses and the splendid poetry of Li Bo and Du Fu, to polo matches and hawking, the Tang's eighth-century elegance masked the increasing bureaucratic and military weakness of the state.

The later years of Xuanzong's reign saw the solid framework of the first century of Tang rule undone by an emperor and bureaucracy meandering aimlessly through more than a decade of a leadership vacuum. This resulted in the command of frontier armies being turned over to generals of questionable loyalty, as well as palace intrigue on a monumental scale. Although traditional historians point out the familiar villains of eunuchs, maternal relatives, and (in this case) a lovely concubine named Yang Guifei, it is clear that a combination of misrule and larger social and economic changes contributed to the mid-Tang crisis. These strains came to a head when An Lushan (d. 757), a Central Asian general, rebelled, leading his troops toward Luoyang and then Chang'an, while Xuanzong and his court fled southward into Sichuan in one of the most famous exoduses in Chinese history.

The An Lushan Rebellion that took place from 755–763 was extremely destructive, and although the Tang dynasty's power was eventually restored, the state was severely weakened over the subsequent 150 years, experiencing increasing difficulties with northern groups and ineffective central institutions. The rebellion's political significance notwithstanding, it is noteworthy to Chinese historians because of its relationship to very important changes in Chinese society. Many historians note that long-term changes—from the suppression of Buddhism to the weakening of early Tang institutions and rapid population growth—are linked to the rich social and economic ferment of the mid-eighth century in the aftermath of the rebellion. As the central government weakened, institutional checks on landlordism and commerce were impossible to maintain. The aristocratic dividing line that had separated the great families of China since the Han dynasty was undermined by waves of social and economic change; the ensuing imperial age would see a vastly different social order.

THE FIVE DYNASTIES (907–959) AND THE KINGDOMS OF LIAO, XI XIA, AND JIN (c. 900–1234)

The slow demise of Tang was abruptly broken by a series of rebellions that led to another period of division, the Five Dynasties. China was again divided between north and south. What are traditionally termed the Ten Kingdoms rose and fell in succession in the south. Each state lacked the strength to consolidate the south, much less unify the empire. Each also modeled itself on Tang-style imperial institutions, but generally enjoyed peace and the fading shadow of late Tang culture. In the north, five dynasties rose and fell, with each lasting only a handful of years. These northern regimes had little time for court culture, and nothing like the means to support them—a far cry from the poetic and artistic extravagance of Xuanzong's early reign. Far more than the dynasties in the south, they single-mindedly concentrated on maintaining what was, in fact, a very fragile military supremacy over other northern leaders and frontier groups, who were amassing increasing strength on China's northern borders. Indeed, it is to these northern states that we must look for much of the flavor of late Chinese political history.

Northern peoples, often referred to by the Chinese as "barbarians," played an enormous role in Chinese history. Throughout the Five Dynasties and the subsequent Song dynasty, non-Chinese states to the northeast and northwest would deeply influence Chinese life. The Liao kingdom to the northeast and the Xi Xia state to the northwest, whose populations were only a fraction of that of China Proper, combined indigenous political and cultural patterns with the Chinese model for state organization during the 10th and 11th centuries. The dynamics of Sinification, or "becoming Chinese," are extremely complex, and hardly a one-way process, as is sometimes intimated in descriptions of cultural contact. On one hand, the Qidan people adopted Chinese practices of ancestor worship, used the Chinese language in official government work, and adopted Chinese-style court regalia. On the other hand, they retained their own tribal organization and maintained their own distinctive styles of food and dress outside of court life. The Xi Xia state of the Tangut people declared its independence from Song in 1038, and its ruler declared himself an emperor on even footing with the Chinese. Its people developed an innovative writing system and adopted Buddhism as their state religion.

Although the Liao and Xi Xia states played a major role in Chinese life during the Northern Song dynasty, neither could withstand the superior power of another northern people, the Ruzhen (often written as *Jurchen*), who created a Jin state that would both annihilate and drive the Song southward below the Yangzi River in the 12th century. From their northern roots in what would later be known as Manchuria, the Ruzhen were unified by a series of charismatic leaders who linked their ability to conquer large regions and the administrative capabilities that were required to rule them.

In spite of all their military power, the core problem for non-Chinese states was how to rule a large land mass populated by Chinese subjects—as many as a hundred million during the 11th century—without losing the cultural identity and nomadic hardiness that helped them to gain power in the first place. We will discuss the particular difficulties associated with this problem when we examine the Mongols, but it is important to understand from the outset that conquering large swaths of China and maintaining rule for long periods of time were fundamentally different tasks, and, in many cases, they were impossible for non-Chinese groups to master. The staccato pattern of northern groups conquering China and then failing to hold it would be seen, in various forms, throughout China's next 10 centuries.

THE NORTHERN AND SOUTHERN SONG (960–1279)

The Song founder, Zhao Kuangyin (r. 960–976), was a capable young general in the 950s who, in a now-familiar pattern, eventually took the throne in place of a child emperor. He and his advisers felt the need for hands-on military leadership in the unstable north, and he was prevailed upon to declare a new dynasty. Creating a lasting political order from the unstable northern and southern politics of the 10th century presented serious challenges for Zhao, who would later be known by his imperial name of Song Taizu, or "Grand Ancestor of Song."

Song Taizu's first priority was solid control in the north. In a break with the policies of previous dynastic founders, he provided his own military supporters with "retirement plans," and thus weakened the possibility of resentment, mutiny, and rebellion. He also replaced regional officials, whose loyalties were not always reliable in times of discord, with officials under his own direction. Finally, he moved the most capable units of the regional armies to his palace army, and put them entirely under his own command. In this manner, he created a military structure that consisted of a powerful, professional army that was under his direct control.

Taizu also expanded the civil service and entrusted government administration to scholar-officials who, although immensely talented, had no power bases of their own. Like other founders who sought to create order after periods of division, he also worked to solidify the infrastructure and create a more central process of collecting taxes and administering local government. Through these actions, Taizu concentrated power in the imperial position, which would have a significant influence on Chinese history.

After solidifying the north, Taizu needed to reincorporate the southern kingdoms. In campaigns launched during the 960s and 970s, he subjugated all but one kingdom, the aboriginal state of southern Zhao, which retained its independence throughout the dynasty. Song Taizu died at the relatively young age of 48, with centralization only partially completed. His younger brother, Song Taizong (r. 976–997), continued the process, moving to solidify the borders (which still constituted a good deal less total territory than Tang at its height) and reunite the lands that were traditionally considered Chinese.

The Liao state offered tribute and became vassals of the Song for a short time. The Xi Xia state, in contrast, successfully held off Taizong's military campaigns. Thereafter, he concentrated on building defenses, and this defensive stance would characterize the Song for the remainder of the dynasty. In fact, many readers of Chinese history are disturbed by the extent to which, during the 11th century in particular, the Song created peace agreements that appear to be very much like tribute payments to what they regarded as barbarian states in order to stave off the possibility of warfare. These gifts began as 100,000 ounces of silver and 200,000 bolts of silk every year. The numbers were later raised in both categories by another 100,000 units, creating what some considered a strain on the economy and limiting the Song court's diplomatic possibilities.

In spite of military tensions, the Song enjoyed internal peace and prosperity during the 11th century, and one can observe growth on several levels. To begin, as part of the long-term changes outlined above, the population reached, by some estimates, 100 million by 1100. New agricultural methods were developed, and a much more sophisticated set of commercial links characterized the growing communication between north and south. Cities, some with more than a million inhabitants, comprised the sites of an elaborate urban culture. A complex system of examinations that led to official positions became the primary vehicle for social mobility and profoundly shaped an increasingly fluid set of class lines. Earlier examination systems in China had benefited land-owning families. The new examination system brought shifting fortunes to many aristocratic families since they were unable to perpetuate power as they had in the past. Finally, the development of printing would have enormous consequences in Chinese history.

Eleventh-century China was immensely prosperous, and that state of affairs would continue as long as the standoff with the northern states lasted. Keeping the indigenous states appeased with payments worked fairly well as long as these states lacked the strength to conquer in their own right. Similarly, the northern states were not united into a single fighting force, and the division worked to the Song's advantage in the short term. This changed with the Ruzhen (*Jurchen*) people's proclamation of a new state, the Jin, in 1115. By 1126, Jin had marched quickly southward, laying siege to the capital. The Song emperor, Huizong, abdicated, and the court moved south. Diplomacy continued for two years, but on terms that were impossibly difficult for the Song to meet. Finally, in 1127, the Ruzhen returned, took the capital again, and carried hundreds of members of the imperial family into captivity.

What remained of the Song dynasty was a distinctly different and much smaller territory, with its capital based in Hangzhou, on the shores of West Lake. The move

---

NORTH-SOUTH CULTURAL DIVISION

Early in Chinese history, what we refer to as Chinese civilization developed in the north in the area surrounding the Yellow River Valley. What we today call southern China was then perceived as a marshy land of barbarian tribes. Even during the first integration of the empire during the Qin and Han dynasties, the north and south were separate. Over the course of two millennia of imperial history, however, there were several periods during which northerners were compelled to move southward from their native homes and begin new lives. Southerners, especially those who traveled for scholarly or economic purposes, often made lives in the north during times of relative peace. There is a vast collection of literature and storehouse of anecdotes in China on the cultures of north and south, with themes ranging from comments on food preferences and weather patterns to pointed personality stereotypes.

---

to a new southern capital marks the dividing line between Northern (960–1127) and Southern (1127–1279) Song. The Song gave up almost all territories north of the Yangzi River, including the Yellow River drainage area that—both practically and symbolically—figured prominently in early Chinese history and culture. They also accepted status as what amounts to a vassal state of Jin, and continued their high payments of silver and silk.

Throughout the almost two centuries of the Southern Song dynasty, the territory under Chinese control was but a fraction of the great dynasties of the past. Emperors of this period were entangled in powerful factional struggles and were too politically weak to create unity at their own courts, much less in the broader arenas required to retake the north. Although the Southern Song was an era of great cultural change, making significant contributions to Chinese philosophy, painting, and poetry, the political story would be defined by reaction to the northern states, and it is to the most prominent of these that we now turn.

THE MONGOLS AND THE YUAN (1234–1368)

Few outsiders have had as powerful an impact upon China as the Mongols in the 13th and 14th centuries. The development of the Mongolian empire under the leadership of Chinggis (Genghis) Khan, and the conquests of much of Europe and Asia, are a significant part of world history. The Mongols annihilated the Jin in 1234, and completed their conquest of the Southern Song in 1279. In the four decades between these dates, the Mongols controlled northern China and solidified their rule of, as the Chinese called their territory, *all under heaven.*

In the early 13th century, a young man named Temüjin led forces that defeated numerous northern tribes. In 1206, as a result of his skillful diplomacy and warfare, he was named paramount ruler of the Mongol peoples as Chinggis Khan. His Mongol troops, led by hereditary leaders trained for lives in the saddle, could

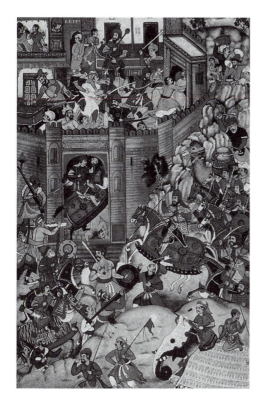

Scene depicting the capture of a Chinese town by Genghis Khan from the 14th-century Persian manuscript Jami al-Tavarikh. *After coming to power in 1206, Genghis launched an invasion of China. It took 20 years to gain complete control of the Jin dynasty. (Corel)*

cover what seemed to European and Chinese observers to be incredible distances. They lived on plunder in raiding to the east and south. It has often been noted that the Mongols' psychological warfare was as effective as their legendary fighting abilities. Stories of terror and devastation preceded them wherever they went, sapping the fighting strength of the mostly agricultural peoples that they conquered. "Man's greatest joy," Chinggis Khan was said to have declared, "is in victory—in conquering one's enemies, pursuing them, depriving them of their possessions, making their loved ones weep, riding on their horses, and embracing their wives and daughters."

During the 13th century, Mongol forces steadily defeated the northern kingdoms before moving on to their conquest of the Southern Song, which fell in 1279. The first Mongol ruler of a unified China was Khubilai (Kublai) Khan, Chinggis Khan's grandson (r. 1260–1294). After an early succession crisis, Khubilai Khan asserted his power over his brothers and various generals, moving the capital to Beijing and declaring a new dynasty named Yuan ("beginning"). Unlike his imperial Chinese predecessors, Khubilai followed his subjugation of the southern regions with aggressive fighting overseas, proclaiming his rule as far as India and Korea, and was hindered only in his attempt to take Japan.

Mongol rule in China combined strong military control with an attempt to negotiate the Chinese bureaucracy. Mongols occupied top posts, but required assistance

REMONSTRANCE

Remonstrance can best be described in the context of Chinese political thought as the *duty* for a junior member of a hierarchy—a son, a government minister, or a young friend—to counsel the senior member of the hierarchy—a father, an emperor, or an older friend—toward proper conduct. Remonstrance is a built-in check on a system that presumes hierarchical leadership. The *Classic of Filial Piety* states that a son *must* correct a father who is doing wrong, and a government minister *must* correct a ruler. Chinese philosophy and political theory engaged the questions throughout the imperial period, with various authors expressing subtle differences in emphasis between forcibly stopping bad behavior and gently persuading without intervention. The classic example, seen in countless poems, plays, and histories, is the remonstrating court official who, upon witnessing misconduct, drags his coffin into court before criticizing the emperor. Knowing that he will be punished, he nonetheless performs his duty. Although the image may seem quaint and literary, one need only think of the lone protestor in front of tanks near Tian'anmen in 1989 to realize how powerful the ideal of remonstrance can be in Chinese culture.

from Chinese officials. Those Chinese who did serve were clearly subordinate to their Mongol leaders and the examination system itself, long considered to be a fair assessment tool of native ability, was altered to produce regional and ethnic quotas that reflected Mongol priorities. Yet under the Mongols, Beijing was a cosmopolitan center, with many foreign travelers and diplomats in the Khan's service—Central Asians, Persians, Arabs, and Russians. The city under Mongol rule is celebrated in the writings attributed to Marco Polo, who mentioned strange, long noodles, black rocks used for fuel, and money made of paper, as well as cities so large that their commercial centers alone would dwarf entire municipalities in his homeland.

The extremely centralized and autocratic government of the Mongols strengthened a trend that had begun with the Song dynasty founder, three centuries earlier: the growth of a strong imperial institution with the potential to be much more brutal and single-minded than any institutions seen in the early empire. The ideal of remonstrance, of a government minister opposing a reflective and understanding emperor (lauded in early writings), was an increasingly quaint ideal.

As the Mongols entered the 14th century, the economy increasingly suffered from corruption and a government that could not reach the lower levels of the administration in an effective manner. Landlord power over tenant farmers became increasingly strong, and economic life was again regionalized in numerous ways. Many Chinese were reduced to the status of tenant farmers—or even to slave status—during this time. The cumulative effect over half a century was the loss of the countryside and, eventually, confusion in the capital. Even the Mongol neglect of agriculture, irrigation, and water control seemed to conspire against them in a form of a series of natural disasters in the 1340s that culminated in the Yellow River breaking its dikes and changing course. The Mongol rulers, whose terrifying fighting abilities combined with the Chinese notion of the Mandate of Heaven to thoroughly occupy China a century earlier, were undone by the very same mandate. Heaven seemingly renounced its will, causing rivers to flood and people to die. For all of their initial terror, the Mongols could not rule all of China for even a century.

THE MING DYNASTY (1368–1644)

Chinese peasants rose in a series of loosely connected rebellions throughout the 1350s, as the Mongols lost control of southern China. In that same region, a Chinese commoner named Zhu Yuanzhang gradually linked his armies with an increasingly wide array of disgruntled groups, and having consolidated the Yangzi River drainage area, declared a new dynasty, the Ming ("bright" or "luminous") in 1368. As with all such foundings, much work remained to be done, and it was not until several years later that the last Yuan emperor was driven back into the steppe of Mongolia.

As the first commoner in 1,500 years to ascend the imperial throne, the man who would become known by the title of his reign as the Hongwu emperor (r. 1368–1398) moved the capital to Nanjing and set out to remedy the harsh conditions in the countryside. He abolished slavery, confiscated large estates, and punished many large landowners. He raised taxes dramatically in southeastern China, where many merchants had benefited enormously from trade networks by land, sea, and river, as well from the almost non-existent checks on trade during the confusion of the late Yuan dynasty. He also returned to the Song model examinations system and sought to raise the status of scholar-officials in his government. Although the gap between the rich and the poor remained great, the effect of the Hongwu emperor's policies (like the Han Emperor Wu and other rulers who sought to level inequities) was to check the worst abuses of landlordism and monopoly that marked the mid-14th century.

The Hongwu emperor[3] was also successful in dealing with the Ming borders and, by the time his reign ended at the close of the 14th century, his government controlled all of what was regarded as China proper, dominating the northern frontier from Inner Mongolia to Manchuria. Because of his success in restoring Chinese rule and his commoner origins, many modern historians have made something of a folk hero out of him. His appealing qualities are clear enough, but there were serious problems with his reign, including a series of bloody purges that ended in the deaths of thousands of officials and their families. Indeed, as he became older, his paranoia and fear of ridicule for his humble beginnings and perceived ugliness—he is known by some as the "bean face emperor" for his pockmarked visage—led him in a direction that strayed far from his founding ideals.

The third Ming emperor, Chengzu (r. 1402–1424), came to power by overthrowing his nephew—the Hongwu emperor's grandson and the son of the Crown Prince—in a tumultuous three-year civil conflict that starkly divided the court. From such beginnings he nonetheless proceeded to, in many ways, create a re-founding for the Ming after the violence of the Hongwu emperor's later years and the conflict that marked his own ascent. He reconstructed the heavily silted Grand Canal, which had become all but unusable after accumulating 800 years of sediment, again linking north-south trade networks. He also moved the primary Ming capital to Beijing in 1421, where

Considered one of the great manmade structures in the world, the Great Wall of China extends about 4,500 miles, from Shanghai Pass to Jiayu Pass. Large parts of the wall date from the seventh through the fourth centuries B.C.E. Much of the wall was built under the Ming Dynasty. (Corel)

it has remained to the present day. Finally, he inaugurated a series of naval missions that went far beyond anything China had seen before or for many centuries since. For a narrow slice of time, from 1405 to 1433, China was Asia's paramount naval power.

This early Ming spirit of travel was not to last, and, for the most part, the Ming could be characterized as an inward-looking empire. There was little of the cosmopolitanism of Tang dynasty Chang'an, or even Yuan dynasty Beijing, with their travelers, musicians, and poets. Indeed, symbolically, if not practically, the building of the Great Wall from fragments of earlier northern walls speaks to a desire to distinguish China from the surrounding world—a breathtaking symbol of imperial isolation, if not an effective check on northern invaders.

By the mid-Ming, serious financial problems had beset the dynasty after decades of poor fiscal management. Eunuchs were the quintessential insiders in traditional politics, and had access to sectors of the palace that duly appointed officials did not. Eunuch management of palace expenditures, according to both traditional and more recent historiography, became a major factor in the weakening of the state. Factional politics, echoing bureaucratic divisions in the Song, also prevailed in the mid- to late-Ming. On a cultural level, the Ming also saw a profound growth in the social, cultural, and intellectual realms, including advances in printing and the growth of the vernacular novel. The population of the north slowly recovered from the Yuan disasters, and the overall population continued a trend that would create serious resource management issues. Throughout the 15th and 16th centuries, one can observe a pattern of increasingly lax governmental administration accompanied by cultural richness and economic growth that led to a long period of late imperial greatness.

The affluence of the mid- to late-Ming dynasty was not equally distributed, and the kinds of abuse that marked earlier ages came to the fore, as well, especially in the form of landlordism. Exploitation of the tax system and the serf-like status of tenant farmers were another component of the problem. The later Ming emperors became increasingly remote. It is difficult for modern American readers accustomed to four- or eight-year presidential administrations to imagine the kinds of problems that *decades* of government mismanagement or neglect might create. In brief, corrupt officials and imperial lieutenants took on enormous authority, and partisan wrangling divided the court. When the central government was most ineffective, landed families and wealthy urbanites were able to act independently, which led to further divisions.

Creating even more serious problems for the Ming was the fact that internal instability coincided with serious northern threats. A domestic rebel, Li Zicheng (d. 1645) seized Beijing in 1644, whereupon the last Ming emperor hanged himself. In the great confusion that followed, regional leaders sought to gain control. The Manchu military forces from the far northeast took advantage of the situation and, with their superior military organization and tactics, acquired power for themselves. The Ming legacy is thus a mixed one. Long-term abuses in the countryside were checked, but only temporarily. By the time the dynasty ended, the Manchu conquerors were welcomed by many Chinese as legitimate holders of power who sought to remedy the problems of greed and abuse among Chinese rulers.

THE QING DYNASTY TO 1800

The Manchus, who, in 1644, founded China's last imperial dynasty, were related to the Ruzhen, whose Jin state had ruled northern China in the 12th and 13th centuries. They adopted the name Qing ("clear" or "pure") and sought to rule China without losing touch with their northern roots. When they gained control of northern China, they cast themselves as preservers of a Chinese culture gone awry, and contended that it was the Ming itself that had lost the Mandate of Heaven and, hence, the right to rule.

The Qing conquest was by no means easy, and it was far from bloodless. Indeed, the massacres that followed them from north to south were a serious point of anger for native Chinese, and stories of Manchu abuses were told for generations. Indeed, the Manchu consolidation took the better part of 40 years, and it was only in the 1680s that all of southern China and Taiwan were reintegrated and various rebel groups were eliminated. This Southern Ming resistance, as it was called, played a prominent role in later criticisms of Manchu rule, and formed an ideal of resistance for many Chinese.

The Manchus organized themselves into a complex banner system, a social and economic institution that organized them into well-ordered fighting troops or disciplined civilians, depending on the needs of the time. The Manchus also set themselves apart from the Chinese by maintaining secret revenues management for the imperial clan and creating a separate Manchu homeland. For at least the first century of rule, Manchu language study was compulsory, and there were restrictions on trade and intermarriage with Chinese. The most dramatic display, however, lay in forcing Chinese men to wear queues, in which the hair was braided and the front of the head shaven. Chinese resistance to this requirement took on various forms, but the Manchus enforced it with the death penalty.

The first 150 years of Manchu rule were marked by the reigns of 3 extraordinary rulers who created a managerial structure that made China, in many ways, the most flourishing of the world's nations. Unchecked by foreign aggression, the Qing enjoyed more than a century of peace and stability, largely through sound, if often harsh, domestic policies, and a clear preeminence over neighboring peoples.

The Kangxi emperor (r. 1661–1722) reigned over China longer than any emperor before him. Although he was actually the second in the sequence of rulers, he has all of the classic qualities of the "good first ruler" in the Chinese political imagination. Raised in the manner of a Chinese heir apparent, he wrote poetry, painted, and enjoyed a wide range of literature. He was also deeply interested in the practical, if not religious, teachings of Jesuit missionaries. Still, he was deeply attached to the Manchurian north, and quite conscious of the unique combination of personal training and insight that was required for him to remain true to his Manchu roots while being an effective Son of Heaven.

The Kangxi emperor carefully regulated the economy and worked for better water control and agriculture. This was no small feat, considering the enormous difficulties the Mongols had encountered with these matters three centuries earlier. He was also a strong military leader who personally completed the consolidation of the empire during the first 20 years of his reign. He planned the campaigns to the south, but also pushed the Qing borders northward to the greatest territorial extent prior to the 20th century.

Where the Kangxi emperor failed was in controlling the succession of his heir. He was eventually succeeded by his fourth son, who would be known as the Yongzheng emperor (r. 1723–1735). Gaining the throne by intriguing against his brothers, the Yongzheng emperor was a wary ruler whose actions demonstrated the potential for autocracy in the imperial institution. His reign seems brief in the context of his predecessor and successor, who each ruled for over 60 years. He carried on the careful management plan of his father, and left the empire in good order for his son, the Qianlong emperor, who would control Qing government until the end of the 18th century.

The Qianlong emperor (r. 1736–1796) was one of the greatest figures in the history of world imperial power. He held power for longer than any Chinese emperor, but abdicated his official role in 1796 as an act of filial devotion toward his grandfather, the Kangxi emperor. For the first 40 years of his reign he was also one of the most capable rulers in Chinese history. Domestically, he continued his grandfather's work as a patron of the arts, and it was his inspiration that led to the creation of

The long reign of the Qianlong emperor was a watershed in the history of China, easily the most wealthy and populous nation in the world in the late 18th century. (Réunion des Musées Nationaux/Art Resource, NY)

several monumental encyclopedic compilations that came to characterize mid-Qing intellectual culture. Militarily, he embarked on 10 campaigns that were meant to preserve and even extend Qing borders, culminating in his destruction of a pesky, resurgent Mongol presence in Central Asia. By the mid-18th century, the power of the Qing military was unchallenged in East and Central Asia.

Two serious flaws, however, damaged the glory of the Qianlong emperor's reign. The first was an extensive inquisition in the 1770s that was designed to suppress subversion in the bureaucracy. The other was the weakening of his will to rule. In the last quarter-century of his reign, he gradually gave power to a Manchu guardsman named Heshen (1750–1799), who controlled the government for the last 20 years of the Qianlong emperor's reign. The combination of the literary inquisition and Heshen's corruption seriously weakened Qing domestic policy and military preparedness. Indeed, in the last 20 years of the century, officers and troops on stipends were forced to subsist on low rations, and often became petty traders or even criminals.

After more than a century of comparative peace, the deterioration of the Manchu military was clearly shown by a large-scale peasant rebellion that, in better times, could have been quickly checked. The same banner forces that had dominated Central Asia for almost two centuries took eight years to suppress the White Lotus Rebellion that arose in the mountainous border regions of Hubei, Sichuan, and Shanxi. Mixing religious strains with an increasingly strong anti-Manchu sentiment, the rebellion was effective both in its wide appeal to the populace and in its nonstandard, guerrilla warfare tactics.

When the Qianlong emperor abdicated in 1796, the Qing's military was spoken of as unrivaled in all of Asia. By the time he died in 1799, the toll of a quarter-century of neglect was increasingly obvious. As China entered the 19th century, it would meet an array of challenges from both within and without for which it was very poorly prepared.

THE EARLY 19TH CENTURY—STASIS, WAR, AND DIPLOMACY (1800–1850)

When the Jiaqing emperor (r. 1796–1820) began to exercise full power in 1799, the Qing government faced enormous challenges, namely addressing the problems of military inefficiency, population growth, and a quarter-century of corruption that had marked central government at the end of the Qianlong reign. Earlier rulers had confronted each of these problems in the past, but when they occurred simultaneously—as they often did at the end of dynasties—the problems were serious indeed. The White Lotus Rebellion was finally quelled in 1804, with a combination of latent military strength and starvation blockades. The long-term effects of the government action, however, would be serious, raising the specter of anti-Manchu resistance.

By the early 19th century, Chinese contact with Western countries was limited to sporadic trade and the memory of Jesuit missionary activities two centuries earlier. There were essentially no diplomatic relations in the form that one could find in European states. The series of conflicts that are often written about as the Opium War had a great deal to do with Britain's (and other nations') desire to open China for much wider trade than the Chinese wished. Just decades earlier, the Qianlong emperor had rejected British interest, reflecting a Chinese governmental world view that, while other nations could come to pay tribute, the Middle Kingdom would not engage them as equals. The British envoy refused to kowtow; the Qianlong emperor stated that "we possess all things." In the late 18th century, it was a standoff. Fifty years later, it would be war.

The war would ostensibly be fought over opium. British traders sought to even the trade balance with China through opium. The Chinese resisted, seeing it as a serious exchange problem, as well as a significant moral issue. A complex series of negotiations and events led to the British Superintendent of Trade turning over British opium stores to the Chinese. When the Chinese ultimately destroyed the opium, British merchants looked to their own government for restitution. There was a great deal of tension on both sides, and the British government felt enormous pressure to take some kind of action. In addition, there were a growing number of conflicts—fights, murders, general misunderstandings between foreigners and Chinese—for which there were no convenient legal mechanisms.

The war itself lasted from 1839–1842. The first phase ended in a tense peace in the summer of 1841, only to be broken soon thereafter. The second phase of the war saw the complete victory of the British, whose cannons were able to fire at will from ships too far away for the Chinese to resist. The defeat itself was humiliating, for it

British ships bombard Canton Harbor during the first Opium War, which started because the British were intent on smuggling opium into China—despite that country's ban on importation and cultivation. (Corbis)

showed that the Qing military forces were backward by international standards, their administration deeply flawed, and, in a time when the rest of the world was capable of sophisticated sea travel and fighting, that China had nothing resembling an able navy. Chinese forces had been defeated before, but not since the Mongols had it been so thoroughly and relentlessly driven into submission.

In the context of later historical events, the diplomatic results of the Opium War are perhaps even more important than China's defeat. The Qing government was forced into concessions it clearly would not have made in the absence of a thorough military defeat. Hong Kong was given to the British. Five treaty ports were opened to foreign consuls, traders, and missionaries along China's southeast coast. The treaty also forced the Qing to pay 21 million silver dollars to Britain, and to give it special diplomatic status. Finally, foreigners were given extra-territorial rights, allowing their home governments to punish them, but preventing the Chinese government from dealing with conflicts on its own territory.

Far from the trade in opium (which remained illegal), the major result of the war was forcing China out of its traditional models of trade and diplomacy. The effects of this outcome were significant, since no amount of classics reading or traditional moral education could help Chinese troops defeat the superior military power of the British. What one sees in the 1840s is confusion that would last for decades, until a wide range of thinkers attempted to resolve the apparent conflict between Western and Chinese ways.

REBELLION AND BEYOND (1850–1870)

Beyond the treaty ports, the Opium War had profound effects throughout southeastern China. The countryside, with a complex local and regional trade network that had grown for centuries, was well connected by land and river to the major coastal cities. In the cities themselves, crime and unemployment increased, as did a simmering resentment of the influx of foreigners. In the countryside, where there had been a long tradition of secret societies linked by fictive kinship ties, religious ideals, and fighting skill, opposition to Europeans broadened to a more general opposition to China's Manchu conquerors.

In this rural context, we can best understand the strange case of Hong Xiuquan, the educated son of a Hakka farmer from just north of Canton. After multiple examination failures, he accepted the pamphlets of a Protestant missionary and Chinese converts. Six years later, he crafted a doctrine of Heavenly Peace and argued that once the Chinese people recovered their "original" religion (for Christianity, in his teaching, was Chinese) by exterminating the Manchus, the "age of great peace" would arrive, uniting the world in universal harmony. Hong would likely have remained an isolated, and somewhat strange, prophet in different times. In this era, however, he found a ready group of listeners in a countryside discontented with massive population growth, restricted resources, official corruption down to the local level, and increased banditry and disorder.

In January 1851, Hong Xiuquan formally declared the Heavenly Kingdom of Great Peace. He declared a new dynasty with the intent of breaking the Manchu hold on China. The Taiping Rebellion represents an important blend of concepts, many of which would play out a century later in the Chinese Communist movement. For the next year, Taiping forces moved north, swiftly sweeping up the indigenous peasantry in the movement. In 1853, they occupied the city of Nanjing, the early capital of the Ming dynasty and a key strategic city. There, they made an enormous tactical error: they stopped moving. They settled in to stabilize and define the kingdom but lost the momentum they had gained in keeping Qing forces off-balance. An even more significant problem also became apparent. Once the Taipings stopped moving, they, not unlike the government they derided, were forced to deal with the complex problems of China's countryside—poverty, overpopulation, and restricted resources. By 1856, the movement was in shambles, with quarreling generals and ineffective administration. Although aided by the brilliant commander Li Xiucheng, the fact that the Taipings remained in Nanjing until 1864 says more about Qing ineffectiveness than any residual strength of the movement.

Coinciding with the Taiping Rebellion, several other rebellions flared throughout the country. By the mid-1860s, more than 20 million people died from warfare, starvation, or natural disasters. Throughout the process, however, the government was also occupied by a series of escalating demands from foreign interests. By 1860, at the Convention of Beijing, 11 new treaty ports were opened, and diplomatic connections with an even wider range of governments and traders emerged. With the Xianfeng emperor (r. 1850–1861) dying and the country enveloped in foreign and domestic crises, the Qing rulers faced challenges that threatened to change the very structure of not only China's government, but of its society and culture, as well.

ATTEMPTS AT RESTORATION AND THE FALL OF QING (1870–1911)

Profound changes resulted from the tumultuous period delineated by the Opium Wars and the Taiping Rebellion. The most important of these is a recurring one: local militarization. From the Warring States period 2,000 years before to the end of the Han dynasty, the An Lushan rebellion, and the fall of the Ming dynasty, there is perhaps no more important ruling theme in Chinese history than this: when the central government found itself overextended, it turned to others for support. Reasserting power was rarely effective. In the wake of the Taiping upsurge and other rebellions, Qing rule was able to survive only by enlisting the support of local militia groups. Over the last decades of the 19th century (and well into the 20th), these local militia groups became increasingly independent actors. Controlling local militia was only a small part of the larger restorative process that a number of late-century thinkers espoused, however.

One of the most significant of these reformers was Prince Gong, the brother of the Xianfeng emperor. He was a talented diplomat with a vision for China's role in world politics. Others who fought for Chinese self-strengthening during this period included Zeng Guofan, who led Hunan armies against the Taiping rebels, Zuo Zongtang, who eventually defeated the Nian rebels, and Li Hongzhang, one of the principal reform leaders throughout the final decades of the 19th century. All of these leaders combined a vision of a modernized society with a deep sense of military preparedness, and many, having regional power bases of their own, displayed the core contradiction of reform—the conflict between a set of national goals and the protection of their own regional interests.

Most of the self-strengthening projects espoused by Qing reformers were meant to balance *ti* and *yong*, "inner essence" and "function," in the modernization effort.

REGIONAL POWER

There is a complex relationship between central power and the local influence of leaders who were familiar with the resources and people in a given territory. Throughout Chinese history, when rule was threatened by uprisings, central governments provided troops and financial resources to commanders who would be tempted to retain control after pacifying the defeated areas. Classic tales in Chinese history often describe commanders and the complex interplay between loyalty to the court and desire to rule that followed their military victories. From the epics of the Three Kingdoms period to the An Lushan and Taiping Rebellions—indeed, well into the 20th century—central power was never secure when "the center could not hold" and rulers gambled by using talented men of questionable loyalty to subdue rebels.

RESTORATION

Restoration is the key idea that a dynasty, once it has begun to spiral toward failure, can be propped up and set aright by a few talented ministers of government acting solely on behalf of the best interests of "all under heaven." When the Han dynasty tottered during the short usurpation of Wang Mang, it could have been lost, according to political thinkers of the time. That it went on to thrive for almost two more centuries is attributed to the determination of talented emperors and ministers to return to the basics of good rule—compassion for the people, proper attention to education, and firm control of the government. Although this may seem to be a dusty old notion from earlier centuries, it remains important in contemporary Chinese politics. Indeed, following the Cultural Revolution and the death of Mao, China's leadership was forced to face the same kinds of restoration challenges confronted by earlier leaders.

They sought to retain the inner core of teachings and moral principles that had shaped three millennia of Chinese life with the sophisticated technology and strategy demonstrated by Westerners. Responding in their own ways to what the Chinese termed the "*tiyong* dilemma," several Japanese thinkers at the same time described this dual focus as "Eastern Ethics and Western Science." Indeed, those were the categories the reformers sought to resolve, as they strived to balance what they saw as integral to their tradition with the need to rise to a competitive scientific level with the West.

This Confucian Pragmatism was applied to military restructuring, economics, education, and social policy. Yet the reforms, in retrospect, were flawed from the outset—no matter how well intentioned they were, there was no systematic restructuring of education to put these blended aims into play for future generations. Traditional-style examinations were held almost until the end of the dynasty, and those who argued most forcefully against the system were often self-educated on reform matters.

By the 1890s, a new kind of critique was taking shape. Far from the pragmatic reforms of Prince Gong and others, these criticisms came in response to China's humiliating defeat in the 1894–1895 Sino-Japanese War, and the subsequent Treaty of Shimonoseki, sparking deep questions about the very basis of traditional ideology. Although traditionally educated, this group, led by Liang Qichao, Kang Youwei, and others, sought not to resolve old and new ways, but rather to abolish the traditional order entirely. They traveled, sought new ideas from the United States, Japan, and Europe, and wrote increasingly virulent attacks on Qing rule and traditional political organization.

For the failures of reform, however, one needs to look back to the end of the Taiping movement when, in the late 1860s, Qing officials proclaimed a restoration that was meant to create a new order without losing their grip on power. When the Xianfeng emperor died in 1861, his son was only five years old. Cixi, the emperor's mother, seized power in a palace coup, with the help of the empress and Prince Gong.

The Dowager Empress Cixi. (Library of Congress)

The complex events of the last decades of the Qing dynasty represent a contradictory combination of Prince Gong's drive to reform and Cixi's desire to retain power at any cost.

During most of the 1870s and 1880s, the court remained under the control of Cixi, the empress dowager. She dominated the young Tongzhi emperor (r. 1861–1875) and (according to legends which take on the misogynistic aura of earlier attacks on the Tang dynasty's Empress Wu) encouraged his excessive ways, leading to his early death at age 19. To maintain her power, she shocked court officials by installing her own nephew, a four year old, on the throne. She continued to rule for the Guangxu emperor (r. 1875–1908) until he came of age in 1889. She removed Prince Gong from power in 1884, and, with reformism cast aside, quietly built her formidable personal fortune.

Several recent historians have argued that Cixi has become a too convenient target for attack in what was an extremely complex, late-Qing political situation. Indeed, she was not the first person to gain power and wealth through nefarious means, nor was she the first to concentrate on retaining power above all else. Some have even argued that *only* such a forceful personality—who broke, in gender and style, the conventions of rule—could control the growing regional armies and the fragile political center. With the situation being extremely fluid, the manipulation of regional leaders was the only way to bring minimal cohesion to the Qing. Restoring central control was out of the question, for the Qing had lackluster military resources of its own.

The dynasty's last major event would combine the 19th-century themes of internal rebellion and foreign influence, and would shake the traditional order to its foundation. The social, spiritual, political, and intellectual tensions that had been building can all be seen in the Boxer Rebellion. The Boxers were resentful of missionary and convert privileges in the treaty ports and the harsh social and economic conditions in the cities and beyond. Holding a deep belief in charms and supernatural powers, the Boxers gained official recognition in their effort to "expel the barbarians" from an unlikely source—the equally "foreign" Qing government. In changing what was at least in part an anti-Qing slogan to one that was anti-Western, the Boxers gained Qing recognition as an official military organization.

In June 1900, they entered Beijing. Eight days later, the Qing court declared war on the treaty powers. Almost 500 foreign civilians and 3,000 Chinese Christians were held under siege in the legation quarters for foreign officials. The gamble failed miserably, and, in many ways, their eventual defeat spelled the end for the Qing government. It had already raised the military readiness of foreign powers, which banded together in an eight-nation alliance. After miscalculating badly, the court fled the capital, and it had to pay a large indemnity to the foreign powers. China's international position was even more thoroughly weakened, and the loss of any realistic power center gave rise to independent action on the part of regional armies. Indeed, during the rebellion itself, several governor-generals refused to follow Qing orders.

In the final decade of the Qing dynasty, there were a series of efforts to prolong, if not save, the political order. The examination system was finally abolished in 1905, and a series of technical schools for Western education were established. The practice of footbinding, which had affected a large portion of women for almost a millennium, began to die out even more quickly than it had taken root in the Song dynasty. Most significant of all, however, was the fact that new groups were asserting collective voices, including students and workers. Indeed, in addition to controlling regional armies and reasserting central government, a new challenge would emerge for future leaders: harnessing the increasingly formidable power of the Chinese people.

REPUBLICAN CHINA AND THE WAR YEARS (1912–1949)

A major revolt in Wuchang on October 10, 1911, sparked a series of uprisings that led almost two-thirds of China's provinces to declare their independence from Qing rule. By December, 17 provinces had sent delegates to Nanjing, where Sun Yat-sen (1866–1925) was named Provisional President of a new Republic of China. Yet only one individual at that time was able to control the burgeoning power of regional armies and negotiate the end of Qing rule: Yuan Shikai, who had the loyalty of government troops, as well as ties to both parliamentarians and the Qing court. The provisional Republican government agreed to give Yuan the presidency if the Xuantong emperor (Puyi) abdicated. The emperor "accepted" (he was barely six years old at the time), and Yuan assumed the presidency in March 1912. Yuan strove to root out opposition, even as his government stated its desire to create a parliamentary system. In 1913, the Guomindang (Nationalist) party, with the help of Sun Yat-sen, won a majority of seats in the national parliamentary elections. Yuan Shikai then plotted the assassination of the party's leader, Song Jiaoren. Later that year, Yuan suspended parliament and amended the constitution, declaring himself president for life. The following year, he declared a restoration of imperial power and proclaimed himself emperor.

The political situation had changed dramatically, even in a few years, and provincial governors throughout China vigorously contested a reassertion of imperial power. Yuan died in June of 1916, and these same governors filled the power void in a manner that has been seen throughout Chinese history during times of division: by combining military and political power on a local level. A dozen different warlords presided over a weak central government between 1916 and 1927, yet none was able to assert lasting power beyond his own territory. During this time, it was the provinces themselves that operated with near-independence from central power. Sun Yat-sen, who had fled to Japan during Yuan's parliamentary crackdown, returned to China in 1917, and founded the Military Government of the Republic of China based in Guangzhou during the next year. In 1920, Sun Yat-sen was elected President of the Republic, but his government remained regional and was not recognized by foreign powers.

At the outbreak of World War I in 1914, Japan (with British complicity) had seized the port of Qingdao in Shandong province, a primary base for German interests in the Pacific. A year later, Japan issued 21 demands, insisting on China's recognition of its claim to Shandong, which would effectively make China a protectorate of Japan. When the fact that the warlord government had secretly acceded to most of Japan's demands became known during the Paris Peace Conference in 1919, student demonstrations ensued; laborers, merchants, and artisans soon joined the demonstrators. A May 4, 1919, demonstration of Chinese students against Japan—now known as the May Fourth Movement—quickly spread to Shanghai and many other cities, becoming a catalyst for change and sparking a New Culture Movement that led to calls for changes ranging from basic modernization to wholesale revolution.

Inspired by these calls for change and influenced by Communist writings, Communist groups developed throughout China. In 1921, a dozen organizers, including Mao Zedong, founded the Chinese Communist Party in Shanghai. By 1927, their membership numbered almost 60,000. At the heart of Mao's philosophy was a desire to harness the power of the people, and of the countryside. Although "the people" had been referred to as an important part of traditional Chinese political philosophy for almost 3,000 years, it was Mao who clearly articulated their role as a true *force* in political power, as demonstrated by his rapid organization of a peasant and worker army.

In 1923, Sun Yat-sen had become the leader of a new coalition government—the National Revolutionary Government, again based in Guangzhou. Sun realized that no central power would be possible without strong military backing. He founded a Revolutionary Army and the Whampoa Military Academy to train officers for war against the northern warlords. Before these plans came to fruition, Sun died of cancer in 1925, and was succeeded by one of his lieutenants, Jiang Jieshi (Chiang Kai-shek). Chiang experienced rapid success and by the end of 1926, the Nationalist Army controlled half of the country. By 1927, Chiang had engineered a bloody massacre of Communist Party members and other opponents in Shanghai and several other cities. By 1928, Chiang's Northern Expedition had reached Beijing, completing the unification process and securing recognition from Western powers.

Between 1928 and 1937, Chiang Kai-shek sought to eliminate the Communists, and used significant resources to achieve that goal. After losing their position within

Photograph shows Mao Zedong (right) and Zhang Guotao standing in the courtyard of the supreme communist headquarters in China, March 1938. (Library of Congress)

major cities, the Communists sought to control the countryside. In January 1932, they established the Chinese Soviet Republic in Jiangxi province, with Mao Zedong as chairman. By 1934, however, Chiang had organized an effective blockade of Communist positions. Seeking to maintain the remnants of its forces, Mao's Red Army evacuated Jiangxi and began the Long March across 11 different provinces covering over 8,000 miles, to move to a new base in Shaanxi. The march began with tens of thousands. Only 8,000 arrived in Yan'an a year later.

While the Nationalist and Communist forces were engaged in civil conflict, Japan seized Manchuria in 1931, establishing China's last emperor of the Qing dynasty as the leader of its puppet government. Although this move generated angry reactions throughout China, Chiang's focus remained on a policy of internal pacification to eliminate the Red Army's presence. The Japanese threat, however, sparked a backlash within the Nationalist Army, and two high-ranking leaders kidnapped Chiang until he agreed to use Nationalist resources for an alliance with the Communist Party against the Japanese.

Chiang agreed and was released. The resulting United Front quickly engaged in full-scale war with Japan. Attacking Chinese troops near Beijing in July 1937, Japan quickly captured the city and then moved to occupy most of China's major coastal cities. The goal of the Allies was to break the Japanese stranglehold on China. It can also be said that a goal of the Allied and Chinese forces was to exhaust the Japanese in the Asian theater. Indeed, some estimates have 70 percent of Japanese casualties coming in China. The challenge was frustrated by poor economic conditions and the coordination of the fighting with what were plainly hostile forces—the Nationalists and Communists—who agreed only on the expulsion of the Japanese. Even their strategic bases were so far apart (Yan'an and Nanjing) that coordination was a difficult task at best for Allied forces. In turn, many Nationalist forces still had strong ties to the warlord armies that had dotted the country for decades. Allied forces had their own competing priorities, with air and ground wars; these in turn played into Nationalist-Communist tension—air strikes did not exhaust ground troops or require closely protected resources. In spite of these challenges, however, the Chinese campaign was able to divert more than a half-million Japanese troops during the Asian conflict.

Both the Nationalist and Communist parties took a two-pronged approach to the war with Japan. Although they each sought to repel the Japanese, they kept wary eyes on each other, and worked to build their own power bases. To this day, both sides blame the other for its lack of resolve in fighting Japan. The acrimony boiled over after the Japanese surrender in 1945. At that time, the Nationalists reoccupied the major cities, while the Communists controlled great portions of the countryside. Over the next four years, the armies would vie for control of China. Although the Nationalist Army, with strong U.S. support, had a seemingly enormous advantage in terms of military resources and urban centers, the Red Army was able to take advantage of ineffective Nationalist strategy and poor morale to gain the upper hand by 1949, when it captured Beijing and moved to solidify the rest of China's mainland. By the end of the year, Chiang Kai-shek's remaining Nationalist forces had fled to Taiwan, where the Republic of China would continue as a government in exile.

THE PEOPLE'S REPUBLIC OF CHINA (1949–PRESENT)

On October 1, 1949, Mao Zedong proclaimed the founding of the People's Republic of China. The first years of his rule were greeted with enthusiasm for an end to decades of conflict and warfare. From the outset, the Chinese Communist Party (CCP) made it clear that a strong, central authority would govern China. All key military and government positions were occupied by party members, and Mao himself served as party chairman, president, and the commander of national forces.

The challenges facing the new government were enormous, and the CCP acted quickly—in the manner of many founding governments before it—to consolidate power and root out opposition. As a people's revolution, however, the dynamics of this solidification differed from those of earlier eras. Although the power of landowners was always a problem for dynastic founders in Chinese history (as we have seen, the Hongwu emperor in the Ming, for one, worked vigorously to check landlordism), the steps taken by the CCP to create genuine land reform were dramatic. In addition, the party launched a series of campaigns to transform China: the campaign to suppress counterrevolutionaries; the "three antis" campaign to root out corruption, waste, and narrow bureaucracy; the "five antis" campaign against bribery, tax fraud, cheating in contracts, public property theft, and economic crimes committed by businesses; and, finally, the Oppose America, Aid Korea campaign. These were more than just political calls to action. During the early 1950s, these campaigns affected the lives of a large portion of China's population, and large numbers were displaced, imprisoned, or executed. Some place the losses in the tens or even hundreds of thousands. In 1956, Mao, embracing the great tradition of political remonstrance, asked for the opinions and criticisms of a wide variety of people, including intellectuals, regarding political policy and the party. Although this Hundred Flowers campaign seemingly had an earnest origin, it was followed in 1957 by a fierce anti-rightist movement that led to the persecution of thousands of intellectuals who had voiced criticisms.

The first decade of the People's Republic also saw two different five-year plans. During this time, the CCP received support from the Soviet Union, and modeled its industrial, banking, and commercial nationalizations on Soviet models as the first of such plans. Thus, the role of the private sector was effectively destroyed. In 1958, the party announced the Three Red Banner Movement—the General Party Line, the Great Leap Forward, and the People's Commune—designed to provide ideological continuity, the maximization of industrial and agricultural output, and the full collectivization of the countryside.

These moves were ineffective at best, and disastrous at worst, given the loss of over 20 million people in the Great Leap Forward, as will be seen in the chapters that follow. Amidst growing domestic troubles, the Chinese and Soviets broke relations after a series of increasingly bitter ideological and territorial conflicts. Mao gave up the presidency in 1959 to Liu Shaoqi, a veteran of decades of struggle who, along with Deng Xiaoping, worked to revitalize the economy through a series of measures aimed to relax state control in key industries and revitalize rural areas. Although many of these policies appeared to be effective, they raised the ire of Mao and others, who saw them as leading toward capitalist actions.

By 1963, Mao had reemerged to launch a Socialist Education Movement to restore teachings on class struggle and people's power. This was just a precursor to a much larger movement that Mao launched in 1966 to solidify support among workers, students, and the army: the Cultural Revolution. In its origins, the Cultural Revolution was a movement against traditional values and ideologies, but it quickly turned into a bitter internal war against many of Mao's political opponents, and opened the door for the settling of a vast number of personal scores at the local level. Many of Mao's earlier associates were demoted or dismissed. Others, including Liu Shaoqi, lost their lives during the conflict. As a result of encouragement from Mao, revolutionary committees were formed to seize power from party and government organizations, and youthful groups of Red Guards were able to act unchecked at local levels and beyond.

The intensity of the first years of the Cultural Revolution diminished by 1969, as Mao gradually extricated himself from its central leadership. From then until Mao's death in 1976, tension between a moderate group led by Premier Zhou Enlai and a radical group led by Mao's wife, Jiang Qing, dominated the party. The deaths in 1976 of Zhou Enlai, China's premier, of Zhu De, the earliest military commander to support Mao, and of Mao himself threw the country into turmoil. Hua Guofeng, selected by Mao as his successor, arrested Jiang Qing's group, which was later vilified as the Gang of Four, removing the strongest proponents of the Cultural Revolution

从政治上思想上理论上彻底批倒批臭中国的赫鲁晓夫

Chinese poster showing artist, peasant, soldier, and Red Guard erasing the image of Liu Shaoqi, represented as a revisionist, hiding inside a crumbling fortress-like structure, 1967. (Library of Congress)

from power. The legacy of the Cultural Revolution persisted in what has been often called a "lost generation" that was characterized by enormous uncertainty, a lack of organized education, and the loss of family connections and local ties.

In the meantime, despite the tensions prevailing within China, dramatic changes had occurred in terms of China's position in the world. In the spring of 1971, the U.S. Table Tennis team, which was in Japan for a tournament, was invited to tour and compete in China; these Americans were the first official American delegation in Beijing in over two decades. In the summer of 1971, U.S. National Security advisor Henry Kissinger held secret meetings in Beijing and established the groundwork for further talks between the United States and China. Richard Nixon's historic 1972 visit to China was an important event in modern American history, and a milestone for a China seeking a broader role in the world. Nixon met once with Mao and accompanied Premier Zhou Enlai to various locations before issuing the joint Shanghai Communiqué, which became the foundation for the United States' and China's relations in the coming decades, acknowledging that there is only one China, and that Taiwan is a part of it. This, in turn, led to the rapid diplomatic recognition of China by many world powers.

Following Mao's death in 1976, Deng Xiaoping, who had been exiled during the Cultural Revolution, gained power in a contentious struggle. Although Deng never held the titles of president or party chairman, he exercised control until his death in 1997. Deng encouraged innovative combinations of communism and capitalism in the countryside. More of a pragmatist than his predecessor, he created profit incentives for businesses and encouraged a limited form of private entrepreneurship. Deng also sought to revitalize the party through a series of purges of Cultural Revolution figures, vowing an end to the political campaigns of the past. He abolished life tenure for senior party members and sought to check corruption at all levels. Under his management, China established diplomatic relations with the United States and created a series of special economic zones to attract foreign investment from multinational corporations. In short, China in the late 20th century was a growing world power that, although still defined by a central party structure, had an enormous and still growing foreign economic presence, as well as a central place in world trade. Many of these themes will be discussed in detail in the next chapters on Chinese politics and economics.

Deng's tenure was not without controversy, and perhaps nothing shows that more clearly than the events that transpired at Tiananmen Square on June 4, 1989. After weeks of student demonstrations that initially marked the death of Hu Yaobang, a popular Party General Secretary who had been dismissed three years earlier for his soft stance on student unrest, the demonstrations in Beijing quickly turned anti-government. By the middle of May, the demonstrators numbered two million, and Deng was confronted with a serious threat to Communist Party rule. Deng ordered a crackdown on the students and, in the early-morning hours of June 4, government troops and tanks expelled the demonstrators, with casualties numbering in the thousands. The aftermath of Tiananmen was no brighter, with mass arrests and reprisals launched among prodemocracy groups.

Two successive leaders—Jiang Zemin and Hu Jintao—who have overseen China's remarkable economic growth and increasing stature in world affairs, have followed Deng Xiaoping. The selection of Beijing to host the 2008 Olympic Games, as well as the choice of Shanghai for the 2010 World Expo, were early indications that China was becoming a significant force in world affairs, and Beijing's extravagant and highly successful Olympic Games point to the opportunities and challenges that China will face in the 21st century. The Games were not without controversy, as will be seen in Chapter 7, "Contemporary Issues." They were, however, China's great opportunity to present itself to the world as a force that—regardless of how one perceives its economic power, record on human rights, or political decisions—will play a major role for decades to come.

NOTES

1. All dates in the text will refer to the Common Era (c.e.), unless specifically noted by "b.c.e." The designation "c.e." will be added throughout the text at points of potential confusion.

2. The reader should note that the Romanized word "Zhou" refers to many different Chinese characters. For the Chinese reader, determining which "Zhou" is being referenced is straightforward. For the Western reader, however, it can be very confusing. There are three prominent "Zhou" references in the history section. There is the degenerate ruler (Zhou 紂 or Zhou Xin (紂辛), the Zhou Dynasty 周, and the Duke of Zhou 周公, an early leader of the same dynasty covered in this section. The later Zhou dynasty of the Empress Wu and the

20th-century Communist official Zhou Enlai represent two other uses of the word, but are unlikely to cause confusion.

3. Readers may notice that multiple titles are commonly used to refer to emperors from the Ming period. "Zhu Yuanzhang" is the proper name (surname first) of the Ming founder. He is also commonly referred to as "Ming Taizu," or "Emperor Taizu of the Ming." The most confusing term for Western readers is another common title. The founder was known as "the Hongwu emperor." This is the name of the period in which he reigned, and it is the format that Qing Dynasty emperors (covered in the next section) followed. It is important to realize that the correct format is "the Hongwu emperor," and not "Emperor Hongwu."

REFERENCES

Abramson, Marc. *Ethnic Identity in Tang China*. Philadelphia: University of Pennsylvania Press, 2007.

Andrew, Anita and John Rapp. *Autocracy and China's Rebel Founding Emperors: Comparing Chairman Mao and Ming Taizu*. Lanham MD: Rowman and Littlefield, 2000.

Bergère, Marie Claire. *Sun Yat-sen*. Palo Alto, CA: Stanford University Press, 1998.

Cohen, Paul. *History in Three Keys*. New York: Columbia University Press, 1997.

Cohen, Warren I. *East Asia at the Center*. New York: Columbia University Press, 2000.

Cotterel, Arthur. *The Imperial Capitals of China*. New York: The Overlook Press, 2008.

Crossley, Pamela Kyle. *A Translucent Mirror: History and Identity in Qing Imperial Ideology*. Berkeley: University of California Press, 2002.

DeBary, William Theodore, and Irene Bloom. *Sources of Chinese Tradition, Vol. 1*. 2d ed. New York: Columbia University Press, 1999.

Dott, Brian. *Identity Reflections: Pilgrimage to Mount Tai in Late Imperial China*. Cambridge, MA: Harvard Asian Center, 2005.

Ebrey, Patricia. *Chinese Civilization: A Sourcebook*. New York: Free Press, 1993.

Elman, Benjamin. *Classicism, Politics, and Kinship*. Berkeley: University of California Press, 1990.

Esherick, Joseph. *The Origins of the Boxer Uprising*. Berkeley: University of California Press, 1987.

Fairbank, John King and Merle Goldman. *China: A New History*. Cambridge, MA: Harvard University Press, 2006

Hansen, Valerie. *The Open Empire: A History of China to 1600*. New York: W. W. Norton, 2000.

Hardy, Grant. *Worlds of Bronze and Bamboo: Sima Qian's Conquest of History*. New York: Columbia University Press, 1999.

Harrell, Stevan. *Chinese Historical Microdemography*. Berkeley: University of California Press, 1995.

Hinton, William. *Fanshen: A Documentary of Revolution in a Chinese Village*. New York: Vintage Books, 1966.

Hoang, Michel. *Genghis Khan*. London: Saqi Books, 1989.

Kuhn, Philip. *Origins of the Modern Chinese State*. Palo Alto: Stanford University Press, 2002.

Kuhn, Philip. *Soulstealers: The Chinese Sorcery Scare of 1768.* Cambridge, MA: Harvard University Press, 1990.

Lewis, Mark Edward and Timothy Brook. *The Early China Empire: Qin and Han.* Cambridge, MA: Harvard University Press, 2007.

MacFarquhar, Roderick and Michael Schoenhals. *Mao's Last Revolution.* Cambridge, MA: Harvard Belknap, 2006.

McDermott, Joseph. *A Social History of the Chinese Book.* Hong Kong: Hong Kong University Press, 2006.

Mote, F. W. *Imperial China: 900–1800.* Cambridge, MA: Harvard University Press, 1999.

Needham, Joseph. *The Shorter Science and Civilization in China: Vol. 1.* Cambridge: Cambridge University Press, 1978.

Perkins, Dorothy. *Encyclopedia of China.* New York: Checkmark Books, 1999.

Roberts, Moss. *Three Kingdoms: A Historical Romance.* Berkeley: University of California Press, 1991.

Schaberg, David. *A Patterned Past: Form and Thought in Early Chinese Historiography.* Cambridge, MA: Harvard University Press, 2001.

Shaughnessy, Edward. *China: Empire of Civilization.* New York: Oxford University Press, 2000.

Sima Guang. *Zizhi tongjian. (A Comprehensive Mirror for Aid in Ruling).* Beijing: Zonghu Shuju, 1956.

Smith, Richard J. *China's Cultural Heritage: The Qing Dynasty, 1644–1912.* 2d ed. Boulder, CO: Westview Press, 1994.

Spence, Jonathan. *God's Chinese Son: The Taiping Heavenly Kingdom of Hong Xiuquan.* New York: W. W. Norton, 1996.

Spence, Jonathan. *The Search for Modern China.* New York: W. W. Norton, 1990.

Watson, Burton. *The Tso Chuan.* New York: Columbia University Press, 1989.

Wilkinson, Endymion. *Chinese History: A Manual.* Cambridge, MA: Harvard University Press, 2000.

Wills, John. *Mountain of Fame: Portraits in Chinese History.* Princeton, NJ: Princeton University Press, 1995.

Wright, Arthur. *The Sui Dynasty.* New York: Alfred A. Knopf, 1978.

Politics and Government

John A. Rapp

FROM TRADITIONAL TO MODERN: THE 20TH-CENTURY CHINESE STATE

Contemporary Chinese politics is both a continuation of traditional Chinese political culture and a reflection of modern Communist political systems. Considering China's three-plus millennia of rich political and cultural history, the country's adoption of Communism in 1949 and its accompanying declaration of itself as the People's Republic of China (PRC) is a comparatively recent event. Communism, a Western import adapted by the Chinese across decades of political, economic, and social upheaval, guided the governance of China for much of the 20th century. Furthermore, China continues to change rapidly in the economic, social, and political realms.

To understand these changes, particularly as they relate to contemporary Chinese politics, we will look at various perspectives that may help the reader explore any era of modern Chinese politics, be it the dawning days of the Cultural Revolution or the country's most recent gestures of openness to international markets and culture. Political events and governmental policies in China often develop and change quickly. For this reason, it is important to provide a sense of the underlying context of Chinese government and politics so that readers are better able to interpret future events for themselves. To help provide that context, we will examine variations in political ideology, party-state structure, and various issues of domestic and foreign policy throughout the history of the People's Republic of China.

As we have seen in the previous chapters, the north-south divide is a longstanding theme of traditional Chinese political culture, and it continues to influence contemporary politics. Since the 19th century, this tension has also often been reflected in the divide between China's coast and its interior. From one perspective, Mao Zedong

Chinese propaganda poster: The Glory of Mao's Ideologies Brightens up the New China. *(Library of Congress)*

led a peasant-based movement aimed at genuine social revolution. However, based on the perspective of the coast-interior divide, in some ways, Mao's movement represented the resistance of northern, interior forces to the corrupting Western influence of Communists based in urban, coastal areas, who were more accepting of economic and other reforms. Thus, Mao's call during the Cultural Revolution to "drag out" those members of the party and state who were "taking the capitalist road" did not represent a mass democratic attempt to prevent elitism and bureaucratism (as some Western and Chinese observers thought at the time). It was, instead, an attempt to enhance Mao's own power base at the expense of other party and state elites.

Mao's paranoid fear of real or imagined rivals echoes that of similar founding rebel emperors from earlier imperial dynasties, most notably Zhu Yuanzhang, the founding emperor of the Ming dynasty, who led his own purge of the bureaucracy in the latter years of his reign in the 14th century. The autocratic policies calling for self-reliance in the Great Leap Forward and the Cultural Revolution are in keeping with the expanded autocracy of rule in China during the Yuan, Ming, and Qing dynasties. Even the attempt to build a third line of industries within the interior to withstand a Soviet or U.S. nuclear attack resembled the neo-isolationist policies of the Ming emperors, who pulled China back from sea exploration in the 15th century and worked to connect the various defenses that would be known as the Great Wall. Another vestige of earlier history and culture that continues to manifest in

---

MAO ZEDONG (1893–1976)

Chairman of the CCP and leader of the PRC until his death in 1976. A founding member of the CCP in 1921 (probably only to represent his home province of Hunan), Mao first came to prominence in 1927, when his "Report into an Investigation into the Peasant Movement in Hunan Province" expressed the heretical view that the Chinese revolution could be based on the peasants. After the Nationalist regime under Chiang Kai-shek massacred the urban-based Communists, the surviving Soviet-backed CCP leaders joined Mao in the countryside, where they pushed him aside, leaving Mao as only the titular head of the Jiangxi Soviet. Mao regained control during the famous Long March when, under the pressure of GMD attacks, the Party retreated deeper into the countryside. Along the path of the march, in the town of Zunyi, Mao gained enough support from other members of the CCP to regain control of the Party. Though Mao did resign his post as Chairman of State in 1961 after the Great Leap Forward, he never again lost control of the CCP and remained China's paramount leader until his death in 1976.

---

contemporary Chinese politics is the influence of *guanxi* (connections), networks of patron-client ties that stretch from the top to the bottom of the Chinese political hierarchy. Though this concept will be examined in more detail in Chapter 5, which examines Chinese politics and social life through the lens of such connections, the ups and downs of individual leaders and policies can be framed in terms of the relationships among the players in China's political structure. In this regard, the Cultural Revolution can be viewed as a temporary triumph of Mao's *guanxi* network over those of his rivals, namely Liu Shaoqi and Deng Xiaoping. Similarly, the failure of Hua Guofeng to solidify his status as Mao's approved successor in 1977–1979 can be traced to Hua's relatively weak and narrow *guanxi* network within the party-state hierarchy, compared to the relatively wide and deep network of Deng Xiaoping, who quickly supplanted Hua as the paramount leader of China after Mao's death.

A final theme that is relevant to both contemporary Chinese politics and the country's earlier political culture is that of the dichotomy between Eastern essence and Western technology discussed in Chapter 2. Nineteenth-century reformers, such as Zeng Guofan, argued that only by combining China's essence and the West's technology (*tiyong*) could China flourish. According to this view, the entire Chinese revolution, from the Opium War to the present day, can be understood as an attempt by a succession of Chinese leaders to maintain a Chinese essence, shifting and varied as that essence might be, by borrowing only enough Western technology to stand up to the West, without being absorbed or corrupted by it. Even after the May Fourth Movement of 1919, when both the Nationalists and Communists felt the need to challenge the "corrupt and decadent" nature of Chinese culture, this dichotomy continued to influence Chinese politics. Similarly, Mao's attempt to adapt Marxism to the Chinese revolution, as well as Deng Xiaoping's efforts to pursue economic modernization without the "spiritual pollution" of "bourgeois" ideas about political reform, can be understood as the continuing (and perhaps doomed) attempt to adapt to the onslaught of Western influence without changing the dominant autocratic and undemocratic strands of China's state tradition.

THEMES FROM COMMUNIST SYSTEMS

Another way to view contemporary Chinese politics is as a variant of Communist political systems. We can understand policy and leadership changes in China from 1949 to the present by examining them in terms of the contradictions and tensions within Marxist-Leninist ideology. Marx had predicted that the proletarian revolution would occur in the mid-19th century within advanced industrial nations. When this didn't happen, Lenin, the leader of the Russian revolution of 1917, explained that the revolution was still immanent, but would occur later and in a different place and on a different scale than Marx had predicted. Imperialism, the exploitation of poorer countries by rich capitalist nations that developed after Marx's lifetime, had delayed the revolution, but it remained inevitable.

"Semi-backward" nations would start to revolt against the major imperialist powers, Lenin promised, when the latter were distracted by wars with one another over their colonies. Though Lenin managed to preserve the ideological credibility of Marxism, he introduced new dilemmas for Communist Party–led regimes. For Marx, the only task of the dictatorship of the proletariat was to redistribute wealth and property among the fully socialist workers in rich countries, after which the state would famously wither away. But for Lenin, because the revolution was expected to occur first in semi-backward areas, the new socialist state would have no wealth to redistribute. The state would have to create wealth in the first place, redistribute the newly created wealth, and create socialist consciousness among a coalition of workers and peasants that was still not fully educated.

The contradictions among these three tasks are what have led to major policy shifts within almost every Communist regime, shifts that are reflected in China's policies at different times in its struggle with communism. The political scientist Edward Friedman has labeled these shifts Stalinist, Titoist, and Maoist. For example, marketeers or Titoists (named after Josef Tito of Yugoslavia, who was the first to break with the Stalinist model) argue for market correctives for central planning and the need to focus on creating wealth, whereas planners or Stalinists argue the need for a strong state to monopolize the ownership of property and wealth in the name of the workers. Lastly, ideologues or Maoists focus on the need to prevent the comeback of capitalism that might arise as a result of inequalities within the socialist state. Because communism came to China through an indigenous peasant-based revolution, rather than in the form of Soviet tanks, as in much of Eastern Europe, China went much further in the Maoist or ideological direction and the Titoist or marketeer direction than most other Communist systems.

A second major theme in Communist systems relates to how the Chinese party-state apparatus works, no matter what formal flow charts might indicate about where power lies and how policy is made. In this model, three terms are used to explain how policy is made and how the party controls the state in all Communist systems: *nomenklatura, kontrol,* and substitution.

The *nomenklatura* is a list controlled by the Communist Party of China (CCP, or the party) that names people loyal to the party and subject to party discipline. The list also names those whom the party appoints to key positions in the party hierarchy, the state, the military, and other mass organizations in order to ensure its control. *Nomenklatura* also stands for the real inequality between the party elite and the masses, based on the non-wage privileges of the top elite, such as access to better housing, automobiles, food and clothing in special stores, and less censored information.

Kontrol is shorthand for the fact that every person in the party-state apparatus is subject to dual and triple mechanisms of oversight and responsibility. A prominent example occurs in the military, where people report not just up the regular military chain of command, but also up a parallel network of political commissars who are ultimately controlled by the party. Substitution conveys the principle that even though, on paper, lower levels elect delegates to higher levels of the party and state, in reality it is the higher bodies of the party that decide policy and personnel issues—decisions that lower bodies merely rubber stamp. Thus, following the Soviet model, in China, it is typically the Political Affairs Bureau (Politburo) of the Central Committee of the CCP that hashes out key decisions. The major exception to this rule occurred during the Cultural Revolution, when Mao called an expanded Politburo meeting to create the Cultural Revolution Group, which, for a time, bypassed the Politburo and the rest of the party leaders in making key decisions.

COMBINING TRADITIONAL AND COMMUNIST SYSTEM MODELS

Of course, in many ways, contemporary Chinese politics is a combination of Chinese state traditions and modern Communist systems. Separating the two helps us to better analyze key issues, but there is actually a rich interplay between them. For example, according to the neotraditional view of Chinese politics, the closed and authoritarian nature of Communist systems encourages the rise of patron-client networks of authority and decision making, networks that serve to revive and intensify the traditional emphasis on *guanxi* in political decision making. Given ordinary peoples' fear of deviating from Marxist orthodoxy and telling the truth to their leaders, all Communist systems lack feedback mechanisms, which top party leaders could use to learn about policy problems and setbacks. Instead, the Chinese regime relies more on informal patron-client ties in which lower-level people are able to report back honestly, without fearing retribution, only to their trusted patrons. Reporting to those whom one has no connections with could be disastrous.

This was especially the case in China after the Anti-rightist campaigns of 1957 and 1959, when Mao clarified his intentions to oppose and purge anyone within society or the regime itself who openly criticized his policies. Likewise, the campaigns against bourgeois liberalization and spiritual pollution of the 1980s succeeded in firming up the *guanxi* networks of individual top leaders in China who differed over the degree of economic reform to be pursued. The imperial Chinese state, however, had a similarly closed structure, and it was only through the ideal of remonstrance

---

GUANXI (SOCIAL NETWORKS)

Nearly all social interactions in Chinese societies can be understood in terms of *guanxi*, which apply to a broad range of relationships, from the family to international affairs. Social relations in China are not simply about getting along well with others. They require building a network of people upon whom you can count (and who, in turn, will count on you) to help make things happen—from finding housing or a job to reserving a seat on a plane or a train during a busy holiday season, acquiring access to good medical care, or being admitted to a top school. Through the continual exchange of both tangible and intangible goods, people develop a sense of mutual obligation that cements their network of social relationships and insures that they are able to get what they need and want. The careful reader will notice these networks in descriptions of Chinese history, politics, economics, and even literature. Indeed, many of the most prominent figures in Chinese history succeeded at least in part because of strong *guanxi* networks on which they could rely.

(sometimes carried out in practice, but usually only by someone who felt he had a strong *guanxi* network) that those on the lower levels of the hierarchy could advise, and even correct, their superiors. The problem of obtaining advice from below one's rank is inherent in the structure of both ruling models.

We will draw upon all of the above themes in examining the shifts and variations from Mao to Deng and beyond in Chinese Marxist ideology, party-state structure, and selected foreign and domestic policy issues.

IDEOLOGY

The government of the People's Republic of China claims to be a socialist state under the leadership of the Chinese Communist Party (CCP). As such, it follows orthodox Marxist-Leninist doctrine, which dictates that Communist parties in semi-backward (and even "fully backward") nations help their citizens finish integrating capitalism—that is, build up wealth and abundance—while, at the same time, work to restrict the inequalities and inequities of capitalism. Besides making this claim of bringing wealth and equality to its citizens, the CCP also took advantage of Marxist-Leninism's fusion of socialism and nationalism. Beginning in its guerrilla days in Yan'an in the 1930s and 1940s, when Communist forces rebuilt their strength in the relative safety of the interior, the CCP claimed to be the truly nationalist party in contrast to the Nationalist Party (or Guomindang, sometimes written as "KMT" in historical and political texts based on an earlier system of Chinese transliteration). The party has carefully protected this mantle of nationalism throughout the radical shifts and changes in official ideology up to and including the present day. In addition, the party claims that it maintains democracy within the one-party state by carefully listening to and taking into account the views of all the various classes. This is remarkably similar to the remonstrance ideal of earlier times, in which listening was idealized but dissent was not tolerated.

Delegates gather for the opening ceremony of the Chinese Peoples' Political Consultative Conference (CPPCC) in Beijing's Great Hall of the People in 2005. The CPPCC is made up of representatives from different political parties and organizations that acts as an advisory body to China's legislature, the National Peoples' Congress. (AP/Wide World Photos)

This claim that the party follows a mass line harkens back to the days when the CCP, under Mao's leadership, forged its basic ruling ideology during the second Sino-Japanese War. Under the Yan'an Line, the CCP claimed to be developing a Marxism with Chinese characteristics that was free of Soviet domination—most importantly, by including several classes among the people. Chinese communism embraced not just the urban workers, but the rural farmers (whom Marx had referred to as a reactionary, petty capitalist class) and even small, medium, and large capitalists, as long as they joined first the anti-Japanese coalition and later the coalition organized against the Guomindang during the civil war.

In the party's Yan'an headquarters, Mao first posited that the CCP was leading China through the New Democratic Revolution and would only much later move on to the socialist revolution, where private property would be collectivized and nationalized. According to Mao, each epoch was shaped by a "principal antagonistic contradiction" between the enemy and the people, which had to be overcome by violent revolution. Nonantagonistic contradictions between the various progressive classes, however, could supposedly be settled by peaceful means. The CCP leaders also took pains to demonstrate that their party was close to the masses, as seen in campaigns to rectify party members' outlook by sending them down (*xiafang*) to live and work among the peasants. The CCP also organized criticism and self-criticism sessions for new party members in Yan'an, not only to push the New Democratic Revolution, but also to enforce party discipline. Scholars now point out, however, that for all its populist rhetoric and democratic claims, the party's rectification campaign in Yan'an served to purge dissent and independent thinking within the party, and served as the impetus for its harsh ideological campaigns and purges after 1949. Most significantly, the people who would be named enemies of the people were determined by the CCP. Later, during the Great Leap Forward and the Cultural Revolution, Mao and his personal followers were the only arbiters of such judgments, thus inevitably undermining the basic principles of true mass democracy.

In 1949, China renamed itself the People's Republic of China (PRC), and its leaders began to refer to this period as "after liberation." At first, Mao and the CCP claimed that the New Democratic Revolution would continue for many years. This could be seen most famously in the Land Reform campaign of 1949–1950, in which peasants were given their own plots of land to till and landlords were eliminated as a class. Though the Land Reform campaign was violent and also served to legitimate the party dictatorship, it was, ironically, an essentially capitalist land reform. Along with allowing small private businesses and joint state-private businesses in urban areas, the campaign incorporated protomarketeer or Titoist policies that would later play an even more important role in CCP ideology.

After a series of campaigns against bureaucratism and bourgeois corruption, the party emphasized its anti-imperialist, nationalist credentials in the Oppose America, Aid Korea campaign in response to the Korean War. In 1952, Mao and the CCP shifted back to a Stalinist version of Marxist ideology, which brought China diplomatically closer to its Western neighbor. Recognizing that China needed help constructing socialism, the CCP suddenly shifted to a line of "leaning to one side," that is, accepting aid and advice from the Soviet Union. The party declared that the New Democratic Revolution was over and that the CCP was now leading China into the socialist phase of the revolution.

As such, throughout most of the early and mid-1950s, China copied the command economy from the Soviet Union, nationalizing all industry and taking on Soviet advisers. Land was gradually collectivized for agricultural purposes, which also adhered to the Stalinist model. The early collectivization of Chinese agriculture took place without as much violence and peasant resistance as there was in the Soviet Union in the 1930s, where millions of lives were lost.

As collectivization progressed, however, Mao and members of the CCP who were more personally beholden to him became emboldened by the seemingly easy success of building rural cooperatives. In 1955, and then after a brief interregnum in the Great Leap Forward of 1958–1960, the party, echoing its Yan'an roots, claimed that socialism could be constructed at the same time as the economy. Mao announced that China's peasants were poor and untouched, and that they had not yet been corrupted by capitalism, meaning that China could leap ahead of the USSR to an advanced stage of communism—the full flowering of social and economic equality—in the very near future.

The goals of the Great Leap Forward aimed to make town and countryside equal, and end the gap between rural farming and urban industry. Production would be increased, the party proposed, not by the coercive methods of the Stalinist five-

美國侵華史

劉大年 著

人民出版社出版
新華書店發行

一百餘年以來美國最初通過別國侵略中國繼之
單獨侵略爭奪霸權最後企圖獨佔中國本書綜述
這四個時期的史實從具體的史實中揭
露美國一貫偽善與兇狠的面貌本書原
名"美國侵華簡
史"經訂補充
後分量較前增
加一倍更名為
"美國侵華史"是
目前同類書中
較完善的一本。

Poster showing a large hand clutching a Chinese flag, pointing at Uncle Sam climbing over a brick wall and carrying a bloody knife. (Library of Congress)

year plans or the private plots and material incentives of the Titoists, but through moral or ideological persuasion. Under this policy, the practice of criticism and self-criticism sessions and the study of Marxism-Leninism–Mao Zedong thought was expanded beyond party members to the masses. Class struggle, rather than efforts to build up the forces of production, was Mao's key emphasis. Mao claimed that the class enemies were not outsiders, but forces within the party who were taking the capitalist road—in other words, anyone who favored market-based economic reforms.

In contrast to the ideological Maoist demand for unanimity, the events of 1956 allowed for a brief moment of sanctioned dissent within the party. This temporary openness came shortly after Nikita Khrushchev's secret speech to the Soviet Communist Party Central Committee, in which he denounced (some of) Stalin's crimes. At the same time, other CCP leaders managed to have the concept of collective leadership incorporated into official party ideology and stressed the idea that class struggle would have to take a back seat to building up the forces of production—that is, wealth and abundance. That year, intellectuals and others were briefly encouraged to speak up and criticize the shortcomings of the regime; this was known as the Hundred Flowers Movement. The events of 1956 had the effect of expanding reform beyond the economy to include the political arena, though only for a short time. Mao turned on his critics the next year, labeling them "poisonous weeds."

Whether Mao was overconfident and expected minimal criticism or was trying to "lure the snakes out of the grass" (i.e., to smoke out his opponents), in 1957, he led what was, in effect, a coalition of Stalinists and Maoists in an Anti-Rightist campaign against all criticism of the party. This amounted to a wide-scale purge of all opposition led and supported by Deng Xiaoping, though Deng later admitted that the campaign went too far. Most observers now view this campaign as the precursor to the Great Leap Forward. It eliminated all potential ideological opposition to Mao outside the party and scared off would-be opponents within the party, paving the way for the radical Maoism of the late 1950s and the Cultural Revolution of the late 1960s. Similarly, the second Anti-Rightist campaign of 1959 against Marshall Peng Dehuai further intimidated any potential rivals or critics from challenging Mao's policies directly. Peng Dehuai's crime was that he had dared to offer internal criticism of Mao's Great Leap policies at the Lushan Plenum of the party.

The Maoists' ideological emphasis on self-reliance during the Great Leap Forward and the Cultural Revolution also produced an ideological break with the Soviet Union, as China declared itself the purest socialist state. Though China continued to denounce U.S. imperialism, the CCP also denounced the Soviet leaders as "social imperialists" and "revisionists" who were taking the USSR back down the road to capitalism. According to the CCP, China represented the most progressive force in global socialism. Thus, under Mao, the CCP could claim that China had not only stood up to imperialism by declaring a new regime in 1949, but had continued to defend a strong national state that would emerge as a world leader.

As noted in Chapter 2, the extreme Maoism of the Great Leap Forward ended in economic disaster, and Mao was forced to retire to the second rank to allow other leaders to try to restore the economy in the early 1960s. From 1961–1963, a coalition of CCP leaders developed a combination of Stalinist central planning, modest market reforms, and other material incentives to help the country get back on its feet. Unlike the Hundred Flowers reform experiment of 1956, these reforms did not accommodate political or intellectual openness. Mao, perhaps reluctantly, went along with this change in ideology, while biding his time for a comeback.

But Mao wasn't interested in lying low for long. He was determined to refocus politics on the ideology of class struggle and launched an ideological counterattack, utilizing the People's Liberation Army (PLA) during the early 1960s under the leadership of Lin Biao, and the Great Proletarian Cultural Revolution of 1966–1976 to do so. Mao built up his own cult of personality and once again stressed the need for continuing class struggle, even after the revolution. This doctrine of continuing the revolution was trumpeted as Mao's main contribution to Marxism-Leninism during the Cultural Revolution. From 1966–1969 in particular, this movement led to great upheaval and even civil war in China, as young students organized into groups known as Red Guards with Mao's approval and roamed across the country, dragging out people in power and ransacking the homes and property of people deemed capitalist roaders. In order to gain the acquiescence of key leaders, such as Prime Minister Zhou Enlai, Mao largely exempted the countryside from the class struggle of the Cultural Revolution, though, in the end, the struggle became especially fierce throughout China.

ZHOU ENLAI (1898–1976)

Premier of the PRC from 1949 to 1976. Zhou first came to prominence as the leader of the Communist movement among Chinese students in Paris, and later became the political commissar of the Whampoa military academy under Chiang Kai-shek. He briefly headed the CCP's Politburo in the 1920s. His switch to support Mao during the Long March was crucial in Mao's rise to dominance. Zhou was careful to remain loyal to Mao thereafter, supporting the Great Leap Forward and the Cultural Revolution. He played a key role in the major diplomatic affairs of the PRC, including the Geneva Conference of 1954 and the rapprochement with the United States in 1972. Zhou is honored in contemporary China for protecting many people during the Cultural Revolution, though recent studies emphasize his role in failing to prevent Mao from starting that upheaval in the first place. Tacitly criticized during the late stages of the Cultural Revolution, Zhou was perhaps on the verge of being purged in January 1976, when he died of stomach cancer.

From 1976 to 1978, under the leadership of Hua Guofeng, the CCP tried to maintain the Maoist rhetorical focus on class struggle and ideological campaigns, while it also built productive enterprises, especially favoring large-scale, Stalinist-style, state-owned industries, such as the Baoshan steel complex and the Daqing oil fields. Given Hua's weak *guanxi* network among administrative leaders, as well as the shortages, bottlenecks, and disincentives that Stalinism brought to the economy, Hua ultimately failed to institutionalize his authority and develop sufficient support for his policies.

Beginning in late 1978, Deng Xiaoping emerged as the paramount leader of the PRC and returned to the ideological approach that emphasized the development of productive forces within the economy. Heralding a return to orthodox Mao Zedong thought, Deng and his supporters announced that the struggle to build up the productive forces was once again a political and economic imperative. According to Deng, Mao's doctrine of the Continuing Revolution was simply a deviation during his later years, when he became divorced from the masses. Deng declared that "practice was the sole criterion of truth" and that the party was not departing from Maoism, but, in fact, continuing the lessons that Mao and others had taught in Yan'an. Deng justified the shift by claiming that the early Communist leaders of China would endorse a departure from Marxist-Leninist orthodoxy in economic matters when Chinese conditions demanded experiment and change.

As the shift toward production unfolded, the party also expanded its attempts to allow positive economic incentives, first in the countryside and later in urban areas. Deng's supporters justified the market reform experiments as being particularly suited to the Chinese definition of socialism. Other significant changes followed. First, intellectuals were relabeled "workers of the mind," as opposed to the pejorative "stinking ninth label" (a category added to the traditional eight bad class elements of landlords, rightists, capitalist roaders, and others), as Maoists referred to them during the Great Leap Forward and the Cultural Revolution. As the market reforms progressed, some

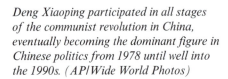

*Deng Xiaoping participated in all stages
of the communist revolution in China,
eventually becoming the dominant figure in
Chinese politics from 1978 until well into
the 1990s. (AP/Wide World Photos)*

Chinese prospered and others did not. To justify the inevitable inequalities produced by the market, the party officially declared the country to be in an early stage of socialism. Interestingly, the PRC now contradicted Mao's earlier doctrine, which worked to restrict inequalities as much as possible during the later stages of the Cultural Revolution. Deng's followers denounced radical Maoist egalitarianism as "eating out of one big pot" that, at best, led the country to an equality of poverty.

At worst, Deng and his followers charged that this radical Maoism only led to hypocrisy. Deng's coalition tried to expose the excesses of top Maoist leaders and put Mao's widow, Jiang Qing, and other Cultural Revolution leaders on trial in 1980. While denouncing the deviations of Mao and his personal followers from Mao Zedong thought, Deng and his group claimed they were the true inheritors of the May Fourth tradition (of those patriotic students in 1919, who first called for opposition to Japanese and Western imperialism) because they stood up for a strong Chinese nation. They claimed that for all the talk of self-reliance, Maoist policies, in fact, nearly bankrupted China and that it was Deng's reform policies that would bring prosperity and strength to the Chinese nation.

Deng's new coalition of Stalinist central planners and economic reformers was not without its own contradictions and tensions, however, as revealed by the ideological campaigns of the 1980s. First, in the Democracy Wall Movement of 1978–1980 outside the party, and later in the inner-party movements of the 1980s, members of Deng's coalition at the middle and lower echelons tried to test the limits of his pro-market line and push the connection between economic and political reform. With

DENG XIAOPING (1904–1997)

The paramount leader of the PRC from 1978 until his death in 1997, Deng became a Communist as a work-study student in Paris in the 1920s, under Zhou Enlai. As one of the CCP members who shifted to Mao's side during the Long March, Deng had a long and varied relationship with the Chairman; he was tasked by Mao to take over the post of General Secretary of the CCP in the 1950s, purged by him in the Cultural Revolution for being the second leading person taking the capitalist road, returned to power in 1973 to restore economic stability, purged again in 1976, after the April Tiananmen protests, and incorporated back into the leadership after Mao's death, where he quickly ascended and started a series of economic reforms, though he never officially claimed a top leadership post. He periodically approved crackdowns on political dissent, most notably the crackdown at the Democracy Wall in 1979–80 and the repression of the 1989 Tiananmen protests. When economic reform seemed to be threatened, he made his last important political contribution in 1992, with his southern tour of Special Economic Zones, which served as a signal to jumpstart economic reform.

support from Deng, political reform was added to the agenda, specifically the separation of party and state, the rehabilitation of past critics of the regime, and steps toward socialist legality and legal reform.

These steps were perhaps necessary to guarantee the permanence of economic reforms to both an internal and external audience. Internally, limited political reforms were required to reassure people who justifiably feared being labeled "bourgeois elements" by some future Maoist backlash if they expanded their private plots or small businesses, or made too much money in the rural or urban responsibility systems. Limited political reform was also necessary externally in order to reassure foreign nations and businesses investing capital in new projects in China that their properties would not be renationalized. Though political reform in China still had its limits, and criticism of China's Communist tradition was still suspect, in 1984, an official editorial in the CCP national newspaper *People's Daily* declared that the works of Marx and Lenin could not solve the problems of the present. A few days later, this statement was partially retracted to read that Marxism could not solve "all" of the current problems.

To take advantage of this possible political opening, throughout the 1980s, certain intellectuals, writers, and artists called for wider and deeper political reforms that might include democratization, human rights improvements, and an end to restrictions on criticism of the regime. Deng, however, remained committed to the hardliner ideological campaigns of the 1980s and against the "bourgeois liberal" elements.

This commitment was illustrated by the 1983 campaign against spiritual pollution in which Wang Ruoshui, a deputy editor of *People's Daily* and a Central Committee-level CCP member, was purged from his post for arguing that alienation continued to exist within socialist China. Drawing upon Marx's early writings, as well as the ideas of the Eastern European Marxist democrats of the 1960s and 1970s, Wang argued that the problem with the Cultural Revolution was its failure to focus on humanism. Humanist goals should have been the main socialist project in China, as Marx's early writings indicated, but instead, people turned on one another in the form of bitter class strife and internecine warfare.

Wang and other critics stressed that the roots of the Cultural Revolution remained intact, however. During the Cultural Revolution, the personality cult of Mao turned him into a god to be worshiped, while the people turned themselves into passive and obedient subjects. Critics from outside the party, such as Wang Xizhe of the Democracy Wall Movement, went further; Wang Xizhe labeled Mao a "feudal fascist emperor." He claimed that Maoism was not a socialist doctrine, but merely the ideology of a rural peasant rebellion that had once opposed tyrannical regimes and, in the end, merely served Mao's personal autocracy and that of his personal followers.

Such attempts by intellectuals to push the limits of the Deng-era ideological line met with fierce opposition, and Deng, again either willingly or out of necessity, allowed periodic campaigns against such critics, most famously the 1989 suppression of student demonstrators at Tiananmen Square. Just as the political reformers pushed the limits of reform, so, too, would ideological hardliners try to exploit crackdowns to push ideology in a Stalinist or even neo-Maoist direction. The fears of backlash materialized. Led by people such as Hu Qiaomu and Deng Liqun, these crackdowns, especially in 1983, 1987, and 1989, turned not just against those who called for democracy and human rights but, increasingly, against those with Western dress or attitudes, or even those making too much money. Whenever such campaigns went too far, Deng, based on his own beliefs or to avoid losing the support of economic reformers, stepped in to limit and end the campaigns, restoring economic reform to a high point. The 1989 student demonstrations at Tiananmen Square and the aftermath of their suppression serve as the clearest examples and culmination of the politics of the 1980s. Initially organized to coincide with the 70th anniversary of the May Fourth Movement of 1919, the demonstrations were moved up after the sudden death of Hu Yaobang from a heart attack.Hu had still been on the Politburo, but was purged as General Secretary of the party in 1987, after being blamed for allowing an earlier round of student demonstrations to get out of hand. Fearing the ascendancy of more Stalinist-inclined hardliners led by the premier, Li Peng, as well as the stalling of Titoist economic and even mild political reforms, university students in Beijing marched to the square to memorialize Hu. They adopted the style of the demonstrations of April 1976 in the same spot that memorialized the popular premier Zhou Enlai and marked the beginning of the end of the Cultural Revolution, a student movement that Deng's regime reevaluated as a revolutionary movement after he came to power in 1978. The 1989 protests quickly expanded and took on a life of their own, given the large foreign media presence in Beijing, which was due to Soviet leader Mikhail Gorbachev's visit to sign a new treaty with the PRC. The demonstrations protested government corruption and included demands for an independent students' union outside of the *nomenklatura* and *kontrol* functions. When ordinary citizens started to support the demonstrations and journalists from state-controlled media outlets began to report honestly on the events, and even join in the demonstrations with demands for their own independent unions, the split in the regime was out in the open. Zhao Ziyang was purged as General Secretary for calling for lenience toward the students, and Li Peng convinced Deng to support labeling the demonstrations as counterrevolutionary, culminating in a violent military crackdown on June 4th that cleared the Square.

The ideological justifications for increases in economic reform and simultaneous limits on political reform varied over the years and were not always explicitly outlined. Some continuing themes, however, re-emerged. First, in 1979, and again during the antibourgeois liberalization campaigns of the 1980s, Deng Xiaoping emphasized the "four cardinal principles" that were forbidden to be criticized: Marxism-Leninism–Mao Zedong thought, socialism, the People's Democratic Dictatorship, and, most importantly, Communist Party leadership. Second, following the line of his protégé, the premier, and, later, the CCP general secretary, Zhao Ziyang, Deng indicated that he favored a view of the PRC as a neo-authoritarian regime in the late 1980s. Almost openly comparing itself to Singapore, South Korea, and Taiwan (the latter two before their liberalization and democratization in the late 1980s and early 1990s), the PRC claimed it had to limit democracy. The party alleged that it needed to limit democracy not to preserve the interest of old elites and stall economic reform, as under Mao, but to carry out economic reforms, which in the short run could lead to inflation, unemployment, and other hardships before their payoffs became clear. The PRC even more openly pointed to the disasters of political reform within those ex-Communist systems as the justification for the continued repression of dissent in China, especially after the fall of the Communist regimes in the USSR and Eastern Europe.

Nationalism played an important role on all sides of the ideological disputes in the Deng era. This is particularly evident in the 1989 Tiananmen demonstrations and their aftermath, in which the students tried to project themselves as patriotic youth who, through self-sacrificing hunger strikes and criticism of official corruption, were the true heirs of the May Fourth Movement of 1919. At the same time, the students implied that the regime was the heir of the weak Qing dynasty of the late 19th century and the warlord governments of the early 20th century (see Chapter 2). The CCP countered by denouncing the students as corrupt lackeys and dupes of Western imperialism, implying that it was the PRC leadership that stood up to the West. In the aftermath of the Tiananmen movement and up to 1992, the regime moved in the most Stalinist and neo-Maoist direction of the Deng era, with stalled economic reform, the denunciation of Western attempts at peaceful coexistence as a secret plan to roll back communism, and a subsequent stall in foreign investment. In 1992, Deng made his last important intervention in Chinese politics in the form of his southern tour of Special Economic Zones, which again jumpstarted Titoist economic reform.

Throughout the 20th century, especially later in the century, China struggled to balance its openness with measured caution about Western influence and interaction with the West. At time, the CCP's ideology briefly slipped into harsh neo-Maoist rhetoric, not only in the aftermath of the Tiananmen demonstrations, but after events such as the bombing of the PRC embassy in Belgrade during the NATO war against Serbia, the missile crises over Taiwan of the mid-1990s, and the downing of

---

JIANG ZEMIN (1926–)

General Secretary of the CCP, 1989–2002, President of the PRC, 1993–2003. Brought to the central leadership in 1989 as a compromise candidate after the purge of Zhao Ziyang, Jiang had been Mayor and then Party chief of Shanghai in the mid- and late 1980s, where he managed to stop student protests without bloodshed. As the head of the third generation of leadership of the PRC, Jiang was a rhetorical supporter of economic reform, but otherwise tacked between Stalinist hardliners and Titoist reformers. After reaching the end of his two terms in office in both positions, Jiang retired in favor of Hu Jintao in 2003, giving up his post, as well as his position as Chairman of the Party's Military Affairs Commission. Perhaps as a consolation, his theory of the "Three Represents" was elevated to a status falling just below the ideologies of Mao and Deng.

---

a U.S. spy plane in 2001. However, given the continuing need for foreign investment and China's new links to the global economy, China's leaders have had to rein in strong language that might jeopardize economic relations with the West.

Even before Deng's death in 1997, but more openly after that time, Deng's initial designated successor, Jiang Zemin, tried to gain approval as the chief representative of the PRC's third generation of leadership. In official ideology, this has included, first, a continuation of the view that China remains in an early stage of socialism that requires economic reforms to further free up markets, as well as the continued privatization of state-owned firms. Second, before retiring, and perhaps as a reward for agreeing to give up his posts, including that of Chairman of the Party's Military Affairs Commission, Jiang was credited with ideological innovations that were nearly on par with those of Mao and Deng for his "Theory of Three Represents." The theory holds that in the contemporary era, the CCP represents the advanced social productive forces, advanced culture, and the interests of the overwhelming majority, which includes what Mao might have termed the "new bourgeoisie," that is, even the large-scale, patriotic capitalists who prospered in the reform era. In this regard, Jiang continued Deng Xiaoping's return to the ideal of the New Democracy of Yan'an, while also extending the Mao-Deng approach to developing a particularly Chinese form of socialism. Early in his first term, Jiang's successor, Hu Jintao, whom Deng designated the eventual leader of the fourth generation of leadership, has announced an ideological line of building a "harmonious society," which perhaps reflects a dim rhetorical survival of the Maoist emphasis on equality among regions and among people in the same region, even if in practice the stress on economic growth based on production for exports continues from the Deng era. As the CCP prepares for another generation of successors after Hu's second term as President ends in 2012, it remains to be seen whether this stress on equality and harmonious development will, in fact, lead to any shift away from the goal of economic growth at all costs, or whether the party will indeed devote real attention to some of the side effects and costs of the reform era, including political corruption, environmental degradation, and growing inequality between winners and losers in the reform era.

China's former president Jiang Zemin. (AP/Wide World Photos)

Whether Hu and his successors can maintain the uneasy ideological balance between political hardliners and economic reformers, or whether Chinese capitalist interests and global economic pressures in the party will eventually splinter the consensus on market-based reform is still not clear. It is impossible to tell whether such internal and external pressures will lead China to return to harsh nationalist rhetoric along the lines of Serbia under Milosevic or other politicians of the far right in Europe, or whether Marxist-Leninist ideology in China will gradually expand to include political liberalization and democratic reform.

PARTY-STATE STRUCTURE

The PRC is, on the one hand, a typical Communist regime in which the party controls the formal and informal levers of power through the *nomenklatura, kontrol,* and substitution principles discussed earlier in this chapter. On the other hand, the PRC contains many neotraditional formal and informal structures inherited from the modern state tradition. Despite major changes in the party-state structure from 1949 to the present, there has been a basic organizational continuity since 1954, when the core organs of state power were set up. Party, state, military, and mass organizational structures all include four levels: national or center, provincial (*sheng*), counties (*xian*), and municipalities (*shi*). But as in the Ming *lijia* and Qing *baojia* mutual surveillance systems, the Chinese Communist Party-State has tried to penetrate society beneath the county and municipal level in both formal and informal ways, as we will see below.

Party

The basic level of the CCP is the Primary Party Organization (PPO), a carryover from the revolutionary cells of the 1930s and 1940s. Under the PPO system, party members in every work unit (*danwei*) officially elect delegates to higher levels of authority. As at all levels, the upper levels of the party enforce discipline against PPO members and limit their real choices. The PPO elects delegates to a Primary Party Congress, which, in turn, elects members of a local party committee, led by a local party secretary.

Officially, the Primary Party Congress sends delegates to the County Congress. This congress then sends delegates to the Provincial Party Congress, which sends delegates to the National Party Congress. Under the Leninist principle of democratic centralism, each of these congresses officially elects a Central Committee, headed by a party secretary and a standing committee of other secretaries. In practice, of course, the upper levels make key decisions that the lower levels largely rubber stamp, and party committees and party secretaries act in the name of party congresses at every level, under the substitution principle discussed earlier in this chapter.

In the reform era extending from 1978 to the present, there has been some experimentation in the form of allowing nominations of more than one person for party elections at the primary and local levels. In addition, during the Maoist periods of the Great Leap Forward and especially the Cultural Revolution, decentralization to local and provincial party levels was emphasized, which often led not to democratization, but to control at the local level by party elites who were loyal to Mao, or "little Maos."

In the early years of the Cultural Revolution, party and state organs were temporarily eclipsed by Paris Commune-type mass organizations based on the model of the abortive 1871 uprising in Paris, which claimed to be comprised of direct, mass democracy. Mao quickly ordered these organizations to be abandoned in favor of revolutionary committees in which three-in-one combinations of military representatives, mass organizations, and returned cadres or officials would supposedly rule together.

When the party-state apparatus was restored in the early reform era, Deng Xiaoping introduced some structural reforms of the party organization, especially at the national level. Today, the National People's Congress meets more regularly than once every five years, as dictated by the party constitution (in fact, during Mao's reign, no Party Congress finished its full term), and officially elects not only a Central Committee typically composed of several hundred members that meets once or twice a year, but also a Central Discipline Inspection Committee (CDIC) that is in charge of investigating party members at all levels for corruption and deviation from party discipline. This organization represents a typical *kontrol* function in which party members report up to dual and triple lines of authority in order to ensure the party's control of the state.

This mechanism can be observed most clearly in the military, where decisions have to be approved not just by the military commander in each unit, but by the political commissar, as well. The CDIC also represents a holdover from the tradition of the censorate in imperial China, which was an administrative unit independent

Then-vice president Hu Jintao is shown during a meeting at the Pentagon in Washington, D.C., in May 2002. On March 15, 2003, four months after former president Jiang Zemin relinquished the role of Chinese Communist Party secretary, Hu became president of China. (Department of Defense)

of the rest of the central bureaucracy, whose function was to maintain loyalty to the center and prevent the rise of mountain-top kingdoms, or decentralized feudal bastions. Likewise, in the PRC, the CDIC represented one institutional attempt to maintain loyalty to the national government in an era of significant economic decentralization.

Another committee officially elected by the National Party Congress was the Central Advisory Committee (CAC), which Deng Xiaoping introduced in order to induce the retirement of key members of the party elite who might resist his reforms. After most of the potential opponents of his reforms were shunted to this committee and then retired or died, the CAC was abolished.

As in most Communist systems, the Central Committee also officially elects a Central Military Commission, which sits at the top of the political hierarchy within the People's Liberation Army and is the main method by which the party maintains control over the military, or, as Mao would say, the way the "party controls the gun."

In addition, the Central Committee officially chooses the general secretary of the party and the various other heads of the party secretariat, which includes Central Committee departments, which mirror the ministries and bureaus of the state. The post of general secretary was held by none other than Deng Xiaoping until the Cultural Revolution, when the post was abolished. When Deng gained control over the party in the late 1970s and early 1980s, he restored the post and gave it to his protégés—first, Hu Yaobang and then Zhao Ziyang, and, finally, after purging both of these men for being too weak against bourgeois liberalization, Deng named Jiang Zemin General Secretary of the Party and President of the PRC, and helped arrange for Hu Jintao to become the Vice-President and Jiang's designated successor.

HU JINTAO (1942–)

Current General Secretary of the CCP and President of the PRC, and former Vice-President of the PRC, 1998–2002. Brought to the Politburo under Deng Xiaoping in 1992 as the first representative of the so-called fourth generation of leadership, Hu had previously been party chief in Tibet, where he presided over a crackdown against demonstrations in favor of the Dalai Lama in 1989, before the Tiananmen protests. Though he was a strong supporter of Deng's economic reforms, in office, Hu has emphasized the policies of ensuring a harmonious society, stressing the need to help the regions and people left behind by market reforms, though he continues to oppose political liberalization. As he was originally put in office by Deng with a separate power base from his predecessor, Jiang Zemin, speculation about a continuing power struggle with Jiang has declined recently, as some of Jiang's reputed supporters in the Politburo have adopted a more independent stance.

Most importantly, the Central Committee elects a Political Affairs Bureau, or Politburo, of 14 to 24 members who meet on a regular basis and formally make key decisions on policy and personnel, which are ratified by lower levels. Departing from the Soviet model, another PRC body, the Standing Committee of the Politburo, comprised of four to seven members who meet weekly (as far as is known, since the committee meets in secret), is truly the most powerful body of the party and includes the key leaders of the PRC, who may also hold dual posts in the state and military apparatus. In the Mao era, there were also chairman and vice-chairman posts in the party, which headed the Politburo and Secretariat. As part of his effort to officially wrest the party from day-to-day control by the state, Deng abolished these chairman and vice-chairman posts in 1982, and restored the general secretary to the official leading role.

As revealed by Zhao Ziyang before his overthrow in 1989, however, with the agreement of the Politburo, Deng Xiaoping remained the paramount leader of the CCP even after he retired, while other retired cadres also maintained influence over the leading bodies of the CCP through their ability to have their protégés appointed to key top posts. This phenomenon was very similar to that of the *genro* who ruled behind the scenes in Meiji Japan, but it also resulted from the Deng-era reforms requiring people to retire from their posts after a set number of terms and/or at a certain age. In fact, Jiang Zemin and other key leaders retired from their party posts in 2002, at the party congress, and from their government positions in 2003, at the NPC Congress, and may hope to maintain influence from behind the scenes by keeping their own protégés in office. There was speculation that Jiang had been reluctant to retire from all of his official posts, a reluctance that may have been behind the delay in the opening of the CCP Party Congress, originally scheduled for September 2002. Even though he did hand over his post of general secretary to Hu Jintao in the end, the fact that Jiang was powerful enough to delay the party congress and at least consider retaining his posts—even in the face Deng Xiaoping's structural reforms— shows that the informal *guanxi* networks, as well as top leaders' need for deep and wide bases of power among Chinese political elites, were still paramount.

State

The structure of the state mirrors that of the party. Of course, despite officially being elected by and responsible to lower levels, all top state leaders are, in fact, subject to party control and supervision. In 1954, the state constitution established a national body to enact legislation, ratify treaties, and elect higher officers—the National People's Congress (NPC). The NPC includes up to 3,000 or so delegates who are officially elected by provincial congresses, chosen every four years, and supposed to meet at least once a year in a plenary session. The NPC has at least nine commissions that meet more regularly, plus a standing committee of 150 or so members that meets on a monthly basis, as well as a chair for that committee. In the Maoist era, that post was known as chairman of the state (a post held by Mao himself until he relinquished it to Liu Shaoqi in the early 1960s and, in turn, abolished the post after Liu's purge during the Cultural Revolution, though he retained his post as chairman of the party). The chairman of the NPC is now treated more as a speaker of the legislature since, in the reform era, Deng Xiaoping introduced the new posts of president and vice-president of China, which theoretically are situated at the top of the NPC hierarchy. The NPC also elects a Central Military Commission, which mirrors the Military Affairs Commission of the party and, in fact, may be identical to it in terms of its membership and meetings.

Finally, the NPC chooses a state council that includes a premier, vice-premier, state councilors, and the heads of other ministries and commissions. The state council also has a standing committee, or an inner cabinet, that works on a daily basis and is responsible to the Politburo and its standing committee. Though the NPC is mostly a rubber stamp, as with the formal legislatures in all Communist systems, greater dissent was allowed in the Deng era, including abstentions and even negative votes against both unpopular ministers (including the premier, Li Peng, after Tiananmen) and controversial policies (including Li Peng's pet project of the Three Gorges Dam on the Yangzi River, which has environmental and reform critics). Observers both within and outside of China speculate that the NPC may be the arena within which real rule by law will develop in the future, but only if the CCP relaxes its *nomenklatura* and other mechanisms, which currently ensure its dominance over governmental institutions.

The central state structure is mirrored at the provincial or municipal, city or county, township, and village or basic levels, at which congresses elect their own standing committees and government leaders. During the reform era, the CCP has allowed some real nominations and elections at village-level posts, which are monitored by international observers, but, so far, it has refused to extend these rights to the township, county, and provincial levels.

Four large cities, Beijing, Shanghai, Tianjin, and, most recently, Chongqing, have the status of provinces, while some provinces, especially those with non-Han ethnic majorities, have the official status of "autonomous regions." There may also be autonomous counties and lower levels within the provinces, but due to the party's control of the state, there is very little actual autonomy in these structures in practice. A new status, Special Administrative Region (SAR), was granted to Hong Kong upon its return to the PRC in 1997, and to Macao in 1999 (see below), a status that the PRC proposes granting to

Taiwan upon reunification. SAR status does include a great degree of real autonomy, though the chief executive of Hong Kong is, in effect, picked by a committee of the National People's Congress of the PRC and is subject to control by the CCP.

Military

Like other organizations, the military is subject to party discipline and control through the party's Military Affairs Commission and General Political Department, which has representatives at all levels of the army, navy, and air force, down to the basic unit. The Minister of Defense of the State Council is the administrative head of the People's Liberation Army (PLA), which includes the service arms of the army, navy, air force, and People's Armed Police. During the late Cultural Revolution, some key Maoist leaders attempted to expand the People's Militia, especially in urban areas, as a counterweight to the PLA, but today, it has largely been relegated to rural areas and placed firmly under the control of the People's Armed Police. In addition to being organized into service arms, the PLA is organized into military regions and districts. Historically, these four to seven regions replicated the main armies of the civil war period and spread across the regular administrative

The Tiananmen National Flag Escort of the People's Armed Police. (Macmaniac/ Dreamstime.com)

boundaries of the state. The *guanxi* networks of top leaders, at least up to the Jiang Zemin era, often had their roots in various field armies and military regions. Top CCP leaders thus periodically shift the commands of these regions and, in the case of Deng Xiaoping, change their numbers and boundaries in order to solidify their own control and prevent the possibility of a military coup.

Mass Organizations

As with most Communist regimes, the PRC officially allows many mass organizations to form—for women, artists, peasants, journalists, and so on—but all of these organizations fall firmly under the control of the CCP through its *nomenklatura* function, which enables the party to name the key heads of those organizations. The peak group of these organizations, the Chinese People's Political Consultative Congress (CPPCC), actually served as China's legislature from 1949 until the creation of the NPC in 1954, and continued to meet after that time based on the CCP's stance that it represented all progressive classes in society. In fact, the CPPCC constituent organizations include non-CCP political parties (even a rump Guomindang, consisting of members who never fled to Taiwan), all of which are subject to CCP control. The CPPCC was eclipsed and repressed during the Cultural Revolution, but has functioned again in the reform era as a rubber stamp advisory body for party congress decisions. As with the NPC, some limited dissent is permitted as long as it does not alter party policy.

Penetration of Society

In addition to the formal structure of the Chinese party-state, other informal or semiformal institutions help to extend the reach of the state to the county or municipal level. In the Cultural Revolution, the People's Communes at the township level formally extended state control beneath the county or *xian* level for the first time in Chinese history—officially as an attempt to build support for socialism among poor peasants. In reality, some observers contend, Mao's real goal was to militarize the peasants and use them as a counterweight to central officials in order to augment his autocratic power, similar to the *lijia* and *baojia* systems of mutual surveillance in the Ming and Qing dynasties. In the reform era, the official line is that commune- and township-level organizations must be officially separated, just as party and state organs should be separated at the higher levels. Nevertheless, other informal or semiformal mechanisms of social control remain, albeit weakened by market-oriented reform policies.

Criticism Groups (*Xiaozu*)

Criticism and self-criticism in workplace and small neighborhood groups (*xiaozu*) were hallmarks of Maoist organization. Essentially extending Communist Party discipline beyond the party and into the workplace, the *xiaozu* were a mass mobilization mechanism designed to ensure that CCP policies were obeyed and carried out by ordinary people. In the reform era, the *xiaozu* have been de-emphasized as both a forum for criticism and self-criticism sessions and a vehicle for mass mobilization. Though they have not been eliminated, they are now used primarily to announce party policy.

Danwei

In the 1950s, the PRC adopted the Soviet model of control through work units, or *danwei*. The *danwei* were an effective method of social control, especially in Stalinist periods, when central planning and the rationing of key goods was emphasized. Workers in state-owned factories gained access to subsidized housing, ration coupons for basic essentials, welfare, and retirement benefits, as well as permission to travel, marry, and have children all through the *danwei*. With the large-scale privatization and foreign investment of the reform era, the *danwei* are also declining in utility and importance, though they will retain at least some importance as a method of social control for the foreseeable future.

Hukou

After 1949, the regime attempted to control movement into the cities so as to prevent the rise of shantytowns and urban blight associated with many Third World countries, and also to maintain social control. As a result, Chinese citizens in urban areas were assigned *hukou*, or urban residence permits, that designated what size and type of urban area they were allowed to live in. Amid the decline of the *danwei* requirement in the reform era, the number of laborers in the cities without the proper *hukou* permits increased dramatically; many Chinese were working in the cities on temporary contracts and thus did not have formal legal access to public education, housing, and other benefits. The possibility for unrest, particularly from peasants in the countryside, who were suffering from overtaxation and extra fees imposed by township- and village-level officials, from this relatively unprotected urban sector was significant. As a result, the regime took steps to officially relax the *hukou* requirement in the 1990s, in effect acknowledging what had already occurred, namely that many people without the proper *hukou* took advantage of nonstate sector jobs and informal support networks, including nonofficial schools, in order to survive, however precariously. The regime continues to control migration to the largest cities, however, where recent urban migrants remain at a severe disadvantage in terms of housing, jobs, public education, and the like, a situation that may yet lead to social unrest in the future.

DOMESTIC POLICY: HUMAN RIGHTS AND DISSENT

According to human rights monitors, such as Amnesty International, Human Rights Watch Asia, and even the U.S. State Department, despite the relative openness of

Chinese policemen stand over a group of men convicted of crimes during public sentencing in front of a train station in China's southern city of Guangzhou, June 20, 2002. The convicted were sentenced to labor camps for "re-education." (Reuters/Corbis)

the reform era, the PRC continues to engage in a number of serious human rights abuses. These abuses include arrest and imprisonment, either through the formal legal system or labor camp (*laogai*) sentences, to which people can still be sentenced to three-year terms by local officials in the absence of a formal trial. Whether in the formal court and prison systems or in the *laogai*, in the reform era, prisoners may be required to work in prison factories for low or even no wages, with some perhaps producing goods for export.

There are several categories of political prisoners, the first among them being the human rights and democracy campaigners from the Democracy Wall and Tiananmen movements, including some who tried to form a new democratic political party. Another prisoner category is religious dissenters, including Catholics loyal to the Pope, rather than the party-controlled patriotic Catholic Church, as well as nonregistered Protestants and devotees of Falun Gong, and other allegedly evil cults based on traditional Buddhist and Daoist health and spiritual practices. This overlapping category of repressed people includes members of ethnic minorities from Tibet and other strategic provinces along China's Central and Inner Asian Frontiers, who are charged with being ethnic separatists. Human rights criticisms also include condemnations of the PRC's use of the death penalty not just for crimes of murder and kidnapping, but for more ordinary economic crimes. The charge has also been made that the regime fails to stop, and even condones, selling the organs of condemned prisoners for transplant operations.

FOREIGN POLICY: CHINA AND GLOBAL POLITICS

Due to political and economic pressures from the international system, Chinese foreign policy has not always varied along the three lines of Communist systems (Stalinist central control, Titoist markets, and Maoist ideological campaigns) or developed in harmony with domestic policy. Nevertheless, over time, there has been change and variation in PRC foreign policy along ideological lines.

In 1945, just before the civil war heated up, and again in 1949, the PRC put out feelers to the United States about improving their relations. But due to the Cold War and Republican accusations that the Truman administration had lost China to communism, U.S. relations with China were frozen, and the United States continued to recognize the Guomindang regime in Taiwan, known as the Republic of China, as the official Chinese government. The Republic of China also retained China's permanent seat on the UN Security Council. The PRC's interest in pursuing relations with the United States cooled with the outbreak of the Korean War (1950–1953), especially after U.S. forces under General Douglas MacArthur advanced to the Yalu River separating North Korea from China. In response, Chinese "volunteers" were sent into Korea to fight the Americans to a costly standstill, and the PRC's rhetoric quickly shifted to an anti-U.S., anti-imperialist line.

China's pro-Soviet stance of "leaning to one side" in the early 1950s led the country to sign a thirty-year Treaty of Peace, Friendship, and Mutual Assistance with the Soviet Union. The United States, in turn, sent the Seventh Fleet to patrol the Taiwan straits, thus preventing the PRC from taking over the island (while also preventing Chiang Kai-shek from launching any attempt to retake the mainland). Throughout the early and mid-1950s, China was heavily dependent on the Soviet Union for protection and support. After a crisis in 1954, when the PRC shelled two offshore islands controlled by Taiwan, the United States signed a mutual defense treaty with Taiwan, which only increased China's dependence on the Soviets.

Beginning in 1953, with the death of Stalin and the July truce agreement that halted the Korean War, the lean-to-one-side policy was moderated. Based on the rapid decolonization of the mid-1950s, under Premier Zhou Enlai, China shifted its foreign policy to support newly liberated colonies in the Third World, even if they did not lean toward the Soviet Union. Most notably, at the Bandung Conference in Indonesia in April 1955, Zhou Enlai announced conciliatory policies toward Third World states in Asia and Africa, and later Latin America. These policies even included a very modest foreign aid program and a stated willingness to start a discussion with the United States. China continued to refer to the "Bandung spirit" in later years as the basis for its claim to leadership of the Third World. Though never clearly translated into concrete institutions or actual leadership, China did receive a great deal of international sympathy and increased formal recognition at the expense of Taiwan due to its efforts during this period.

In the late 1950s, China shifted its foreign policy even further away from that of the Soviet Union, culminating in the official Sino-Soviet split of 1960. The reasons for this major split were numerous and complicated, but, at its root, the PRC was based upon an indigenous rural revolution that succeeded without much Soviet aid and support, and indeed, at times, China succeeded when it opposed Soviet advice. After the Soviet Union refused to give the PRC nuclear weapons in its dispute with Taiwan and the United States over the offshore islands, after Khrushchev denounced some of Stalin's crimes in his 1956 speech and announced polices of peaceful coexistence with the capitalist world, and after the Soviets denounced Mao's Great Leap Forward and pulled out their advisers, the stage was set to extend Maoist policies of self-reliance to the foreign policy arena.

This new policy included support for national liberation wars in the Third World, including, perhaps, support for the attempted coup d'état by the Communists in Indonesia and support for opposition parties and movements in Africa and Latin America. China also fought a war with India in 1962 over a border dispute and, although China won militarily, its involvement in the war prompted other nations to take notice. When China began testing its own independently developed nuclear weapons in 1964, it aroused fears and undermined its support in the Third World. By 1965, the Afro-Asian conference was postponed indefinitely after China failed to exclude the Soviet Union.

During the early years of the Cultural Revolution, China's foreign policy left it extremely isolated, with Albania as its only official ally. China's Red Guards criticized the official foreign policy establishment for being too influenced by bourgeois tendencies. To express dissent, the Red Guards attacked the foreign ministry itself and launched a brief seizure of the British embassy and other violent incidents in a number of foreign embassies, including Hong Kong. Chinese foreign policy was paralyzed for a time, and all of its ambassadors were recalled, save for the Egyptian ambassador. The Soviet Union was denounced at this time as a revisionist and social imperialist country that was led by capitalist roaders (an ironic accusation in retrospect, since any real market-based reforms that might have occurred in the Soviet Union were quashed by Leonid Brezhnev after his purge of Khrushchev in 1964). Tension with the Soviets increased to the point that border skirmishes in the Northeast occurred in 1968–1969, including a serious one in the Ussuri River in March 1969, when Chinese border guards fired on their Soviet counterparts, who responded in kind. This incident led to further border clashes in the Central Asian provinces bordering the USSR. For a time, rumors were rife throughout the world of a possible preemptive Soviet strike against China's nuclear facilities in Xinjiang province, and China was increasingly isolated from the global community.

Mao and other CCP leaders began to see the Soviet Union as the main enemy and came to favor reengagement with the rest of the world in the late 1960s, including the return of most ambassadors to their posts, as well as apologies and even some restitution for the attacks on foreign embassies during the height of the Cultural Revolution. Most famously, China initiated a new policy of rapprochement with the United States in the early 1970s, beginning with the "ping pong diplomacy" of April 1971, when an American table tennis team was allowed to visit China. The United States acquiesced to the PRC taking over the Chinese seat in the UN and acquiring a permanent seat in the Security Council in October 1971. In 1972, U.S. President Richard Nixon visited the PRC, and China shifted its policy away from isolation

A Chinese soldier poses next to a portrait of Mao Zedong in April 1969 on the border between China's Xinjiang province and the Soviet Republic of Kazakhstan, one of several sites where the two nations clashed in 1969 over border disputes. (AFP/Getty Images)

and toward rapprochement with the United States. This occurred even as the United States was involved in the war in Vietnam and the Cultural Revolution was officially continuing. The chief impediment to the full normalization of relations between the United States and the PRC, however, was the Taiwan issue. In the famous Shanghai Communiqué issued jointly at the end of President Nixon's 1972 visit, the United States and the PRC declared "all Chinese on either side of the Taiwan Strait maintain that there is but one China and that Taiwan is part of China. The United States government does not challenge this position." This public statement did not incite a public outcry in Taiwan at the time because of the Guomindang's tight control and repression of any pro-Taiwan independence sentiments percolating within its borders. Today, a democratized Taiwan is home to many outspoken proponents of an independent Taiwan, which may lead to greater tensions and possibly even war in the Taiwan straits.

In the early 1970s, however, President Nixon agreed to reduce U.S. military support for Taiwan, and began a process of normalizing relations with China. This started with the establishment of a liaison mission headed by George H. W. Bush and culminated in the establishment of full diplomatic relations on January 1, 1979, during the Carter administration. America pulled its military advisers from Taiwan, abrogated the U.S.-ROC Mutual Security Treaty, and markedly increased its trade,

U.S. President Richard Nixon meets Chinese Communist Party Chairman Mao Zedong during Nixon's historic visit to China in 1972—the first such trip by a U.S. president. The visit provided a memorable symbol of the thawing of Cold War tensions and initiated cultural exchanges between the two nations. (National Archives)

cultural, and other contacts with China. In response, the U.S. Congress passed the Taiwan Relations Act in April 1979, which some analysts believed gave Taiwan more promises of aid than the previous security treaty. In any case, the act codified into law previous executive branch pledges to sell defensive weapons to Taiwan to prevent the PRC from attacking it.

This full normalization of relations with the United States occurred at the beginning of Deng Xiaoping's reform era in China. In 1974, Mao's view divided the world into three camps: the United States and the Soviet Union; Japan, Europe, and Canada; and China, along with the entire continent of Africa, the rest of Asia, and Latin America, though, according to this view, China acted against the hegemony of both First World powers, and Deng reformed China's policies to move closer to the United States. Trade and investment from the United States and Europe greatly expanded in the Deng years as China joined the World Bank and the International Monetary Fund, and began long negotiations that culminated in it joining the World Trade Organization in 2002. This tilt toward the United States and the West started in 1979, after China fought a war with its communist neighbor, Vietnam, and after that country invaded Cambodia and expelled the Pol Pot regime allied to the PRC.

China proceeded to further distance itself from the Soviet Union. After the Soviet Union subsequently allied itself even more closely to Vietnam and obtained military bases in Cam Ranh Bay, the PRC abrogated its 1950 treaty with the USSR, and after the Soviet invasion of Afghanistan, China suspended talks aimed at negotiating a new treaty. In the 1980s, however, Chinese frustrations with the United States increased as American arms sales and military transfers to Taiwan continued and as the United States continued to put restrictions on Chinese textile imports. As a result of these frustrations, China adopted a more equidistant policy between the United States and the Soviet Union, a policy that culminated in Mikhail Gorbachev's visit to Beijing in May 1989. A new Sino-Soviet treaty was signed, the two countries' longstanding border disputes were settled, and a mutual demilitarization of the Sino-Soviet and Mongolian-Soviet borders was declared. Deng Xiaoping perhaps intended this treaty to be his final crowning achievement in foreign policy, but, of course, Gorbachev's visit was completely overshadowed by the Tiananmen demonstrations of April–June 1989. After June 4, 1989, when the demonstrations were brutally repressed, China's image and relations with the rest of the world were temporarily damaged. In 1992, the world's interest in relations with China resurfaced when Deng Xiaoping toured southern China and ordered market reforms to be enacted more quickly, including a greater openness to Western investment.

Despite the end of China's isolation from the rest of the world and the opening up of its economy to foreign trade and investment, some observers fear that China may again become an enemy of the West and a threat to world peace in the new century. Evidence for this new alleged threat includes increased Chinese missile sales and nuclear-related exports to Algeria, Pakistan, Syria, Iraq, and Iran. China has also raised international concerns due to its aggressive territorial claims of islands in the South and East China seas, which could lead to military tensions with Japan and the nations of Southeast Asia. The country's close ties and support of the repressive military regime in Myanmar (formerly Burma) are also a source of concern. Tensions with the United States spiked upwards in recent years, first with the U.S. bombing of the Chinese embassy in Belgrade during the NATO war against Yugoslavia in 1999, and later with the shooting down of a U.S. spy plane over the Taiwan Strait in 2001. In 2008, the PRC regime again whipped up nationalist rhetoric in response to foreign calls for boycotts of the opening ceremony of the Beijing Olympics over complaints about China's treatment of Tibetans and the PRC's support of unsavory regimes in Sudan, Burma, and elsewhere. Others, especially in the PRC, would argue that China is only assuming its rightful place in Asian and world leadership and that, despite possible future conflicts over oil and other natural resources, China's need to continue to improve its peoples' living standards by participating in the global economy will prevent it from becoming a military threat.

In the past decade or so, Chinese foreign policy has perhaps been most significantly affected by Taiwan. As Taiwan liberalized and democratized its own political system from the late 1980s onward, and shifted to a more flexible diplomacy in which it increasingly welcomed contacts and relations with countries who recognized the PRC, the threat of Chinese military action against Taiwan—ironically—increased. After the selection of the first native Taiwanese, Lee Tenghui, as president of the Republic of China (ROC) and the resulting Chinese fear that he held a secret independence agenda, despite his then-leadership of the Nationalist Party, or Guomindang, China began a series of missile tests and war games in the Taiwan Strait in 1995–1996, which led the Clinton administration to send U.S. aircraft carriers into the strait.

With the subsequent rise to power of President Chen Shui-bian of the opposition Democratic Progressive Party (DPP), at least half of whose members favor eventual Taiwanese independence, there were periodic revivals of tensions in the Taiwan Strait during the early years of the new millennium. Continuing international tensions and domestic politics on all three sides (China, Taiwan, and the United States), in which politicians often have to play to their hardliners and prove their nationalist credentials (or, in the case of the United States, anti-Communist credentials), guarantee that this issue will be a contentious one well into the future. U.S. President George W. Bush's first-term announcement to end the U.S. policy of "strategic ambiguity" (as to whether the United States would always come to Taiwan's aid in the event of an attack) and his reference, mistaken or not, to the "Republic of Taiwan" may yet serve to increase tensions.

Upon his election as president of the ROC in Taiwan in 2000, Chen Shui-bian announced that he would not declare Taiwan independent or even call for a referendum on the issue in the future, and he agreed to open Taiwan to direct trade and contact with the mainland, which helped to allay the fears of the United States and increase Taiwan's support in Washington. Later in his second term, however, Chen Shui-bian declared that Taiwan is already a de facto independent country and that it may have to consider calling a referendum on independence in the future if the PRC threatens reunification by force. As a result, talks between Taiwan and the PRC stalled, though tensions did not heat up to the point that they did in the late 1990s, perhaps due to the PRC's need to maintain relations with the United States and the Western world in order to continue to improve its economy. Chen Shui-bian also seemed to be wary of opening up further trade with the mainland, a policy shift that seemed to hurt his party, as the Guomindang blamed Chen and the DPP government for a relative slowdown in Taiwan economic growth during Chen's second term. In the presidential election of 2008, Chen managed to add a referendum to the ballot seeking UN admission for Taiwan, which further inflamed China, though the issue failed to pass, as the winning Guomindang urged its voters not to participate in the referendum, leading to what may be a thawing of relations between Taiwan and the PRC in the near future (see below).

Nevertheless, after the repression of the Tiananmen demonstrations, and continuing with the crackdowns against Falun Gong and regional autonomy or separatist advocates in the 1990s, CCP leaders became even more dependent on nationalism as a strong component of the regime's legitimacy. If Chinese economic growth and development falter in the near future, the PRC regime may be tempted to play the nationalist card over Taiwan in order to maintain its legitimacy. Again, the question is whether China's need for global trade and investment will outweigh the need of its leaders to prove their nationalist credentials, leading instead to a more demilitarized foreign policy.

GREATER CHINA ISSUES

A major component of the reforms enacted by Deng Xiaoping was his changing of official PRC policies on Hong Kong and Taiwan (as well as on the former Portuguese colony of Macao, which is now mostly a gambling haven), the only parts of China that were officially colonized by Western powers in the 19th century.

Hong Kong

Though Hong Kong island and the adjacent Kowloon peninsula were ceded to Great Britain in perpetuity in the Opium Wars of 1839–1842 and 1860, the new territories that Britain leased from China for 99 years in 1898 were due to go back to China in 1997. People on all sides realized that Hong Kong as a whole was not a viable colony without those territories and that China could bring Hong Kong to a standstill merely by turning off the water. As a result of pressure from businesspeople and those concerned about long-term leases and other business deals, in the early 1980s, Great Britain began to negotiate with China about Hong Kong's return to the PRC, culminating in the Basic Agreement of 1984, in which Britain agreed to hand over Hong Kong to Chinese sovereignty in 1997, and China agreed to a policy of "one country, two systems," under which Hong Kong would be declared a Special Administrative Region (SAR) of the PRC and be allowed to keep its capitalist economy and autonomous political system for at least 50 years after accession. The PRC openly announced that this policy was meant to serve as an example to Taiwan, which it offered a similar deal under even more generous terms, under which Taiwan's SAR could maintain Guomindang control and even its own military as long as it agreed to officially declare itself a province of the PRC. In Hong Kong, by contrast, People's Liberation Army troops replaced the British as the main police force when the colony became a SAR. Hong Kong and Taiwan, however, have key differences that so far have resulted in different outcomes for the "one country, two systems" offer.

In the first place, Hong Kong was a British colony that never had pretensions of being an independent state, and second, it was never a democracy. A British-appointed governor ruled Hong Kong, advised by an appointed executive council and an appointed and mostly indirectly elected 60-member Legislative Council (LegCo). When the last British governor of Hong Kong, Christopher Patten, increased the number of directly elected seats, China strongly protested this action as an abrogation of the Basic Agreement. When China promulgated the Basic Law (Hong Kong's mini constitution), it returned the number of directly elected seats to 18 and declared China's National People's Congress as the final site of appeal for Hong Kong's courts. Since Hong Kong's return to the PRC in 1997, the feared mass exodus of its citizens has not materialized, but CCP decisions indicate to many that Hong Kong's real autonomy may be eroding. These decisions include overturning lower Hong Kong court decisions on issues such as rights of abode in Hong Kong for certain immigrants, the resignations of civil servants and journalists, proposed new laws limiting the rights of free assembly, and the denial of visas for Falun Gong members and others. Hong Kong only slowly recovered from the Asian financial crisis of the late 1990s, and may

The raising of the Chinese flag in Hong Kong in June 1997 marked the moment the territory reverted to Chinese rule. (AP/Wide World Photos)

also be threatened by the revival of Shanghai as a site of international investment and banking now that China has joined the World Trade Organization. With the sudden resignation of SAR Chief Executive Tung Chee-hwa in 2005, under pressure from the PRC, a constitutional crisis ensued, given the lack of procedures in place under the Basic Law to deal with a mid-term replacement. Beijing finally managed to engineer the selection of respected former civil servant Donald Tsang to fill out Tung's term on an interim basis and then had the pro-Beijing electoral college, which selects the Chief Executive, choose Tsang for a full term of his own in 2007. Beijing has let it be known that it will not allow full direct elections for the Chief Executive and LegCo until after the 2012 elections, further disrupting the democracy movement in Hong Kong.

Taiwan

Taiwan was a colony of Japan from the end of the first Sino-Japanese War in 1895 to the end of World War II in 1945. After a brief period of rule by a corrupt Guomindang governor from 1945 to 1949, which included a massacre of the Taiwanese after a riot in 1947, Taiwan became the site of the national Guomindang government under Chiang Kai-Shek when it lost the civil war on the mainland in 1949. With the rise of the Cold War in Asia, the United States committed itself to defending Chiang's regime and sent its Seventh Fleet into the Taiwan Strait to prevent a PRC takeover (and, less widely known, to prevent Chiang from attacking the mainland, as noted above).

Far from being the bastion of Free China that its advocates in the China lobby in the United States proclaimed, from 1949 until its liberalization in the mid-1980s, Taiwan was a one-party military dictatorship in which martial law was declared and all independent political activity outside the Guomindang was banned, with Taiwan independence advocates being especially subject to arrest, imprisonment, and torture.

The Guomindang did carry out a series of economic reforms, beginning with land reform that resulted in an economic miracle and huge development on the island, aided by industrial infrastructure that was first built by Japan, heavy amounts of U.S. aid in the key early years, and a free trade environment for its exports into the 1960s. Under the rule of Chiang Kai-shek's son and eventual successor, Chiang Ching-kuo, Taiwan gradually started to liberalize its political system in the mid-1980s, due also to heavy pressure from *dangwai*, or independent nonparty forces. Eventually, this led to democratization in the 1990s under Chiang's Guomindang successor, the native Taiwanese Lee Teng-hui, who eventually legalized non-Guomindang parties, including the Democratic Progressive Party, at least half of whose members favored Taiwanese independence. As noted above, this democratization process culminated in the election of the DPP's Chen Shui-bian as president in 2000, followed by the loss of the Guomindang's majority in the legislature for the first time in 2001.

Lee Teng-hui changed Taiwan's policy from the "three no's" (no contact, no negotiations, and no compromise) with the PRC to one of flexible or substantive diplomacy, as the PRC's image suffered after Tiananmen, and as the democratization of Taiwan increased. International sympathy and support for Taiwan increased and global public perceptions of Taiwan as intransigent and the PRC as conciliatory reversed. Nevertheless, the rise of the DPP and the end of the rule of the CCP's old enemy, the Guomindang, ironically increased tensions between the two sides since the ruling party in Taiwan no longer had any stake in claiming to be the sole legitimate government of all of China and represents mostly native Taiwanese (descendants of immigrants from southern China from the 17th to 19th centuries) who have no identification with either the CCP or Guomindang. In 2008, with the victory of the Guomindang in the legislative elections and the election of their leader, Ma Ying-jeou, as President, relations between the PRC and Taiwan almost immediately seemed to ease, with discussions held between PRC President Hu Jintao and Taiwan Vice-President-elect Vincent Siew on opening up more trade and commercial ties.

Under both the DPP and the Guomindang, Taiwanese investment in the mainland greatly increased, just as the Taiwanese economy improved to the point where it lost its cheap labor advantage and needed to move investments offshore. Although China is much less dependent on Taiwanese investment given its much larger size, any action against Taiwan—such as a missile blockade, if not an outright invasion—could severely reduce investment and trade from other countries. It is in this light that global public opinion and sympathy for Taiwan's democratization plays such a large role; nowhere is the relation between economic liberalization and political reform more apparent and obvious. Whether Taiwan will prove to be an example of how China itself will democratize in the future, or whether tensions between the PRC and Taiwan will lead to military hostility and war, will be the main question regarding Chinese politics and foreign policy in the years to come.

REFERENCES

Amnesty International. 2007. Annual Report for China. Reprinted at http://www.amnesty usa.org/annualreport.php?id=ar&yr=2007&c=CHN.

Andrew, Anita M., and John A. Rapp. *Autocracy and China's Rebel Founding Emperors: Comparing Chairman Mao and Ming Taizu.* Lanham, MD: Rowman & Littlefield, 2000.

Bernstein, Richard, and Ross Munro. *The Coming Conflict with China.* New York: Alfred A. Knopf, 1997.

Dittmer, Lowell. "Bases of Power in Chinese Politics." *World Politics* 31, 1 (October 1978), pp. 26–61.

Dreyer, June Teufel. *China's Political System: Modernization and Tradition.* 6th ed. New York: Pearson Longman, 2008.

Friedman, Edward. *National Identity and Democratic Prospects in Socialist China.* Armonk, NY: M. E. Sharpe, 1995.

Gurley, John G. *Challenges to Communism.* San Francisco: Freeman and Co., 1983.

Hammer, Darrell P. *The USSR: The Politics of Oligarchy.* 3d ed. Boulder, CO: Westview Press, 1990.

Human Rights Watch World Report 2008: *Events in China in 2007:* Reprinted at http://china. hrw.org/press/other_news/hrw_world_report_2008_events_in_china_in_2007.

Kelly, David. "The Emergence of Humanism: Wang Ruoshui and the Critique of Socialist Alienation." In *China's Intellectuals and the State: In Search of a New Relationship,* 159–182. Edited by Merle Goldman, Timothy Cheek, and Carol Lee Hamrin. Cambridge, MA: Harvard University Press, 1987.

Lieberthal, Kenneth. *Governing China: From Revolution through Reform.* New York: W. W. Norton, 1995.

McCormick, Barrett L. *Political Reform in Post-Mao China: Democracy and Bureaucracy in a Leninist State.* Berkeley: University of California Press, 1990.

People's Republic of China and United States. "Joint Communique." February 27, 1972. Reprinted in *Peking Review,* March 3, 1972, p. 5.

Saich, Tony. *Governance and Politics of China.* 2nd Edition Revised and Updated. New York: Palgrave MacMillan, 2004.

Schurmann, Franz. *Ideology and Organization in Communist China.* 2d ed. Berkeley: University of California Press, 1968.

Solinger, Dorothy, ed. *Three Visions of Chinese Socialism.* Boulder, CO: Westview Press, 1984.

Walder, Andrew G. *Communist Neo-Traditionalism: Work and Authority in Chinese Industry.* Berkeley: University of California Press, 1986.

Wang, James C. F. *Contemporary Chinese Politics: An Introduction.* 6th ed. Upper Saddle River, NJ: Prentice Hall, 1999.

Wang Xizhe. "Mao Zedong and the Cultural Revolution." In *On Socialist Democracy and the Chinese Legal System: The Li Yizhe Debates,* 177–260. Edited by Anita Chan, Stanley Rosen, and Jonathan Unger. White Plains, NY: M. E. Sharpe, 1985.

The Modern Chinese Economy

Warren Bruce Palmer

Any understanding of the economic challenges and choices faced by China today must incorporate an appreciation of the magnitude of China's population. The economic well-being of one-fifth of the world's population depends on the performance of the Chinese economy; more than 1.3 billion people are making their living in this ancient land, which possesses less than 7 percent of the world's cultivated acreage.

In the 18th century, China's economy was the largest in the world, accounting for 25 percent of global output. China's wealth was admired and its social organization praised. Yet after a short time, the industrializing world left China behind, and it tumbled into a long period of domestic crisis and relative economic stagnation that was exacerbated by foreign invasion. In the first half of the 20th century, China was called "the poor man of Asia." One-fourth of the world's population lived in China, but by 1949, its economy produced only 5 percent of global output, and hundreds of millions of China's citizens lived in terrible poverty.

The 1949 triumph of the Chinese Communist Party in its civil war with the Nationalist Party produced the most effective national government in over 100 years. The new government achieved some remarkable successes, particularly in public health, raising life expectancy from less than 40 years in 1949 to nearly 70 years by 1978. Yet, the economic record was very mixed.

By the late 1970s, China had established itself as a major industrial power by employing the Soviet development strategy, but its industry was inefficient, producing inferior products with antiquated technology. Meanwhile, its market-oriented East Asian neighbors excelled at producing the newest consumer products with advanced, efficient technology.

China's industrial expansion served mainly to expand heavy industry, not to increase consumption or rapidly improve living standards. Even in urban China, which received preferential treatment, consumer goods were low in quality, lacking

*At night, a distant view of the Huangpu River, the Bund, and the Puxi area in Shanghai.
(iStockPhoto.com)*

in variety, and hard to obtain, even with ration coupons. In rural China, which accounted for 80 percent of the nation's population, the growth of agricultural output barely kept pace with the growth of the population, and in the 1970s hundreds of millions of China's rural citizens still lived in severe poverty.

However, since instituting a series of economic reforms, beginning in 1979, the Chinese economy appears to be on a spectacular roll. According to its official statistics, China's economic output, as measured by real gross domestic product (GDP), grew 9.6 percent per year between 1978 and 2005. Because the population grew 1.1 percent per year over the same time period, economic output per person in China has grown about 8.5 percent per year—the equivalent of the per capita GDP doubling every 8.5 years.

These results are the best ever recorded by any economy over such a long period of time. Such rapid growth has lifted more people out of severe poverty in a shorter period of time than ever before. Officially, 200 million people living just above the starvation level have escaped dire poverty since the enactment of the economic reforms.

In terms of purchasing power, China already has the world's second-largest economy, and the fourth-largest, based on a comparison of GDPs using exchange rates. Using this data, China could have the world's largest economy by at least 2035, if it sustains this rapid growth in the future. In purchasing power terms, China's GDP could be the world's largest by 2015. Whichever method is used to compare GDP across nations, the message is clear: As a major actor, China has arrived to stay on the world's economic stage. Consider the remarkable fact that China contributed more to global economic growth in 2007 than the United States, a trend that is likely to continue for some time to come.

MODERN ECONOMIC GROWTH

Real gross domestic product (GDP) is the inflation-corrected, market value of final goods and services produced in a nation in a year. Modern economic growth is sustained growth in real GDP per person for successive generations and has only been achieved in the past 250 years.

Modern economic growth results from the development and application of new scientific, technical knowledge to the continual transformation of production. A modern economy consists of mechanical production systems powered by inanimate energy, especially electric power and liquid fuels, and linked together by mass transportation systems that rapidly move goods and information at a low cost. These systems greatly magnify human effort, and their continual development is caused by and results in the continual invention and refinement of new products and production processes.

Since 1949, attaining and maintaining modern economic growth has been the most important goal of the Chinese Communist Party, and is one of three pillars of the continued legitimacy of CCP rule, along with maintaining domestic order and national integrity. Any annual growth rate below 6 percent threatens the maintenance of domestic tranquility.

China has gone from having one of the world's most closed economies to having one of the most open economies. China is the world's third-largest trading nation and will soon be the second largest. Following Deng Xiaoping's slogan that some must become rich first, the super-rich now call China home. With the 2008 Summer Olympics, China announced that it is back to being one of the world's top nations.

These basic statistics tell the story of China's great economic success. However, considered alone, they oversimplify the story of China's modern economic development—which, in fact, is a dramatic, complicated saga rooted in China's past that is still unfolding and reshaping the fate of one-fifth of the world's population. The longer story that follows traces the rise of China's traditional economy, its subsequent and relative fall, and its eventual success with establishing robust, modern economic growth in the world's most populous nation.

CHINA'S TRADITIONAL AGRICULTURAL ECONOMY

Worldwide, the pre-industrial, traditional economy was a rural, agriculture-based economy powered almost entirely by animate energy—human and animal muscle power. The traditional economy did not support sustained growth of output per person over successive generations. In the traditional economy, most people lived in the countryside and worked in agriculture. The pattern of the seasons, the demands of farming, and the power of local customs ruled people's lives. Economic relationships and practices changed slowly over time, much more slowly than in the modern economy.

Yet, even before the modern era, Chinese civilization attained high levels of achievement, based on its traditional agricultural economy. This agricultural economy produced sufficient surplus beyond the basic needs of farming families to support

Farmers tend to the rice harvest in southern China. (Corel)

large urban populations, extensive government organizations, major public works, standing armies, and active intellectual and artistic elites. For centuries, China had the world's most advanced civilization, judged by its achievements in literature, art, government, science, and production technology. Yet, as Chapter 2 demonstrated, China's economic success was repeatedly disrupted by war.

China's Population Before 1850

In times of peace, China's population probably grew at a fairly constant rate of 1 percent per year, doubling every 70 years. However, until 1000 C.E., China's population failed to surpass the peak of 60 million recorded in 2 C.E. because periods of war repeatedly interrupted the relatively short periods of peace (see Figure 4.1). The population then contracted as large numbers of soldiers and civilians died violently and even more succumbed to the famine and pestilence caused by the wartime economic disruption. This pattern changed in the 150 years of sustained peace during the Northern Song dynasty (960–1127) when the population grew to 120 million. Two dramatic population contractions occurred thereafter during periods of invasion and civil war, but the peacetime population had grown so large that 60 million represented its lower limit. Then, long periods of peace in the Ming (1368–1644) and Qing (1644–1911) dynasties resulted in large population growth. By 1850, China supported almost half a billion people with agricultural technology that was largely developed 1,000 years earlier.

THE CITY IN SONG CHINA

Song China produced the largest city that China, and perhaps the world, had ever known before modern times. The capital of the southern Song, Lin'an (today's Hangzhou), had a population of between one and two million. The accomplishments of a civilization can best be judged by its cities. The city concentrates human energy and intelligence, leading to significant achievements in arts, literature, and science, and requiring high levels of economic surplus to support concentrated, non-agricultural populations. In addition, by concentrating people in a relatively small area, stable cities require both complex public health systems to prevent epidemics and sophisticated social systems to maintain public order. Song China's urban development was supported by such high levels of technological and commercial development that scholars have long pondered why China's industrial revolution did not begin in the 12th and 13th century. Many Chinese inventions from that period later became important components of the European industrial revolution.

China has had a long history of advanced urban development. The total urban population, living in 36 large cities and 500 smaller cities, numbered about 4.3 million in 300 B.C.E.—more than 14 percent of the population. Chang'an, the capital during the Tang dynasty (618–907), had more than 800,000 residents. Lin'an (present-day Hangzhou in Zhejiang Province), the capital of the southern Song dynasty (1127–1279), may have reached a population of 2.5 million in the early 1200s, including its suburbs.

These cities throughout the country were much more than administrative centers; considerable productive activities were centered in the cities. Highly developed workshops existed for the production of all manners of goods that were used by both rural and urban residents.

As Figure 4.2 shows, the share of China's population living in cities and towns reached a peak in the 1200s and declined thereafter, falling by 1800 to a level that

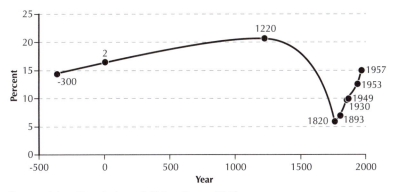

Figure 4.1. *Population of China, 2 C.E.–1850*

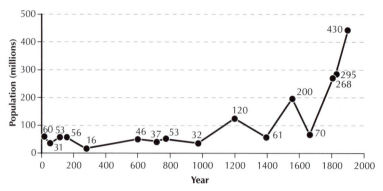

FIGURE 4.2. *Percentage of China's population living in urban areas, 300 B.C.E.–1957*

was lower than the one achieved 2,000 years before. The total number of urban residents probably did not increase after the early 13th century, and the countryside absorbed the increased population. As the urban percentage of the population fell, the number of smaller towns increased and the largest cities held fewer people than in the Song dynasty.

The Family: The Foundation of the Traditional Economy

The ability of rural China to absorb more and more residents derived from the economic flexibility of rural families. By the 1700s, China's population had grown so large that neither rampant disease, natural disaster, nor massive civil war could reverse its growth trend—so long as the willingness to found and expand families continued unabated. This willingness formed the bedrock of Chinese tradition and culture, which places the highest value on family, the central economic and religious institution in China, and on the perpetuation of family through the birth of male heirs.

Family members existed to serve the living family and to worship their ancestors. Even the poorest of young men sought early marriage and the birth of sons to continue their family lineage. Early marriage was almost universal for Chinese women. The cultural family imperative resisted deteriorating economic conditions. The rural Chinese responded by supporting growing families on smaller and smaller farms, rather than limiting the size of the family.

The average farm size in China had been generally decreasing for centuries. Even in the 11th century, the average Chinese household farmed about 5 acres, while the typical English peasant tilled 30 acres. Yet, up to the 12th century, the Chinese were still inventing labor-saving agricultural implements. Thereafter, technological efforts were more focused on increasing output per acre than output per worker. The central economic task for the Chinese farm became how to utilize a growing population.

The rural Chinese family was a complex economic unit that uniquely tolerated overpopulation. The Chinese family system coped with the worsening land-people

Farmers working in a grain field (page from Bianmin tuzuan—Ming dynasty). (Library of Congress)

ratio by intensifying its agricultural efforts and diversifying its economic activities. Small-scale handicraft production for home use and for the market became an increasingly important part of the rural economy and replaced much of the urban production. This development increasingly drew farm families into a market economy, and this, in turn, spurred further development of the market economy, including the proliferation of smaller towns mentioned above. These towns served to collect the peasant families' output and to supply them with the production and consumption goods they could not produce themselves. Paradoxically, the relative decline of large cities coincided with a greatly expanded population engaged in greatly expanded market activities in the 18th century.

China's Economy in the 18th Century

China's traditional agricultural economy reached its high point in the 18th century as China reached its largest geographic size, and its economy accounted for approximately 25 percent of global economic output. During the Qing dynasty, an extended period of peace, the introduction of new crops, improvement to traditional crops, and expanded irrigation allowed China's population to grow and expand into formerly uncultivated lands. China's population doubled in the 1700s, reaching perhaps 310 million by the end of the century. At the same time, the economy became increasing commercialized, and GDP growth seems to have at least kept pace with population growth.

Such sustained population growth for a period lasting over 100 years might seem indicative of modern economic growth, yet China achieved this wealth without the help of an industrial revolution, such as the one that began to transform European economies in the mid-18th century. Still, to Europeans, China represented the pinnacle of success. Europeans idealized and envied China's social organization and greatly coveted its fine silks, exquisite porcelain ware, tea, and other products.

China was, at best, a reluctant trading partner of European nations, even though it maintained a trade surplus during the 1700s. The influx of silver from European merchants buying Chinese goods, especially from the British buying tea, helped fuel the economic expansion and the increasing commercialization of China's economy. Europeans strove to overcome China's reluctance to trade and strove to develop closer economic ties to this fabled land. Officially, China spurned its impatient European suitors. In a famous rebuff to a mission from Great Britain, the Qianlong emperor dismissed the mechanical marvels of Britain's emerging technical and industrial prowess as being irrelevant to China, a tragic miscalculation.

In this instance, China was a victim of its own success. Even though they controlled an empire that encompassed most of East Asia and historically faced threats to peace and prosperity from the interior, not the sea, they were riding a wave of great success as both the population and economy continued to grow. Heir to 2,000 years of imperial history and a social system capable of ruling a vast nation, China's leaders, unsurprisingly, did not understand either the promise or the threat of new inventions from the industrializing West.

Why didn't China launch an industrial revolution on its own, before Great Britain, Europe, North America and Japan, either during the 1700s or under earlier dynasties, such as the Song, when China clearly led the world in inventiveness? Scholars have proposed several answers: the foot binding of Chinese women that hobbled half of the population; the civil-service examination system that diverted intellectual efforts away from science, invention, and commerce, and toward literary studies; the sustained population growth and the decline of farm size, which eliminated the demand for labor-saving inventions; or the poorly defined property rights that undermined the initiative of entrepreneurs, who experienced the arbitrary confiscation of their wealth. All of these factors probably played some role in China's failure to develop an indigenous industrial revolution and its failure to recognize the threat posed by ambitious Westerners.

Despite the outward success of the 18th-century Qing government, by the late 1700s, China was headed toward social crisis. The Chinese government maintained peace during most of the century, but failed to respond in any meaningful way to the challenges of expanding population and commercial activity. The doubling of the population did not occur alongside any corresponding increase in government personnel or institutions. The government failed to support the significant increase in commercial activity by developing supporting governmental institutions, such as a unified system of weights and measures, or expanded transportation systems. A costly war against internal rebellions in the late 1700s focused the government's attention inward. However, on the other side of the globe, European ambitions regarding China were ripening in the direction of aggressive expression as the industrial revolution brought technological developments at a quickening pace, transforming production, transportation, and war.

Economic Change in the 19th Century

Economically speaking, in many ways, the 19th century continued the main trends of the 18th century. Output continued to grow through the application of traditional agricultural methods to existing resources, but now the entire economy and social system staggered under the burden of the large and growing population. The annual population growth rate was about 0.8 percent in the 18th century. It probably declined to 0.4 percent in the 19th century. Still, by 1850, China had a population of more than 400 million—a remarkable achievement for a traditional agricultural economy. GDP was probably still growing, but more slowly than the population. From 1839 onward, China's government slowly succumbed to internal discord and rebellion, as well as to external political pressure and military defeat.

For much of the 18th century, British and other European traders had paid for Chinese goods in silver because Europe produced no product that China needed in large quantities. This balance of trade began to change when the British discovered an appetite for opium in China. The British East India Company produced opium in India and exported the product to China. The flow of silver into China reached a peak of about one million kilograms in the first decade of the 19th century, but the growing market for opium soon reversed the flow. By the 1830s, China saw a silver outflow of almost 400,000 kilograms. This outflow contracted China's money supply, causing severe deflation and recession. As described in Chapter 2, Chinese officials' belated attempts to stop the opium trade ended when Great Britain declared war and then defeated China through the use of superior military technology—cannons,

Beijing in 1861. (The Illustrated London News Picture Library)

INFLATION, DEFLATION, AND WAR IN QING CHINA

The Qing economy's 18th-century expansion benefited from an unplanned and unexpected increase in the money supply: European merchants paid in silver for Chinese goods that were in high demand in Europe. The increasing money supply and mild inflation spurred the rise in commerce that helped to facilitate China's 18th-century population increase. British merchants, however, wanted to buy Chinese goods without spending silver, and in opium, they discovered a good that could reverse the silver flow. The Chinese appetite for opium grew rapidly, and as it did, silver money flowed out of China, producing deflation and recession. In the 1820s, Qing leaders reacted to this destabilizing shift in China's money supply by banning the sale of opium, which triggered the Opium War with Great Britain. Britain's victory marked the triumph of opium and the surrender of China's monetary supply to outside forces.

---

rifles, ships of war—made possible by the West's industrial revolution. Economically, the most important result of the Opium War was not the robust growth of Britain's opium trade, which remained illegal in China, but the forced opening of China to a permanent foreign presence in the form of five treaty ports and foreign trade expansion.

For most of China, the Opium War was of little direct consequence. Of greater importance was the continued growth in population and the pressure it placed on agricultural lands. This pressure helped incite large-scale internal conflicts and rebellions, which dwarfed all foreign military incursions. The largest revolt, the Taiping Rebellion (1850–1864), almost toppled the increasingly ineffective national government. The Taiping rebels occupied Nanjing, one of China's most important cities, controlling much of the rich Yangzi River basin. Local armies loyal to the Qing government ultimately defeated the rebellion in a series of attacks that left many of China's richest counties devastated and depopulated. Perhaps 20 million Chinese died during the Taiping Rebellion, but China's population grew with such momentum that this loss was rapidly replaced and the empty counties were repopulated.

Foreign military and political pressure on China's government continued. In response to a string of military defeats, the Chinese government signed a series of treaties in the 19th century that progressively opened China's economy to foreigners, who introduced new business practices and new technologies into the traditional economy.

The wealth and size of China beguiled foreign commercial interests, which dreamed of the profits that could be generated by selling to the huge Chinese market. Foreign merchants founded modern European communities and commercial activities in the treaty ports. These cities were designated for special development and allowed Europeans special privileges. Shanghai and Hong Kong, the most prominent treaty ports, as well as lesser known treaty ports, grew rapidly in response to foreign commercial activity. By 1850, the population in China's cities began to increase faster than the overall population, reversing a 600-year trend. In the treaty ports, the foreigners began building a modern industrial and commercial economy that, over time, became intertwined with the traditional Chinese economy. Some Chinese entrepreneurs acquired new technological skills and prospered from conducting business with foreigners.

Many Chinese resented foreign commercial activities and blamed them for damaging China's economic interests. Certainly, the foreign incursions into China demoralized a people long accustomed to viewing themselves as the center of the world and exacerbated the political weakness of the government. From a modern perspective, the foreign powers perpetrated grave injustices against Chinese sovereignty and the Chinese people. Nevertheless, it is hardly credible to blame imperialism for China's economic woes in the 19th century. Providing for a very large and growing rural population continued to constitute the main long-term challenge faced by the Chinese economy.

A common charge is that mass-produced European goods destroyed China's handicraft industry. A closer analysis reveals that rural households shifted labor away from spinning, buying machine spun thread instead, and transforming the former spinners into weavers. The handicraft production of textiles actually expanded and improved their quality.

Another charge was that foreign imperialism and its economic manifestation prevented indigenous Chinese industrialization. But the Chinese economy worked with and incorporated foreign economic elements, particularly in the latter 19th century, when an industrial base that was part foreign and part Chinese developed in China in response to the forced opening of the Chinese economy. Chinese financial institutions began evolving to meet the challenges of new commerce, and Chinese transportation systems, particularly water transport systems, expanded and changed to meet the increasing demand for commercial transport. (One notable transportation failure was the slow development of rail transport, but here, only government intervention could possibly solve the property rights challenges of building long-distance rail lines.)

Some regional leaders who had been instrumental in defeating the Taiping Rebellion tried to adopt foreign technology and construct modern armament and other military industries. These leaders, such as Li Hongzhang and Zeng Guofan, strove to build up modern iron and steel works, to develop coal mines, and to develop machine tool factories. Their goal was to equip a Chinese army with modern weaponry and to create a modern navy. They were well aware that a rapidly modernizing Japan was doing the same with greater effectiveness and imperial support, and that Japan cast a covetous eye upon Chinese and Korean territory.

This budding industrial development was obstructed by the Qing dynasty, which failed to strengthen either the economy or the military by effectively and consistently sponsoring industrial development. In one instance, Qing officials ordered the removal of the first train line installed in China. The central government also opposed early efforts at electrification. In another notorious case, the Empress Cixi, who sided with more conservative leaders opposed to adopting foreign technology, diverted funds intended to create a modern Chinese navy into rebuilding her summer palace, which was destroyed by the British in 1860.

Interior of an industrial fiber factory in China, about 1900. (Library of Congress)

The contradictory responses of China's leadership to the foreign technology of war culminated in a disastrous defeat in 1895 by the modernized Japanese army and navy. In the Treaty of Shimonoseki, the Chinese government ceded its influence over Korea and its control of Taiwan to Japan, while agreeing to pay Japan's cost of waging the war. Other nations took advantage of China's weakened state to occupy or claim expanded spheres of influence in China.

Still, at the grass roots level, the Chinese government's failures did not halt the growing connections provided by a new class of Chinese entrepreneurs between the foreign-dominated modern sector and the traditional economy. The early beginnings of Chinese industrial development were underway by the end of the century. Three sectors led the way: steam-powered transportation, manufacturing, and commercial banking. Nevertheless, most Chinese still followed the ancient patterns of traditional agriculture.

THE CHINESE ECONOMY, 1900–1949

After the demise of the Qing government in 1911, China entered an intensified period of political chaos and fragmentation that only partially concluded with the Nationalist Party's establishment of a new national government in 1929. The new government only weakly controlled many regions that were still under the control of local warlords, who often battled among themselves. In addition, the government expended great effort trying to eradicate Communist control of rural bases. Japan's seizure of Manchuria in 1932, and then its complete invasion of China in 1937, extended China's political chaos and fragmentation. Japan's surrender in 1945 gave China only a brief respite from war. Soon, China's extended civil war resumed as the

---

ELECTRIC POWER IN REPUBLICAN CHINA

Electric power is the quintessential fuel of modern economic growth. Generating electricity from fossil fuels involves thermodynamic losses relative to the direct combustion of the fuels. But the properties of electricity make the conversion highly desirable. Electrical energy is the most flexible, transmissible, adaptable energy source. Electrification in the U.S. economy produced a productivity boom through much of the 20th century, and every developing nation, China included, has tried to mimic U.S. development. China experienced rapid growth in the modern sector from 1912–1936, with the electric power industry as the fastest-growing sector. In 1927, for example, electricity sales in Shanghai were greater than in any English city. Still, the development of China's electric power industry lagged behind that of its chief rival, Japan, even at comparable stages of development. Japan's electrical output in 1930 was seven times greater than China's—a clear indicator of China's weakness compared to Japan.

Nationalists and Communists fought for control of China, culminating in a Communist victory in 1949.

If we pay attention only to the political history of 1900–1949 and ignore economic history, China appears to be a complete disaster in this period. Most Chinese continued to live at subsistence levels or worse after the mid-1930s. Yet, over this period, both the population and economic output continued to grow at about the same rate, so GDP per person did not decline. The period from 1912–1936 saw some remarkable modern economic growth, considering the political disorder of the era.

World War I produced a boom in Chinese exports and spurred modern economic development in China. Economic growth continued in the 1920s, despite the highly unsettled political environment, and the worldwide depression in the 1930s had less of an impact in China than elsewhere. Over the entire 1912–1936 period, modern industry expanded at an annual average rate of eight percent per year. Yet, even by the late 1930s, the modern industrial sector accounted for less than five percent of GDP, while traditional handicraft production generated more than seven percent. Traditional agriculture continued as the main source of production.

The development of the modern and traditional sectors complemented one another; both produced outputs that the other sector used as inputs and both produced primarily consumer goods. Heavy machinery and other producer goods designed to expand industry primarily came from abroad, but the modern sector did begin to diversify its production. "By 1933, chemicals, non-metallic minerals, basic metals and metal products accounted for 15 per cent of manufacturing output" (Richardson, 1999:65). The Nationalist government established state-run enterprises in heavy industry and mining. Recent research even suggests that the average output per person in China may have increased between 1913 and 1936 because of industrialization. The Japanese invasion of China greatly altered this development.

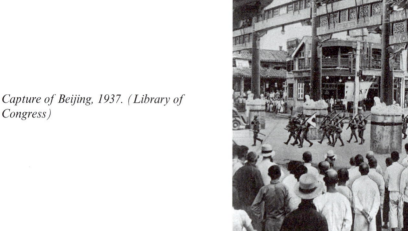

Capture of Beijing, 1937. (Library of Congress)

Until 1945, Japan occupied large parts of China, including the coastal areas, which had been responsible for most modern production. The war crippled production in these areas. The Nationalist government retreated into the hinterlands, carrying much of the industrial equipment with it. Cut off from normal transportation networks and suffering from Japanese attacks, significant industrial development in the Chinese-controlled regions was difficult. In Manchuria, however, industrial development accelerated under Japanese rule.

Japan had possessed considerable influence in Manchuria since its victory in the Russo-Japanese War in 1905. Russia surrendered all of its interests in Manchuria to Japan. Under Japanese influence, Manchuria became one of China's most important industrial areas, comparable to treaty ports such as Shanghai or Hong Kong. During 1931–32, the Japanese military seized complete control of Manchuria, which already produced 14 percent of China's manufacturing output. Thereafter, Japan further expanded industry in Manchuria, planning to make it a major source of manufacturing for Japan's imperial expansion. By 1945, Manchuria was the most industrialized part of China.

These industrial facilities would have provided a good base for Chinese industrialization after World War II. However, in August 1945, the Soviet Union declared war on Japan and invaded Manchuria. When the Soviet forces returned home after Japan's surrender, they took a large part of Manchuria's industrial plant with them.

In addition to the Soviet confiscation of Manchuria's industry, economic revival after 1945 was also disrupted by civil war between the Communist and Nationalist parties. The Nationalist government's inept and corrupt policies undermined the urban economy, producing hyperinflation that left almost all urban residents scrambling for the most basic means of survival. The Nationalist government's economic failures greatly contributed to the military victory of the Chinese Communist Party.

CHINA'S ECONOMY: THE MAO ERA, 1949–1978

On October 1, 1949, Mao Zedong, Chairman of the Chinese Communist Party and the architect of its victory over the Nationalist Party, announced the founding of the People's Republic of China, claiming that "the Chinese people have stood up."

This statement seemed more like bravado than reality. The economy, at least, was on its knees. Agricultural output in 1949 was 70–75 percent of its pre-war peak and industrial output was 56 percent. Inflation of 100–500 percent per month crippled the urban economy.

However, the new government backed Mao's boast with action by getting the economy back on its feet during a three-year period of reconstruction, even with China's entry into the Korean War in October 1950. Hyperinflation was halted in 1950, and prices were stable by 1952. By then, the production of basic foodstuffs had returned to or exceeded its pre-war peak output. Food grain production was 11 percent higher than the best previous harvest, and industrial output exceeded prewar peak production by 25 percent.

Still, the new government faced great economic challenges. Traditional peasant agriculture dominated the economy: 89 percent of the population lived in the countryside, and agriculture produced 60 percent of economic output. The typical farm was tiny. Farming resembled gardening, requiring intense hand cultivation using simple tools. Even with industry restored, its output was quite low. For example, in 1952, electricity production averaged 13 kilowatt hours per person—one kilowatt hour will light a 100-watt bulb for 10 hours—and only cities had electrical service.

The new government had great ambitions. The Communists wanted to build a socialist economy that eliminated free markets and private enterprise. They also wanted to build an advanced industrial economy that was able to equip modern armed forces and raise people's living standards. National defense required the expansion of those heavy industries—coal, steel, electric power, petroleum, and heavy machinery—necessary for manufacturing the weapons of modern warfare. Improving living standards required expanding consumer goods industries, developing retail and wholesale commerce, and constructing new housing, hospitals, medical clinics, schools, and other infrastructure. All of this development also required agricultural output to grow considerably faster than the population.

As a very poor country, China lacked the investment resources to launch rapid industrialization. What it had in abundance were unskilled workers who needed jobs. China's natural advantage thus lay in labor-intensive production that required relatively little investment. China could produce consumer goods and agricultural products at a very low cost for its own population and for export throughout the world, which would produce both jobs and profits. The profits could then be invested in building up other sectors of the economy, including heavy industry, which required

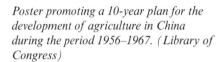

Poster promoting a 10-year plan for the development of agriculture in China during the period 1956–1967. (Library of Congress)

relatively large investments and produced relatively few jobs. Developed economies around the world had followed just such a path in their economic development. The United States had initiated its rise by exporting raw materials, agricultural products, and consumer goods to Europe. Japan followed suit in its economic growth, both prior to World War II and during its economic recovery in the 1950s. Other Asian economies—South Korea, Singapore, Hong Kong, Taiwan, Thailand, and Malaysia—would then all follow in Japan's footsteps. In all of these nations, economic growth and urbanization coincided, as farmers with low productivity left the countryside for urban jobs with higher productivity.

This same transformation had begun in China, but had been interrupted by the war with Japan. A China that was once again at peace could have returned to this development path. However, socialist goals, international events, and particular political developments in the Chinese Communist Party eliminated this strategy in China between 1949 and 1978.

Even at its founding in 1949, China's new government had few friends and many enemies. During the civil war, the United States had strongly supported the Nationalist government. In addition, the Communist Party's nationalist, anti-imperialist politics jeopardized Westerners' investments in China. Finally, China's entry in October 1950 into the Korean War against the United States and its allies left it with the support of only one major power: the Soviet Union. During the Korean War, the Soviet Union gave China financial and military support. China also began following the Soviet Union's advice on economic planning and development.

In the 1930s, under Stalin's leadership, the Soviet Union launched an all-out campaign to expand its heavy industry by placing the entire economy under central command. Other governments have taken control of vital economic sectors in times of war, but the Soviet Union under Stalin was the first nation to do so in peacetime and to extend this method to its entire economy, creating a centrally planned economy.

This economy matched the anti-market inclinations of socialists, but was primarily invented on the spot to carry out the top leaders' investment plans and to protect their political power.

In the Soviet Union, the state owned all enterprises and controlled them through a bureaucracy of industrial ministries. A central planning office created five-year plans that set the general course of the economy based on the top leaders' priorities. Central planners and the ministries then created annual plans for the actual operation of the economy. In principle, these plans told enterprise managers what outputs to make and what inputs to use. In practice, the plans were quite incomplete and left enterprises scrambling to meet their plans, using semi-legal, quasi-market means to obtain the inputs needed for production, maintaining high inventories of inputs or inefficiently making the inputs themselves. The plan's failure even to balance inputs and outputs meant that little attention was focused on efficient production. Still, the planned economy achieved its main goal of building heavy industry while severely restricting the production of consumer goods. The state set wages and the prices of agricultural goods, industrial goods, and consumer goods to limit consumers' incomes and direct money flows into heavy industry investment.

The new Chinese government adopted a similar economic system. With the help of the Soviet Union, China launched its first five-year plan in 1953, and began centralizing the economy under state control.

China's First Five-Year Plan

China's previous government had already paved the way for national economic planning by nationalizing much of China's modern economic sectors. By 1948, the Nationalist government controlled most of the production from the metal, electric power, railroad, and petroleum industries, and 33–45 percent of coal, cement, and shipping. The new Communist government nationalized all foreign-owned firms by the end of 1952. However, at first, the Communists moved slowly in taking over Chinese-owned enterprises, encouraging their owners to stay in business and run their companies. In 1953, privately owned firms produced 40 percent of modern industrial output. This changed during the first five-year plan. By 1957, all enterprises were under state control as most private commercial activity was outlawed and suppressed. For the next 30 years, state-owned enterprises thoroughly dominated the Chinese economy, absorbing the bulk of investment funds.

China contracted with the Soviet Union for the design and construction of 156 key projects in heavy industry, including ". . . seven iron and steel plants, twenty-four electric power stations, and sixty-three machinery plants" (Riskin, 1988:74). The Soviet Union supplied entire factories in some cases, and designed other projects, trained Chinese personnel, and sent engineers to supervise construction and start-up.

The structure of the Chinese economy changed with the emphasis on heavy industry. In 1952, industry accounted for only 20 percent of economic output, and light industry produced more than 64 percent. By 1957, industry's share of economic output had risen to 28 percent, and heavy industry produced almost 50 percent.

The rapid growth of heavy industry reflects the high investment rates achieved by China's new command economy. The state channeled 24 percent of current economic output into investment, with heavy industry receiving about half. China paid for its industrial imports through exports and short-term loans provided by the Soviet Union at favorable interest rates. Much of the resources had to come from agriculture, which still produced half of China's economic output. The state needed surplus agricultural output to feed the increased urban population, to provide raw materials for industry, and to pay for its loans and imports from the Soviet Union.

Land Reform and the Collectivization of Agriculture

Delivering on promises to its peasant supporters, between 1950 and 1953, the Communist government confiscated land and tools from rural landlords and gave the property to poorer peasants. Even peasant women received similar rights to land as men—truly a revolutionary move in a society where women had possessed few, if any, rights. By 1953, land reform was essentially completed. About 10 million rural households lost some portion of their land and household property, while about 300 million peasants each received about one third of an acre.

Land reform in and of itself was not a step toward socialism. Land was not nationalized, socialized, or collectivized in the initial land reform. In the short run, the land reform primarily strengthened the peasant market economy by expanding the number of private landowners. But the land reform movement gave the new government great prestige among the peasants and created a political organization in the countryside to carry out the step-by-step collectivization of agriculture, which, by 1958, would take away almost all land from the peasants. This collectivization would be reversed in the early 1980s.

Land reform did not solve the basic problems of Chinese agriculture—small, fragmented fields, a lack of modern inputs, highly labor-intensive technology, the continually falling ratio of land per rural family, and intense poverty. Land reform also complicated the government's efforts to gain enough of the peasants' agricultural output to use for export, feeding a growing urban population, and as inputs into expanding industry. Newly landed peasants had a strong incentive to increase production since they would own the increased output, but if they consumed the increase instead of selling it, urban agricultural supplies would be threatened.

In the 1920s and 1930s, about half of agricultural production was marketed, largely due to the rents peasants paid their landlords, but with the land reform's abolition of rented land, this ratio fell to less than 30 percent in 1953. In order to extract enough grain from peasants, the state enacted taxes that had to be paid on agricultural output and required peasants to sell an additional part of their output at low, state-set prices. The state banned all private purchases of grain, forcing peasants to deal only with the state trading organizations. These policies increased the share of agricultural output flowing to the state, but decreased peasants' incentives to expand production. The state still needed more agricultural output.

The state could have expanded agricultural output by investing in agriculture, expanding irrigation, providing improved seed and chemical fertilizer, and mechanizing

*Unidentified workers plan their day's chores on a collective farm, May 1, 1958, China.
Machines are self-propelled combines purchased from the Soviet Union. In an effort to boost
sagging food production, the communist Chinese government confiscated nearly 120 million
acres of land between 1950 and 1953 and parceled it out, with machinery and animals, to the
peasants. (AP/Wide World Photos)*

agriculture. But it did not want to divert scarce investment resources from industrial development. Instead, the state hoped to increase agricultural output through the socialist transformation of agriculture.

Following land reform, party leaders first encouraged peasants to pool their resources into mutual aid teams. In keeping with party and government policy, local officials then encouraged, led, and coerced the formation of lower- and higher-order collectives. At each stage, the number of families in collectives increased. In the early stages of development, peasants received incomes in proportion to the land (to which they retained the title), tools, and labor they contributed. In the larger, higher-order collectives, income was based on labor, not on ownership of land and tools. However, peasants did retain about five percent of their land in the form of small plots for personal production. Peasants farmed their small plots intensively, producing 20 to 30 percent of farm income and 80 percent of pigs in 1956 through their private efforts.

By 1957, almost 94 percent of peasant households were members of higher-order collectives, each larger than a traditional village. China had good harvests in 1956 and 1957. Agricultural output achieved the production targets set in the first five-year plan, but industrial growth greatly exceeded its planned targets, increasing the demand for agricultural products. Unfortunately, from the point of view of the planners, the level of agricultural products extracted from the countryside scarcely changed from 1953–1957.

The Great Leap Forward, 1958–1960

In 1958, China embarked on the Great Leap Forward—Mao's plan to propel the economy to a new level of development by arousing the socialist enthusiasm of the people. China veered away from detailed central planning because of the low rate of agricultural growth and because Mao distrusted the growing bureaucracy of the centralized economy, fearing that it undermined socialist goals and his own power. Starting in 1957, the new strategy decentralized much of the economic planning and control to lower government levels and tried to replace careful planning with political fervor.

The collectivization of agriculture rapidly advanced as the countryside was organized into rural communes that combined political and economic power in a single entity. The intention was to use China's greatest resource—the agricultural labor force—to transform the rural economy through brute force. During the winter of 1957–1958, vast armies of peasants armed with shovels, baskets, and wheelbarrows constructed reservoirs and irrigation systems across China. As the Great Leap Forward moved into high gear, local leaders and political campaigns also directed peasants' energies into local industrial construction.

However, large-scale heavy industry remained the main focus of development. Although the planning and control system was partially decentralized, the goal of rapid industrialization remained paramount. The rate of investment jumped from 25 percent of economic output to 40 percent or more, and the share going to heavy industry increased from 47 percent in the first five-year plan to over 56 percent 1958–1960. Many new projects were begun. Existing facilities operated more intensively, damaging some industrial equipment when it was operated at capacities beyond its design limits. The excessive growth rates and weakened coordination caused bottlenecks throughout industry. Still, according to official statistics, industrial output grew 57 percent in 1958. This growth was entirely in heavy industry, where output more than doubled, while light industrial output declined from 1958–1960. These figures overstate actual growth since many factories running at breakneck speed produced low-quality or unusable products.

A messianic fervor spurred on by Mao and other top leaders gripped the country. Mao believed that the selfless, socialist enthusiasm of the people could accelerate the pace of economic development to a level higher than any economy had previously achieved. The development goals rapidly became more grandiose in 1958 and 1959. To doubt the goals became politically suspect, and even a sober statistical statement of economic outcomes was viewed as evidence of treason.

Leaders at multiple levels reported inflated production figures. Based on highly exaggerated agricultural production figures, Mao and China's other top leaders called for even faster development. More workers were shifted out of agriculture into local water control and industrialization projects. Many peasants went to work expanding industrial facilities in the cities, increasing the urban population by one-third in three years.

Banners and a portrait of Communist Party Chairman Mao Zedong adorn the front of this strange-looking freight train making its first run in Yuxian County, Shanxi Province. According to information supplied by the Chinese Communists, the 125-mile railroad was built by the people of the county to carry coke to the Yuhsien power equipment plant. The locomotive, powered by a converted automobile engine, pulled six cars, each loaded with three tons of coke, August 5, 1958. (Bettmann/Corbis)

The drain of farm workers prevented the harvesting of a significant part of 1958's actual bumper crop. But the extreme overestimates of agricultural yields at first made unharvested fields seem unimportant. Unfortunately, state agricultural procurements went ahead, based on the highly inflated production figures. Many communes were left with very low stockpiles for the coming winter, even though peasants were working longer hours than ever before. In the winter of 1958–1959, peasants on the communes began starving.

The Great Leap Forward continued on through 1959 and 1960. Peasants continued to be diverted from agriculture and made to work at a pace that available food rations could not support. Bad weather hampered agriculture and aggravated the problem. China's leadership reacted slowly to the developing disaster. No unbiased statistics existed to clarify the true state of agricultural production and supplies. Actually, grain output fell in 1959 and 1960 to a level that was 25 percent below production in 1958, but state acquisitions of grain jumped almost 40 percent in 1959, leaving many communes without enough food to get through the winter. In 1959, the one top official, Peng Dehuai, who dared to criticize the development program lost

---

THE GREAT LEAP FORWARD AND THE ELECTRIC POWER INDUSTRY

As the previous sidebar stated, electric power plays a pivotal role in modern industrial development. China's new rulers gave its development the highest priority and very rapidly expanded its capacity. But the Great Leap Forward put politics, instead of engineering, in command. China's generating equipment, much of which was of pre-1949 European origin, was operated in excess of its rated capacity because the ratings were products of "bourgeois thinking." The over-stressed equipment failed, though such failure was avoidable. Electric power systems throughout the world are subject to careful planning and operation to avoid unnecessary equipment failure and to serve expected increases in demand. Long-term planning is a hallmark of the electric power industry in market and planned economies alike. The electric power industry in China was the most appropriate sector for central planning. The failures in its electric power system indicate exactly how dysfunctional the Chinese economy was from 1958–1961.

---

his job. By the time the Great Leap was officially abandoned, the damage was done. Famine swept the country, and China lost 20–30 million people.

Recovery, 1961–1965

The setback in population growth was only temporary. In 1953, China's first modern census had counted a population of 588 million, an increase of about 200 million over 1800. By 1957, China had added 60 million new citizens. In 1962, the population was growing again and at a faster rate than in the 1950s. (Because Mao rejected population control programs as reactionary, China's population would continue to grow rapidly through the 1960s.)

The economic setback, although quite severe, was temporary, as well. Mao relinquished control over economic policy to more pragmatic leaders, such as Liu Shaoqi and Deng Xiaoping. In 1978, Deng would emerge as China's top political leader (his political and economic career would take many turns before then) and would institute economic reforms that were first experimented with during recovery from the Great Leap Forward.

China abandoned the Great Leap Forward strategy and recentralized economic planning. The state shut down many industrial construction projects and increased the priority of light industry. About 20 million of the new urban residents were forced to return to the countryside. The communes remained, but China abandoned the mass organization of production. The work team, a unit of production smaller than a village, became the main production unit. Liu and Deng reintroduced individual economic incentives, allowing peasants once again to farm small garden plots, raising vegetables and livestock for their own use and for sale at markets. In a foreshadowing of the economic reforms in the 1980s, their policies introduced the household responsibility system, a modified form of family farming, in some areas. After declining for three years, economic output rebounded, growing at double-digit rates between 1963–1965.

Ten Years of Disorder, 1966–1976

Mao Zedong's power and prestige had been diminished by the Great Leap Forward debacle, but not his ambitions to shape economic and political policy. In 1966, Mao Zedong reasserted control by initiating the Cultural Revolution, a political movement aimed at top party leaders, who had engineered the recent economic recovery, especially Liu Shaoqi and Deng Xiaoping. Mao disapproved of their economic programs and resented their political prominence. In retaliation, he claimed these Communist leaders were leading China back to capitalism and incited rebellions across the country against the "capitalist roaders."

Over the next 10 years, Mao and his allies dominated economic policy. They revived many features of the Great Leap Forward. The greatest similarity between the two periods was the extreme politicization of economic decision-making. The "redness" of one's actions and words became more important than actual economic results. Again, economic planning and enterprise control were partially decentralized to lower levels. In the countryside, private market activity was once more repressed, although the level of repression ebbed and flowed. Communes were urged to pursue self-reliance by creating small-scale industry and becoming self-sufficient in grain production.

Communes were urged to become self-reliant partly to avoid the challenges of supplying the countryside with the required industrial inputs and partly to prepare for invasion. In the event of invasion, each locale would be better able to resist if it was largely self-sufficient. This policy of communes and local government funding their own development also freed central resources for a program to build military-industrial facilities in China's hinterland.

Third Front Investment Program

Beginning in 1964, China secretly launched a crash industrialization program to prepare for invasion by either the United States or the Soviet Union. If there was an invasion, China's leaders planned to retreat from the coast, the first front, and the lower lands within 400 miles of the coast, the second front, into remote, mountainous regions, the third front. From there, China would wage a prolonged war of resistance against any invader.

Since much of China's industry was concentrated on the coast, the leaders endorsed a highly centralized investment plan to build new industrial facilities in these remote regions. Between 1964 and 1971, this military-industrial program absorbed the majority of China's new investment. The program moved existing factories from the coast and created complete heavy industrial systems able to produce all manner of military equipment in rugged interior locations.

The turmoil of the Cultural Revolution and the administrative decentralization of the rest of the economy did not hinder the third front investment program. It moved ahead at great haste, initiating many projects before planning was complete and scattering many new facilities in remote valleys to protect them from air attack. As a defense strategy, perhaps the program made sense, although the scale of many of the projects was so large that they would not be completed and placed into production for many years. However, in the absence of invasion, the investment program had a high economic cost. Many of the new industrial plants would have been cheaper, easier to build, and more useful if they were located elsewhere.

Assessment, 1949–1976

By the mid-1970s, the shortcomings of China's economic development were brought into stark relief by the successes of other East Asian economies. Starting first with labor-intensive industries, Japan had quickly grown into a technological and industrial powerhouse. Other countries followed its lead: South Korea, Thailand, and Singapore. Taiwan and Hong Kong in particular achieved great success, growing rapidly while transforming their industrial structure.

Annual investment rates of almost 40 percent had failed to transform the lives of most people. The Maoist industrial system, with its emphasis on politics, self-reliance, and administrative decentralization, failed to wisely invest the economy's savings. Excess capacity existed in many industries, but investment in new ventures continued, creating new facilities that incorporated old technologies. For example, each province had at least one truck and automobile plant, even though some produced only a few vehicles per year. State-owned enterprises dominated the economy, but had no incentives to produce efficiently; their managers often lacked technical training and had to pay more attention to political concerns than efficient production. Industrial workers had guaranteed lifetime employment, and their compensation, frozen since the late 1950s, bore no relation to their economic effort. Many factories produced output that was either not needed or of poor quality. Stockpiles of industrial output equaled almost a year's worth of production. Economic results were simply not very great for all of the effort and sacrifice that had been made.

China was still fundamentally a poor, rural economy. The creation and development of communes and communal industries had created larger fields amenable to mechanization, greatly expanded irrigated land, and developed small-scale chemical fertilizer plants. In addition, China had independently developed and popularized high-yield, short-stalk rice. Still, the institutional and technological transformation of agriculture had failed to increase agricultural output much faster than population growth. Extreme poverty persisted, with most rural residents living near the absolute poverty level.

The poor agricultural performance resulted directly from Maoist policies emphasizing self-reliance, restricting markets, and encouraging bureaucratic interference in local decision-making. These policies prevented farmers from using their specialized knowledge to select the products and processes that were best suited to their local conditions. For example, the policy requiring each commune to be self-sufficient in grain production and preventing the market transfer of grain between communes lowered cotton production, as high-yielding cotton fields were planted in wheat. Other locales, specialists in growing wheat, devoted land to local cotton production. Both wheat and cotton production suffered.

Two Chinese women tune their machines at a tool plant, 1956. (Library of Congress)

The policy of local self-reliance achieved the opposite result on the national level. By the mid-1970s, China relied on imported grain to feed 40 percent of its urban population and was a major importer of other crops, such as cotton and edible vegetable oils, which it should have excelled in producing. China's production of grain per person had just kept pace with its population. The real income of rural households had barely increased since 1956.

Even in the relatively highly favored urban areas, people's economic lives were bleak on the day-to-day level. Government-run stores were poorly stocked. Consumer goods, rationed by a complex system of coupons, remained in short supply, of poor quality, and lacking in variety. Even basic foodstuffs were rationed. Monetary incomes were low. Wages and promotions had been frozen since the late 1950s. Still, people saved money because there was so little to buy. The major consumer goods in the 1970s were bicycles (rationed), wristwatches, and sewing machines—a far cry from the goods that were available in Hong Kong and Taiwan, for example.

ELECTRIC POWER SHORTAGES IN THE CHINESE ECONOMY

Recall the importance of a growing electric power industry to a growing economy. According to Chinese sources, China suffered electric power shortages almost continuously from 1970 through the early 1990s. In the early 1970s, political zeal and above-capacity use again damaged about 5 percent of thermal generating capacity. The damage was repaired, but shortages did not disappear. Poor planning kept demand for electricity growing faster than supply in the 1970s. In a 1980 report, the U.S. Central Intelligence Agency predicted that electric power shortages would limit China's GDP growth to 3 percent per year from 1980–1985. Other Chinese and non-Chinese analysts made similar predictions in the 1980s, when China's electric power industry did grow slowly. But the reforming economy broke through the electricity constraints and grew three times faster than predicted. The Chinese economy was rapidly changing, and a little electric power went a long way in the new labor-intensive workshops springing up in China's urban and rural areas.

On September 9, 1976, Mao Zedong died. Within a month, top Maoist leaders, "the Gang of Four," were arrested and China entered a period of uncertainty. Hua Guofeng, the new top leader picked by Mao on his deathbed, stressed self-reliance in word but not in action. The new leadership adhered to the Soviet development model and tried to revive Soviet-style central planning. At the same time, the lost economic opportunities of the previous 10 years made the leadership impatient for improved growth. A new great leap began in the countryside. As before, rural authorities organized armies of peasants for mass construction projects with the goal of mechanizing agriculture by 1980.

Agricultural mechanization required rapid industrial development, but this time, instead of relying on the Soviet Union, China planned to import industrial plants from the most advanced capitalist economies and to pay for the imports with income from oil exports. For a while in the 1970s, China believed that its oil resources would rival those of Saudi Arabia. With the development of the Daqing oil field in the Northeast, oil production had grown rapidly. The increased production combined with the high price of crude oil in the 1970s rapidly increased China's export earnings. China's leaders decided to abandon efforts at technological self-reliance and to instead leap to the frontiers of technology by importing advanced industrial plants.

In 1977–1978, the Chinese government set off on a buying spree around the world, planning to spend over $12 billion on imported plants for heavy industry. The actual contracts that were signed greatly exceeded this amount, as individual ministries made deals without central coordination. The buying binge was predicated on the continual discovery of new oilfields and greatly expanded crude oil exports. However, great efforts at exploratory drilling in 1978 produced no major discoveries, jeopardizing increased oil output. China was not Saudi Arabia, and could not expect rising oil revenues to pay for the heavy industry shopping spree. China's exports were not nearly sufficient to cover the jump in imports.

ECONOMIC REFORM, 1979–1989

In December 1978, Deng Xiaoping finally established his position as China's top leader. He greatly scaled back Hua Guofeng's expensive development program and launched a reform program that was radical for China, but actually rather modest in scope. The early reforms addressed three areas: agriculture, foreign trade and investment, and state-owned industry. Ironically, the early steps at reform had unexpected and unintended consequences that set China's economy on the road to a market economy.

In agriculture, the state raised the price paid for grain, permitted the revival of market-oriented household handicraft production, and granted agricultural collectives greater freedom to make economic decisions. This reform began to change the incentive systems for rural workers, directly linking individual effort to individual reward through a revival of traditional household economic activity, in which farm families produced consumer goods for the market using surplus labor in the household. The reforms also permitted the poorest districts to experiment with household responsibility systems. Initially a minor element in the reform, the household responsibility system permitted individual households to lease land from the commune. The household guaranteed to deliver a fixed amount of output to the commune, keeping everything else for itself. The household responsibility system amounted to nothing less than a return to family farming, and although official decree limited its application to only the poorest regions, the implementation of this reform slowly spread into other areas between 1978 and the first half of 1981. Then, in the second half of 1981, the adoption of the household responsibility took off like a prairie fire, racing ahead of the leaders. As word of the system spread, communes in richer regions switched to the new system, and within one year, 70 percent of communes had adopted the new system without approval from higher leaders. But the leaders let the change stand, as agricultural output boomed under the new system. By 1984, the commune system was dead, and farm families once again tilled China's earth.

During 1978–1984, the growth rate of grain output averaged five percent per year, more than twice the 1957–1978 growth rate, while the annual growth rates of other major agricultural products grew even faster. The surge in production improved Chinese diets and reduced agricultural imports. The growth in agricultural output plus the growth of handicraft production caused rural incomes to increase substantially for the first time since the mid-1950s.

The second element of the early reforms experimented with foreign trade and foreign investment in China. China set up Special Economic Zones (SEZs) in areas isolated from most of China, but with close ties to the outside world. The plan was to attract foreign investment and technology, and to earn foreign currency through exports. The SEZs became grand experiments in economic reform, using their unusual freedom to introduce many market-based initiatives. Along with the SEZs came the reform of China's trade system. The SEZs and the reform of China's trade system signaled an increasing opening to the world. Soon, foreign tourists and foreign investors flocked to China in increasing numbers, and China, in turn, sent students around the world to study at top universities.

STEPS TO A WELL-FUNCTIONING MARKET

According to Dwight Perkins, one of the world's top experts on the Chinese economy and economic development, there are five key steps required for a well functioning market that ". . . also describe the concrete steps that a Soviet-type command economy must take if it is to evolve into a functioning market economy. The five steps are: (1) achieve macro stability, meaning an acceptable level of inflation and a balance of payments not in serious disequilibrium; (2) make inputs and outputs available for purchase and sale on the market, rather than allocated administratively through a state bureaucracy; (3) free up prices to reflect relative scarcities in the economy; (4) remove barriers to market entry so that competition between firms in different localities becomes possible; (5) change key elements of the institutional framework so that decision-makers in the production unit (farms and industrial or service enterprises) have an incentive to maximize profits by cutting their costs or raising sales" (Perkins, 1994).

The third element of the early reforms expanded the autonomy of state-owned enterprises and improved their material incentives, first on an experimental basis with a few enterprises, and then quickly across the nation. State-owned enterprises were given more control over their financial flows and partially rewarded for improving profits.

A firm responding primarily to the profit motive has a strong incentive to lower its costs through innovation and to produce products that customers actually want to buy. Both the input and output effects improve profitability and efficiency. But to get enterprise managers to truly behave according to "a prosper or perish" formula, firms must really face the possibility of failure and must really experience the rewards of success. If a poorly run firm can turn to the government for a bailout, then the incentive for efficiency will be weak.

Chinese state-owned enterprises could legitimately argue that they could not possibly show a profit, given the socialist price system, which had intentionally distorted prices to help the state raise investment revenues. Consequently, profitability varied widely across sectors. Without changing prices, the reforms could not get firms to behave as if profits and efficiency really mattered.

Managers used the ability to control resources to pay bonuses to workers. China's industrial workers had long-term grievances about their wages. Under Mao, wages and promotions were frozen. Managers could not fire disgruntled workers, so a wise manager did what was necessary to keep workers happy. In the 1980s, state-owned enterprises also increased expenditures on employee benefits, especially housing.

The state also relaxed its monopoly over retailing. This reform was enacted in response to a growing problem of urban unemployment. Thousands of urban youth sent to the countryside during the Cultural Revolution flooded back to their homes in the cities and were permitted to set up restaurants and other service enterprises. In addition, the state encouraged collective enterprises spawned by state-owned enterprises in the 1960s and 1970s to expand into commercial activities. Peasants resumed selling their produce and other wares in the cities as the government relaxed the prohibition against such marketing.

The 1978–1984 reforms dramatically changed the distribution of annual economic output in China, transferring 10–15 percent of disposable income from the state to Chinese households. Rural households were the biggest recipients of this change. Household savings rates also increased, so all of this increase did not immediately flow back out of the households as increased consumption. Instead, the rate of household savings increased from 3 percent of household income to 15 percent or more. Still, the increased income financed increased consumption expenditures by rural and urban households on a growing variety of consumer goods. China's consumers bought goods from newly expanded markets, and their purchases, in turn, encouraged further market expansion. Rural residents and state-owned enterprises also invested greatly in improved and expanded housing, further improving the quality of life.

Not all party members favored the reforms, particularly those reforms that breathed new life into the market economy, which the Maoists had done their best to kill. Despite strenuous efforts during the Cultural Revolution, extinguishing people's "propensity to truck, barter, and exchange one thing for another" (in Adam Smith's words) proved impossible. Local officials supported reforms that increased local autonomy, and rural households embraced reforms that increased their economic independence. Reformers seldom knew for sure where a reform would lead, but proceeded based on the reforms' success at spurring production and creating jobs. More conservative party leaders disliked these trends, wanting instead to stay with central planning as the economy's main coordinating mechanism.

The struggle between the reform faction and the central planning faction created a business/political cycle as the policies of first one group and then the other attained temporary ascendancy. When expanded reforms produced enough negative side effects, such as inflation, the central planning faction tried to re-exert control. But each time, their restriction of market-oriented activities caused an economic slowdown and met with considerable resistance. The inability of weakened planning institutions to solve the problems of an economy that was rapidly growing in both size and complexity then set the stage for a new round of reforms. With each cycle completed, the scope of economic reform expanded.

The pace of change initiated by the first set of reforms caused increased inflation and a corresponding backlash from the central planning coalition. Although the rural economy continued to change with the expansion of the household responsibility system, 1981—1983 was a period of retrenchment for reform in the urban economy.

A second round of reforms between 1984—1988 built on the success of the earlier reforms and tried to solve problems that were created by or not sufficiently addressed by the earlier reforms. Some reforms increased the participation of state-owned enterprises in both the input and output markets. The government froze the scope of the state plan so that firms could sell above-plan output at market prices, but they also had to buy above-plan inputs on the market. The lower prices for plan inputs and outputs served mainly as subsidies or taxes. Firms made decisions to increase or decrease production in response to market factors. The frozen plan meant that, over time, the industrial economy would grow out of the plan.

In the second round of reforms, the former commune enterprises took on a new life. With the increased economic freedom, these enterprises quickly reoriented their

TOWNSHIP AND VILLAGE ENTERPRISES

In 1987, Deng Xiaoping, China's top leader, reportedly admitted, "In the rural reform, our greatest success—and it is one we had by no means anticipated—has been the emergence of a large number of enterprises run by villages and townships" (Wu, 2005: 183). Huang (2008: 102) argues that broadly based growth created by private, rural entrepreneurs did more to increase the income of average citizens than urban-dominated growth after 1994. Huang persuasively argues that China's economic successes in the 1980s resulted from political leaders allowing rural commerce to follow market imperatives. The result, according to Naughton (1996), was China's "growing out of the plan": the market-oriented production of state-owned enterprises (SOEs) and TVEs increasingly dwarfed output set by the plan, but the growth of the SOEs was greatly eclipsed by the TVEs whose output grew from ". . . less than 6 percent of GDP in 1978 to 26 percent of GDP in 1996" (Naughton, 2007: 274).

production from agricultural inputs to consumer goods for the newly expanding markets. The increased prices for agricultural output and the increase in small-scale production raised rural incomes, which, in turn, increased the demand for consumer goods and the revenues of rural enterprises. Spurred by profit opportunities, local government created tens of thousands of new enterprises. These township and village enterprises (TVEs) produced a wide range of products for the domestic market and, in the coastal provinces, for export. The growth rate of these TVEs soon exceeded that of state-owned enterprises and became the major source of employment for surplus rural workers.

China's participation in the world economy advanced rapidly under the second set of reforms. The government expanded the number of cities and regions open for foreign investment and greatly expanded the ability of Chinese firms to engage in foreign trade. The reforms opened the Chinese economy to increased imports and foreign investment.

The Tiananmen Incident and its Economic Aftermath

In 1988, the Chinese economy boomed and inflation accelerated to levels that caused great complaint and fear among urban residents. At a Fall Communist Party meeting, more conservative party leaders curtailed the powers of the top reformer, Premier Zhao Ziyang, and began a new retrenchment and attempted strengthening of central control. This effort gained greater momentum with the violent repression of the Tiananmen Square protests and the removal from power of Zhao Ziyang and other reformers. After the June 4, 1989 attack on the protestors remaining in Tiananmen Square, the hardline leadership restricted economic, as well as political, freedom. Leaders who favored the command economy gained ascendancy. At last, the planning faction had the freedom to return the economy to greater central control; it increased planning and tightened control of market activities.

A sea of student protesters gathers in Tiananmen Square on May 4, 1989. They were asking for greater freedom of speech and democracy. (Peter Turnley/Corbis)

Planners froze total investment in 1989 at the same level as in 1988, but since prices had been rising rapidly, this was a decrease in the real value of investment. The new policies refocused investment on state-owned firms, giving particular priority to energy industries. Planners imposed strict controls on loans to non-state firms, hitting rural industries quite hard. Planners' efforts to halt inflation exceeded their expectations and abilities. Many workers in the non-state sector lost their jobs, and consumers became much more cautious in their expenditures. Some prices began to fall, and China entered a recession between mid-1989 and mid-1990.

Although state-owned firms were seemingly given preferential treatment under the recentralization, they did not prosper. The planners decreased the emphasis on profitability and decreased managers' autonomy. Planners increased their interference in SOEs operations, requiring them to help meet social goals, such as retaining excess workers to restrain unemployment. Firms' costs rose, but sales of above-plan output suffered due to the recession. Large state firms' losses climbed and became a burden on the state budget, rather than a source of revenue.

The efforts at recentralization were short-lived. Economic conditions changed too fast for the slow central planning apparatus, and important local officials opposed policies that weakened non-state firms. The dynamic TVEs in coastal provinces had become important sources of local government revenue, and provincial officials resisted planners' efforts to restrict or roll back the growth of TVEs. Even in 1990, the planning faction began to backtrack on the efforts at reviving the centrally planned economy. Economic circumstances showed that even a partial return to the planned economy could not deliver the one thing that was most important to the continued legitimacy of Chinese Communist rule: economic growth. This proved to be the last serious effort to return to the centrally planned economy.

In early 1992, Deng Xiaoping signaled his approval of renewed economic reforms and his disapproval of conservative economic policies by touring South China, including Shenzhen, which had most embraced market development, and by calling for renewed reform. At the 14th Party Congress that October, the Communist Party officially announced the goal of establishing a socialist market economy, marking the first time since reforms began that creating a market economy was the expressed goal. Since then, China's leaders have announced a whole series of reform efforts, including permitting private business owners to join the Communist Party. China's movement toward a market economy is not yet complete, but it is an irreversible reality. Even if it wanted to, the Chinese Communist Party has lost the power to put the market genie back in the bottle.

The Chinese Economy Today

The results of China's market reforms are obvious: under its market-based economic reforms, the Chinese economy has now grown at a faster pace for a longer time than any other nation, even somewhat exceeding the performance of other remarkable Asian economies, such as Taiwan, South Korea, and Japan. This rapid growth could well continue with some moderation for another 10 to 20 years. This section provides a snapshot of the Chinese economy today. Alas, fairly and completely describing China's economy requires more words than space allows for in an introductory volume such as this one. The final section of this chapter can only sample some of the highlights of the ongoing story of the evolving Chinese economy. For more thorough treatments, see the suggested readings at the end of this chapter. Many excellent studies on the Chinese economy have been published just recently, and this chapter has benefited from their insights and thorough analysis.

RESOURCES

A nation need not be rich in natural resources to become wealthy, as Japan or Singapore have shown, nor will a nation that is rich in natural resources automatically become a wealthy country, as Nigeria has demonstrated. Overall, though, a nation is better off possessing a generous endowment of natural resources; such riches have been important in facilitating the growth of economic well-being in the United States, for example. Since the geographical areas of China and the United States are almost identical, this section often compares the two nations' natural resource endowments.

Mineral Resources

In absolute terms, China is blessed with a rich endowment of mineral resources that is roughly in proportion to its land area. In relative terms, China's mineral endowment is considerably diminished when evaluated on a per capita basis, lagging far behind that of the United States simply because China's population is 4.3 times larger than the United States' population. As Barry Naughton (2007: 28) notes, China's "mineral reserves per capita are typically half or less of world averages."

In recent years, China has achieved considerable success in developing its mineral resources. According to the U.S. Geological Survey, in 2006, China "was the leading producer of aluminum, antimony, barite, coal, fluorspar, graphite, iron and steel, lead, rare earths, tin, tungsten, and zinc" and the top exporter of "antimony, barite, coal, fluorspar, graphite, rare earths, and tungsten" (USCGS, 2006).

Despite its mineral riches and mineral exports, China's overall mineral development has not kept pace with its economic development, so that China is one of the world's largest importers of many key minerals, importing 30 percent of the mineral resources consumed each year, including copper, chromium, cobalt, iron ore, manganese, nickel, petroleum, and potash. According to the U.S. Geological Survey, "Mineral trade accounted for 21.6 percent of the country's total trade in 2006" (USCGS, 2006). In the first half of 2008, iron ore and other minerals accounted for almost 35 percent of China's imports by value and had increased almost 75 percent compared to the same period in the previous year.

China's rapid economic growth helps drive demand for additional global production of many raw materials. As the world's workshop, China claims large portions of the global incremental output of raw materials, and its growing demand for these inputs has greatly contributed to the rapid rise of commodity prices in recent years. For example, in 2004, China absorbed half of the world's incremental demand for metals and one-third of its incremental demand for oil. Ensuring access to these vital inputs is a key driver of Chinese foreign policy.

China's accelerating demand for raw materials is driven by massive construction projects throughout the nation and its accelerating industrialization. China also ships a considerable share of its industrial output overseas, so world demand for China's low-cost exports partially explains the country's rapid growth in demand for raw materials. As more Chinese enter the middle class and as per capita incomes rise, some analysts believe that China's demand for metals, minerals, and energy will further accelerate as personal consumption claims a larger share of economic output. Garnault and Song, for example, predict that China will maintain its high rates of economic growth for at least another decade and that this growth will be more resource intensive, following the economic development paths taken by already developed nations. According to Garnault and Song, per capita demand for metals and energy increases markedly when GDP per capita reaches $2,000—$5,000. China's per capita income has attained this level, and even the Chinese government is encouraging Chinese consumers to increase their consumption expenditures. In this income range, the demand for resource-intensive goods expands faster than the demand for less resource-intensive services, so China's growth will continue to place growing

Miners at the Qingciyao coal mine wait for an elevator at the end of their shift, some 750 feet (230 meters) underground on May 30, 1996. The state-owned mine, near Datong in China's Shanxi province, has more than 7,000 employees, including 2,700 miners who work eight-hour shifts. China is already the world's top producer and consumer of coal. Experts say it will use at least twice as much coal, the only fuel it has in plentiful supply, by 2020. (AP/Wide World Photos)

demands on its own mineral resources and those of mineral producers around the world. The same is true of China's demand for energy.

Energy Resources

China's energy endowment, particularly in per capita terms, lags behind that of the United States in every category, except for hydropower. China has the largest hydropower potential in the world, but the location of hydropower resources matches up poorly with that of the country's electric power load centers, with much of the unexploited potential situated in the remote, mountainous areas of Tibet and Southwest China. Still, China has rapidly developed its hydroelectric potential, with annual output increasing eight-fold since 1980, boosted by the construction of numerous new dams, including the Three Gorges Dam, the largest hydropower generator in the world. Hydroelectricity supplied 15 percent of electrical generation in China in 2006, more than double the average share in the 1980s, and the equivalent of hydroelectricity's worldwide share in electricity production. China will be hard-pressed to maintain hydroelectricity's share in electricity production, even given its rich hydropower potential, because electricity demand is growing so quickly and the construction

THE THREE GORGES DAM

The construction of the $30 billion Three Gorges Dam, the world's largest hydroelectric project, demonstrated China's ability to plan, finance, and execute ambitious projects on a world-class scale. Intended to prevent all but the largest downstream floods, the dam, reservoir, and locks allow 10,000 ton vessels to reach Chongqing, located 400 miles upstream, and to produce about 100 terawatt-hours of electricity annually, avoiding the annual burning of 40–50 million tons of coal. International critics charged that the project's cost was understated and its benefits exaggerated, and doubted China's ability to successfully complete the project. Some of these fears were fulfilled. For example, the relocation program for two million displaced people was flawed, with the poorest people suffering the most. But fears about China's ability to finish this project proved to be unfounded. Along with completing the Three Gorges Dam, China launched and completed numerous major construction projects, including an interstate-style highway system that rivals the United States' in length, the architecturally daring projects for the Beijing Olympics, plus countless other large-scale infrastructure projects. Today, no experienced observer doubts China's ability to design, finance, and build numerous visionary projects simultaneously throughout the country.

China's Three Gorges Dam, the world's largest hydroelectric dam. The dam's construction had long been supported by Chinese officials for its financial benefits, and long been opposed by environmentalists, historians, and human rights groups for the flooding of the gorges and Chinese villages along the Yangtze River. (Bimuyu503/Dreamstime.com)

times required for hydropower projects are much longer than for thermal power projects. But China's rising concerns over greenhouse gas emissions provide a strong motivation for continued hydropower development and also explain China's push into other renewable energy forms, such as wind and solar.

Coal Resources

Both the United States and China have rich coal deposits that will be sufficient for hundreds of years. There is no looming peak coal problem resembling that predicted in the near future for oil. The United States' coal reserves are more than twice as plentiful as China's and between them, the two countries possess 42 percent of the world's coal reserves. China is the world's largest coal producer, and while its per capita production lags behind that of the United States, per capita coal production in China is only half that of the U.S., indicating how coal-intensive the Chinese economy is. China's energy endowment and consumption are skewed heavily toward coal, with relatively little natural gas use. In fact, China relies on coal for almost 70 percent of its energy supply, and too much of the coal is burned inefficiently, causing severe air pollution problems. The transport of the bulky fuel challenges China's rail system, and mine safety is an acute concern, with much of its incremental output coming from small-scale mines lacking modern mining technology and safety equipment and procedures. Moreover, China's reliance on inefficiently burning increasingly large quantities of coal has now made it the world's largest incremental source of greenhouse gas emissions and the second-largest source of greenhouse gases overall.

Oil Resources

As new oil fields were found in Northeast China, Chinese officials in the 1970s dreamed of being the next Saudi Arabia. This dream was shattered by stagnant oil production in 1978 and 1979, which played an important role in persuading Chinese leaders to launch economic reforms, rather than rely on disappearing oil riches to fuel a boom in imported industrial plants. Instead, as discussed earlier, China's leaders switched to a policy of economic reform that set China on the road to rapid economic growth.

For much of the time since reforms began, China was self-sufficient in oil production and was even an oil exporter. This changed when China's growth accelerated after the turn of the century and the absolute level of economic output reached globally significant levels: the growth of industry, public transportation, freight hauling, and private car ownership causes demand for petroleum products to grow much faster than domestic production. Today, China is mimicking the oil development path of the United States, not Saudi Arabia, by increasingly relying on imported oil to meet the growing domestic demand. China's oil reserves are two-thirds those of the United States and major oil finds both inland and off-shore have so far eluded zealous exploration by Chinese and foreign firms. China imports more than half of the petroleum it consumes, and Chinese authorities subsidize gasoline and diesel prices to avoid the price shocks and social unrest they anticipate that fluctuating energy prices would cause. Many other nations also subsidize fuel supplies, short-circuiting their economies' ability to adapt gradually to changing energy prices, and forcing the government to make large expenditures to subsidize petroleum consumption.

Since 1949, the Chinese economy has periodically experienced energy crises, particularly electric power shortages. Prior to 1978, some of these shortages were caused by central planning failures and misguided political campaigns. In the late 1970s, a slowdown in the growth rate of the electric power industry prompted the CIA to predict that the Chinese economy would grow no faster than 3.5 percent per year in the 1980s due to constricted electricity supply. Of course, the Chinese economy grew much faster than this. The CIA was correct in predicting slower than normal growth of electric capacity because the early reforms shifted investment resources away from heavy industry. What was not predictable was the degree to which market reforms would improve economic efficiency in China, enabling a significant increase in output per unit of electricity consumed. The command-style Chinese economy used energy very inefficiently. The new emerging economy used energy more economically as it expanded labor-intensive production. Electric power shortages have also periodically plagued China during the reform period, but this is not an unusual phenomenon for a rapidly developing nation. During periods of particularly rapid growth, the new demand for electricity grows faster than the new supply; new factories, shopping malls, apartment buildings, and other users of electric power can be built in a fraction of the time required to construct a large-scale electric power plant and bring it into operation. So, times of rapid growth in China have been plagued by rolling blackouts as dispatchers rationed supplies to customers. Such shortages also occurred in the South Korean and Japanese economies during their high-growth periods. However, the electric power industry has continually and rapidly added new capacity, and electric power shortages have eased whenever China's economic growth rate has moderated.

Overall, the Chinese economy uses energy less efficiently than it could. The energy intensity of the economy has declined a great deal since economic reforms began, but it has a long way to go in reducing its energy intensity to the level of the United States, which has a higher energy intensity than most other advanced economies. Energy drives all modern economies, and almost all nations import a portion of their energy supplies. The logistics of importing energy are challenging, and importing energy carries a greater risk of supply interruption based on political instability in energy exporting nations. China's growing demand for energy moves world markets. In recent years, China consumed 10 percent of global petroleum output, but this share is increasing since growing oil demand in China accounted for 30 percent of the increase in world oil consumption.

Agricultural Resources

China's natural resources lag far behind those of the United States. First, China is a much more arid, mountainous nation with fewer water resources that are poorly matched to China's population centers. Precipitation in North China, one of the nation's important granaries, is much less frequent and more variable than that found in comparable areas of the United States, such as the Midwest.

China's arable land per capita is less than 20 percent that of the United States. In addition, much of China's farmland has been cropped for more than 2,000 years, while most of the farmland in the United States has only been brought into cultivation in the last 200 years. Chinese farmers have struggled for centuries with maintaining soil fertility. Still, even though China's cropland area is only 75 percent of the U.S. total, China produces about 30 percent more crops and livestock than the United States due to intensive cultivation. China feeds 20 percent of the world's population, largely from the output of its own farmers. It is the world's largest producer of cereals, meat, cotton, tea, and fruit, the third-largest producer of sugar cane, and the fourth-largest producer of soybeans. It is a net exporter of agricultural products. However, a tension exists between maintaining agricultural output and expanding urban economies. Today, existing farmland is under increasing pressure from alternative uses: builders of highways, cities, homes, and factories compete with Chinese farmers for scarce land.

Desertification threatens marginal agricultural lands in China. Over 30 percent of China is desert and the agricultural lands subject to intermittent rainfall in the north and northwest are prone to erosion and desertification, which affects 400 million people. Over-grazing and cropping fragile lands can ruin their productivity.

Water Resources

Water is a perennial problem in China. Statistically, China's water endowment is only eight percent less than that of the United States. This does not sound like much of a difference, but this smaller quantity serves a billion more people in China than in the United States. Water shortages are particularly acute in Northern China, where rivers often run dry and excessive ground water pumping leads to ground subsidence and declining water tables. To solve this problem, China is planning a massive water diversion from the Yangtze River to North China. Additionally, water pollution plagues most of China's rivers and many cities lack adequate sewage treatment facilities.

Forest Resources

China possesses about four percent of the world's forest cover. Vigorous reforestation programs have increased China's forest cover from 12 percent to 18 percent over the last 20 years, with a national goal of reaching 23 percent by 2020, approaching the forest coverage found in the United States. In comparison, U.S. forests cover 25 percent of the country, and the United States has over six times as much forest per capita as China. Heavy snowfall damaged 10 percent of China's forests, according to Chinese news articles, in the winter of 2007–2008.

The above discussion could be continued by reviewing other natural resource endowments in China. The bottom-line for all of these discussions would be the same: China is poorly endowed with natural resources in per capita terms because China contains about 6 percent of the world's land area and 20 percent of the world's population. But natural resource endowment is neither a necessary nor sufficient condition for economic development. Japan demonstrates how economic development does not require rich natural resource endowment, and many poor nations in Africa illustrate the fact that rich natural resources do not produce wealth and well-being. The more important resources are human resources and the social, economic institutions that foster innovation and encourage the creation and expansion of profitable, creative farms and firms.

CHINA'S ECONOMIC SYSTEM

Remember communism, the social movement pioneered by Marx, who envisioned a proletarian revolution abolishing capitalism, injustice, and inequality by establishing a classless society in which the state would wither away? Inspired by this vision, communist parties around the world produced the greatest revolutions and social upheavals of the 20th century. As late as 1988, about 30 percent of the world's population lived in countries ruled by communist parties. Then, in a few short years, the rule of almost every communist party withered away, replaced by new governments that quickly began dismantling the state-run economic system, with many using what came to be known as the Big Bang approach. China is the only major nation still ruled by a communist party, and notably, it adopted a much more gradual, experimental approach in reforming its economic system, while eschewing political reform.

The Chinese Communist Party remains firmly in control of China, repressing all challenges to its political power, but that power, too, probably would have failed, as it has throughout the world, with the exception of Cuba, Vietnam, and North Korea's hermit communist state, had the Chinese Communist Party not engineered the most successful transition to a market economy achieved by any of the formerly Soviet-style economies. As Nicholas Kristoff of the *New York Times* observed, "China may claim to be Marxist-Leninist, but it's really Market-Leninist." According to Barry Naughton (1996), a leading U.S. expert on the Chinese economy, "The market is now the predominant economic institution in China" (p. 5). In his view, China has largely accomplished the transition from a command to a market economy; now, the challenges for China's economic system are the challenges of development: China is still relatively poor, and it needs to develop institutions to support continued, stable growth. Much has been accomplished in 30 years of economic reform, yet much still needs to be done for China to have a complete set of economic institutions to support its growing market economy.

One sure sign of the change in China's economic system is the enormous expansion in the economic freedom of the typical Chinese. The reforms have not increased political freedom, but ordinary citizens now have the freedom to order their personal economic lives in ways that the pre-1979 economic regime repressed and punished. What matters is not simply how fast the economy grows, but what it produces and who receives the output. Unlike pre-reform growth, China's recent growth has expanded consumer incomes and consumer choice, thus lending an expanded scope to private lives.

Prior to China's economic reforms, the lives of China's urban citizens were remarkably homogenous, as were the lives of rural citizens, with a large gap separating urban and rural. For both groups, the state restrained incomes and restricted the variety, quantity, and quality of goods and services on which Chinese citizens could spend their income. In addition, neither urban nor rural residents had any control over where they worked; China had no labor market. Prior to China's economic reforms, the state assigned young urban residents to work units, which would offer them their only possible job for life and the source of their well-being. Urban residents depended on their work units for the basics of everyday life. The work unit provided workers' families with housing, health care, education, and access to consumer goods. Thus, the choices available to a typical urbanite were controlled by their workplace and were highly subject to political movements and personal connections; personal economic effort had little impact on one's income and future prospects. Rural residents were forced to live and work in the village where they were born, except for women, who typically married outside of their own village—the husband's village became their permanent place of residence. Rural residents had essentially no chance of moving to cities and obtaining the better-paying urban jobs; a system of internal passports tightly controlled movement within the country, effectively halting the rural-urban migration that is usually the norm for a developing economy. The fate of Chinese peasants was tied directly to their work teams' economic output. The lack of personal incentive combined with the state policy of underpricing agricultural output kept the countryside extremely poor. The poverty of China's peasants precluded expenditure on personal consumption, and economic planners deliberately restricted the range, quantity, and quality of consumer goods. Government policies prevented urban and rural residents from exercising individual initiative to increase either their incomes or the supply of consumer goods. Neither urban nor rural residents could start a business, even to produce consumer goods that were in tight supply. Little or no change in wages, plus the deliberate restriction of consumer goods production, starved Chinese appetites for goods and services readily available elsewhere in Asia.

Since the start of the reforms, China's citizens have enjoyed greatly expanded personal incomes, and greatly expanded choices in consumer goods. The Chinese responded to new market freedoms and new market choices with gusto. They abandoned the drab blue clothing and black cloth shoes of the Mao years for stylish clothing and fancy footwear. Restaurants scarcely existed in pre-reform China; now, Chinese citizens have the option of dining at Chinese restaurants, grabbing a snack from the innumerable food carts on the street, or eating at an American-style fast food restaurant. Bicycles were once the only means of private transportation. Now, Chinese consumers are buying automobiles in increasing numbers for local transportation, and even go on long, American-style road trips. (A former Chinese student of mine emailed me photos of his road trip from Beijing to Tibet in his Jeep Cherokee.) In China today, both urban and rural residents can own their homes, and home decorating has become a nation pastime with the appearance of Home Depot-style stores in the large cities. Young urban couples devote a great amount of time and money to personalizing their living spaces. Rural residents have constructed elaborate multi-story homes.

Both consumer choice and consumer sovereignty now reign in China. Chinese consumers can shop for the item they want to buy, guided by personal taste within

Shopping mall in China. (Shariff/ Dreamstime.com)

the limits of their financial resources, and Chinese firms respond to the preferences shoppers reveal through their purchases. Firms that make the goods Chinese consumers want to buy at the prices they want to pay succeed and grow in the new Chinese marketplace, while firms making the wrong goods or charging too high a price wither and fail. Noted economist Josef Schumpeter labeled these twin phenomena, the emergence and expansion of firms that meet buyers needs and the decline and disappearance of firms that do not, "creative destruction," and the existence of this process is a sure sign of a functioning market economy.

All of these changes in the economic lives of the typical Chinese are powerful signs of just how much China's economic system has left the planned economy behind and replaced it with a flourishing market economy. However, a great deal of work on the economic system is still required to ensure continued growth and economic outcomes that favor continued social stability.

Developing and maintaining the right institutions to maximize economic growth and well-being in a market economy is no easy task; it is a continuing challenge, even for nations with long-established market economies, as the recent world financial crisis made clear. In a democratic, market economy, special interest groups constantly promote economic policies that will benefit their constituencies at the cost of the overall economy and to the detriment of the average citizen. In the United States, for example, both Congress and state legislatures face unremitting pressure from lobbyists to shift economic regulations in favor of one group or the other. This results in a maddening mixture of policies that often clearly favor the few, harm the many, and retard economic growth and well-being. Cases in point include federal farm legislation, subsidies for corn-based ethanol, and government bailouts of failing financial firms that avoid paying the full price for their reckless lending practices.

It is not surprising, then, that much work remains to develop a complete, well-functioning market economy in China. Since 1979, Chinese reformers have had to recreate a market economy after Chinese officials' vigorous efforts to abolish all normally functioning markets in the last 30 years. The reform method has been one of gradual change coupled with a great willingness to experiment and learn from mistakes. No other Soviet-style economy has done nearly as well in its transition from a command economy to a market economy.

As in the United States, wealthy, powerful factions strive to mold the changing economic environment for their own personal benefit, sometimes at the cost of decreased economic efficiency. Complaints about corruption are endemic in China today, and present ongoing threats to social stability. Other continuing challenges to fuller development of the market economy are conditioned by China's socialist past and the continued dominance of the Chinese Communist Party. Yet, the Chinese Communist Party and China's government have shown a remarkable willingness to experiment with the economic system and officially recognize the need for its continued development.

Some of the biggest challenges to continued development include the economy's incomplete system of property rights and its faulty banking system, which makes too many loans on the basis of politics instead of profits.

INTELLECTUAL PROPERTY RIGHTS

A well-functioning market requires clearly assigned property rights and an orderly system to enforce and exchange these rights. Two key areas that require improvement in China are first, the effective enforcement of intellectual property rights, and second, the clear assignment and enforcement of property rights to agricultural land.

China's lack of intellectual property rights (IPR) enforcement has been a continuing source of tension between the country and its trading partners. IPR is probably second only to China's exchange rate policy as a continuing irritant in the United States' and China's economic relations. In a 2005 report, the Office of the U.S. Trade Representative labeled IPR enforcement one of China's greatest trade shortcomings. International copyrights, trademarks, and patents are constantly violated by entrepreneurs in China. No academic research is required to verify this claim; any traveler to China can casually observe the ubiquity of counterfeit products that range from low-quality knock-offs of trademarked apparel to exact replicas that are exported abroad and sold as genuine articles. Bootlegged CDs and DVDs are easy to find in China, and they flood out of the country into markets around the world. "In 2004, more than 60 percent of the counterfeit goods seized in U.S. ports by Customs authorities were of Chinese origin" (Bergsten, 2006: 97). Stories of manufacturers stealing the designs of foreign firms are common. For example, Toyota, Honda, and

Chinese customs agents with weapons stand guard over counterfeit CDs, DVDs, and CD-ROMS readied for destruction by the Chinese authorities in Zhuhai, Southern China, in August 2001. Sixteen million counterfeit items were destroyed during the event held in a region known both as a major export-manufacturing base and the heartland of China's piracy industry. (AP/Wide World Photos)

Nissan are suing Chinese automakers for violating copyright and patent protection. This problem is not a new one. On a research trip to China in 1988, I gained access to any number of ministry offices in my quest for research data, but when I tried to go to the second floor of a major public bookstore, a guard stopped me, saying that foreigners were forbidden entry. A friend explained that the second floor contained English books reprinted in violation of their copyright. During later trips, I observed pirated materials that were openly displayed for sale in many shops and little kiosks on the street.

As Chinese firms and inventors develop more of their own designs and inventions, intellectual property right protection will become increasingly important to maintaining economic growth in China. Intellectual property rights will hopefully give innovators monopoly profits from their innovations. Research and development is expensive and risky; success is never guaranteed. The rationale of intellectual property rights is to create incentives for innovation by allowing inventors the exclusive right to use their creation for a specific period of time. China has mechanisms for granting and enforcing patent rights in the country, and both Chinese and foreign inventors are filing patent applications in increasing numbers. The number of annual patent applications in China more than tripled between 2000 and 2006, increasing by 44 percent in 2005 and another 20 percent in 2006, ranking China as one of the top ten patent-filing countries. U.S. firms operating in China are also increasing their investment in research and development, signaling increased confidence in intellectual property right protections in China.

Rural Property Rights

China's fantastically successful economic reforms got their start in early tentative changes in the countryside. For 20 years prior to the reforms, the growth of agricultural output barely kept pace with population growth: there had been little change in average grain per capita, and rural people, comprising 80 percent of China's population, lived very hard lives, many of them with incomes hovering around the absolute poverty level. All of the collective investment in terracing fields, constructing irrigation systems, developing new strains of rice and wheat, and locally producing chemical fertilizers had not resulted in acceptable growth in agricultural output. Political interference in cropping decisions and misaligned incentives prevented better agricultural performance, but great potential existed in the countryside, just waiting for the right institutions to release it.

The initial economic reforms relaxed tight controls on individual economic activity, and the long-repressed entrepreneurial instincts of China's peasants burst forth, producing a wide range of new, simple consumer goods to meet the pent-up demand of both rural and urban dwellers for basic foodstuffs, household implements, furniture, and all sorts of basic consumer goods that the planned economy had failed to produce in sufficient quantity or acceptable quality. Of course, once permission was given to disband the collective farm and return to household farming, this revolution rolled through China, well ahead of leaders' expectations. Yet, so immediate was the jump in output that no effort was made to halt, let alone reverse, the spread of the household responsibility system.

For the first time in many years, the peasants' economic incentives were aligned with the economic goal of the nation to increase agricultural output. Peasants had to deliver set amounts of output to the state, but all output beyond this lump-sum tax was theirs to use or sell. Peasants got to keep 100 percent of their incremental production. Smart, industrious peasants could really prosper and pursue Deng Xiaoping's slogan, "It is alright for some to get rich first." In a surprisingly short time, rural incomes began to catch up with urban incomes.

Unfortunately, rural property rights were only partially reformed. The collective or village still owned the land; individual plots were leased to peasants on long-term leases that eventually had terms as long as 30 years. These long leases might have given farmers sufficient incentive to make long-term investments in developing the productivity of their farms, except for peasants' uncertainty over the reliability of their leases. The leases could be broken by village leaders and, too frequently, they were broken. The collective land could be reallocated to improve the distribution of land in response to changes in village population. Too often, village leaders sold farmers' land to developers who wanted the property for non-agricultural uses.

Such transfers of land from agricultural to non-agricultural use represent exactly what must occur in a rapidly developing economy, building new factories, new towns, new commercial centers, and new roads—all of the infrastructure required for an urbanizing society. Economically speaking, such transfers are efficient if they are priced correctly: the land transferred from agriculture might be much more valuable in its alternative use.

However, the transfers lacked equity and, sometimes, even efficiency. Farmers who lost their land were paid its value as farmland, not its value based on the new, more productive use. On some occasions, the displaced farmers were paid little or nothing for the loss of their land. Wu Jinglian (2005: 27) notes that "low-priced farmland requisition caused at least RMB 2,000 billion worth of losses to farmers whose land had been occupied with no or inadequate compensation." Even considering the bribes paid to local leaders, the owners of the new industrial facilities still paid low prices for their land, encouraging excessive expansion and contributing to the recent excess capacity in heavy industry.

Land confiscations of this sort have been one of the biggest causes of social unrest in China. Peasants who have lost their land have little else left to lose in protesting their treatment. China is, indeed, a totalitarian state with effective and ubiquitous police. Still, each year, tens of thousands of demonstrations are reported, and these are likely the tip of the iceberg of the complaints and resentments expressed by displaced farmers. In traveling through China, one is struck by how much is new and how much has been built on such a grand scale in such a short time in places where one previously saw nothing more than farmers tending their fields. One wonders what inequities and grievances are simmering throughout China over these land transfers.

Here is one form of the corruption that pervades the Chinese economy: village leaders pocket the profits from the land transfers. The transfer may be efficient in the narrow sense, but the side effects of these transfers hinder better, faster development in the countryside. Many problems could be solved by carrying forward the reform of rural property rights. The household responsibility system failed to grant sufficient property rights to farmers. Complete property rights to plots of land would improve farmers' incentives to find the most productive use for their land, and would help them realize the gain from selling the land for other uses, removing one of the biggest sources of discord in the countryside. Farmers could also use the land as collateral on loans secured to shift their efforts into other productive activities on or off the land. Farmers wishing to permanently relocate to urban areas could sell their land and use the proceeds to fund a more successful move, or farmers could sell or lease their land to other farmers trying to create larger fields that are more amenable to mechanizing operations. Even for farmers with no desire but to continue farming, more secure property rights would increase the likelihood of long-term investments to improve the productivity of the land.

The Chinese Communist Party and the Chinese government are not oblivious to these problems or to the social problems caused by arbitrary land transfers that disenfranchise farmers. The length of lease terms has been increased over time. According to Wu, a new law enacted in August 2002 promised to protect "the long-term stability of rural land contract relations" and that "the state protects the rights of the party awarded the contract" to be fully compensated when transferring the contract (Wu, 2005: 27).

Establishing a new law and actually implementing it in each village is a different matter, and peasants' dissatisfaction with property rights has continued. In late 2007, this dissatisfaction achieved new expression as peasant demonstrators called for the privatization of land, a move that directly contradicted the party's insistence on the collective ownership of agricultural land. Farmers in Shaanxi and Heilongjiang called for land privatization, using the Internet to publish their demands, aided by journalists, academics, intellectuals, and political activists who supported their efforts. Some protesting farmers were detained and a Xinhua news article quoted a top official who rejected privatization and insisted on continued collectivization.

Still, this is currently a very active issue in China. After all, China's current top leaders have proclaimed the importance of improving rural living standards. On October 12, 2008, top party leaders announced new initiatives designed to raise rural income. A major component of the new policy eliminated the 30-year time limit on land leases, making them open-ended. The policy will also constrain local leaders' ability to arbitrarily reallocate land from agriculture, formalize the process, and require compensation based on the market value of the land. The new policies establish a more formal land registration system and would allow peasants to engage in the unrestricted trade or sale of land-use contracts. If they are enforced properly, such efforts will move China's farmland a long way toward privatization and will likely provide the high-powered incentives needed for farmers to maximize their incomes from land holdings. Perhaps this change will once again begin to close the urban-rural income gap and provide the right price signals for land transfers out of agriculture.

CHINA'S FINANCIAL SYSTEM

Prior to reform, China's financial system was a rudimentary one fashioned in the typical Soviet style of planned economies, where a mono-bank, the People's Bank of China, carried out the financial aspects of planned economic activities. Although it accepted consumers' savings deposits, the bank did not function as a true financial intermediary, which makes business loans based on the expected profitability of the loan applicant and thus plays an important role in firm governance. Before reform, independent agents could not apply for loans because no independent economic activity was permitted.

Early in the reform period, the State Council directed state-owned enterprises to gradually shift to using bank loans to finance working capital and fixed-asset investments; the government moved away from providing investment funds as grants from its own budget. At the same time, market-oriented township-village enterprises (TVEs) grew rapidly by using local government investments and increasingly retained earnings from their profitable operations.

Justin Yifu Lin, vice president and chief economist of the World Bank. (Laurent Gillieron/epa/Corbis)

The banking sector was transformed in successive waves with the creation of new banks. The People's Bank of China became China's central bank and four additional commercial banks were created from the old banking system: the Industrial and Commercial Bank of China, the Agricultural Bank of China, the Construction Bank of China, and the Bank of China. These big four banks are tightly connected to the party and government, which influence their lending practices, and together, these banks own over 50 percent of the country's total bank assets. Three additional policy banks were created to pursue specialized government goals: the China Development Bank, the Export-Import Bank, and the Agricultural Development Bank. Over time, the number, types, and functions of small banks have grown to include joint-stock banks, city commercial banks, rural and urban credit cooperatives, and foreign-funded banks.

Thanks to changes in the savings behavior of Chinese citizens, China's banks receive a steady flow of new deposits. The household savings rate was quite low at the start of the economic reform period at about 5 percent, but it climbed to over 40 percent as personal incomes rose and Chinese citizens saved for targeted purchases and precautionary purposes. Including all sources, the national savings rate reached 50 percent in 2005. Total household savings deposits rose from 6 percent of GDP in 1978 to 77 percent in 2005.

China's financial system is actually over-reliant on the banking system. The Shanghai and Shenzhen stock exchanges are relatively small compared to the overall size of the Chinese economy, and the corporate bond market is relatively unimportant, as

CHINESE ECONOMISTS

As China embraced the market economy, Chinese students flooded into economic graduate programs around the world. Today, professional Chinese economists hold positions at top universities and think tanks around the world, publishing in top professional journals. Chinese economists trained in the West have returned to China, reforming economic education, working in top banks, supporting economic policy making, and founding economic research organizations. One of the earliest graduates of a top U.S. economics department, Justin Yifu Lin, joined Beijing University in 1987, and in 1994, founded the China Center for Economic Research, China's top economic think tank. He also helped found Beijing International MBA at Beijing University, the first joint international MBA program in Beijing. In June 2008, Dr. Lin became a Senior Vice President and the Chief Economist for the World Bank, the first economist from a developing nation to hold this position.

well. Thus, Chinese firms heavily rely on their retained earnings and on bank loans for their financing—if they have good connections, for the lending process is highly politicized. State-owned enterprises (SOEs) and former SOEs receive favorable treatment in their loan applications. The commercial component of China's banking system has been slow to develop. Too often, banks made loans without regard to the borrowers having a viable business plan; instead, the banks granted loans based on the political connections and political value of the borrower. Non-performing loans became a serious problem for China's banks in the late 1990s, constituting 40 percent of total lending, and required national government intervention to remove bad loans from the banks' balance sheets and ensure that the banks were adequately capitalized.

While they were funding the unprofitable ventures of large firms, the banks neglected small private firms that needed financing for highly profitable projects. Huang (2008) argues that in the 1980s, China's banks did a good job helping fund township-village enterprises (TVEs), which were the most market-oriented, most entrepreneurial, and fastest-growing part of the Chinese economy. According to Huang, in the 1990s, banks increasingly favored the large, well-connected firms and restricted purely private firms' access to bank financing. One sure sign of China's underdeveloped commercial banking is the irregular financing mechanisms that fill the gap left by the banks. For example, viable private firms use pawnshop-style financing to meet short-term financing needs because lines of credit are unavailable from the banks.

The prejudice against private enterprise continues, but the restructuring and recapitalization of the large banks put China's top banks on much more solid footing from 2002–2008, according to Nicholas Lardy (Bergsten, Bates, Lardy, & Mitchell, 2008). He reports that nonperforming loans declined to only 6.7 percent in 2007, and that "the banking sector as a whole" had a return on equity (net income/stockholders equity) of almost 17 percent. This period coincided with very rapid growth in the Chinese economy, based to a surprising degree on the expansion of heavy industry. Low, even negative, real interest rates spurred a borrowing binge and a building binge. New infrastructure projects required steel, cement, and other heavy industry products, and Chinese firms rapidly expanded to meet this demand, building excess capacity in the process; increased exports only partially absorbed this excess capacity.

Thus, as the world plunges deeper into financial crisis, and as both demand and prices fall, the profitability of Chinese firms will fall, as well, with some facing large losses. China's banks will again see a rapid increase in nonperforming loans, and all the while, other profitable lending opportunities may continue to be neglected, given the prejudice against private firms, as documented by Huang.

Trade

This section focuses primarily on foreign trade, foreign direct investment, and China's exchange rate policy, with particular reference to trade relations between the United States and China. But first, we should note that this foreign trade and foreign investment would not be possible without progressively freer domestic trade in China. An essential element of China's shift from a command economy to a market economy is the replacement of bureaucratic transactions with market transactions between willing partners. External trade and foreign direct investment receive the most attention outside of China, but in sheer volume, China's internal trade matters most. Domestically, trade is flourishing in China in a multitude of forms, most of which are good for the participants, good for society, and good for the continued development and enrichment of the nation and of the world.

Although trade within China advanced rapidly after the introduction of reforms, more remains to be done. The degree of openness to interprovincial trade in China has been the subject of some debate among experts on the Chinese economy. For example, Alwyn Young (2000) argued that the process of economic reform actually "led to the fragmentation of the domestic markets," with local governments creating local monopolies and obstructing the free flow of goods between regions. In a recent paper, Brandt, Rawski, and Sutton disagree, noting that "domestic trade barriers are no longer a central economic issue in China's economy" citing data on interprovincial flows in railway freight and the creation of an interstate-style highway system. This is not to say that private Chinese firms face no administrative barriers to their operation; as already noted, private firms struggle to obtain bank financing and face residual prejudice due to past ideological campaigns. Huang (2003, 2008) amply documents this continuing official discrimination against home-grown, private entrepreneurs. Still, private Chinese firms are prospering and expanding despite these restraints. Private firms, SOEs, and foreign-funded firms are developing national brands and undertaking cross-provincial mergers. Chinese consumers, in turn, are increasingly buying goods shipped from around the nation in nationally branded stores.

The Growth of Foreign Trade

Once upon a time, U.S. policy makers worried about China exporting revolution. Now, policy makers worry about China's trade revolution, in which low-priced

Chinese goods flood into the United States, pushing the U.S. trade deficit with China to greater and greater heights. Under the leadership of the Chinese Communist Party, China switched from exporting communism to exporting toys, clothing, and other labor-intensive consumer goods. China is currently moving up the value chain into more capital- and technology-intensive products. Today, firms and governments around the world worry about the commercial competition created by China's low-price exports, while consumers across the globe benefit from lower prices and increased variety. At the same time, foreign firms compete to invest in China and to sell their goods and services to Chinese customers.

Trade liberalization was an early, fundamental element of China's economic reforms. Although originally initiated with caution, China's international trade soon took off. China quickly changed from being one of the world's most closed economies to being the world's most open large economy. International trade openness is measured by the trade-to-GDP ratio—the ratio between a nation's total foreign trade (exports plus imports) and its GDP. When economic reform began in 1978, China's total foreign trade was about $21 billion, and its trade-to-GDP ratio was about 10 percent, one of the lowest in the world. By 1990, China's total trade had increased by 500 percent, and its trade-to-GDP ratio was about 25 percent, a ratio that was already greater than that of many other large nations. From 1990 to 1995, China's total trade grew almost 20 percent per year, or more than twice as fast as the overall economy, with its trade-to-GDP ratio reaching almost 45 percent in 1994. The rate of increase in foreign trade declined in the second half of the 1990s, as Chinese economic growth slowed and the trade-to-GDP ratio declined. In 1998, at the time of the Asian financial crisis, the ratio stood at about 30 percent. From the relative low point of 1998, China's foreign trade and its trade-to-GDP ratio has risen rapidly, particularly following China's entry into the World Trade Organization (WTO) in December 2001.

Between 2000 and 2007, China's economy grew 187 percent, or almost 10 percent per year, but its international trade grew even faster, with exports increasing almost 490 percent, while imports grew 425 percent. In the period from 2004–2007, China's trade-to-GDP ratio averaged 69 percent, according to statistics from the WTO. For comparison, in the same time period, the United States' trade-to-GDP ratio was only 26 percent. Remarkably, China's trade-to-GDP ratio exceeds that of France (53%) and is quickly catching up to that of Germany (77%), the most open large economy in the world. For comparison, consider India, the world's second-most populous nation, which is also enjoying rapid economic growth; it has a trade-to-GDP ratio of only 42 percent, again highlighting the remarkable growth and size of China's international trade.

In terms of total trade volume, China became the third-largest trading nation in 2004, supplanting Japan, and in 2008, China surpassed Germany to become the world's second-largest trading nation, with the United States still in first place. If current trends continue, China's economy will be larger than the U.S. economy within 25 years, if not sooner, and before then, China will have become the largest importer and exporter in the world. China is already one of the major drivers of world economic growth. Between 2000 and 2005, China "accounted for about 12 percent of the growth in global trade," contributing more to international trade growth than the United States, even though the U.S. economy is many times larger than China's. China's role in world growth is more important now than ever, as the world enters the uncharted territory of global financial crisis. The manner in which China responds to this crisis will greatly impact the severity of the crisis, not just in China, but around the world. China's relatively strong financial condition gives it an unprecedented opportunity to pursue game-changing leadership, both at home and abroad, as we will discuss in the conclusion.

CHINA'S TRADING PARTNERS AND CHINA'S TRADE BALANCE

The United States is China's largest trading partner. According to U.S. statistics, the flow of imports and exports between the two nations totaled over $386 billion in 2007: China imported $65 billion from the United States, while exporting $321 billion, leaving the United States with a bilateral trade deficit of $232 billion. Nevertheless, China has been the fastest-growing export market for U.S. firms. From 2000–2007, U.S. exports to China increased 300 percent, while U.S. exports to the rest of the world grew 44 percent. Generally, the growth rate of U.S. exports to China is greater than the growth rate of Chinese exports to the United States, but since China's exports are so large, the U.S. trade deficit with China is still growing.

The fact that the United States runs a large international trade deficit cannot be attributed to Chinese policies alone. In 2006, the total U.S. trade deficit was $838 billion, while its trade deficit with China was $232 billion. From another perspective, while China runs a trade surplus with the entire world, it actually would run a deficit if it were not for its trade surplus with the United States. For example, in 2006, China's trade surplus with the world was $177.5 billion, and its surplus with the United States was $232 billion. In other words, China's trade deficit with the rest of the world totaled $54.4 billion. One could make a similar argument with regard to China and the European Union (EU). China's trade surplus with the EU is about the same size as its trade surplus with the United States. China's trade surplus with the EU has grown very rapidly in recent years, partly because of China's exchange rate policy, which will be discussed below.

Trade statistics that focus on bilateral trade overlook important regional patterns. Consider the 10 nations with the largest volume of trade with China. Seven of these are located in Asia, including Japan, Hong Kong, South Korea, Taiwan, Singapore, and Malaysia. Other Asian nations also have large volumes of trade with China. For China, trade within Asia is the most important component of its international trade, and China runs a trade deficit with many of these nations. Why? Because China is the final assembler of products produced in Asian production systems that span multiple nations. With the rise of China and its vast pools of low-wage labor, production systems throughout Asia have been transformed. Nations such as Japan, which once exported finished goods directly to the United States, now route the final assembly of many goods through China. U.S. statistics count the entire value of the final product as a Chinese export, but, in fact, the value added in China may comprise only a small

Stacking shipping containers at a container terminal on Victoria Harbor, Hong Kong. (iStockPhoto.com)

part of the product's price; 65 percent of the Chinese goods exported to the United States are assembled from imported components. While the U.S. trade deficit with China has been increasing, it has been decreasing with other Asian nations. In 1985, for example, exports from Japan, Hong Kong, Korea, Taiwan, and China accounted for 52 percent of the U.S. trade deficit. In 2004, exports from Japan, Hong Kong, Korea, Taiwan, and China accounted for 40 percent of the U.S. trade deficit. China's share had grown dramatically, but direct exports from Japan, Hong Kong, Korea, and Taiwan had comparatively declined, thanks to the new Asian production systems that used China as the final assembler.

Composition of Foreign Trade

When China first began to rejoin the trading world, 50 percent of its exports were primary goods—agricultural products, raw materials, and minerals. As China's exports rapidly grew in the 1980s—slowly at first, but more quickly as the decade progressed—the share of primary goods shrank to 26 percent of total exports in 1990. During the 1980s, China's manufacturing exports grew rapidly, with much of this growth occurring in the labor-intensive light industry sector.

In the 1990s, China's exports grew in fits and starts, increasing at double-digit rates in six of these years, but barely growing at all in 1996 and 1998. Still, the major trends in the composition of trade continued, as exports of primary goods declined to just 10 percent of total exports. Today, primary products comprise less than 5 percent of China's exports. Since 2000, China's exports have grown at an average annual rate of 25 percent per year. (China's export growth rate was slowing throughout 2008, and China may well see no growth in its exports in 2009, as a world-wide recession appears most likely.)

Today, China has become the world's workshop, churning out a vast array of consumer and producer goods across almost the entire range of manufactured products. "Made in China" is the ubiquitous label on the clothing, tools, and toys filling the Wal-Marts and Targets in the United States. But China is not content to be the final assembler of toys, clothes, and simple household appliances. Its goal is to internalize the production of more of the products it assembles and to switch from manufacturing low-tech consumer goods to designing and manufacturing high-tech and high-quality producer and consumer goods, continuing to follow the development path blazed by Japan, Taiwan, and South Korea. Apparently, China's goal is to become a major exporter of all major products. Chinese firms are building international name brands that will eventually have reputations comparable to that of top U.S., European, Japanese, or Korean firms. Lenovo brand computers already possess world-wide recognition and a reputation for high quality and reliability. China's Haier Group is the world's fourth-largest manufacturer of major home appliances, serving both the large internal Chinese market and the rest of the world in the form of exports. Chinese automobile firms are rapidly expanding within China and planning to launch their brands, even in the U.S. market. China is actively pursing the design and manufacture of passenger airplanes, and is already exporting small regional jets. The ambition of China's leaders and its firms is to shift from imitating the designs and production processes of leading foreign firms to being the innovator of new products and processes.

A surprising aspect of China's recent growth is the rapid growth rate of key heavy industries since 2000: iron and steel, aluminum, cement and glass, paper and pulp, and chemicals. The growth in production of these industries is directly related to China's massive infrastructure investments in new roads and buildings. The increase is also connected with the weakening of the U.S. dollar to which the Chinese renminbi has been closely pegged. Thus, as the dollar weakened after 2001, the renminbi weakened against many currencies, as well, decreasing the price of Chinese exports. Spurred by the low real interest rate charged by banks, heavy industry greatly expanded its capacity. In 2006, China produced almost 50 percent of the world's flat glass and cement, 35 percent of its steel, and 28 percent of its aluminum. Most of the expansion served the booming internal market, but excess capacity has been exported. For example, China's net steel exports in 2006 totaled 24 million tons; by comparison, total steel production in Japan, the world's second-largest producer after China, was 112 million tons in 2005.

Foreign Direct Investment

How has China progressed so rapidly in the last 30 years? Beginning as an ailing economy with agriculture barely able to keep pace with the population and with antiquated industry, much of which was based on Soviet designs that were out of date even in the 1950s, when China imported key industrial plants from the Soviet Union, China has dramatically transformed its economy. A visit to any major city in China presents the visitor with a cityscape that appears entirely new, featuring high rise buildings, some with very flamboyant designs, which seem to sprout like mushrooms overnight. Of course, the explanation for all of these changes is quite complex, as this survey suggests, but to the casual observer, foreign direct investment seems to be a major driving force behind some of this change.

Certainly, the presence of foreign firms and foreign products in major cities reinforces this view. A superficial summary might explain China's spectacular transformation as being funded by the massive inflows of foreign investment and facilitated by an equally massive transfer of technological and managerial expertise. Indeed, the volume of foreign investment and technology transfer lends some support to this assessment. But the actual impact of foreign investment is more complex, nuanced, and even contradictory than casual observation suggests.

Early in the reforms, China's leaders very cautiously opened the door to foreign investment in special economic zones (SEZs). The intention was to attract foreign capital and know-how that would utilize Chinese resources to process goods for export. China-savvy investors from Hong Kong and Taiwan responded to the early invitation and the desired result ensued, so more areas were opened to foreign investment during the 1980s. Guangdong and Fujian, in particular, were rapidly transformed. In the 1990s, the scale of foreign direct investment increased considerably, and more and more of China was opened to foreign investment. As a share of GDP, foreign direct investment increased from about one percent in the 1980s to about four percent of GDP in the 1990s, and has been around three percent from 2000–2007. Given China's unexpectedly rapid growth after 2000, three percent of GDP means that the volume of foreign direct investment in China remains quite high.

Viewed only as a source of investment capital, foreign direct investment appears to be a curious, even unnecessary, phenomenon because China has a very high domestic savings rate. The nation generates enormous capital flows out of its current production, with savings rates between 35–40 percent and higher. In addition, because China has a net trade surplus, it is continually adding to its foreign exchange holdings, which are then invested in foreign financial assets, such as U.S. Treasury bonds, in order to stabilize the exchange rate. China is in the curious position of being a relatively poor nation exporting capital to the world's most advanced economies. In particular, The Peoples Bank of China, China's central bank, is investing large sums in the debt instruments of the United States, the world's richest nation, and is now the largest foreign holder of U.S. government debt.

Thus, the main purpose of foreign direct investment cannot be to provide scarce investment resources. Instead, foreign direct investment serves multiple transformative roles in the Chinese economy. First, foreign investors bring knowledge of foreign market opportunities, knowledge of products that will find markets abroad, and transfers of managerial and technological knowledge. Foreign-funded firms also provide competition for Chinese firms, inducing improvements in Chinese competitors, particularly state-owned enterprises (SOEs) and descendants of SOEs. Joint

A Chinese man relaxes beside a statue of Ronald McDonald in front of a Starbucks coffee shop in China. (Corbis)

ventures can help transform existing Chinese enterprises, as well. Finally, Huang (2003) argues that political leaders prefer foreign-owned firms because they wish to restrict the success of private, home-grown enterprises and he argues that it is easier for foreign capital than domestic capital to flow between regions in China.

Whatever the reasons for foreign direct investment from the Chinese side, foreign investors' goals are clear: they want to establish themselves in one of the world's most dynamic economies in order to sell to its domestic market and participate in its burgeoning export trade.

China's Exchange Rate Policy

In recent years, China's exchange rate policy has become a source of discord between China and the United States. Recently, the European Union joined in these complaints, particularly as the dollar weakened against the Euro from 2002 until the spring of 2008. When China pegged the renminbi (RMB) to the dollar in the 1990s, China's exchange rate was not a source of global concern. In fact, during the Asian financial crisis of 1997, China resisted devaluation and helped its Asian neighbors by maintaining its fixed exchange rate. However, matters are quite different today.

U.S. experts estimate that the RMB is undervalued by 40 percent compared to the dollar and by an average of 30 percent or more compared to the currencies of its trading partners. China's central bank has made gradual efforts to revalue its currency since 2005, but these efforts have not been sufficient to redress China's large trade surplus. To prevent the trade surplus from forcing a rise in the RMB, the People's Bank of China continually intervenes, buying foreign currency and investing in U.S. Treasury Bonds, as well as in the debt of other nations.

China's exchange rate policy supports the competitiveness of its exports abroad, but it undermines other goals, particularly that of increasing personal consumption expenditures in China. As a share of GDP, consumption in China is at a very low relative level: 38 percent of GDP in 2005, a decline of 8 percentage points from its average in the 1990s. The declining share of consumption has been taken up by surging investment and net exports. Allowing the RMB to appreciate would help shift China toward being a more consumption-based economy. Another good reason to appreciate the RMB would be to head off protectionist pressures that are building up within the United States, where some politicians use China's economic success as a convenient scapegoat for regional economic woes. How and when China should more seriously revalue its currency is complicated by the unfolding global financial crisis.

China's Future Economy

Today, China's economy is the world's second largest, and it is modernizing at a rapid pace. But it is still a relatively poor economy in per capita GDP terms, and its recent economic success has come at a very high price in terms of its environment. Chinese cities are some of the most polluted on earth, and China is now the largest source of greenhouse gas emissions in the world. What will China's economy look like in the future? The apparent answer today is that it will look like much of the rest of the world, as increasing numbers of its citizens move into the middle class. If so, the price to China's and the world's environment may be very high.

China recently announced a major stimulus package to counteract the 2008 global financial crisis. This crisis will leave no country untouched, but it offers Chinese leaders an opportunity for bold, global leadership that could launch China toward an alternative future. China must grow its economy. It must enlarge its cities and build new ones, as another 200–300 million people migrate from rural to urban environments. All of this growth requires energy to produce the construction materials needed for new homes, schools, roads, commercial centers, and factories. If China relies on its traditional energy source, coal, to fuel this expansion and modernization, it will surely contribute to global climate change, to which China is particularly vulnerable.

Already, the glaciers in Tibet are shrinking. These glaciers feed all of the major rivers of Asia, and when these glaciers are gone, China and the rest of Asia will face much more variation in river volumes. North China currently faces severe water constraints and global climate change, combined with economic growth and urbanization, will only make this problem worse. China can do a great deal to rationalize water use through proper water pricing, but decreased summer flows in the Yellow River and the Yangtze River will have severe impacts.

SOLAR ENERGY IN CHINA

Today, China is conquering one traditional industrial sector after another. Will China become a major supplier of renewable energy equipment tomorrow? Hopefully the answer is "yes," for China needs expand its electricity production without digging more coal. China needs to deploy utility-scale solar generating plants and can only build these on the necessary scale by relying on Chinese firms, such as Suntech. Founded in 2001 by Dr. Zhengrong Shi, Suntech was the first private Chinese firm to list on the New York Stock Exchange and has become one of the world's largest manufacturers of photovoltaic panels. Suntech's output goal is to have a capacity of 1.4 GW by 2009 and 2GW by 2010. In 2008, China added about 55 GW of new coal-fired power plants. Solar energy companies, like Suntech, need to scale up very fast to slow down China's accelerating rate of coal mining. Given all of the negative environmental consequences of mining and burning coal, this is a task that China's leaders should embrace; they have the increasing assistance of entrepreneurs and firms in taking on this challenge.

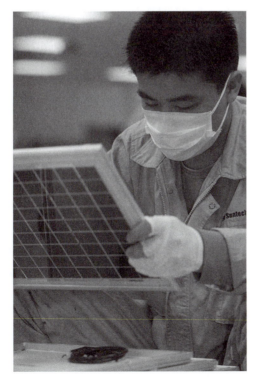

Workers assemble solar power panels at the Suntech factory in Wuxi, China. China has recently set new laws for the generation of renewable energy, including financial subsidies and tax incentives for the development of renewable energy sources. (Qilai Shen/EPA/Corbis)

The current financial crisis offers the Chinese government an opportunity to take a giant step toward solving its energy problems, its air pollution problems, and its contribution to climate change, while establishing China and Chinese firms as world leaders in the new industries required in the 21st century. To stimulate its economy, China could metaphorically build a new Three Gorges Dam by investing a similar amount into utility-scale solar power generation. China already has some of the world's largest solar companies. The biggest problem for these firms and for solar power in general is that the demand for solar power has not reached the economies of scale where solar electricity can compete with coal-fired electricity. A Three Gorges-style commitment by the Chinese government would change that and build on the industrial foundations that China already possesses. Such a program would move China into a position of imaginative world leadership that would parallel its dawning role as the world's largest economy.

REFERENCES

Bergsten, C. Fred, Bates Gill, Nicholas R. Lardy, and Derek Mitchell. (2006). *China: The Balance Sheet.* New York: Public Affairs.

Bergsten, C. Fred, Charles Freeman, Nicholas R. Lardy, and Derek Mitchell, (2008). *China's Rise: Challenges and Opportunities.* Washington, DC: Peterson Institute.

Brandt, Loren and Thomas G. Rawski, *China's Great Economic Transformation.* New York: Cambridge University Press.

Eastman, Lloyd E. (1988). *Family, fields, and ancestors.* New York: Oxford University Press.

Fairbank, John King. (1992). *China: A New History.* Cambridge, MA: Harvard University Press.

Garnaut, Ross and Ligang Song. "China's Resources Demand: At the Turning Point." Rio Tinto-ANU Partnership, 2007.

Huang, Yasheng. (2003). *Selling China: Foreign Direct Investment During the Reform Era.* New York: Cambridge University Press.

Huang, Yasheng. (2008). *Capitalism with Chinese Characteristics.* New York: Cambridge University Press.

Lardy, Nicholas R.(1983). *Agriculture In China's Modern Economic Development.* New York: Cambridge University Press.

Lardy, Nicholas R., (1992). *Foreign Trade And Economic Reform In China, 1978–1990.* New York: Cambridge University Press.

Lardy, Nicholas R. (1998). *China's Unfinished Economic Revolution.* Washington, DC: Brookings Institution Press.

Lin, Justin Yifu. (1995). "The Needham Puzzle: Why the Industrial Revolution did not Originate in China," *Economic Development and Cultural Change*, 43.2 (January 1995), pp. 269–292.

Lin, Justin Yifu, Fang Cai, and Zhou Li. (2003). *The China Miracle Development Strategy and Economic Reform,* Hong Kong: The Chinese University Press.

Myers, Ramon H. (1991). "How Did the Modern Chinese Economy Develop? A Review Article." *The Journal of Asian Studies* 50, no. 3, (August 1991): 604–628.

Morgan, Stephen L. "Richer and Taller: Stature and Living Standards in China, 1979–1995." *The China Journal,* 44 (July 2000).

Naughton, Barry. (1996). *Growing Out Of The Plan: Chinese Economic Reform, 1978–1993.* New York: Cambridge University Press.

Naughton, Barry. (2007). *The Chinese Economy: Transitions and Growth.* Cambridge, MA: The MIT Press.

McGregor, James. (2005). *One Billion Customers: Lessons from the Front Lines of Doing Business in China.* New York: Free Press.

Perkins, Dwight. (1994). "Completing China's Move to the Market" *The Journal of Economic Perspectives* 8, no. 2 (Spring 1994), pp. 23–46.

Richardson, Philip. (1999). *Economic Change in China, c. 1800–1950.* New York: Cambridge University Press.

Riskin, Carl. (1988). *China's Political Economy.* New York: Oxford University Press.

Spence, Jonathan D. (1990). *The Search for Modern China.* New York: W. W. Norton & Company.

U.S. Central Intelligence Agency. *The World Factbook: China.* Accessible online. https://www.cia.gov/library/publications/the-world-factbook/geos/ch.html.

Wang, Shaoguang, and Angang Hu. (1999). *The Political Economy Of Uneven Development: The Case Of China.* Armonk, NY: M. E. Sharpe.

Wang, Yan and Yudong Yao. (2001). "Sources of China's Economic Growth, 1952–99," World Bank Policy Research Working Paper 2650, July 2001.

World Bank. *China Quarterly Update.* Available online, excellent overview of current developments in Chinese economy. http://web.worldbank.org/WBSITE/EXTERNAL/COUN-TRIES/EASTASIAPACIFICEXT/CHINAEXTN/0,,contentMDK:20652127~pagePK:141137~piPK:141127~theSitePK:318950,00.html

Wu, Jinglian. (2005). *Chinese Economic Reform.* Mason, OH: Thomson Southwestern.

Young, Alwyn. "The Razor's Edge: Distortions and Incremental Reform in the People's Republic of China. *The Quarterly Journal of Economics* 115, no. 4 (November 2000), pp. 1091–1135.

Society

Religion and Thought

Robert André LaFleur

The English word "religion" does not begin to convey the wide range of attitudes and ideas pertaining to the spiritual practices found in China. Aside from Christianity, Judaism, and Islam (none of which enjoy full freedom of observance in China today), religious practices tend not to be concentrated in just one place, such as a local church, a single temple, or a mosque. In China, Taiwan, and for overseas Chinese throughout the world, many family homes have shrines for what are often called "Confucian" family rituals. Temples and pilgrimage sites also serve as localities for veneration, offering a complex mixture of Buddhist, Daoist, and Confucian themes. It is not unusual for the first-time traveler to China to ask the question, "What kind of temple is this?" The answers are often as confusing as the question, since one of the first things one learns is that the vast majority of temples are *working* temples. In short, they are places where people make offerings, and they reflect a mixture of doctrines that are as diverse as the Chinese history behind them.

The key word is "syncretism," or the blending of three traditions—Confucian, Daoist, and Buddhist—into an active whole. There is a memorable, four-character Chinese phrase that best conveys the blending of the syncretic ideal: 三教合一, which translates as "the three teachings unite as one." Relationships between adherents were not always easy, and they struggled against one another for ascendancy throughout Chinese history, as noted in the history chapter, with the suppression of Buddhism in the eighth and ninth centuries being quite severe. Monasteries were occupied, property was confiscated, and Buddhist practitioners were vilified. This kind of suppression has affected all of the major religious and philosophical traditions in

SYNCRETISM AND LIFE AS LIVED

The ideal of "the three teachings blending into one" was often described in memorable ways to represent a day in the life, or a life itself. In the morning, it is said, we are bustling, frenzied Confucians, striving for order in our lives and hoping to accomplish a great deal. By afternoon, as we begin to tire, we take on the thoughts of a Daoist, wondering what the rush and hurry is all about, and perhaps trying to find a way to perpetuate the afternoon relaxation. Finally, by evening, we tire and will soon be asleep; the Buddhist focus on the transience of life overtakes us as we drift off to sleep. Similarly, as youths, we strive for success. Toward middle age, we start to ask questions about all the hustle and bustle. As we become old, we start to contemplate why we struggled in the first place. Whether described in terms of a day or a life, the intertwined doctrines of China have withstood the test of time. Many people still tend to think of their lives as reflecting a blend of traditions, rather than a single overarching one.

China at some point, including Confucianism, which was held up for denunciation and ridicule during the Cultural Revolution of the 1960s and 1970s. The doctrines of Buddhism, Daoism, and Confucianism have competed with one another throughout the last two millennia of Chinese history, but their greatest rival may well be the central rule of the Chinese state, which, through the centuries, has sought to mold and manipulate them for its own purposes.

By the later imperial age of the Ming and Qing dynasties, however, the three teachings theme had become a component of everyday life. This doctrine of syncretism clearly illustrates the role of the individual and the family in Chinese religious practice, for it shows that, in stark contrast to Western religious experience, which tends to focus on a single doctrine, very few people would have described themselves as "a bit" Catholic and Protestant, and no one would have described herself as Catholic, Protestant, Muslim, and Jewish—all at once. Yet, in China, portions of each major doctrine influence the way that people relate to their families, execute their various roles in life, and manage the complexities of living.

Not even the new ideas that took root in China in the late 1940s, with the rule of the Communist Party, have shaken the power of syncretism in daily religious life. One can see it most prominently at the sites that comfortably combine all three traditions in one place—the five sacred peaks of China mentioned in Chapter 1. On the eastern peak of Mount Tai, for example, thousands of pilgrims climb the 7,000 steps to the summit every day. There are distinct temples of all kinds winding their way up the mountain, and on the spacious mountaintop, as well. People tend to be eclectic in their offerings, which include Buddhism, Daoism, and Confucianism, with many people visiting all three sites and paying their respects in ways that are both generic and welcoming.

There is a dramatic difference between the ritual practices of the average visitor from the People's Republic of China at a holy site and those of visitors from Taiwan, Singapore, or Hong Kong (or even overseas Chinese)—people who were

Tourists walk through the arch of the "Heavenly Street" near the summit of Mount Tai, a sacred mountain near Jinan, in China's Shandong province. The mountain is the most famed of China's mountains and was where the country's former emperors once came to offer sacrifices to the spirits of heaven and earth. (AP/Wide World Photos)

raised outside of the Chinese mainland, often in traditional households. In today's China, which offers relatively free travel to famous pilgrimage sites from locations all over the world, it is not unusual to see travelers from, for example, Taiwan watching the clumsy temple behavior of their mainland Chinese brethren with amusement and horror. Almost everyone who grows up in Taiwan has a reasonable comfort level in a ritual setting (Hong Kong and Singapore are similar in this regard), since spiritual practice is as much a part of everyday life as going to school or work. That is not the case in the People's Republic, where quite dramatic changes have taken place, even in the last few decades, in terms of the everyday attitude toward religion and what some people regard as superstition. For that reason, textbook temple behavior, such as having perfectly lit incense stick embers casting a small plume of smoke (not the flaming torch, laughter, and amusement that one quite often observes from the inexperienced) is not as common a sight as it is in other parts of the Chinese-speaking world.

The point is an important one—and more telling than an image of flaming torches at otherwise serious temples—if we are to understand the manner in which religious and philosophical traditions are perpetuated. As we shall see below, the three traditions have long histories in China, albeit broken at times by persecution or other problems. We will also see that the traditions have evolved over time and accommodated a range of outside ideas. In short, we can learn a great deal from the relative gap that has occurred in the People's Republic of China with regard to religious practice.

Traditional religious practices were condemned and their adherents persecuted during the Cultural Revolution, and thousands of holy sites, both large and small, from temples on Mount Tai to street-side shrines, were smashed and often destroyed. Traditional thought, not the least of which is the work of Confucius himself, was criticized and mocked. All of this had a deep effect on those who cared about traditional doctrines, sacred sites, and the perpetuation of tradition.

Still, those who argue that Communist ideology has terminated what we call religious beliefs in China misunderstand the issue on at least two fundamental levels. First, it is an extremely shortsighted perspective. All of the major religious practices—Buddhism and Daoism in particular—have endured fierce persecutions, only to emerge later with renewed strength. The second half of the 20th century was arguably not even the harshest period that such religions have endured. Second, to assert that religion has ended in China reflects a profound misunderstanding of the way that religious beliefs are intertwined with life as it has been lived in China for centuries, even millennia. Family rituals that comprise a great deal of what we might call Confucian religious beliefs are such an integral part of living as a father or a son (or any other family relationship) that it is difficult to imagine them dropping from sight. To be sure, the one-child policy and economic changes have had an impact, but this is not the first period in Chinese history in which traditional practices have been challenged.

Another example is the examinations that will be discussed in the education section. Five hundred years ago, in the middle of the Ming dynasty, parents and loved ones would go to temples to pray for the success of an aspiring candidate. Today, one sees similar practices aimed at ensuring that a son or daughter (or grandson or granddaughter) will emerge successfully from the college entrance examinations or even gain admission to one of the most prestigious universities. A rhetoric of fate and future is alive in these practices, and they are far from needing churches or other edifices to function; they are built into the practice of daily life. Chinese religion and thought are grounded in the family and the extended family network, and they are perpetuated in much the same way. One does not choose so much to *believe* in this or that ritual as one lives according to its tenets (or tolerates the tenets espoused by one's grandmother or grandfather, or cousin or parent). It is not very different from the experience that anyone might have in a traditional, extended family setting anywhere in the world. A great deal of tradition is perpetuated merely as a by-product of living.

Another subject worth addressing is the role of religious groups that the Chinese government is most worried about. Falun Gong has received a good deal of press, and the outside observer might well wonder why a powerful government would be concerned about it. A martial arts cult with supernatural overtones is something that many Westerners might think of as an exotic, idiosyncratic side issue when it comes to matters of political power and religious belief. Yet, just such groups have often alarmed Chinese governments in the past, and several have directly contributed to the overthrow of dynasties. Secret societies tied to various martial arts and supernatural powers were significant parts of the Red Eyebrows movement of the first century, the Yellow Turban uprising in the second century, and countless others throughout China's imperial history.

In just the past 200 years alone, in fact, there have been significant threats from the White Lotus Rebellion (late 18th century), the Taiping Rebellion (mid-19th century), and the Boxer Rebellion (early 20th century). Even if overthrowing the current order was not their goal, such groups have often had a highly destabilizing effect, and have worried the central power. The government's wariness about Falun Gong is in keeping with these historical themes. Few things have concerned the Chinese central government—in both imperial and modern times—as much as the combination of kinship ties, supernatural beliefs, and the pursuit of social causes. The point here is not to condone the Chinese government's harsh actions toward such groups, but rather to place them in a historical perspective that gives them context. It is sometimes difficult for Westerners to see why *organized* religious movements send warning signals to those in power, while the individual practices Westerners would also call religious are mostly seen as a normal part of daily life. Groups are perceived as powerful and, potentially, as threats. By gathering in groups, whether for the purpose of sharing political opinions or common worship, individuals become greater than the sum of their parts, and the Chinese government has always taken notice of this status. We will return to the theme of religious tradition and gathering at the end of this chapter. First, however, it is necessary to learn more about the individual traditions themselves.

THE HUNDRED SCHOOLS OF THOUGHT
(c. 700–200 B.C.E.)

In order to understand the foundation of Chinese thought, we must go back more than two millennia to a turbulent time in China's past. As can be seen from the history chapter in this volume, those who lived in China from the sixth through the third centuries before our era—a time of dramatic social and historical change—perceived a world in disarray, with small, independent territorial governments striving for ascendancy. They armed themselves and bitterly disputed their borders. Allies turned against one another and as many states were brought down from within as from without. Through it all, a number of major thinkers stubbornly addressed questions of how best to rule, and their works still have an enormous influence on Chinese life. Several philosophers imagined a better life for future generations by looking far back into the Chinese past. Others argued that people need only look at the present, and then calmly follow the path (or Way) of least resistance. Still others argued for strict, harsh laws that compelled people to maintain a life of order in service to the needs of the state. Every strand of those traditions (and Buddhism, which would emerge later) can still be found in China today.

Confucius and Confucian Thought

Political and philosophical views were highly contested in the centuries before political unification (221 B.C.E.), and conflict on the battlefield was only part of a larger struggle in early China—the struggle to define ideas that would shape how people ruled was inextricably linked to warfare. Even the most practical advisers understood

Statue of Confucius in the temple of Confucius in Beijing. Confucius's philosophy has dominated Chinese society and intellectual development for well over 2,000 years. (Sofiaworld/Dreamstime.com)

that winning on the battlefield had to be followed by effective rule, and that guiding concepts were necessary to make that rule effective. Confucius (551–479 B.C.E.) taught that the breakdown of social order lay in a lack of attention to the fundamentals of family, state, and social life. A native of the small state of Lu in present-day Shandong province, he taught groups of disciples who eventually compiled his lessons into a slender volume known as the *Analects*. In his middle-age years, he spent the better part of a decade traveling throughout north China in the hopes of persuading territorial lords to put his teachings into practice. Several key concepts emerge from a careful reading of the *Analects*. One of the most significant is the importance of achieving social and political harmony through proper attention to the hierarchical roles one plays in society. As one entry puts it, "Fathers must be fathers and sons son; rulers must be rulers and ministers ministers" (Analects 12.11).

One of Confucius's great contributions was to rework core concepts that had been used for centuries, giving them new moral dimensions through his discourses. The most important of these concepts are ritual, benevolence, sincerity, trustworthiness, loyalty, filial piety, and righteousness. These English translations do not do justice to the ethical subtleties of the terms discussed by Confucius, but the clear and persistent articulation of a limited number of important terms lies at the heart of Confucius's teachings. One can almost think of the *Analects* as a text on the fundamentals of a well-led life. Confucius cast himself as a transmitter of the old ways that had been practiced by the Duke of Zhou. His teachings were, from his perspective, merely a restatement of the core ideals practiced by the three sages—Yao, Shun, and Yu—and the early leaders of the Zhou dynasty during which Confucius lived. He deplored the deterioration of his society and sought to reassert the core values that, he argued, would revitalize the human order.

Working in a tradition that would become known as *ru*, and what we call Confucianism, was another great philosopher, Mencius (372–289 B.C.E.). Although Confucius's teachings were set down in the form of pithy moral maxims that were often no more than a few sentences long, Mencius expanded upon those concepts with full historical and cultural examples that run many pages. He promoted the concept that people are basically good, and that by paying attention to what he saw as the core ideals in human nature—not the flawed realities of what people actually did— leaders could create order in their domains and assert their dominance peacefully throughout the empire. Mencius taught that people's positive natures could be seen if one stripped away the detritus of social norms and false expectations. Goodness, he claimed, was always there, waiting to be rediscovered and replenished. More than any other early philosopher, Mencius asserted that the heart of rule lay in promoting the welfare of the people. Mencius's attitude can best be summarized by his statements that all a ruler needs to do to succeed is exude goodness. If the good ruler did that, the people from other states would take notice and flock to him. It is as easy, he taught, as turning over the palm of one's hand.

Daoism and Daoist Thought

The texts that took shape in the late Zhou period, which encompassed the sixth through third centuries B.C.E., were not written in isolation. They were the products of intense intellectual conflict, and the fervor with which philosophers argued their points about human nature and ruling reflected, on many levels, the contentious environment within which the territorial lords operated. Many of the texts from this period specifically attack the writings of the other schools. States needed advisers, and all of these philosophies, even those dealing with somewhat esoteric subjects, address the problem of ruling—of managing a complex state and managing others.

The Daoist thinkers, of whom the most prominent are Laozi and Zhuangzi, argued in pointed opposition to Confucian thinkers. Indeed, in Zhuangzi's writings, Confucius often appears to be a bumbling character who is unclear about how to operate in the world around him. At the core of Daoist thinking is the concept of the Way. *Dao* literally means "road" or "path," and the concept of the Way can be extended to human action within and beyond government—the path of life, as it were. The term was also employed by philosophers from other schools, but the articulation of the concept by Daoists took on a power that persists to this day, well beyond the borders of China. The major disagreement Daoists had with Confucians was that Confucians opposed the Way or flow of nature. Daoists maintained that all a ruler had to do was just *be*. Numerous examples in the writings of Laozi and

Statue of Laozi, ancient philosopher and a central figure in Daoist thought. (Kenliu/ Dreamstime.com)

Zhuangzi explain that trying too hard or thinking too much destroys the flow of life. One of the most famous Daoist passages of all articulates this point in a memorable fashion:

> Duke Huan was reading upstairs in the hall while Pian the wheelwright was hewing a wheel in the courtyard below. Pian set aside his chisel and went upstairs, where he said to Duke Huan, "Dare I ask what words are in the book my Duke is reading?" The Duke responded: "They are the words of the sages." "Are these sages alive today?" asked the wheelwright. The Duke answered, "They have been dead for some time." The wheelwright said, "Thus what your Excellence is reading is like the dregs of dead sages!"
>
> Duke Huan said, "How may a wheel chiseler have opinions about my reading? Explain, and I will allow it; if you cannot explain, you will die." The wheelwright replied, "I, your servant, understand things from the perspective of my own work. When I chisel a wheel, if I move slowly, it will not stay put; if I go fast, it will not carve. I find the way somewhere between a pace of fast and slow—I grip the chisel in my hands but respond with my heart. I cannot articulate it, yet something is contained within me. Your servant cannot teach it to his son, nor can his son learn it from him. In this manner I have put this into practice for seventy years, growing old carving wheels. Men of antiquity could not pass on what they practiced, and died. Because of this, what your Majesty is reading is the dregs of men of antiquity." (Zhuangzi, 1998, 5.13)

From the perspective of the wheelwright Pian, the Duke is glued to the past, and the books that he reads are no more than dregs. The significant act, he argues, is living and doing, which cannot be passed on in books or enshrined in temples.

More provocative still is the Daoist concept of *wuwei*, or non-action. This is the extreme political statement that a good ruler does nothing. According to this philosophy, by *not* categorizing, *not* making rules, and *not* ordering the people, order will, in fact, be achieved. Although there is an element of argumentativeness directed at Confucians in such rhetoric, many have found truth in it. Most everyone has seen the results of a competent manager who lets members of the workforce work within the flow of their jobs, the kind of leader who *seems* to do little, yet the work is accomplished, and well. Hence, the Daoist statement: "Through not doing, nothing is left undone." There is a pointed nature to Daoist critiques of Confucians, but one must remember that it, too, is a doctrine meant to teach people how to manage themselves, their families, and even the state. The message is a complex one, but it is useful to remember that many Daoist teachings from this period stress that in trying too hard, in organizing too much, everything falls apart. It is a minimalist philosophy meant to challenge the doctrines of the Confucians, and the opening line of Laozi's *Classic of the Way (Daodejing)* perhaps explains it best: "The Way that can be articulated is not the constant, true Way." Once it is made into a phrase, a rule, or a teaching—once one is no longer engaged in just living and doing—the Way is gone.

Legalism and Legalist Thought

The Legalists formed the most practical pole in early Chinese philosophy, one that aimed unashamedly at ordering society for the sole purpose of creating a unified state that would ultimately rule the empire in a way that was never previously achieved. Xunzi (c. B.C.E. 300–235) was an exponent of Confucian doctrine who inspired later Legalist thinkers. Arguing against Mencius's contention that human nature is inherently good, Xunzi noted that humans are intrinsically flawed; it was only through proper attention to education, memorizing the classics, and articulating the great teachings that people became good. Much has been made by later philosophers of this disagreement about human nature. There is room for agreement, however. Both Mencius and Xunzi asserted a common thread: people stayed good or became good through attention to core values and teaching. Their differences lay in whether goodness was innate, and the moral implications of that. For both, education lay at the heart of moral and practical statecraft.

Xunzi's crisp rhetorical style and careful patterns of argumentation deeply influenced thinkers for 1,000 years, and it was only relatively recently that the words of Confucius and Mencius were deemed superior, as Chinese philosophy took on new shapes in later times. At the heart of Xunzi's thought is an expansion of those two thinkers' idea that people are only as trustworthy as their actions. Xunzi focused on such actions and the practical elements of ruling, and it was this focus that later Legalist thinkers would expand. In opposition to the other schools, Legalist thought concentrated on what the people *must* do, no questions asked. Opposing other thinkers who concentrated on the people, or on just being, Legalists focused on what must be done to make the state prosper. It was an amoral philosophy that articulated the regimentation of society for the purpose of bettering the state itself.

What mattered to Legalists was power. For them, administration was the difficult art of manipulating people by taking advantage of their selfish interests and making it profitable for them to do what served those interests. It is not a philosophy that relied, as did Confucius's thought, on trust—not even on that of family members. The enforcement of law itself was meant to be so swift, so automatic, and so dreadful that it appeared to be a part of the natural order. Above all, one sees no strains of sentimentality in Legalist writings. The people were meant to be molded to the needs of the state. The same was true of administrators and even the ruler himself. The challenge of Legalism was to actually put it into practice, to go beyond the ordering of ideas, and to manage an actual state. The results were mixed: utter failure, if one looks to the fate of the Qin state, which, as can be seen in the history chapter, was unable to rule as a unified empire for even two decades; or some success if one sees that Legalist thought, with a somewhat more harmonious rhetoric than the Qin's, has influenced Chinese governments for well over two millennia.

BUDDHISM AND RELIGIOUS DAOISM DURING THE PERIOD OF DIVISION (c. C.E. 200–600)

The Introduction of Buddhism in China

The most significant political and intellectual change during China's Period of Division (the third through sixth centuries C.E.) was the entrenchment of Mahayana Buddhism as an intellectual and, indeed, political force from the upper classes down to the common people. Because it was a set of doctrines created in South Asia and brought to China, many Chinese saw Buddhism as a foreign doctrine that disrupted important aspects of family ritual and harmony. By shaving one's head and rejecting one's family, a monk or nun went against some of the most basic ideas of filial piety known in China. Early Buddhist advocates in China argued that it was necessary to look beyond these differences, and to focus on a message—profoundly original in the Chinese intellectual context—that addressed human suffering and the impermanence of life.

The Three Treasures of the Buddha—the Buddha, dharma, and sangha—opened a window onto a way of thinking about life and religion that was new to China. The Buddha offered the ideal of enlightenment to all people; the *dharma* articulates the universal laws of human life, while the *sangha* refers to practicing communities—people who have gathered together to follow the Buddhist way. Buddhism's Four Noble Truths state that life is suffering, and that the ways of the world do not bring happiness. Craving lies at the root of suffering, and suffering can only end when the cycle is broken. Finally, the Eightfold Path is a means of ending suffering that requires right perspective, right thought, right speech, right action, right life-path, right effort, right mindfulness, and right concentration. The goal, albeit a distant one, is nirvana—not an explosion of joy or lands of milk and honey, but rather an extinguishing, as when two fingers put out the flame on a candle.

Buddhism found an immediate audience in China, and it has persisted for almost two millennia. It took root not merely by winning over ordinary converts in addressing the concerns of those masses forgotten in much of Chinese religious teaching. A large part of its success lay in converting, or at least influencing, the powerful. After the fall of the Han, in the changed political climate of the northern and southern dynasties, Buddhism became a way for states to distinguish themselves from their predecessors and create a cultural and ideological identity that marked their kingdoms' rule, as each vied for control of larger swaths of land. Buddhism thoroughly penetrated the north, and its popularity would eventually serve as a form of glue through which the north and south could reconnect in the future. It is no small irony that one of the most persistent integrative forces in Chinese history came from afar.

Buddhism in China developed in the accepting environment of the Period of Division and early Tang dynasty (the third through seventh centuries C.E.). During that time, one of the great, ongoing translation projects in the world's history took place, as complex texts from South Asia were translated into Chinese for their use in specialized teaching and lay instruction. Trips to India for scriptures often brought long-lasting fame, as in the cases of the monk Fa Xian, who gathered texts in the fourth century, and Xuanzang, who returned to the Tang capital from India in 645. These journeys are also the stuff of legend. Every Chinese reader knows of the *Journey to the West*, loosely based on Xuanzang's travels, and the exploits of the Monkey King as he helped (and hindered) the monk on his journey. The religious texts themselves presented monumental difficulties for translators, and one fascinating result was that many of the key terms from South Asian Buddhism were translated using concepts from early Daoism.

During this welcoming five-century period, Chinese Buddhism strongly influenced Chinese artistic culture, and Buddhist monastic sects enjoyed an expanded role. Temple design blended traditional architecture and Buddhist themes, but nothing in China's artistic past prepared it for the great statues that would be carved into hillsides throughout the country, and which can still be seen today.

Sectarian developments also characterized this formative period, as various schools arose. The Tiantai sect taught the Lotus Sutra, while the Chan school practiced meditation and focus as a way of gaining insight leading to enlightenment. The Pure Land school, on the other hand, focuses to this day on the repetition of the name of the Amitabha Buddha. Pure Land teaching has always been the most inclusive and popular of Buddhist teachings, stressing that the route to the Western Paradise (and, ultimately, enlightenment) can be found in recitation.

Religious Daoism and Daoist Practice

Although it would never have the enormous influence of Buddhism on all levels of society, religious Daoism played a significant role in the diverse intellectual climate of the time. Its focus on astrology, breathing techniques, mysterious sexual rituals, and the ingestion of materials for immortality formed a religious tradition that deeply influenced many rulers and practitioners in later China. The same Period

Longmen Grottoes. (Dreamstime.com)

of Division that saw Buddhism come to the fore as a force in Chinese religious life lent significance to the writings and practices of groups of Daoist adepts in China. Venerating Laozi as a deity, and raising many other figures into the pantheon, the practices, lineages, and writings of what is often called religious Daoism have only a loose connection to the more philosophical teachings of Laozi and Zhuangzi discussed above.

Daoist sects were organized in a number of ways. The Celestial Masters sect was founded by Zhang Daoling in the second century of the Common Era. His purported role in healing the sick is still evident today in a popular section of the Chinese Almanac, and the connection to healing provided a distinctive message for early Daoists. The healing themes have figured in several key events in Chinese history, and the Celestial Masters sect still has adherents today (a sect named Supreme Peace also figured prominently). Two fourth-century sects, Maoshan and Lingbao, were instrumental in combining textual study, the production of numerous original texts, and ever-more-esoteric ritual practice. The history of religious Daosim shows a good deal of cross-fertilization and adaptation, with the Celestial Master sect absorbing many of the others over time.

Many of the deepest teachings of religious Daoism, and the various sects, can be found in the *Daozang*, an enormous compendium referred to in English as the Daoist Canon. The compilation began in the fourth century as a way to bring together varying strands of Daoist thought and practice. It remains a vital source for both

---

PHILOSOPHICAL AND RELIGIOUS DAOISM

Many readers sense a great contrast between the classical Daoist works of Laozi and Zhuangzi, on the one hand, and the seemingly more mystical writings and practices of later Daoists. Scholars have traditionally made a specific distinction between the "philosophical" works of the early Daoists and the "religious" character of later Daoism (beginning in the last decades of the Han dynasty and continuing with intellectual traditions and schools throughout the imperial period and up to the present). Some scholars have recently asserted that such a distinction obscures as much as it clarifies, and they persuasively point to a creative interplay between these themes throughout the history of Daoism. Readers can see elements of this lively debate in some of the texts listed in the References section below.

---

practitioners and scholars today, even though its contents are enormously diverse, containing well over a thousand scrolls and thousands of discrete texts. The Three Grottoes—authenticity, mystery, and spirit—comprise the major themes, followed by a dense series of talismans, commentaries, genealogies, rituals, biographies, and the like. These, in turn, are followed by four supplements that explicate major texts.

Finally, it should be noted that both Buddhism and religious Daoism developed alongside a plethora of other changes in government, literature, and society that mark the comparatively unstudied Period of Division. A vibrant new style of literature and strange stories took root, and the period saw a wide array of innovative medical techniques and artistic creations (both as a part of Daoist practice and independent work). Indeed, from religious change to the development of techniques in what today we call the arts and sciences, China has rarely seen a more diverse and exciting period.

NEO-CONFUCIAN THOUGHT

It would not be an exaggeration to say that Confucian thought has dominated China since the beginning of the Han dynasty (206 B.C.E.–C.E. 220), and that it played a central role in the organization of the state and the education of China's elites throughout the imperial period. China is even experiencing something of a revival of Confucian teachings in the present day, with television specials and best-selling books devoted to the explication of the doctrine, and even cautious attempts by government officials to use the rhetoric of harmony, cooperation, and stability to articulate its long-term vision of the country beyond the 2008 Beijing Olympics.

Confucian thought did not remain static over two millennia. It has been adapted for use by the state, in conjunction with the arrival of Buddhism and the popularity of Daoist religious practices. Throughout, Confucianism has shown a suppleness that readers of only the earliest Hundred Schools texts might not have anticipated. Over the centuries, a brand of Confucian teaching that we often refer to in the West as

Neo-Confucianism began to take hold. It, too, is hardly of a single piece, but it shows a remarkable resiliency in the face of changes throughout Chinese history.

As we have seen, China experienced profound developments in religion and thought during the Period of Division. By the time the Tang dynasty began (C.E. 618–906), China had established well-developed monasteries and academies devoted to Daoist, Buddhist, and Confucian teachings. The Sui (C.E. 581–617) and Tang states each promoted a blending of doctrines that was meant to support their claims to rule and perpetuate their own command of the territory. By the ninth century, after the disastrous rebellion of An Lushan (C.E. 755–763), a number of influential thinkers in the Confucian tradition began to articulate a new vision of their teachings. These scholars saw Buddhism, in particular, and Daoism as undermining the core teachings of Confucianism, on which (they argued) Chinese civilization was built. They roundly condemned the financial benefits given to Buddhist and Daoist sects, as well as their lucrative landholdings.

The backlash had political, economic, and intellectual implications. Many landed estates were confiscated, and the organizational strength of the various sects, if not their ongoing connections to wide groups of believers, was dealt a severe blow. The practical implications of the backlash are important, but the intellectual resurgence of Confucianism needs to be understood, as well. The perspective was articulated forcefully in an influential essay written by the 11th-century scholar Ouyang Xiu (1007–1072), who saw both a past that was problematic and the potential for a powerful future. He points to the disorder created after the fall of the Han dynasty, and asserts that the time was ripe for foreign doctrines that would harm China.

> Then Buddhism, entering at this juncture, trumpeted abroad its grand, fantastic doctrines to lead them, and the people could do no other than follow and believe. How much more so when from time to time kings, dukes, and great men sang its praises, declaring that Buddhism was truly worthy to be believed and followed. Could our people then still doubt and fail to follow? . . . What then can be done? I say there is nothing so effective in overcoming it as practicing what is fundamental . . . rites and righteousness are the fundamental things whereby Buddhism may be defeated. If a single scholar who understands rites and righteousness can keep from submitting to these doctrines, then we have but to make the whole world understand rites and righteousness and these doctrines will, as a natural consequence, be wiped out. (DeBary, 2000, 594–595)

Ouyang's negative vision of Buddhism's influence is clear. His positive vision is equally clear, beginning with the essay's title itself: *Discourse on Fundamentals*. The way forward, he argued, lay in a commitment to a spirited rethinking of the original Confucian vision. The profound intellectual diversity that would follow differed from traditional Confucianism in degree, not in kind. It was a creative synthesis of classical Confucian scholarship and the realities of life in a later era. It was not so much a break with the classical past as a reconception of it. Song dynasty Neo-Confucians sought to apply what they perceived to be the original vision of thinkers such as Confucius and Mencius, and to reform life around them. We might well say that the concern of Chinese philosophers at this time was the fusion of contemporary government with the ideal of a moral society. It was grounded in the study of ancient texts. A scholar named Li Yanzhang wrote in 1112:

> If scholars are made to concentrate their attention solely on the classics and are prevented from slipping into the study of the vulgar practices of later generations, then the empire will be fortunate indeed! (Hartwell, 1971, 691)

Several key figures and the reforms they made set the course for a Neo-Confucianism that still casts a formidable shadow in Chinese political and intellectual debate. The first group appeared in the late-Tang, Five Dynasties, and Northern Song periods (the 8th through early 12th centuries). A Tang scholar, Han Yu, wrote a forceful condemnation of Buddhism that criticized the emperor for deigning to venerate a finger bone of the Buddha. We have already identified Ouyang Xiu's anti-Buddhist rhetoric in his *Discourse on Fundamentals*. The prominent 11th-century scholar Sima Guang, who was discussed in the history chapter of this volume, articulated a Confucian vision of regulating the self, the family, and, eventually, "all under heaven." His massive historical study, *A Comprehensive Mirror for Aid in Ruling*, presents a picture of the Chinese past that Sima hoped later rulers would use to better understand how to benefit the people and the state. In the 11th and early 12th centuries, other scholars, such as Shao Yong, the Cheng brothers (Cheng Hao and Cheng Yi), and the Su family (Su Xun, Su Shi, and Su Che) wrote essays and spoke about the *Book of Changes*, numerology, and the need for a comprehensive approach to intellectual and political change.

It was in the Southern Song, Yuan, and Ming periods (the 12th through 16th centuries C.E.) that what we now call Neo-Confucianism truly became the foundation of education and the political order. The first major innovation came in the form of a fundamental reordering of education. Zhu Xi (1130–1200) showed the same zeal for returning to the original Confucian vision as the early reformers. He was much more interested in questions of morality, legitimacy, and correctness than his predecessors, and showed this by creating a curriculum of study that would prevail as the foundation for all education in the imperial period—up until the last imperial examinations in the early 20th century.

This education was grounded in what are still called the *Four Books* (*sishu*), and the aspiring student was to memorize them at an early age. It is difficult to overstate the effects of this change in the way that students prepared for their careers. Although people had read these books in the past (Confucius and Mencius had, in particular, always been extremely influential), the combination of the *Four Books* and the enormous influence of the examination system meant that almost every reader in the later empire began, after studying several primers to learn the basics, with the same readings. In a positive sense, this helped to create a shared world of knowledge. In a more insidious sense, it pushed other writings to a less prominent position. No longer would the supple writings of the Warring States thinker Xunzi influence the average reader the way that they had before. Even Buddhist and Daoist practitioners often had a foundation in *Four Books* teachings. In short, a curricular change that became rooted in all education helped to give Neo-Confucian thought a kind of ascendancy in the 700 years that followed Zhu Xi's time.

THE FOUR BOOKS (SISHU)

The Four Books that formed the core of late imperial Chinese education were Confucius's *Analects*, Mencius's philosophical works (*Mengzi*), and two smaller sections from the *Book of Ritual* (*Liji*). The first is often translated as the *Great Learning* (*Daxue*) and the other is entitled *Doctrine of the Mean* (*Zhongyong*). These four books of uneven length (the Mencius is much longer than the others) became the key to examination success in the centuries that followed. This curricular innovation by the scholar Zhu Xi maintained, in effect, that the path to government service lay in mastery of these classical works, and that good government depended on them. Their influence was all the greater for the fact that they were memorized early in life. In almost any essay written during the last dynasties of the imperial era, one can find the cadences and passages from the *Four Books*, which were to create the pathway to success in the later empire.

Another scholar, Wang Yangming (1472–1529), shows the powerful impact that syncretism—the theme with which we began this chapter—had on later religious and philosophical thought. Wang sought to bring knowledge and action together into a unified doctrine. Focusing on the text of the Mencius, Wang articulated the idea of "innateness," in which every individual, at her very foundation, knows the difference between right and wrong, and good and evil. Wang taught that this knowledge was intuitive, and lay beyond complex doctrinal arguments or rationalizations. From there, one developed as a person in a subtle dance of knowledge and action. Wang argued that there was no such thing as first learning and then applying lessons. Echoing arguments made by Mencius, mixed with traces of Daoist and Buddhist teachings, Wang asserted that learning and being were of a piece. Finally, Wang's approach to what we might call perception is equally innovative, yet grounded in classical Chinese arguments. In an almost Kantian set of statements, Wang taught that the mind creates objects—creates the world, as it were. Such was the influence of Buddhism and Daoism; Wang taught a kind of meditation to steady the mind for perception.

In short, what China experienced in the millennium before the 20th century was a complex interplay—occasionally antagonistic, but usually played out in the realm of doctrine—between China's three major religious traditions, with a smattering of influences beyond them, including Christianity, Islam, and the religious traditions first encountered along the Silk Road. Chinese teachings would also have a significant effect on the intellectual growth of Korean, Japanese, and some Southeast Asian religious and philosophical teachings, including Chan Buddhism (Korean: *son*; Japanese: *zen*) and the teachings of Zhu Xi and Wang Yangming.

RELIGION, THOUGHT, AND
THE POWER OF GATHERING

We return at the conclusion of this chapter to an idea that deserves greater attention than it usually receives in surveys of Chinese religion and thought: the social nature

New Year celebration, Hohhot, China. (Corel)

of religion and the power of social gathering. It will serve us well to briefly examine the work of Marcel Granet (1884–1940), an early-20th-century scholar of China who focused on the theme of gathering in his classic work, *The Religion of the Chinese People*. His is a poetic and sometimes fanciful description of religious life in early China, and of the power of festive gathering for the rural Chinese. Granet argued that to understand the fundamentals of all religion in China, one must return to the foundations of social gathering and seasonal celebration. Granet's mentor, the French sociologist Emile Durkheim, taught that all religions need the regeneration that is created by bringing people together for periods of communal excitement.

> It is at moments of collective ferment that are born the great ideals upon which civilizations rest . . . [and religious] ideals could not survive if they were not periodically revived. This revival is the function of religious or secular feasts and ceremonies, public addresses in churches or schools, plays and exhibitions—in a word, whatever draws men together into an intellectual and moral communion. (Durkheim, 1974, 91)

Marcel Granet describes Chinese peasant communal activity in the same context of *moral communion*. Peasants gathered at seasonal festivals to mark the beginning and end of agricultural work. Much larger—and infinitely more complex—gatherings would, in time, characterize the feudal nobility and later imperial court in China. Nonetheless, for Granet, the peasant gathering constitutes the beginning of all later Chinese religion, and he is hard-pressed to restrain his ethnographic and literary enthusiasm.

GATHERING AT THE GRAIN SHRINE

Gathering (會 *hui*) is a key element of Chinese religion and thought. Indeed, the very word for "society" used in China and Japan today—*shehui* and *shakai*—has its roots in the concept of gathering. To *hui*—to gather, coalesce, congregate, or commune at the *she*, the grain shrine to Earth—is to form something greater than the individual, something that moves, thinks, and acts differently than a single human mind or body ever could. In early agricultural society, the grain shrine was a place to meet, to plan, and to coordinate activities that extended far beyond the individual family's interests. It was also a place to pay reverence to the soil that provided all people sustenance. Gathering at the grain shrine, then, implies a concept in which the individual is part of something far larger, and much more profound, than his own private thoughts. It is profoundly social and, for some thinkers, constitutes the heart of Chinese religiosity.

It was only on exceptional occasions that the individual family could feel itself mastered by the vision—then sudden and dazzling—of higher interests never clearly seen in ordinary circumstances. Their rhythmic life provided the Chinese peasants with these occasions at two points every year: when they finished and when they began domestic work and labor in the fields, when men and women, their activity alternating, changed their mode of life, at the beginning of spring and at the end of autumn. . . .

In these solemn meetings of families usually withdrawn into themselves and shut up within the circle of their daily cares, each of them—becoming aware of its power at a time of plenty and feeling it to be increased by its public display—lost its usual feelings of enmity towards the neighboring families at the moment when its self-confidence was carried to its highest point. The mingling of the different groups was more intense, more moving, more intimate, and more absolute for their isolation and self-containment in ordinary times. (Friedman, 1975, 40)

This is not a church or temple religion. It is one that is as much a part of the campfire and the agricultural calendar as it is of ritual. This is not to say that ritual is absent, but religion was intertwined with the practitioners' very sense of being, their very sense of acting and moving. For Marcel Granet, early Chinese peasants represented China's elementary forms of religious life, and their greatest communion and greatest shared joy could be found in the very act of gathering at the seasonal festivals each year, where they became, for a moment, something other—something larger and more powerful than themselves.

These festivals of peasant harmony . . . snatched people suddenly away from their monotonous lives; they sharply awoke within them the profoundest hopes to be conceived by an agricultural people; they excited the creative activity of inner life to the highest degree. The practices and beliefs born of this extraordinary activity governed the development of Chinese religion: public and family cults, ancestor and agrarian cults, even the cult of heaven, emerged from these festivals of human and natural fertility in which the domestic spirit was revealed in all its strength while the sense of society was created. (Friedman, 1975, 40–41)

Here, Marcel Granet is the poet of social gathering and dispersal, but the foundations of his lyric lie in a theme that should not be forgotten, even when we focus on particular Chinese thinkers and their doctrinal differences (as we must in our study of complex thought). Granet's point resonates with the greatest joys of communal activity and the greatest fears of government figures. Indeed, if one adjusts one's perspective slightly from a focus on what we normally think of as religion—ritual, temple or church attendance, and differences in doctrine—it is easier to understand the power of the gathering idea, and to realize its all-too-often forgotten importance in understanding China.

The great religious festivals in present-day China are examples of gathering, communal activity, and sharing in every case. Throughout Chinese history, the gathering has taken place within the extended family setting. Even today, one can see it in action in the great celebrations at the New Year, when ordinary life ceases for family celebrations, and people gather from all over the country, sometimes for their only opportunity to see family members all year long. It can be seen in the great Qingming festival of the third month, when families gather together to share meals and attend to the graves of their ancestors. Finally, in the autumn, at harvest time, families come together for the mid-Autumn Festival to celebrate the harvest and the full moon, even if their families have not been on a farm in generations. In short, religion and thought in China can be seen in the most esoteric doctrines and ritual practices, as well as the most common foundations of social life.

REFERENCES

DeBary, William T. *Sources of Chinese Tradition* V.1. New York: Columbia University Press, 2000.

Durkheim, Emile. *The Elementary Forms of Religious Life*. Edited by Karen Fields. New York: Free Press, 1995.

Durkheim, Emile. *Sociology and Philosophy*. New York: Free Press, 1974.

Graham, A. C. *Disputers of the Tao*. La Salle, IL: Open Court Publishing Company, 1989.

Granet, Marcel. *The Religion of the Chinese People*. Edited by Maurice Friedman. New York: Harper & Row, 1975.

David Hall and Roger Ames. *Thinking Through Confucius*. Albany, NY: SUNY Press, 1987.

Hartwell, Robert. "Historical Analogism, Public Policy and Social Science in Eleventh and Twelfth Century China," *American Historical Review*, 76:3 (June, 1971), 691.

Ivanhoe, Phillip J. *Readings in Chinese Philosophy*. Indianapolis, IN: Hackett Publishing, 2000.

Lopez, Donald C., ed. *Religions of China in Practice*. Princeton, NJ: Princeton University Press, 1996.

Yu, Anthony C. *State and Religion in China.* La Salle, IL: Open Court Publishing Company, 2005.

Zhuangzi. *Zhuangzi.* Edited by Sun Yongzhang. Taibei: Jianan Chubanshe, 1998.

Social Classes and Ethnicity

Robert André LaFleur
Tamara Hamlish

PEOPLE

The population of China is largely composed of Han Chinese, an ethnic group that traces its origins to the early inhabitants of the Yellow River Valley. By far the dominant ethnic group in contemporary China, comprising nearly 92 percent of the current population, the Han live in the most densely populated regions of China, along the eastern coast and throughout the river valleys. The remaining 8 percent of China's population consists of over 50 government-designated minority groups. The differences between Han and these non-Han minority groups are often readily apparent in the way people dress, the languages they speak, the foods they eat, the architecture of their homes and other buildings, the images and materials used in their art, and in the organization of their family lives. Government-designated ethnic minorities often live apart from their Han neighbors, either in small communities within larger Han communities or in one of the five more remote, autonomous regions. Despite significant diversity among ethnic Chinese minorities, from the hill tribes in the mountains of the southwest to the horsemen of the northern steppes, the richness of particular cultures is often obscured by the simple opposition between the Han majority and non-Han minorities.

Yet, even within the Han majority, there is tremendous cultural variation. One of the most prevalent oppositions is the classic rivalry between north and south China. Northerners see themselves as honest, hardworking, loyal, and trustworthy, whereas southerners tend to regard northerners as slow, stupid, rude, and arrogant. Conversely, southerners see themselves as smart, sophisticated, educated, and cosmopolitan, whereas northerners are quick to describe them as sneaky, and prone to lying and cheating. Southerners have a reputation for being talented in business, and northerners are said to dominate the political landscape. Beyond these kinds of rivalries, more practical differences exist between the north and south in people's daily lives. For example, despite common Western stereotypes of rice as a staple at every Chinese table, inhabitants of the northern plains generally rely on wheat-based staples, such as noodles or steamed breads. The labor-intensive industries of the

Mother and son. (Corel)

south—especially the rice cultivation and silk production industries—often require the cooperation of large extended families that operate as corporate groups, as opposed to the smaller, more loosely organized family groups of the north.

Although it remains one of the most powerful oppositions in Chinese culture, the north-south rivalry is occasionally overlooked by highly educated, urban sophisticates, who see themselves as part of a cultural elite, rather than as part of regional communities. This is not to say that the north-south rivalry disappears, but rather that it takes a backseat to the more important distinction between elite and popular culture. Although this distinction is often discussed in terms of geographical differences between city dwellers and village peasants, geography has become far less important in contemporary society than it was in earlier periods. As China has become increasingly industrialized, and sophisticated systems of transportation and communication have made it easier to move around the country with greater ease and speed, the difference between elite and popular culture has become less a question of the difference between urban and rural ways of life and more a question of people's attitudes and daily habits. Local folk culture—including home-style cooking, decorative arts, such as papercuts and woodblock prints, and extended families living under a single roof—not only reflects the social and economic position of China's lower classes, but gives us a window onto their attitudes and beliefs about family, society, and the workings of the universe. Members of the urban elite are familiar with these aspects of rural life, but they often dismiss this lifestyle as crude, old fashioned, or steeped in superstition.

Detail of Scholars from Northern Qi Scholars Collating the Classic Texts, *traditionally attributed to Yan Liben. (Burstein Collection/Corbis)*

Not surprisingly, Americans are most familiar with the elite culture of what is often described as "traditional" China—the habits and customs of China's scholars and government officials. The members of this group produced and perpetuated a rich legacy of fine art, including literature, calligraphy, painting, porcelain, and poetry. They were charged with developing and maintaining social order through elaborate educational and political structures. The elites were known for their sense of refinement and their dedication to leisure through activities such as the appreciation of fine teas and culinary delicacies, or the construction of elaborate homes, gardens, and temples. In contemporary China, these continue to be important qualities of elite culture. One of the most striking differences, however, is the impact of globalization and the subsequent struggle to make sense of China's high culture, not only in contrast to high culture from other parts of the world, but also in the context of the popular culture of Hollywood movies, fast food, and the mass production and commodification of consumer goods.

One of the greatest challenges for members of today's Chinese elite is to find a place for the rich legacy of China's past in the globalized world of the present and the future. The tensions between these cultural spheres bring with them a vibrant cultural synthesis seen, for example, in contemporary Chinese film, cuisine, fashion, and architecture, as well as in the daily habits of people who shift between several worlds of shared customs and beliefs—without leaving their homes and offices in Beijing or Shanghai. Chinese tourism has sought to negotiate the same set of challenges, showing the great displays of modernity to be found in Shanghai, Beijing, and other cities alongside such cultural attractions as the terra cotta soldiers, the Great Wall, Mount Tai, and the Yangzi River Valley.

The impact of globalization is not limited, however, to the elite. Successive waves of emigration have created strong ties between Chinese who have settled in other countries and their family and friends who remain in China. Within these overseas communities, people create informal associations with others from the same place, in part because they speak the same local dialect, enjoy the same kinds of food, and, most importantly, have an immediate bond of trust based on shared networks of family and friends back in China. Overseas workers often send money home to help support aging parents or spouses and children who remained in the village. Families use these funds to demonstrate the success of their overseas relations by building new houses, buying cars, or funding public works projects, such as local clinics and schools, or, most recently, providing the necessary capital to start small businesses. In China's rural villages in particular, those who return home bring with them not only material goods, but their experiences of another world and certain changes in the habits and expectations of their daily lives. Finally, they support future waves of emigration when they help family and friends navigate the intricacies of immigration, apply to foreign colleges and universities, or find jobs. One hundred years ago, Chinese peasants who wanted to move up the ladder of success had few options beyond the traditional civil service examination system. Today, with the influx of cash from overseas, and the opportunity to follow others who have emigrated, the simple distinction between "popular" and "elite" is becoming far less rigid.

All of these differences, however, highlight a more broadly encompassing sense of the Chinese people since these differences are not irreconcilable, but, instead, are clustered around similarities. Similarities, in turn, often reveal subtle yet important differences. The ability to understand when and how people call upon these similarities and differences— how they use them to express where they stand in relation to someone else—most clearly symbolizes the complexities of Chinese culture. We will look first at class and status issues in China, today and in the past, and then turn to China's ethnic minorities.

WEALTH, CLASS, AND STATUS IN CHINESE HISTORY

China has often been characterized as a society that allows the free movement of individuals and families through its reward system. Indeed, the idea of social mobility exerted itself with a good deal of force throughout Chinese history, and the ideal of moving from poverty to the highest realms of government was the stuff of anecdotes, legends, poetry, and plays in Chinese literature. The children's primer *Three Character Classic* is filled with examples of hardworking children of modest means who succeeded through determined efforts.

> One young child opened bamboo rushes and plaited them together
> Another scraped tablets of bamboo so they could write
> These students had no books
> But they knew how to exert themselves
> One tied his head to the beam above him to stay awake
> Another pricked his thigh with an awl so as not to doze

They could not afford teachers and tutors
But studied hard of their own accord
Then there is the child who put fireflies in a bag to read at night
And another who read by the white glare from snow
Although their families were poor
These individuals studied unceasingly

(Chen, *Sanzijing*, 44–45)

The actual path to success in imperial China was often determined by the examination system, which provided individuals, families, lineages, and clans with the means to attain and even perpetuate success, although its influence varied under different dynasties and even under the reigns of different individual emperors. One of the greatest challenges for family groups was to ensure success over generations. For the wealthiest of families, that required placing sons in the higher ranks of the imperial administration; for less affluent families, it meant exerting administrative influence at a regional level. Far from the ideal of the hardworking young scholar making good on his family's hopes and achieving high positions, another, more cynical picture of the official who worked to benefit influential families (and curry favor with them) took root.

He Qingming's "Ballad of the Government Granary Clerk" contrasts favoritism for the elite with disdain for the less fortunate. It begins with descriptions of the "piles" of grain given to the wealthy, and ends with the following lines:

A hungry man from the countryside . . . wants to come forward for grain, but the clerk just curses at him.

(Mair, 1994, 276)

Although students of lesser means did sometimes rise to the highest levels of government, the Chinese ladder of success, as it has been termed by one prominent scholar, was literally grounded. Land, more than any other feature in the social and economic equation, was the factor that separated the rich from the poor, and families of moderate means from families of ample means. Westerners were introduced to the relentless logic of land acquisition through the narrative of Pearl Buck's *The Good Earth*, in which the protagonist slowly gains land and moves from poverty to comfort to status as one of the richest men in his region. It is only as a secondary process that he gained status through shrewd decisions in marital alliances, the acquisition of a concubine, and the education of his sons. Chinese readers heard countless stories with the same themes, published century after century in the imperial era, and even those who could not read a character knew that rented land was only a way of making ends meet in the best of times—it was never a path to comfort or increased status.

Pitying the Farmer Li Shen (780–846)

Working the grain beneath the heat of day
Sweat drips down to the grain-bearing soil.
Who can comprehend—that of the food in one's bowl
Every single grain comes with great toil? (http://www.lckps.edu.hk/chi/poems/p15-1.htm)

Chinese wash drawing of the interior of a tea merchant's shop, about 1800. (Library of Congress)

The despair-filled tone of Li Shen's poem gives the lie to the classic four-level schema that persisted in China into the 20th century regarding the status of various occupations. First in the order was the scholar, followed closely by the farmer. Both were said to work in primary occupations, using their own bodies and minds to change the world around them, and thereby benefiting the larger society. Artisans were a somewhat more distant third in the idealized classification. They built houses, furniture, instruments, weapons, and other products that were necessary, by extension, for the working of the world. The last of the four rungs in the hierarchy—and so distant from the others in the scheme as to be off the chart—was occupied by merchants. In the idealized rhetoric of human work, the merchant benefited from the toil of others, merely moving around and reselling the grain (or the artisanal products or even books) that were acquired by acting as parasites on the hardworking primary occupations.

Stereotypes of merchants often painted them as despicable and amoral creatures. Western readers will surely recognize several of the stereotyped themes when they ponder their own societies' ideas about mercantile activity and those who sold goods for profit. The stereotype has persisted in China into the 21st century, but it is accompanied by what has become an equally strong vision of the merchant as representative of ultimate success. Indeed, the four-level schema, with scholars on the top and merchants on the bottom, always provided fodder for irony in Chinese

---

MERCANTILE REVENGE

Some of the best expressions of the irony of the traditional four-fold classification can be found in literature, especially in the poems and plays of the later imperial period. Zhang Yu's (1333–1385) poem about "the merchant's joy" exposes the inadequacies of the outdated classification system. The poem begins with a description of the pleasures of travel and notes that the merchant loves traveling on the rivers and lakes, engaged in trade and not pinned down by the tax authorities. He has enormous wealth, the pleasure of friends wherever he goes, and the attentions of his concubines. The poem concludes with the following lines. It would be difficult for a struggling scholar of modest means to read them without irony.

There are many houses of pleasure on both banks of the Yangtze . . . he has passed through them all!

What other human is as happy as the merchant: aside from stormy weather, what problems does he have? (Mair 1994: 262–263)

---

history. Western sayings stress ideas such as "Living well is the best revenge," meaning that ample resources can take the sting out of the lack of status the newly rich might feel. In China, such sayings (and there were many) were accompanied by a powerful generational and family logic. Merchants lived well, it was often said, and enjoyed wealth that scholars could not even dream of. More importantly, though, they had the resources to perpetuate their success and raise their status by paying for the best teachers for their sons, creating the ultimate revenge—fabulous wealth combined with the highest levels of education and government service in just two or three generations.

As we have seen, few things were more important than land in ensuring the success of Chinese families during the imperial era. Beyond that, the commercial interests of enterprising individuals were a key to success, and mercantile activity was a significant factor in the growth of families, not to mention regional and national economies. It would be a mistake, however, to assume that such concerns dominated equally in all areas and at all levels of society. Throughout Chinese history, and to this day, there is a persistent thread of thought and social behavior that says, in effect, "I will work the earth, sustain my life, and do as I please"—a refreshing contrast to accounts of Chinese life that focus only on the center, whether that center is dominated by an imperial government or the Chinese Communist Party.

Ground-Thumping Song (Anonymous, Han Dynasty)

When the sun comes up we work, when the sun goes down we rest . . .
The Emperor and his might—what are they to us?

(Mair, 1994, 444)

WEALTH AND STATUS IN CONTEMPORARY CHINA

The enormous social and political changes that took place in China between the mid-19th and mid-20th centuries have altered class and status distinctions in profound ways. One of the most lasting impressions of the Chinese Communist Party's ascent to and consolidation of power in the 1940s and 1950s, as well as of the Cultural Revolution of the 1960s and 1970s, is the overturning of class and status distinctions based on land, which represented a complete rethinking of the relationship of people to the land. Landed families were among the biggest losers in the equation, and the reapportionment of land was one of the most dramatic social and economic changes ever to be undertaken—and on a massive scale—in human history.

Even in the wake of the economic reforms of the 1980s and the burgeoning Chinese economy of the 1990s and 2000s, the relationship of Chinese families to the land is fundamentally different from the pattern that previously dominated for millennia. Wealth and status in today's China have their roots in China's rapidly growing economy and Communist Party membership. The two are not necessarily allied, and the economic changes have created multi-millionaires where such opportunities did not exist 30 years earlier. On the other hand, party membership remains a route to success, along with the kinds of *guanxi* connections that have always been significant in doing business in a state-influenced economy. Particularly at the highest-ranked universities, students often feel the pressure of deciding whether or not to combine party membership with their elite educations as they ponder the opportunities they might have in the future.

It is also necessary to consider the success of the family unit in today's China. No longer are extended lineages or clan groups influential in the manner that dominated social and economic choices in the imperial era. The key unit in the success equation in today's China is somewhat larger than the nuclear family, but a great deal smaller than the extended family grouping that dominated earlier historical eras. In a similar fashion, the abrupt break between agnates and affines (the father's and mother's sides) is not nearly as pronounced as it was even 100 years ago. A family group's path to success in present-day China might well rely on, for example, the party connections of a father-in-law and the business opportunity provided by a cousin. While such a situation could have manifested at any point in Chinese history, those who benefit today are sharply different, and the group is a great deal smaller. Indeed, the commonly stated equation for child rearing in contemporary China might be the best way of envisioning the opportunity structure, as well. This equation is 4–2-1: four grandparents, two parents, and one child. Within that slender network (amplified by *guanxi* relationships and strategic kinship connections) lies the path to success for the enterprising individual.

Wealth and status in today's China are arguably even more fleeting than during the tumultuous centuries of China's examination system. While there is a greater range of opportunities for individuals (from academic pursuits to business careers and from modern agriculture to sophisticated commerce and an increasingly service-centered economy), the social network is smaller and more tenuous. As we saw earlier in this chapter, these networks still exist, and they remain enormously important on the ladder of success. Still, the combined effects of governmental population policy, economic growth, and geographical mobility have created a substantially new dynamic for families who seek—as Chinese families always have—to gain and perpetuate wealth and status.

ETHNICITY AND OUTLYING PEOPLES IN EARLY CHINESE THOUGHT

As we saw in the history chapter, China has had a complex relationship with its neighbors to the north, west, and south, having been overrun several times in its history (especially from the north), and absorbing—through military aggression or gradual acclimation—peoples in what were originally foreign territories. The earlier chapters showed that the Zhou political system (c. 1050–221 B.C.E.) was concentrated in the Yellow River drainage area, and that what we see today on maps of China as the west or the south were territories so far removed from that political order as to be beyond negotiation. Far from being recognized as distinct minority groups, foreign peoples were referred to as indistinct collections of people clustered according to directions—the Di peoples (north), the Yi (east), the Rong (west), and the Man (south).

Early Chinese thought regarding territory was dominated by what might be called the mythology of the center. Early texts, such as the one we encountered in the "Imaginative Geography" section, adopted the appearance of a mythological universe of sorts. The Chinese territories were centered in this literature, and imbued with a higher level of prestige—the term often used is *de*, or "virtue"—than surrounding lands. In this system, it was the relationship to heaven (*tian*) that gave these areas their value, and it is fitting to recall at this point that the term commonly used throughout Chinese history to refer to what we today would call "the state" or "the country" was "all under heaven" (*tianxia*).

This conceptual break in physical space in Chinese literature and philosophy is evident in countless texts, a few of which serve as examples below. The world "under heaven" is stable and ordered. Outside territories bring images of difference—the sky, a vaulted yurt—at best, and discord and ruin at worst.

> *Tchirek Song (Altun C.E., 486–566)*
> Tchirek River
> Lies under the Dark Mountains
> Where the sky is like the sides of a tent
> Stretched down over the Great Steppe.
> The sky is gray, gray:
> And the steppe is wide, wide:
> Over the grass that the wind has battered low
> Sheep and oxen roam.
>
> (Waley, 1918, 72)

On the way from the periphery to the center of these symbolic territories, one encounters images of a humanized world: learning and morality, restrained military

---

KEY TERMS IN THE TRADITIONAL CLASSIFICATION OF OUTSIDERS

Even a cursory reading of texts describing outsiders shows a number of key oppositions that persisted throughout imperial Chinese history. The most important of these oppositions divide all under heaven from the bordering nations.

Under Heaven	*Outside*
culture	nature
order/harmony	chaos/disharmony
hierarchy	anarchy
virtuous people	criminals
government	tribes
agriculture	nomadism
peace	war

There are two significant spheres of mankind in these writings: the peripheral one, consisting of nomads, barbarians, and criminals, who enter the texts in a negative manner by disrupting the harmony of the Middle Kingdom, and the center—the Nine Provinces, imbued with the Way of Heaven. In this rhetoric, those who lived under heaven had a responsibility to higher values; virtue and humility governed their actions, as is apparent in the following quotation from the *Book of History*:

"It is virtue that moves Heaven; there is no distance to which it does not reach. Pride brings loss and humility receives increase. This is the Way of Heaven."

---

strength, government hierarchies, agriculture, cities, and capitals, which suggest the existence of an ordered world governed by higher values.

As the *Book of History* makes clear, the cultural world under heaven was carved out of the raw physical world. The Middle Kingdom was created along the lines of heaven. As the *Book of History* states, "Order was effected and the lands made habitable" by early sage-kings. Created in accordance with divine values, the geography and society of the Middle Kingdom shared in that divinity. The bordering nations, however, did not, as we can see in the pointed wording of a memorial to the throne from the third century of the Common Era.

[A minister of government], Lu Mao, sent up a memorial:

"I have heard that in controlling distant barbarians, a sage Sovereign holds only nominal suzerainty and does not exercise a constant sway over them. Thus, when such domains were instituted in antiquity, they were called 'wild domains,' which means that they were between being and non-being—inconsistent—and could not be kept [under Chinese control]. Now [the rebel outsider] Gongsun Yuan is an insignificant thing among the Eastern Barbarians, cast away at the far corner of the sea; though he has a human face, he is no different from birds and beasts." (Fang, 1952, 408)

The official's critique maintains that the sovereign could not govern the distant barbarians (and their leader, Gongsun Yuan) precisely because, since they were not subject to the moral force of heaven, and unendowed with conceptions of propriety, they would not interact with moral officials on their own terms. Definitions of humanity in this remarkably persistent worldview were intimately related to definitions of geography. One who lived, as Gongsun Yuan did, outside of the core of the Nine Provinces was something less than human—culture and nature mixed, combining a human face with the conduct of a beast. Barbarians were represented, as the memorial states, as beasts with human faces; those who inhabited the "wild domains" were only marginally attached to life under heaven. Just as the bordering peoples played a rather small role in the vast literature of imperial China, so, too, was their role in the symbolic order limited to tales of disruption. They were not part of the moral order under heaven, although, in the course of history, they sometimes played a role in disrupting it, as we have seen above.

ETHNIC MINORITIES IN MODERN CHINA

The highly symbolic and largely negative perspective of outsiders that is evident in the literary tradition should not be confused with an equally persistent desire on the part of Chinese rulers to extend their territory to the further reaches of the continent, as they perceived it—particularly east and south. By the Song dynasty (C.E. 960–1279), the vast southland had been brought largely under Chinese control, and the clearest indication of that process was the removal of the Song court from Kaifeng (in Henan province, near the Yellow River) to Hangzhou (in Jiangsu, south of the Yangzi River). The court's movement, appropriately enough, was forced by northern armies that had taken over the Yellow River area, but moving the capital proved to be a boon for the flourishing economy and the burgeoning industries of the south. At the same time, Chinese influence was slowly moving west, as peoples in the southwestern provinces of Guizhou and Yunnan were brought under the successive control of the Yuan, Ming, and Qing governments.

Today, the Chinese state recognizes more than 50 minority groups of widely varying populations. Most of these groups are concentrated in the very regions that were referred to as being outside the territory "under heaven" 2,000 years ago. Of course, today's Chinese government has a different approach to such groups, and finds itself striving for the integration of minority groups, on the one hand, and celebrating the diversity that they bring, on the other. Indeed, today's map of China shows startling territory differences from the maps of the early Chinese states during the Zhou, or even during the first dynasties of the imperial era. The minority groups in the most recently acquired areas (such as Tibet and Xinjiang, not to mention Yunnan) are the least completely integrated, and in some cases—most notably, in Tibet—they have been the subject of a great deal of dispute regarding sovereignty and independent status.

Although China's ethnic minorities have blended with the Han population in many cases, they are still often thought of as living in distinct regions—from the Manchus and Mongols in the north to the Uyghurs and Hui in the west and the Zhuang in the south. According to the most recent census, China's minority groups range from ten million or more (the Zhuang, Manchu, and Hui) to several groups numbering only a few thousand. In fact, the top 9 groups together number over 80

Thousands of Muslim worshippers depart Id Kah Mosque after service at the end of Ramadan, Kashgar, Xinjiang province. (Pniesen/Dreamstime.com)

million, while the remaining 46 groups do not even approach half of that number. These population figures can be found in the Facts and Figures section at the end of this book.

China has five autonomous regions that are administratively distinct from the various provincial governments. A significant percentage of China's ethnic minorities live in these regions, and there is little doubt that such a residential format separates minority groups from the rest of the population, even as it allows them some autonomy in their religious and social lives. As many Westerners who are familiar with the issues surrounding Chinese influence in Tibet know, the autonomous regions also have the potential to mask conflict and keep news (and reporters) from those areas under tighter control than would be possible in the more developed areas around the Yellow and Yangzi rivers.

Even from an anthropological perspective, the autonomous regions create challenges for the interpreter since what is shown to outsiders is often highly structured and organized to convey a set of images that are expected and even celebrated in the wider Chinese world. A good example of these displays can be found in the festivals and clothing that characterizes each of the major ethnic groups. While many of these events are an integral part of long-held, independent cultural traditions on the margins of Chinese culture, they play a distinctive role today as markers of diversity and ethnic celebration. The dual rhetoric of demarcation and inclusivity can be seen in some of China's museums, where meticulous displays show the proper male and female festival clothing for many of the country's largest ethnic minority groups, even if the festivals themselves have become a combination of seasonal celebration and tourism.

We have seen the importance of territory—both physical and imagined—in China's relationship to its minority groups. Perhaps the most important distinction, however, is language. Although all Chinese students encounter Mandarin during their school years, even the Han Chinese speak at least seven major languages (depending on how one counts languages), including Mandarin in the north and Cantonese (Yue) in the south, as well as an entire cluster from Shanghai (Wu) to Taiwan (Minnan). By contrast, almost all of China's ethnic minority groups are distinguished by their own languages, which provides a far greater sense of social integration—and separation from other groups—than differences in clothing, occupation, or even faith. One of the most significant questions in 21st-century China will be whether such groups will maintain their independent identities, even as they function within the larger Chinese political and economic realm.

REFERENCES

Chen Xiujun, ed. *Sanzijing [Three Character Classic]*. Taibei: Yuwentang shuju, 2001.

Fang, Achilles. *The Chronicle of Three Kingdoms*. Cambridge, MA: Harvard University Press, 1952.

Mair, Victor. *The Columbia Anthology of Traditional Chinese Literature.* New York: Columbia University Press, 1994.

Sima Guang. *Zizhi Tongjian [Comprehensive Mirror for Aid in Ruling]*. Beijing: Zhonghua shuju, 1956.

Watson, James and Rubie Watson. *Village Life in Hong Kong*. Hong Kong: Chinese University Press, 2004.

Women and Marriage

Robert André LaFleur
Tamara Hamlish

WOMEN IN CHINESE SOCIETY

There is another aspect of social life in Chinese society in which the importance of social networks is revealed, this time by its relative absence: the situation of women in China. In many respects, Chinese women enjoy opportunities that are lacking for women in other parts of the world. In the first decades of the 20th century, during the early years of the new Chinese nation, women's rights were an important priority. Women were encouraged to obtain an education and to pursue their professional ambitions. They became doctors and research scientists. Marriage laws were enacted to protect women from being forced into arranged marriages, to enable them to leave marriages in which they were being abused, and to protect their property rights and give them some control over their own resources.

Although these reforms brought about significant changes in the status of women in China, they had little effect on women's cultural value—their importance to the perpetuation of Chinese culture and society. As Carma Hinton points out in her documentary film *Small Happiness*, female children are welcomed into the family as a "small happiness," while boys are received as a "great happiness." The ratio of men to women in China differs from the global averages, a difference that is often attributed to abortion, the abandonment of female children, or unconfirmed accounts of female infanticide. Despite the social reforms that now make it possible for women to work outside the home—especially before they are married—and to contribute more money to the household, they are still largely seen as a drain on family resources. It is expected that a daughter will eventually marry and that her education, talents, and labor will then benefit her husband's family. In addition, women often earn less money and have fewer opportunities to advance in their careers, a scenario that also encourages a preference for sons, who will likely earn more and advance further in their professions.

Historically, women who were articulate, talented, and well-educated often did not marry, but instead became the highly valued and much-adored concubines of wealthy and powerful men. Those who did marry pursued their interests within the confines of the household. Today, successful or ambitious women may encounter similar difficulty finding a spouse who understands and supports their professional goals. And like women the world over, those who do marry often have difficulty balancing their domestic and professional responsibilities. All of the efforts that have been made to afford women equal opportunity in the workplace have generally not been matched with efforts to demand equal work from men in the home. Chinese women continue to be held responsible for shopping, cooking, cleaning, and caring for both children and elderly parents at the same time that they are expected to take advantage of opportunities to contribute to the household economy through wage work outside the home. It is not uncommon for women in China to note that equality has amounted to a full-time job outside of the home, followed by another full load of housework.

Although social reforms have introduced significant changes for women's lives in contemporary China, they have not yet resulted in deep and lasting changes in society. Most importantly, they have not changed the ways that women participate in the vast networks of social relationships that form the foundation of Chinese society. We see this quite literally in the term *neiren*, a word for wife that means, translated directly, "insider." When a woman marries, she moves from being a stranger or outsider to standing at the very core of the household. She takes on the obligations of wife, mother, and daughter-in-law in exchange for the benefits of becoming a family insider, who is represented to the rest of society through her husband and eventually her sons. This social structural pattern has been dominant in China for many centuries, and only in the larger cities is it showing signs of adjusting to the new realities of women's lives.

Social activists and scholars often debate the reasons for women's limited social networks in a changing China. Some point out that women's household and family

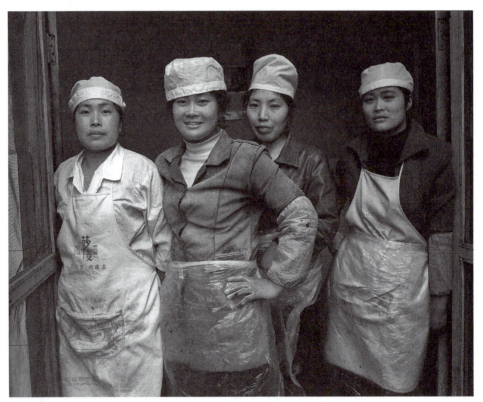

Bakery employees, Chengdu, China, 2007. (Robert van der Hilst/Corbis)

responsibilities leave them little time to cultivate social relationships with people outside the family. Others protest the idea that women are fundamentally different from men and do not possess the same qualities of trustworthiness, endurance, or respectability. Finally, some maintain that women have simply not been given sufficient opportunities and that social reforms concerning education, marital laws, and professional advancement will naturally lead to an expansion of their social network. Although women may maintain a small, local network of friends and colleagues, they are largely dependent on the social network of their husbands to fulfill their own needs and desires, as well as the networks of their own families. This is especially true outside of China's largest cities. We will obtain a clearer picture of the challenges faced by Chinese women, as well as a perspective on their opportunities for change, if we look more carefully at the marital and family system that dominated China for many centuries, as well as the dramatic changes that occurred in the 20th century.

MARRIAGE AND FAMILY IN TRADITIONAL CHINA

Anthropologists emphasize the importance of the marriage alliance for understanding kinship, gender, and family issues in society. Men and women do not live in a vacuum when they interact, but, rather, function within a complex network of social

A bridal procession in the streets of Beijing, about 1902. (Library of Congress)

forces that provide them with opportunity in some cases and restrict social movement in others. At its most basic level, marriage is a way to diversify the social fabric, and in China (as in many societies) the movement of women between families was the social lubricant that enabled traditional society to continue thriving. The French scholar Marcel Granet has described the situation in stark terms, as closed-off village units exchanging "hostages" for the revivification of the social unit.

> [In ancient China] the two sexes took it in turns to labor: the work, regulated by an alternating rhythm, was modeled on the succession of wet and dry seasons well marked on the plains of eastern Asia. Throughout the year, in fields cultivated in common as in their shut-off villages, the peasants had dealings only with their kinsmen. A village enclosed a close-knit unit and homogeneous great family. . . . The large undivided family, which, as the days went by, was self-sufficient and lived in isolation, was, however, neither completely independent nor always closed. The alternating distribution of work went with a strong opposition between the sexes expressed also by the prohibition on marriage within the group of kinsmen. (Granet, 1975, 38–39)

The only way to create real integration and a continuing social regeneration is through exchange, and this is precisely why marriage lies at the very heart of the social order.

From the perspective of most marriage scholars, it is not merely a useful social practice: it is absolutely necessary at all levels of the social order. The exchange of women creates one kind of social integration (even though men could theoretically be exchanged just as easily, this exchange became the norm in most early societies). The practices that lead to that integration are not without conflict by any means, but in the case of marriage, there is a biological price to pay for keeping kinship systems closed. Marcel Granet and other social theorists stressed that the social cost is almost as great.

How did Chinese peasant villages in early China achieve social integration? The short answer is that they traded half of the village's children in each generation to other villages, integrating the children of those villages into their domestic units. The social structural necessity of this arrangement should not mask its pain for individuals and families. Many sources, including the classic *Book of Poetry*, convey the misery of young women leaving their families and villages to become daughters-in-law in far-away villages. Even 20th-century accounts depict similar themes. Necessity does not equal ease, and exchange was accompanied by great pain in many cases. Granet continues:

> In each generation one half of the children, all those of one sex, had to leave the familial village to go to marry into a neighboring village, being exchanged against a group of young people of the same sex and of another name . . . the exchange was of girls: the most pathetic plaint in the old songs is that of the bride forced to go to live in a strange village. (Granet, 1975, 39)

Regeneration comes from a mixing of names even more than from a mixing of blood (in the popular imagination, at least). The most idealistic picture has the young women of one village bringing new life, on numerous levels, to what was a closed system of gender-divided labor and a single surname. Of course, it is not quite as clean as the model suggests. In every generation a full exchange must take place, and the actual movements occur on a smaller scale every year or so, even in the tiniest of villages. Regeneration then, even at its most orderly, was as painful as it was necessary.

We now can see the combined effect—economic, agricultural, and social—of marital connections between villages. Marcel Granet's phrasing is memorable, for it links the crossing of families (with blood ties and differing surnames) with the crossing of furrows for agricultural work, which was an important theme in early Chinese texts. Regeneration, in short, requires *crossing*, whether that be on the plane of crop fields or marital exchange.

> The essential point was that marriage was made by a crossing of families, just as the field were made by a crossing of furrows. By this practice each hamlet received a group of hostages from a neighbor and in turn furnished it with one. These periodic exchanges, by which a family group obtained pledges giving it a hold upon another group, also caused a foreign influence permanently to penetrate its inner life. They made evident the dependence of the domestic communities and the supremacy of the local community, a wider grouping of another kind. (Granet, 1975, 39)

THE ROUND FAMILY IDEAL—FIVE GENERATIONS UNDER ONE ROOF

The traditional ideal for a Chinese household was to have a "round" family—five generations living together under one roof. How often that ideal was met is a matter of some conjecture, but it is fair to say that the two- or three-generation patrilineal unit of parents and children—and often grandparents—was by far the most common. In a society that experienced high levels of infant mortality and early death, the forces working against even the four-generation family were often overwhelming. That the five-generation family remained idealized in literature and oral stories is striking, yet these stories had a cultural resonance that exerted great influence on the way that families were idealized and ordered.

Exchanges also demand pledges, which, in turn, provide a hold upon another group. Above all, such exchanges (which Granet describes as "hostage" situations, highlighting the power of the hold on the other group) permanently alter the closed interactions that would have constituted the ultimate death of the domestic order.

"Causing a foreign influence permanently to penetrate its inner life," the closed domestic order grudgingly (and necessarily) welcomed "foreign influence." This action was not conducted happily on either side. One village gave up its young women and received another group whose members were influenced by different ways. Usually, neither village was as inviting as it might have imagined itself, precisely because each was dominated by an in-group mentality. Ultimately, the domestic group was dependent upon these exchanges because they created something larger through their alliances. The new blood also offered new ideas, social networking, and names. The progeny that were generated as a result expanded the limited influence of the original family unit far beyond what could have been accomplished without such a traumatic exchange of people.

This is the complex network of social alliances within which women's lives were conducted in traditional China, and too often it is not considered in analyzing the challenges that they faced—in the past or the present. Throughout Chinese history, raising daughters was perceived as labor for uncertain gain. Some have compared it to watering another family's plants, while others have likened it to working in their fields. Before moving to an examination of women's issues in contemporary China, though, we first need to look at life within the traditional household unit.

TRADITIONAL MARRIAGE AND FAMILY LIFE

Ban Zhao's *Admonitions for Women* is often quoted as an important early advice text written in the style of many of the behavioral texts that mainly targeted men by the beginning of the Common Era. Ban Zhao (C.E. 45–116) was a successful historian and accomplished scholar who felt the need to give advice to her daughters, as well as a wider audience of female readers and listeners. In *Admonitions for Women*, her opening passages about the need for humility speak directly to the marital politics considered above.

> On the third day after the birth of a girl the ancients observed three customs: first to place the baby below the bed; second to give her a potsherd with which to play; and third to announce her birth to her ancestors by an offering. Now to lay the baby below the bed plainly indicated that she is lowly and weak, and should regard it as her primary duty to humble herself before others. To give her potsherds with which to play signified that she should practice labor and consider it her primary duty to be industrious. To announce her birth before her ancestors clearly meant that she ought to esteem as her primary duty the continuation of the observance of worship in the home. These three ancient customs epitomize woman's ordinary way of life. . . . Let a woman modestly yield to others; let her respect others; let her put others first, herself last. Should she do something good, let her not mention it; should she do something bad let her not deny it. Let her bear disgrace; let her even endure when others speak or do evil to her. Always let her seem to tremble and to fear. (Mair, 1994, 535)

It is difficult for readers today to conceive the manner in which such advice was intended: as a way to ease a young woman's transition into a very difficult situation. A woman's options were limited, especially after marriage. In order to find her place within a strange household, she would have to show respect to her new kin. In order to cement her position, she would have to bear one or more sons. In order to make a permanent place for herself in the family, she would have to become a grandmother and mother-in-law. As harsh as the patrilineal system was, those who gave birth to sons and extended the generations benefited from its peculiar reward system. Those who fought the system or, through nothing more than bad luck, failed to give birth to sons had a much more tenuous fate.

The film *Raise the Red Lantern*, which depicts a fictitious early 20th-century family with a wealthy man and four wives, lays out the structural elements of the multiple-generation, multiple-partner family in tremendous depth, even as its story is the stuff of chance and fiction. The first wife, old and seemingly unappreciated, is the success of the family; she has raised a son who has grown to a marriageable age. The second wife has a daughter, and the third wife has a son. The fourth wife strains against the rules and regulations of the household. The deeper social lessons of the film are often lost on viewers as they watch the slow unwinding of this family's social fabric. The sad story behind relative success in the social network is that it is achieved by keeping to the margins and providing what the patrilineage needs. It is in this context that we can see what Ban Zhao is arguing in her *Admonitions for Women* when she concludes with advice on women's conduct and the necessity of obedience.

It is not as though such expectations of women went unnoticed or uncriticized. One of the barometers of social awareness is the poetry that has persisted through the ages. A prominent theme is the frustration of women within the male-based social structures of the extended family, and many poems speak to the limited opportunities for fulfillment within that setting. Perhaps the most dramatic internal critique of the

---

BAN ZHAO ON CONDUCT AND OBEDIENCE

Conduct—A woman ought to have four qualifications: (1) womanly virtue; (2) womanly words; (3) womanly bearing; and (4) womanly work. To guard carefully her chastity; to control circumspectly her behavior . . . this is womanly virtue. To choose her words with care . . . may be called the characteristics of womanly words. To wash and scrub filth away . . . may be called the characteristics of womanly bearing. With whole-hearted devotion to sew and to weave . . . may be called the characteristics of womanly work.

   Obedience—Whenever the mother-in-law says, "Do not do that," and if what she says is right, unquestionably the daughter-in-law obeys. Whenever the mother-in-law says, "Do that," even if what she says is wrong, still the daughter-in-law submits unfailingly to the command. Let a woman not act contrary to the wishes and the opinions of parents-in-law about right and wrong; let her not dispute with them what is straight and what is crooked. Such docility may be called obedience which sacrifices personal opinion. Therefore the ancient book, *A Pattern for Women*, says: "If a daughter-in-law who follows the wishes of her parents-in-law is like and echo and shadow, how could she not be praised?"

   (Mair, 1994, 534)

---

treatment of Chinese women comes in the form of a fictional tale from the Ming dynasty. Entitled "In the Country of Women," the text tells the story of a shipwrecked sailor who is found on the shore of a far-off island. He is taken in by the island's inhabitants—all of whom are women—and made into an object for their pleasure. First, they rouge his cheeks and pierce his ears. He weeps from the frustration and pain, but never more so than when they begin the process of binding his feet into dainty little objects of admiration. The criticism is pointed in its gender reversal and its fictional portrayal of men trapped in a closed system.

> Having finished binding his feet, the maidens hurriedly made a pair of large red slippers with soft soles and put them on for him. Lin Chih-yang's tears flowed for a long time. His thoughts flew back and forth, but he could think of no plan, all he could do was entreat the palace maidens: "My brothers, I beseech you, put in a word for me before your ruler: I am a married man, I have a wife, how can I become a concubine? And these big feet of mine . . . how can they bear restriction? I beg you, let me go, and then my wife as well will be filled with gratitude." But the maidens replied, "Our ruler has just now given us the order to bind your feet and then invite you into the palace? Who then would dare to raise her voice in protest?" (Birch, *Anthology*, 189)

The subject of footbinding is a difficult one, and not only because of its physical cruelty. Women of ancient and early dynastic China walked about on unbound feet, and even Ban Zhao's strictures were written for women who never conceived of such an institution. The origins of footbinding are hazy, but what had begun as a practice

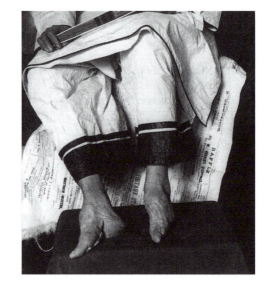

Early-20th-century photograph of a woman's bound feet. (Library of Congress)

limited to the pleasure quarters and teahouses of China's vast cities in the late-Tang and Northern Song dynasties (the 9th, 10th, and 11th centuries) became one of the prime movers of marriage politics by the 13th century. It persisted for the better part of seven centuries, before dying out—almost as quickly as it began—in the late 19th and early 20th centuries.

During the Yuan, Ming, and Qing dynasties, however, bound feet had a serious impact on women's desirability for marriage, beginning at the elite levels of society and working down to the ever-more humble levels. Indeed, as time went on, rural families of even quite modest means were faced with difficult choices regarding their daughters. Young women with unbound feet would be far more able to help with work in the household, but they would also be doomed to very limited options in marriage, which would, in turn, limit the family's potential alliances. It was the women of the family who set about binding children's feet at relatively early ages.

This is perhaps the most striking element of footbinding for today's reader. Conventional wisdom paints the practice as a pattern of male domination, a way of keeping women in their places, especially in the inner quarters of elite households. No careful observer would deny this. The problem is that the critique often does not go far enough. Footbinding was a pattern of domination that not only enabled male sensibilities to dominate those of women, but one that simultaneously allowed older generations (male and female) to benefit from the painful binding of younger generations' feet. Perhaps the most telling criticism of the practice can be found in the way that it was carried out—with men having far from anything to do with the procedure. Women initiated and carried out all aspects of the operation. This fact has sometimes been used to add layers of feminine complicity to an already difficult narrative, and occasionally to argue that men were complete outsiders in the process. It is not difficult to see through such contentions, however. This most gendered pattern of domination was one that benefited men enormously, even as women were placed in a position in which they could benefit only by following narrow rules (not unlike their positions within patriarchal households).

Additional depictions of women's lives within traditional household settings can be found in the great fictional works of the Ming and Qing dynasties, as well as in a genre of texts that have remained relatively neglected by Westerners: the household management manuals that were enormously popular in the later imperial period. *The Plum in the Golden Vase* is a 100-chapter fictional narrative that depicts the life and household of the protagonist Ximen Qing and his six wives. It is a relentless portrait of family instruction in reverse, as it were. The battles within the family are so brutal—and so overwhelming to all of the characters, each of whom eventually meets a sorry end—that during the Qing dynasty some Chinese critics commented that it is precisely the story of how *not* to lead one's life, and how *not* to run a family.

The *Plum in the Golden Vase* is the first Chinese literary work to provide full and detailed portraits of its female characters, which was noted by Cao Xueqin (1715–1763), who, two centuries later, wrote what is still considered China's finest work of traditional fiction, *The Story of the Stone*. Deeply influenced by the poetry and structure of *The Plum in the Golden Vase*, Cao's novel is a more delicately told tale of the slow decline of a prominent family, and the love (and love lost) of one of the most tragic couples in all of Chinese literature. The portraits of women—from the young women of the family to the distant imperial concubine; from the wives of the middle-aged men to the old matron, who represented femininity's great success—are among the finest from the Chinese literary tradition. The lessons that could be drawn by a Qing dynasty reader, however, do not substantially differ from those taught by Ban Zhao 18 centuries earlier. Women who were able to operate within the system through proper conduct and the appropriate humility were able to benefit. Those who stepped outside the boundaries of proper conduct, as well as those who were unlucky enough to be in the wrong situation at the wrong time, had a very limited future, indeed.

WOMEN IN CONTEMPORARY CHINA

Historical context is important in examining any aspect of Chinese life, and it is of primary importance in discussing the role of women in contemporary China. In many respects, everything has changed, even as many of the most persistent aspects of patriarchy remain, especially in rural areas. As we have already observed in several sections of this book, the largest urban centers in China are undergoing rapid change. It should not be surprising, then, that Beijing, Shanghai, Chengdu, and other cities have the largest numbers of women with independent careers and increasingly independent lifestyle choices, one of which is to avoid marriage for as long as possible. It should be clear by now, however, that even independence does not operate in a vacuum, and that every young woman in China still operates within a network of agnatic and affinal connections that have social, economic, and educational implications.

In the early 21st century, a number of reports from China have noted the changing nature of marriage, especially for urban women. Urban marriages are increasingly likely to come with stipulations about how much, and for how long, a woman might wish to continue working, and even (in some cases) whether or not a woman is willing to have children, at least soon after marriage. Such stipulations would have been unheard of in earlier eras, and it is necessary to point out that they are still quite unusual today, even in urban settings and among young professionals. Nonetheless, one of the newest features of recent marriages is the recognition of the role of the bride's family in the proceedings. While this might come as a surprise to many Western readers, accustomed as they are to the bride's family playing a significant ritual and economic role in the wedding ceremony, including the father of the bride walking her down the aisle, Chinese marriage ceremonies have traditionally been almost exclusively dominated by the husband's side, and it was common for a young woman to be taken alone from her natal home in a sedan chair financed by the groom's family. The ceremony itself was dominated by the groom's side—from venerating the husband's ancestors to providing an appropriately bridely pose for the groom's male and female relatives.

Some weddings in China today have taken on a more even-handed approach, giving the bride's family a role in speaking, toasting, and "giving away" the bride. While this is certainly a sign of the growing significance of women in Chinese society, as well as an acknowledgment of the kinship realities of a one-child family system, it is also a major step toward a neutral setting for young couples starting their own nuclear families. Urban, professional women are the most likely to insist on concessions from their prospective husbands and their families, and it is not as though they lack leverage. The birth rate in China remains significantly out of step with normal biological rates, with the male to female birth ratio reaching 1.11/1.00 in 2007. Boys may still be preferred, overall, by prospective parents, but women enjoy a relatively strong strategic situation because of this preference, even more than two decades after the implementation of the policy.

Just one sign of that change is the greater role women's families play in some wedding ceremonies, but changes can also be seen in venue and work opportunities. The most enterprising and financially secure urban women tend to prefer a nuclear family setting that is free from the direct influence of their own or their husbands' parents. Similarly, they often negotiate agreements that allow them to continue working well into their marriages. In turn, many urban families do not share the common preference for a boy to continue the family line. The social and economic dynamic has changed so significantly in Chinese cities that the idea of perpetuating the male line is often no stronger there than in Western countries. While this idea is not insignificant in Chinese cities, the urban setting creates far more fluid situations than one finds in more rural settings. It should also be noted that it has become fairly common for some parents today to state a preference for a girl, especially in urban areas with one-child policies. Anecdotes to this effect have been in circulation since at least the late 1980s, and the change is the product of a simple rethinking of the changing dynamics of kinship, economic opportunity, and status. Many families have come

A woman feeds her baby daughter in a market in Beijing, 2005. Government figures show 117 boys are born in China for every 100 girls, a gap attributed largely to a policy limiting most couples to one child. (AP/ Wide World Photos)

to the conclusion that they prefer a girl if they are only able to have one child. The reasoning is direct: a girl today, at least in an urban setting, is more likely to stay close to her parents and provide them (together with an urban husband and grandchild) what they need for a prosperous life than a boy, who could move abruptly and be out of contact with the family.

The new preference for daughters should be taken seriously, but the example should not be extended too far. China remains dominated by male kinship relations, and it is only in urban centers, such as Beijing and Shanghai, that we see significant numbers of people adapting wedding ceremonies, expressing preferences for daughters, and choosing to remain childless for years rather than months. In smaller cities and rural areas, the traditional pressures remain stronger, and the most recent innovations are far less likely to be found. Nonetheless, it would be a mistake to characterize the differences that have arisen in China regarding gender issues as simply a traditional versus modern conflict. The gendered terrain is changing almost by the month, and the dynamics promise to contribute powerfully to China's future.

REFERENCES

Birch, Cyril. *Anthology of Chinese Literature: Volume II: From the Fourteenth Century to the Present Day*. New York: Grove Press, 1994.

Göran Aijmer. *New Year Festivals in Central China in Late Imperial Times*. Hong Kong: Chinese University Press, 2005.

Granet, Marcel. *The Religion of the Chinese People*. Edited by Maurice Friedman. New York: Harper & Row, 1975.

Hinton, Carma. *Small Happiness*. New York: Ronin Films, 1984.

Ko, Dorothy. *Cinderella's Sisters: A Revisionist History of Footbinding*. Berkeley: University of California Press, 2007.

Lévi-Strauss, Claude. *The Elementary Structures of Kinship*. Boston: Beacon Press, 1971.

Mair, Victor. *The Columbia Anthology of Chinese Literature*. New York: Columbia University Press, 1994.

Pruitt, Ida. *Daughter of Han*. Stanford, CA: Stanford University Press, 1967.

Education

Robert André LaFleur

Today, China has almost 400 million students, a number that surpasses the total population of the United States. Nine years of education are compulsory, followed by competitive placements in senior secondary and university educations. The 2000 census figures showed a literacy rate in China of just over 85 percent, with literacy defined as knowledge of 1,500 Chinese characters in rural locations and 2,000 characters in urban ones. Due to the sheer size of China's population, this still means that 150 million Chinese fall below these fairly minimal literacy rates. Women lag slightly behind men, although the gap is narrowing. Fairly optimistic Chinese government projections show China climbing to a 97 percent rate in 2010, and a 99 percent rate in 2015. Chinese education has made enormous strides during the past few decades, yet the system still faces formidable challenges on several levels, as we will see below.

LANGUAGE AND LOCALITY

The language of education in China is Mandarin. This is also true of education in Taiwan and of much Chinese instruction in Southeast Asia. Nationwide Mandarin instruction was an important step toward creating an integrated educational experience for citizens in China. As we have seen, China is made up of a number of distinctive regions, each with its own geographical, historical, linguistic, and cultural peculiarities. To paraphrase an old saying in China, when one travels 10 miles, speech becomes fuzzy; when one travels 50, speech is incomprehensible. Regional patterns of speech, cuisine, and custom vary enormously in China. If one thinks of the multiple languages, customs, and tensions that can be found in a smaller area, such as Western Europe, one begins to understand how difficult an integrated educational system can be to create. Chinese teachings, both in China and abroad, tend to stress

---

ENCULTURATION AND ACCULTURATION

Enculturation is often defined as the means by which an individual is taught to be a member of a particular society. The process begins as soon as the child is born, and everything from the singing of nursery songs to watching plays or television is a part of it. Acculturation generally refers to the process by which an individual learns about another culture. The two ideas are powerfully intertwined. Learning to be Chinese and learning to be a part of the larger world are closely connected—one need only consider the 2008 Olympic theme of "One World, One Dream" as an example. The message of pride in Chinese culture is combined with a theme of welcoming the world and its various cultural traditions. The term "acculturation" is sometimes used as an umbrella term to cover both aspects, and we will use it that way here.

---

themes of integration. However, a large percentage of Chinese people today speak a different language at home and do so throughout their lives, a powerful reminder of how difficult the integrative challenge can be to overcome.

In light of this, it is significant that the northern dialect of Mandarin (*guoyu*, "national language," or *putonghua*, "everyday language") is used in all instruction. It was, for centuries, the language that united scholar-officials from all over the realm, and functions on an even more powerful level today: almost everyone who has gone through the school system can converse with another person in Mandarin. This can be observed most clearly at popular tourist destinations and pilgrimage sites, such as the Great Wall, Beijing's Forbidden City, or China's preeminent mountain, Mount Tai. Hiking up the curving steps to the 1500-meter (almost mile-high) summit, family groups can be heard to talk amongst themselves in Cantonese, the Shanghai dialect, Taiwanese, and many other variations. When speaking to others or encouraging faltering hikers, they invariably speak in Mandarin. The common language in the educational curriculum—instituted long before Chinese citizens were allowed to travel freely, as they are today—has contributed considerably to a wider integration and public culture in China.

Regional dialects figure in social life and local business culture, but they have little role to play in the educational system (with the exception of Hong Kong; see below). The curriculum is standardized; the books that students read during their academic careers are determined by the Ministry of Education. They are produced based on general requirements—down to the characters to be taught at each grade level—throughout China. The system is a good deal more open today than it was in the past, when students throughout the country read the same textbooks. Today, regional companies create books used by various city or provincial educational bureaucracies. There is still a high degree of standardization, though. It might best be expressed as follows. In Hunan (south), Shandong (east), and Shanxi (midwest), the first story in, for example, the language arts readers used during the second semester of the third grade will all be different. The characters used, and required for memorization and composition, are exactly the same throughout the country, however.

EDUCATION AND ACCULTURATION

It has long been understood that educational systems play a dual role in building upon a family identity and the first years of experience in that private setting and helping to create a wider public identity that will serve the student, family, and society in the future. When a child begins first grade—in China and every other developed country in the world—she does so with a foundation of five or six years of spoken language, knowledge of etiquette and behavioral expectations, and a storehouse of general information about the world around her. In short, she does not begin learning in first grade (or kindergarten, or even preschool, for that matter). A child is taught to integrate what she already knows with a system of knowledge created to extend far beyond her immediate needs. When studying the first lessons of the Beijing first-grade reader, a young student learns pinyin Romanization (the same system used to render terms such as *Beijing* throughout this book). This is precisely the same way that a foreign student in a beginning Chinese college course will start— with the sounds and structures of the language. There is an enormous difference, though. The first-grade textbook, unlike the college textbook, is filled with words that most college students do not learn until much later in their educations, words such as "lotus," "ostrich," "butterfly," "winding," "planting," and "etiquette." The elementary-school textbook takes a half-decade of lived experience and begins to teach the student to read it, write it, and think about it in new ways. If family life is the first step in acculturation, beginning school is surely the next significant one.

Chinese children listen to their teacher during a reading class in Yanmaidi village, in China's southwest Sichuan province, 2005. (AP/Wide World Photos)

As in other educational systems, the acculturation process continues throughout the school years (and, indeed, throughout one's life). Examples of this process in educational instruction during the past three decades demonstrate a much more direct interest in traditional Chinese culture and the stories behind significant events in Chinese history, something that was not embraced warmly in the early decades of the People's Republic, when many traditional teachings were deemed "backward looking" and even reactionary. Moreover, textbooks show an appreciation for (and a clear statement of China's role in) a wider world history, economy, and culture. Textbooks and bookstores' educational sections today offer a wide range of translated stories from Europe and the United States, and one can clearly glean the assertion of a positive personality type: the individual who functions well, and with sensitivity, in her own culture, yet who is also comfortable in a global setting, based on her knowledge of everything from classical (Western) music to Olympic sports—a fully acculturated person.

TRADITIONAL EDUCATION

There are significant continuities and contrasts in earlier forms of education in China. The idea of a standard 6-, 9-, or 12-year educational program for all members of society was rather late in arriving. It was not quite as elitist, however, as general textbooks sometimes imply. As early as the Song dynasty (960–1279), private academies and clan-based charitable organizations were developed that often held the ideals of educating all young men in their family grouping. Still, even with these charitable institutions, there were significant gaps in access to education. Women, in particular, had far fewer opportunities than men, and it was not unusual for families to teach women the domestic arts, but not reading and writing. The ideal for many households of means was for women to spend their lives in the inner quarters, not venturing out into the broader world, except for very special events.

There are significant exceptions, though. As we have seen, Ban Zhao (C.E. 45–116) was one of the foremost minds of her time. Educated at home alongside her talented brothers, she wrote poetry, essays, and, with great skill, finished the monumental historical work begun by her father and continued by her brothers, the *Hanshu* (*History of the Han*). Yet, as we saw in the preceding section, she is as widely known for her statement that a woman should devote her life in submission to three men: her father, her husband, and, ultimately, her son. Given her educational achievements, such a statement is surprising, but it remains the case that it was the rare woman in imperial China who exerted intellectual influence beyond her family unit.

Li Qingzhao (1084-c. 1150), a Song dynasty poet, is another great example of exceptional talent in the literary arts. Her poetry has long been anthologized, and her pieces flow with grace and elegance. She was raised in a literary family and had an unusually close relationship with her husband, whose literary interests she shared until his death in 1129. Only about 70 of her poems survive, but they show a depth of learning and emotion that few poets attained. There are many more examples of such talent, but what unites them is the exceptional nature of their educations. They had access to the greatest works and the finest instruction

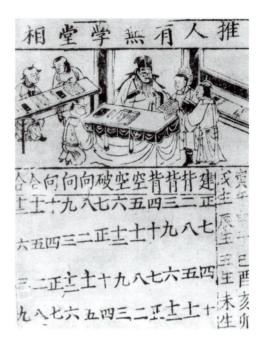

Teacher in a classroom with young students, from the Song Dynasty (960–1279). (Library of Congress)

because they had fathers who were willing to educate their daughters and were affluent enough to do so. By the Ming and Qing dynasties, highly educated women were not unusual. Still, it was not until the 20th century that women attained equal legal access to education.

In a similar fashion, access to education was difficult in the past (and often is in the present) for working families. In fact, so rare was the ascent from working in the fields to the higher reaches of the examinations in imperial China that it became something of a distant ideal, not unlike the "from a log cabin to the White House" ideal found in earlier American history. Yet, even though the reality was often quite different, examples of perseverance work their way through many of the books that Chinese children studied in their early years, and stories of perseverance are gathered in textbooks in China, Taiwan, Singapore, and other locations where Chinese education flourishes.

In the later imperial era, the *Three Character Classic* was one of the first books that a child would memorize, at the age of six or seven. Although arranged in a singsong fashion with an emphasis on brevity (each line is three characters long), this book is filled with the educational ideals espoused during the later imperial period, particularly diligence and commitment. The opening lines address the famous philosophical debate over whether people are born good or become good through learning. The text then goes on to address education, which starts in the home and continues with strict teaching and diligent study:

To raise children without instruction
This is the father's error
To teach children without strictness
This is the teacher's indolence.

If children fail to study
This is inappropriate
If they don't learn in youth
What will happen when they are old?
If jade is not carved
Its potential is incomplete
If people do not study
Righteousness cannot be known.

(Chen, *Sanzijing*, 5–6)

The text goes on for hundreds of characters to describe key points in Chinese history and philosophy, before closing with the lines excerpted below, which again exhort students to remain diligent and to study for the sake of their families and the good of society. As we saw in the Social Classes section, it particularly addresses the concerns of those who do not have the means to obtain a good education. Whether they include people making their own books for composition practice, remaining awake after a hard day of work, or reading by natural light, the *Three Character Classic* offers examples of dedication. Learning, we are told, is what separates us from the rest of the natural world; it is what makes us human. Just as the culture heroes described in Chapter 2 transformed the world around them into a place of order and continuity, so, too, must the diligent child learn while young, serving the sovereign and people with superior knowledge:

Silkworms emit silken thread
Bees produce honey
If people do not study
They are not equal to the animals.
Learn in youth
Put it into practice when grown.
Above, influence the ruler;
Below, aid the people.

And finally, another exhortation to the student:

Perseverance leads to success
Idleness has no benefits
Be ever vigilant
And exert your strength!

(Chen, *Sanzijing*, 51–53)

Until the last imperial examination was given in 1905, a traditional education consisted of memorizing basic beginner texts, such as the one above, and moving quickly on to the *Four Books* discussed in the Religion and Thought chapter. From there, students would read philosophy, history, poetry, and the like, with the goal of passing the many levels of examinations that began at the local level, continued

---

THE EXAMINATION SYSTEM IN LATE IMPERIAL CHINA

Early in Chinese history, education was the exclusive domain of wealthy families, who were able to gain access to the appropriate texts, tutors, and government positions. By the Song dynasty, however, an examination system had taken root that was to become the prime determinant of one's position in political life in the later imperial period. Although there were quotas under the Mongols and, to a lesser extent, the Manchus, the system was meant to evaluate prospects solely on the basis of their abilities. The curriculum became standardized as early as the Southern Song, with students beginning with simple texts, such as the *Classic of Filial Piety*, and advancing to memorization of the *Four Books*. The examinations themselves were a grueling series of tests that began at the local level and eventually moved the most talented (or the best test-takers) to the imperial level. Memorization and competitive examinations remain a key to scholarly success today, even though the subject matter has broadened enormously since the last imperial examination was given early in the 20th century.

---

through various county and provincial levels, and ended in the imperial examinations given once every three years in the capital. Those who passed were the superstars of Chinese society, and both they and their families spent years preparing for the day that they would begin their official careers.

CONTEMPORARY EDUCATION

One might ask what possible connection there can be between a traditional education in China and today's educational system. To be sure, China has made enormous strides in educating its people, and the literacy rate grew tremendously in the 20th century. The current Chinese education system provides six years of primary school and six years of secondary school (taking a student through the equivalent, in years, of an American junior high and high school education). There is also a state-organized university system, with key campuses (and fierce competition for admission) at Beijing University and Qinghua University in Beijing, Fudan University in Shanghai, Nankai University in Tianjin, and Zhongshan University in Guangdong. In addition to these major centers of higher education, each province has its flagship campus, not unlike land-grant colleges in the United States. There are also thousands of institutions, large and small, of higher education that specialize in technical training throughout China.

The curriculum has changed a great deal from earlier times, although a Chinese student still receives thorough instruction in history, philosophy, and literature through middle school. Science and math are also a very important part of the curriculum, and the Ministry of Education has put a good deal of emphasis on building technical expertise—the very kind that 19th-century reformers wanted as part of a new set of skills that could be used to challenge the West. One thing that has remained consistent, however, is competition. Admission to the university system takes place in the form of a nationwide competition, and the students' jockeying for position

Beijing University quadrangle, 2007. (Bruce Connolly/Corbis)

is intense. The stress on family members—from grandparents and parents to the students themselves—is equally great, and some say that it is more intense with one child than with many. There is also a significant urban-rural divide in educational access. Rural schools have far less flexibility in terms of attracting quality teachers, and even educational funding remains, for the most part, a local concern beyond the urban centers. Even within a locality, different schools with different rankings (and criteria for admission) influence the ladder of success in China.

Education in contemporary China places a decided emphasis on language, writing, and scientific skills, including mathematical literacy, and this can be seen clearly in the curriculum through middle school. After that point, the system continues to emphasize the core skills that are necessary for the students who are fortunate enough to test well and enter good high schools and universities. For many other students, however, the educational path after middle school is a great deal more vocational. Training schools and job-specific education play a very large role in the education of millions of Chinese young adults, and are an integral part of the growing Chinese economy. These schools do continue to teach the core curriculum, but the focus is much more directly on job training.

Finally, many Westerners wonder whether the Chinese educational system is able to accommodate students who are unable to keep up with the demands of their programs or have serious learning disabilities. For the latter, there is a strong, if imperfect special education system (the same can be said for any major industrial country) that seeks to train and integrate students with learning disabilities into the wider society. This is particularly well organized with the education of mentally handicapped students. The educational training and social integration of students challenged with other disabilities is far more mixed. The social and organizational role of the Chinese classroom has never been very accommodating for students who are unable adapt to its fairly rigid structures. As in the West, but arguably with greater force, the system privileges those who adapt, and too often loses contact with those who do not.

EDUCATIONAL CURRICULA

Two subjects—language/culture (*yuwen*) and mathematics (*shuxue*)—dominate the educational landscape from first grade through high school graduation. To be certain, other subjects are integrated into the curriculum and comprise dominant strands of instruction. These include English, science, and social studies at the primary level, and philosophy, history, geography, chemistry, and physics at the higher levels. There are only two subjects, however, for which an anxious parent can buy a complete review of important primary-school themes in preparation for middle-school exams: language/culture and mathematics. The first day of school can be said to begin with them, and the last day of school will end with them.

Mathematical education in China is focused and workmanlike. There is an assumption that students can "do math," and that the skills required should be evident in any educated person. It is often remarked that Chinese (and other countries') students advance far more quickly in mathematics than American students. It is a fact that is almost beyond dispute, and the reason lies in relentless focus and persistence. That same focus and persistence can be seen from the first day of first grade in the language/culture readers, as well. After learning *pinyin*, students begin a process of learning to read and write Chinese characters at a rate that will have them reading at formidable levels by the sixth grade. Students begin by learning to recognize 400 Chinese characters in the first semester of first grade, and to write 100 of them. This variable pace continues well into one's education, and it is only quite late in the process that people are able to write almost everything that they can read or say. This is such a far cry from education in Western languages that the point needs to be underlined. Knowing how to *say* something in (Mandarin) Chinese is only tenuously related to knowing how to *write* it. One cannot sound out a character, except in the roughest manner.

The educational process from first grade forward is a delicate balancing act between reading and writing. It is also a balancing act between regional dialects and Mandarin. It is one thing to be able to speak Mandarin grammatically; it is another thing to iron out strong regional pronunciations that create confusion when people with other home languages try to communicate in Mandarin.

The lessons in Chinese textbooks can often be seen beyond the text, as it were. History texts are often the most scrutinized educational materials, and the last century of Chinese history certainly causes Chinese authorities a great deal of concern (this situation is, of course, not unique to China). If one thinks back to this volume's history chapter, such basic events as the Sino-Japanese War (1937–1945) are fraught with difficulty as one attempts even a simple recitation of events. Nationalist, Communist, and Japanese forces all saw matters differently 70 years ago, and time has

---

REGIONAL PRONUNCIATIONS OF MANDARIN

Chinese language arts textbooks focus on a key series of pronunciations that cause great difficulty for speakers from some dialect groups, such as Cantonese. There is a popular phrase—none too polite—to this effect: "I fear not heaven or earth; I only fear Cantonese people speaking Mandarin!" Among the persistent problems are the pronunciations of words that start in "sh" and those that start in "s." An example is the number 44, which, in Mandarin, is pronounced "sishi si" (suh sure suh). For speakers of southern dialects, it often comes out "sisi si" (suh suh suh).

Other tongue twisters are zh/z, ch/c, and n/l. This is not a very difficult problem for foreign learners, but textbooks in China focus relentlessly on the matter because it is a problem that extends beyond language and understanding. It is an issue of integration and identity, as well, and it is a point of pride for the educational system when a southern speaker (notoriously challenged with these issues by very different regional dialects) perfectly pronounces Mandarin words and communicates in a wider Chinese setting.

---

done little to soften their perspectives. What is more striking is that getting the tone to work is a challenge for textbook writers beyond their core audience of school children; in a sense, they are also writing for the internal secondary audience of teachers and parents. It might be possible to find approval regarding the events surrounding World War II, but any treatment of the Cultural Revolution is potentially incendiary.

In light of these challenges, it is significant that the Ministry of Education has recently deemphasized some of the more hotly disputed elements of recent Chinese history (and, as a result, subtly deemphasized important elements of the Communist past). It has placed far more emphasis on world history and themes in China that formerly received little attention, from environmental awareness to the social and cultural themes connecting China to its indigenous inhabitants and the larger world. One might argue that this curriculum is the result of changing perspectives over the past 20 years. It could also be argued that the curriculum is, at least in part, driving it—that China has opened itself to change and has promoted that change as a way of participating in a broader fashion with a changing global culture.

EDUCATION IN TAIWAN AND HONG KONG

Students in the Republic of China in Taiwan follow the same general pattern of education as students in the People's Republic of China. They attend six years of primary school, three years of middle school, and three years of high school. Over the course of the past 50 years, the most significant issues separating students in Taiwan from those in the People's Republic have been language and politics. The language of education in Taiwan is also Mandarin, but students all learn the traditional characters that are explained in detail in the Language chapter of this book. This means that even when they read the same story about a Chinese cultural figure, the language used is different enough that two primary-school students from Beijing and Taipei would likely be confused.

Over time, students in the People's Republic become acquainted with and facile in their recognition of the traditional characters. Indeed, those who specialize in traditional culture need to do so since simplified Chinese characters are a very recent development. The situation in Taiwan is somewhat different. The only people who become thoroughly acquainted with simplified characters are those doing business in China or students studying scholarship written by contemporary academics in the People's Republic. It is important not to overstate the issue, however. Language policies in the two systems have created a gulf, but it is far from insurmountable, as business people from Taiwan manage to work effectively in China, and classical scholars are able to read traditional texts in the People's Republic.

A larger issue in Chinese education in Taiwan lies in politics. The island's peculiar political situation has played an enormous role in the education of its students during the past 60 years. During the 1950s and 1960s, in particular, the Republic of China described itself as the legitimate source of political power in China, even though it happened to possess only the single province of Taiwan. In the world of diplomacy, such an assertion needed to be couched and modified. In the world of primary education, the message was anything but subtle. A perusal of a series of textbooks used in Taiwan in the 1970s and 1980s reveals distinctly political themes, even in primary school texts. Inserted alongside the standard teachings on social cooperation, harmony, family life, and student diligence are a large number of readings showing a Chinese (not a Taiwan-based) identity. A representative text from the 1985 second-grade reader makes the identity clear, even before one sees the illustration of two children and a large Republic of China flag beneath the text.

> I am Chinese.
> My roots are in China.
> I love China
> With a love that runs deep
> (*Guomin xiaoxue guoyu*, 1985, 2a.27)

It is perhaps less surprising that one finds many stories about the founding heroes of the Republic in these textbooks. There are stories about Sun Yat-sen in his youth, and several about Jiang Jieshi (Chiang Kai-shek), the president of the Republic until his death in 1975. One shows a young Jiang in army school standing up for his homeland when a Japanese teacher criticizes China. The contents that outside observers might find most startling, however, are the directly political stories that were included for every grade level. For example, one text in the 1985 third-grade reader shows an emaciated man surrounded by skulls and a sign that reads "People's Commune." The text is titled "The Place Where There is No Sun," and describes life for our "unfortunate brethren on the mainland." Another third-grade text shows a large drawing of two children giving away piggy banks. The text begins:

In December 1978, American President Carter suddenly broke ties with our country (The Republic of China on Taiwan); every freedom loving Chinese (citizen) was enraged.

(*Guomin xiaoxue* 1985, 3a. 25)

It goes on to tell the story of two primary-school children who, upon hearing the news, contributed their savings to a fund-drive at National Taiwan University in order to protect the country.

Despite the directly political educational messages during the first four decades of Republican rule in Taiwan, the texts were no less serious for that. Even today, after major curricular changes were made (none of the stories mentioned above survives in today's elementary readers), adults who grew up with the older books often say that they were tougher and did a better job of teaching language, history, and culture. Be that as it may, the clear message is that education has a great deal to do with creating identity, and the Ministry of Education in the Republic of China took that work very seriously. Even though the message is much more nuanced today, the work of identity creation—now with a greater emphasis on Taiwanese history, language, and culture—continues.

The educational situation in Hong Kong is very different, and has been buffeted by forces that are both similar and dissimilar to Taiwan and the People's Republic. Language and politics also dominate the educational challenges in Hong Kong, but the situation is much more complex. In the People's Republic of China and Taiwan, Mandarin Chinese is the first language of education, and English holds an overwhelmingly important position as *the* foreign language. Other languages, from French and German to Japanese and Korean, are a distant third in priority, and students often do not begin to study them until they specialize in a university or work setting. In Hong Kong, however, three languages dominate, creating a difficult logistical situation for textbook writers, teachers, administrators, and students. English was integral to the curriculum for as long as the British were in Hong Kong, and the situation remains similar today, more than a decade after Hong Kong was returned to Chinese control. Cantonese has always been the Chinese language of instruction in Hong Kong, and has dominated the curriculum, as well as business and social life, throughout Hong Kong's modern educational era. The new wild card is Mandarin, which has achieved a very high level of influence in the past few decades, with business interests in the People's Republic streaming to Hong Kong, and vice versa. Some parents, in particular, fear that students will be at a disadvantage at English, American, and Chinese universities if students are unable to concentrate on a primary language.

Politically, Hong Kong textbooks have changed somewhat over the last few decades, but not nearly as much as those in Taiwan. The British influence from a century and a half of colonial presence (which only ended in 1997) can still be felt, but there is a distinct quality of Chinese cultural appreciation in the texts that might be said to have been somewhat more muted in the past. Indeed, one might even say that the textbooks reflect the generally positive attitude that many Hong Kong residents have taken toward Chinese stewardship. The attitude is not unambiguous, however, and the challenges for educators lies in building a Hong Kong identity that is both global—reflecting, in particular, the British past—and Chinese—reflecting the river of culture.

EDUCATIONAL CHALLENGES

When one returns one's focus to the People's Republic of China, the first challenge that arises is the sheer size of the country and the population. Although the strides that the Chinese Ministry of Education has taken toward national educational integration and equal access are notable, there remain a number of significant challenges. The most obvious is that, since the end of the imperial examination system just over 100 years ago, China has gone through turbulent changes in terms of its economic and political fortunes. One can look at the past century and say that it is only in the 1980s, 1990s, and 2000s that there has been the kind of consistent policy and institution building that takes many decades, and several generations of students, to bear significant results. Even a cursory reading of the last sections of Chapter 2 will show that the fall of the Qing dynasty, the ensuing period of warlordism, the war of resistance against Japan, and the civil war with the Nationalists have not been conducive to building continuity in education. The history of the People's Republic has been equally eventful, with major breaks in the system through the Great Leap Forward and the Cultural Revolution. In fact, many survivors of those eras refer to themselves as "Lost Generations," and it is education to which that loss most often refers.

The challenges for the Chinese government include continuing to make strides in integrating urban and rural, male and female, and rich and poor into a system that provides a stable educational base for a large percentage of students and the facilities to provide for high-level training, as well. As we have seen in previous chapters, the theme for all of the institutional goals in contemporary China remains similar: in order to build institutions, continuity is needed. The apocryphal Chinese curse, so often quoted by Westerners—"May you live in interesting times"—was remarkably pertinent to China for much of the 20th century and has resulted in a formidable challenge for educators of all kinds.

REFERENCES

Chen Xiujun, ed. *Sanzijing [Three Character Classic]*. Taibei: Yuwentang shuju, 2001.

Chafee, John. *The Thorny Gates of Learning in Sung China*. Albany, NY: SUNY Press, 1995.

Elman, Benjamin. *A Cultural History of Civil Examinations in Late Imperial China*. Berkeley: University of California Press, 2000.

Elman, Benjamin. *Education and Society in Late Imperial China*. Berkeley: University of California Press, 1994.

Hsiung Ping-chen. *A Tender Voyage: Children and Childhood in Late Imperial China*. Palo Alto, CA: Stanford University Press, 2005.

Postiglione, Gerard. *Education and Social Change in China.* Armonk, NY: M. E. Sharpe, 2006.

Miyazaki Ichisada. *China's Examination Hell: The Civil Service Examinations of Imperial China.* New Haven, CT: Yale University Press, 1981.

Walton, Linda. *Academies and Society in Southern Sung China.* Honolulu: University of Hawaii Press, 1999.

Republic of China Ministry of Education. *Guomin xiaoxue guoyu.* Taibei: 1985.

Wang Xiufang. *Education in China Since 1976.* Jefferson, NC: McFarland & Company, 2003.

Culture

Chinese Language

Shin Yong Robson

To those who do not know Chinese, the appearance of the Chinese language is altogether novel: instead of neat rows of alphabetic letters, there are thousands of unique characters, many of which seem incredibly intricate. The diversity of these characters is also fascinating, both visually and aurally. For example, the word "China" requires two characters (see Figure 6.1, a and b). But one may also render the word "China" with the two characters in Figure 6.1, c and d, using the simplified version of character 1b (character 1d). Cantonese Chinese pronounce this word *junggok*; people from Shanghai pronounce it *zonggoh*; and Mandarin speakers say *zhōngguó* or *chūngkuó*. Which is the correct form and pronunciation for the word "China"?

In fact, all of them are right. Chinese is not as "simple" as English, which has a five-letter word representing the name of the largest country in Asia. Variety is what the Chinese language is about, and all aspects of this variety have evolved through China's long history. The respective pronunciations for the word China—*junggok* in Cantonese, *zonggoh* in Shanghaiese, and *zhōngguó* in Mandarin—represent three of the eight major dialects of China.

THE HISTORY OF WRITTEN CHINESE

The legendary Cang Jie (c. 2500 B.C.E.), the official historian of the Yellow Emperor, is often credited with the invention of the earliest Chinese characters. According to folklore, Cang Jie had an extra pair of eyes that brought him extraordinary discernment. Inspired by the natural objects around him, particularly by the footprints of

221

Figure 6.1. *The word* China *in Chinese writing.*

a. b.　　　c. d.

YELLOW EMPEROR

The Yellow Emperor, called *Huangdi* in Chinese (a.k.a. Xuan Yuan), is one of remote antiquity's five legendary rulers. He and the Yan Emperor (a.k.a. Shen Nong [Divine Peasant]), are regarded as the mythical ancestors of the Han people. Thus, the Chinese regard themselves as *Yan Huang zi sun*, descendants of Yan and Huang Emperors. The Yellow Emperor reigned, according to the great historian Sima Qian (145 B.C.—90 B.C.), from 2497 B.C. to 2398 B.C. He is credited for many accomplishments, such as the principles outlining traditional Chinese medicine, the use of herbal medications, and the inventions of silk and the lunar calendar.

---

birds and animals, he ostensibly created the pictographic symbols that marked the beginning of the Chinese written language.

The actual origin of such a sophisticated writing system is, of course, less simple. The early pictographs were reflections of daily life, and they developed gradually from various sources. Thus Cang Jie can be considered the collector and organizer of existing signs and symbols, rather than the genius who successfully and single-handedly created an intricate communication method. Still, the legend surrounding his contribution remains—the first computer program for building characters that were not yet in the vocabulary pool, developed in the 1980s, was named after Cang Jie.

The oldest form of the Chinese written language can be found in the oracle bone inscriptions called *jiǎgǔwén* (see Figure 6.2a). Carved on tortoise shells and mammal bones during the Shang dynasty (c. 1600–1100 B.C.E.), these inscriptions recorded royal events and documented divinations. Each symbol represented a concrete image: a number, an animal, a tree, a mountain, the sunrise, and so forth. These early inscriptions demonstrate the inconsistencies found in primitive writing: an idea can be carved with many strokes or with just a few. Likewise, character size varies, and character positioning can be upright, sideways, or reversed. The strokes of these symbols mainly take the form of straight lines with sharp ends made with forceful carving knives.

During the late Shang dynasty and throughout the Zhou dynasty (c. 1100–256 B.C.E.), bronze inscription, *zhōngdǐngwén*, prevailed (see Figure 6.2b). This form of inscription refined oracle bone inscription. Although its earliest characters resembled the oracle bone inscriptions, curved lines are common in bronze inscriptions. Characters in this form were more regular in size and mainly upright. The number of characters was also greater: the large text inscribed on a single piece of bronze in the Zhou dynasty could contain as many as 500 characters.

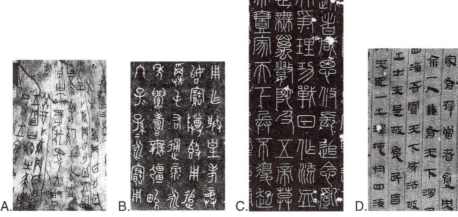

FIGURE 6.2. *A. Oracle bone inscription. B. Bronze inscription. C. Small seal script. D. Clerical script.*

The standardization of Chinese characters began under the First Emperor of the Qin dynasty (221–206 B.C.E.), who founded the first unified Chinese empire and ordered the unification of the written language. This standardized writing, called the Small Seal script (*xiǎozhuàn*), was the official national script designed by the court of the Qin (see Figure 6.2c). The characters in the Small Seal script are highly stylized, with each confined to a vertically oblong shape. The lines are even, thin, and wiry; the space is carefully regulated, and the pictorial elements of earlier writing forms are not apparent. Although the Small Seal script was crisply distinctive, its composition required patience and skill, so it was inconvenient for daily use.

The Clerical script (*lìshū*, Figure 6.2d) began to appear at the end of the Qin dynasty and was adapted as the formal writing form during the Han dynasty (206 B.C.E.–C.E. 220). As its name suggests, the Clerical script was initially used by clerks for the daily documentation of government records in the early Han. Reaching the height of its popularity in the Later Han period (C.E. 25–220), it simplified the complicated curves of the Small Seal style and replaced them with straightened lines and angles for clarity in reading and ease of writing. The Clerical script marked an important change in Chinese writing, for, hereafter, Chinese characters progressed from ancient symbols to their modern form.

Following the Clerical script was the Regular styled script (*kǎishū*, Figure 6.3), which came into use at the end of the Han dynasty (C.E. 220). It is an austere script that eventually replaced the Clerical for daily official functions. The Regular has been the formal script and remains the standard printing type in China today. Its major features are clarity and legibility—every character has a definite form and a square shape, and only minor variations are allowed. Each character in the Regular script clearly displays the basic strokes of Chinese writing that Chinese school children learn and practice.

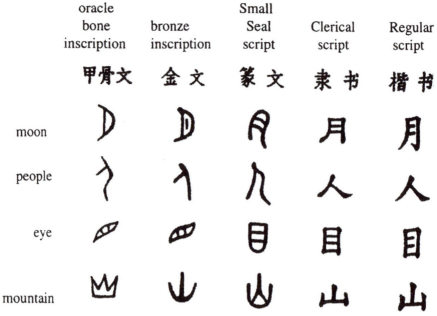

	oracle bone inscription	bronze inscription	Small Seal script	Clerical script	Regular script

FIGURE 6.3. *Evolution of written Chinese.*

It is technically true to say that Chinese writing reached its modern form as early as C.E. 200 because the basic principles of Chinese writing have remained unaltered for more than 1,800 years. A Chinese school child today can read and write the characters written by a clerk in the Han court because the contemporary Chinese script (Regular script) is so closely related to its literary past (see Figure 6.3).

FORMATION OF THE CHARACTERS

To an untrained eye, Chinese characters may look like many small, square-shaped pictures. Chinese characters, in fact, are written with strokes (see Figure 6.4). Some of the basic strokes—dot, hook, and turn strokes—enable variations. The number of strokes for a character may range from 1, such as for the word "one," to 17 (or more) for the word "dragon" (Figure 6.4).

Contemporary Chinese dictionaries commonly arrange characters by their recurrent parts, which are called radicals. For example, the characters for juice, pond, river, sea, and soup all have a radical called "three drops of water" on the left side of the character. The three–drops-of-water radical derives its name from the three dot strokes that resemble water drops. Similarly, the characters for snow, cloud, thunder, frost, and dew share a "rain" radical (on the top). This radical is the miniature of the pictographic character for the word "rain," which illustrates raining under the sky. A dictionary normally begins with a section that lists categories based on 214 radicals. The radicals are arranged in ascending order of stroke numbers. In this arrangement, the three-drops-of-water radical, which contains three dot strokes, comes

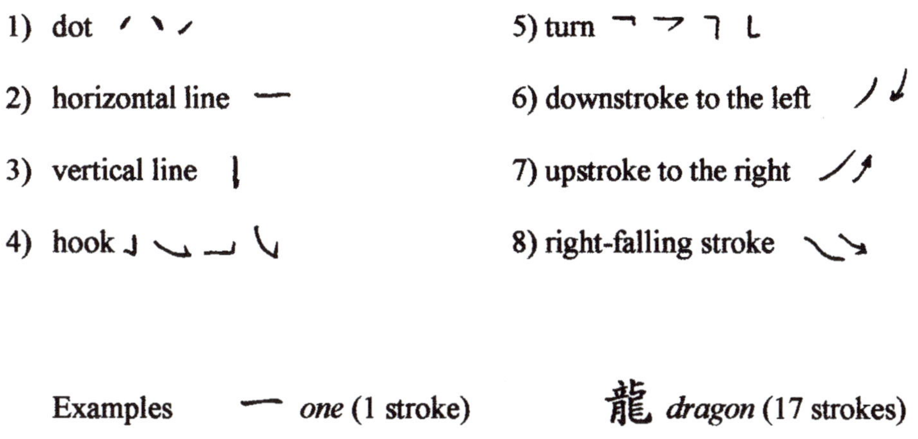

1) dot ✓ ＼ ✓

2) horizontal line —

3) vertical line |

4) hook ⌙ ＼ ⌣ ⇃

5) turn ⏋ ⏗ ⏞ ∟

6) downstroke to the left ╱ ⌡

7) upstroke to the right ╱⌠

8) right-falling stroke ＼ ⬎

Examples — *one* (1 stroke)   龍 *dragon* (17 strokes)

FIGURE 6.4. *Eight basic strokes of the Chinese characters.*

RADICAL NAME	RADICAL	CHARACTERS				
three drops of water	氵	汁	池	河	海	湯
		juice	*pond*	*river*	*sea*	*soup*
rain	雨	雪	雲	雷	霜	露
		snow	*cloud*	*thunder*	*frost*	*dew*

FIGURE 6.5. *Examples of the character arrangement.*

before the rain radical, which has eight strokes. The characters under each category of radicals are arranged in ascending order of the number of the remaining strokes (that is, the strokes other than those of the radical). For example, in the section on the three-drops-of-water radical, the five characters listed in Figure 6.5 would appear in this order: juice, whose remaining part (on the right) contains two strokes; pond, with three strokes in its remaining part; river, with five; sea, with seven; and, finally, soup, which has nine strokes in its remaining part.

The number of Chinese characters has increased over time. The first dictionary compiled by Xu Shen in the late Han dynasty (c. C.E. 100), *Explanations of Graphs and Analysis of Characters* (*Shuō Wén Jié Zì*), contains 9,353 characters. The *Kangxi (K'ang-hsi) Dictionary,* the largest dictionary compiled in Chinese imperial history, was completed in 1716, at the request of the Kangxi Emperor and lists 47,035 characters. The Grand Chinese Dictionary published in 1986 lists 56,000 characters. The increased numbers of characters in the later dictionaries (after the Han dynasty) arose from an attempt to capture dialects, geographical names, colloquial expressions, and variant forms. The most commonly used 8,000 characters, however, are collected mainly in Xu Shen's *Explanations of Graphs and Analysis of Characters.*

In modern times, a person who knows 3,000 characters is able to read a newspaper and handle the ordinary events of the day. Chinese characters generally originated in four ways (see Figure 6.6). The first group contains image shapes (*xiàngxíng*). These are imitative symbols, meaning that each character resembles an object's shape. The character for mountain shows three mountain peaks (Figure 6.6a). The character for door shows a door with two swinging panels (Figure 6.6b). The eye character is a vertically standing eye (Figure 6.6c). The sun and moon characters are also included in this category (Figures 6.6d and e). The wood character shows the branches and roots of a tree (Figure 6.6f).

The second group of characters, "pointing to matters" (*zhishi*), is used to indicate abstract meanings. The characters for one, two, and three are simply one, two, and three lines. The meanings of "up" and "down" are clearly indicated by their characters, as are the meanings of the characters for "convex" and "concave." The character for "dawn" shows the sun rising above the horizon.

The third group of characters, the "meeting of ideas" (*huìyì*), includes logical compounds. Two or three ideographic symbols are joined to form a new character that reflects the compounded meaning. For example, wood was originally an imitative symbol (Figure 6.6f). Two wood characters are combined to make "grove" (Figure 6.6g), and three are combined to create the character for "forest" (Figure 6.6h). The combination of the sun and moon characters is similar. The original form of *sun* shows the sun with an added short line, and it has been changed to reflect the modern script (Figure 6.6d). The character for *moon* has also been changed from its original form, which is easily recognized as a crescent moon, to the script used today (Figure 6.6e). The combination of (Figure 6.6d) and (Figure 6.6e) is (Figure 6.6i), the character for "bright."

The fourth and largest group of characters is "shape-sound" (*xíngshēng*). These characters are comprised of two parts: a radical that indicates the meaning of the character and another character (usually on the right) that represents the pronunciation. For example, the character for "green" is pronounced *qing* (Figure 6.6j). The five other characters (Figures 6.6k–o) that are written with additional strokes, but share the same character green (on their right), are also pronounced *qīng*. While the right-hand character *green* identifies the pronunciation of these five characters, their meanings are indicated by their left-hand radicals, as shown in Figure 6.6.

SIMPLIFIED CHARACTERS

The mainland Chinese write certain characters differently than the standard form established more than 1,800 years ago, using fewer strokes for some characters. For example, they use the simplified second character in the word "China" (Figure 6.1d). Characters with reduced strokes are known as simplified characters (*jiǎntizi*), as opposed to complex characters (*fántizi*), or traditional characters.

The simplified characters are the products of the script reform initiated in 1956 in the People's Republic of China to promote universal literacy and to enhance the

FORMATION CATEGORY	EXAMPLES
Image shapes (*xiàngxíng*)	a. 山 b. 門 c. 目 d. 日 e. 月 f. 木 *mountain door eye sun moon wood*
Pointing to matters (*zhǐshì*)	一 二 三 上 下 凸 凹 旦 *one two three up down convex concave dawn*
Meeting of ideas (*huìyì*)	木 + 木 → g. 林 *grove* 木 + 木 + 木 → h. 森 *forest* 日 + 月 → i. 明 *bright*
Shape-sound (*xíngshēng*)	j. [qīng] 青 *green* 氵 (*water* radical) + 青 → k. [qīng] 清 *clear, unmixed* 日 (*sun* radical) + 青 → l. [qíng] 晴 *fine, sunny (day)* 言 (*speech* radical) + 青 → m. [qǐng] 請 *to request* 忄 (*vertical heart* radical) + 青 → n. [qíng] 情 *feeling, sentiment* 魚 (*fish* radical) + 青 → o. [qīng] 鯖 *mackerel*

FIGURE 6.6. *Formations of the characters.*

efficiency of writing. The second edition of *A Comprehensive List of Simplified Characters*, published in 1964, is the official guide for the simplified characters used in the PRC today. This list contains 2,236 simplified characters, which account for about one-third of the 8,000 most commonly used characters in modern Chinese. In other words, about one-third of the total number of characters commonly used in modern Chinese have two written versions: the traditional form and a corresponding simplified form. In the case of the two characters for China, the first character does not have a simplified version, whereas the second character (Figure 6.1b) does have a simplified equivalent (Figure 6.1d).

Simplifying the traditional characters usually means reducing the number of strokes in complex radicals or side components. For example, although the character "door" (Figure 6.7a) is simplified, it is also simplified when it serves as the radical or side component of another word. Consider the three characters that follow *door* in Figure 6.7, in which *door* serves as a radical (Figures 6.7b and c) and as a side component (in Figure 6.7d). Sometimes, only one part of a traditional character remains and the rest of the character is simply deleted, as in the characters in Figures 6.7e and f. When the shorthand forms replace the traditional forms, the simplified

TYPE	EXAMPLES					
	a.	b.	c.	d.	e.	f.
Traditional	門	問	閑	們	習	飛
Simplified	门	问	闲	们	习	飞
	door	to ask	not busy	suffix that turns single pronouns plural	practice; exercise	to fly
	g.		h.	i.	j.	k.
Traditional	萬		厲	礪	勵	邁
Simplified	万		厉	砺	励	迈
	ten thousand		strict	whetstone	to encourage	to stride

FIGURE 6.7. *Traditional and simplified characters.*

characters look entirely different, such as the character "ten thousand" (Figure 6.7g). When this simplified character *ten thousand* appears in other characters as a side component, those characters also look very different from their traditional counterparts (see Figures 6.7h–k).

Although publications aimed at overseas Chinese are often written with traditional characters, simplified characters were officially adopted as the standard writing within the PRC. Since the 1960s, almost all books and newspapers in mainland China have been printed with simplified characters, as are textbooks for school children. Chinese educated before the 1960s and using the traditional characters have added the simplified forms to their visual repertoire, whereas those educated thereafter have only learned the simplified characters.

PROBLEMS OF SIMPLIFICATION

The simplified characters may take less time to write, but their use causes linguistic confusion and difficulties for non-natives studying the language. One illustration of simplified characters cut from their historical roots is the simplified version of "country," which is the second character of the word *China* (see Figure 6.1). The ancient pictogram in the bronze inscription for the idea *country* is a character representing an ancient weapon defending a town surrounded by a fence (see Figure 6.8a). In the Small Seal script, this character is enclosed in a larger square that indicates the surrounding boundary of a state. From this conception, the traditional character for *country* evolved (Figure 6.8b), and later, the character was adopted in Regular script (Figure 6.8c). Another character for *territory/region* (Figure 6.8d) also derived from the ancient pictogram for *country* (Figure 6.8a), in which a radical representing *earth/dirt* is added to its left. In other words, the ancient pictogram (Figure 6.8a) represents the origin of two characters: *country* (Figure 6.8c) and *territory/region* (Figure 6.8d).

Just as one easily relates the meanings of "country" and "territory," one also connects the characters that represent them. There is a simplified form for *country* (Figure 6.8e), which replaces the ancient pictogram for *country* (Figure 6.8a) with the character *jade* inside a large square. Ideology replaced history in this case. The reasoning behind this simplified character (Figure 6.8e) is that *jade* here represents the jade imperial seal, the representation of a state, and when it is enclosed by a large square, the meaning of *state* is expressed. This equation of *jade* and *country*, however, is far from obvious. The character for "territory" (Figure 6.8d), on the other hand, does not have a simplified version. Breaking the historical and linguistic link that has existed for centuries, the simplified character for *country* has no connection to the character *territory.*

In many cases, by recreating the characters, the reform has broken the logic behind the structure of the traditional characters. For instance, many characters related to trading share the character "shell," which was the valuable item used in trading in ancient China before money was invented. The character *shell* (see Figure 6.9a) was originally an imitative symbol, which serves either as a radical or a side component in characters related to trading. Some of the characters containing the "shell" radical have an obvious semantic connection to its ancient origin (see Figure 6.9c–i). When the character *shell* is simplified (Figure 6.9b), the other characters with the "shell" radical are correspondingly changed, as demonstrated by the differences between the top and bottom lines of Figure 6.9c–g. But two of the most important characters in this sequence, "buy" and "sell," (Figures 6.9h and i) lose both their historical and logical contexts since their simplified versions adopt shorthand forms in which the radical *shell* is completely abolished. These two simplified characters thus have no connections to other members of their philological family. People who learn only simplified versions of these two characters may never relate them to other characters that share the "shell" radical.

For non-native students of the Chinese language, character simplification has not made study easier, but, on the contrary, more burdensome and confusing. Certain radicals and characters, for example, are hard to distinguish in their simplified forms. One such problem is the resemblance between the two simplified radicals "metal" and "food." The traditional radical metal is the miniature of the character for *gold*

FIGURE 6.8. *The characters for* country.

TYPE	EXAMPLES
	a. Evolution of the character for *shell*. (oracle bone) → (bronze) → (Small Seal) → 貝 (Regular) 貝 (traditional) → b. 贝 (simplified)
Traditional **Simplified**	c. d. e. f. g. h. i. 財 貴 費 資 貸 買 賣 财 贵 费 资 货 买 卖 *wealth* *expensive* *fee* *capital* *loan* *buy* *sell*

FIGURE 6.9. *Characters related to trading.*

(Figure 6.10a). Characters sharing the metal radical (on their left) refer to objects made of metals, such as needles, nails, and pliers, or to natural elements, such as silver (see Figure 6.10). When the radical *metal* is simplified (Figure 6.10b), the characters that contain this radical also change. Similarly, another traditional radical "food," which is the miniature of the character for "food" or "to eat" (Figure 6.10c), is also simplified (Figure 6.10d). Characters sharing the *food* radical, which is normally related to food names or eating, are correspondingly simplified. Consider the contrast between the traditional and simplified versions for the characters "dumpling," "pancake," "restaurant," and "be hungry" in Figure 6.10. To many non-natives, the two radicals *metal* and *food* are very similar in appearance after they are simplified (Figures 6.10b and d). In writing, students often erroneously substitute the simplified radical *metal* for the characters related to food or vice versa. For them, these two simplified radicals seem like entirely new symbols that are no longer related to their origins—the characters for *gold* and *food*.

The confusion is not necessarily less pronounced for those who prefer to study only simplified characters. For example, one simplified part may replace various, different parts in different traditional characters (Figure 6.11) and the pattern of such replacements is hard to grasp. While a number of simplified radicals are completely new creations (i.e. extra segments that students must learn), they do not always remain consistent in replacing their traditional counterparts. The simplified radicals *metal* (Figure 6.10b) and *food* (Figure 6.10d) represent two such examples. Two other common radicals, *silk* (Figure 6.12b) and *speech* (Figure 6.12d), cause similar confusion. Simplified versions of these radicals are only used on the left side of a character, as the *silk* radical is used in characters "yarn," "paper," and "silk fabric," and the *speech* radical used in the characters "to record," "word," and "poem" (see Figure 6.12). If, however, such radicals appear in any other part of a character, the traditional version remains. Hence, the characters for "rope," "purple," and "numerous" still have the traditional *silk* radical at the bottom, whereas the characters for "alert," "vow," and "letter" still have the traditional *speech* radical at the bottom and the right side.

TYPE	RADICAL NAME	RADICAL	EXAMPLES			
Traditional	*metal*	a. 金	針	釘	鉗	銀
Simplified		b. 钅	针	钉	钳	银
			needle	*nail*	*pliers*	*silver*
Traditional	*food*	c. 食	餃	餅	飯館	餓
Simplified		d. 饣	饺	饼	饭馆	饿
			dumpling	*pancake*	*restaurant*	*be hungry*

FIGURE 6.10. *Radicals for* metal *and* food.

TYPE	SIMPLIFIED PART	REPLACED PARTS	EXAMPLES				
		(b) (c) (d) (e)	b.	c.	d.	e.	
Traditional		漢 菫 雚 對	嘆	僅	歡	對	
Simplified	a. 又		叹	仅	欢	对	
			to sign	*only*	*merry*	*correct*	
		(g) (h) (i) (j) (k)	g.	h.	i.	j.	k.
Traditional		重 軍 曾 宣 溫	動	運	層	壇	醞
Simplified	f. 云		动	运	层	坛	酝
			to stir	*to carry*	*layer*	*altar*	*to brew*

FIGURE 6.11. *One simplified part replaces various parts.*

Which is better.

Generally speaking, character simplification has not carried consensus among Chinese for being simpler and therefore better, and it remains controversial. Despite its original intention of making writing simpler, in practice, this reform has complicated matters. While for highly educated Chinese residents of the PRC, switching gears between the simplified characters and the traditional characters is a common practice, and average citizens may master traditional characters by reading classical literature, this mixed use is difficult for those overseas. Unlike people inside the PRC, who are mainly exposed to simplified characters, the Chinese who live outside the PRC routinely encounter publications in traditional characters from outside the PRC and publications in simplified characters from the PRC. They consequently must learn both the traditional characters and the simplified characters to accommodate their constant encounters with publications reflecting both versions. To most readers outside the PRC, learning a large set of characters in addition to an already existing and

TYPE	RADICAL	EXAMPLES					
Traditional	a. 系	紗	紙	綢	索	紫	繁
Simplified	b. 纟	纱	纸	绸	索	紫	繁
	silk	*yarn*	*paper*	*silk fabric*	*rope*	*purple*	*numerous*
Traditional	c. 言	記	詞	詩	警	誓	信
Simplified	d. 讠	记	词	诗	警	誓	信
	speech	*to record*	*word*	*poem*	*alert*	*vow*	*letter*

FIGURE 6.12. *Radicals for* silk *and* speech.

familiar written language has been burdensome. Hence, publications in simplified characters from the PRC are not popular in Chinese communities overseas.

As a result, although China's simplification of characters is known throughout the world, it is habitually avoided outside of the PRC. Traditional characters are commonplace for street signs and for printing in Chinese communities overseas. Taiwan and Hong Kong allow simplified characters for informal communications, but use traditional characters in virtually all printed matter. In Singapore, newspapers print simplified characters, but traditional characters dominate most other communications. Accordingly, the *People's Daily*, the official newspaper of the PRC, regularly provides an overseas edition in traditional characters.

In the meantime, simplified characters have not completely replaced traditional characters in mainland China. The traditional characters are still preferred for such activities as the printing of historical documents and classical literary works. Since the PRC opened its doors to international trade in the 1980s, business exchanges between mainland China, Hong Kong, and Taiwan have increased, with the result that the use of traditional characters in trademarks, products' logos, signboards, and advertisements has become commonplace.

In recent years, an increasing number of scholars in the PRC have addressed the linguistic confusions caused by simplification and the problems related to this mixed use of the traditional and the simplified characters. Some scholars point out that in these technological times, Chinese needs another era of *shū-tóng-wén*, translated as "writing in the same language" and referring to the standardization of characters that the First Emperor of the Qin envisioned 2,000 years ago. For Chinese all over the world, that would mean reading, writing, and computer-inputting a single version of the characters. There is hope that this issue will be handled seriously. Since its beginning, Chinese writing has served as an unvaryingly reliable vehicle for chronicling the breadth and depth of Chinese civilization and has provided an unbreakable bond uniting readers of Chinese across the span of centuries and the space of the worldwide

Chinese diaspora. For Chinese, this new normalization would be of great significance in preserving the status of this living heritage.

PRONUNCIATION

Throughout their long history of language, the Chinese have used ideographic writing featuring characters rather than phonetic symbols (alphabetical letters). To native Chinese, the idea "He is Chinese" is conveyed by a five-character sentence. This sentence is pronounced *tā shì zhōng guó rén*. A listener who wishes to write Chinese, but who is unable to write the characters, must use a phonetic script to represent this phrase. Using the Roman alphabet, the phonetic script can record Chinese pronunciations, but this phonetic writing is difficult for native Chinese and non-natives to read. So, let us explore the system of Chinese pronunciation.

Every Chinese character represents a syllable comprised of three parts: an initial consonant, a single or a compound vowel, and a tone (which indicates inflection). For example, in *mài*, the "m" represents the initial consonant, *ai* the compound vowel, and [`] the tone. In *chéng*, the "ch" is the initial consonant, the "eng" is the compound vowel, and ['] is the tone. If any one of these three parts changes, the sound and meaning of the syllable changes, as well.

Tones are a distinctive feature of Chinese, and are as important as the other two parts of a syllable. They represent one of the chief differences between Chinese and English. In English, a speaker expresses affirmation with "Yes," a question ending with "Yes?" and a reluctant agreement in the form of "Y-e-s." Unlike the expressive intonation of English, Chinese tones are used to distinguish word meanings. Thus, the Chinese term *mǎi* means "buy," but *mài* means "sell." Consider another example. The English word "fee" has the same meaning in a question "Do they charge a fee?" with a rising intonation and in the statement "We need to pay the fee," which has a falling intonation. The meaning of the Chinese word *fei*, however, depends on the tone that is used. Spoken with a high, level tone, it means to fly (*fēi*); with a rising tone, it means fat (*féi*); with a very low tone, it means bandit (*fei*); and with a falling inflection, it means fee (*fèi*).

Tone is the movement or holding of the pitch of the voice within the time span of the syllable. Every syllable in Mandarin belongs to one of four tones: high and level, rising, low, and falling. To further complicate things, there are hundreds of homonyms in Chinese—that is, characters that are written differently and have different meanings, but have the same sound and the same tone. For instance, the sound *fēi* with the high, level tone can mean to fly, but it can also mean imperial concubine, wrong, door leaf, or Pacific herring. The sound *qián* can mean money, front, or pliers. If one considers full words rather than single syllables, the problem is certainly compounded. For example, without tones, it is rather difficult to determine, even from context, whether the two-syllable word *shiyan* is *shíyán* (salt), *shìyàn* (test), *shìyǎn* (rehearsal), *shíyàn* (experiment), or *shìyàn* (oath, pledge). Because most Chinese words have two or more syllable combinations, pronunciation without tones produces chaos. On the other hand, even though the tones provide the words with a distinguishing feature, to native Chinese, only the characters represent the language in pronunciation and in meaning.

PHONETIC WRITING (ROMANIZATIONAL) SYSTEMS: PEKING OR BEIJING?

The phonetic system for Chinese that uses the Roman alphabet is called Romanization. Of several alphabetical systems used to transliterate Chinese to English, the Wade-Giles system was the most widely used international system until 1979. After 1979, the pinyin system gradually replaced Wade-Giles for Chinese pronunciation in matters pertaining to China. This switch has puzzled some Westerners. For example, does one say Peking or Beijing? The latter. Was Guangzhou once Canton? Yes. Do Chiang Kai-shek and Jiang Jieshi refer to the same person? Yes. Many Chinese names and terms that were once familiar to Westerners are now transliterated to pinyin and may no longer look familiar.

The Wade-Giles system originated in 1859 with Sir Thomas Wade (1818–1895), a British military and diplomatic official in China in the mid-19th century and, later, a scholar of Sinology (Chinese Studies) at Cambridge University. His system of Romanization was revised by Herbert Giles (1845–1939), a prolific writer and a translator of Chinese literature at Cambridge, in his *Chinese-English Dictionary*, published in 1892.

For many years. the Wade-Giles system was used in publications, including newspapers and maps. What made Wade-Giles widely acceptable to Westerners was its ease of use. Supposedly, any English speaker could pronounce a Chinese syllable without serious inaccuracy and without extensive study. For example, a Westerner would probably find *t'a shih chung kuo jen* easier to capture than *tā shì zhōng guó rén* and Chiang Tse-min less exotic than Jiang Zemin. In both cases, the earlier transliteration is Wade-Giles; the latter is pinyin. To Chinese speakers, however, the latter transliteration more accurately represents the standard pronunciation in each case.

Pinyin was officially adopted in the PRC in 1958, and has had a growing number of uses: teaching character pronunciation, transliterating proper names in the press, transcribing some minority languages, and teaching people to speak Mandarin. It is also used in dictionaries and textbooks. In 1979, the government of the PRC began to replace Wade-Giles with pinyin in publications designed for foreign distribution.

Although the same linguistic principles apply to Wade-Giles and pinyin, Westerners may find it more difficult to pronounce pinyin script because some consonants in the system are pronounced quite differently from what Westerners would expect. For instance, the "Q" in Qing is pronounced like the English "ch," and *xiao* is pronounced *hsiao*. To some Westerners, many of the familiar names become unfamiliar under the pinyin system. But to Chinese ears, pinyin produces a more accurate pronunciation of the language. Pinyin was quickly accepted as the standard transliteration for Chinese terms in linguistics, science, and in textbooks. Since the 1980s, pinyin has been gradually adapted in all of the humanities fields and has become the dominant transliterational system. Nowadays, readers are more familiar with the term "Daoism" (which used to be "Taoism") and understand that tofu is actually pronounced *dòufù*.

Most sounds in Mandarin are not difficult to pronounce. Those that might be unfamiliar to Westerners include the pronunciation of some consonants, such as j, q, x, z, c, zh, and r, which, although they may appear puzzling to a Western eye, are not impossible to manage. "J" is a tight sound that is somewhat similar to the first three letters in jeep; "q" is sounded out as "chee" in "cheer"; "x" is sounded out like the English "c" pronounced with a smile and with the teeth almost closed; "z" is pronounced "dz"; "c" is pronounced "ts"; "zh" is sounded out like the "G" in "Gerry"; and "r" is pronounced like the "r" in "run." To say "The Chinese speak Chinese" in Mandarin, one would state: *zhōng-guó-rén shuō zhōng-wén*.

MANDARIN VERSUS DIALECTS

When people talk about the Chinese language, they are usually referring to the language used by the Han people, who make up more than 90 percent of the Chinese population. Correspondingly, the term for Chinese characters is *hànzì*, or "the Han characters." Other Chinese languages used by China's minority ethnic groups, such as the Mongolians and Manchus, are entirely different from the one used by the Han.

Although all Han Chinese read and write the same characters, some Chinese speak Cantonese, Taiwanese, or Shanghaiese, and so forth. The Chinese language possesses eight major dialect systems, most of which developed because the country was divided by natural barriers. These so-called dialects are all Han languages that differ from one another in terms of pronunciation, much as French differs from other Romance languages. Named for the main areas in which they are spoken, the dialects are Northern division, Wú (in regions of Jiāngsū-ZhéJiāng provinces), Yüè (Cantonese dialect), Xiāng (Húnán dialect), Hakka (spoken by the descendants of northern immigrants, who are widely scattered from Sìchuān to southeastern China), Gàn (Jiāngxī dialect), Northern Min (Northern Fukienese), and Southern Min.

To standardize communication, the government of the PRC decided in 1955 that the northern dialect based on the Beijing pronunciation would be the official means of communication. It is known by Western people as Modern Standard Chinese or Mandarin. Mandarin was originally a term used by Europeans to refer to a public official in imperial China; its Chinese equivalent is *guān*. The original term for the Mandarin language was *guānhuà*, which means "speech of the official class." After the fall of the Manchu regime in 1911, the term *guóyǔ*, meaning "national language," was used to refer to Mandarin until 1949, when the PRC was established in mainland China. The term *guóyǔ* is still used in Taiwan. In the PRC today, the term referring to Mandarin is *pǔtōnghuà*, or "common (people's) speech." So, when a Chinese friend says "I speak *guóyǔ*," and another one says "I speak *pǔtōnghuà*," these two are actually telling you the same thing—that is, "I speak Mandarin." From the term they use to identify Mandarin, you know that the first person is from Taiwan and the second is from mainland China.

The most obvious difference between the dialects and Mandarin is pronunciation. For instance, the numbers one through five in Mandarin are pronounced *yī, èr, sān, sì, wǔ*; in Cantonese, they are *yah, yee, sam, say, hmm*. "How are you?" in Mandarin is *ni hǎo*, which in Cantonese is *lay hoe*. Such differences exist between all of the dialects. Chinese people who speak any one of the dialects ordinarily cannot be understood by those speaking other dialects, or by people using Mandarin. Mandarin remains the standard language taught in schools and used in all of the media in the PRC. Educated Chinese usually learn Mandarin in addition to their native dialect. Although Mandarin is also the official language in Taiwan and in Singapore, most people in Hong Kong speak Cantonese, which was long the dominant dialect of Chinese communities in the United States and Canada. In the 1980s and 1990s, and especially since 1997, when Hong Kong was taken over by the PRC, Mandarin became more and more common in these previously Cantonese-speaking communities.

USEFUL CHINESE EXPRESSIONS

Hello!

Hǎo a!

Bye!

Zài jiàn!

Good morning!

Zǎo!

How do you do? Pleased to meet you.

Ni hǎo!

May I ask what your name is?

Qingwèn, nín guì xìng?

What is your name (to a young person/child)?

Ni jiào shénme míngzi?

I am Mary.

Wo shì Mary.

Thank you. You are welcome.

Xièxiè. / Bú xiè.

Excuse me! Sorry!

Duì bù qi!

OK!

Hǎo!

That is fine. There is no problem.

Méi wèntí.

Is that so?

Shì ma?

Excuse me, where is the bathroom?

Duì bù qi, cèsuo zài nǎr?

Is there a cafe around here?

Zhè fùjìn you méiyou kāfēi guǎnr?

Please, no MSG.

Duì bù qi, bú yào wèijīng.

Delicious food!

Zhēn hǎo chī!

Cheers!

Gān bēi!

Bill, please.

Duì bù qi, zhàngdān.

How much does it cost?

Duōshǎo qián?

Can you help me?

Néng bù néng bāngbāng máng?

I understand a little Chinese

Wo dong yìdiǎnr zhōngwén.

Sorry, I do not speak Chinese.

Duì bù qi, wo bù shuō zhōngwén.

Does anyone here speak English?

Zhèr yǒurén shuō yingwén ma?

Please speak more slowly.

Qing ni shuō de màn yìdiǎnr.

I do not understand.

Wo bù dong.

I do not know.

Wo bù zhīdào.

What time is it?

Xiànzài ji diǎn?

What did you say?

Ni shuō shénme?

REFERENCES

DeFrancis, John. *The Chinese Language: Fact and Fantasy*. University of Hawaii Press, 1986.

DeFrancis, John. *Visible Speech: The Diverse Oneness of Writing System*. University of Hawaii Press, 1989.

Kane, Daniel. *The Chinese Language: Its History and Current Usage*. Tuttle Publishing, 2006.

Norman, Jerry. *Chinese*. 11th printing. Cambridge University Press, 2005.

Ramsey, S. Robert. *The Languages of China*. Princeton, NJ: Princeton University Press, 1989.

Tsien, Tsuen-hsuin. Written on Bamboo and Silk: The Beginnings of Chinese Books and Inscriptions. 2nd ed. Chicago: University of Chicago Press, 2004.

Social Relationships and Etiquette

Tamara Hamlish
Warren Bruce Palmer
Robert André LaFleur

NESTED BOXES

Most Americans have encountered some piece of Chinese culture without ever traveling to China. In nearly every town across the country, we find the familiar aromas of Chinese foods in Chinese restaurants. We recognize the highly stylized architecture of Chinese arches and pagodas from the Chinatown districts of major U.S. cities. We can puzzle over the subtleties of Chinese paintings on the scrolls that are housed in American museums. While these small slices of Chinese culture may be familiar to us, they also remind us of the tremendous differences between our cultures. Encountered in the form of isolated occurrences against the backdrop of daily life in the United States, Chinese culture often seems even more distant, more exotic, and more mysterious. We are often aware of the great changes in our own society (imagine making cell phone calls or paying at the pump just 20 years ago), but encounter fragments of other cultures as timeless essences. In this section, we will explain aspects of Chinese social behavior and etiquette to put those isolated fragments of culture into the context of the larger whole of contemporary Chinese society—which is itself undergoing profound changes here in the early 21st century.

The image of Chinese boxes nested inside one another, with each one opening to reveal not just one more box but another perfectly matched set, is an image that works well when considering the complexities of Chinese culture. Although human society and social behavior are never so perfectly matched and organized, this image is useful because it reminds us that cultural differences are relative. Each box may be useful, or interesting, or beautiful in its own right, but it is also appraised in relation to the size and shape of neighboring boxes. Similarly, cultural differences between, for example, China's north and south (which we have already encountered in several chapters) only make sense in relation to the bigger box of China as a whole and to the smaller boxes of local and regional cultural practices.

SOCIAL RELATIONSHIPS—*GUANXI*

If, as we saw in the preceding section, language is at the center of Chinese culture, then social relationships are at the very core of Chinese society. It is in the area of social relationships that the metaphor of nested boxes may be most useful because it can help in visualizing the system of social relations that extends outward from each individual, shifting in size and complexity over the course of one's life. Nearly all social interactions in Chinese societies can be understood in terms of *guanxi*. It would be difficult to overstate the significance of these networks, since they apply to a broad range of relationships, from the family to international affairs. In fact, some scholars suggest that conceptions of *guanxi* even extend to the supernatural, or unseen, world of gods, ghosts, and ancestors, where good connections ease the pressures of life in the "real" world.

It cannot be overstated that social relations in China are not simply about getting along well with others; they are about building a network of people upon whom you can count (and who, in turn, will count on you) to help make things happen—from finding housing or a job to reserving a seat on a plane or a train during a busy holiday season, acquiring access to good medical care, or being admitted to a top school. Through the continual exchange of both tangible and intangible goods, people develop a sense of mutual obligation that cements their network of social relationships and ensures that they are able to get what they need and want.

This attitude toward social relationships is unfamiliar to many Westerners, who clearly distinguish between relationships based on seemingly rational, economic needs (that is, one's relationship with the clerk at the local grocery store) and relationships based on emotional needs and desires (that is, with a spouse, children, close friends). The Chinese system of *guanxi* may seem like a cold and calculating approach to personal relationships based on what a person can get out of them. But the calculations are not as utilitarian as they may appear, and relationships are always mutual, with a clear expectation that both parties will give and receive. In fact, the fundamental principles of Chinese social relations are abstract qualities that have more to do with a person's character and integrity than with material resources.

Enduring concepts, such as *ren* and *xin*, refer to qualities such as trustworthiness, credibility, endurance, tolerance, and respect, and have been an important part of Chinese definitions of the individual for millennia. The concept of *mian* ("face") is perhaps familiar to many Americans, although it is not always fully understood. One has the ability to enhance the reputation of others (to "give face" to others), as well as the desire to preserve one's own reputation (to "save face"). In other

---

FILIAL PIETY AND BEHAVIORAL EXPECTATIONS

The overarching quality of filial piety (*xiaoxun*) signifies the importance of the family as the model for all social relationships, both in the abstract and in more practical assessments of someone's integrity and character. In one of his landmark studies of Chinese culture and society, the anthropologist Fei Xiaotong notes that social responsibility in China begins and ends at the gate to the family home. Family loyalties take priority over all other relationships, and family background is a key factor in determining an individual's place in society. Family resources are pooled, with all family members expected to devote at least a portion of their labor or other resources to the family, under the expectation that individuals will use these resources in ways that will enhance the well-being and the reputation of the family as a whole. It is therefore easy to see why people's behavior inside the family is taken as a good indicator of how they will behave outside of the family.

---

words, relationships are not entered into casually, nor are they considered short term. *Guanxi* requires a deep commitment and a long-term investment of time and energy, and, like all social relationships, offers the potential to reap considerable returns.

SOCIAL RELATIONSHIPS—FAMILY

The words that are used to identify kin are extraordinarily complex, in part because they are an expression of the nature of family obligations. Relationships are clearly and precisely defined on the basis of gender, age (birth order), and generation. Hierarchical values are attached to each category, with senior-generation, first-born males ranking highest. Unlike English, where the term "cousin" includes all of the children of all of the siblings of both parents, Chinese kinship terms identify each individual through a specific term that traces the relationship through distinctions between mother and father, the sex and birth order of the (parent's) siblings, and the sex and birth order of the children of the siblings. Thus, when someone talks about a cousin in Chinese, it is immediately clear who the actual person is, even without mentioning a name.

This complex system of kinship terms speaks to the importance of knowing one's place within the wider family—and the wider social world. Families are organized hierarchically, and older men are treated with the most respect, even if the man's actual power has been usurped by his sons or his spouse. Although changes in Chinese laws over the past 45 years have given women more rights, family property, wealth, and other family resources are still often transferred to sons before daughters. In rural areas, where agriculture is still the primary livelihood, this is often justified by the fact that young couples generally move in with the groom's parents after they are married, and it is in that household that both husband and wife offer their greatest investments of time and energy. Although this scenario has changed dramatically among urban families in China today (and the situation is in flux all over the country because of the One-Child Policy), many families continue to privilege sons over daughters.

Elderly men visit in Lijiang, China. (Travel Pictures Gallery)

In the past, marriages were arranged and were seen as alliances between family groups. Today, despite the disappearance of formally arranged marriages, many people still rely on introductions from family or friends in their search for a spouse. Unlike marriage and family in European and American society, which focuses on the sexual relationship between husband and wife, the primary bonds in Chinese families are intergenerational, between parents and children. Resources, including children, are regarded as belonging to the family, without much emphasis on individual ownership. In urban areas, families often live in nuclear units (parents and children) with aging parents close by, in part for space and privacy, and in part because (as wage earners) they may seek to establish some independence. Still, families in China are far less independent than nuclear families in the United States. Extended family (grandparents, aunts, and uncles) often participate in decisions about disciplining children, making major purchases, choosing a school, or changing jobs—in other words, anything that will affect either the resources or the reputation of the family as a whole. In rural areas, families may live with several generations under a single roof, or children may live with their grandparents while their parents go to the city or overseas in search of better economic opportunities. Although it is certainly easier to control resources when people live together—or at least in close proximity—the cultural value of *xiaoxun* brings with it a strong sense of obligation that is not diminished by long distances or infrequent visits.

SOCIAL RELATIONSHIPS—BEYOND HOME

The principles that govern relationships within the family can also be seen in social relationships that extend beyond the family in the social networks that emerge at school, at work, and in the local community. In many of these contexts, kin terms are used to express respect, admiration, or the desire to sustain the relationship into the future—classmates are referred to as brothers and sisters, or neighbors may be addressed as "Auntie" or "Grandpa." The fact that, for example, a younger male might call an older female friend "Big Sister" (*dajie*) does not imply that the relationship is meant as a substitute, or even an extension, of actual kin relations. What these relationships do suggest are the kinds of parallels among these different networks—in terms of age, gender, or generation, for example—and the principles that define the responsibilities and obligations of the people involved.

The social networks that connect classmates provide a good example of both the parallels between kin and other kinds of social relations, and of the nested-box quality of social relations in general. Although elementary school is obligatory for all children, the kind of school a child attends depends in large part on his or her family background and academic abilities. Children who attend local village schools often know their classmates in other contexts, as well, and the school relationship simply adds another dimension to an existing relationship. Children in urban areas who are sent to specific schools in order to build a foundation for future academic endeavors begin to establish a different kind of social network. As their education progresses, however, children are channeled into schools that are believed to match their abilities and talents.

There, they encounter others who share similar talents and interests, and who they will likely eventually encounter in a professional context. As students move into higher education, they become part of a highly select group, drawn together from various places and family backgrounds to prepare for their future as educated professionals. The networks of relationships that are formed in this context produce extremely strong lifelong ties and loyalties. Unlike the alumni associations of U.S. universities, which are formal networks built on a sense of loyalty to an alma mater, relationships among Chinese students form an informal network that grows out of shared interests, experiences, and expectations.

For those who do not attend college, important networks are built in the workplace or work unit, especially when people have recently migrated from a rural to an urban area. Residence in a workers' dormitory or other kinds of shared housing, the rhythms of daily life and work schedules, and the shared experience of the work that they are doing all contribute to establishing relationships of mutual dependence and obligation. Much like college students, young factory workers or shop clerks may use kin terms, such as "brother" or "sister," to define and express the nature of their relationship. But these networks often do not endure in the same manner as the networks established by college students, in part because they grow out of the

People walk past a billboard encouraging couples to have only one child. The one-child policy, as it is known in the Western world, refers to the regulations concerning birth control in China. (Corel)

activities of daily life, rather than out of shared academic experiences or intellectual interests.

In recent decades, the Chinese government instituted the One-Child Policy in order to curb the very rapid growth of the population. Families were limited to one child, a rule that was enforced by requiring parents to pay for medical care, schooling, and other needs for additional children. This policy, however, has also had an effect on social networks. In a culture where family is always the first priority, and extended family provides a ready-made extended social network, the One-Child Policy has reshaped the nature of social networks in China in ways that are not yet wholly apparent. Some studies have suggested that only children become spoiled after being the center of attention for six adults—mother, father, and two sets of grandparents (a dynamic often referred to as "four-two-one" in Chinese). Other studies suggest that these children are smarter, more focused, and well rounded because families have sufficient resources for a better education and a more sophisticated lifestyle. Although the first full generation to be born under this policy is just now coming of age, it is difficult to assess the long-term impact of a society full of sibling-less children. Yet, it is clear that extended social networks, whether formed through school, work, or local communities, will become increasingly important. Certainly, the extensive use of terms like brother, sister, or auntie will shift as the kin relations become more limited. That is why the principles that define relationships, rather than the relationships themselves, are so important for understanding social networks and social behavior in China.

SOCIAL RELATIONSHIPS—PRACTICAL ETIQUETTE IN CHINESE SOCIAL SITUATIONS

It is important to understand the role of the family and an individual's wider social context if one is to act with composure in Chinese social situations. Books on etiquette in Chinese social situations often give only prescriptive advice ("Don't blow your nose;" "Don't be aggressive") without providing the wider context for why such behavior might be considered offensive. The preceding paragraphs should help the reader to understand the deeper cultural context for social etiquette in China, and to realize how each of the components below fits into the larger whole of social harmony.

By now, the reader's understanding of Chinese history, economics, politics, and society has surely improved, yet there remains the practical challenge of traveling in China without giving offense through blunders in etiquette or, from another perspective, needlessly taking offense at behavior rooted in cultural differences. The following advice will serve a reader well in her travels in China. It represents a beginning cultural grammar that can be built upon as travelers get to know China better. First, let us start by comparing and contrasting China and the United States. As we have seen in this book, China has a very long history and an ancient culture that has evolved over thousands of years, and of which the Chinese are very proud. The United States has a very short history by Chinese standards (it was settled in the Qing dynasty, China's last imperial era) and has a constantly changing, evolving culture born of immigrant interaction. Chinese society is strongly based on hierarchical relationships, and (as we have seen) almost 60 years of Communist rule has not eliminated the importance attached to knowing one's place in the family, in personal networks, and in the larger society.

U.S. society is relatively egalitarian, in principle, where economic and social mobility based on ability is believed to be both possible and desirable. Chinese society relies on personal relationships and networks to achieve personal ends to a much greater extent than U.S. society, which relies much more, in both theory and practice, on rules and laws that are ideally applied impersonally and fairly to all people. Finally, communication in China is much more indirect and face saving, whereas frank, direct speech is—at least in principle—more highly valued in the United States.

Considering these contrasts, we can easily imagine the unintended insult that typical behavior in the United States might produce in China, and vice versa. A businessperson from the United States, who is well respected at home for frankness and being a "straight shooter," might well be considered rude, overbearing, and uncultured in China. Polite, circumspect, face-saving behavior in China might seem indecisive or even dishonest in an American context. Chinese and Americans both have distinctive patterns of communication and interaction, with many layers of experience and memory, that create vast cultural differences. An awareness and appreciation of differences in each nation's cultural norms and communication styles can help to limit misunderstandings and promote a richer set of interactions than would have otherwise been possible.

Saving Face

The key to good relationships and good communication in China is respect. People in China place great weight upon "face"—attaining and maintaining self-respect and the respect of others. "Saving face" is of paramount importance in China, and in the East Asian world in general. Face consists of reputation, trust, and influence—how one appears and wants to appear to others. It depends upon social position, personal ability, economic status, and social ties. But, above all, face depends upon how others treat you. If you cause someone to lose face, then you have behaved rudely and have lost face, as well. The following activities or gestures threaten a person's face and may provoke shock, embarrassment, and defensive reactions:

Being openly challenged
Being openly disagreed with
Being openly criticized
Being openly denied

When communicating a "no" to someone in China, one should be less direct than is normal in the United States. How do you say "no" or even know when a request of yours has been denied? The following phrases avoid a blunt denial, saving face while leaving open future possibilities. They will blend so nicely into the flow of your interactions in China that they will soon become second nature.

We'll see what we can do.
We'll do our best.
Let us think about it.
It may be difficult.
We'll try.
Let us talk about that later.
We need to discuss this with my supervisor.

If a conflict does arise, one should avoid reactions that cause a loss of face. In particular, avoid finger pointing or assigning blame. In addition, avoid losing your cool, no matter how angry you feel. This is not just a matter of being polite in another cultural context; it is a practical issue, as well. Americans in particular have a reputation (fair or not) for becoming quite heated in their interactions. The authors of this volume have all seen the effect—the official taking abuse from a foreigner becomes embarrassed, then shuts down, and sometimes becomes defiant, making all wrath completely counterproductive. Instead, a good strategy is to focus on common ground and seek a resolution without an absolute winner or loser. Particularly if you are involved in a conflict where you feel you are clearly in the right, diligently seek a face-saving way to allow your counterpart to correct the mistake. Direct confrontation will almost certainly lead to failure, even in a one-time situation. If one must depend upon the person being confronted in the future, it could be disastrous.

Names and Titles

The first name is usually the family name, followed by the given name of one or two syllables. For instance, in the name "Li Jianguo," "Li" is the family name that you would normally use with a title—Mr. Li, for example. In the United States, we address people by their given names much more often and much more casually than in China. For the U.S. traveler in China, the best rule is to address a person by his or her family name plus title, and to resist using first names until one becomes very familiar with an individual. Even in a friendship, it is better to err on the side of formality. In a business setting, it is always a good idea to exercise formality. One does not create a more fluid working relationship in China by being on a first-name basis, as we often assume in the United States. Doing so is, in fact, often quite counterproductive.

It should be mentioned that Chinese women in the People's Republic of China do not, as a rule, take their husbands' surnames. It sometimes causes at least mild embarrassment when a visitor describes a couple as "the Zhangs," as she might "the Smiths" or the "Johnsons," or Mr. Li's wife as "Mrs. Li." It is usually understood that foreign visitors might not understand this custom, especially since it is quite common in Taiwan, Hong Kong, and Singapore to take the name. Visitors should at least be as aware of the Chinese custom, however, as they are of the norms for such social encounters in the United States.

Gifts

The giving and receiving of small gifts is much more common in China than in the United States, and one can see evidence of this internal trade in the large bags of gifts—from cigarettes to local foods—that travelers carry after even the shortest of trips. When visiting China, small items that are distinctive in your region of the United States make good gifts, and you should be clear that your intention is to give the recipient a sense of your own cultural setting with the gift from your home area. Do not give knives or other sharp objects, clocks, white flowers, or handkerchiefs. Some of the contexts behind these prohibitions can be seen in the popular culture section, below. There is, in fact, a set of customs surrounding gift giving in China that is so complex that it can bewilder a foreigner. Chinese gift recipients certainly understand that you will not know all of the rules of gift giving, but pay attention to the clues you receive. Here are the three most basic rules: First, give and receive gifts with *both* hands. One will see this courtesy in almost every exchange in Chinese society, including handing over one's credit card to be scanned. It will go far toward showing one's sincerity in trying to maneuver through the rules of Chinese etiquette. Second, do not unwrap—or ask the recipient to unwrap—the gift in your presence. Third, if you later give a gift in return for a gift you have received, reciprocate with a gift of equal or (slightly) lesser value.

Eating and Drinking

Dining represents a social occasion that builds relationships and, as we have seen, is at the heart of social relationships within and beyond the family. Drinking is a social activity, as well, and foreign visitors sometimes cause confusion by assuming that it is an individual act. Westerners often drink as they please while dining, and assume that toasting is a formality. Pay careful attention to the culture of drinking on social occasions, and be aware that your companions will often seek to drink with you. For dining, the most basic advice is to learn to use chopsticks well, and—in the vast majority of situations—not to eat food with your hands. Western rules usually apply in

Western-style fast-food restaurants, such as Kentucky Fried Chicken or McDonalds, and one will occasionally see patrons eating Beijing Duck roll-ups with sauce and scallions with their hands. Even here, it is worthwhile to observe carefully, however. Even with what Westerners regard as finger food, Chinese diners almost never touch the food directly with their hands, preferring to use wrappers or utensils.

Certain behaviors may be surprising to Westerners. Expect your host or hostess to put food into your bowl (often reversing the chopsticks to their "clean side" for this purpose) or to fill your glass. Eat with a hearty appetite, but beware of cleaning your plate or emptying your glass, for each is a signal of continuing hunger and thirst. When you have had enough, leave some food in your bowl and beverage in your glass. If in doubt, follow the lead of your host and other guests. Finally, never stick your chopsticks into your rice bowl, even if you don't know where else to put them; it is far better to rest them on a dish or even on the table, but never stuck in a bowl of rice. A rice bowl with chopsticks in it represents a way of making an offering and conjures up the ideas surrounding death and family rituals. It does not fit well with the festivities of a meal.

Conversation

Because meals are social occasions, not simply times to "fill up the tank" or "strap on the ol' feed bag," good conversation is a necessary component of them. Conversation topics that are always suitable include family, the meal, food in general, shopping, the distinctiveness of the locality, and other topics of general interest. Open-ended questions that allow people to speak about their lives or their country are a good way to learn more and allow your hosts to show themselves in a positive light. Avoid initiating conversations on politics and religion, in particular, and do not ask questions, even if well intended, that might put a person on the spot. For example, many Americans may desire to tell about their country, but might be embarrassed to be asked about particular details of history and geography, about which they may be rather unclear. Seek a balance with your questions and answers; this is not unlike the balance found in a fine meal. Finally, you should expect an atmosphere in a restaurant that is *renao*. This translates to something like "hot and noisy," but it will quickly be recognized when one sees large tables filled with festive conversation and toasts, as well as children playing between tables and a busy atmosphere filled with movement, noise, and tables full of food. There is a line between liveliness and rowdiness in Chinese social situations that becomes easier to perceive with experience. The foreign visitor would do well to err on the side of measured liveliness, at least until she has spent enough time in China to interpret social situations more accurately.

Respectful Behavior

The norms of respectful behavior in China sometimes seem to be the exact opposite of those in the United States. As we have discussed, the frank and straightforward talk so often praised (at least in theory) in the United States can seem rude and dis-

Wenshu Monastery restaurant, Chengdu.
(Travel Pictures Gallery)

respectful in China. For example, a Chinese host will not praise a meal when he or she serves it, as we might do in the United States (for example, "I think you will love this dish"). Rather, the host will often apologize for serving such plain food. Further, you should respond to a compliment not with a simple "Thank you," as in the United States, but with counter compliments that the host will then defer.

Compliments are greatly appreciated in China, possibly even more than in the United States, and are used much more frequently in polite speech. However, Western visitors to China (and most other part of East Asia) will quickly realize that no compliment they receive should ever be allowed to stand without self-effacement. To wit, if you compliment a host or hostess in China for an excellent meal, the response will be "Oh, not at all, I am sorry I could not serve you a better meal." You, of course, would repeat your praise a time or two more to communicate your thanks, while your host or hostess would say, "Don't thank me," or "It was nothing," or make similar self-deprecating remarks. Be sure, though, that you are giving and gaining face by trying to fit your behavior to Chinese standards, and do not be like the American boyfriend in *The Joy Luck Club*, who agrees with his girlfriend's mother that her cooking was "a little too salty." Westerners might also find self-deprecation in Chinese contexts to be somewhat startling. It is not unusual for a Chinese man, if someone gives praise to his capable, efficient, beautiful, or intelligent spouse, to respond with polite denials. This remains in keeping with values of familial modesty, and is not meant as a criticism of his spouse.

The Chinese Art of Apology and Thanks

In China, the apology is used frequently. Sometimes, an apology may simply be part of a ritual—"Please excuse my poor English," a translator may say to you in perfect English. In Chinese, a request or question often is preceded by *duibuqi*—"Please excuse me"—serving merely as a polite sound. Other times, the apology may be quite sincere. You can use both types in order to follow local custom or to cover your ignorance and lapses in Chinese etiquette. No rulebook can describe all of the nuances of proper behavior in any culture, and even if it could, who could remember all of the details? Any traveler in a foreign land is bound to make mistakes. When you blunder in China, apologize.

"Please excuse me for not speaking Chinese, do you speak English?"
"Pardon me for bothering you, but do you know how I can find ____?"

Finally, Westerners might be somewhat surprised that they are often perceived as being overly effusive with their thanks, and many Chinese are puzzled by being thanked when they perceive that nothing more than an ordinary transaction has occurred. To be sure, it is important to learn how to say "Thank you" (*xiexie, duoxie*), as noted in the language section, and one should always express thanks whenever there is a social relationship involved (having dinner in someone's home, being given a gift, receiving a favor, and so forth). It is always better to err on the side of thanking too much rather than too little. It is not necessary, however, to say "Thank you" after paying for a newspaper or a soft drink. Recently, a traveler who had a store clerk help him find books in an out-of-the-way corner of a little bookstore reported that he had said "Thank you for all of your help." The clerk's response? "Don't thank me; I did what I ought to do." As one spends time in China, one learns to say *zaijian* ("Goodbye") after a taxi ride or to nod appreciatively after purchasing goods and being given the polite standard parting words "Go slowly" (*manzou*). Learning to thank and apologize, much like other Chinese social behavior, requires persistence, patience, and careful observation.

REFERENCES

Eastman, Lloyd. *Family, Fields, and Ancestors: Constancy and Change in China's Social and Economic History, 1550–1949.* New York: Oxford University Press, 1988.

Diamant, Neil J. *Revolutionizing the Family: Politics, Love, and Divorce in Rural and Urban China, 1949–1968.* Berkeley: University of California Press, 2000.

Hinton William. *Fanshen: A Documentary of Revolution in a Rural Chinese Village.* New York: Monthly Review Press, 2008.

Mayfair Mei-hui Yang. *Gifts, Favors, and Banquets: The Art of Social Relationships in China.* Ithaca, NY: Cornell University Press, 1994.

Mobo C.F. Gao. *Gao Village: Rural Life in Modern China.* Honolulu: University of Hawaii Press, 2007.

Literature

Daniel Youd

INTRODUCTION: CONTINUITY, DISCONTINUITY, AND DIVERSITY

When people talk about Chinese literature, what are they referring to? Generally, they have a wide array of verbal artifacts in mind, from poetry to essays, prose fiction, and drama, all of which have been produced in various versions of the Chinese language over a span of some 3,500 years. Historically, the tradition begins with the oldest poems of the *Classic of Poetry* (*Shijing*), some of which may date to as early as the 10th century B.C.E., and it continues without interruption to the present day.

Two widely recognized aspects of Chinese literary history deserve immediate and critical comment: first, the tradition's length; next, its continuity. Both relate to the perceived perdurability of Chinese civilization, its values, and its assumptions. They also depend, in no small measure, on the unifying power of the Chinese script—as does the very notion of a unified Chinese civilization itself.

Throughout the millennia, the written form of the Chinese language has enabled a remarkable compression of both space and time because it is largely independent of phonetic change. That is to say, the use of Chinese characters has long encouraged inhabitants of a vast geographic area, many of whom speak mutually unintelligible dialects, to imagine that they share, among other things, both a common language and a common literary heritage. Not surprisingly, a palpable sense of the connectivity between the past and the present is an abiding feature of Chinese literary history.

The length and continuity of Chinese literary history should not, however, mask the fact that the canonical genres of classical poetry and literary prose engage in complex and even contradictory ways with the historical and cultural milieu in which they are embedded. When the canon is expanded to include the voices of more women and non-elites, as well as works written in the various Chinese vernaculars and regional dialects—to the extent that such material survives—the perception of the variability of the tradition will only increase.

THE CLASSIC OF POETRY

Almost all histories of Chinese literature begin with the *Classic of Poetry*, which, as already mentioned, contains some of the oldest poetry written in the Chinese language. Just because there is general agreement that the Chinese literary tradition begins here, however, does not mean that there is any agreement on exactly what these poems are or what they mean.

The poetry in the *Classic of Poetry* touches on a vast variety of themes related to life in early China. A large number of poems appear to be hymns that were sung in

---

CLASSIC OF POETRY

The *Classic of Poetry* is one of the five *jing*, or classical texts of Chinese intellectual civilization. Modern scholarship maintains that this collection of 305 poems reached its present form by about 600 B.C.E. Tradition holds that all of the poems were selected and edited by none other than Confucius himself. Under these circumstances, it is no wonder that the interpretation of the *Classic of Poetry* encompasses much more than the mere appreciation of the belletristic qualities of the poems, although many of them are remarkably beautiful, as the first two stanzas of the first poem in the collection demonstrate:

> Guan! Guan! cry the fishhawks,
> From an island in the river.
> Fair maiden, most demure,
> A fit match for a prince!
> Uneven grows the vetch,
> We pluck it, left and right.
> Fair maiden, most demure,
> I seek you while awake and in my dreams.
> . . .

---

the courts of Chinese feudal lords. These poems—or, more accurately, songs—were intimately connected to the rituals of ancestor worship. Other poems recount crucial episodes in the founding of the Zhou dynasty. One notably tells the legendary story of how the first ancestor of the Zhou royal house was born after his mother stepped on the footprint of a god. Some poems may have been peasant work songs. Some appear to be related to love, courtship, and marriage.

The exegetical tradition that grew up around this text stressed its political and ethical significance, often connecting specific poems—regardless of their original, or apparent, significance—with events in the lives of important figures from classical Chinese history.

Rejecting traditional interpretations of the *Classic of Poetry*, more recent scholarship has often focused on the text as a valuable collection of early folk poetry. Indeed, the poetry is rich with the imagery of farming and animal husbandry. Midnight trysts and mulberry-grove assignations are not uncommon. A handful of poems, moreover, give voice to the resentments many peasants must have felt toward their feudal overlords.

Despite traditional interpretations that find a political message in this poem, the poem is also an undeniably attractive love ballad. It describes a young man pining for his beloved. Perhaps, like the young man, the fishhawks on the island are also calling out for their mates.

THE SONGS OF CHU

The *Songs of Chu* (*Chuci*) is another early poetry anthology of great importance. The "Chu" in the work's title refers to an ancient kingdom from which this poetry is believed to have originated. Located in the Yangzi River Valley a considerable distance to the south of the center of Zhou dynasty civilization, this kingdom maintained its independence and own distinctive culture until the third century B.C.E. After the kingdom's political destruction, its unique poetic heritage—exemplified in the *Songs of Chu*—continued to serve as a counterpoint to the dominant culture of the north.

One of the greatest significances of the *Songs of Chu* lies in the ways that it differs—stylistically, temperamentally, and thematically—from the *Classic of Poetry*. The lush, fantastic world of the *Songs of Chu* seems far removed from the more austere and realistic concerns of the *Classic of Poetry*. Not surprisingly, the simple juxtaposition of the one work with the other is often used as a convenient shorthand to indicate the cultural divide that—perhaps even to this day—separates northern from southern China.

Judging from the *Songs of Chu*, shamanism was a key feature of this early southern culture. Of the various nature deities referred to in these poems, of particular importance were the water goddesses, who were believed to inhabit the many rivers and lakes that define the fecund south. Numerous poems describe how ritual adepts attempted to achieve religious-sexual union with these deities, seducing them with music, dancing, jade pendants, beautiful clothes, blossoms, and fine-smelling herbs. In these poems, shamans frequently undertake marvelous spirit journeys in search of their divine lovers. All too often, however, their love is rejected and their quest fails, as in "The Lady of the Xiang River":

> The lady does not go, she tarries.
> Who is it bids her stay on river isle?
> Mysterious beauty, finely adorned!
> Towards her swiftly I steer my cassia boat.
> I command the waves of the Yuan and Xiang to be still,
> and placid the waters of Jiang.
> I look for her, but she does not come.
> I play my pipes, but for whom?
> . . .
> I relinquish my jade ring into the river,
> And leave behind my pendants at the mouth of the Li.

This poem is perhaps best understood as describing a ritual propitiation of the goddess of the Xiang River—the "lady" of the poem. Rowing his boat onto the river, the shaman approaches the lingering deity. He recites a spell to still the waters. Next, he plays her music. Despite earlier indications to the contrary, she does not respond. The shaman then drops his ring and pendants into the river as an offering. Coy seduction, ecstatic pursuit, mysterious rebuff, deep yearning, and resentment: all of these themes, worked and reworked in many different contexts, remained hallmarks of Chinese love poetry throughout the centuries, long after their origins in shamanistic rite were obscured.

EARLY PROSE

The high attainments of early Chinese poetry were matched by developments of equal sophistication in two areas of prose literature: historical narrative and philosophical discourse. At first sight, it may seem unusual for literary history to concern itself with the qualities of either historical or philosophical prose, but from the Chinese perspective, both history and philosophy belong unquestionably to the realm of *wen*. Lacking an adequate English equivalent, this term is sometimes translated as a pattern or aesthetic refinement. At other times, it is referenced by the word "literature" itself. When applied to historical narrative and philosophical discourse, it indicates an intimate relationship between substance and style. As Confucius is credited with remarking, "If words lack *wen*, they will not go far."

Historical Narrative: The Records of the Historian (*Shiji*) by Sima Qian (ca. 145–ca. 85 B.C.E.) remains the signal achievement of the long and illustrious tradition of Chinese historical writing. This truly monumental work, embracing all of Chinese history, from its legendary beginnings up to the reign of emperor Wu of the Han (i.e., the present day for Sima Qian), includes the annals of various ruling houses, chronological tables, essays, and—most significantly—the narrative biographies of specific individuals. To this day, the biographies remain a touchstone of elegant classical prose style.

The circumstances of the composition of the *Records of the Historian* only enhance its greatness. The conception of the *Records of the Historian* began not with Sima Qian himself, but with his father, Sima Tan. As a clerical functionary in the court of emperor Wu, Sima Tan decided, of his own volition, to write a comprehensive history of China, based upon materials in the palace archives to which he had access. At his death, the project remained unfinished. Not only did Sima Qian inherit his father's official position, he also assumed responsibility for seeing this great scholarly endeavor to completion. As he worked on the *Records of the Historian*, however, disaster struck: by taking up the cause of a defeated general at court, Sima Qian incurred the emperor's wrath. The punishment was castration. In effect, this was a death sentence. Faced with the prospect of so ignoble a fate, men of honor were expected to commit suicide or beg for execution. But for Sima Qian, death was not an option. In his own words, he explained:

> The draft version [of the *Records of the Historian*] was not yet completed when this misfortune befell me. I could not bear that it not be completed, so I submitted to the most extreme punishment without showing my ire. When I have actually completed this book, I will have it stored away on some famous mountain, left for someone who will carry it through all the cities. Then I will have made up for the blame that I earlier incurred by submitting to dishonor. (Owen, 1996, p. 141)

Thus, Sima Qian devoted the remainder of his days to the writing of the *Records of the Historian*, "enduring [the] contempt . . . [of] the inferior sort of people," subject to grave misgivings concerning the course he had chosen for himself, yet adamant that his achievements as an historian would one day redeem him.

Ancestral temple of Chinese historian and writer Sima Qian, Hancheng.
(Zgsxyc/Dreamstime.com)

We would be wrong, of course, to reduce the *Records of the Historian*—a work of truly vast scope—to the details of its author's biography alone. At the same time, no one can read Sima Qian without calling to mind the dramatic events of his life. It is surely no coincidence, moreover, that many of the most famous and moving passages from the *Records of the Historian* depict conflicts of honor and duty, and touch profoundly on the meaning of death and fate.

Philosophical Discourse: It is commonly noted that the military confrontations among the early Chinese kingdoms paralleled an equally intense—if less bloody—confrontation of ideas. In this battle of ideas, words played an integral role. Over time and born of necessity, the forms of argumentation became more complex, as ideas were first asserted, next rebutted, and then defended. The effects of this process are clearly evident, for example, within the *ru*—or Confucian—tradition. Thus, in the *Analects* (*Lunyu*), or conversations of Confucius and his disciples, passages are usually very brief, even cryptic. They offer conclusions, but rarely do they provide much insight into the processes of reason and argumentation that must have been employed to reach those conclusions. Several generations later, however, when the views of Confucius came under attack from various rivals, Mencius, a staunch upholder of the *ru* tradition, launched a spirited and explicitly argued defense of his ideals. The result, the *Mencius*, is a text of far greater length and clarity than the *Analects*. It is also a work of remarkable rhetorical sophistication, showcasing all of the persuasive tactics that were common to the milieu of court debate, such as clever metaphor, argument by analogy, and the liberal use of apposite anecdotes.

With the refinement of the persuasive arts in the realms of both speaking and writing, a growing awareness of what might be termed the "problem of language" emerged, which was namely that arguments could be persuasive without being true. In other words, the clever use of language could deceive just as easily as it could illuminate. Among a number of well-known language-based paradoxes of the period was Gongsun Long's (ca. 325–250 B.C.E.) celebrated proof that "A white horse is not a horse." Some have argued that sophistry of this kind may have been little more than the early Chinese equivalent of a clever parlor trick. Nevertheless, in the hands of Zhuangzi, one of the period's most profound thinkers, such language games serve a far more serious purpose, while, at the same time, retaining their charm and wit. The epitome of both Zhuangzi's philosophy and literary style—the two are really inseparable—is found in his essays, such as "On Seeing All Things As Equal," in which the philosopher parodies the sophists' rhetoric to challenge the most basic assumptions that we make about ourselves and our world.

HAN DYNASTY POETRY

We turn our attention now back to poetry, which flourished in various forms during the Han dynasty. Court poets, such as Sima Xiangru (179–117 B.C.E.), were well known for their *fu* (conventionally translated as "rhyme-prose"), long and florid compositions that often took as their theme the praise of imperial power and virtue. In order to provide music and song for official ceremonies and the emperor's pleasure, the Western Han court also maintained a music bureau—the *yuefu*. Significantly, not unlike many of the folk poems in the *Classic of Poetry*, certain examples of Western Han *yuefu* poetry show signs of popular origin. By collecting verse from the common people, the music bureau followed a precedent set by the various feudal courts of the Zhou period.

The interaction between elite and popular culture during the Han dynasty had lasting consequences for the history of Chinese poetry. During this period, a new kind of folk poetry, which was formally distinct from both the verse that had preceded it and from the poetry of the court, began to attract the attention of the elite. We know of this poetry through a collection called the *Nineteen Old Poems*, likely dating to the Eastern Han. Here is the beginning of the first of these poems:

> I travel on and on, and on some more.
> Though alive, yet separated from you.
> More than ten thousand *li* divide us,
> each at one extreme of the world.
> The road between: blocked and, what's more, long.
> Who is to say when we will ever meet again?
> Horses of Hu lean into the north wind;
> Birds of Yue nest in southern branches . . .

In addition to being charming in their own right, the *Nineteen Old Poems* are the earliest extant examples *shi* poetry. One cannot overstate the importance of *shi* poetry in the history of Chinese literature. From its humble beginnings in the *Nineteen Old Poems*, it became, by the Tang dynasty, *the* dominant mode of elite literary expression in China. For this reason, some of *shi*'s most basic formal elements—already visible in the *Nineteen Old Poems*—deserve our attention.

A defining feature of the *Nineteen Old Poems* is the five-character line, as opposed to the irregular line length of the *Songs of Chu* and the dominant four-character line of the *Classic of Poetry*. In time, *shi* poems with seven characters per line also appeared. In either case, poets paired lines of equal length, of five or seven characters, to form couplets. When combined, couplets created entire poems. Rhyme lent an overall sense of unity to a given composition, most often at end of even-number lines (i.e., at the end of each couplet). Individual couplets also tended to exhibit different degrees of verbal parallelism, as in the following well-known example from the poem excerpted above:

A: 胡馬依北風
B: 越鳥巢南枝

Literal translation:

A: Hu horse lean north wind,
B: Yue bird nest south branch.

Translation:

A: Horses of Hu lean into the north wind;
B: Birds of Yue nest in southern branches;

The parallelism here is perfect, if rather simple. Grammatically, both lines follow the same pattern: adjective—noun—verb—adjective—noun. (The latter literal translation should make this more evident.) Note also how the words in parallel positions in lines A and B fall into the same categories—Hu and Yue are both geographical locations; horses and birds are both kinds of animals; leaning and nesting each convey a sense of "seeking refuge"; north and south are both directions; and the wind and tree branches are both kinds of natural phenomena. Within individual categories, moreover, objects and qualities may form identical or opposing pairs. Thus, Hu, a region to the north of China, is the opposite of Yue, China's southernmost region, and north is the opposite of south. Significantly, verbal patterning of this sort highlights relationships of separation and proximity and difference and similarity, thereby grounding the metaphor of the Hu horses and the Yue birds in the theme of the poem: two people at *opposite* ends of the world united in a *common* longing.

Over time, the formal features of *shi* poetry became more elaborate. Taking advantage of one of the distinguishing qualities of the Chinese language, certain kinds

XIANG YU

Sima Qian's account of the death of Xiang Yu, erstwhile contender with Liu Bang (the first emperor of the Han dynasty) for the imperial throne, is an excellent example of the emotional power of the *Records of the Historian* (*Shiji*). Pursued by the Han army to the banks of the Yangtze River, Xiang Yu declines a villager's offer to ferry him to the other side, saying:

"It is Heaven that is destroying me. What good would it do me to cross the river? Once, with eight thousand sons from the land east of the river, I crossed over and marched west, but today not a single man of them returns. Although their fathers and brothers . . . should take pity on me and make me their king, how could I bear to face them again? Though they said nothing of it, could I help but feel shame in my heart?" . . .

Xiang Yu then ordered all his men to dismount and proceed on foot, and, with their short swords, to close in hand-to-hand combat with the enemy. Xiang Yu alone killed several hundred of the Han men, until he had suffered a dozen wounds. Looking about him, he spied the Han cavalry marshal Lü Matong. "We are old friends, are we not?" he asked. Lü Matong eyed him carefully and then pointing him out to Wang Yi, said, "This is Xiang Yu!"

"I have heard that Han has offered a reward of a thousand catties of gold and a fief of ten thousand households for my head," said Xiang Yu. "I will do you the favor!" And with this he cut his own throat and died. (Birch, 1965, v.1, p. 121)

of couplets required precise tonal balancing in addition to verbal parallelism. For obvious reasons, this aspect of *shi* poetry is impossible to translate; it is even difficult for modern Chinese speakers to appreciate, as it requires knowledge of medieval pronunciation. It is adequate to realize, however, that the formal tendency of *shi* poetry to invest complementary and oppositional pairings with particular significance had a lasting effect on the Chinese poetic heritage.

ONE POET FROM THE PERIOD OF DIVISION: TAO QIAN

The years 220–581 define China's Period of Division. The first date corresponds to the dissolution of the Eastern Han dynasty; the latter date indicates the year in which the first emperor of the Sui dynasty brought all of Chinese territory back under unified imperial rule. For the roughly 400 years during which China was governed by a succession of regional dynasties, political chaos was a constant of Chinese life. Daoism and a newer belief system introduced from India—Buddhism—offered solace to many who were disaffected with their era. These cultural forces are clearly visible in one of the period's most important poets, Tao Qian (365–427).

Tao Qian, who is also often referred to by his sobriquet, "Tao Yuanming," remains to this day one of the most well-known of all Chinese poets. As a younger man, he held minor government postings under the Jin dynasty. At 35, however, he made a decisive break with his past: no longer would he strive for wealth and station. Instead, he was determined to seek a simpler, more natural life by returning to dwell among his gardens and fields. Tao Qian's decision was not unique. Chinese history and literature are replete with examples of those who, in order to escape treacherous times, retreated to the mountains and the hills, choosing Daoist or Buddhist reclusion over Confucian social engagement.

But Tao Qian's poetry cannot be reduced to political commentary alone; it is also the embodiment of an intensely personal vision of transcendence. Of equal importance are the ways in which it employs the developing resources of the poetic tradition to convey this vision. The following poem, number five in a series, is perhaps Tao Qian's single most famous piece:

Drinking Wine (No. 5)
I make my home in the world of men,
but am undisturbed by the sounds of horse and carriage.
How so? you ask:
My heart being distant, my place is thus remote.
I picked a chrysanthemum by the eastern hedge,
And off in the distance gazed on south mountain.
At dusk the mountain mists are radiant in the setting sun,
As birds on the wing return in flocks.
In all of this there is a profound meaning,
But when I come to speak of it, the words are gone.

At first, the first two lines of this poem seem to describe the consequences of the poet's withdrawal from political life. No longer a man of any importance, he has no visitors; gone, too, is the noise from the horses and carriages that these visitors would have parked outside his home when they came to call on him. The second couplet offers a different possibility: perhaps the poet is describing the conditions under which he took a mental retreat from the noise of human existence, while simultaneously continuing to live among his fellow creatures. This idea is illustrated in the third and fourth couplets, as the poet first draws the reader's gaze to the near-ground—the chrysanthemums—and then projects it to the distance—the birds and mountains. Whether occupied with objects close at hand or far away, the mind is always capable of finding repose. The last two lines are surely ironic: Tao Qian has not lost the words to expound on the true significance of his feelings—they exist in his poetry.

TWO POETS FROM THE TANG: LI BO AND DU FU

A recipient of universal acclaim, the Tang dynasty (618–907) signals a high-water mark in the history of Chinese literature. The range and depth of the period's poetic

After a bout of drinking, the Tang poet Li Bo (center) finds his balance with the help of two servants. (Julia Waterlow; Eye Ubiquitous/Corbis)

achievement is so stunning that it resists facile summary. Nevertheless, in the Chinese imagination, two poets, each with his own distinctive voice and poetic personality, have come to epitomize the age. They are Li Bo (701–762) and Du Fu (712–770).

Although he is now known as one of China's most famous poets, Li Bo was most likely of non-Han parentage. Evidence suggests that, in addition to Chinese, he also spoke Turkish. There are numerous theories concerning Li Bo's birthplace: according to some, he may have been born in Central Asia, whence he moved to Sichuan as a very young child. Others maintain that he was born in Sichuan, which was situated far from the center of Chinese culture. In either case, exotic origins contributed to his reputation for eccentricity and uncouth behavior.

In his poetry, Li Bo embraced a number of different roles, most notably the knight errant, the Daoist sage, and the hedonistic reveler. Sometimes, all of these personae combine in one poem, as in "Watching the Dancing Girls at Handan's South Pavilion":

Boys from Yan and Zhao sang and drummed,
While the beauties from Wei strummed resounding strings.
Powdered faces shone like the brilliant sun.
Fluttering sleeves spread out like flowering branches.
I offered wine to a lovely girl,
And asked her to sing me a Handan tune.
While pure notes of the zither hung in the air,

The hair of the girl cascaded down.
Where now is the Lord of Pingyuan,
That tadpoles bread in his palace ponds?
Of his three thousand brave retainers,
Whose name is remembered today?
If we fail to make merry now,
Worthy will we be of the pity of generations to come.

The atmosphere of the first half of the poem is one of extreme warmth and sensuality. Its emphasis on wine, women, and song is typical of Li Bo. But so, too, is the more philosophic turn of the poem's latter half. The city of Handan and its music cause the poet to think of the gallant Lord of Pingyuan, who established a reputation for providing generous hospitality to men of heroic virtue during the Warring States period. Li Bo deeply admired the martial ethos of these ancient knights, seeking to embody it in his own poetry and deeds. At the same time, his Daoist sense of the impermanence of all things cautioned him against placing too much stock in worldly fame. Rather than leading him to despair, however, these thoughts spurred him on to take pleasure in the moment.

For most readers, stark contrasts differentiate Du Fu from Li Bo. Li Bo, with his strong Daoist sympathies, is daring and unconventional. Du Fu is more timid and restrained; his sense of social responsibility is archetypically Confucian. The usefulness of this schema cannot be denied. We would do well to remember, nevertheless, that the two poets evidently respected each other's work. Indeed, Li Bo's poetry exhibits moments of incisive social critique. Similarly, Du Fu experimented with fantastic images and a more heroic style, especially in his early work.

Above all else, Du Fu used poetry as a means of autobiographical expression. He captured his most intimate thoughts and feelings in verse. The major events of his life, therefore, are best related with reference to his poetry. One work in particular, "Traveling from the Capital to Fengxian: A Song of My Sorrows," is vital to our understanding of Du Fu. The poem describes Du Fu's thoughts as he journeys from Chang'an to visit his family in Fengxian. It is a masterpiece that combines many moods, from the apologetic to the self-critical to the outraged. Its conclusion is simply harrowing.

The poem begins with Du Fu recalling how he has spent his life to that point, just prior to the An Lushan rebellion. "How naïve in all I have dedicated myself to do!" he cries. As a young man, he had high hopes of passing the civil service examinations and obtaining a post in the imperial bureaucracy. Having failed, he is now a man of middle age, but still dressed "in commoner's clothes." As such, he is "mocked by old men, fellow students of my youth." He, in turn, is not above sneering back at "this generation of ants,/who can do more than seek their own holes." He is, moreover, appalled at the extravagance of his age:

. . .

In vaulted halls goddesses dance;
Silk clothes, like mist, shroud their jade-like forms.
Sable wraps warm the guests,

While mournful pipes harmonize with pure strings.
Plied, are they, with camel-hoof soup,
and frosted oranges stacked on fragrant tangerines.
From crimson gates, the stench of wine and meat;
While along the roads the bones of those who have frozen to death.
Opulence and despair cheek to jowl!
Disconsolate, I can say no more.

. . .

The strength of this prescient social criticism culminates in personal tragedy as Du Fu reaches home:

. . .

Entering the gate I heard the wails of grief:
Dead of hunger, my youngest son!

Sadly, this crushing loss did not mark the end of Du Fu's sorrows. Not long after he finished "A Song of My Sorrows," the entire fabric of Chinese society—already fraying at its edges—was torn apart by the An Lushan Rebellion. Du Fu was once again separated from his family. Stranded in the devastated capital city, the poet anxiously followed reports from the battle front and waited for news from home. His poems from this period are best known for the way they mingle descriptions of events of great national significance with the poet's own private emotions. "Spring View" is a representative example:

The kingdom destroyed, yet its mountains and rivers survive.
Springtime in the city: lush the grass and trees.
Moved by the times, I spatter the flowers with my tears.
Distraught by separation, the birds startle my heart.
The beacons of war have burned for three months;
A letter from home would be worth ten thousand pieces of gold.
I've scratched my white hair so short,
It almost will not hold my hairpins.

The final couplet exemplifies Du Fu's genius: with the "kingdom destroyed" and loved ones parted, there is indeed much that seems at the breaking point—that "almost will not hold."

CI POETRY OF THE SONG DYNASTY

In Li Bo's "Watching the Dancing Girls at Handan's South Pavilion" (quoted above), the poet depicts a common scene from Tang dynasty life: a man enjoying the company of a professional female entertainer. Indubitably, women of this sort sold sexual favors. But they also amused their clients in other ways: by singing, dancing, writing poems, or engaging them in witty repartee. Thus, offering a cup of wine, Li Bo engages a "lovely girl" to sing him "a Handan tune." At other times, it is quite

LI QINGZHAO

Li Qingzhao lived during the transition from the Northern to the Southern Song. Her father was both a scholar and an official, as was her husband, with whom she had an extremely loving, although complex, relationship. Her husband was a noted antiquarian and bibliophile, and Li Qingzhao shared his interests. After her husband's death, she wrote an epilogue to his scholarly work on epigraphy, in which she describes her family's harrowing escape to the south in advance of the invading Jin army. Along the way, most of her husband's precious books and antiques were destroyed.

Li Qingzhao's surviving work, although limited, is divided into two periods. Her early poetry is more carefree; her latter work, reflecting the change in her family's and the dynasty's fortunes, is more melancholy. In the following example, we find Li Qingzhao in a lighthearted mood:

Tune: "Rouged Lips"
Hopping off the swing,
She rises, and spreads her delicate hands.
Like a slender flower weighed down with heavy dew,
Slight perspiration penetrates her light gown.
An unknown man enters.
Wearing only socks and with hairpins all askew,
She retreats bashfully.
But then leans against the gate and turns back her head,
As if to smell the green plum.

likely that Li Bo asked similarly attractive women to sing him tunes of Central Asian origin, as they were very much in vogue then. Although these songs began as a form of popular entertainment, they gradually attracted the more sustained attention of elite poets, many of whom had begun to feel hemmed in by the regularity and seriousness of the *shi* form. For them, the varied metrical patterns of popular song offered new possibilities for poetic expression. To differentiate them from *shi* poetry, these new poems were called *ci,* or "lyrics." Li Bo himself wrote *ci* poetry, but the greatest practitioners of this art flourished in the dynasty that followed the Tang: the Song (960–1279).

It is important to realize that *ci* poets did not write new songs. Rather, they composed their verses by adding new words to old songs. That is to say, the corpus of *ci* poetry is constructed from a number—albeit a fairly large number—of specific tunes. The tunes are known by generic titles that may or may not have a bearing on the content of the poem. The real significance of the title is that it indicates meter. The irregularity of line length within a given *ci* poem certainly allowed for a greater latitude of expression than sometimes seemed possible with the uniform five- or seven-character format of the *shi*. The form of each *ci* tune remained, nevertheless, prescribed.

The subject matter of *ci* poetry could be greatly varied. Reflecting its origins as a form of popular entertainment, however, themes of love, longing, delight, and loss were perennial favorites. In addition, since these songs were originally sung by female entertainers, when male poets wrote *ci* lyrics, they often adopted a female voice. It seems eminently appropriate, then, that one of the great *ci* poets of the Song dynasty was a woman: Li Qingzhao (ca. 1084–1151). Her poetic feat was to re-appropriate the genre's affectation of female subjectivity and make it her own.

What is so delightful—even shocking—about this poem is how the poet combines feigned—or is it real?—naïveté with brash eroticism. One cannot tell if Li Qingzhao is depicting a young virgin's flight from a potential ravisher or a scene of seduction. The ambiguity is intentional.

FICTION: TALES AND SHORT STORIES

The closest word in the native Chinese vocabulary for "fiction" is *xiaoshuo*, which translates literally as "trivial chatter." From this point of view, poetry and the higher genres of prose—narrative history, philosophical discourse, the literary essay, and the like—define the literary tradition. Starting as early as the Ming dynasty (1368–1644), however, a small number of literary historians began to offer a contrary perspective. For them, *xiaoshuo* was a vital form of literary expression. Taking their lead from these early pioneers, modern scholars have moved decisively to place the various genres of the *xiaoshuo* more squarely at the center of the Chinese literary heritage. Fully developed narrative fiction appears for the first time in the Tang dynasty in both the literary and vernacular forms of the Chinese language.

Tang Classical Tales

Tang dynasty classical tales are so designated in English because they were written in a refined literary idiom that bore little or no resemblance to the spoken Chinese of the day. In Chinese, such tales are known as *chuanqi*, or "stories that transmit the remarkable." Just what makes a Tang classical tale remarkable? In many cases, they narrate supernatural events; in others, they depict strange twists of fate, or exceptional acts of selflessness. Still others deal with that most remarkable force of all: love.

Indeed, the single most famous Tang classical tale is a melancholy love story: Yuan Zhen's (779–831) "Yingying's Story" (*Yingying zhuan*). The story tells how a certain young man, Zhang, initiates a passionate affair with the beautiful and sensitive Yingying. The lovers' idyll is cut short when Zhang must travel to Chang'an to take the imperial civil service examinations. On their last night together, Yingying releases Zhang from his pledge of fidelity to her. More than a year passes. Zhang fails his examination, but remains in the capital. Eventually, both Zhang and Yingying marry other people.

"Yingying's Story" is a tour de force of psychological realism that is thoroughly grounded in the details of mid-Tang life. Since the story is reputed to be auto-biographical, the author's rather unflattering portrait of the faithless hero is also noteworthy. As with many other *chuanqi*, "Yingying's Story" was retold many times. Most famously, it provided the source material for Wang Shifu's *The Romance of the Western Wing* (*Xixiang ji*). A romantic comedy for the stage, Wang's play—while a masterpiece in its own right—retains only a tenuous relationship to the original.

Transformation Texts

In the context of Chinese literary history, the term "vernacular literature" designates a corpus of texts written in a manner that approximates, to a greater or lesser extent, the spoken language. Classical—or, more precisely, literary—Chinese was maintained as a written standard until the early part of the 20th century, and the formal characteristics of vernacular literature must be understood in this context. Whereas the literary language is pithy and allusive, the vernacular tends to be less compact and more explicit.

The written vernacular was also less prestigious than the literary form of the language. As a result, less care was taken to preserve texts written in this form. In fact, the earliest extant examples of vernacular fiction that survive have been transmitted to the present day by chance. These texts—the so-called *bianwen*, or "transformation texts"—were discovered with a hoard of other manuscripts in a hidden cave library outside the western Chinese oasis town of Dunhuang. They date to the Tang dynasty.

Bianwen are sometimes referred to as "prosimetric" fictional texts because, formally, they consist of alternating section of prose and verse. While the connection is not completely clear, the transformation texts are related in some manner—whether as scripts or as transcriptions of performances—to a kind of oral storytelling that employed illustrations—*bianxiang*, or "transformation images." Some surviving transformation texts retell stories from the indigenous Chinese tradition, but others showcase Buddhist narratives. One of the most significant *bianwen*—"The Transformation Text on Mulian Rescuing his Mother from Hell"—provides unique insight into the processes of cultural accommodation and appropriation that characterized the Chinese experience with Buddhism. The hero of the story, Mulian—or "Mahāmaudgalyāna" in Sanskrit—is an Indian Buddhist monk who is moved by filial piety—that quintessentially Chinese virtue—to seek out his sinful mother in hell and free her from its torments.

Ming and Qing Vernacular Stories

Before the fortunate rediscovery of Tang dynasty transformation texts, stories printed in the Yuan and early Ming dynasties were believed to be some of the earliest surviving examples of vernacular fiction. A number of these stories—for example, those set in the Northern and Southern Song capitals of Kaifeng and Hangzhou—may have even earlier origins. Elite interest in this previously marginalized form of literature expanded in the 16th and 17th centuries. Connoisseurs collected and edited older stories; a large number of literary men of the period also wrote new ones.

The basic narrative model of the vernacular short story derives from the context of oral storytelling. As narrators build suspense, dispense advice, and pass moral judgment on the characters in their stories, they adopt the persona of the oral story teller addressing an audience of teahouse patrons. It is important to realize, however, that this is a fictional conceit. Vernacular short stories are the product of a written, not oral, literary culture.

The thematic range of the vernacular short story was broad: collections include ghost stories, heroic legends, and Daoist and Buddhist hagiography. Other stories have a more mundane focus, centering on the lives of merchants, trades people, and the lower level literati. Deeply enmeshed in the sophisticated urban society that had taken root in China in the Southern Song and that had experienced a revival and expansion in the mid- to late Ming, these stories display a keen interest in the circumstantial realities of daily life. Crime narratives and love stories are common, and characters are regularly swayed to ill-considered action by greed and lust. Unashamedly didactic, these stories are governed by a strict morality, the guiding concept of which is the notion of *bao*, or "recompense": all good and bad deeds receive their just rewards.

DRAMA

Chinese drama stands at the intersection of fiction and poetry, combining elements of both. As with fiction, the drama has a long and complicated pre-history, which, due to space limitations, cannot be rehearsed here. For our purposes, we will pick up the story in the Yuan dynasty (1279–1368), as it was during this period that various performance traditions first merged to form a fully realized dramatic literature: *zaju*, or variety plays.

Zaju

A typical variety play consists of four acts with an optional interlude—called a "wedge"—inserted somewhere in between. The two most important formal elements of *zaju* are the poetic arias and the (mostly) prose dialogue. In performance, the arias were sung with musical accompaniment by a single member of the cast. As is still the case with Beijing opera, actors specialized in role types: male roles, female roles, comic roles, and the like.

The composition of dramatic arias was not all that different from the composition of poetry. As you will recall, *ci* poets added new words to pre-existing songs. Playwrights did the same, except that the tune patterns they used—known as *qu*—were different. Individual *qu*, just like *ci*, could stand alone as poems in their own right. Not surprisingly, the most accomplished and prolific *zaju* playwright, Guan Hanqing, was also a virtuoso *qu* poet. In each act of a *zaju*, however, individual *qu* formed suites of songs that were, in turn, linked together by dialogue. The song suites were the most important part of the drama, and they were composed by the playwright. The dialogue, which was of secondary importance, was often left to the actors to improvise. As a result, in the extant editions of Yuan *zaju*, the dialogue has often been edited, expanded, or provided in its entirety by later Ming dynasty editors.

TANG XIANZU

Tang Xianzu (1550–1617), is best known for his *Peony Pavilion* (*Mudan ting*), a lengthy *chuanqi* drama. For many, *Peony Pavilion* is *the* definitive statement on love or sentiment (*qing*) in the Chinese literary tradition. The genius of Tang Xianzu lies in his ability tell a magical story in the most artful way, while, at the same time, investing it with profound psychological and philosophical significance. The plot of *Peony Pavilion* concerns a young girl who dreams of love, pines for her dream lover, and then dies. Meanwhile, the dream lover, who is an actual living man, happens upon the spot where she is buried. He sees her portrait, unites with her in his own dream, and exhumes her body. At this point, the girl comes back to life, and the young couple has the difficult task of convincing the once-dead girl's parents that marriage is appropriate. After much fuss, all ends happily.

Generally speaking, *zaju* plots overlap with those of the oral storyteller and the various genres of fiction. Some plays feature events from Chinese history. Others elaborate on episodes in the careers of legendary heroes and outlaws. Then, too, there are romances and justice dramas, which feature the sagacious and ever-upright Judge Bao. Slapstick comedy mingled freely with profound tragedy on the Yuan stage, and many see a strong strain of social criticism in these plays.

Chuanqi

The center of *zaju* performance was in northern China in the Yuan capital of Dadu, or present-day Beijing. During the Yuan and early years of the Ming, a different, although not unrelated, tradition of dramatic performance developed in the south, eventually becoming known as *chuanqi*. Not only does this dramatic form share its Chinese name with the Tang classical tale, it also shares a similar set of plots. In fact, many *chuanqi* plays are based directly on Tang classical tales.

Chuanqi drama differs from *zaju* in a number of ways. First, there was no restriction on *chuanqi* length; plays of 50 to 60 scenes are quite common. (As the performance of an entire work in a reasonable period of time became impossible, a tradition of performing selected scenes arose.) Second, the requirement that only one character per play could sing, which was typical of the *zaju*, was abandoned. In the *chuanqi*, everyone could sing, and they could sing to and with each other. Finally, as a result of the aforementioned two differences, *chuanqi* plots reached a new level of complexity—or convolution—and sophistication. During the late Ming and early Qing, the genre became the perfect vehicle for effervescent romantic comedy.

MING AND QING NOVELS

Traditionally, six novels from the Ming and Qing dynasties are singled out as undisputed masterpieces. They are: *Romance of the Three Kingdoms* (*Sanguo yanyi*);

Outlaws of the Marsh (*Shuihu zhuan*); *Journey to the West* (*Xiyou ji*); *The Plum in the Golden Vase* (*Jin Ping Mei*); *The Scholars* (*Rulin waishi*); and *Dream of the Red Chamber* (*Honglou meng*). Like the vernacular short stories discussed above, almost all of these novels are written in a variety of vernacular Chinese, with the exception of *Romance of the Three Kingdoms*. Like the short stories, these novels also rely on the simulated rhetoric of oral storytelling for their narrative model. They are, nevertheless, products of literati culture and, despite their frequent use of more popular sources, reflect literati values.

Dream of the Red Chamber, also known as *Story of the Stone* (*Shitou ji*), is the single most important masterpiece in the Chinese novel category. A work of immense complexity, the novel offers readers an encyclopedic depiction of 18th-century Chinese society. Its author, Cao Xueqin (c. 1715–c. 1763), came from an extremely wealthy family that had distinguished itself in the service of the Kangxi emperor. Sometime during Cao's youth, however, the family ran afoul of Kangxi's successor, the Yongzheng emperor, and their wealth and property were confiscated. Cao Xueqin alludes to his former life of luxury in this psychologically revealing explanation of the novel's genesis:

> Having made an utter failure of my life, I found myself one day, in the midst of my poverty and wretchedness, thinking about the female companions of my youth. As I went over them one by one, examining and comparing them in my mind's eye, it suddenly came over me that those slips of girls—which is all they were then—were in every way, both morally and intellectually, superior to the 'grave and mustachioed signior' I am now supposed to have become. The realization brought with it an overpowering sense of shame and remorse, and for a while I was plunged in the deepest despair. There and then I resolved to make a record of all the recollections of those days I could muster—those golden days when I dressed in silk and ate delicately, when we still nestled in the protecting shadow of the Ancestors and Heaven still smiled on us. (Cao, 1973–1986, v.1, p. 20)

Not surprisingly, the novel's hero, Jia Baoyu, bears a certain resemblance to Cao Xueqin himself, and Jia Baoyu's female companions are assumed to have been drawn from the "slips of girls" mentioned above. Despite these compelling autobiographic connections, the novel is also a clever recasting of *The Plum in the Golden Vase*'s story of family disintegration—condemned by some as pornographic—into a more refined register. Similarly, the novel's obsession with the intricacies of sentiment hearkens back to Tang Xianzu's *Peony Pavilion* and other touchstones of the romantic tradition. After working on his novel for a decade, Cao Xueqin died in 1763, his masterpiece unfinished.

THE MODERN AND CONTEMPORARY PERIODS

Since the First Opium War (1839–1842), China's response to and interaction with the Western world has became a dominant theme in its history. Some mid-19th-century literary works, while still adhering to traditional generic conventions, depict changes

Chinese novelist Mo Yan. (Sophie Bassouls/Corbis)

in Chinese society, including the devastating effects of widespread opium addiction among the Chinese population.

The influence of European and American literary works on Chinese writers became particularly strong in the late 19th and early 20th century as more translations became available. In fact, one of the earliest modern Chinese plays was an adaptation of Harriet Beecher Stowe's *Uncle Tom's Cabin*, which was first performed in 1907, under the title *Heinu yu tian lu* (*The Black Slave's Appeal to Heaven*). Themes such as political reform and self choice in marriage (as opposed to arranged marriage) became prominent in the literature of the period.

One of the most significant trends in late-19th and early-20th-century Chinese literary history was the rejection of the classical, or literary, language in favor of a new vernacular style in both fiction and poetry. Not only an issue of literary style, the triumph of the vernacular language also represented a refutation of the Chinese cultural and political tradition as a whole, which was seen by many as irredeemably corrupt and decadent.

One of the most important advocates and practitioners of the new vernacular literary style was Lu Xun (1881–1936). His masterful short stories and essays in social and literary criticism have earned him a reputation as China's most accomplished 20th-century writer. Other writers of note from the same period include the romantic poet Xu Zhimo (1897–1931), whose scandalous relationship with the already betrothed Lin Huiyin embodied his revolutionary literary ideals, and Lao She (1899–1966), whose depictions of Beijing life combine humor with searing social commentary.

While fierce pressure to conform to Communist Party orthodoxy dominated mid-20th century literature in mainland China, writers such as Zhang Ailing (Eileen Chang, 1920–1995), who spent most of her adult life in Hong Kong and the United States, produced fine works of great feeling and psychological subtlety. Since the 1980s, and the emergence of a more liberal political climate, a number of authors of note have appeared in mainland China. Many of their most well-known works have been adapted to the screen, including Mo Yan's (1955–) *Hong gaoliang* (*Red Sorgum*), Su Tong's (1963–) *Da hong denglong gaogao gua* (*Raise the Red Lantern*), and Yu Hua's (1960–) *Huozhe* (*To Live*). While some complain that the new commercialism and materialism of contemporary Chinese society threatens to undermine the appreciation of serious literature, writers continue to respond to the quick-paced changes in mainland China with creativity and insight.

REFERENCES

Birch, Cyril, ed. *Anthology of Chinese Literature.* 2 vols. New York: Grove Press, 1965.

Birrel, Anne. *Popular Songs and Ballads of Han China.* London: Unwin Hyman, 1988.

Cao Xueqin, *The Story of the Stone: A Chinese Novel in Five Volumes.* David Hawkes and John Minford, trans., 5 vols. London: Penguin, 1973–1986.

Crump, James I. *Chinese Theater in the Days of Khubilai Khan.* Tucson: University of Arizona Press, 1980.

Dolby, William. *A History of Chinese Drama.* New York: Barnes & Noble, 1976.

Edwards, E. D. *Chinese Prose Literature of the T'ang Period.* London: A. Probsthain, 1938.

Hanan, Patrick. *The Chinese Vernacular Story.* Cambridge, MA: Harvard University, 1981.

Hanan, Patrick. *The Invention of Li Yu.* Cambridge, MA: Harvard University, 1989.

Hawkes, David. *Ch'u Tz'u: Song of the South.* Boston, Beacon Press, 1962.

Hawkes, David. *A Little Primer of Tu Fu.* Oxford: Clarendon, 1967.

Hsia, C. T. "Time and the Human Condition in the Plays of T'ang Hsien-tsu." In *Self and Society in Ming Thought.* edited by Theodore de Bary. New York: Columbia University Press, 1970.

Hung, William. *Tu Fu, China's Greatest Poet.* Cambridge, MA: Harvard University Press, 1952.

Li, Wai-yee. *Enchantment and Disenchantment: Love and Illusion in Chinese Literature.* Princeton, NJ: Princeton University Press, 1993.

Liu, James J. Y. *The Art of Chinese Poetry.* Chicago: University of Chicago University Press, 1962.

Liu, James J. Y. *Chinese Theories of Literature.* Chicago: University of Chicago University Press, 1975.

Mair, Victor, ed. *The Columbia Anthology of Traditional Chinese Literature.* New York: Columbia University Press, 1994.

Owen, Stephen. *The Great Age of Chinese Poetry: The High T'ang.* New Haven, CT: Yale University Press, 1980.

Owen, Stephen. *The Poetry of the Early T'ang*. New Haven, CT: Yale University Press, 1970.

Owen, Stephen. *Readings in Chinese Literary Thought*. Cambridge, MA: Harvard University Press, 1992.

Owen, Stephen. *Traditional Chinese Poetry and Poetics: Omen of the World*. Madison: University of Wisconsin, 1985.

Owen, Stephen, trans. and ed. *An Anthology of Chinese Literature: Beginnings to 1911*. New York: Norton, 1996.

Plaks, Andrew. *Archetype and Allegory in the Dream of the Red Chamber*. Princeton, NJ: Princeton University Press, 1976.

Plaks, Andrew, ed. *Chinese Narrative: Critical and Theoretical Essays*. Princeton, NJ: Princeton University Press, 1977.

Plaks, Andrew. *Four Masterworks of the Ming Novel*. Princeton, NJ: Princeton University Press, 1987.

Schafer, Edward. *The Divine Woman: Dragon Ladies and Rain Maidens in T'ang Literature*. Berkeley: University of California Press, 1973.

Strassberg, Richard E. *The World of K'ung Shang-jen: A Man of Letters in Early Ch'ing China*. New York: Columbia University Press, 1983.

Waley, Arthur. *The Book of Songs*, 1937. New ed. New York: Grove Press, 1987.

Waley, Arthur. *The Poetry and Career of Li Po*. London: G. Allen and Unwin, 1950.

Watson, Burton. *Chinese Lyricism*. New York: Columbia University Press, 1971.

Watson, Burton. *Early Chinese Literature*. New York: Columbia University Press, 1962

Watson, Burton. *Records of the Grand Historian: Chapters from the Shih Chi of Ssu-ma Ch'ien*. 2 vols. New York: Columbia, 1961.

Wong, Timothy C. "Self and Society in T'ang Dynasty Love Tales." *Journal of the American Oriental Society*, 99.1 (1979).

Yu, Pauline. *The Reading of Imagery in the Chinese Tradition*. Princeton, NJ: Princeton University Press, 1987.

Chinese Art

Kenneth S. Ganza

It is as difficult to generalize about the arts of China as it is to encapsulate its political history, literature, or philosophy, except perhaps to observe that, like China's language, its art often seems unintelligible to the Western observer. The themes, media, structures, patterns, and purposes of Chinese art forms frequently appear to offer no familiar frame of visual reference to anyone grounded in the expectations of art as it developed in Western culture. In other words, when pressed, Western viewers of Chinese art will often admit that Chinese art looks odd to them, even if they can't exactly put their fingers on why that is the case. But just as those other facets of China's history—politics, literature, philosophy, language—are keys that can unlock our understanding of Chinese culture, with a bit of explanation, the visual arts can open doors to a deeper appreciation of who the Chinese were throughout history and who they are today as a result of that history.

A detailed examination of all of Chinese art through all of Chinese history is obviously too much to take on in this small space. But by dividing this weighty subject into three themes whose ubiquity and longevity dominate the overview of Chinese art history, we can impose an economical structure upon it without, one hopes, doing too great an injustice to its complexity and richness.

CHINESE ART AND THE SUPERNATURAL WORLD

Thanks to exhaustive work by Chinese and Western archaeologists and scholars in the 20th century, we know that the earliest expressions of Chinese art, like those from many cultures throughout the world, were intimately tied to ceremonial function, religious ritual, and communion with the world beyond death. The forms and the decorations on the objects discovered in ancient burial sites throughout China help to shed light on what the earliest cultures believed about life after death and what they deemed most important about that hidden world.

Ceramic wares from graves dating as far back as China's Neolithic period (ca. 5000–3000 B.C.E.), for example, suggest that the people who crafted them believed: (a) that material objects from the world of the living would be useful to the dead; and (b) that the unique context of the grave required special objects, employing technology and artistic craftsmanship beyond the level of the everyday. So, unlike the simple, undecorated, low-tech earthenware food storage vessels that archaeologists found in Neolithic dwelling sites, the objects recovered from graves exhibit more sophisticated ceramic technology and more elaborate artistic design.

This is most strikingly apparent in the painted earthenware vessels found at a number of middle Neolithic period sites in north central China. Exhibiting both abstract, geometrical patterns and proto-representational imagery, the painted designs on these bowls, pots, and jars offer important clues as to the spiritual beliefs and artistic predilections of China's earliest civilizations. The vessels are made of hardened, burnished earthenware, and the designs have been applied by brush. The intricate, flowing patterns of the abstract designs suggest an early preference for and mastery of linear motifs in Chinese art, and indeed, the visual power of *line* emerges as a dominant aesthetic force throughout Chinese history.

Representational motifs indicate the religious importance of the Neolithic vessels, for they depict designs that have been interpreted as expressions of shamanistic spirituality or portrayals of the supernatural creatures that populate the invisible world beyond the grave. The presence of this kind of imagery on ancient funerary ceramic vessels transforms the vessels themselves into sacred objects—things that

Neolithic storage jar found in Gansu province, China, about 2500 B.C.E. (Kimbell Art Museum, Fort Worth, Texas/Art Resource, NY)

have no function or meaning in our world, but which equip their dead owners with the passports they require to travel easily among the spirits of their ancestors and the beings whose likenesses are portrayed on those objects. Some scholars, in fact, have traced the roots of certain significant motifs and ideas in later Chinese folklore and philosophy to the beliefs embodied by the imagery on Neolithic grave pottery.

The predilection for decorating funerary objects with spiritually significant linear imagery survived from China's prehistoric period into the earliest dynasty for which we have recorded evidence—the Shang dynasty (ca. 1700–1027 B.C.E.)—but with dramatic advances in the sophistication of both the technology and the artistry. While ceramic vessels have been recovered from Shang tombs, just as they were from Neolithic period graves (though they were considerably more elaborate in terms of both aesthetic complexity and ceramic manufacture), a more spectacular expression of Shang spirituality through material objects is evident in the bronze vessels.

Shang society was apparently stratified into a rigid hierarchy, with the king as the sole occupant of the topmost tier. In this unique position of power, the king was the only mortal with sufficient status to offer sacrifices to the Supreme Being—his counterpart in the supernatural realm—on behalf of his people. In addition, it was the king's duty to solicit blessings and protection from his royal ancestors, again for the welfare of all Shang people. These sacrifices of food and wine were offered in vessels of cast bronze, which were also used in funerary ceremonies and buried with deceased royalty in their tombs. The artistic evolution of these objects throughout the Shang dynasty and the centuries that followed provides a barometer of the aesthetic development and philosophical change that characterized the early period of Chinese art.

THE YIN/YANG CREATURE

One of the most intriguing artistic clues about the nature of early Chinese spirituality is the existence of certain images that seem to combine male and female characteristics androgynously on single figures. Certain motifs painted onto Neolithic Yangshao pottery, for example, seem to blend elongated, angular phallic shapes with their visual and conceptual opposite, the circle. Small jade figures from the Shang dynasty have also been found to have a male figure on one surface and a female on the reverse side. Some Chinese scholars have termed such imagery "yin/yang creatures," after the philosophical female/male forces underlying the entire universe, which became such a significant component of Chinese philosophy throughout history.

The earliest Shang dynasty bronze vessels, dating from the 19th to the 16th centuries B.C.E., are notable for their relative paucity of decoration. When present, decorative motifs occupy only a minor portion of the available surface, and they consist primarily of abstract linear patterns rather than any kind of representational forms.

But by the time the Shang dynasty ended in the 11th century B.C.E., a significant evolution in bronze vessel decoration had occurred, in which designs became prominent rather than tangential and representational rather than abstract. Over the centuries—like ribbons of fog congealing into solid shapes—amorphous lines turned into stylized figures of animals or parts of animals, with some originating in our world and some existing only in the realm of the spirits. Shapes of fantastic creatures and fantasized animals represent the Shang vision of what awaited the deceased in the supernatural world. Their presence on funerary vessels effectively transforms those objects into spirit channels, bridges that link the shores of the living with those of the dead.

The Shang concept of the afterworld, though it paralleled the hierarchy of the earthly realm, emphasized the vast gulf between the worlds of the living and the dead and reinforced the idea that actions in the natural sphere could affect reactions from the supernatural. But during the dynasties that followed—the Zhou, the Qin, and the Han (11th century B.C.E.— C.E. 2nd century)—different views on the workings of the universe and the nature of the afterlife created changes in peoples' attitudes regarding the role of the objects that archaeologists had discovered beneath Chinese soil and, consequently, led to changes in their appearance.

Shang sacrifices had been performed in order to placate and influence a supreme being, a personal deity, albeit a figure whose specific characteristics were not outlined in detail. When the Zhou dynasty replaced the Shang, the Zhou concept of the divine replaced the Shang's devotion to a personal supreme being. The Zhou believed that the governing source of the universe was not an anthropomorphic divine figure, but, rather, an impersonal, abstract force—a cosmic principle of rightness that enabled the world to run its proper course simply by virtue of its very existence. It was not a divinity to whom mankind could appeal for favor through ceremony, and

Carving of a phoenix or crane. These birds are the symbols of good fortune and protection. In the Chuci, The Anthology of Poetry of the Kingdom of Chu, *they protect the spirit of the dead during the celestial travels. Eastern Han, 25–220 C.E. Wood. (Werner Forman/Art Resource, NY)*

accordingly one of the primary purposes for bronze sacrificial vessels was simply undercut.

The Zhou had adopted the conceptual practice and technological methods of casting bronze vessels from the Shang, but the change in cultural context meant a new usage for bronze objects and a resultant change in their appearance. While the Shang had used bronzes as channels of communication with the spiritual world, the Zhou transformed them into tools of political statecraft in the worldly realm. Objects that had once been offered to deities and the spirits of departed ancestors were awarded as symbols of alliance and political reward to clans whose loyalty the Zhou rulers wished to solidify. Their function was no longer religious but secular; during the Zhou, the decorative motifs that charged Shang vessels with spiritual significance evolved into patterns that were no longer recognizable as totemic symbols, but appealed to the Chinese based simply on their visual beauty.

It is possible to see the vestiges of Shang designs, stylized, abstracted, and bled of their representational qualities, in the decoration of Zhou vessels. Since these designs were created to please the eyes of the living, rather than to represent the spirits of the afterworld, the vessels themselves were no longer employed as funerary objects. Whereas Shang vessels were recovered from archaeological tomb sites, Zhou bronzes were, for the most part, discovered in treasure troves—pits in which noble families had hidden these trophies of their aristocratic status during the tumultuous periods of dynastic decline and widespread warfare. Visual luxury for the eyes of the living, not spiritual meaning for the realm of the dead, distinguishes Zhou decorative motifs from the earlier styles of the Shang.

Advances in the technology of luxury only reinforced the trend that the Zhou had initiated. More elaborate forms were combined with techniques of inlay in gold, silver, and semiprecious minerals as the Zhou dynasty gave way to the Qin and the Han by the third century B.C.E. The elaborate tombs from these periods have yielded remarkable discoveries, indicating that the tradition of interring the dead with special funerary goods did not dissipate over the course of centuries. But though the practice continued, a significant shift had occurred in the philosophy behind the practice. While the Shang funerary practices had highlighted the gulf between the worlds of the living and the dead—and accordingly fashioned goods for the grave, which served as a bridge between the two—the objects from later dynasties signify the belief that the familiar objects of this world will continue to have meaning and function in the world beyond.

It was held that the corpses of the departed needed to be supplied with the accoutrements of status and ease that they had enjoyed before death, and so later tomb objects are remarkable for the degree to which they duplicate the material culture of the living world; in this pursuit of realism, the physical form matches the philosophical intent. Whereas more ancient burial practices armed the dead for their journey through mysterious paths in an unknown world, the Qin and Han philosophy was that you can (and should) indeed take it with you. It represented a more humanistic view of the world, a view suggesting that human beings and their material possessions would continue to have a role to play on the stage of the afterlife.

The most spectacular expression of this belief is the famous collection of earthenware warriors interred as guardians for the tomb of the first emperor of China, the ruler of the Qin dynasty. Reproduced with meticulous fidelity to individual physical reality and assembled to replicate a Qin military formation, the underground army guards the emperor's tomb from the east, the direction toward which Qin's army marched on its path of conquest in life. On a lesser scale, whether they were designed in the relatively unassuming medium of glazed earthenware for simple landowners or in exquisitely wrought, costly materials like jade and bronze for the nobility, Han tombs continued the practice of furnishing their occupants with replicas and reminders of the good things that they had enjoyed in life.

Even today, in parts of China where traditional customs are revered, one may witness funerals in which special mortuary money, paper models of homes and luxury cars, or other status symbols are ceremonially burned for the afterlife benefit of the departed. Such practices illustrate the depth to which the ancient Chinese attitude about the afterlife is rooted in cultural consciousness and how it is expressed and served by objects of material culture.

NATURE IN CHINESE PICTORIAL ART

One of the most enduring themes in several facets of Chinese culture is a reverent affinity for the rhythms, structure, and metaphysical transcendence of nature. Shaped by the everyday realities of an agrarian society and fortified by philosophical traditions that explored the relationship between the natural world and the social fabric, Chinese culture found diverse ways to explore what nature is, how it looks, and what it means to mankind. In the visual arts, primarily the art of painting, we can think of nature as a barometer that measures what Chinese artists wanted to do, what they were capable of doing, and what they believed at various times about the function of art. During different periods of Chinese history, painters viewed nature as a motif to be decorated, a reality to be described, or a vehicle to be transformed for the purpose of self-expression or to make a statement informed by historical knowledge.

Chinese pictorial art was born in the context of Chinese decorative art. The earliest motifs depicting elements of the natural world are treated simply as such: motifs rendered with an eye for formal impact rather than for visual fidelity, and organized to create a surface pattern rather than to suggest the illusion of natural space. Precious metal inlays on bronze or stone relief sculptures lend themselves well to visual opulence, though not to pictorial representation, so Chinese craftsmen in the earliest centuries considered color, shape, and design first, and concern for natural reality secondarily, if at all.

By the fourth century, even when painting on silk with brush, ink, and color began to develop as an artistic medium, nature was treated almost as a pictorial afterthought, a stage setting to enhance a narrative whose primary concern was the figures telling the story. Some of the earliest examples of Chinese painting deal with subject matters drawn from literature or history, so figure painting, the artist's primary focus, achieved greater artistic sophistication sooner than landscape painting. Even when landscape was incorporated into early paintings, it was rendered not as it appears in the real world, but as it might look if it were shaped in the hands of a skilled craftsman: highly artificial, impossibly colorful, and unnaturally ornamental.

However, beginning in about the 10th century, a dramatic shift started to occur in the Chinese artistic and cultural attitude toward landscape and nature. At this time, the glorious Tang dynasty—a three-century period during which China could arguably have been called the most prosperous, powerful nation on earth—took its last breath. The fall of the mighty Tang taught a bitter lesson about the inevitable transience of human accomplishments in the grand scope of time, and as a result Chinese philosophers, writers, and artists sought refuge in nature, which is constantly changing but unfailingly constant. The 10th century, therefore, marked the beginning of a grand tradition of Chinese landscape painting in which artists developed techniques to render the majesty of nature as realistically as possible to capture an encounter with real mountains, valleys, trees, rocks, and streams on a few yards of silk.

In the Northern Song dynasty (960–1127), landscape painters like Li Cheng (919–967) and Fan Kuan (late 10th—early 11th century) produced virtual recreations of monumental mountainous topography on hanging scrolls and invited the viewer to lose himself within their painted paths. Never before this time had Chinese artists been so adept at affecting the illusion of solid, textured objects, separated by palpable space, and organized into visually logical compositions. It was truly an era of artistic realism. Visually complex and daunting in scope, these epic landscapes dwarfed

Detail From Going Up-River at the Qing Ming Festival, *Zhang Zeduan.*
(Pierre Colombel/Corbis)

the human figures or architectural structures that may be found tucked away at the foot of some grand mountain or in the hollow or some misty valley. For the artists of the time, they represented not only a physically realistic portrait of topography, but a more philosophically accurate expression of the balance between mankind and nature in the grand scheme of life.

The intense pursuit of realism revealed itself not only on the scale of majestic landscape vistas, but on the small scale, as well, for this same period saw the rise of intensely naturalistic representations of artfully posed flowers, birds, and other animals. This style of painting regarded nature as a source of familiar personal enjoyment rather than of imposing grandeur, and it was energized by the patronage of one of China's emperors, Huizong (1082–1135). The emperor was not only a patron of realistic painting, but one of its most accomplished practitioners. His incredibly precise brushwork and faithfully observed coloring created beautifully accurate representations of nature and served as an inspiration for other Song-dynasty artists working in this style.

Still other realistic artists found their inspiration not in compositions of flowers and wildlife, but in the activities of everyday people. Genre painting flourished in the late 11th century, reflecting the patronage of tradesmen, petty bureaucrats, and other members of what might be termed the Chinese middle class of the day. Artists who worked in this style have given us virtual, visual time capsules capturing the material culture of Song dynasty China, recording reality without editing or altering it for visual impact. Works such as Zhang Zeduan's incredible *Spring Festival on the*

ARE CHINESE LANDSCAPE PAINTINGS REAL?

A comment frequently overheard by visitors to China when they view its terrain is, "I feel as if I'm in a Chinese landscape painting." There is an otherworldliness in the impossibly craggy peaks, magical mists, and dizzying perspectives seen in many Chinese landscape paintings, which is only confirmed when experienced in person. But how much of the Chinese artist's vision arises from visual observation and how much is the product of imagination? Unlike Western painters, Chinese artists did not carry their materials into the wilds, set up before inspiring vistas, and capture what was before them. Rather, they rambled through landscapes, absorbing both the appearance and the feeling of places, so that when they returned to their studios, they could recreate the *experience* of nature, along with its outward form. Topographical reality could be expendable. Occasionally, it was important for the artist to record the literal layout of some location as a record of what he experienced while traveling. Other times, the artist might transform the outward appearance of actual topography to make it express a personal feeling. Frequently, the only way to discern the difference between the two is to read the artist's inscription on the painting.

River handscroll are mind boggling in their almost cinematic unfolding of physical detail. Such realism was the other side of the coin from the artifice of bird and flower compositions, but both sides reveal the prominence given to visual truth in the Chinese painting of the period.

Soon thereafter, though, Chinese artists began to regard nature with a more poetic than prosaic eye. Beginning in the 13th century, landscape artists pursued not the physical reality of nature in its vastness, but an emotional impression of nature with a sense of intimacy. While painters from a few centuries earlier described the appearance of nature in precise detail, artists in the later Southern Song dynasty captured the feeling of nature through suggestion, leaving as much to the viewer's imagination as to his eye. The human figure played a larger role in these portrayals of nature: the figures occupied more of the picture space, on an equal footing with the natural elements, and artists would usually find some way of drawing the viewer's attention to the figure. A popular technique was to frame the figure in the embrace of arcing pine branches or curved rock surfaces. The relationship between the human element and the natural landscape shifted from an imbalance that favored nature to a more equal and enjoyable partnership.

At the same time that landscape painters were crafting these monumental or poetic visions of nature, however, different groups of artists were planting the seeds of an entirely different view of the relationship between painting and reality, which would later have a revolutionary effect on the history of Chinese painting. One of these groups consisted of scholars whose primary vocation was within the government bureaucracy and who painted only as amateurs, while the other was comprised of artists who followed the Chan school of Buddhism (better known to Westerners by its Japanese designation, "Zen").

The former group was termed "literati" because its members' careers as government officials steeped them in the written word—official documents, records, memoranda, edicts, and reports. The culture of the brush-written word informed their off-duty lives, as well, for they prided themselves on their devotion to literature, calligraphy, and painting. The revolutionary idea that the literati introduced to Chinese painting was simply that the purpose of art should be self-expression rather than the faithful reproduction of physical appearances. They approached picture making as they approached calligraphy: just as everyone's handwriting is a unique expression of one's individual personality, a painting should not slavishly mirror some physical reality. Though every Chinese character has an objective, orthodox form, superior calligraphy does not merely copy that form, but infuses it with the stamp of the individual's interpretation. So, objects in nature might begin with empirical physical forms, but they should be transformed through the filter of the individual's unique personality, character, and expression. Their paintings of landscape, figures, or bamboo appear odd, amateurish, sketchy, and unfinished because their intention was to deliberately expunge any polished, picturesque, or emotional qualities from their work that, while attractive to the eye, hide the individual's hand behind a veil of physical reality. They introduced paper as an alternative painting ground to silk because its more absorbent surface was better-suited to inky, non-descriptive brushwork, and it was, after all, the staple of their everyday work as bureaucrats.

Chan Buddhist artists also rejected the reproduction of objective forms, but for very different reasons. At the heart of Chan doctrine is the belief that empirical reality is an illusion, a smoke and mirrors shadow of the true reality, and that when we cling to the illusion of outward form, we keep ourselves mired in a world of deception and desire, and so never achieve an enlightened experience reflecting our true natures. Like literati artists, Chan painters believed that physical realism was not only unnecessary in painting, but represented exactly what painting should not attempt. So, with quick, spontaneous, dynamic brushwork, they created human figures or landscape scenes that do not look the way they're "supposed" to be, because their images are intended not to please the eye, but to direct the mind to an understanding of non-objective reality. It is thus possible for a literati painting and a Chan painting to have a great deal in common while embodying distinctly unrelated artistic aims.

The revolutionary conception of painting as a means of self-expression became solidly entrenched in the Chinese artist's consciousness during the Yuan dynasty (1279–1368), when China was under the rule of the Mongols. Chinese literati painting truly came into its own during this time, while the creative torch of Chan painting was passed to Japan, where Japanese Zen students returning from China enthusiastically brought the technique and its canon home with them. Literati masters of this era, like Huang Gongwang (1269–1354) and Ni Zan (1301–1374), painted highly individualistic interpretations of the Chinese landscape that were so stylized by their personal brushwork that, in fact, it might be more appropriate to call them "inkscapes" than landscapes. Indeed, they are meant to be read not as visions of nature, but as the revelations of the artists who created them.

Literati painting never entirely replaced realistic, descriptive styles, but, instead, coexisted with them, especially in the Ming dynasty (1368–1644), when both schools

Jade carving discovered in Fu Hao's tomb. Fu Hao was a consort to King Wuding during the Shang dynasty and is reputed to have served as a military leader. Her tomb at Anyang was untouched when discovered in 1976. (Corbis)

enjoyed a fertile period of revival and reinterpretation. In fact, the later history of Chinese painting has often been characterized as a yin-yang rivalry between the scholar amateurs and the professional, naturalistic painters. The true picture is not as clear-cut, though, because painters from both groups were struggling with the same problem: paying homage to the past masters of one lineage or the other without relinquishing their individual creativity as artists. This dynamic artistic problem makes later Chinese painting a complex tapestry whose threads are still being traced and analyzed by scholars today.

CHINESE DECORATIVE ART

China has contributed some of the most significant technological developments in world history, including paper, gunpowder, the compass, and block printing, among others. At the same time, Chinese technological innovation has historically been combined with aesthetic sophistication to produce captivatingly beautiful decorative arts in a number of media.

Foremost among these is the rich and complex development of Chinese ceramic wares, from basic earthenware objects in the Neolithic era to the discovery of true porcelain and a myriad of decorative techniques employing pigments and glaze. As observed earlier, earthenware objects with painted decorations are among the earliest indications of Chinese belief in the special status of the tomb, for they employ a more advanced technology than any required for utilitarian objects, and they exhibit forms that exceed the demands of simple function. The earthenware objects from Yangshao archaeological sites dating to the third millennium B.C.E. were fired within a kiln to a temperature of about 1,020 degrees Celsius in an oxygen-rich atmosphere, producing a relatively hard ceramic body with a reddish color. A thousand years later, Chinese ceramic artists had mastered the use of the potter's wheel and advanced control of kiln temperatures to sustain levels high enough to produce thin-bodied objects that were almost sculptural in their elegance.

The first historically recorded Chinese dynasty, the Shang (ca. 1750–1050 B.C.E.), witnessed the development of three significant milestones in ceramic production, and it can be argued that all later innovations were simply extensions and refinements of these breakthroughs. The first was the ability to reach kiln temperatures as high as 1,280 degrees Celsius, a level at which the body of specially refined clay achieves a sufficient degree of hardness to be labeled stoneware. The special property of stoneware is that its denseness makes it impermeable to liquid, and, in some cases, the body actually vitrifies to a certain extent, which nudges it closer to the category of actual porcelain. Another aspect that adds impermeability to a ceramic vessel is the application of a glaze—which is, essentially, a glassy coating that helps to seal the body—and this, too, was developed during the Shang dynasty. The addition of a glaze not only makes a ceramic object more functional as a vessel, but it opens the door to an almost limitless range of possibilities for adding decorative beauty to even the most pedestrian of objects.

The third significant development in the Shang dynasty was a major discovery that would be lost and later reclaimed by the Chinese several centuries later: the production of a high-fired ware made from white clay and containing a high degree of a material called kaolin, which is very low in iron content. The presence of iron in clay is one of the chief factors that causes it to change color when fired. These white, hard-bodied, nearly vitrified wares almost fit the definition of true porcelain, and we are left wondering how the Chinese might have expanded on the potential of this discovery were it not for the interruption of cultural developments forced by the vagaries of historical change. In fact, though, it was not until nearly two millennia later, in the Tang dynasty (618–907), that the Chinese did develop a white ware in which the glaze was fused with the body, and thus porcelain was born.

It would take far more space than is available here to catalog the myriad developments in the decorative ceramic wares that the Chinese worked with, such as variations in painting, glazing, enameling, and other techniques. Perhaps the two that are most recognizable to Western eyes are the Tang dynasty tomb objects colored with energetic splashes of blue, green, cream, and yellow glazes and the refined porcelain objects of the Ming dynasty (1368–1644) that are decorated with cobalt blue floral, animal, and figural motifs painted beneath a clear glaze. But over the centuries, Chinese potters achieved virtually the full range of possibilities in the aesthetic spectrum, from classically elegant shapes in pure, restrained monochrome glazes, to robust sculptured forms in boldly contrasting hues of glazes splashed vigorously and spontaneously over their surfaces, to complex shapes abundantly ornamented with a visual overstimulation of pastel enamel. The technical and aesthetic brilliance of Chinese ceramic techniques spread influentially eastward into Korea and Japan, and westward into Europe. Collectors around the world still eagerly seek out Chinese porcelains and stoneware.

One of the decorative art forms most readily associated with China is the carving of jade, and this art also has a long and venerable history in Chinese culture. The word "jade" is really an umbrella term applied to two stones with different mineral compositions. One of these is nephrite, recognizable by its relatively matte colors and waxy surface, and the other is jadeite, the harder of the two, with a brilliant, glassy surface that better lends itself to intricate carving than nephrite. Green is the color we most commonly associate with jade, although brown and black nephrite and white, red, or even purple jadeite examples do exist.

Jade is usually classified as a semiprecious stone, but to the Chinese, it has always possessed a virtually magical property. Archaeological discoveries from the Neolithic era have brought to light jade objects with clearly spiritual, ritual significance. For centuries, jade was believed to have properties designed to promote longevity and even immortality. The spiritual cachet of jade never entirely disassociated itself from the mineral, even when, in later centuries, carved jade objects were more treasured for the intricacy of their carving and the jewel-like dazzle of their color. It is an extremely difficult mineral to work, often containing flaws around which the crafts-man must navigate to avoid losing his entire creation in one ill-directed movement of the carving drill. Some of the most brilliant examples of jade carvings are those that manage to incorporate flaws or color variations of the unworked stone into the finished piece.

Traditional-style porcelain production in Jingdezhen city, Jiangxi province, China.
(Ariel Steiner)

THE IMPERIAL PORCELAIN KILNS AT JINGDEZHEN

Richly blessed with the natural resources for ceramic production and conveniently situated near a major transportation artery, the town of Jingdezhen in Jiangxi province, near the Yangzi River, became a significant pottery center as long ago as the 11th century. It was the primary source for the stoneware and porcelains used at the imperial court, and by the 18th century, its products were being exported to Europe and influencing the nature of porcelain manufacture in various centers around that continent. It is one of the few centers of Chinese material culture that can boast that it served both emperors and the leaders of the Chinese Communist hierarchy, and it remains an actively productive manufacturing complex today.

Over the centuries, Chinese craftsmen have employed a wide variety of materials to create intricately decorative objects for the imperial palace or the scholar's studio: gold, silver, ivory, bamboo, glass, enamel-inlaid metals (known as *cloisonné*), and such exotic media as rhinoceros horn or hornbill beak. The inherent beauty of these materials and the skill with which those materials were fashioned gave the noble or the scholar a place of visual repose whenever he needed to divert himself from the demands of everyday life, and they may perform the same function for us today.

REFERENCES

Barnhart, Richard, et al. *Three Thousand Years of Chinese Painting*. New Haven, CT: Yale University Press, 2002.

Chang, Kwang-chih, and Pinfang Xu. *The Formation of Chinese Civilization: An Archaeological Perspective*. New Haven, CT: Yale University Press, 2002.

Clunas, Craig. *Art in China*. Oxford, New York: Oxford University Press, 1997.

Farrer, Anne, et al. *The British Museum Book of Chinese Art*. Edited by Jessica Rawson. New York: Thames & Hudson, 1996.

Li, Zehou. *The Path of Beauty: A Study of Chinese Aesthetics*. New York: Oxford University Press, 1995.

Rawson, Jessica, ed. *Mysteries of Ancient China: New Discoveries from the Early Dynasties*. New York: George Braziller, 1996.

Sullivan, Michael. *The Arts of China*. Berkeley: University of California Press, 2000.

Thorp, Robert L, and Richard Ellis Vinograd. *Chinese Art and Culture*. Upper Saddle River, NJ: Prentice Hall, 2001.

Wen Fong, ed. *The Great Bronze Age of China: An Exhibition from the People's Republic of China*. New York: Metropolitan Museum of Art, 1980.

Wen, Fong, and James C. Y Watt. *Possessing the Past: Treasures from the National Palace Museum, Taipei*. New York: Harry N. Abrams, 1996.

Music in China

Ann L. Silverberg

INTRODUCTION

All types of music can be heard in modern China. From karaoke to Western classical music, from popular songs blending hip-hop and rock styles to traditional music, which includes Beijing opera and a wide variety of ethnic folk song, dance, and instrumental music, the Chinese enjoy an enormous variety of musical entertainment. China has historically experienced a continuing flow of musical influences from within and without its borders in both the past and present, despite the fact that during various periods, outside influences were shunned. The long and diverse history of China has brought over 50 officially recognized ethnic groups together under one flag over the course of 5 millennia, with the majority Han Chinese now representing over 90 percent of the population. Since Opening Up (*gaige kaifang*) began in the late 1970s, the mix of musical styles in China has grown exponentially. Some of the current popular

Two Chinese men blow their suonas *to accompany a group of folk dancers on a Beijing sidewalk, during the city's first snow of the winter—November 1997. (AP/Wide World Photos)*

A CHINESE GOLDEN OLDIE: THE MUSIC OF TERESA TENG (DENG LIJUN)

A Chinese Golden Oldie: The Music of Teresa Teng (Deng Lijun)

Born in Taiwan in 1953, Teresa Teng became the darling of Taiwanese listeners and gained a great following in mainland China as well. Known for her sweet voice and sentimental lyrics, she toured widely and enjoyed Elvis Presley-like fame. Her song melodies continue to be well known and are omnipresent on Chinese karaoke lists. These include "Yueliang Daibiao Wo de Xin ("The Full Moon Is Like My Heart"), a love song with a waltz-like lilt. Teng was fortunate to enjoy her fame just as the Opening (*gaige kaifang*) began in the late 1970s, enabling her music to be heard and marketed in the People's Republic. She died suddenly in 1995.

---

songs heard in China would be almost equally at home on radios in the Western hemisphere, were it not for the Chinese lyrics; in fact, some popular music is identical in both markets: more and more Western music can be heard on Chinese radio and television than ever before.

Judging from the music-making that can be observed in China's municipal parks, and from the tremendous growth in the number of music classes and lessons available in urban China, Chinese of all ages seem to be more active in making music for themselves than many Americans. Small children take music and/or dance lessons in great numbers (with the most popular instrument being the piano), and on walks through city parks in many of China's metropolises, one can hear middle-aged or elderly citizens practicing music: a group of saxophone players here, a small combo of drums, trombone, and clarinet there, and several people playing *erhu* (bowed fiddle) in unison in still another place. Along a river or a canal, one can often hear someone practicing the *dizi* (bamboo flute). Recorded and broadcast music is pervasive in urban China, just as it is in the West, but the variety of music played in China is greatly enriched by distinctively Chinese sounds. This essay will introduce some of the factors that make traditional Chinese music sound uniquely Chinese, and discuss several types of Chinese music. In addition, this chapter will provide a simplified outline of Chinese music history, focusing on some of the musical types that are unique to China. Finally, it will mention some of China's most influential musicians and suggest a few sites in China that are of particular musical interest. The goal of this essay is to provide readers some basic knowledge about Chinese music that will improve their understanding and appreciation of it.

DIFFERENCES BETWEEN CHINESE AND WESTERN MUSIC

Why does Chinese traditional music often sound profoundly different from most Western music? In short, Chinese music sounds distinctively non-Western because it is governed by aesthetic, theoretical, practical, and musical-cultural Chinese criteria.

These criteria developed over long periods of time in ways that are quite dissimilar from Western cultures. Five basic factors make the bulk of traditional Chinese music sound distinctively Chinese, foreign, and exotic to listeners steeped in popular and classical Western music. These five factors are: 1. the pitches (notes or tones) used; 2. the vocal and instrumental tone quality (timbre) presented; 3. the musical instruments employed; 4. the combinations of simultaneous sounds (harmonies) and textures (simultaneous layers of music) heard; and 5. the manner in which music is organized (the shape or form of the music as it unfolds). Finally, the meaning of traditional Chinese music—its significance and its reason for existing, as well as its function in society—is, in many cases, quite unlike the meaning, significance, and function of music in the West, despite the fact that these concepts are very hard to define precisely in any society. In traditional Chinese music, pitch, timbre, instruments, harmonies, form, and meaning are manipulated in ways that differ significantly from Western music on the whole. For this reason, many Westerners find traditional Chinese music difficult to appreciate, understand, and enjoy, and they often consider some Chinese music, such as Beijing opera, unpleasant. Understanding why the music sounds very different to so many listeners can help us to begin to understand it, allowing us to hear Chinese music from a more informed perspective.

Pitches (Notes) and Melodies

One basic difference observed in traditional Chinese music is the use of five-note (pentatonic) scales. The vast majority of popular and classical Western music uses the eight-note (diatonic major) scale familiar to many people as "do, re, mi, fa, sol, la, ti, do" (ascending); in contrast, the more typical Chinese scale can be represented by the syllables "do, re, mi, sol, la" (ascending): only five pitches, without the notes "fa" and "ti," and with no repetition of "do" at the top. While this is an oversimplification, as one can certainly find traditional Chinese music that includes the "fa" and "ti" pitches, it is nevertheless true that the pentatonic scale is the most prevalent in Chinese traditional music. (It should also be noted that just as some Chinese traditional music does use "fa" and "ti," some Western music, especially folk songs, uses the pentatonic scale.) Tuning (temperament) is usually different in Chinese music, as the pure intervals of just intonation are often preferred to the equal temperament that is commonly used in the West. This type of tuning gives Chinese instruments a particularly clear, resonant sound, and it also means that certain pitches (such as "ti," when it is employed) may sound out of tune to ears accustomed to equal temperament. Finally, bends, curves, or glissandos (which smear pitches up and down) are prized features in a great deal of Chinese traditional music. These methods of handling pitches are not at all common in the West, where musicians are usually taught to sound a pitch straight on and stay on that pitch until moving to next pitch, at which point the musician makes a precise, quick change to a distinct new pitch. In traditional Chinese music, there may well be some blurring or sliding between pitches instead; in some cases, the second half of a pitch may be altered up or down.

Sound or Tone Quality (Timbre)

Sound or tone quality, also known as timbre, refers to the acoustic properties of tones (pitches) that make it possible to distinguish between instruments and voices, even when they produce the same pitch, permitting very fine distinctions between individual instruments and/or voices. Given sufficient exposure, most listeners can distinguish between a pitch played on the flute and the same pitch played on a trumpet, piano, or harp. A highly trained pianist or violinist may be able to tell individual instruments apart based on their tone quality alone. The timbre of the human voice is as individual as a fingerprint due to the uniqueness of each person's vocal cords in combination with other organic characteristics of the human body, such as the precise configuration of the lungs, mouths, lips, and so forth. Over time, cultures come to prize certain tone qualities in voices and instruments above others.

In vocal music (singing), and in instrumental music, traditional Chinese music has generally developed an aesthetic that favors timbres that are tense and nasal, rather than full and relaxed, pure and straight, rather than oscillating in pitch (technically, having vibrato), and bright—in acoustic terms, emphasizing higher harmonics—rather than dark (or emphasizing lower harmonics, resulting in more complex resonance patterns). Thus, voices and instruments in the higher ranges create clear, pure, and sometimes even piercingly bright tones that are typically produced without vibrato, and tend to be favored in Chinese music.

Chinese Musical Instruments

Chinese musical instruments have a long history; some are indigenous to China, while many others were imported long ago from other lands, and, in most cases, these instruments have taken on specifically Chinese characteristics as they have continued to be used in China. Historically, Chinese musical instruments were categorized into eight groups, according to the material from which they were made: bamboo, clay (earth), gourd, metal, silk, skin (animal hide), stone, and wood. Some instruments use combinations of these materials and, in some cases, it can be difficult to ascertain their proper category; thus, this discussion of Chinese instruments categorizes them based on the manner in which they produce sound: with blown air (wind instruments), through bowed or plucked strings (string instruments), or by striking (most percussion instruments). The complete Chinese instrumentarium includes hundreds of instruments, some of which are unique to specific ethnic groups, geographic regions, or time periods. Only the most prominent and distinctive Chinese musical instruments will be discussed here. These are the musical instruments that a visitor to China might well encounter in a tourist-oriented performance.

Wind Instruments

The *dizi*, or side-blown bamboo flute, and the *suona,* or Chinese oboe, are the two most commonly heard Chinese wind instruments. The *dizi* is held, fingered, and sounded much like the Western transverse flute, which is held roughly parallel to the ground, and slightly to the right of the player's body, with the fingers of both hands covering holes along its length. However, the *dizi* is made of bamboo, rather than of metal, and its sound tends to be breathy or buzzy and nasal, particularly because one of the holes in the instrument's side is neither blown into nor covered with a finger; rather, it is covered with a thin, flexible membrane that vibrates and adds a certain fuzz to the pitches produced.

The *suona* is sometimes called the "Chinese oboe," but because its sound is quite loud and its bore (tubing) is conical, ending in a metal bell, it might also be called the "Chinese trumpet." *Suona* players blow air through a pair of small reeds (paper-thin pieces of wood tied together) to create sounds that are amplified and adjusted as air is pushed through the rest of the instrument, much like the Western oboe. Overall, the sound of a *suona* is buzzy and bright: it may be likened to a car horn's beep. This instrument is commonly heard in outdoor processions and can also be heard in Beijing opera.

The *sheng* might be called the "Chinese mouth organ": it has the unique feature of playing more than one pitch simultaneously, resulting in harmony. Sounding a bit like a small pipe organ, the *sheng* looks like a small bowl with an array of pipes (cylindrical tubes) of various lengths standing up vertically inside the bowl. The lower part of the bowl has a metal tube attached to it, and the player blows air through this tube, with the air flowing into and across the pipe openings (inside the bowl). On the outside of the bowl, numerous finger holes (for the fingers of both hands) allow the player to change pitches by covering or uncovering various holes. The simultaneous pitches (harmonies) the *sheng* produces do not correspond at all to Western concepts of consonant (stable, sweet-sounding) and dissonant (unstable, harsh-sounding, or clashing) chords. The *sheng* adds a truly unique sound to the ensembles in which it is heard.

Bowed and Plucked String Instruments

The *erhu* (literally "two barbarian") is by far the most popular and commonly encountered Chinese bowed string instrument. Sometimes called the "Chinese bowed fiddle," the *erhu* originated outside of China, probably among the Mongolians, though it has been in use in China for centuries. Its name is thus derived from its origin and from the fact that it has two metal strings. The strings are attached to a wooden pole (neck) approximately two feet long, with pegs holding the strings taut at one end; the other end of the neck is attached to the body of the instrument, an octagonal or sexagonal wooden box that is perhaps five inches in diameter and three or four inches deep; the top side of the box is covered with snake skin and the two strings are stretched across the skin and fastened to the far end of the wooden box.

To play the *erhu*, the body of the instrument is placed on the performer's left thigh (players usually sit to perform); the left hand presses the strings to change pitches, and the right manipulates a bow that consists of horse hair stretched tight along a wooden stick and attached to both ends of the stick (like the bows used by Western orchestral

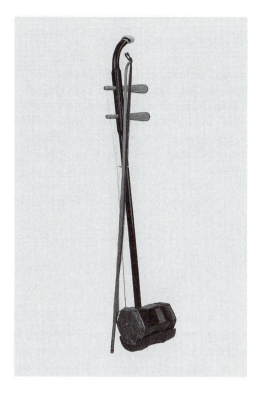

Erhu, *the "Chinese bowed fiddle."*
(iStockPhoto.com)

string players). The bow's horsehair is dragged across the strings to produce sound in a manner analogous to playing the violin. As with the violin, obtaining a good sound on the *erhu* demands careful control of the bow's pressure on the strings, its friction, and its speed as it moves across the strings; precise control of the left hand as its fingers move up and down the strings is also necessary.

The *erhu* is capable of great expression, and because the neck or pole has no frets, the slide or glissando is frequently heard between pitches and is characteristic of performances featuring this instrument. A large repertory of traditional Chinese *erhu* pieces exists, but an increasing number of Western pieces of music have also been adapted for the *erhu*. The *erhu* has many relatives that are both larger and smaller, with some found in ethnic groups within China and others in nations abroad. Most of the Chinese variants are constructed and played like the *erhu* and some have the word *hu* in their Chinese names: they include the *jinghu*, a high-pitched *hu* often heard in Beijing opera, and the *matou hu*, a *hu* with a carved wooden horse head at the end of the neck that is often used in Mongolian folk music.

Plucked string instruments abound in Chinese traditional music. The most commonly heard of these are the *pipa*, the *sanxian* ("three strings"), and the *yueqin* ("moon lute"), all of which are held on the lap and have hollowed-out bodies analogous to the Western guitar or lute. The shape of these three instruments is a distinguishing characteristic: the body of the *pipa* is teardrop-shaped; the *sanxian*'s body is oval or round, with a pole-like wooden neck several times longer than the diameter of

---

THE *GUZHENG*: GROWING IN POPULARITY DAILY

The *guzheng*, sometimes translated as "Chinese table harp," is a 21-stringed half-tube zither (resembling a long, narrow wooden box with a convex top) that has been played in China for at least 2,000 years. Played for entertainment purposes, the *guzheng* was often heard at court banquets; pictures from the Tang dynasty show female performers playing the *guzheng*. Unlike its relative, the *guqin*, the *guzheng* has wooden bridges that suspend the instrument's strings above the soundboard. Played with fingerpicks attached to one or both hands, the *guzheng* is growing more and more popular in China. In major cities, classes for children and adults can be found, and *guzheng* schools have been established in many cities abroad, including New York, San Francisco, and Chicago.

---

the instrument's body; and the *yueqin*'s body is circular (like the full moon), with a relatively short neck. Both the *pipa* and the *yueqin* have four strings. The *pipa* is a popular solo instrument in China, and is thought to have been imported into the empire centuries ago, over the Silk Road: its relatives in other lands include the Arabic '*oud* and the European lute, both of which have a teardrop-shaped bodies, though the *pipa*'s body is far shallower than the '*oud* or lute. The most characteristic *pipa* sound is the roll, a sound made by hitting the same string repeatedly with the fingers and thumb of the right hand; the motion is outward, away from the palm, and the technique is a great challenge to master. The *pipa*, *sanxian*, and *yueqin* are often played in ensembles with other instruments.

China is home to several types of plucked zithers, which are string instruments structured so that the strings stretch across all or most of the instrument's resonating cavity; they lack the solid wood poles or necks characteristic of the *erhu*, *pipa*, *sanxian*, and *yueqin*. The *qin* (or *guqin*: roughly, "old lute") is a plucked string instrument indigenous to China, featuring seven strings stretched over an oblong wooden box; it is deeply revered for its association with literature and the elite class of educated Mandarins across thousands of years of imperial Chinese history. Learning to play the *guqin* was a mark of cultivation and good taste in imperial times. Far from being a concert instrument, the *guqin* was normally played in solitude for the enjoyment of the player or in a small circle of intimate friends, most or all of whom also played the instrument. Because of its association with the upper class and with traditional literature (in classical Chinese), the *guqin* by and large fell out of favor in 20th-century China. The number of *guqin* students is now very small, although there are associations for the study of the *guqin* and its music in China and in other nations. Many Chinese landscape paintings (*shanshui*, mountains and rivers) show a gentleman on his way to a place of seclusion, accompanied by a servant carrying a *guqin* in cloth wrappings; some paintings of this type also show a *guqin* being played. Confucius was said to be a *guqin* practitioner.

A Chinese woman in traditional dress performs on the guzheng, *a long zither.*
(Linqong/Dreamstime.com)

Struck Instruments

The struck instruments used in China include a hammered trapezoidal dulcimer, along with numerous types of drums, chimes, clappers, cymbals and gongs. The *yangqin* (hammered trapezoidal dulcimer) is a string instrument, but because it is played by striking the strings with bamboo hammers, it is included here amongst other instruments sounded by striking. In general, the *yangqin* is thought to have its origin outside China, probably in the Middle East, where several related hammered dulcimers have historically been played. The sound of the *yangqin* is unusual in its metallic, pitched, rather loose or rattle-like sound; the sound might be likened to tapping the strings inside a piano. *Yangqin* players sit behind their instrument, which is perched on a stand with the upper, shorter edge of its trapezoidal shape positioned at an angle somewhat higher than the longer, lower edge, which is nearest the player. The player holds bamboo sticks or mallets in each hand that are about a foot long, and quite flexible.

Chinese percussion instruments include bells, chimes, cymbals, clappers, drums, and gongs of many types, some indigenous to China, and some with distant origins. A few salient features of this large group of musical instruments will be discussed here. Bells, many of which are struck from the outside with a metal or wooden rod, rather than through an internal clapper, and tuned chimes of stone and metal have been unearthed at many archaeological sites, testifying to their importance in ancient times. Striking bells is said to invoke good luck, and thus, numerous tourist sites, including temples of various types, have bells that can be struck by visitors, often for

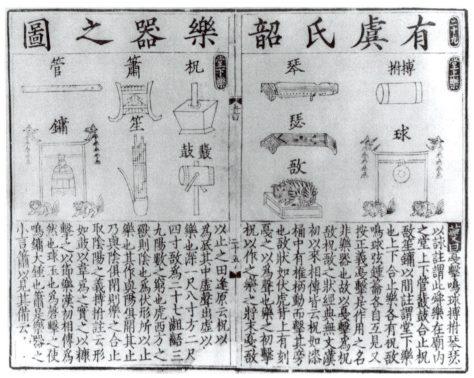

Chinese musical instruments, about 1190. Illustration from the Song Dynasty.
(Library of Congress)

a fee. Bell and drum towers were historically important in many Chinese cities and some of these structures are open to visitors. The sounds of bells and drums were used to mark divisions of time (the night watches and times of day, for example) and to summon troops. Tuned sets of bells and chimes can be heard in performances of ritual music. The modern Chinese composer Tan Dun made use of the tuned bells unearthed in the tomb of the Marquis of Yi in Hubei Province, which date back to approximately 500 B.C.E., in his *Symphony 1997: Heaven, Earth, Mankind*.

Cymbals are relatively flat, circular plates of metal that are typically played by being crashed or struck together. Some Chinese cymbals are smaller than the palm of one's hand, while other types may be close to a foot in diameter. Gongs are also metal and circular, but may have a turned-under rim. Gongs are often hung on wooden racks and they are normally played with a metal or wooden beater. In ensembles, a set of tuned gongs called *yunluo* (literally "cloud gong") may be heard; these are small gongs several inches in diameter, and ten *yunluo* are hung on a single wooden rack. Chinese opera often features hand-held gongs that rise or fall in pitch. Wooden clappers and wood blocks are commonly heard in Chinese instrumental ensembles and in accompaniments to vocal music; their timbres are typically hard and brittle. Near the beginning of a great deal of vocal music, one can hear a wood block tapping in increasing speed. Chinese narrative song is often accompanied by hand-held wooden clappers, which add to the music's rhythmic vitality.

Simultaneous Sounds: Textures and Harmonies

Chinese traditional music has a characteristic manner of combining the sounds of instruments and/or voices. Musicians usually produce the same melody at the same time, but not actually in unison: each musician adds rhythmic or melodic decoration to the basic melody, without falling behind or running ahead of the other musicians. This performance style gives the melody performed a certain characteristic thickness, but an experienced listener can often pick out the sounds of various instruments. The technical term for this type of single-melody, uniquely embellished ensemble music is heterophony. Heterophony is much more characteristic of Asian music than Western music, which has long favored polyphony. Polyphony may feature contrasting melodies that are heard at the same time, or voices or instruments imitating a single melody in a canon or round (such as when "Row, Row, Row Your Boat" is sung by several people, with some singers waiting for planned time intervals before beginning).

Form

Form refers to the way the music is organized—the shape of the music as it unfolds. As an aural art, listeners recognize repeated or returning patterns of sound, which create coherence; the patterns of repetition are heard in juxtaposition with contrasting sounds, which provide novelty and maintain interest. Western music tends to feature short passages that recur frequently, perhaps like a poem with a repeating line at the end of each stanza, while in traditional Chinese music, the emphasis is on contrast, rather than repetition. Chinese music tends to move on from its starting point more like a narrative prose paragraph than a poem with lines that repeat. For Western listeners used to hearing frequently recurring sonic patterns, Chinese music may not seem to cohere; it may sound disorganized, and its form may be difficult to follow.

CHARACTERISTIC TYPES OF TRADITIONAL CHINESE MUSIC

Scores of English-language books and articles have been written about the myriad types of traditional Chinese music. References at the end of this chapter will guide the reader to sources where this wealth of information may be explored. Only a very few types—those a visitor might encounter live on a visit to China—will be described here.

Beijing Opera

Beijing opera has been called "the essence of Chinese culture," and it is clearly a fascinating attraction for many visitors. Beijing opera is one of many regional types of dramatic music practiced in China, but it has become the most nationalized and easily recognizable. Known for its colorful costumes, elaborate makeup, amazing acrobatics, and surprising music, Beijing opera is now performed throughout China and in many of the regions reached by the Chinese diaspora. While many Chinese deplore a supposed decline in the popularity of Beijing opera, live, broadcast, and

Chinese opera performer in elaborate costume. Traditional theater costumes are all more or less loosely based on Ming dynasty imperial attire. (Corel)

recorded performances continue to command attention and sales, and some young people participate in Beijing opera singing contests and Beijing opera interest groups at Chinese universities. Still, it must be said that while Beijing opera is regarded as a national treasure, it is not widely popular, particularly among young people.

Beijing opera shares several traits with its Western counterpart: it is narrative, dramatic music performed by singers dressed up as characters in costume, and largely sung. Its accompaniment is an orchestra, though the number of orchestral musicians is much smaller than in a Western opera orchestra. Solo sections of singing (arias) are its most important musical feature, and these typically feature drawn-out texts that express emotion. Especially capable singers extend certain syllables at great length, to the delight of their audiences, but it is not uncommon for Chinese listeners to have difficulty understanding the texts being sung, as pronunciation is generally quite distorted in performance. Some theaters (such as the Chang'an Grand Theatre in Beijing) have supertitles in Chinese and English to facilitate greater audience comprehension. Unlike Western opera, the Beijing opera orchestra is usually positioned onstage (often at stage left), the melodies of many arias are traditional, remaining the same from opera to opera, rather than being composed individually, and costuming and makeup identify the performers of stock characters. Finally, Beijing opera commonly includes acrobatic feats executed by the singers, and opera stories are drawn from legend, myth, and history.

The striking, elaborate costumes and makeup worn by Beijing opera performers allow audiences to determine the sort of character being portrayed; role types have associated actions and acrobatic moves, as well. The gorgeously dressed young

A GREAT BEIJING OPERA STAR

Mei Langfang (1894–1961) is famous for being one of the four founders of modern Beijing opera. He specialized in performing *dan* (female) roles, and toured Japan, Russia, and the United States. Mei is said to have perfected the imitation of female gesture, with some of his work having been filmed. He was credited with bringing Beijing opera to the wider world, and even with influencing Western performers' portrayals of women.

woman with an elaborate headdress is invariably portraying a *dan* role, usually a flirtatious young lady of high rank. Historically, *dan* roles were performed by young men singing in their highest (falsetto) range. Male warriors with black, white, and red paint covering their faces, along with elaborate headdresses and costumes with pennants worn on the back, are performing *jing* roles. The visual, vocal, and orchestral characteristics of Beijing opera combine to produce one-of-a-kind effects.

Tea-House Music

Among the kinds of performers who might be heard at a modern Chinese tea house are players of the *guqin* or *guzheng* or small groups of instrument players, such as *jiangnan sizhu* (Silk and Bamboo Ensemble). "Silk" refers to the stringed instruments, usually including the *erhu*, *pipa*, and *yangqin* (their strings were formerly made of silk) and "bamboo" refers to wind instruments, such as the *dizi*, made of a single bamboo tube, and the *sheng*, which has many tubes. The music performed by such ensembles is often intended as much or more for the enjoyment of the players than for the pleasure of other listeners. Heterophonic in texture, the melodies played are often variants of well-known basic tunes with specific numbers of beats, such as Lao Liu Ban (Old Six Beats).

Temple and Ritual Music

Active Confucian, Daoist, and Buddhist temples incorporate some degree of music into their rituals, most commonly chanting. Chanting may range from less musical types, such as the reading of sacred texts and prayers aloud, perhaps with a steady metrical accent and some pitch variation, to more musical sorts emphasizing the singing of repeated pitches, but still showing some pitch variety within a narrow range and involving a few instruments, such as a drum, small cymbal, or gong. Temple music performed by instrumental ensembles is less common, and may include the *yunluo*, drum, *dizi*, and *guanzi* (a type of end-blown wind instrument). Some temples, such as the Zhi Hua Temple in Beijing, frequently present tourist-oriented performances featuring instrumental music.

Folk Song and Dance

China's 50-plus ethnic groups present a rich treasury of folk song and dance. The song lyrics may be in non-Mandarin dialects or in *fangyan*, which is similar to Mandarin, but with some distinctly non-Mandarin pronunciations. While many of the melodies and texts of folk songs and dances are passed on in an oral/aural tradition, a great deal of effort has been made to collect, transcribe, and teach folk songs in Chinese schools. In conservatories, student musicians are typically required to learn to sing folk songs from a variety of regions. Yunnan province in southwestern China is especially rich in minority ethnic groups, some of which produce tourist-oriented performances. One such group is the famed Naxi Orchestra, which performs in Lijiang Town, Yunnan. Such groups often travel, so it may be possible to partake of folk performances in many of China's major cities. Folk dance and folk music programs are ubiquitous on Chinese television stations.

Traditional Orchestras

The People's Republic is home to several traditional orchestras, all of which were founded after the establishment of the republic in 1949. These include the National Traditional Orchestra, the Hong Kong Chinese Orchestra, and the Shanghai Traditional Orchestra. Each of these groups is a large ensemble composed of traditional Chinese instruments and led by a conductor. The most numerous instrument in these ensembles is the *erhu*. The creation of these traditional orchestras may be seen as the Chinese answer to the Western classical orchestra, but they also boast impressive performances by large numbers of instrumentalists. The small *jiangnan sizhu*-sized ensemble of perhaps eight or a dozen players is, however, more in line with historically accurate performance practice. Still, the large traditional orchestra is attractive in its own right. Performances may feature virtuoso soloists on instruments such as the *erhu* and *pipa*.

Chinese Music History

During much of China's imperial history, dynasties supported a Music Bureau (*Yuefu*) that controlled music in the empire. The size of these organizations is legendary: at one point, the Music Bureau was reported to employ more than 10,000 individuals in Beijing alone. The functions of the Music Bureau are not completely known or clear, but is it said that the structures of instruments and the pitches they produced were controlled by the Music Bureau, which also controlled the means by which musicians with official positions were educated. What sorts of roles did musicians have in the various dynasties? Two important functions immediately spring to mind: first, the role of music in the many rituals observed by the court required multiple, highly trained musicians to produce the correct music; and second, a very large group of musicians and dancers were employed to entertain various members of various courts, and some of these musicians also taught courtiers to play instruments and to sing. When imperial rule came to an end, the reign of the Mandarins and their associated arts (such as *guqin* music) was dealt a serious, nearly mortal blow. As Republican China emerged, its new rulers made an effort to have the arts serve the public at large, rather than being accessible only to the socially and economically elite.

LANG LANG AND YUNDI LI: YOUNG CHINESE PIANISTS AT LARGE

Yundi Li (from Chongqing) and Lang Lang (from Shenyang) were both born in 1982, and are now international artists of the first order who have taken the world of classical Western music by storm. Trained in China, Yundi Li was the first Chinese pianist to win the International Frederick Chopin Piano Competition in Warsaw, Poland (2000), and went on to make his debut in the United States in 2003. Lang Lang began his training in China, but he journeyed to America to study at the Curtis Institute of Music in his late teens. Since performing with the Chicago Symphony Orchestra in 1999, Lang has traveled the world performing with orchestras and in solo recitals. Li and Lang have made it clear that Chinese pianists have arrived.

Soon after the fall of the Qing dynasty in 1911, a vast change in the way music was approached in China unfolded. The Republican government emphasized access to education, including music education, so many famed Chinese musicians (such as Xiao Youmei and Xian Xinghai) began to work toward the founding of schools of music and the establishment of music pedagogy in China. When the People's Republic of China was established in 1949 and the Communist Party was installed as its chief authority, a new wave of reforms was enacted, with many of them based on Mao Zedong's 1942 Yan'an talks on art and culture. The arts were to serve the masses, and historical art forms were to be mined to bring forth fresh, relevant work. As a result, new musical repertories sprang up, including songs meant to be sung by large groups in unison.

The Cultural Revolution was a period during which musical progress and production was nearly halted. The strictures on music during the Cultural Revolution were devastating: a fierce effort was made to return all cultural manifestations to the people—meaning the rural farmers—and to avoid anything that was Western (or, specifically, non-Chinese). Because music almost by its very nature involves specialized study that often results in honoring a few highly skilled musicians, it was quite easy to label most musicians (and most music) elitist and therefore deserving of no status in Chinese society. Musical productions were strictly limited, and only a few model operas were heard. Such forces brought China's cultural development to a near standstill. After Deng Xiaoping began to expound on the views underlying the *gaige kaifang* in the late 1970s, an intense revival of all of the arts began. Soon, a large number of Chinese musicians (especially students) began to travel to Europe, Australia, and the Americas for extended musical training.

In many of China's cities, music conservatories are now educating thousands of college-age musicians every year. While many of these young people are studying classical Western music (the piano and violin are particularly popular), most of the conservatories also offer training in Chinese traditional music, including folksong and dance. Some also offer training in electric piano, jazz, music technology, the craft of building and repairing instruments, and popular music. The unique curricula these students undertake include studies of Chinese music history, Chinese folksong and *changshuo* (traditional song-speech), and courses in political theory. Like their counterparts in American music schools and departments, students majoring in music in China take lessons, study music theory and analysis, ear training, sight singing, and Western music history. Given China's massive population advantage and current prosperity, the future of every type of musical art is bright there, and will likely grace international stages in the decades to come.

REFERENCES

Jones, Stephen. *Folk Music of China*. Oxford: Clarendon Press, 1995.

Lau, Frederick. *Music in China: Experiencing Music, Expressing Culture*. New York: Oxford University Press, 2008.

Miller, Terry E., and Andrew Shahriari. *World Music: A Global Journey*. 2nd ed. New York: Routledge, 2009.

Nettl, Bruno, Charles Capwell, Thomas Turino, and Isabel Wong. *Excursions in World Music*. 5th ed. Upper Saddle River, NJ: Pearson, 2007.

Provino, Robert C., Yoshiko Tokumaru, and J. Lawrence Witzleben, eds. East Asia: China, Japan, and Korea. *The Garland Encyclopedia of World Music*, Vol. 7. New York: Routledge, 2002.

Rees, Helen. *Echoes of History: Naxi Music in Modern China*. Oxford: Oxford University Press, 2000.

Stock, Jonathan. *Musical Creativity in Twentieth-Century China: Abing, His Music, and Its Changing Meanings*. Rochester, NY: Rochester University Press, 1996.

Thrasher, Alan R., Joseph S. C. Lam, Jonathan P. J. Stock, Colin Mackerras, Francesca Rebollo-Sborgi, F. Kouwenhoven, A. Schimmelpenninck, Stephen Jones, Han Mei, Wu Ben, Helen Rees, Sabine Trebinjac, and Joanna C. Lee. China, People's Republic of. In *The New Grove Dictionary of Music and Musicians*, 2nd ed., Vol. 5. London: Macmillan Publishers Limited, 2001.

Witzleben, Lawrence *Silk and Bamboo Music in Shanghai: The Jiangnan Sizhu Instrumental Ensemble Tradition*. Kent, OH: Kent State University Press, 1995.

Food

Robert André LaFleur
Tamara Hamlish

FOOD IN CHINESE CULTURE

Although food has only occasionally been a subject of scholarly study in China, it constitutes a central element of Chinese culture, as suggested by the standard greeting

Steamed buns are a typically northern dish. (iStockPhoto.com)

of "Have you eaten yet?" (*"chibaole meiyou"*). The proper response is a perfunctory "Yes"—any other response will result in extensive efforts to feed you, whether or not they are for profit. Outside of China, the sweet tastes of Guangzhou (Cantonese) and the spicy flavors of Sichuan (Szechwan) are familiar to many. In China itself, however, the differences between regions are far more significant. Some of those differences depend upon the availability of certain kinds of foodstuffs that have, at least traditionally, been specific to an individual region.

Contrary to popular Western belief, not all Chinese survive on rice. In the arid northern plains, wheat is a staple grain, and noodles, steamed buns, and a plethora of other wheat products are the standard fare. In the south, where both rice and labor are plentiful, one finds elaborately produced *dim sum*. Southern cuisines have a reputation for being more adventurous than northern ones, with a broader range of ingredients that include delicacies such as snake or rat, as well as donkey and pigeon. Northerners enjoy lamb, and they also appreciate strong flavors in a wide variety of wheat-based dishes, including dumplings, wontons, pancakes, and steamed, boiled, baked, or fried buns. Deservedly famous is Beijing (Peking) duck, as well as *mushu* pork and Mongolian beef.

Cooking methods also vary across China. Although electric and gas ovens were virtually unknown in China until the last few decades, there has always been a broad range of possibilities for cooking over an open wood or coal fire. Breads, as well as other foods, including dumplings and some noodles, are often steamed in wooden or metal baskets that sit atop a stove, and one will find them along almost any street or alley one travels in China. Foods are also fried, with the style ranging from deep fried in the south to lightly sautéed in the north. Sweets, other than manufactured candy or fresh fruit, are not often part of a Chinese meal, and there is nothing that resembles a sweet, Western-style desert at the end of a meal (which many Chinese feel overpowers the balance of the meal just eaten).

The focus is on providing a balance of flavors that comes from both the primary ingredient and the spices that are utilized. Like the art of calligraphy, cooking takes place in one single motion; it happens quickly, over a hot fire, with little room for contemplation or for error. Although stir-fried dishes routinely accompany the staple food in national Chinese cuisine, the cooking styles of these dishes vary by region. Chinese roughly divide the cuisine into four regions: the northern region above the Yellow River; the coastal region, which features fish dishes and fresh vegetables; the inland region, which includes the Hunan and Sichuan provinces; and the southern region, which is best known for the cooking varieties of Guangdong province. The cultural consensus is that coastal cuisine is relatively sweet, for native residents like to put a bit of sugar in the dishes; that northerners favor salty dishes; and that Hunan and Sichuan dishes are very spicy.

Three meals a day is the Chinese custom. The breakfast is relatively simple: a steamed bun, a sesame-seed pancake, or a pair of deep-fried dough sticks (*youtiao*) with a bowl of soymilk for a northerner, or rice porridge with pickled vegetables for a southerner. Far more elaborate, however, is the Cantonese restaurant breakfast of dim sum, a veritable feast of perhaps 50 dishes from which a group of friends will choose perhaps a dozen. In large restaurants, these dishes come by in carts from which patrons choose dishes that suit them. In smaller venues, they can be ordered at the table. The possibilities include braised Chinese mushrooms stuffed with pork and water chestnuts, egg rolls with shrimp and pork, and steamed buns with roast pork fillings or steamed crabmeat dumplings.

In China, the major daily meals are lunch and dinner. A typical major meal for a family consists of a staple, such as rice, plus three or four stir-fried dishes, including a meat dish (pork, chicken, lamb, and sometimes beef, as well as seafood in areas where it is plentiful) and several predominantly vegetable dishes. One of the distinctive aspects of Chinese cooking lies in the countless ways that meats and vegetables can be combined; the traditional Western notion of a meat dish balanced by separate helpings of vegetables is quite foreign to China.

Feasts and family banquets are more infrequent, and far more elaborate. The hospitable Chinese habitually invite friends home for meals. For a planned family treat, the feast starts with various alcoholic beverages that are often quite refined, and a few cold appetizer dishes, such as roast pork, exquisitely cured duck eggs, called thousand-year-old eggs, jellyfish, asparagus salad, and fried peanuts, which accompany the varied beverages. After the cold appetizers are consumed, 10 to 12 hot courses are served, followed by a final soup course. During the banquet, Chinese hosts constantly encourage guests to eat and drink more. They continually add food to a guest's plate and bowl, and the complement to this hospitality by the host is the guest's obligation to accept the endless supplements. It is a custom that Chinese hosts would never want to see a guest's plate become empty. During a typical two-hour meal, course after course of food is served. Visitors to China are sometimes surprised by the impossible amount of food—always sampled, but rarely finished—on the table at the end of a banquet-style meal. The experienced banquet diner in China learns quickly (almost from birth, if one is born in China) to pace herself and to enjoy the unfolding of flavor and appearance that characterizes the dishes over the course of several hours. Most Chinese agree that the stages of the meal in and of themselves constitute one of the greatest aesthetic pleasures of Chinese cuisine.

The liquid complement to any meal in China is tea. With some 250 varieties from which to choose, there is a tea for every regional cuisine or individual preference. Everyday tea is like *vin ordinaire*, or table wine, and fine tea (like fine wine) is expensive. In a Cantonese restaurant, tea boys carry a huge kettle with a long spout on each arm. When they notice a teapot with the lid upright, they refill it with fresh boiling water. The tea boy usually stands a foot away from the table. As he raises a kettle, the steaming hot water travels gracefully through the air in a two- or three-foot arc into the open tea pot before him. When the pot is nearly full, the tea boy withdraws his arm, and the pouring ceases without a drop being spilled. For the visitor, trust is necessary.

The Chinese believe that food reflects multiple forms of balance that all represent their pursuit of the ultimate form of balance, *yin* and *yang*. Balance is achieved by matching hot dishes to cold weather, and vice versa, and by the proper proportion of *fan* and *cai*—the staple food (rice or noodles, for example) and all other dishes. Within *cai* (other dishes), one must also have balance. Thus, neither meats nor vegetables are cooked whole, but cut appropriately and blended carefully. Depending on the mode of cooking—steaming, braising, stir-frying, or boiling—certain ingredients should be cut thinner or thicker, in slices or cubes. Ultimately, every dish should satisfy three standards: good appearance, good scent, and good taste. The best food strikes a perfect balance that is blended with the weather, the foods around it, and even a kind of cosmological harmony that can be explored further in the Popular Beliefs chapter.

FOOD IN CHINESE HISTORY

Food has played an enormous role throughout Chinese history, from the immensely practical to the highly esoteric. China has been, and remains today, a predominantly agricultural society. Agriculture has been a foundation of the economy, and everything from family and lineage organizations to the central government has been organized around it. Farming technique and food preparation records dating as far back as the Shang Dynasty (the second millennium B.C.E.) show that wheat and rice cultivation comprised staples of the Chinese diet even then. A significant variety of domestic animals were raised, including cattle, chicken, pigs, and sheep, and these still constitute the major meat groups on a Chinese menu. Fishing and hunting were prevalent, as well, and alcoholic beverages (*jiu*) were an accompaniment to many meals. Indeed, the connections to the present go a great deal further; culinary techniques, such as frying, steaming, and even baking, were already in use in that early era. Moreover, the Shang banquet table, based on archaeological evidence, featured a wide array of utensils used for the preparation, cooking, and consumption of meals.

As written and archaeological sources on the Zhou era (the first millennium B.C.E.) become more numerous, we can observe a rapid diversification of foodstuffs and agricultural techniques that would define Chinese history and, in many ways, the character of the Chinese state, which relied upon agricultural productivity above all to support a tendency toward political and even economic centralization. With regard to the history of food, two of the greatest technological innovations were increasingly sophisticated storage techniques and mills for the grinding of grains. In early eras, storage techniques consisted of underground cold storage areas and, in later times, of granaries. Storage allowed families and communities to protect grain supplies for longer periods, and even today, in the Chinese calendar proscriptions against opening granaries on inauspicious days, one can see a cautiousness that, in all likelihood, is linked to the early concerns of villages over using stored grains in a well-planned manner.

The Chinese state recognized the importance of storage, as well, creating an increasingly sophisticated set of granaries and even a storage bureaucracy, so important was a well-fed people to the aims of the state. Similarly, the development of mills to grind grains during the last centuries before the Common Era facilitated significant advances in Chinese cuisine. In the Shang and Zhou, crops were unprocessed or processed in rather crude ways. The invention of the stone mill allowed people to grind grains to create such modern products as steamed bread, alcohol, beancurd, and the like. This, in turn, stimulated further innovation and experimentation in cuisine.

This process continued throughout the first millennium of the Common Era, with the greatest changes taking place south of the Yellow River. As we have already seen in several places in this book, north and south have always been significant and distinctively different regions in the Chinese imagination. Through the study of food and agriculture, we can see the enormous bounty that China discovered as the south was slowly opened, settled, and then populated over the course of the last 2,000 years of Chinese history.

Innovations included rice-growing technology, terraced landscaping, and one of the greatest benefits of all, double-cropping, which allowed farmers to expand their yields dramatically to feed a growing population. Indeed, it is hard to speak about food in China without referring to population growth, which we first encountered in the geography section. China's population grew steadily through the first millennium of the Common Era, with only temporary setbacks, and at a dramatic rate through the second millennium. Much of that growth took place in the ever-expanding south, which served both as a place of new settlement (as territories considered to be uncivilized and foreign were opened over the centuries) and, eventually, rural and urban development.

The opening of the south played an even larger role when, in an era long before train or truck transport, the Grand Canal—which followed a north-south trajectory—served as a major economic linkage between the Yellow and Yangzi rivers. For the first time, it was possible to ship goods efficiently between regions, and, as part of the overall effect of economic exchange, for a wider number of people to sample distinctive foodstuffs from the north and south. In a similar fashion, goods traveled from west to east along the Yangzi and Yellow rivers, both of which originate in the

---

CHINESE REGIONAL CUISINES AND CHINA'S URBAN CENTERS

Chinese cuisine is ever-changing and benefiting from experimentation. Nowhere is this more obvious than in the most international Chinese cities in Asia—Beijing, Shanghai, Hong Kong, and Taipei. The trend began in the 1970s and 1980s, making Hong Kong and Taipei into veritable sampling centers for the best Chinese cuisine. Over the past two decades, Beijing and Shanghai have become places where there are fine restaurants serving each of the cuisines. Increasingly sophisticated storage and transport techniques have made this possible, as has the mobility of experienced chefs. As we study the various regional cuisines, it is good to keep in mind that these cuisines, and their areas, are not etched in stone; they are in a constant state of change and regeneration as China undergoes a culinary revolution in the 21st century.

---

mountainous Qinghai province. Moreover, China boasted a sophisticated coastal trade that covered significant distances along China's coast, from the Bohai Sea to the Gulf of Tonkin and locations between.

Beyond water travel, there was the Silk Road, which steadily carried goods from Inner Asia into Chinese territory, including grapes, carrots, walnut, garlic, and pomegranate, to name only a few. In the last 1,000 years in particular, China has also been intersected by an increasingly sophisticated network of overland routes—the precursors of today's railway lines and highways. The shipping (both river and coastal) and caravan routes are important components of our themes of Chinese national and regional cuisine because they show that, even in early eras, the exchange of goods (more often, perishable goods) and experimentation with flavors and ingredients both represented constant learning processes in China's culinary history. As we have already seen, the process of discovering new ingredients, which was often aided by shipping routes, food preparation, including grinding and storage, cooking techniques, and even the organization and aesthetics of the dining experience benefited from a history and culture of constant discovery, trade, and innovation that covered enormous swaths of territory, from the Yellow Sea to the Mediterranean.

CHINESE REGIONAL CUISINES

Northern Cuisine

As noted above, wheat products prevail over rice in China's northern provinces. Many varieties of noodles and dumplings make up the northern diet, and they often have a high caloric content, as much to ward off the cold as to provide fuel for labor. Westerners will likely recognize *jiaozi* (steamed dumplings) and *chunjuan* (spring rolls), as well as a variety of roasted meats, the most famous of which is *Beijing kaoya* (Peking duck). The duck should be ordered whole, unless the party is very small indeed, and (in contrast to some Western restaurant customs) the diners should pay

A famous Chinese dish, Peking Duck is a flattened roast duck dish with crispy skin, usually eaten with small pancakes, a sweet sauce, and a kind of finely shredded spring onion. (Travel Pictures Gallery)

attention to the showmanship associated with slicing the duck at the table. The first cuts will be especially tender (and somewhat greasy) skin, which should be picked up with chopsticks and dipped lightly in sauce, then eaten without accoutrements. After that, plates will emerge to accommodate virtually every part of the duck, some of which skittish travelers may find challenging. The more mundane meat from the duck should be wrapped pancake-style and eaten with sauce and scallions. There will be at least one (and usually more) soups made from the duck, and a wide array of dishes on the menu that can accompany the meal. There is a large Beijing Roast Duck chain in northern China and China's larger cities called Quanjude. It provides consistent quality, but it is worth sampling smaller duck restaurants, as well, since they are found throughout Beijing (and beyond), and provide wonderful opportunities to observe cooking and serving distinctions.

Other northern cooking relies less on seafood than freshwater fish, and poultry dishes are also quite prevalent. One of the most memorable is Mongolian hot pot, a specialty with origins in China's west, influenced by the cooking techniques of Chinese Muslims. Several soup stocks start the process, as the pot comes to a boil on a charcoal burner (or electric stove) in front of patrons. Pieces of mutton or, occasionally, other meats are cooked along with a wide variety of vegetables, such as bamboo shoots, mushrooms, *doufu* (tofu), and cabbage. As with Beijing duck, there is a dependable chain—Dong Lai Shun—in Beijing and beyond, but it is well worth the effort to find distinctive, small hot pot restaurants, as well.

Those from China's south and west tend to think of northern cuisine as bland, and it is often perceived as food that may fill the stomach but leave little to remember. The assessment seems rather harsh if one has eaten some of the specialties mentioned above, but it is true that the combination of dumplings, vegetables (especially cabbage), and meats make it a good fit for the hardy northern conditions, where winds blow throughout the year and the chill of winter is fierce. In fact, many northerners pride themselves on the enormous possibilities afforded by the use of wheat in their diets and consider rice somewhat one-dimensional for a meal. The possibilities for noodles and dumplings are seemingly endless, and the only way to begin to grasp the wonders of wheat is to sample these foods at every opportunity.

Southeastern (Coastal) Cuisine

The bountiful coastal areas of China's southeast provide a rich array of culinary opportunities. The farmlands are subtropical, so the southeastern cook has a range of vegetables far richer than those to the north or west. The cuisine from Fujian, Jiangsu, and Zhejiang provinces tends to be too oily for the tastes of most northerners, but it is a rich blend of steamed, deep-fried, boiled, and braised vegetables and meats. The balance of fish, meats, and vegetables is impressive, as are the soups, which blend the same ingredients in innovative ways. A southeastern cab driver recently said that he pitied the northerners, with their predictable array of foods and endless cabbage dishes. On the coast, he said, he could sample not only fish from the sea, but the rich variety of fish from the Yangzi River. That opinion represents a common one among coastal diners, who see the combination of fresh vegetables, new ways of cooking common meats, and seafood as the very stuff of culinary excitement.

The same individual went on to say that the oil in southern cooking was healthier than the dry diet of the north, and that a little bit of oil in the diet was good for one's appearance. Indeed, the coastal cuisine is exciting, and not only in terms of the wide array of ingredients. Vegetables are plentiful, and one can sample *doumiao* and *bocai* (tasty bean sprouts and leafy spinach) in ways that have only recently become available to northern residents, thanks to improvements in produce trucking. Shrimp, prawns, and crabs are plentiful, as well, and it is only the experienced diner who is able to eat all of the tasty parts of a very large crab. Indeed, as one begins to understand regional variation in Chinese cooking, one is confronted with the challenge of cracking, prying, chewing, and even gnawing (not unlike a visitor to Maine with a lobster on his plate). All are necessary skills to master coastal cuisine. It is an art of sorts to make one's way through a crab, and a skill that few Westerners possess (those who do have practiced), to get the tender meat off a bone-filled fish cube in an otherwise delicate dish, such as West Lake Fish. The same goes for true appreciation of another specialty of the region: Dongpo pork, named after the Northern Song scholar Su Shi (Su Dongpo) (1037–1101), who served as an official in the beautiful city of Hangzhou in the 11th century. Dongpo pork consists of a meaty portion of pork on the bone, wrapped in a generous layer of pork fat. Part of the enjoyment comes from knowing how to eat it, and that is, indeed, part of the enjoyment of Chinese cuisine of all kinds. One watches, learns, and gains experience.

Western (Inland) Cuisine

Many Westerners are familiar with Sichuan (Szechwan) and Hunan cooking, and many think of them (along with some Americanized dishes from the south) as encompassing much of the range covered by Chinese food. Even those familiar with such restaurants in the United States will be amazed by the rich possibilities in the hot, spicy dishes of the west. For quite obvious geographic reasons, seafood will not be encountered inland as often as poultry, freshwater fish, soybeans, legumes, and a wide variety of vegetables cooked together in heavy seasonings. Tiny dumplings in hot, spicy sauce (*chaoshou*), hot pepper dishes with chicken or other meats (*gongbao; kung-pao*), and spicy beancurd and pork (*mapo doufu*) are among the dishes most familiar to foreigners, but they only scratch the surface of culinary possibilities, and it is fair to say that they are rarely prepared in everyday American restaurants the way that they are in western China or China's urban centers.

As mentioned above, there are very fine Sichuan restaurants in all of the major cities in China, and the influence of Sichuan cooking can be seen on almost every small-town restaurant menu, which tends to have at least a version of *gongbao* chicken, twice-cooked pork, or other popular western Chinese dishes. It is less likely that one will find some of the other superb dishes of the region outside of the largest cities or Sichuan province itself, though. One famous dish in Sichuan is fried string beans. They are cooked over a hot flame and served in what looks to be a withered form that masks a distinctive taste. Even the more familiar Sichuan and Hunan dishes are likely to arrive at the table much spicier than those found in any but the most authentic and hardy restaurants outside of China. One of the spiciest dishes in the cuisine is a fish stew in which a whole fish is cooked in hot, red oil with an enormous bowl full of peppercorns. One dips one's chopsticks into a stew of oil, peppercorns, and red peppers to find the tender pieces of whole fish below. The only reason the fish can even be found, however, is because the server, using a large ladle, removes at least three cups of red peppers from the serving bowl before the diners begin.

Sichuan and Hunan are landlocked locations with abundant produce, animals, and farmland. They have always been agricultural centers of China, and the cuisine has developed to complement both the climate (cold in winter and extremely hot in the summer) and the conditions (flowing terrain with distinct changes in elevation). Chongqing is known as one of China's "three furnaces" in the summer, but it can become very cold in the autumn and winter. Moving to the east in the region, Hunan cuisine has a slightly different range of spices, but the dishes are equally spicy, and the array of vegetables and meats utilized also varies somewhat. This is not bland food, though, and (as travelers often learn) one must work very hard to choose dishes that will allow more sensitive palates to survive the meal. Some people who are averse to spicy food order milk or yogurt before every Sichuan or Hunan meal, with generally favorable results. It is worth stressing, however, that not all Hunan and Sichuan foods are spicy, and even this cuisine prides itself on balance. In fact, travelers who enjoy spicy food will often be scolded by restaurant personnel that their choices contain "too much hot." Balance, as in calligraphy, poetry, dance, and song, is the key.

Southern Cuisine

This style of Chinese cooking is the most familiar to the Western world since, prior to the 1970s, most immigrants had ties to Guangdong or neighboring southern provinces. The weather in Guangdong is hot in the summer and still warm in the winter. It is humid, and there is a great deal of rainfall (unlike the western and northern regions of China). The possibilities for combining vegetables and meats are enormous in this climate, and they tend to be stir-fried or steamed so that they maintain their taste as much as possible. Southern cuisine is justly famous for dim sum and its seemingly endless variety of dishes that subtly echo the cuisines of the various regions of China. The dim sum meal is more than a time to eat, though. The Chinese characters for dim sum (Mandarin: *dianxin*) represent "a spot on the heart," meaning that one talks, eats, enjoys one's companions, and eats some more. It is a festive occasion that has become a weekend ritual for many Chinese and Westerners in restaurants throughout the world.

A regular dinner of Guangdong cuisine, though, can include some of the following dishes. It can be a bland cuisine (according to some tastes) if one sticks to sweet and sour dishes and the array of menu items found in many Western restaurants. In many ways, however, Guangdong cuisine is the most daring in China. In addition to an enormous variety of green vegetables, often combined with mushrooms, one will

Several bamboo steamers and plates of dim sum. (Shoutforhumanity/Dreamstime.com)

find both river and sea fish, including eel backs with eggplant, prawns prepared in multiple ways, stewed pigeon (with meat that only emerges for the most determined diner), and even camel (a culinary stretch if one considers the improbability of such sources in southern China). It is best to refrain from even trying to offer a sample of the most truly exotic southern cuisine (some of which has persisted in the West in the form of urban dining legends). Suffice it to say that the cuisine of the south has wonders that can only be sampled by repeated dining.

Guangdong cuisine has adapted to other cuisines in China, even as it has made endless innovations of its own. The south was, as we learned in earlier chapters, one of the last parts of China (beyond the far west) to be developed fully. Travelers from other regions settled in the south and brought their cooking techniques with them. At the same time, the array of ingredients that were possible in the south often stunned landlocked people from the (relative) north. Seafood was abundant from the coast, as well as from rivers, and the possibilities of fish, game, and cultivation (in the humid southern climates) were enormous. From that rich set of possibilities came one of the most distinctive, broad, and aesthetically pleasing cuisines in the Chinese world.

TEA CULTURE AND CHINESE FESTIVAL FOODS

As we complete our investigation into the history and culture of food in China, it is necessary to mention a number of distinctive themes that do not fit easily into regional patterns: fine teas and festival foods. Both figure prominently in Chinese life throughout the year, and both are connected to some of the most significant cultural patterns of Chinese life, from the everyday sampling of ordinary teas to the enjoyment of the rarest of them; from one year's New Year's dumplings to that same year's Autumn Festival moon cakes. Through it all, the very rhythms of the year and of social life are punctuated by distinctive food and drink.

Tea has been a tradition in China for 3,000 years, and is often associated with the great contributions of the early culture heroes we encountered in the History chapter. Tea serves as an offering in China, as well as an everyday beverage, and virtually everything in-between. It has played an important role in various philosophical traditions. It is said to calm and open the mind, which was something that Neo-Confucian, Buddhist, and Daoist thinkers admired. Tea has been widely perceived to have health benefits, some of which have been confirmed through scientific findings in the last few decades. Its role in trade was also enormously important to China in both positive and negative ways; Chinese tea figured prominently in some of the great diplomatic crises—even wars—of the 18th and 19th centuries.

All of the great Chinese festivals are associated with food on at least two levels. First, it is plentiful because the great festivals are all gatherings of family, as we learned in the chapter on Religion and Thought. Great feasts have occurred during the holidays throughout history, and this is only slightly less true today since families tend to be smaller and extended kin networks not quite as influential as they were in imperial times. Family and food have always gone together, though. Second, many

Tea steward refilling a teacup with a special long-spout kettle while the local opera troupe performs at the Yiyuan Tea House in Chengdu, 2004. (Corbis)

of the festivals are associated with particular foods, and the assumption is that they will be prepared (or purchased) and consumed by the participants. For example, dumplings are an expected treat during the New Year in the north, and it is the rare birthday celebration that does not have a bowl of longevity noodles for the celebrants—the noodles' length gives a sense of longevity. There are succulent offerings of wine and food at the Qing Ming festival in the third month, with a festive meal after the ancestors have (in the format of the ritual) "eaten."

Perhaps the most famous food festival examples are to be found during the Dragon Boat Festival (the fifth day of the fifth lunar month) and the mid-Autumn Festival (the full moon of the eight lunar month). During the Dragon Boat Festival, a special sticky rice treat wrapped in bamboo leaves (*zongzi*) is eaten in remembrance of Qu Yuan, an ancient official who drowned himself in the Miluo River as a protest. Unable to locate his body, the people were said to throw *zongzi* into the river to keep the fish from eating his body. Today, as dragon boats race along rivers (in China and the West), *zongzi* frames the culinary experience of the festival. The mid-Autumn Festival provides a similarly memorable food. With the moon at its brightest, harvest point, Chinese tradition is that families will tell stories about the moon and the maiden Chang'e in the moon with her rabbit. Through it all, people sip tea and eat the moon cakes that are as much a part of the holiday as the stories themselves.

As one festival—and one season—gives way to another, there is a subtle interplay of social rhythms and culinary distinctions, not unlike the American experience of

---

TEA CULTURE IN CHINA

Today, in China, teashops still flourish, and tea culture is one of the refinements that many people seek to enjoy in their lives. Whole books are devoted to tea culture, from the *Classic of Tea* (eighth century) to hundreds of specialized volumes on bookstore shelves. The many varieties of tea include green teas, black teas, and oolong teas, as well as white teas and scented teas (such as jasmine). Each of these varieties has tens, even hundreds, of sub-varieties, and one can find oneself with an array of choices for tasting that would take many years of disciplined sipping. All aspects of tea preparation and consumption are part of a complex process of assessment and enjoyment, much like the tasting of fine wines. There are distinctive ways of washing the tea leaves, pouring, and steeping. Sipping the tea itself is no ordinary process. Many people state that one needs three sips to enjoy fine tea at its best. The first prepares the palate. The second engages the drinker. The third creates a lasting aftertaste. Those associated with wine culture will surely notice parallels, and the world of tea is every bit as mysterious and compelling for many enthusiasts.

---

negotiating the foods and gatherings associated with contemporary festivals, such as the great secular holiday surrounding the Super Bowl, as well as Easter, Memorial Day, Independence Day, Labor Day, Thanksgiving, Christmas (or other winter holidays, such as Hanukkah or Kwanzaa), and New Year's itself. One need not stretch one's imagination too far to see that—in almost any family setting and over a period of years—distinctive foods and social gatherings merge to lend a distinct culinary and social feel to the calendar. In China, these patterns have endured for millennia, forming one of the most lasting festival traditions in the world.

REFERENCES

Anderson, E. N. *The Food of China*. New Haven, CT: Yale University Press, 1990.

Chang Kwang-chih. *Food in Chinese Culture: Anthropological and Historical Perspectives*. New Haven, CT: Yale University Press, 1981.

Dunlop, Fuchsia. *Shark's Fin and Sichuan Pepper: A Sweet-Sour Memoir of Eating in China*. New York: Norton, 2008.

Farquhar, Judith. *Appetites: Food and Sex in Post-Socialist China*. Durham, NC: Duke University Press, 2002.

Huang, H. T., ed. *Science and Civilisation in China*. Vol. 6, *Biology and Biological Technology*. Part 5, *Fermentations and Food Science*. New York: Cambridge, 2001.

Jun Jing, ed. *Feeding China's Little Emperors: Food, Children, and Social Change*. Palo Alto, CA: Stanford University Press, 2000.

Lam, Kam Chuen, Lam Kai Sin, and Lam Tin Yu, eds. *The Way of Tea: The Sublime Art of Oriental Tea Drinking*. Hauppauge, NY: Barron's Educational Series, 2002.

Simoons, Frederick. *Food in China: A Cultural and Historical Inquiry*. Boca Raton, FL: CRC Publishing, 1990.

Leisure and Sports

Robert André LaFleur
Tamara Hamlish
Kevin Latham

A WALK IN SHANGHAI

With the growing affluence found in many households within China today, many new forms of entertainment are now available. This is just one of the reasons why such pursuits as composing poetry, attending operatic performances, and reading long, 100-chapter novels has been supplemented by television, radio, magazines, and that import from Japan, karaoke. As with other topics covered in this volume, however, there is both great change and impressive continuity at work. A good way to illustrate this might be to follow just one of the paths open in a major city on a summer night. One such walk—starting from the area called the Bund along the Huangpu River in Shanghai—reveals a great array of popular leisure activities, from bookstores and high-end retail shops to television, skateboarding, museums, and alley food sellers. There are certainly more activities than one would have been found five centuries ago or, perhaps more significantly, even 50 years ago, yet many remain consistent with decades—even centuries—of Chinese tradition.

This particular walk begins on Nanjing East Road, which is rife with the effects of globalization and evidence of China's role in a changing world economy. The department stores are stocked with new fashions, and Western fast food restaurants are mixed with venerable Chinese establishments, some dating back to one of Shanghai's heydays in the 1920s and 1930s. It is also where one encounters what can only be called a tribute to shopping—a bronze statue of a woman with a large purse and a child in tow, which is a popular photo spot for Chinese and Western tourists.

Walking quickly through side streets filled with fruit stands, dumpling sellers, and little barbershops, one comes to Fuzhou Road. There, in front of a modern, high-rise office complex (closed for business by sunset), sit perhaps 40 men and women in their fifties, sixties, and seventies on folding lawn chairs, fanning themselves and watching passersby. When the skies open for brief showers, as they often do, they hurry under an overhang with their chairs to wait it out before moving back into the open when the skies clear again. Further down the road, which is lined by stationery stores and sign-makers, stands a six-story bookstore called Book City filled with people reading guidebooks for travel within China and beyond, cookbooks, traditional literature (including at least a dozen different editions of the Ming novels discussed in the Literature section), English-language works, and how-to manuals. Many shoppers have large plastic grocery baskets of books at the checkout counters, and full bags of newly purchased books as they leave.

Nanjing East Road. (Shutterstock)

From there, one can weave through the major shopping networks and thorough-fares. There are Western-style, 24-hour convenience stores, which are common throughout Asia, selling snacks, toiletries, newspapers and magazines, as well as a wide variety of drinks, including beer and wine from Europe and the United States. There are also small storefronts open well into the night, selling an assortment of fruits, snacks, and Chinese-style liquor. In passing by businesses that had been open just hours before, half-closed sliding doors allow glimpses of tables and people play-ing cards, impromptu games of guess fingers, or mahjong. Many have televisions on, and some watch intently, even as other chat, relax, or doze. Walking back through trendier sections, there are all-night bars, karaoke centers, and late-night noodle and dumpling counters.

In short, such a walk around Shanghai on a summer evening provides an array of sights that, in some ways, one might find walking through any other major city in the world. Only the details are different, such as an office address number boldly written as "666" (an unlucky number for many Westerners, but one considered auspicious in China, as we will learn in the next chapter), whole ducks hanging in side-street stalls, or the distinctive look of a horde traveling en masse across the street, as if to provide protection against traffic. In rural locations, one sees less variety, yet even a dusty dirt street on the outskirts of a medium-sized city will still have half a dozen or more little shops selling sundries. Ordinary people shape their days and structure their activities in ways that we often take for granted when we study the big picture of geography, history, politics, and economics. There are rhythms built into the day, the week, the month, and the year in China that are little known to Westerners. The aforementioned activities are only the outer shell of these patterns. Readers will surely note the way that their own lives are paced through a weekday, a workweek, or a weekend. More importantly, there are yearly patterns that we often take for granted, yet they have an enormous effect on the way we structure our personal and social lives.

Far from being a thing of the past that died with the arrival of a more modern China, there remains a style of life for many people that is tied to the cycles of the moon. This is certainly true in Hong Kong, Taiwan, Southeast Asia, and many cities in the West with large Chinese populations. The yearly pace—leading from one New Year through a cycle of festivals and family events all the way to preparations for the next—is guided by daily, weekly, and monthly rhythms. The great French sociologist Marcel Mauss once wrote that such cycles, with their interweaving of work and relaxation, are the very substance of social life. Indeed, he taught that one cannot understand leisure without understanding work, and that work makes little sense without a profound understanding of leisure. Our lives need patterning, or they lose their meaning. They require gathering together, as well as dispersal. They need the excitement of the group and the sanctuary of relative privacy. It is in that spirit that we will examine the alternating patterns of work and leisure in Chinese life. One should not be understood without the other.

DAILY LIFE IN CHINESE SOCIETIES

The rhythms of daily life in Chinese societies reflect China's social structures and networks of social relations. For example, while people in China draw distinctions between home and office, or between friends and colleagues, as different networks of social relations, these two spheres do not differ dramatically in the kinds of activities they offer. In other words, there is no sense of job-related work as a distinct kind of activity, nor is there a sense of leisure as we now perceive it in the West. Working or taking care of business (*gongzuo, zuoshi*) is contrasted with resting (*xiuxi*). Resting refers not only to brief breaks during the day, but also to vacation days, closing time, and going to bed. In agricultural communities, it can also refer to seasonal changes in activity. In other words, the cycle of daily activity is defined not so much by where things are done, or with whom one happens to be in contact, but rather by the activity itself. The contrast between work and rest is found throughout Chinese society, among office workers and small businessmen, and among laborers in factories or in agriculture.

In urban areas, where people work in offices or run small businesses, the Chinese workweek often extends through midday Saturday and there is little time for leisure activity as we know it in the United States. Yet, for many Chinese, the workday is far less stressful than for their American counterparts because it is punctuated by frequent breaks. Midday naps are common—it is not unusual to walk into a post office, a bank, or a department store in the middle of the day and find people with their heads down on their desks resting, with no intention of interrupting their naps to work. Meals are also a resting time. Even if a person eats out of a container at her desk, she rarely works at the same time. Job-related events that take place in the evening

---

BICYCLING AS WORK AND LEISURE

One activity that almost no Chinese individual, until recently, would call a sport or exercise is bicycle riding. Far from being a leisure activity for most people, it has been a means of transportation, and quite often a logistical challenge during traffic-filled times of day. Today, one more than occasionally sees people on the equivalent of an evening bicycle stroll, but this pales in comparison to commuter cycling. The health benefits, at least when smog is left out of the equation, are potentially great, but its linkage to work makes bicycle riding anything but leisure for most Chinese. In an earlier era, not long ago, bicycles were the primary means of transportation for most people, and the air and roads were cleaner. Bicycling, even then, was most often perceived as a means to an end, not a way to define and shape the body.

---

and might be characterized as social activities—for example, a birthday celebration for a colleague—are instead seen as an extension of work. In most cases, spouses and families do not participate, and, even when coworkers truly enjoy each other's company, they tend to keep these two spheres of social relationships distinct.

This alternating cycle of work and rest extends beyond the workplace. Without many of the conveniences available in the largest cities—such as a large refrigerator to store a week's worth of food, a private car to run a quick errand, or an automatic washer and dryer to wash clothes, to name just a few—much of any day is engaged in taking care of business. Job-related work is seen as just another kind of work that must be completed over the course of the day, and this remains true for the vast majority of people, even in urban settings such as Shanghai and Beijing.

Factory workers may face a more tightly regulated work schedule, dictated by the demands of a long assembly line and supervisors who are far-removed from the factory floor. Breaks are determined by the pace of the entire factory, and the length of the workday depends on the demand for the goods being produced. Because many of these workers are young and unmarried, they often live in dormitories on the factory campus. They eat their meals together in a common mess hall and spend the greater part of the day standing together on the line, running machinery. The beginning and end of the workday are marked by announcements and music played over a loudspeaker that can be heard throughout the factory grounds. Many factories, especially state-run enterprises, resemble small villages, with schools, clinics, movie theaters, and athletic facilities on the factory grounds. In this highly structured, all-encompassing environment, workers often form close ties with one another as they move through the cycle of daily life in unison.

For those engaged in agricultural work, the cycle of daily life is embedded in a larger cycle of seasonal changes. Much like farmers throughout the world, periods of work and rest follow the seasons. During periods of intense activity, the day begins before the sun comes up and ends after the sun has set. Much of the agricultural work in China is still done by people rather than machine, and therefore requires that each member of the household contribute to the process. Activities must be carefully

People on bikes on a Hong Kong city street. As people in China were becoming more financially comfortable in the 1990s, many began turning to motorized scooters as a form of city transportation. (Corel)

coordinated among household members so that each step is accomplished on time and things move smoothly into the next stage. Labor-intensive activities, such as harvesting or threshing, may require cooperation among several households, and an entire community may pull together for an intense cycle of work. People are heavily dependent on one another, and a strong network of social relations—either extended family or neighbors or both—that can be called upon whenever they are needed is critical for survival in Chinese agricultural households.

In contrast to this continuum between work and rest, Chinese clearly distinguish between public and private spaces in daily life. Great care is given to activities and relationships that occur inside the family or among colleagues or coworkers. Within these places, there is a great deal of attention devoted to keeping order and observing the responsibilities and privileges that go with rank and status. Once outside these environments, however, order and civility are replaced by determined self-interest and a strong sense of anonymity, whether jostling for a place on the bus, negotiating the line at the market, or disposing of scrap paper in the garbage. This public anonymity is one of the most difficult things for an outsider to understand, and Westerners are often shocked to see abrupt or even what they might call "rude" behavior in public venues. In a fashion that resembles the contrast between the cycle of work and rest, daily life in China is also punctuated by a constant cycle of public and private behavior, between roles clearly defined by family or work unit and the anonymity of the world at large. As we shall see below, these distinctions set the boundaries of daily life, as well as the possibilities for activities and events that are set apart.

Inside the perpetual cycle of work and rest that comprises daily life, a smaller allotment of free time can be found. For most Chinese, daily life leaves little time for leisure activities. Typically, free time is spent with family, including married siblings, children, and parents. When the weather is nice, families generally head outside to a park or other public space for an outing and a leisurely meal. On Sunday afternoons in most Chinese cities, towns, and villages, public spaces are crowded with multiple generations of families simply spending time together. In China's big cities, large shopping malls provide a diversion for all ages, while small-town public squares give families a place to sit and relax. At home, families spend time watching television or playing cards or games such as *mahjong*.

Celebrating family events, such as a wedding, the birth of a child, or the birthday of an aging parent, involves a larger circle of family, friends, and colleagues. At these times, the boundaries between home and work are blurred, and invitations are extended to all who are part of the daily life of the host. Most families try not to flout the ideals of a Communist society, even as they find ways to mark important life-cycle events. They strive to maintain a careful balance between celebrations that are too small and simple and those that are too elaborate and ostentatious—although the line has been blurring in many urban settings. In all cases, detailed records are kept to ensure that proper social relationships are maintained, and that gifts and invitations to future family events are adequately reciprocated—one of the most important functions in all social relations in China. Finally, distinctive and symbolic food, drink, dress, and activities distinguish these times as profoundly different from the work-rest cycle of daily life.

In addition to celebrating family events, Chinese families often prepare elaborate holiday celebrations. The Chinese calendar includes both national holidays and ancient lunar holidays (based on the cycles of the moon). National holidays include National Day, marking the founding of the nation (October 10 for the Republic of China and October 1 for the People's Republic of China), Teacher's Day (September 28, the birthday of Confucius), and International Labor Day (May 1). These dates are fixed on the solar calendar. As we have seen, lunar holidays, such as the Lantern Festival, the Dragon Boat Festival, the mid-Autumn Festival, and the Double Yang Festival are observed through ritual foods and activities, such as lantern displays, dragon boat races, or family moon viewing.

But the most elaborate holiday observance is the Spring Festival, commonly known in the West as the Lunar New Year, which falls between mid-January and mid-February. Businesses close for an extended holiday—sometimes up to two weeks—and nearly everyone travels home to be with family. Starting the new year with the family symbolizes wholeness and bodes well for the coming months, so most families make a concerted effort to have everyone at the table for the elaborate ritual meal that is supposed to begin late in the evening and continue well past midnight. Mothers serve their families symbolic foods such as fish (*yu*, a homonym for "plenty"), noodles (symbolizing long life), and eggs (symbolizing family unity). Some of the most extravagant fireworks displays take place at midnight of the Lunar New Year. In addition, gifts are given, often in the form of money bundled in red envelopes, from parents to their young children and from adult children to their parents.

It is customary for a married woman to spend New Year's Eve and the first day of the New Year with her husband's family, and then travel on the second day to see her own family. Similarly, after the first day, people head out to visit friends or invite extended family and friends into their own homes. Days are spent eating, playing cards or mahjong, watching television extravaganzas and variety shows that have been produced for the occasion, napping, strolling through the neighborhood, and chatting with visitors. Shops and offices are closed, and virtually no business occurs during this time, although growing participation in a global economic community has resulted in greater pressure to get back to business sooner rather than later.

Daily life in China is thus regulated by the contrasts between work and rest, and between one's public persona and one's personal, private identity. Routine is punctuated by holidays and lifecycle events that offer a notable contrast between the mundane and the exceptional. This contrast is further accentuated by the traditional beliefs and symbolism that are found throughout holiday and family celebrations, despite the fact that these beliefs and symbols have often been lost in the rush of a frenzied new daily life, particularly among those who are living and working in large urban areas. In order to understand Chinese leisure activities, such as tourism, exercise, and even entertainment—activities that punctuate the mundane—one must break with the common Western habit of focusing on individual and activity, when a much greater insight is gained by concentrating on where the activity fits in the pattern of a life, a year, a month, a week, or a day.

PILGRIMAGE AND EVERYDAY ACTIVITIES

In the paragraphs that follow, we will examine two fundamental poles of leisure activity in China—one that is often considered more or less once in a lifetime, and another that happens almost every day. In between are the punctuations of life that might be considered cyclical, such as family celebrations, national holidays, and so forth. We will take a brief look at the activities that many people hope to do once, as well as those that (while still considered leisure activities by the participants) are as common as the rising or setting sun. Let us begin with an example of where leisure activity might fit into the pattern of one's life.

Once-in-a-Lifetime Travel

China is filled with memorable destinations that have been justly famous for centuries, even millennia, and many of them are spoken of as places that a person *must see* in order to appreciate the country and have led a full life. While no destination in China quite fulfills the role of Mecca for a devout Muslim or Jerusalem for a Christian, several approximate it and are tourist locations at least as important (and lucrative for the growing companies that specialize in intra-China travel) as Compostella, Lourdes, or other destinations. Shandong province's Mount Tai, as well as Confucius's birth-place of Qufu an hour away, are significant pilgrimage destinations, and have served as such for over two millennia of Chinese history. The almost 7,000 steps to Mount Tai's summit, leading through stone arches and passing more than 1,000 poetic in-scriptions carved into the rock face, have constituted a trek of a lifetime for many Chi-nese travelers, including countless emperors, not to mention virtually every important Communist Party leader in the last half-century. Over the centuries, tour groups from other provinces have flocked to Shandong province to climb the steps of Mount Tai, and see the world the way generations of poets, officials, and humble travelers saw it. Busloads of pilgrims come to Mount Tai every day, and climb the stone steps to the South Heaven Gate (very often surrounded by family) to reach what, metaphorically at least, is a high point of Chinese civilization and their own lives.

Further south, the city of Suzhou is known for its canals and beautiful, elaborate gardens, which dot the city in some of the most unexpected places. Several hours to the south lies Hangzhou, which is dominated by the spectacular beauty of West Lake. A popular saying about West Lake and Hangzhou is that:

晴西湖不如雨西湖
雨西湖不如霧西湖
霧西湖不如雪西湖

A clear West Lake does not compare to a rainy West Lake
A rainy West Lake does not compare to a foggy West Lake
A foggy West Lake does not compare to a snowy West Lake

The clear implication is that it is a place that must be seen. For that reason, Suzhou and Hangzhou are both tourist destinations of the first order, and trips there have represented a lifetime achievement for many. It goes without saying that the more affluent travelers today would not see matters in quite this manner, but it is important to remember that such travel, especially from locations far to the north or west, is not a minor matter for many people. Adding to the aura of the destinations is a popular saying about the singularity of Suzhou and Hangzhou:

上有天堂 下有蘇杭

Above, there is the heavenly palace
Below, there are Suzhou and Hangzhou

Even beyond the financial arrangements lie the problems of finding time for va-cations amid a work or school schedule that runs from Monday through noon on Saturday for most of the year, with vacation time shared by almost all workers and students in the country, clogging railway cars, bus seats, and the public highways. There is even a further issue that readers may well have guessed by now. All of the temporal and financial challenges of tourist travel are exacerbated by the fact that trips such as these for Chinese travelers are almost never meant to be for an indi-vidual alone, and rarely for just a pair or a small group. Group travel (the ideal is the extended family) is something to which people aspire, and going to the great

Silhouette of visitors to West Lake, Hangzhou. (iStockPhoto.com)

once-in-a-lifetime locations is never more pleasurable than when one is sharing the experience with a lively group of family members.

Foreign tourists traveling alone are often asked "Are you *alone*?" and many Chinese have said that such an enterprise seems distinctly lonely. For a perspective on this attitude, one need only look at the major tourist destinations—from the Forbidden City and Temple of Heaven in Beijing to the Great Wall, the Terra Cotta soldiers in Xi'an, and the famous pilgrimage mountains of ancient lore—and see throngs of tourists, traveling together, often wearing matching caps as they follow a tourist guide with a pennant.

Chinese travelers often say that this is what travel means to them: a festive, family environment that embodies the same qualities one finds in a banquet overflowing with food and cheer—a frenzied, lively atmosphere that recalls the *renao* we encountered in the Social Relations section. It is in that spirit, which is well in keeping with the themes introduced thus far, that we can interpret the opposite side of the pole—those activities that are common and truly occur every day.

Everyday Leisure Activities

Many Chinese begin their days with exercise, and it is common to see large crowds of people, even before daybreak, taking a morning walk or practicing their *taijiquan* or *qigong* movements. Almost any open area, and certainly any patch of green, is seen as a place to begin the day's exercise. Almost all of the most popular morning activities, other than a morning constitutional, have some connection to the Daoist-

Group of tourists with matching caps in Beijing. (iStockPhoto.com)

inspired breathing techniques and bodily movements that have become a part of Chinese martial arts. These forms of full-body exercise emphasize the relationship between breath, mindfulness, and physical movement. The emphasis is on posture, bearing, and sculpted movement. It is necessary to point out that such activities as jogging, power-walking, and fitness cycling are not very popular among average Chinese citizens. To be sure, health clubs are growing in urban centers, and a more Western (some would say American) vision of exercise is taking root in some areas. Still, for many Chinese, the idea of being out of breath is distinctly unharmonious and they feel that it has a negative impact on the rhythms and harmonies of the body and the circulation of energy. While this may seem to be an overstatement, there is great cultural resilience in it. Almost all of the most popular (and these remain traditional) exercise forms take as their foundation the yin-yang or five-phase patterning and philosophy discussed in the Traditional Beliefs section of the next chapter.

Informal Sporting Activities

In addition to organized sports, participatory sports also include the various informal games played by people using work, school, or college facilities, as well as commercial facilities. Students are some of the most active informal sports participants in China. Within minutes of walking through a university or college campus, one will find informal games of soccer, basketball, table tennis, badminton, and tennis. On campuses with pools, swimming is also a very popular pastime, and students are often willing to get up for early-morning swimming sessions. Even small and less wealthy colleges and universities usually have at least one running track available to students and such basic outdoor gym equipment as horizontal bars. Similarly, one can usually expect to find children—particularly boys—playing soccer or some other ball game during their school breaks.

It is also not unusual at any relatively large organization, whether it be a factory, newspaper offices or government departments, to find some kind of sporting facilities for employees. Workplace sports facilities are important because they give people the chance to participate in sports with minimal organizational effort. Apart from workplace sports, there are basically two kinds of participatory sporting opportunities open to Chinese people, some of which are free and others of which are increasingly provided commercially. Going out to try one's hand at a golf driving range might be an alternative to going to a disco or a bowling alley for some. For free sporting opportunities, however, China's parks are among the main venues. Early in the morning, up and down the country, it is common to see groups of people practicing *taijiquan* or other callisthenic exercises.

Taijiquan and other martial arts also fit into contemporary Chinese popular culture in a variety of ways. They are commonly practiced by individuals or groups ranging from students keen to perfect combative martial arts to elderly Chinese who practice *taijiquan* to improve their health. Learning martial arts is usually done under a master,

Wang Hao (China), world champion, on attack in the final against Korea in the 2008 World Team Table Tennis Championships, Guangzhou, China, in 2008. (Grosremy/Dreamstime.com)

TWO DECADES OF THE MONKEY KING—JOURNEY TO THE WEST

In 1986, CCTV released a television drama that would captivate television audiences for more than two decades. A 25-part series, the drama captures the major scenes of the epic novel *Xiyouji (Journey to the West)*. As it aired through 1987 and 1988, it achieved the highest viewer rating in Chinese television history, and is known to almost everyone in China—from the memorable theme music to the cast of characters. As noted in the literature chapter, *Journey to the West* is a powerful tale of travel and adventure in pursuit of Buddhist scriptures from the West. The monkey king character (played by Liu Xiao Ling Tong) has become one of the most prominent in China today, a powerful example of an early-modern literary figure claiming a major role in a much later era. It has been replayed in syndication throughout China for two decades, and has spawned at least one sequel (1996).

---

someone who is already expert in a particular tradition of martial arts. With combative martial arts, this is often accomplished through one-on-one training or small group tuition. *Taijiquan*, on the other hand, is often learned by joining one of the many large groups of early-morning practitioners. Forms of *qigong* are also popular, and those who become experts can take on students and, if they are able, offer therapeutic services.

Reintegrating Leisure and Sport

Having established the significant connection of everyday exercise to the rhythms of body and universe, it is necessary to note that there is growing interest in competitive sports in China. Although it still represents a tiny minority of participants when compared to more traditional forms, sports such as table tennis and badminton have grown exponentially in the past few decades. Some Americans are aware of Chinese skill in table tennis from the historic ping-pong diplomacy of the 1970s. Fewer are aware that table tennis is a popular televised sport in China, with close-ups of coaches, fans, concentrating players, and even multiple-angle replays of excellent points—often punctuated by announcers' exclamations of *piaoliang (beautiful)*. It is a sport that the Chinese have dominated for decades, and the results of the 2008 Beijing Olympic Games show that influence at its height. Not only was the medal competition dominated by the People's Republic of China, but the quarterfinals and semifinals (and even the lower rounds) showed the influence of Chinese table-tennis dominance, with expatriates from China playing for nations such as Australia, the United States, and several European countries.

Badminton has become a popular participatory and spectator sport, as well. Equipment costs are relatively low, and one can play anywhere there is open space. One location where one often sees badminton games is in Tiananmen Square, at least on relatively slow days.

With our focus on everyday leisure, it is worth mentioning several activities that fit both parts of that phrase, without necessarily being about physical activity. Sitting and chatting is one of the most common everyday activities of all. In rural areas, one can see people squatting comfortably in the shade and passing time as they talk with neighbors. The gregarious Westerner might be surprised by the difference between chatting while sitting at a table and an equally engaged conversation while squatting.

In other places, people chat on benches and comment on the world going by. In upscale locations in major cities, sitting and watching may take place in a coffee shop, a teahouse, or a Western fast-food chain. The pace is unhurried in all instances, and there is an air of camaraderie and patience. Even though it would seem to go against the generally healthy habits thus far discussed, it must also be mentioned that two-thirds of Chinese men smoke, and the time spent smoking in the smoking area of a train, the lobby of a building, or by the side of a parked car is one of the most often-observed leisure activities in all of China. Sharing cigarettes is a common gesture between almost any group of two or more men who spend even brief moments of time together.

Finally, as the day draws to a close, most evening leisure in China remains dominated by the television. Television dramas remain popular and riveting, and the Westerner who is truly interested in contemporary Chinese culture would do well to spend time watching them (they are available conveniently and affordably on DVD, although very few are subtitled with anything but Chinese characters). For Chinese viewers, television dramas are, to echo the words of the late American anthropologist Clifford Geertz, "the stories we tell ourselves about ourselves." These stories are not told to an outside (Western) audience, as some of the most famous movies from China are. Sometimes, the most fascinating view of culture can be what one sees when no one cares who is paying attention.

Chinese television dramas are not the stuff of world cinema, nor are they meant to be. They are well filmed and acted, though, and the result is that many television series speak to the concerns, fears, and joys of a Chinese public still just over 30 years removed from the Cultural Revolution and only 20 years from the beginnings of an almost unimaginable growth in the economy. Their content and their structure make them one of the most common and powerful leisure activities in China.

Unlike American television series, which appear for a half-hour or an hour once a week until their cancellation, Chinese television series are produced and taped for one major showing, followed by syndication. What that means is that a television drama is a family affair, and a whole evening at that. A typical series might consist of 30 total episodes that are televised (without repeat) for 3 hours in a row for 10 straight days. It is no wonder that the television has remained a fixture at the center of Chinese leisure life.

SPECTATOR SPORTS AND THE OLYMPIC GAMES

From once-in-a-lifetime events to everyday activities, we have obtained a glimpse of leisure in China from a perspective that many Westerners might not have considered

---

FOOTBALL (SOCCER) IN CHINA

A fundamental milestone in the transformation of Chinese sport was the founding of the first national professional soccer league in 1994. This established soccer as a major spectator sport, a commercial venture, a popular cultural leisure activity, and one of the most widely followed sports in Chinese media. With an average of 18,000 spectators per home game in the country's top Jia A league in 2001 (ranging from 1,000 to 51,000), China had developed a following for the game comparable with some of the leading European leagues in a relatively short space of time, and soccer has become the largest spectator sport in the country (Jones 2004: 60–61). The sports sections of Chinese newspapers are often dominated by soccer coverage of both domestic Chinese and foreign games. In addition to Chinese games, Chinese soccer fans can also watch Italian Series A, English Premiership, and German Bundes league matches, often live, throughout the European season.

---

before. Now, we will take a look at the spectator sports that are becoming increasingly prominent in China, and which are sure to gain interest in the wake of China's successful 2008 Olympic Games. Beyond table tennis, badminton, and the other sports that China has traditionally dominated lies a vast organization meant to develop Chinese athletic talent at the international level. Chinese basketball has already shown significant growth, both with the national teams and with the successes of individual players, such as Yao Ming and Yi Jianlian, who have enjoyed successful careers in the National Basketball Association (NBA). Football (soccer) is also a sport of great national interest, even though China has struggled to attain rapid success in an arena that has been dominated by Europe and Latin America, with soccer traditions that stretch from small localities all the way to the highest realm of international competition.

It is the Olympic Games themselves that will likely have the greatest impact on spectator (and, quite possibly, mass-participation) sports in China in the coming decades. Not only were the 2008 Beijing Games spectacularly successful in terms of world attention, but Chinese viewers were riveted by the medal competitions for sports in which Chinese athletes showed promise. From a gold medal in women's weightlifting on the first day of competition through impressive results in shooting, archery, judo, diving, gymnastics, and the aforementioned strengths of table tennis and badminton, the Chinese team earned 100 medals—51 of them gold. The medal count, which outpaced all but the United States (110) in total medals and far surpassed all nations in the gold, was a point of national pride in the summer of 2008. It represented much more than that, though. The medal count was the result of careful planning on the part of the Chinese Olympic Federation, whose plan since the early 1990s, when China first bid for the Olympic Games, was to maximize medals in relatively obscure Olympic sports.

This is not to say that the Chinese team eschewed the dominant Olympic sports of athletics (track and field), swimming, basketball, and soccer. The Chinese team was

Sign for the 2008 Olympic Games in Tiananmen Square in Beijing, China. (Etherled/ Dreamstime.com)

the largest of all participating countries, and many athletes, even in sports that were relatively new to Chinese competition, have shown a great deal of progress since the country's concerted effort toward Olympic dominance began. Several Chinese commentators have noted that China has excelled at "small ball" (*xiaoqiu*) sports, such as table tennis and badminton, but has struggled in major sports, such as basketball, soccer, and the track and field competitions. Some early successes, such as Liu Xiang's gold medal and world record in the 2004 Athens Games' 110-meter men's hurdles, created enormous expectations for the 2008 Games—pressure that proved to be too much for an athlete who had been injured for much of the season. The significant pressure to repeat played itself out in several events in which athletes had dominated in 2004, and an eager public had counted on—one could almost say assumed—a repeat performance.

Nonetheless, the success of the Chinese team in 2008 bodes well for China's Olympic hopes, and there is little doubt that Olympic success will guide the planning for China's sporting future. Even in sports for which China has found key marketing opportunities, such as the National Basketball Association in the United States, the focus remains on building a national team capable of competing at the highest reaches of world competition.

The export of China's best basketball player, Houston Rockets' center Yao Ming, to the NBA has created great interest throughout China, where Houston's games are often broadcast live, and are almost always shown the evening after they were played (there is a 13- to 16-hour Standard Time difference between China and the various time zones of the continental United States). Still, the enormous success of

THE NATIONAL ANTHEM OF THE PEOPLE'S REPUBLIC OF CHINA

The Chinese National Anthem was heard more often than any other nation's at the 2008 Beijing Olympics as 51 Chinese athletes (or teams) ascended the podium to receive the gold medal in their sport. The *Guoge*, or March of the Volunteers, was composed by Nie Er, a left-wing composer, based on words previously written by Han Tian. The song became wildly popular when it was used in the 1934 film *Children of the Hour (Feng Yun Er Nu)*. The song is always heard with its instrumental introduction and includes lyrics that refer to the Great Wall and the building of the new China, calling on the people to brave the worst as one.

the NBA in China, along with the budding Chinese Basketball Association, pales in comparison with the national interest when China plays internationally in the Asian Championships, World Basketball Championships, or the Olympic Games. Even players with valuable contracts, such as Yao Ming, are expected to compete for their home country, and to use their off-season to help build the Chinese basketball program.

Bronze mirror with kickball scene, about 960–1279.

Football (soccer) is perhaps the greatest sports organizational challenge that the Chinese face, even greater than making inroads in the multiple single-event contests that make up the athletics and swimming categories of Olympic competition.

Although the origins of a Chinese form of football or kickball can be traced to the Song Dynasty (960–1279), the Chinese arrived rather late to the world's most-loved sport, and developing the talent—even from a nation over a billion strong—to compete with the world's soccer powers is enormously difficult. Without access to the highest levels of competition that are found in Europe and Latin America, the Chinese team is forced to rely upon Asian competition and struggling Chinese feeder leagues. The system that works so well to tap talent in individual or small team sports— finding youthful talent and training the athletes relentlessly, with ample funding from local organizations and the state—is unable to create the level of competition that a large team needs to rival even mid-level teams, such as those of England, the Czech Republic, and the United States, much less elite teams, such as those from Germany, Argentina, Brazil, and Italy.

China's hopes for influence based on the outcome of the Olympic Winter Games is perhaps the longest stretch of all, even though some planners have marked out strategies to field competitive teams beginning in 2010 and continuing though the 2020s. On the other hand, China's Summer Olympic future looks very bright indeed, and its dominant medal counts are likely to continue for many more Olympiads into the future. By focusing on a number of sports and events that benefit from the careful selection and rigorous training of China's youth, China has developed a very deep reservoir of talent that is capable of yearly regeneration. The larger issue remains the growth of classic individual sports and the most popular team sports. The future looks to be a great deal murkier, especially with regard to its soccer and basketball teams, as China seeks to create world-class competitors in an environment that does not yet lend itself to the highest levels of competition. The powerful sports ministry of the People's Republic will have to find a way to send more of its very best athletes abroad for high-level competition, even as it strives to maintain its competitive roots and enthusiastic fan base at home.

REFERENCES

Dong Erwei. *Leisure Lifestyles in Urban China*. Saarbrücken, Germany: VDM Verlag, 2008.

Dong Jinxia. *Women, Sport and Society in Modern China: Holding up More than Half the Sky*. London: Routledge, 2002.

Dott, Brian. *Identity Reflections: Pilgrimages to Mount Tai in Late Imperial China*. Cambridge, MA: Harvard University Asia Center, 2005.

Frank, Adam. *Taijiquan and the Search for the Little Old Chinese Man: Understanding Identity through Martial Arts*. New York: Palgrave Macmillan, 2006.

Guoqi Xu. *Olympic Dreams: China and Sports, 1895–2008*. Cambridge, MA: Harvard University Press, 2008.

Jones, R. "Football in the People's Republic of China." In *Football Goes East: Business Culture and the People's Game in China, Japan, and South Korea*. Edited by W. Manzenreiter and J. Horne. London: Routledge, 2004.

Lo, Benjamin P. *The Essence of Tai Chi Chuan: The Literary Tradition*. Richmond, CA: North Atlantic Books, 1993.

Schultheis, Eugenia Barnett. *Hangchow, My Home: Growing Up in Heaven Below*. Fort Bragg, CA: Lost Coast Press, 2000.

Wang Jing. *Brand New China: Advertising, Media, and Commercial Culture*. Cambridge, MA: Harvard University Press, 2008.

Popular Culture and Traditional Beliefs

Robert André LaFleur
Kevin Latham
Tamara Hamlish

In the sections that follow, we will touch upon a few major themes in popular Chinese culture and belief that have remained continuous from early times all the way to the present, as well as several that represent a marked break with the past. We will look at the role of the Internet, as well as cinema, popular literature, and religion, before moving on to examine the calendar, lucky (or auspicious) days, lucky directions, and feng shui, as well as the concept of lucky numbers. Some of these practices represent a distinct break with past culture; others have deep philosophical roots in early China, and have been studied by some of the greatest minds in Chinese history. As the contributors to this book have emphasized throughout these pages, the government one finds in China today represents both a break with the past and a powerful continuation of it. It is no different in popular culture than it is in politics, economics, or history.

THE INTERNET, GAMING, AND COMMUNICATION

What can be considered China's contemporary popular cultural landscape is constantly and, in some areas, very rapidly changing. New technologies and new consumer opportunities, as well as changing regulatory, political, and social contexts, allow new popular cultural practices to emerge regularly, and some of those discussed in this volume will become outdated in the relatively near future.

The Internet and telecommunications have had a fundamental impact on contemporary Chinese popular culture in recent decades—since the end of the 1980s, in the case of telecommunications, and since the mid-1990s, in the case of the Internet. They have changed the ways in which people interact and communicate with one another and have offered a wide range of new forms of leisure and entertainment. With the advent of the Internet, Chinese people—particularly young people—have started communicating using email and instant messaging services, in chat rooms, on bulletin boards, and through short messaging services (SMS) to mobile phones. They now enjoy access to endless sources of information—from online newspaper

POPULAR CULTURE

Translating the term "popular culture" into Chinese is difficult. There are several possibilities, but each of these has a different range of connotations and none overlaps exactly with the flexible and wide-ranging English term. For instance, one common translation is *liuxing wenhua*, with *wenhua* being the conventional translation for "culture." *Liuxing* is usually translated as "fashionable," hence in *liuxing wenhua*, the sense is of transient or contemporary popular culture that may be a passing fad or fashion. Another translation is *tongsu wenhua*, where *tongsu* means "popular" in the sense of being widespread among the people, but can also carry connotations of vulgarity, low value, or commonality. Other less common translations include *dazhong wenhua* and *minjian wenhua*. The former—"mass culture"—cannot escape from the connotations of the Maoist past and the latter—"among-the-people culture"—is more like folk culture and tends to conjure up ideas of folklore, folksongs or folk music, dance, myths, and legends.

articles and news portals to government Web sites and cultural associations—that could not have been imagined just 20 years ago.

Chinese Internet users have access to a wealth of information, but this does not mean that the Internet is a free area of uncontrolled and unrestricted interaction. There is a range of ways in which the Chinese authorities in particular, but also others, control Chinese Internet access and content. These include blocking sites, the use of commercial pressures, requirements for self-censorship and regulation, restrictions on online news production and reporting, and the arrest of online dissidents. Indeed, deterrence is a key feature of Internet control in China.

The Chinese authorities regularly block access to foreign sites, particularly prominent news sites like CNN or BBC News or sites expressing views that are unacceptable to the Chinese government, including advocacy for Taiwanese or Tibetan independence or human rights Web sites. The authorities have introduced a number of filtering devices that screen sites for particular phrases and vocabulary to help them block the ones they do not like. In addition to government censorship, there is also the matter of language. Most Chinese people utilizing the Internet use Chinese-language Web sites and services, and although many users will have some basic working knowledge of English and other languages, the majority of Chinese Internet users are not suitably proficient in English to be able to use the English-language Internet as a matter of routine. Thus, just as important as site-blocking, if not more so, is the use of other forms of regulation and self-censorship in shaping Chinese Internet content. Web site operators are responsible for what appears on their sites under the threat of losing their licenses and being closed down. In this way, the kind of self-censorship regime that operates in other media sectors was fairly successfully introduced to some areas of the Internet.

Online gaming has become a popular leisure activity among young people, particularly in the cities; e-commerce is starting to offer alternative ways of shopping

Chinese youths work at their computer stations in an Internet cafe in Beijing, China, 2006. (AP/Wide World Photos)

and consuming; and broadband is offering new ways of enjoying films, music, and television. These are changes that have affected many parts of the world in recent years. However, the impact in China is all the greater because up until the 1980s, the country was largely closed to the outside world and people had limited leisure time, disposable income, and entertainment opportunities, and lived within a regime that closely guarded information of all kinds. Netbars, or Internet cafés, became very popular, particularly with young people, in the early 2000s. They are places where young people go to play online and other computer games, to socialize with their friends and make new acquaintances, and to surf the Internet. In this way, netbars play a significant role in contemporary Chinese youth culture as a location for social interaction in addition to providing Internet services.

There are other ways in which the Internet plays a key role in youth culture and social interaction, particularly through the possibilities that it offers for new kinds of communicative practices. The Internet provides new forms of communication, including email and instant messaging. Unlike in other parts of the world, however, email is relatively lightly used in China. One reason for this is the popularity and accessibility of mobile phones; text messaging in particular has offered an easier, more flexible alternative to email. Bearing in mind that more people have mobile phones than computers at home, combined with the portability of mobiles, it is not surprising that SMS and speaking to people on the phone is often preferred over email, which requires the more cumbersome use of a computer terminal and an Internet connection.

HIGH CULTURE AND POPULAR CULTURE

A useful distinction can be made between high culture and what may be considered popular culture. Much of what is categorized as pop culture in the English-speaking world, from television and pop music to instant messaging and mobile phone downloads, does not generally qualify for consideration as high culture in China, which is commonly associated with traditional watercolor painting, poetry, literature, philosophy, calligraphy, and some forms of music and theater. Defining popular culture against high culture may offer a useful shortcut that bridges the apparent similarities between notions of culture common in the West with those of China. However, it is also potentially misleading, as forms of traditional Chinese high culture have always been broadly popular with the masses and have, at different times and in very different contexts, pleased audiences across social classes, from illiterate peasants up to high-ranking officials and emperors.

It could be argued that telephones, pagers, faxes and mobile phones have had a more fundamental and far-reaching effect than the Internet on Chinese social interaction in the last two decades. Chinese people are generally far more likely to have seen their lives changed by telephones than by the Internet. The kind of interpersonal communication that telephones, particularly mobiles, facilitate has opened up new informal sources of information transfer—whether through calling friends or relatives overseas, talking with work colleagues in another part of the country, or by enabling on-the-spot accounts of news events as they happen—that offer a fundamental alternative to centralized mass media.

The growing digital divide in China between rural and urban areas and between the wealthier, more economically and technologically developed eastern coastal provinces and the central and western hinterland provinces gives an indication of the kinds of differences that telecommunications can make in people's lives. Any visitor to China's large metropolitan centers will be struck by the range, diversity, and ubiquity of telecommunications, particularly the highly visible mobile phone. Mobile and fixed-line phones have become such a common feature of everyday life in the towns and cities that they have transformed many of the ways in which people interact socially.

FILM AND CINEMA

Chinese cinema has become one of the most internationally visible areas of contemporary Chinese popular culture. Such film genres as martial arts films, historical films, thrillers, comedies, documentaries, educational films, and propaganda films are all created and viewed by the Chinese populace. Since the mid-1980s, when young filmmakers of the so-called Fifth Generation started making films that hit cinema screens throughout the world, Chinese cinema has established a recognized position on the

Workers travel past a big advertisement of the U.S. film Cold Mountain *and the Chinese film* Brothers, *in Shanghai, China, 2004. (AP/Wide World Photos)*

international cinema circuit of film festivals, competitions, and arthouse cinema distribution. However, it is not only in the last 20 years that cinema has become an important feature of Chinese popular culture. Since the 1930s, cinema has had a crucial role to play in formulating and embodying ideas of Chinese modernity; in the development of revolutionary Chinese intellectual and political movements; in entertaining, educating, and informing ordinary Chinese citizens; in promoting the policies of the CCP; and in raising the profile of Chinese artistic production on the international stage. Chinese cinematic production is a fundamental component of China's recent historical and contemporary artistic, entertainment, and political heritage.

Apart from much of the period under Mao, Chinese people both earlier in the 20th century and at the end of the 20th and beginning of the 21st centuries have been watching many films that were not made in mainland China or even by Chinese people at all. Unsurprisingly, at different times, the Hollywood film industry has played a key role in the history of Chinese filmmaking and film viewing. However, at other times, so, too, have European and other international films. Hong Kong cinema in particular has enjoyed a special relationship with mainland Chinese film watchers during the post-Mao reform era.

Cinema, like other media in China, is considered to be part of the state and party propaganda machine, but also like other areas of Chinese, media is undergoing reform aimed at least in part at greater commercialization and international competition. There are ways in which film content is directly censored, including the compulsory preapproval of screenplays before films are made. However, it has often been easy for filmmakers, in the post-Mao era at least, to stray from the original script without being stopped in the process. This may be due to the lax implementation of supervisory procedures, broadly sympathetic studio managers, or other contingent factors. Thus, films considered sensitive can still be made by state-owned, state-run, state-financed, and state-controlled film studios.

Prior to World War II, cinemas, as a new technology, constituted a key feature of modernity, with strong foreign associations and a flavor of luxury in the buildings themselves and on-screen that was not necessarily part of the everyday lives of Chinese people. After the war, a newly enhanced political role and the function of film in society transformed cinema-going from a relatively independent, individual act of consumer choice to one of political engagement. In the 1960s and 1970s, watching films became an organized experience of mass political participation. Work units organized trips to the cinema for their workers or showed films in dining halls or theatres at their workplace. Watching films could also be accompanied by discussion in political meetings before or after the viewing. Work units were equipped with projection facilities, and new projection teams were set up to travel around showing films where there were no cinemas, including many rural areas where the inhabitants had never seen a film in the past.

In the late 1970s and early 1980s, after the political turmoil of the Cultural Revolution period had died down, cinema-going peaked once again with record audience levels attracted by more interesting films, a more relaxed political environment, and a relative lack of other forms of entertainment. A fundamental shift since the 1980s has seen more Chinese people watching films at home on video, VCDs, or DVDs than at the cinema and cinema-going itself has also changed enormously over the years. By the second half of the 1990s, it was easy to buy pirated VCDs of the latest Hollywood films, as well as of Hong Kong and Chinese films, often before they hit the cinemas either in China or other parts of the world. In the 2000s, VCDs largely gave way to DVDs, the quality of pirated copies improved, and the cost of legal copies of films came down.

In addition, from the 1980s onward, a whole range of other entertainment possibilities has gradually developed, from discos, music, and dancing to sports, theatre, dining, bowling, and other public activities. Consequently, for many in China, film watching has gradually become separated from the notions of cinema-going and public activity. Film watching is an increasingly flexible, personal, and domestic experience.

POPULAR RELIGION

One area in which increased consumption in the post-Mao period has generally been greater in the countryside than in the cities is popular religion. Under Mao, all religious activities were suppressed and traditional weddings, funerals, temple festivals, and other popular religious celebrations disappeared. However, in the post-Mao era, many families, villages, and communities have started staging more elaborate ceremonies and celebrations again, drawing to varying degrees upon people's memories and knowledge of how things were done in the past. This kind of popular religious renaissance has entailed new forms of individual, family, and community consumption.

Over the last 30 years, thousands of village temples and ancestral halls have been renovated and some of their roles in village affairs have been reinstated. Much of the expenditure for renovation has come from private sources, usually with large contributions from wealthy businessmen or peasants and combined smaller contributions from less wealthy families. The renewed position of village temples in village life has also seen renewed expenditure on temple visits, with incense, food, drink, and paper money offerings made to deities or donations given in return for divining services and consultations. Temple festivals can also involve considerable expenditure on offerings, theatrical performances, or entertainment and banquets, and although not every village and temple is involved in such expenditures, many are.

Expenditure on popular religion is not confined to festival, ceremonial, and celebratory consumption, however. In the post-Mao era, Chinese peasants have increasingly returned to what the government would call feudal or superstitious practices, like fortunetelling, horoscope readings, exorcisms, geomantic consultations, healing, and almanac use. This kind of consumption is frowned upon by the authorities, who see such practices as unscientific, but the practices continue nonetheless and involve not only payment for services rendered, but also for books, calendars, offerings to deities, and other accompanying expenditures. Many people also buy and set up shrines in their own homes to kitchen gods, ancestors, or popular deities. Such shrines are often found in business premises set up by proprietors to protect and bring good fortune to their businesses.

We will now take a closer look at some of the beliefs that have experienced a resurgence in the late 20th and early 21st centuries.

CALENDARS AND ALMANACS

Chinese almanacs and calendars have been published for centuries. Indeed, it is true that the calendars one can buy today in Hong Kong, Singapore, or Chicago are similar in overall form to those printed during the Ming dynasty 500 years ago. Calendars available for purchase elsewhere in China or in Taiwan have a different appearance, but much of the information within them is similar. When examining a traditional Chinese calendar and almanac, what strikes the observer first is the initial section, printed in red characters, that contains a cowherd and the spring festival ox, giving a general picture of the coming year's weather, not unlike what one might see (without the ox and cowherd) in an American *Farmer's Almanac*.

One has to turn to the back of the volume to find the actual calendar, with a separate column for each day of the year, and characters in red and black ink. It is the reason people need to buy new almanacs in the late months of the year, and it is still the job of calendar specialists to put together an accurate and, one might say, compelling calendar for personal and family reference. One can find them in the autumn and winter throughout China, Hong Kong, Taiwan, or Singapore, as well as in almost any city in the world with a sizable Chinese population.

Complete with month-by-month and day-by-day breakdowns, the current calendars are divided into as many as eight sections. The calendar has traditionally

Two performers wait to take part in the Dragon Altar temple fair ceremony welcoming the Year of the Horse in Beijing, China, on February 12, 2002. (AP/Wide World Photos)

figured prominently in everything from family decisions and business negotiations to government activities and the planning of large events. For example, the calendar was (and often still is) consulted about days on which one would get engaged, marry, or hold a funeral, even if a person felt that the book was superstitious. One might ask why this was so, especially if some people simply didn't believe in lucky days for events. The answer is an important one in terms of understanding the perpetuation of cultural beliefs. Even today, because so many others follow the practices, it is difficult (without appearing arrogant and uncaring) for an individual to choose an unlucky day for an important event. In the past, as well, it mattered to others, even if it did not for the individual. It would not be difficult to think of a similar situation in American society. Imagine an atheist among very devout Christians. How easy would it be to have a nondenominational funeral service for a beloved family member? By no means did everyone accept such customs, even in earlier centuries. Social pressures helped perpetuate practices as much as the beliefs themselves, as they do today.

The most important parts of the Chinese calendar for popular cultural practices are the items to avoid and the items best suited to any given day. There are several days a month on which it is unlucky to cut one's hair or clip one's nails. Mixing sauces or digging wells also have prohibitions. In fact, it is startling to see how popular the almanac and calendar remain in urban areas, such as Hong Kong, Taipei, Singapore, Shanghai, and Beijing, when a large proportion of the activities in these sections are clearly linked to life in an agricultural setting. The "activities to do" section on any given day might well include study (*ruxue*). In fact, after looking at every almanac for the past two decades, and many from much earlier periods, one realizes that not once has a day appeared on which the calendar notes that it is unlucky to study. There are good (and bad) days to move one's house, bury the dead, go on long (or short) trips, and put up beams in a shed. These activities give a fascinating perspective of daily life and its domestic rhythms. A sampling of the categories from a Lunar Year 2008–2009 calendar follows. Note that the categories (other than study) can appear under either heading; it is the timing that is important, not the activity.

Avoid	*Appropriate*
Opening granaries	Marriage ceremonies
Erecting (roof) beams	Meeting with friends
Taking long trips	Engagements (marriage)
Paying mourning respects	Placing beds (for *fengshui*)
Discarding clothing	Cutting/patterning hair
Moving earth	Studying

The almanac's middle sections contain descriptions of dreams, omens, bad luck, small-business management, and numerous fortune-telling charts. There is even an English pronunciation guide that gives a distinctive flavor of Hong Kong in an earlier era, complete with Chinese characters used to simulate the correct pronunciation (using Cantonese) of English words. It is a mixed proposition, at best. In the almanac's illustrations, one sees a clear connection between text and picture, often in the *bantu* (half-picture) format that made the book at least somewhat accessible for a wide range of people in a household, even those who couldn't read well. They do not constitute great art, by any means, but they do create a linkage between literate and oral cultures that was profoundly significant in Chinese history well into the 20th century.

In addition to the sections on charms, agricultural information, and folk wisdom mentioned above, one finds a series of divination sections of widely varying seriousness. Many of these sections are intended, from their own introductions, to give a small glimpse of the characteristics of future events in a person's life. It is easy to mistake many of these activities (and their corresponding almanac sections) for extremely serious inquiry into the future. Most of them are meant to be somewhat playful. That does not diminish the role that professional astrologers have played in Chinese society over the centuries. A professional with books and treatises, not unlike some of those discussed in the Daoism section of Chapter 5, would go far beyond the sections of the almanac to link personal fate and future for their clients.

Given that China is well into the scientific age, and that there have been harsh reprisals against practitioners of superstition in the People's Republic within living memory, why would anyone in China today buy a calendar or go to a fortune teller? Admittedly, it is easier to find fortune-tellers in the trade centers of Hong Kong, Singapore, Taipei, or even large cities in the Western world than it is in Shanghai, Beijing, or much smaller cities. They exist, however, in spite of the protestations one might hear that these beliefs are dead. A brief anecdote from the author's research and two further examples will have to suffice.

When I was working for a computer company in Taiwan 20 years ago, I had a female colleague who had recently graduated from college and was a true asset to the company. I thought of her as very modern, yet she would often return from lunch with her latest reading from a fortune teller. I found that shocking at the time (long before these matters began to make sense to me in the larger pattern of Chinese culture). I asked her pointedly how someone so well educated could believe such "nonsense." Her answer intrigued me, and has since led me to study what some people call "superstition" in Chinese and Western culture and what I have come to think of as a rhetoric of fate and future. She said that she enjoyed being single, but that her family was pressuring her to marry. She wanted to "get a feel" for what might come next in her life. The phrase struck me, and made me wonder how one could get a feel for something in the future.

There is nothing logical about the matter, but the Chinese almanac (as well as the full fortune-telling booths in Taiwan, Hong Kong, and out-of-the-way places in the People's Republic) is filled with sections that do just that: playfully lead an individual to get a feel for the future. If one considers the matter seriously, one might ask whether a person feels comfortable, say, walking under a ladder. Many answer "yes," but a surprising number of people say "No . . . just to be safe." It is an illuminating answer. Further, what role do glances at newspaper horoscopes, plucking petals from a flower (s/he loves me, s/he loves me not), and even checking betting odds for sporting events play in life, if not to provide just a glimpse, or "feel", for the future?

In the People's Republic of China, people still talk of the ill-fated double-eight year of 1976 (a common feature of the lunar calendar in which a month is repeated to bring it in line with the solar calendar). That year, Mao Zedong died and there were major floods throughout China. Almost 20 years later, people speculated that 1995 might be the year of Deng Xiaoping's death—it was the first double-eight year since Mao died, and Deng was ailing (he lived for two more years, dying in 1997). Another very common example is the pictures taxi drivers in Beijing had of Mao in the 1980s and 1990s. He had become a minor god of taxi drivers since, it is said, a driver survived a horrific accident because he was one of the few to have had a picture of Mao on his dashboard at the time. Word spread quickly, and the Mao pictures followed. Perhaps the most startling example could be seen at the most prominent cultural event in modern Chinese history: the Opening Ceremony of the Beijing Olympics. It was scheduled to begin, by official government decree, precisely at 8:00 p.m. on August 8, 2008 (8/8/08 at 8:00). As we will see below, numerical symbolism is prominent in China. Still, the official homage to "superstition" for a watershed event is telling.

NUMBERS AND DIRECTIONS

Such ideas are also displayed by the fact that businesses pay a great deal of money for auspicious phone numbers that play on the numerical symbolism of early Chinese thought, and that geomancy, known as *fengshui,* has become an international phenomenon. Although the social and political landscape has changed dramatically, and there is by no means a unified voice in these matters, the language of fate that I referred to earlier in this section is a vital part of everyday life in China. This can be seen in cultural ideas about directions and numbers.

PRACTICALITY AND SUPERSTITION—MORE CHALLENGING THAN ONE MIGHT THINK

As a test of the popular belief propositions mentioned in this chapter, I have often asked students and colleagues in the West, particularly the United States, if they can think of one person who is so "bottom line," so obsessed with making a profit, that superstition would *never* enter his or her thoughts. The vast majority of respondents—even without prompting—say "Donald Trump." Almost 20 years ago, though, CBS News ran a feature on a Trump business enterprise in New York's Chinatown. The apartment complex had failed to sell out, and it remained half-empty. In the end, the practical, hard-nosed, and bottom-line Donald Trump spent $250,000 to call in *fengshui* experts to improve the buildings' directional influences, and the apartments started selling. One would be hard-pressed to find a better example of popular belief overriding even the staunchest of critics.

It seems that there are as many English-language books these days with *fengshui* in the title as *Dao (Tao)*. It has become associated with what many call Eastern thought. What is *fengshui* and why has it captured so many imaginations? It would be no exaggeration to say that the best thinkers in earlier Chinese society studied matters of *fengshui* and, at the same time, criticized non-scholars who used it. They often described the methods of determining burial directions as confusing and deceptive—a waste of the people's energy. Yet, the Ming tombs just north of Beijing are laid out in exquisite geomantic (*fengshui*) fashion, with nothing left to chance. One of my friends has noted that party members always seem to have houses with excellent *fengshui* and lucky telephone numbers. Finding the right directional influences for furniture, homes, and even graves lies at the heart of popular geomancy. Just as in the Daoist sense of breath and the cyclical flow of essences discussed in Chapter 5, the key idea of *fengshui* is that the world is composed of forces that need to be harmonized. The path to harmonization is challenging, and experts are often sought out.

Numbers are also a powerful cultural issue in China (and are a larger part of Western life than many realize). As early as the third century B.C.E., several thinkers were articulating the power of numbers. The categories of yin and yang were at work in these conceptions, but they ran much deeper to include ideas contained in the challenging text, the *Book of Changes* (*Yijing; I-Ching*). What we call "even" numbers are yin, and "odd" numbers are yang. Just as in the West (but for completely different reasons), the number three is a powerful symbol of, in this case, yang strength. Numbers related to it carry even more power. Thus, the number nine is one that holds great symbolic value, because it is three squared. The number 27 is also seen as one that, in its combinations of threes and nines, represents something "more than counting." Still, it is the number 81 (3^4) that packs an even more powerful punch in Chinese life. Some novels have 81 chapters, while others have 81 challenges that the hero must face. Finally, 72 may well be the most perfect number of all in numerical thought, since it is a powerful blend of *yin* and *yang*—$3^2 \times 2^3$. China's southern cosmological mountain, Mount Heng, is said to have 72 peaks, and the number figures in countless stories and anecdotes.

An even more current example can be found in hotel rooms and phone numbers. The number four is a homonym for "death." The characters don't look anything alike, yet they are pronounced the same way. For that reason, saying or hearing "four" in most dialects can make people uncomfortable. The fourth floor is traditionally skipped (as some Western buildings do with the 13th). Even more perplexing is the habit of putting Westerners on the fourth floor. A traveler told me the story of a trip to Beijing, when she was put in room 2442. In some dialects, that sounds like "You dead, dead—you," and it is the reason why some hospitals change room number 244 ("You dead dead") to 2C4 or something similar.

When the traveler mentioned this to a Chinese friend (after hearing numerological explanations like the ones above), she got a very interesting response. "True, but that's our culture. It's not yours." The Chinese friend interpreted it not as an act of ill will, but, rather, as a cultural anomaly that no Westerner would take seriously. Another example is the fascination in China with the lucky number 666, which, in Western culture, holds a Satanic reference that renders it disliked by some. Those numbers, however, are the essence of yin beauty in China, and it is an address or phone prefix to which companies aspire. They also pay large amounts of money for good numbers. No cab company wants 4444, of course. A beautiful mix of yin and yang numbers is not just a superstitious way of feeling good; there really is a bottom line to it. Companies pay very large amounts of money today—in a China that has ostensibly eschewed superstition—for phone numbers and even addresses that will be good for business, and in 2006, a man paid a million yuan (about $125,000 at the time) for the luckiest cell phone number in China.

YIN-YANG, THE FIVE PHASES, AND COLOR SYMBOLISM

All of these ideas relate on several levels to the complex symbolic interplay of yin-yang and what are called the five phases. Learning about Chinese medicine, *fengshui,* the calendar, and various popular beliefs presumes knowledge of the way that the yin-yang dyad and the five phases interact. The first thing to understand is that yin and yang are not opposites. The original meaning of yang is the sunny side of a slope, while yin referred to its shaded side. This simple, original definition shows clearly the changeability of yin and yang. They are not black and white, good and evil. They change in a methodical fashion. In the morning, one side of a slope is yang. By late afternoon, that same slope is yin. The same principle of change flows from the five phases. It is common for Westerners to think of the various phases as elements, along the lines of Greek thought. The five phases, although they are associated with items in nature, are in constant motion, and their power in Chinese thought depends on that understanding.

These phases move endlessly around the calendar, the seasons, and other aspects of culture and nature. They are associated with the directions (north, south, east, west, and center), colors, and the seasons. One has to learn to think in patterns of five, and the great cosmologist of the Han dynasty, Dong Zhongshu, classified the vast

Cosmological symbols carved in stone: yin/yang and animals of the Chinese zodiac. Qingyanggong temple, Chengdu, Sichuan, China. (Felix Andrews)

bulk of the world's categories according to the five phases. Chinese dynastic history is said to move in the patterns of the phases, as do the seasons, and the days of the calendar itself.

The seasons may represent the best way to understand these categories and the idea of change. Everyone knows the feel of a hot summer day or a cold winter one. In order to understand the cycles of the phases, one must think of a winter day and the way that it will progress, in time, inexorably toward warmer weather. Along the way to spring and summer, the weather may show discrepancies. There might be an unusually cold spring or summer day. Everyone knows, however, that the progress or phasing is toward warmer weather. These are the yang months of warming and heat. Just as inexorably, the yang months will turn slowly to yin and the growing warmth will give way to cooling. The process continues, on and on, into eternity.

This is phase thinking, and it has dominated Chinese thought for millennia. It can be prominently observed today in the way that foods and tastes are classified, in colors and directions, and even in ways of counting. Colors are an area of cultural discernment that many outsiders find perplexing, but, at their base, they are related to the changing seasons and the cardinal directions of China. Green, the color of beginning and renewal, is associated with Mount Tai, spring, and the east—the land of the rising sun. Red, the color of intense heat and power, is associated with summer, the southern mountain (Mt. Heng), and the southern realm. The color yellow is associated with Mt. Song, the center, and the timeless period between the six yang and six yin months. White is associated with Mt. Hua, the west, and the autumnal changes. Finally, black is associated with the north, another Mt. Heng, and the cold of winter.

These lofty cosmological ideas may seem to be a long stretch from popular beliefs, but they are related, at least in a tenuous fashion. Dynastic Chinese history was dominated by the colors and the symbolism noted above. One of the most influential texts in the Chinese cosmological tradition provides a detailed account of these issues by noting what the ruler should wear, eat, and listen to at each point in the calendar. The *Spring and Autumn Annals of Mr. Lü (Lüshi chunqiu)* can make for difficult reading, but it sums up the yin-yang, five-phase themes admirably. The idea is to understand how things *correspond* (animals to mountains to musical tones), not what they are in and of themselves.

The first month of spring

During the first month of the spring, the sun stays in the constellation *ying* (Pegasus . . . Its first day has the cyclical combination *jiazi* [beginning], and the animals of this month bear scales on their body. The corresponding sound is the note *jiao*, and the temper of the pipes corresponds to the tone *taicu*. Its corresponding number is eight, the corresponding flavor is sour, the corresponding smell is animal odor. . .

The son of Heaven moves to the apartments going to the green side (east), he rides a chariot decorated with green phoenixes and bells, he steers a bluegreen dragon (horse) team, his chariot shows the green banner. He is clothed in green clothes, he is adorned with green jade. He eats grain and lamb, the pattern of his bowls is wide and reaching everywhere . . .

[Warning] If the king should mistakenly give orders belonging to summer, wind and rain will come in untimely fashion, the plants will too early wither and give damage to the country. If he should give orders belonging to autumn, pestilence will befall people, strong wind and great rain will appear, and the fruits of the field will not be ripe in their time. If he should give orders belonging to winter, cold water will appear as an enemy, frost and snow will attack everyone, and the grain will have no ears. (John Knoblock and Jeffrey Riegel. *The Spring and Autumn Annals of Lü Buwei.* Stanford University Press, 2000)

Today, color symbolism dominates in China just as it did in the past, but with very different messages and a rather more scattered philosophical patterning. Nonetheless, it remains strong. Red is generally considered an auspicious color, and is prominent at celebrations. Traditional Chinese wedding dresses are a bright red, and even the grooms bear a red sash or bow. Because of red's auspicious overtones, it is the color of important books, such as the almanac and Mao Zedong's reflections. It is also the color of fertility and growth. In traditional times, red-dyed boiled eggs were given to friends and relatives as fertility-laden gifts.

White is a color of death and mourning, and is one that more than a few Westerners have misidentified in China in thinking of Western weddings. Funeral flowers and

Newlyweds tour on boats during a group wedding of traditional Chinese style in the Shajiabang Scenic Spot in Changshu, east China's Jiangsu Province, 2008. The couples wear the traditional red. (AP/Wide World Photos)

wreaths are white, and one never gives white flowers as a gift, particularly to someone who is ill. So important is the prohibition on white that it is especially unseemly to wear pins or medallions of that color, particularly in one's hair. Black can also carry a somber message, but it borders on serious in much the way that a black suit or dress conveys a tone of great seriousness. Black is not limited to such seriousness, though. Boys were traditionally dressed in black, and it is a particularly auspicious color for a car. Finally, green is a color of growth, renewal, and liveliness, as one can see in the first-month prescriptions in the *Spring and Autumn Annals of Mr. Lü*. One modern and arbitrary meaning of the color is known by everyone, though. A man should never wear a green hat or cap. No matter how fashionable it may seem, it sends the signal to everyone in China that he is a cuckold.

LANGUAGE AND POPULAR CULTURE

A final category that should be discussed is connected to the subtleties of the Chinese language. Language provides us with tremendous insights into popular culture and society, in part because it defines the boundaries of communities of people who are able to communicate effectively with one another. It also has a profound effect on how people live, what they recognize as important, and how they relate to the people around them. This is certainly true of the central role of language in popular Chinese culture, which is always changing to adapt to new situations, yet remains grounded—as we have seen in cosmology and the calendar—in core traditions.

There is a fascinating interplay in Chinese life between written and spoken language. For people who use an alphabetic writing system, this distinction is often

He Wenjun, a local calligrapher, writes a gigantic brushwork of the Chinese character "niu," meaning ox, *at a size of 20 meters (66 feet) in length and 9 meters (30 feet) in width, with a 54-kilogram (119-pound) weight and 3.8-meter (12-foot)-long brush, at a square in Nancong, southwest China's Sichuan Province, January 17, 2009, ahead of Chinese Lunar New Year celebrations. (AP/Wide World Photos)*

difficult to grasp, yet it is crucial to understanding the significance of language in Chinese culture. Chinese traveling throughout the country can read a street sign, a menu, or a local newspaper as if they were in their native county. Spoken language, in contrast, varies dramatically, sometimes even across extremely short distances. Regional differences in spoken languages—often defined as dialects—can range from slight differences that require little translation to differences so extreme that no one outside the local community could possibly decipher what is being said. Although the written language permits communication despite differences, spoken languages emphasize those differences and clearly define the boundaries of local communities.

The boundaries of those local communities are evident in the way that popular sayings are used in various locations, so that a northerner will pronounce a series of numbers in one distinctive way, while a southerner will pronounce them in another. The difference goes beyond mere communication, as we will see. It is bound up in the way people speak, the way they make puns and jokes, and even in the way that they negotiate. Beyond the practical functions of communication, and the symbolism of cultural identity, there is yet one more dimension to the richness of Chinese language, seen most clearly, perhaps, in the sister arts of calligraphy and poetry. It is in poetry and calligraphy that we can truly begin to understand the implications of some of the distinctive characteristics of Chinese language—characteristics that

---

SPOKEN AND WRITTEN SAYINGS

The themes of culture and communication are evident in some of the most common sayings and images in the Chinese world, many of which are linked to either the spoken or written language. We already learned about the unlucky number four, which is a homonym for death. Other examples include "fish" and "abundance" (both pronounced "*yu*"); gifts of fish or pictures of fish are common at New Year, with the unspoken wish for abundance being clear to everyone. The same goes for pictures of bats, which a Westerner might find surprising. Good luck (*fu*) is being conveyed through the medium of the bat (*fu*). The situation works in the other way, too. It is considered particularly inauspicious for someone to give the gift of a clock. It has nothing to do with the object itself. "Clock" (*zhong*) and "end" (*zhong*) are connected by speech. The list goes on and on, and the above examples only give a sense of the associations that have lasted for centuries, even millennia. Many more pass through popular culture in several years or, at most, a decade, not unlike fashionable phrases and statements in other parts of the world.

---

lend both beauty and depth to these uniquely Chinese art forms. In both calligraphy and poetry, every character is carefully chosen so that the sound, the meaning, *and the visual form* are in harmony.

What makes this even more unusual is the fact that both poetry and calligraphy are generally improvised—that is, they are created spontaneously in response to a particularly emotional event. They are a part of a lived experience, and are interpreted in that living, popular light, rather than as remnants left in books. Once an artist has either composed a poem of his own or called to mind a well-known poem that conveys the sentiments of that particular moment, he picks up his brush to capture it all on paper. Calligraphy involves the use of delicate brushes loaded with ink and applied to highly absorbent paper, a technique that leaves no room for error. The piece must be completed in one continuous movement, without pauses or hesitations, in order to portray the immediacy and urgency of the moment, captured at the intersection between the spoken language and the written language.

It should be clear by now that what we commonly think of as the Chinese language is, in fact, a complex system for creating cultural communities through both writing and speech. Yet, despite this seeming complexity, the various dimensions of Chinese language are part of the everyday activity of communicating with others in every Chinese community. People draw upon the resources of the language to express themselves—to bargain at the market, chat with a friend, close a business deal, or create a work of art. This can be seen in most social interactions, where even a brief conversation is generally accompanied by hand gestures that depict the corresponding characters in order to add emphasis or to make something clearer. It is not unusual to see people using their index finger to write on the palm of the opposite hand or trace a character in mid-air. You might even be able to judge the seriousness of a conversation by the moment at which pen and paper are pulled out and verbal exchanges are accompanied by the writing of entire phrases (as opposed to single characters being casually scribbled in the air).

Meaning in Chinese language is not just about the meaning of words, but also about whether words are spoken or written, whether they are the local dialect or standard pronunciation, and whether they are formed in the air or carefully inscribed with a brush. It is not only the meanings of words that matter, but which words are chosen and through what medium they are conveyed.

The notions of popular culture and popular beliefs may seem to be catchalls intended to round out more practical matters of history, economics, politics, and society, yet this is far from the case. Indeed, the calendar, glimpses of the future, cosmology, numerology, and popular language lie at the heart of a changing China. The themes are interwoven in ways that cannot easily be explained, but are too important to ignore if we are to understand China at a deeper level. Like the nested Chinese boxes we encountered early in this Culture chapter, each discovery—from lucky numbers and the spontaneous use of language—brings with it a new opportunity. The past is dead, as many critics from the 19th century onward have claimed (or hoped), and the past is everywhere. The only constant is a flowing river of continuity and change.

REFERENCES

Granet, Marcel. *La pensée chinoise*. Paris: Albin Michel, 1934.

Latham, Kevin. *Pop Culture China!: Media, Arts, and Lifestyle*. Santa Barbara, CA: ABC-CLIO, 2007.

Lindquist, Celia. *China: Empire of Living Symbols*. Reading, MA: Da Capo Press, 2008.

Eberhard, Wolfram. *A Dictionary of Chinese Symbols: Hidden Symbols in Chinese Life and Thought*. New York: Routledge, 1988.

Contemporary Issues

Anita M. Andrew

CONTEMPORARY CHINA: ECHOES OF THE PAST

The year 2008 was an important one for American news coverage about China.

There was such a wealth of information available on the Internet, television news, and in print newspapers about China's political, economic, and societal conditions that most Americans could say with confidence that they were at least familiar with some aspect of Chinese history, politics, or culture.

Although there were both positive and negative reports about China in 2008, what most Americans remembered more than anything else was the Beijing Olympics held from August 8–24, 2008. That was fine with China, since its government longed to use the international games as a way to highlight its accomplishments to the world in a setting that it could control. This was China's show and it intended to make the most of its time in the spotlight.

China's government sought to increase its share of the international tourist market. China's official Xinhua News agency reported in June 2008 that the Beijing Olympics would be just the beginning of China's tourism boom and estimated that by 2015, China would be the world's leading tourist destination. China counted on its centralized sports system, which identified and trained potential stars at a very young age, to prove that not only could its athletes compete with the best in the world, but that they would win more gold medals than any other nation. To reach this goal by the 2008 Olympics, China instituted a strategy known as "Project 119" to identify those Olympic sports in which China had not excelled previously, but which offered the possibility of a cachet of medals if they increased their competitive edge, especially with the United States.

View of fireworks launched over the National Stadium, known as the "Bird's Nest," during the opening ceremony for the Beijing 2008 Olympic Games in Beijing. (Guimahky/ Dreamstime.com)

To accomplish these goals, the Chinese state poured enormous amounts of money, time, talent, and technology into the opening and closing ceremonies to produce an awe-inspiring spectacle intended to demonstrate that it had become wealthy, technologically proficient, and modern in every respect. It was not surprising to many observers that China was able to accomplish such feats with respect to the Olympics.

It did seem surprising to many that China cared what the world thought of it. It can be argued that China's main motivation with the Beijing Olympics was to draw the most powerful nations of the world into its own arena, where it, not they, dominated. This idea was not a new one at all. Throughout most of China's long history, the West had dreamed about contact and trade with China. Prior to the twentieth century, Western diplomats, merchants, and missionaries did not initially realize that any interactions with China were typically orchestrated by China from a position of strength. From China's perspective, no country or ruler was China's equal. As we have already noted in several chapters, such an attitude of cultural superiority had been the cornerstone of Chinese foreign policy for thousands of years. Yet, in 2008, China was hardly an imperial monarchy any longer. The Olympic Games, however, resounded with some echoes from the country's past.

The purpose of this chapter is to address a number of key contemporary issues that motivated China's desire to operate on the national stage from a position of strength. The most significant news about China in the Olympic year was related to environmental problems with coal mining, pollution, the monumental dam project across the Yangzi River, the poaching of endangered species, the Chinese government's crackdown against political protests by Tibetans and Uighurs, tainted Chinese products exported to other countries, the Chinese adoption industry with the West, and the Beijing Summer Olympics themselves.

These events had a number of points in common. First, they revealed that China had largely succeeded in convincing the West that China did not have to play by the same rules of engagement that applied to the Western industrialized nations in order to get what it wanted. China insisted on doing things its own way and it expected the West, especially the United States, to accept its position. Second, even when these same nations voiced criticism of China, they did not sanction China for its behavior. Instead they undertook great efforts to avoid confrontation with China over ideological or policy differences, proving that the country exercised a significant amount of control over the nature of interaction with the West.

CHINA'S TRADITIONAL WORLDVIEW

China's international behavior did not develop suddenly. Rather, it was the result of China's determination to assert itself from a position of strength in a unique manner that drew on its past. Throughout Chinese history, the country's rulers and officials viewed their civilization as a source of immense pride. As we have seen, the Han peoples were the ethnic majority in China, as well as the most important group of citizens in China. With the exception of two periods in Chinese history, the Mongol era that began in the 13th century and the Manchu period that began in the 17th century, the Han controlled China's many ruling houses, called "dynasties." As the officials who ran the Chinese empire and wrote the official histories, they also dominated the educated elite. The Han dynasty (206 B.C.E.–C.E. 220) was one of the strongest, longest-lasting dynasties in Chinese history. This era was also when China's dominant patterns of dealing with foreigners were developed.

Because of their dominance, the Han tended to have an exalted self-image. They called their country the "Middle Kingdom" and their rulers "Sons of Heaven." They did not accept foreign governments, peoples, or cultures as equal to their own and they insisted on being in control when dealing with outsiders. As we saw above, those who were not ethnically Chinese were considered "barbarians." Han rulers utilized a unique foreign policy strategy that they referred to as "using barbarians to check barbarians," one which sought to keep rivals divided so that they would not have enough strength to challenge the Chinese state.

China became accustomed to dealing with foreigners on its own terms. Until the mid-19th century, China was the oldest and most powerful country in East Asia. In relations with other countries and peoples, China expected visitors to understand that they could not measure up to China's importance and accomplishments. Westerners saw this as a form of cultural arrogance, but the Chinese simply expected visitors to accept their worldview without question. Such cultural arrogance did not pose a significant problem until the 19th century because China had the political, military, and economic power to back up its assertions and to deal with any challenges to its dominance. China's 19th-century rulers—focused as they were on an earlier worldview—did not understand, or seek to assess, how to deal with formidable Western nations who were determined to establish trade with China on their own terms. They seriously underestimated the threat those nations could pose.

EUROPEAN MARITIME POWERS AND THE QING DYNASTY

When Western merchants from Great Britain and the Netherlands first attempted to establish trade and diplomatic relations with China in the early 17th century, China treated their emissaries as they would any other group of visiting "barbarians."

The British and Dutch were, by this time, two very powerful maritime nations. They came to China to buy exotic goods they knew they could sell at home. By the end of the century, tea was the mainstay of the British trade. These early European entrepreneurs expected the Chinese government to recognize their importance and throw open its doors to trade with them. The Chinese did not oblige. China did permit trade, but its rulers made sure that they controlled all aspects of the trade. Again, this policy was nothing new; China had always treated "barbarians" this way.

The interesting twist on the Chinese attitude toward foreign policy was that the rulers of this period were not Chinese at all. The Qing dynasty (1644–1911) was created by the Manchus, who originally comprised a society of pastoral nomads in the region later known as Manchuria. The Manchu conquest of China in 1644 was only the second time in Chinese history that foreigners were able to conquer the entire Chinese empire, both north and south. Yet, even foreign conquerors could not superimpose their customs and authority on China. They may have been able to conquer China, but in order to gain the assistance of the Chinese scholarly elite for the monumental task of ruling the country, they had to adapt to the ruling patterns of the Chinese state.

Until the 1840s, China had significant control over who came into China and what they did there. Foreign trading companies, such as the British East India Company, were restricted to one port city in China and they had to abide by Chinese rules when conducting trade. This was the southern coastal city of Guangzhou in Guangdong Province, which Westerners called Canton, the name derived from the French, Italian, and Latin terms for a section of territory.

Under what historians have called the Canton System, foreigners who wished to engage in trade with China were isolated so that they could not freely move about in China. This system of trade subjected foreigners to fees that were levied at the discretion of the Chinese government and their middlemen. All the economic benefits of the Canton System went to China.

Perhaps the most difficult notion for the diplomatic and business emissaries who came to China under the Canton System to accept was that it treated them as its vassals rather than as equals. Dynastic rulers simply assumed that all who wished to make an official state visit to the emperor's court did so to demonstrate their government's awe of and submission to China, the undisputed military, cultural, and economic center of East Asia. Thus, all those who wished to negotiate with the

Engraving of George Macartney's mission to China in 1793. The mission was an attempt on the part of the British government to persuade the Qianlong emperor to open new opportunities for British trade and accept a permanent British ambassador in Beijing. (AFP/Getty Images)

government were required by protocol to perform a symbolic gesture in the presence of the emperor. This gesture was the "kowtow," a term which literally meant to "knock the head."

Such an act must have been difficult for visitors to China to endure, but it was absolutely necessary from the Chinese perspective. Any government wishing to have contact with China was expected to direct its representatives to comply with Chinese requirements. As demeaning as the kowtow must have been for the foreign dignitaries who visited China in the 18th and 19th centuries, none made an issue of the requirement until the British arrived in China and attempted to establish trade relations with China on their own terms.

A turning point in China's interaction with foreigners occurred in the late 18th century when the Qing Dynasty's Qianlong emperor (who reigned from 1735–1796) received the first British Ambassador to China, Lord George Macartney. Lord Macartney's arrival in China in 1793 created the first of many misunderstandings between China and the West that would cause China to insist that foreigners accept its worldview without question. The Chinese government treated Lord Macartney and his entourage as it would any other group of foreigners under its traditional tribute system. The British mission even referred to its purpose as bringing gifts to the Qianlong emperor in honor of his 83rd birthday. From the Chinese state's perspective, this constituted very traditional behavior for its vassals to follow. It expected foreigners to behave as subordinates in return for the recognition bestowed on them by the emperor, with the most obvious acceptance of their status being the kowtow.

The Qing Emperor Qianlong received Lord Macartney in 1793. Macartney stated that he would not perform the kowtow, but he was able to negotiate a compromise of bending one knee after explaining that it was how he showed respect to his own ruler. The British recorded this remarkable event as follows:

> As soon as the monarch was seated upon his throne, the master of the ceremonies led the ambassador [Lord Macartney] toward the steps. The latter approached, bent his knee, and handed, in a casket set with diamonds, the letter addressed to His Imperial Majesty by the King of England. The emperor assured him of the satisfaction he felt at the testimony which His Britannic Majesty gave him of his esteem and good will in sending him an embassy with a letter and rare presents; that he on his part entertained sentiments of the same kind toward the sovereign of Great Britain, and hoped that harmony would always be maintained between their respective subjects. He then presented to the ambassador a stone scepter, whilst he graciously received the private presents of the principal personages of the embassy. He was perfectly good-humored, and especially pleased with the son of Sir G. Staunton, who talked a little Chinese, and received as a token of imperial favor a yellow plain tobacco pouch with the figure of the five-clawed dragon embroidered upon it . . . (Tappan, 1914)

If Lord Macartney actually believed he had achieved a successful beginning to regular and mutually advantageous British trade relations with the Qing dynasty as a result of his audience with Qianlong, he was mistaken. He did not yet understand what China required of foreigners. The emperor himself set the record straight in his own letter to King George III of England, dated 1793. In it, Qianlong stated:

> Yesterday your Ambassador petitioned my Ministers to memorialise me regarding your trade with China, but his proposal is not consistent with our dynastic usage and cannot be entertained. Hitherto, all European nations, including your own country's barbarian merchants, have carried on their trade with our Celestial Empire at Canton. Such has been the procedure for many years, although our Celestial Empire possesses all things in prolific abundance and lacks no product within its own borders. There was therefore no need to import the manufactures of outside barbarians in exchange for our own produce. (Long, 1793)

The emperor's response could not have gone over well in King George's court. The situation between the two countries became even more strained when another British ambassador to China, Lord William Amherst, arrived in China in 1816. Lord Amherst was far more direct in his refusal to perform the kowtow. The Qing government responded by refusing to receive him at court. The British and other foreigners who hoped to open trade to China undoubtedly expected China to recognize their accomplishments, but neither the Qianlong emperor nor subsequent Chinese rulers in the 18th and 19th centuries sensed any real use for these foreigners or their goods. All trade with this latest group of "barbarians" favored China, and the assumption was that this state of affairs would continue.

The real problem that developed between the Chinese and the British in the late 18th and early 19th centuries, however, was that neither country understood the other or was even willing to accept the other as an equal. Their competing worldviews ultimately made it impossible for the two countries to negotiate a workable trade relationship for one simple reason: the British wanted trade on their own terms and the Chinese wanted it their way. There was little room for compromise. By the 1830s, it was the British who were in a position of strength. As we saw in the history chapter, China did not yet realize it had reached the limits of its power. What gave the British the edge in their quest for a trade advantage in Asia was their control of the cultivation and distribution of opium in India, coupled with its maritime dominance.

THE OPIUM WAR, 1839–1842

Historians Timothy Brook and Bob Tadashi Wakabayashi have described the issues surrounding the British importation of opium to China and the actions of various Chinese governments to oppose it as representing a pivotal point in modern Chinese history. Although opium had long been regarded as a medicinal drug used to treat a number of ailments, by the 18th century, the Qing government was aware of the economic and societal dangers of opium smoking as a recreational activity far before it went to war with England.

The British had chafed under the Chinese-dominated trade of the Canton System for many years, as all of the profit went to China. The British had not been able to find a commodity that China would want until they became involved in the opium trade. Opium became the means of finally overturning the Chinese advantage. By the turn of the 19th century, the British had a vigorous trade in opium that paid premium prices set by the British. The Qing government tried to stop the trade, but it could not, although it issued many edicts between 1800 and 1839 about the opium crisis for China. Yet, the clash between the two nations was not even principally about the moral impact of opium on Qing society, but rather about who controlled the opium trade and how that trade operated.

The tensions between China and England escalated in the spring of 1839, when Lin Zexu (1785–1850) became the Imperial Commissioner in charge of dealing with the opium problem. Commissioner Lin even took the bold step of trying to send a letter directly to the British sovereign, Queen Victoria (r. 1837–1901), about his concerns. There is no record of a reply. Although Lin made a reasoned appeal in his letter, he did refer to the British opium importers as "barbarians." He might have chosen another term, but it is significant that Lin used it. Did he know that the East India Company was directly linked to the British government? To the 21st-century reader, it is startling to conceive of such a direct form of address being made to a foreign power. Did Lin notice such matters?

At first, China attempted to deal with the British according to its traditional method of dealing with "barbarians." By the 19th century, the British were far more

JOHN QUINCY ADAMS, "ADDRESS ON THE OPIUM WAR" (1841)

In 1841, former president John Quincy Adams asserted—while the Opium War was still going on—that China brought the war upon itself by the way it treated the West.

. . . It is a general, but I believe altogether mistaken opinion that the quarrel is merely for certain chests of opium imported by British Merchants into China and seized by the Chinese Government for having been imported contrary to Law. This is a mere incident to the dispute; but no more the cause of the War than the throwing overboard of Tea in Boston Harbor was the cause of the North American revolution . . . The cause of the war is the pretension of the Chinese, that in all the intercourse with other Nations, political or commercial, their superiority must be implicitly acknowledged and manifested in humiliating forms . . . (page 314)

. . . Which has the righteous cause? You have perhaps been surprised to hear me answer Britain. Britain has the righteous cause. But to prove it, I have been obliged to show that the opium question is not the cause of the war, and my demonstration is not yet complete.

The cause of the war is the Ko-tow! the arrogant and insupportable pretension of China, that she will hold commercial intercourse with the rest of mankind, not upon terms of equal reciprocity, but upon the insulting and degrading forms of the relation between lord and vassal . . . (p. 324)

powerful militarily than China and they were determined to have *their* way with the opium trade. Neither was willing to back down. The two countries went to war from 1839–1842. The war itself came as no surprise to other Western nations, including the United States. Former President John Quincy Adams (the sixth President of the United States from 1825–1829) even called it a "righteous cause" in an address he had written about the war in 1841 (Adams, 1910).

During the war, China discovered that it was not modern or powerful enough to defeat the British "barbarians" and by 1842, the British had forced China to sue for peace. The opium trade continued into the 20th century.

Beginning in 1842, China signed a series of "unequal treaties," first with England and then with France, Germany, Russia, the United States, and, by 1895, Japan. The so-called Treaty Port System replaced the old Canton System. For the first time, however, the West controlled trade with China. The Treaty of Nanjing (Nanking) ended the Opium War in 1842, imposed an indemnity of 21 million Mexican silver dollars on China for the cost of the war, and opened the port cities of Canton (today known as Guangzhou), Amoy (also known as Xiamen), Fuzhou (referred to in the treaty as Foochow), Ningbo (referred to in the Treaty as Ningpo), and Shanghai, and permanently ceded the island of Hong Kong to England.

In 1843, the British Supplementary Treaty of the Bogue established the provision of extraterritoriality, a legal protection that permitted the British and, later, other foreign nationals to be tried according to their own country's law in criminal cases involving Chinese nationals. It also guaranteed other Western nations the same rights and privileges that were originally given to the British in the unequal treaties with China by means of a provision known as the "most-favored-nation" status. These two treaties began what Chinese governments, activists, and historians of the 20th century often refer to as the Century of Humiliation, which China endured at the hands of foreigners and their governments.

THE *CENTURY OF HUMILIATION*

The *Century of Humiliation* lasted from 1842–1943 and took the form of an armed occupation of parts of China by a shared consortium of nations (Great Britain, France, Germany, Italy, Russia, the United States) that controlled China's territory and trade for over 100 years. The Century of Humiliation, a term used in China to express frustration with foreign influence, became an important rallying point for Chinese nationalism throughout the 20th century, as China struggled to regain the ability to control its own trade, as well as its own destiny, without foreign interference.

In the period leading up to the Beijing Olympics, numerous commentators cited the Century of Humiliation as a key part of China's motivation to ensure the success of the 2008 Summer Games. The most representative voice of this group of China specialists, who offered one explanation of why China acted the way it did in 2008, was Professor Orville Schell of the Asia Society Center on U.S.-China Relations. Professor Schell spoke and wrote quite often in 2008 about what he thought Americans needed to know about China and its Olympics.

As compelling as this theory may be, it is also important to recognize that it focused primarily on the notion of China as the victim of Western imperialism. The Century of Humiliation did give rise to many manifestations of Chinese nationalism in the 20th and 21st centuries, but it was not the only factor to consider when assessing China's behavior in 2008. China did not define itself this way for most of its history. As we have previously seen in this chapter, prior to the 19th century, China was an empire and culture characterized by brilliance and strength. The Century of Humiliation finally ended in 1943.

The Chinese Communist Party may have owed its formation, at least in part, to the impact of imperialism on China, but its victory in 1949 was over Chiang Kaishek and the Nationalists, rather than a colonial government. The country we refer to as China, and the People's Republic of China today, was divided by politics in 1949. The Chinese Communist Party ruled mainland China and established the People's Republic of China, and the Nationalist Party fled to Taiwan and established the Republic of China. Both claimed to be the legitimate government of China and that has caused countries throughout the world to take sides since 1949. The United States publicly backed the Nationalist government in Taiwan until 1978. This caused many mutual misunderstandings between the United States and China during the Cold War era and after this period due to differing worldviews, traditions, and political ideologies.

In other chapters of this book, readers learned how the leaders and policies of the People's Republic of China dealt with other nations and ideologies. During the Cold War era, China and many Western nations viewed one another with great suspicion and distrust. The main impetus for China's reaction to the West after 1949 was its rejection of everything that China associated with the West's political agenda. What Mao Zedong (1893–1976) and other Chinese Communist leaders never acknowl-

Men of the 9th U.S. Infantry Regiment camp inside the Forbidden City, Beijing (Peking), China. The group formed part of an international expeditionary force called in to counter the Boxer Rebellion in 1900–1901. The foreign forces in the Chinese (Qing) capital contributed to negative Chinese perspectives regarding the Century of Humiliation. *(Library of Congress)*

edged, however, was the often unspoken, but still deeply rooted, traditional Han Chinese notion of cultural pride. Yet, as we have seen above, when dynastic rulers dealt with outsiders, cultural pride was also fused with disdain.

How China handled the Olympics and other issues in the news in 2008 demonstrated that it was not only driven by current political ideology and goals. Echoes of history were evident, as well. But what aspects of the past were most relevant? In the lead-up to the Olympic Games, Chinese government officials repeatedly demonstrated that they cared little about what outsiders thought of them or how they dealt with a wide range of issues that affected their own citizens. Such behavior seemed to have far more in common with imperial China's historical views of foreigners than any motivation it had to prove itself in the aftermath of the Century of Humiliation.

The sections that follow will focus on key contemporary issues to illustrate how China has sought to establish a distinctive way of dealing with foreign and domestic matters, summarily rejecting the views of outsiders in what it considered its internal affairs. These issues have created significant disagreement between China and many

Western countries, and the rhetoric on both sides has often been pointed. They are also among the issues that are most likely to appear in news stories in the coming years.

ENVIRONMENTAL PROBLEMS

At a current population of over 1.3 billion people, China was in great need of housing, food production, industrial output, and energy needs to fuel its economy. China had already attained status as an economic and nuclear superpower, but it also continues to face an environmental crisis from which it may not be able to recover. A *New York Times* article from August 2007 stated that China was "choking on growth."

> Environmental degradation is now so severe, with such stark domestic and international repercussions, that pollution poses not only a major long-term burden on the Chinese public but also an acute political challenge to the ruling Communist Party. And it is not clear that China can rein in its own economic juggernaut. (Kahn & Yardley, 2007)

This was only one of many dire predictions of disaster coming both from around the world and within China. Activists have attempted to raise awareness about the extent of China's environmental problems, but that does not mean that the Chinese government accepted the criticism or pledged to act to alleviate the problems. Efforts from organizations such as the World Trade Organization (WTO) linked China's participation to greater attention to fair trade, environmental improvement, and human rights, but China has been resistant to change and has ultimately fallen short of the WTO's requirements for member nations. China has been a member of the WTO since December 2001. According to the WTO's own Ministerial Conference, "China has agreed to undertake a series of important commitments to open and liberalize its regime in order to better integrate in the world economy and offer a more predictable environment for trade and foreign investment in accordance with WTO rules" (World Trade Organization [WTO] News, 2001). It did so with the strong endorsement of the United States, yet there were no requirements that China's admission or continued membership in the WTO be tied to commitments to significant changes in China's record on human rights and environmental policy.

It was not until quite recently that China began to face open criticism from its citizens about its serious environmental problems. Chinese activists came forward from many sectors of Chinese society to expose environmental problems, as well as the Chinese government's actions on environmental issues. The government often took a hard line in dealing with them, however, and has used imprisonment and other punishments in an attempt to silence them.

POLLUTION

Pollution has been a serious problem in China for decades. China's 1.3 billion people comprise the largest population on earth. China became the third-richest economy in the world in 2007, and much of its growth is tied to industrial development. The

Two environmentalists wearing masks and holding a huge dummy face with a mask march through a Hong Kong street in April 2002, to call on the government to curb Hong Kong's air pollution. The demonstration was held on the eve of Earth Day. (AP/Wide World Photos)

Chinese government has not adequately regulated its industries, however. There has been rampant illegal dumping of industrial chemicals in landfills and waterways, and the air quality of Chinese cities ranked as the most polluted in the world.

In 2008, China sought to showcase its wealth and modernity through its preparation for the Olympic Games, yet, even in its showcase, there remained serious problems. The issue of pollution in Beijing and other venues was such a concern for Olympic athletes that many refused to train in China in the months leading up to the Summer Games. There was also a separate organic food support provided for the athletes to ensure that there would be no question about the quality or safety of the food served. Chinese officials made many public assurances of the safety of the Olympic food supply. Even amid this public demonstration of quality assurance, however, there were reports and questions about the safety of China's regular food supply.

Most news reports from this period raised concerns that China had not done enough to allay fears about food safety—not just for the Olympic athletes, but also for its own citizens. There was ample evidence that the Chinese government was still not fully committed to making its air, water, and food supplies safe for its citizens. Chinese citizens have been concerned about the quality of the air they breathe for decades, Chinese have traditionally boiled their water, but scientists estimate that hundreds of millions of people do not have safe drinking water. Sharp increases in respiratory diseases, cancers, and birth defects in recent years have all been linked to pollution. Pollution did not just have a significant human cost; its economic impact also affected 5.8 percent of China's Gross Domestic Product in 2008.

The problem of combating widespread air and water pollution in China is made even more difficult by the Chinese government's insistence that foreign governments and non-governmental organizations were interfering in China's development and trying to hold China to standards that did not apply to Western countries, especially the United States, when they went through their own 20th-century economic boom. These arguments carry a certain moral and historical weight (one country pollutes and prospers, as another is held back), yet the sheer size of China's population makes the matter extremely sensitive.

COAL DEPENDENCE AND MINING DANGERS

Coal has been China's source of energy for thousands of years. According to American University's TRADE & ENVIRONMENT DATABASE (TED) (1996), "The coal resources in China have been exploited since 476 B.C., and it is estimated that even with all the years of coal exploration, China has total coal deposits of 4,490 billion tons which are as deep as 2,000 vertical metres."

Westerners first learned about China's use of coal from the Venetian explorer, Marco Polo, in his controversial book *The Book of Ser Marco Polo*, dating from approximately 1300 C.E.; readers were quite skeptical about the fantastic tales of the exotic East. Polo described coal as having unusual qualities:

> It is a fact that all over the country of Cathy [an early Western name for China] there is a kinds [sic] of black stones existing in beds in the mountains, which they dig out and burn like firewood. If you supply the fire with them at night, and see that they are well kindled, you will find them still alight in the morning; and they make such capital fuel that none other is used throughout the country. It is true that they have plenty of wood but also, but they do not burn it because those stones burn better and cost less. (Yule, 1903)

Henry Yule, the editor and translator of the 1903 edition of Marco Polo's account, further explained in a note that, "There is great consumption of coal in Northern China, especially in the brick stove, which are universal, even in poor houses. Coal seems to exist in every one of the eighteen provinces of China, which in this respect, is justly pronounced to be one of the most favored countries in the world." (Yule, 1903)

Today, Shaanxi, Shanxi, Inner Mongolia, and Hebei provinces produce the richest reserves of coal. China's plentiful deposits of these black stones powered China's economic boom. By 2007, coal produced at least 70 percent of China's massive—and growing—energy needs. Typical estimates reveal that China builds a new coal-fired energy plant every week just to keep up with demand.

Many news stories from 2008 focused on the fact that China's coal dependence made it a very significant source of polluting energy. Yet, China also made progress on this front. The country signed and ratified the Kyoto Protocol, which committed member nations to significantly reduce greenhouse gas emissions by 2012. It also concluded a ten-year U.S.-China Energy and Environment Cooperation Framework in June 2008 "to foster extensive collaboration over a ten-year period to address the challenges of environmental sustainability, climate change, and energy security" ("U.S., China to Cooperate on Energy and Environment" 2008). Nevertheless, the vast number of news accounts still focused on the number of mining disasters that occurred in 2008, the great dangers China's coal miners faced working in the mines, and the deplorable treatment many received at the hands of greedy and unscrupulous mine owners.

Even in the mines that were officially licensed by the government, working conditions were precarious at best and there were reports of many more mining operations that operated illegally and without any oversight at all. Tim Wright, a specialist on the Chinese coal industry at the University of Sheffield (England), suggested in a recent interview that "There's no doubt that Chinese mining is much more labor intensive than Western mining. There's no doubt that [it] puts workers at risk" (Lelyveld, 2009). Another problem revealed in the stories of 2008 was that the Chinese government has sought to minimize the impact of these mining disasters, including the casualty reports. It was not until 2005 that the Chinese government publicly acknowledged the "'astonishingly serious' corruption, chaotic management and lax enforcement of safety rules in investigating coal mine disasters that have killed thousands of Chinese workers" (Cody, 2005).

Since that time, reports of mining accidents have appeared with quite alarming frequency in the international media, but there is also widespread skepticism about the accuracy of the casualty numbers provided in these reports. As Sharon La Franiere reported in the *New York Times* in April 2009, "Work-safety officials in Beijing complain that even more than in other industries, death tolls from accidents at coal mines are often ratcheted down or not reported at all. That is because of the risky profits to be made—by businessmen and corrupt local officials—exploiting dangerous coal seams with temporary, unskilled workers in thousands of illegal mines" (LaFraniere, 2009). *The People's Daily*, China's main Communist Party newspaper, issued a statement in February 2009 that the official death toll in China's coal mining accidents for 2008 was 3,215, down from 3,786 in 2007, according to the State Administration of Work Safety (SAWS). Chinese officials pointed out that the conditions of its legal mines had improved in recent years, but such claims are difficult to verify, since China still does not allow international mine safety organizations or their representatives to inspect its mines.

THREE GORGES DAM CONTROVERSIES

The Three Gorges Dam project has figured prominently in news reports during the last decade. This project was one of the most significant in Chinese history and it involved the third-longest river in the world, after the Nile and the Amazon. Known as the "Long River," the Yangzi cuts through China's middle section and flows from its source in the Tibetan plateau of Qinghai province to the city of Shanghai on the East China Sea. The Yangzi is over 3,900 miles long.

The name of the project is derived from the region of the Yangzi River Basin, which winds around three steep-walled mountains, the Qutang Gorge, the Wuxia Gorge, and the Xiling Gorge, known collectively as the "Three Gorges." The area encompasses some of the most beautiful scenery in China. Historian Lyman Van Slyke noted that the Three Gorges have "inspired awe and captured imagination" since the Han Dynasty (VanSlyke, 1988).

The Three Gorges Dam is located at Sandouping near Yichang city in Hubei province. It began as the pet project of former Prime Minister Li Peng, who served the Deng Xiaoping administration from 1987–1998. Li was the Chinese official who was referred to as the "Butcher of Beijng" after the government crackdown on the protestors who participated in the Tiananmen demonstrations of 1989. He used his influence in the early 1990s to push the project through the National People's Congress, the Chinese Communist Party's highest group of representatives. Yet, even in this group, which regularly supported the leadership's policies, there was widespread opposition to the project.

Government officials justified the project as a way to bring much-needed hydroelectric power and economic prosperity to western China once the dam was operational. The dam itself is one and a half miles wide and more than 600 feet high. It will create a reservoir hundreds of feet deep and nearly 400 miles long. This will be the biggest dam and hydroelectric project in the world, capable of producing over 18,000 megawatts of power.

The Yangzi Gorges Dam is a project that is considered as large and important to China as the control of the Yellow River in the north was to ancient China. The Yellow River was the location of the earliest-known Chinese settlements dating back to prehistoric times, perhaps as early as 4000 B.C. The Yangzi River became the key to economic development between the 13th and 15th centuries, as it was an important way to transport people and goods between south and north China.

In the 21st century, the Yangzi River is clearly the most important river in China. The Chinese government has touted the Dam project as the key to new jobs, improved navigation, and flood control along the Yangzi River. The project began in 1994, with an expected completion date of 2009.

This entire project has been plagued by problems for the past 15 years, however. Critics of the project both within China and elsewhere in the world have complained of cost overruns, corruption, failure to remove toxic building materials from construction sites, poor quality control, the impact on wildlife, the effects of sediment build-up, the forced resettlements of millions of people, and the incalculable loss of historic and archaeological sites.

China has responded to criticism from Chinese environmental activists by arresting and imprisoning its leaders, such as journalist Dai Qing, in order to silence their opposition to the Dam project. It also rejected statements about the project's hazard until September 2007. There has been widespread speculation that Chinese leaders took this unprecedented stand to begin to distance themselves from the project in case something went wrong.

POACHING OF ENDANGERED SPECIES

Poaching, the illegal hunting of endangered animals linked to China's traditional medicine industry, has been a serious problem in China for years. Chinese medicine has long used plant, mineral, and animal ingredients to treat a myriad of conditions

The giant panda is an animal of great significance in Chinese cultural lore. It remains a symbol of peace to the Chinese, and the government has made gifts of giant pandas to other countries to signify peaceful relations. However, even the pandas have suffered loss of environment and poaching. (Kldy/Dreamstime.com)

and diseases. Of particular concern are the body parts of tigers, rhinoceros, and bears, which are used to treat inflammation and infections.

Long before China and Taiwan had any official commercial or diplomatic ties, the black market in traditional medicines from China was a well-known enterprise that operated through Hong Kong. Yet, until the last decade, the Chinese government was very slow to respond to calls to protect endangered species that were part of this industry. China did not implement or sign the Convention on International Trade in Endangered Species of Flora and Fauna until 1981, or enact its own Law on the Protection of Wildlife until 1988. In 2006, its State Forestry Administration of China even explored the idea of auctioning hunting licenses to foreigners to hunt some endangered animals. One commentator referred to profit as the chief motivating factor in this decision.

International organizations, such as the World Wildlife Federation (W.W.F.) and the International Union for World Conservation (I.U.W.C.), have launched coordinated campaigns to publicize the continuing problem of tiger, bear, deer, tortoise, and even giant panda poaching. In fact, China even featured ivory carvings and chopsticks from African elephant poachers in state-run friendship stores throughout the 1980s, without apology or explanation to the foreigners who purchased these items. It was not until 1989 that a worldwide trading ban on ivory was imposed. Yet, in a startling development in the summer of 2006, the Convention for International Trade in Endangered Species permitted China to buy ivory again for commercial purposes. That sale was delayed until the summer of 2008.

As of 2009, there is still an active and very profitable illegal trade in endangered species, which are illegally hunted for their body parts and fur, centered in China and the Chinese government has not yet stopped the poaching of endangered species.

TAINTED PRODUCTS FROM CHINA

Concerns about the safety of Chinese food products have been in the news for several years now. On May 20, 2007, Rick Weiss of the *Washington Post* wrote about the range of tainted foods from China, identifying "dried apples preserved with a cancer-causing chemical; frozen catfish laden with banned antibiotics; scallops and sardines coated with putrefying bacteria; mushrooms laced with illegal pesticides" (Weiss, 2007).

The scandal of tainted foods from China first surfaced in March 2007, and involved the contamination of many brands of dog food sold in the United States. Laboratory analysis revealed that wheat gluten produced in China and sold to American companies contained melamine, which was found in the foods. Melamine is an industrial chemical that, according to the U.S. Centers for Disease Control and Prevention, "is a synthetic chemical with a variety of industrial uses including the production of resins and foams, cleaning products, fertilizers, and pesticides. It does not occur naturally in food" (CDC, 2008).

A woman with her baby looks at powdered milk products with notice boards of "no melamine" displayed inside a supermarket in Chengdu, Sichuan province, China, October 2008. China's quality watchdog has said no traces of the industrial chemical melamine were found in new tests of liquid milk sold domestically, amid official efforts to restore public trust in milk supplies. (AP/Wide World Photos)

Melamine was supposedly used by Chinese companies to boost the protein levels in foods, yet the manufacturers did not voluntarily reveal the use of melamine in their products. That fact led to speculation about how long melamine has been used in food products from China, as there was no previous testing for this contaminant. It was not until early 2008 that a U.S. federal grand jury indicted both Chinese and American businesses for their suspected connection to the tainted pet food.

The fall of 2008 again brought Chinese products into focus, with the discovery of the industrial chemical melamine in Chinese baby formula, powdered and fresh milk products, and even candy, cookies, and drinks made with Chinese milk powder and sold throughout Asia and many countries in the West. The worldwide popularity of Chinese foods made such an alert necessary, since the products are no longer available only in specialty import food markets, but on many supermarket shelves. The Chinese government made no effort to pass the alerts along to importers, however. Neither the importers nor the retail stores in the United States routinely alert consumers to the potential dangers of the melamine-tainted foods. In most stores in America, the products were stocked on shelves without any warnings about the problem.

LEAD PAINT PRODUCTS FROM CHINA

Americans are always surprised to learn how connected we are to China in terms of the everyday goods we buy and use. Chinese products may be found everywhere, from those toys sold in gum machines to the treasures that stock most dollar stores to the textiles, electronics, jewelry, dishes, and clothing sold at popular retail stores. In 2008, they dominated the American market because of their generally lower prices. Many Americans did not realize that many of these products had very high levels of lead, however. Chinese manufacturers routinely used lead-based paints on their exports. Lead contamination has been detected in all of these products from China.

As a direct result of the lead contamination, there have been recalls in the United States since 2007, due to the hazards lead exposure poses to small children. China and the United States signed an agreement September 2007 to ban lead from toys, electronics, lighters, and fireworks. There remained concern about the level of enforcement from China, however. There were also concerns that the 2007 agreement did not include painted jewelry intended for children. In July 2008, Congress passed the Consumer Product Safety Improvement Act, which regulated the allowable levels of lead and other substances for children's toys. President George W. Bush signed the bill in August 2008. It took effect in February 2009.

The lead contamination of products made in China and sold on the American market caused a crisis in confidence about their safety. No trade sanctions were imposed on China, however. The Bush administration continued to follow a policy of economic engagement, a strategy recommended by the Clinton administration in 2000. The idea behind this strategy is to do business with China, and draw China into the international community with incentives, rather than punishments.

The impact of recent legislation on the Chinese toy industry remains to be seen. American consumers have learned much in the past year, however. As news stories have shown, many U.S. parents and other consumers have begun to read the labels on goods and have become wary of buying toys or other products made in China.

POLITICAL EVENTS IN CHINA: CHINA'S GOVERNMENT CRACKDOWN AGAINST POLITICAL PROTESTS BY TIBETANS AND UIGHURS

On March 10, 2008, Tibetan monks began to protest against the 49th anniversary of an unsuccessful attempt to overthrow the Chinese occupation of Tibet. The protests began peacefully, but quickly polarized Tibetans and Han Chinese nationals in Tibet and China, who saw the protests as a challenge to Chinese control in Tibet. China has occupied Tibet since 1959. The monks took advantage of the opportunity this period afforded to demand independence from China before the Beijing Olympics. They did so because they knew the world was watching and they might not have such an opportunity again.

Tensions between the Chinese and Tibetans continued to escalate throughout the spring and summer of 2008, and even threatened to disrupt the Beijing Olympics when pro-Tibet demonstrators demanded that the Olympic torch route not travel through Tibet. The Chinese government responded first by arresting and jailing monks. By March 15, it had also responded with the force of the Chinese army and imposed severe restrictions on foreign journalists who attempted to cover the crackdown.

The human rights group, Amnesty International, issued the following statement about the crackdown in March 2008:

> The Chinese authorities should allow an independent UN investigation into the events of the last week in Tibet, particularly in the light of the sealing off of the region in recent days and the long-term restrictions on human rights monitoring there. The situation also demands attention by the Human Rights Council at its current session. (Amnesty International, 2008)

There were swift condemnations of the Chinese crackdown from the European Union and the U.S. Congress. There was no public comment from President George W. Bush, however. Both the U.S. House of Representatives and the Senate passed non-binding resolutions condemning China's use of force in quelling the demonstrations in Tibet and urging China to hold talks with the Dalai Lama about the future of Tibet. Nancy Pelosi (D-California), Speaker of the U.S. House of Representatives, offered one of the strongest statements about the crackdown: "If freedom-loving people throughout the world do not speak out against China's oppression in China and Tibet, we have lost all moral authority to speak on behalf of human rights anywhere in the world" (Stolberg & Sengupta, 2008).

China rejected the criticisms and stressed that the issue was an internal matter. It also launched a campaign to implicate the Dalai Lama as being responsible for the Tibetan protests. Chinese Communist Party leaders and newspaper referred to supporters of the Dalai Lama as the "Dalai clique" and to their goals as "separatists." Chinese President Hu Jintao issued a statement on April 12, 2008.

> Our conflict with the Dalai clique is not an ethnic problem, not a religious problem, nor a human rights problem. It is a problem either to safeguard national unification or to split the motherland. (President Hu, 2008)

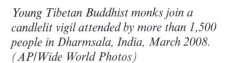

Young Tibetan Buddhist monks join a candlelit vigil attended by more than 1,500 people in Dharmsala, India, March 2008. (AP/Wide World Photos)

Another indication of minority discontent with China erupted in anti-Chinese demonstrations in March 2008. This time, it involved Uighur Muslims (Muslim minorities originally from Central Asia) in China's Xinjiang Province. China has controlled the Xinjiang region since the mid-18th century. The Uighur minority population is some 16 million people and most live in Xinjiang, but call it East Turkestan.

Uighurs have increasingly called for independence from China and claim that the Chinese government is trying to eliminate their culture. China has dealt harshly with all Uighur demonstrations and demands by citing them as evidence of separatism, an offense punishable by death. In May 2008, Chinese actions against Uighurs were again in the news because of the local reaction to the government's attempt to route the Olympic torch relay through western Xinjiang province.

In an attempt to garner international support for its actions, the Chinese government pointed out that the Uighur demonstrators were actually Muslim terrorists linked to Al Qaeda, which it claimed planned to disrupt the Beijing Olympics. Unlike the situation in Tibet, there was little foreign reaction to the Uighur protests or China's response.

THE CHINESE ADOPTION INDUSTRY

The year 2008 marked the 18th year of a very fragile, but enduring, diplomatic and immigration arrangement that has permitted foreign parents to adopt children from China. The children available for adoption were mostly infant or toddler girls, and all of them became available for foreign adoption as the result of the population control efforts that

Two American adoptive mothers hold their new daughters in Guangzhou, China, October 1998.
(AP/Wide World Photos)

have been in place since the early 1980s, known as the One Child Policy. The United States quickly became the leading destination for many of China's abandoned children. More than 50,000 Chinese children have become Americans since then by way of adoption.

Adoptive parents in the United States looked to China as a reliable source of "waiting children," particularly girls and boys with special needs. China offered single parents and older parents a unique opportunity that was not usually available in domestic adoptions. Many adoptive parents were also drawn to China because they sincerely believed they were saving a child's life.

Since the beginning of China's involvement in international adoptions in 1992, it has been very clear that the Chinese government strictly controlled the entire process. Chinese adoption laws from 1992, 1993, 1998, 2005, and 2007 spelled out in very specific terms what sort of foreigners could adopt its children. By far, the most restrictive regulations were enacted in 2007, which established requirements about the health, income, and marital status of potential adoptive parents.

Despite the rules China set for international adoption, foreign parents readily accepted the terms for these adoptions, including the requirement of travel to China, the necessity of spending weeks in China to complete the adoption process, a required cash "donation" to the child's orphanage, and the promises they were required to provide regarding the welfare of the child. As costly and inconvenient as the trip to China would be for most American adoptive parents, two main factors made China a good choice: the adoptions were finalized in China, providing automatic citizenship for the child, and the issue of dealing with a birth parent would never arise since all of the children available for adoption by foreigners were officially classified as "abandoned" by China.

Since 1994, there have been numerous accounts in the media about how the adoption of children from other Asian countries, particularly Cambodia and Vietnam, has often been plagued by corruption, but that was not the case with China. Adoptive parents in America considered China a safe bet, supposedly due to the steps the government itself takes to ensure that each child is indeed legally available for adoption. In reports issued by the Chinese government, prospective parents are told when the abandoned child was brought to the orphanage and that efforts to locate the child's parents were unsuccessful. There was no reason to question the Chinese government's conclusion or methods.

By 2008, there was mounting evidence that China had not only had its own problems with baby trafficking as early as the 1990s, the same time that its own foreign adoption boom occurred, but that it also did not report such cases, either in the Chinese press or to the U.S. State department or the Immigration and Naturalization Service. A revealing documentary directed by Jezza Neuman aired in the United States during the summer of 2008, first on the HBO network and then on many public television stations in the nation. It was called *China's Stolen Children* and it sent shock waves through the community of parents in America who had adopted Chinese children. It was difficult enough for adoptive parents to try to make sense of the One Child Policy, abandonment, and what to tell a daughter of China about her birth mother without the possibility of a black market in babies.

Every aspect of transnational adoption from China since 1990 has hinged on the assumption that the children placed in American homes were abandoned. American immigration law specifically classified an abandoned foreign child as an orphan for adoption purposes. It suggested no hint of ties with the birth parents, and enabled adoption agencies and adoptive parents to justify removing the child from her or his homeland and taking her or him to a new life in America. If this central aspect is called into question, however, then the future of international adoption from China may be in jeopardy.

The response from the U.S. government has been curious and disturbing. The State Department Web site on international adoption still makes no mention of baby trafficking in China, even though the site is updated often and is quite pointed in its criticism of similar practices in both Cambodia and Vietnam.

THE BEIJING SUMMER OLYMPICS

This chapter ends as it began: with the issue of the Beijing Summer Olympics.

The spectacle of the Olympics gave the world a unique opportunity to examine China for this most important sports international competition. Yet, such views were perhaps the most calculated and controlled in the history of the Olympics. A catchy Olympic song sung on video by China's most popular recording artists (*Beijing huanying ni*, or "Beijing welcomes you"), cartoon mascots, and the opening and closing ceremonies were all designed to awe the world.

Two of the world's most notable film directors were hired by the Chinese government to co-produce the ceremonies, American Steven Spielberg and Chinese Zhang Yimou. Spielberg resigned in February 2008, after expressing his frustration about trying to convince China to do more to use its influence and friendship with the Sudan to intervene in the humanitarian crisis in the Darfur region in Western Sudan, where hundreds of thousands have been killed and millions were forced to flee their homes by the ethnic violence. Human rights activists have used the term "genocide" to describe the conflict that has raged there for five years. Spielberg was not the only person to use his influence to try to convince China to do more to aid the peace process in Darfur. On February 14, 2008, an international coalition of Nobel laureates, Olympic athletes, government officials, business leaders, human rights activists, and public advocates sent a petition to the Chinese government.

Many felt that China's role in the peace process was essential. China did not agree. China's response to the Spielberg resignation in the international press was defensive, yet it did not address the issue in Chinese newspapers. The government's action indicated that it would not allow any issue of its links to Sudan to interfere with the Olympics. The BBC reported in February 2008 that China had imported $4.1 billion worth of goods from Sudan in 2007, including 500,000 barrels of oil per day.

There was discussion of a boycott of the Olympics, not only because of the Darfur issue, but also due to China's handling of the demonstrations by Tibetan monks and the Uighurs. Ultimately, this boycott did not materialize.

After Spielberg's departure, Zhang Yimou's role as chief director/producer of the opening and closing ceremonies became even more crucial. Zhang was well known for the visually stunning films he made; China counted on him to make the world stand in awe of China's athletes, as well as China's history, wealth, and power. China invested an enormous amount of money into advertising campaigns shown on television in Western countries. It also created a sophisticated Olympic Web site. There was much emphasis placed on state-of-the art venues and facilities. The Beijing Olympic site even featured a curious link called "Preserving the Charm of Beijing" about the *hutong*, the traditional alley communities that used to populate Beijing before China began to ready the city for the 2008 event. Yet many *hutong* were eliminated in the years leading up to the Games as part of Beijing's Olympics redevelopment since they were considered inefficient in some areas, while others did not provide the modern and sophisticated image China hoped to convey.

Prior to the opening of the Games, there was something of a media volley from both China and the West. Western news reports often focused on construction accidents associated with Olympic venues, traffic problems, construction accident cover-ups, air pollution, the blood doping of athletes, crackdowns on political dissidents, the elimination of the poor and homeless from Beijing, and the tearing down of traditional houses and neighborhoods.

China's response was to defend its interests and to point out that those making criticisms did not know China. Indeed, the domestic press' hostility to those criticizing China was often intense, and it was followed by public reactions to the boycotting of the French superstore Carrefour and demonstrations against Western ignorance about Tibet (Cody, 2008). The world did notice that there was a great difference between the images China wanted them to see and the reality of life in China. As the Olympics drew closer, there was increased pressure on the International Olympic Committee (IOC) to take stern action against China, but this action did not materialize.

As it turned out, Americans watched the Olympics with great interest. Viewers were indeed impressed by the opening ceremony. China was still in the news, but it was not the sort of publicity that the country wanted; the coverage concerned the attacks on two American relatives of an Olympic coach, scandalous revelations about the opening ceremony, and speculation about China's sports system, particularly in women's gymnastics. China tightly controlled information until after the success of the opening ceremony. Nine-year-old Lin Miaoke did not really sing her rendition of "Ode to the Motherland" at all, but simply lip-synched it. The global community also learned after the fact that a female dancer had been seriously injured during rehearsal for the ceremony and that China had kept this incident a secret.

Even these issues, coupled with the other issues outlined in this chapter, did not seem to affect how most Americans felt about the Beijing Olympics. According to a poll conducted by the Associated Press-Ipso during the first few days of the Beijing games: "By 55 percent to 34 percent, respondents said the International Olympic Committee's selection of China was the right choice rather than a mistake, a sentiment expressed evenly across party and ideological lines" (Most Americans, 2008). During the two weeks of coverage, viewers were more concerned about American Olympic stars, such as Michael Phelps and Shawn Johnson, than about China. It was as if China had become irrelevant to the Olympics by that time.

CONCLUSIONS

All of the recent issues introduced in this chapter are linked by a common theme that highlights China's ability to control the image, something it expected the rest of the world to accept. Despite the negative press about environmental coal-mining problems, pollution, the monumental dam project across the Yangzi River, the poaching of endangered species, the Chinese government's crackdown on political protests by Tibetans and Uighurs, tainted Chinese products that were exported to other countries, the Chinese adoption industry, and even the problems associated with the Beijing Summer Olympics, China definitively showed the world that outsiders must take China on China's terms and not expect to change China.

In the news stories discussed in this chapter, we have also seen that China did not take well to criticism from other nations about its problems. It most often responded to such criticism by pointing a finger back at the criticizing country and saying that that country already went through the same type of stage for which they criticized China. China has not easily or quickly moved to change based on feedback from outsiders. It unapologetically defended itself against such onslaughts. In all of the issues examined in this chapter, we saw a China that acted from a position of strength to have its own way. That is why China refused to be swayed by what it dismissed as American interference in its internal affairs in the months leading up to the Olympic Games. It behaved not as a country that suddenly found its voice and power to stand up to an oppressor, but as a country that had, for thousands of years, made demands on foreigners and expected those demands to be met.

Finally, the themes we have covered in this chapter serve to underscore China's ability to handle outsiders. There was no Olympic Games boycott in 2008. Tourists still flocked to China. Americans stores still featured Chinese products. The American government did not impose sanctions on China for its trade policies and human rights record. Adoptive parents still contracted to adopt Chinese children and were willing to do as China demanded and to wait as China instructed them to wait.

From a Chinese perspective, the real triumph of the Beijing Olympics was that it gave China the opportunity to deal with foreigners from a position of political and economic strength. China's attitude recalled its approach to foreign policy under the tribute system of the imperial past. It showed that, in the wake of the Olympic Games, China still did not kowtow to the "barbarians."

REFERENCES

Adams, John Quincy. "Address on the Opium War." (1841), reproduced in the Proceedings of the Massachusetts Historical Society, February meeting, 1910, page 324.

Amnesty International Press Release, March 15, 2008: http://www.amnestyusa.org/document. php?lang=e&id=ENGPRE200803154215.

Centers for Disease Control and Prevention (CDC), Frequently Asked Questions (FAQ): "Melamine in Food Products Manufactured in China," October 7, 2008: http://www. bt.cdc.gov/agent/melamine/chinafood.asp.

Chang, Chun-shu. *The Rise of the Chinese Empire: Nation, State, and Imperialism in Early China, ca. 600 B.C.–A.D. 8*, Ann Arbor: University of Michigan Press, 2007.

Cody, Edward. "Chinese Government Discloses Corruption, Mismanagement in Mining Sector." *Washington Post*, December 23, 2005 http://www.washingtonpost.com/wp-dyn/content/article/2005/12/23/AR2005122300728_pf.html.

Cody, Edward. "For Chinese, a Shift in Mood, From Hospitable to Hostile," *Washington Post* Foreign Service, Tuesday, April 29, 2008; Page A10 http://www.washingtonpost.com/wpdyn/content/article/2008/04/28/AR2008042802238.htm.

Emperor Qian Long: Letter to George III, 1793, Chinese Cultural Studies: http://academic.brooklyn.cuny.edu/core9/phalsall/texts/qianlong.html.

Kahn, Joseph and Jim Yardley. "As China Roars, Pollution Reaches Deadly Extremes." *The New York Times*, August 26, 2007: http://www.nytimes.com/2007/08/26/world/asia/26china.html?_r=1.

La Franiere, Sharon. "Graft in China Covers Up Toll of Coal Mines," *New York Times* April 10, 2009: http://www.nytimes.com/2009/04/11/world/asia/11coal.html.

Lelyveld, Michael. "China's Miners Pay Price for Poor Safety," Radio Free Asia, 3–02–09: http://www.rfa.org/english/energy_watch/mine-safety-03022009164225.html.

Littlefield, Angie. TED Case Study #234 CHINCOAL, "China Coal Use and Environmental Impacts, TED Case Studies, American University, Volume 5, Number 1, January, 1996://www1.american.edu/TED/chincoal.htm.

"Most Americans back holding games in China," MSNBC, August 13, 2008: http://www.msnbc.msn.com/id/26170515/.

Mungello, David E. *The Great Encounter of China and the West, 1500–1800* Lanham, MD: Rowman & Littelfield, 2005.

President Hu. "Tibet problem entirely internal issue of China." *People's Daily Online,* April 12, 2008: http://english.people.com.cn/90001/90776/90785/6391334.html.

Stolberg, Sheryl Gay and Somni Sengupta, "Bush Silent, but Others Speak Out on Tibet Crackdown." *The New York Times*, March 22, 2008: http://www.nytimes.com/2008/03/22/world/asia/22prexy.html.

Tappan, Eva March, ed. "The Reception of the First English Ambassador to China, 1792." In *Modern History Sourcebook, China, Japan, and the Islands of the Pacific,* Vol. I of *The World's Story: A History of the World in Story, Song, and Art.* Boston: Houghton Mifflin, 1914, pp. 189–192. Scanned by: J. S. Arkenberg, Dept. of History, Cal. State Fullerton. Prof. Arkenberg has modernized the text. http://www.fordham.edu/halsall/mod/1792macartney.html.

Teng, Ssu-yu and John Fairbank. *China's Response to the West.* Cambridge, MA: Harvard University Press, 1954.

"U.S., China to Cooperate on Energy and Environment"—http://www.america.gov/st/text trans-english/2008/June/20080619150612xjsnommis0.6257855 html#ixzz0FSjthWXo &A.

Van Dyke, Paul A. *The Canton Trade: Life and Enterprise on the China Coast, 1700–1845.* Seattle: University of Washington Press, 2007.

Van Slyke, Lyman P. *Yangtze: Nature, History, and the River.* Reading, MA: Addison-Wesley Publishing Company, 1988. 28.

Weiss, Rick. "Tainted Chinese Imports Common." *Washington Post*, May 20, 2007: Washington Post.com: http://www.washingtonpost.com/wp-dyn/content/article/2007/05/19/AR2007051901273.html.

Worden, Minky. China's Great Leap. *The Beijing Games and Olympian Human Rights Challenges.* New York: Seven Stories Press, 2008.

World Trade Organization News. 2001 PRESS RELEASES, Press/243 17 September 2001, "WTO successfully concludes negotiations on China's entry," http://www.wto.org/english/news_e/pres01_e/pr243_e.html.

Yule, Henry, ed. and trans. *The Book of Ser Marco Polo, the Venetian Concerning the Kingdoms and Marvels of the East,* Book II: *Concerning the Black Stones that are Dug in Cathay and Burnt for Fuel,* Chapter 30., New York: Charles Scribner's Sons, 1903, 442.

Glossary

Beijing Opera (*Jingju*) Beijing opera is one of many regional types of dramatic music practiced in China, but it has become the most nationalized and easily recognizable one. Known for its colorful costumes, elaborate makeup, amazing acrobatics, and surprising music, Beijing opera is now performed throughout China and in many of the regions where overseas Chinese have settled.

Boxer Rebellion (1900) The Qing dynasty's last major event, the Boxer Rebellion, combined the 19th-century themes of internal rebellion and foreign influence. The Boxers resented missionary and convert privileges in the treaty ports, as well as the harsh social and economic conditions affecting China. The Boxers gained recognition from the Qing court as an official military organization to support the court against foreign influence, and laid siege to the foreign legation in Beijing. Eight days later, the Qing court declared war on the treaty powers. The siege was lifted on August 14, 1900, and the resulting defeat was a major blow to the Qing and China's reputation in the international community.

Century of Humiliation The Century of Humiliation lasted from 1842–1943 and took the form of an armed occupation of parts of China by a shared consortium of nations (Great Britain, France, Germany, Italy, Russia, and the United States), which controlled a significant portion of China's territory and trade for over 100 years. The Century of Humiliation became an important rallying point of Chinese nationalism throughout the 20th century, as China struggled to regain the ability to control not only its own trade, but also to control its own destiny without foreign interference.

Chinggis (Genghis) Khan (d. 1227) The paramount leader of the Mongols during their rise to power in the 13th century, Genghis Khan was one of the world's great military organizers. He led Mongol troops to conquests reaching both east and west. Although the Southern Song would not fall to the Mongols until 50 years after his death, his conquest was evident throughout Asia and Europe.

Confucius (551–479 B.C.E.) A native of the small state of Lu, Confucius taught groups of disciples who eventually compiled his philosophy into a slender volume known as the *Lunyu*, or *Analects*. Confucius cast himself as a transmitter of the old ways that had been practiced by the Duke of Zhou, and he argued that the states of his day were corrupting key ritual practices and usurping the authority of the Zhou dynasty. Confucius was traditionally believed to have written or edited many classical works, including *The Book of History*, *The Book of Poetry*, and *The Spring and Autumn Annals*, a history of his own state of Lu.

Criticism Groups (*xiaozu*) Hallmarks of the Maoist organization, these groups extended Communist Party discipline beyond the party and into the workplace. They were mechanisms of mass mobilization designed to ensure that CCP policies were obeyed and carried out by ordinary people.

Cultural Revolution (1966–1976) This series of events was a social and political movement with roots in the Communist Party's factional leadership struggles that spread to a much wider scale of conflict, affecting individuals even on a local level. Mao Zedong's role was muted in the later years, but the movement, with its echoes of "continuing revolution" from Red Guards, affected China for more than a decade. The Red Guards often dealt harshly with those suspected of having rightist tendencies, and demonstrations with thousands of students and other young people occurred frequently at its height. Virtually the entire Chinese leadership was affected in some way by the changing political climate.

***Danwei* (work units)** An effective method of social control in the early decades of the People's Republic, the *danwei* work units have declined in utility and importance with the large-scale privatization and foreign investment of the reform era.

Democracy Wall Movement (1978–1979) In the years after the Cultural Revolution, Mao's death, and the incarceration of the Gang of Four, a number of cities saw the rise of what has become known as the Democracy Wall Movement. The most prominent of these movements was in Xidan, just west of the Forbidden City in Beijing, where posters and magazines served as notice boards for people dealing with the effects of the Cultural Revolution and striving to articulate a future for the country. The movement prompted the kind of public discussion of political events that had been lauded in theory, but often punished in practice.

Eightfold Path The Buddhist Eightfold Path as a means of ending suffering requires right perspective, right thought, right speech, right action, right life-path, right effort, right mindfulness, and right concentration. The goal, albeit a distant one, is nirvana—not an explosion of joy or lands of milk and honey, but rather an extinguishing, as when two fingers put out the flame on a candle.

Face (Saving Face) People in China place great weight upon face, or attaining and maintaining self-respect and the respect of others. Saving face is of paramount importance in China, and in the East Asian world in general. Face consists of reputation, trust, and influence—how one appears and wants to appear to others. It depends upon social position, personal ability, economic status, and social ties. But, above all, face depends upon how others treat you.

Fengshui **(Geomancy)** *Fengshui* is a kind of directional symbolism at the heart of a great number of popular cultural practices in China and the West. Literally "wind-water," *fengshui* places natural and cultural objects in an ordered pattern, and is said to enhance (or detract from) the flow of energy in the world.

Five Phases (Correlative Cosmology) The five phases move endlessly round the calendar, the seasons, and other aspects of culture and nature. They are associated with the directions (north, south, east, west, and center), colors, and the seasons. The great cosmologist of the Han dynasty, Dong Zhongshu, classified the vast bulk of the world's categories according to the five phases. Chinese dynastic history is said to move in the patterns of the phases, as are the seasons and the days of the calendar itself.

Five Sacred Peaks The five sacred peaks make up a temporal and spatial template for the early Chinese state. To this day, they remain prominent features of Chinese geography and are popular destinations for tourists.

Four Noble Truths Buddhism's Four Noble Truths state that life is suffering and that the ways of the world do not bring happiness. Craving lies at the root of suffering, and suffering can only end when the cycle is broken.

Genre Painting Genre painting flourished in the late 11th century, reflecting the patronage of tradesmen, petty bureaucrats, and other members of what might be termed a Chinese middle class of the time. Artists who worked in this style have given us virtual visual time capsules of the material culture of Song dynasty China. Works such as Zhang Zeduan's *Spring Festival on the River* handscroll create an almost cinematic unfolding of physical detail.

Grand Canal The Grand Canal is a major waterway connecting the Yellow and Yangzi rivers. The canal is actually a connection of man-made and natural sections that were linked by engineers beginning in earnest in the Sui Dynasty (581–617).

Great Leap Forward (1958–1960) The Great Leap Forward reflects Mao's plan to propel the Chinese economy to a new level of development by arousing the socialist enthusiasm of the people. The plan sought an unprecedented rise in industrial production and reflected Mao's frustration with Soviet-style five-year plans and his growing distrust of the bureaucracy that handled them. Production goals were raised dramatically, and the entire population was urged to help with steel production. Peasants continued to be diverted from agriculture and to work at a pace far beyond available food rations. Bad weather hampered agriculture and aggravated the problem. China's leadership reacted slowly to the developing disaster. By the time the Great Leap was officially abandoned, the damage was done. Famine swept the country, and China lost 20 to 30 million people.

Guanxi (Connections) Social relations in China are not simply about getting along well with others; they are about building a network of people upon whom you can count (and who, in turn, will count on you) to help make things happen— from finding housing or a job to reserving a seat on a plane or a train during a busy holiday season, getting access to good medical care, or being admitted to a top school. Through the continual exchange of both tangible and intangible goods, people develop a sense of mutual obligation that cements their network of social relationships and insures that they are able to get what they need and want.

Han Wudi; Emperor Wu of Han (r. 141–87 B.C.E.) One of the most effective rulers in Chinese history, Emperor Wu made major changes in Han policy with its neighbors and within its borders. He strove to eliminate the growing regionalizing tendencies of territorial lords, and he asserted Han control over the Xiongnu tribes to the north. Emperor Wu's reforms would not be carried through by his successors, and the dynasty was lost in the early years of the Common Era, during the interregnum of Wang Mang.

Hongwu Emperor (r. 1368–1398) The founder of the Ming dynasty was the second emperor to rise from commoner status to occupy the imperial throne. An orphan, Zhu Yuanzhang was raised in a Buddhist monastery. During the tumultuous last decades of Mongol rule, with the countryside in confusion, Zhu effectively gained control of the Yangzi River Valley region near Nanjing and was able to solidify power by the late 1360s. The Hongwu emperor's reign was marked by a reassertion of Chinese cultural values (including a revived examination system) and measures undertaken to check the activities of landowning families, as well as merchants in large coastal cities. The later years of his reign cast a negative shadow, with violent purges that affected a large number of officials and their families.

Hukou (Urban Residence Permits) After 1949, the PRC attempted to control movement into cities, so as to prevent the rise of the shantytowns and urban blight associated with many Third World countries. Chinese citizens in urban areas were assigned *hukou* that designated the size and type of urban area in which they were allowed to live. Restrictions were relaxed in the 1990s, but the PRC continues to control migration to the largest cities.

Hundred Schools of Thought (c. 700–200 B.C.E.) Referring to the intellectual diversity and engagement of the Spring and Autumn and Warring States periods of the Eastern Zhou, the Hundred Schools ("hundred" here means "many") reflect the struggles between states vying for ascendancy in a complex social and military situation. Philosophers addressed the problems of state and personal management that have influenced thought to the present day.

Hundred Surnames A listing of the most common surnames in China (totaling over 500 in many editions) and their original locations. The Hundred Surnames (again, "hundred" refers to "many") are frequently published in small books, but they also constitute a prominent section of Chinese almanacs, including contemporary almanacs published in Hong Kong.

Jie and Zhou ("Bad Last Rulers") Known to later readers as degenerate rulers who brought their early dynasties to terrible ends, Jie and Zhou became synonymous in Chinese political writings with self-gratification and rulers who pay no mind to the people's problems. They form the very model of bad last rulers in the traditional interpretation—those who worried more about their own comforts and lost control of the empire.

Kangxi Emperor (r. 1661–1722) The second ruler of the Qing dynasty, the Kangxi Emperor reigned longer than any emperor in Chinese history. Exercising full power on his own by the age of 15, the Kangxi emperor solidified Manchu rule in China and oversaw the full north-south integration of Chinese territory, including the island of Taiwan. The last years of his reign were marked by a bitter factional struggle among his sons as they sought to succeed him.

Land Reform (1950–1953) Delivering on promises to its peasant supporters, between 1950 and 1953, the PRC government confiscated excess land and tools from rural landlords and gave the property to poorer peasants. About 10 million rural households lost some portion of their land and household property, while about 300 million peasants each received about a third of an acre of land.

Laojia ("Old Home;" "Venerable Home") Laojia is the term used in China to refer to the place of one's family origin. The term refers not so much to an individual's birthplace or hometown as to the (often quite distant) historical location with which a particular kinship group identifies.

Liu Bang (r. 202–195 B.C.E.) Also known as Han Gaozu ("Lofty Ancestor of Han"), Liu Bang was the first emperor to come from among the people. He established central rule after only 15 years of Qin rule threatened to return the territory to a system of territorial leaders vying for power. The first emperor of the Han dynasty was said to have been a coarse individual (it was written that he urinated into the official cap of a minister of government when he grew impatient with his speech), but one who knew how to accept critical advice from members of his government.

Long March The Long March was a large-scale military retreat by Communist forces in China to evade the power of the Nationalist army in the mid-1930s. Actually a series of retreats, the Long March is usually linked with the 8,000-mile retreat from Jiangxi to Shaanxi undertaken by Mao Zedong, Zhou Enlai, and other figures.

May Fourth Movement (May 1919) After the Paris Peace Conference, in which the fact that the Chinese warlord government acceded to Japanese demands became known, demonstrations of students and workers spread throughout China, sparking a New Culture Movement, which led to calls for wholesale change in Chinese policy. In a broader sense, the New Culture and May Fourth movements represent a rethinking of traditional culture on several significant levels.

Mencius (372–289 B.C.E.) A Warring States period political thinker, Mencius advised the kings of several states that were pursuing unification of the fractured Zhou dynasty order. Whereas Confucius's teachings were set down in the form of pithy moral maxims that were often no more than a few sentences long, Mencius expanded on these concepts in the form of full historical and cultural examples that ran for many pages. He promoted the concept that people are basically good, and through paying attention to what he saw as the core ideals in human nature—not the flawed realities of what people actually did—leaders could create order in their domains and assert their dominance peacefully throughout the empire.

Neo-Confucianism In the aftermath of the An Lushan Rebellion (C.E. 755–763), China saw a spirited rethinking of the original Confucian vision. The profound intellectual diversity that followed differed from traditional Confucianism in degree, not in kind. It was a creative synthesis of classical Confucian scholarship and the realities of life in a later era—not so much a break with the classical past as a re-conception of it. They sought to apply what they thought to be the original vision of thinkers such as Confucius and Mencius, and reform life around them.

Non-Action (*wuwei*) Non-action (*wuwei*) is the extreme political statement that a good ruler does nothing. By *not* categorizing, *not* making rules, and *not* ordering the people, order is, in fact, achieved. The quintessential Daoist statement follows from this: "Through not doing, nothing is left undone" (*wuwei er wubuwei*).

Oracle Bones The oldest form of the Chinese written language can be found in the oracle bone inscriptions. Carved on tortoise shells and mammal bones during the Shang dynasty (c. 1600–1100 B.C.E.), these inscriptions recorded royal events and documented divinations. Each symbol represented a concrete image: a number, an animal, a tree, a mountain, the sunrise, and so forth. They are a magnificent source of information about early China.

Radicals (Chinese Language) Chinese dictionaries commonly arrange characters based on recurrent parts called "radicals." A dictionary normally begins with a section that lists categories according to the 214 radicals. The radicals are arranged in the ascending order of stroke numbers. They form a key component of Chinese characters, and often hint at the general meaning of the character. One prominent radical is "person," which is often used in characters dealing with individual or social ideas and attributes. Another radical is "earth," which is found in characters dealing with land, such as dikes, embankments, and so forth.

Regency Regency is the practice of ruling in the place of a young heir to the throne until that individual is able to exercise power on his own. The model for regency is the Duke of Zhou, but Chinese history is rife with many examples of power grabs by regents.

Remonstrance Remonstrance is the concept in Chinese political philosophy that the junior member of a hierarchy has a responsibility to correct, or admonish, a senior member if the latter commits errors. In practice, remonstrance was carried out imperfectly, but the ideal remains to this day.

Shanghai Communiqué (1972) Issued at the end of President Nixon's 1972 visit, the United States and the PRC declared "all Chinese on either side of the Taiwan Strait maintain that there is but one China and that Taiwan is part of China. The United States government does not challenge this position."

Sima Guang (1019–1086) A major Song dynasty official and writer of history, Sima Guang is still known for his role in one of the great bureaucratic debates of Chinese history: a clash with Wang Anshi over the use of government resources in aiding the people and dealing with northern threats. Sima completed one of the richest works of history in the Chinese tradition. His *Zizhi tongjian* (*Comprehensive Mirror for Aid in Ruling*) is a thorough, chronological account of China's past from 403 B.C.E. to C.E. 959, and covers, in recent editions, almost 10,000 pages of text.

Sima Qian (c. 145–86 B.C.E.) Arguably China's most innovative historian, Sima Qian's works are still read by many, as much for their literary qualities as for their portrayals. The best way to contrast the Two Simas (see above) to a Western audience would be to call to mind Herodotus and Thucydides. The former was known for his fantastical, but deeply memorable, accounts of the lands in present-day Greece and beyond. So, too, is Sima Qian an author who brings vivid accounts to the page, even 21 centuries after he wrote the works. The 130 chapters of his history are filled with portrayals of sage kings, emperors, and even quite ordinary people, such as money-lenders and fortune-tellers.

Simplified Characters (Chinese Language) The mainland Chinese write certain characters differently than the standard form established more than 1,800 years ago, using fewer strokes for some characters. Characters with reduced strokes are known as simplified characters (*jiǎntizi*), as opposed to complex characters (*fǎntizi*), or traditional characters. The simplified characters are the products of the script reform begun in 1956 in the People's Republic of China to promote universal literacy and increase the efficiency of writing. The simplification has resulted in over 2,000 characters that have 2 forms for reading media produced in different parts of the world.

Special Administrative Region (SAR) A new status granted to Hong Kong upon its return to the PRC in 1997, and to Macao in 1999. The PRC has also proposed the status to Taiwan in the hopes of an eventual reunification.

Southern Ming (c. 1640–c. 1685) With Manchu power growing in China, and many northern territories already taken, some families fled to the south and southeast. The resistance movement figured prominently in the far southern provinces, in Taiwan, and in areas of Southeast Asia, including Vietnam. It took almost 40 years for Manchu forces to subdue the rebels, and the loyalist movement lived on during the Qing dynasty in subtle, but often deep-seated, resistance to the Manchus.

Syncretism In the context of Chinese thought, this term refers to the blending of three traditions (Confucian, Daoist, and Buddhist). A popular phrase states that "The three teachings blend into one" (*sanjiao heyi*).

Taiping Rebellion (1850–1864) The Taiping Rebellion foreshadowed, in many ways, the people's movements of the 20th century in China. Part religion, part social movement, and part political force, the Taiping rebels moved north from their southern roots to capture the city of Nanjing in 1853. Although they were eventually subdued by government forces, the challenge they had posed to both the traditional political and social orders was profound. The human cost was enormous, with more than 20 million lives lost during the rebellion.

Third Front Investment Program Beginning in 1964, China secretly launched a crash industrialization program to prepare for invasion by either the United States or the Soviet Union. In case of invasion, China's leaders planned to retreat from the coast, the first front, and from the lower lands within 400 miles of the coast, the second front, into remote, mountainous regions, the third front. From there, China would wage a prolonged war of resistance against any invader. The program moved existing factories from the coast and created complete heavy industrial systems that were capable of producing all manner of equipment in rugged interior locations.

Three Dynasties—Sage Kings Yao, Shun, and Yu (23rd century B.C.E., traditional) Key figures in early foundations myths centering on the Chinese state, Yao, Shun, and Yu were said to rule in the period preceding the Xia Dynasty. Legend has it that Yao, after ruling for a century, chose a commoner, Shun, to be the next ruler. After a similarly successful period of rule, Shun chose another outsider, Yu. Yu faced quelled great floods, stabilized rule, and, eventually, instituted imperial succession through his own heirs.

Three Gorges Dam The Three Gorges Dam is a major water control project initiated by the Chinese government and expected to become fully operational in 2011. The project led to mass relocations and the loss of numerous cultural sites along the Yangzi River.

Three Kingdoms (220–280) The period in Chinese history best known to students, the Three Kingdoms is, to this day, the stuff of legend. From at least the year 180 onward, the Han was crumbling, and several men, including Dong Zhuo and Cao Cao, sought either to control or solidify the dying empire. The territories that emerged were centered in the north (Wei), the west (Shu Han), and the south (Wu).

Three Treasures (of the Buddha) The Buddha offered the ideal of enlightenment to all people; the dharma articulates the universal laws of human life, while the sangha refers to practicing communities—people who have gathered together to follow the Buddhist way.

Tiyong Tiyong refers to the attempt to maintain a Chinese essence, even while borrowing technology and other ideas from the West, which is sometimes described as "Eastern ethics and Western science." Nineteenth-century reformers, such as Zeng Guofan, argued that by combining (Eastern) fundamentals with (Western) usages, a new future could be achieved.

Treaty Ports After the Qing government's defeat in the Opium War, China was forced by the Treaty of Nanjing (1842) to make major concessions to the British (and, in turn, other foreign powers). The original five ports were in Canton, Fuzhou, Ningbo, Shanghai, and Amoy (Xiamen).

Treaty of Shimonoseki (1895) In the peace treaty that marked the end of the 1894–1895 Sino-Japanese war, the Chinese government ceded its influence over Korea and its control of Taiwan to Japan, while agreeing to pay Japan's cost of waging the war. Other nations took advantage of China's weakened state to occupy or claim expanded spheres of influence in China. Chinese have regarded their defeat and the subsequent treaty as a low point in their modern history, and as an example of how fragile the imperial order and traditional methods in education, military, and government had become.

Xuanzang's Travels Travels to India for scriptures often brought long-lasting fame, as in the cases of the monk Fa Xian, who gathered texts in the 4th century, and Xuanzang, who returned to the Tang capital from India in 645. The texts themselves presented monumental difficulties for translators, and a fascinating result is that many of the key terms from South Asian Buddhism were translated using concepts from early Daoism.

Zeri (Day Selection) The traditional Chinese calendar has figured prominently in everything from family decisions and business negotiations to government activities and the planning of large events. For example, the calendar was (and often still is) consulted about days on which one would get engaged, marry, or hold a funeral. That such practices persist in modern times and in China's urban centers is a testament to the power of kinship connections and social pressures.

Zhao Mengfu (1257–1322) A scholar-official and painter during the transition from Southern Song to Yuan, Zhao was a descendant of the Song dynasty's first emperor. He served the Mongol-ruled Yuan dynasty as a writer of memorials and proclamations, and is an example of the key to effective ruling on the part of outside peoples in China. Without the collaboration of Chinese administrators, negotiating the bureaucracy and managing the empire would have been impossible for the Mongols. Zhao came to regret his decision to aid the Mongols, and he was vilified by many historians for it. He excelled at landscape painting and was a skilled calligrapher. He is well known for his paintings of bamboo, which are often perceived as being resilient in the face of the elements—a none-too-subtle allusion to a Chinese spirit that would bend, but not break, in the face of outside pressures.

Facts and Figures

The following tables present facts and figures about the People's Republic of China. These statistics begin with basic facts about the country and continue with the country's demographics (including population, ethnicity, and religion), geography, economy, communications and transportation, military, and education. Following these basic facts and figures, more detailed data of interest are presented as a series of tables, charts, and graphs.

TABLE A.1. Basic Facts and Figures

	Country Info
Location	China spans much of east Asia, bordering the East China Sea, Korea Bay, Yellow Sea, and South China Sea, between North Korea and Vietnam.
Official name	People's Republic of China (Zhonghua Renmin Gongheguo)
Local name	China (Zhongguo)
Government	Communist state
Capital	Beijing
Weights and measures	Metric system
Time zone	13 hours ahead of U.S. Eastern Standard
Currency	Chinese yuan

(continued)

TABLE A.1. Basic Facts and Figures *(continued)*

	Country Info
Head of state	President Hu Jintao
Head of government	Prime Minister Wen Jiabao
Legislature	National People's Congress—operates in accordance with the will of the Chinese Communist Party
Major political party	Chinese Communist Party

Sources: ABC-CLIO World Geography database; CIA World Factbook (https://www.cia.gov/library/publications/the-world-factbook); U.S. Department of State—China: Background Note (http://www.state.gov/r/pa/ei/bgn/18902.htm)

DEMOGRAPHICS

This table features information about the people of China, including statistics on population, religion, language, and voting.

TABLE A.2. Basic Facts and Figures

	Demographics
Population	1,354,146,000 (2010 est.)
Population by age	(2010 est.)
0–14	22.4%
15–64	70.5%
65+	7.1%
Median age	(2010 est.)
Total	34.2 years
Males	33.1 years
Females	34.1 years
Population growth rate	6.1% per year (2010–2015 projection)
Population density	361 people per sq. mile (2010 est.)
Infant mortality rate	20.4 deaths per 1,000 live births (2010–2015 projection)
Ethnic groups	Han Chinese 91.5%; Zhuang, Manchu, Hui, Miao, Uighur, Tujia, Yi, Mongol, Tibetan, Buyi, Dong, Yao, Korean, and other nationalities, 8.5% (2000 census)
Religions	Daoist (Taoist), Buddhist, Christian 3%–4%, Muslim 1%–2%. (2002 est.) *Note: China is officially atheist.*
Majority language	Mandarin Chinese (Putonghua)

(continued)

TABLE A.2. Basic Facts and Figures *(continued)*

Demographics	
Other languages	Cantonese (Yue), Shanghainese (Wu), Minbei (Fuzhou), Minnan (Hokkien-Taiwanese), Xiang, Gan, Hakka dialects, and minority languages
Voting age	18 years
Life expectancy (average)	72 years (2005–2010 projection)
Fertility rate	1.8 children born per woman (2008 est.)

Sources: ABC-CLIO World Geography database; CIA World Factbook (https://www.cia.gov/library/publications/the-world-factbook); U.S. Department of State—China: Background Note (http://www.state.gov/r/pa/ei/bgn/18902.htm)

GEOGRAPHY

The following table provides general facts and figures on the geography of China.

TABLE A.3. Basic Facts and Figures

Geography	
Land area	3,695,500 sq. miles
Arable land	10%
Irrigated land	210,797 sq. miles (2003)
Coastline	9,010 miles
Natural hazards	Earthquakes, typhoons, sandstorms
Environmental problems	Air pollution and acid rain (from reliance on coal), water pollution, water shortages, deforestation, desertification
Major agricultural products	Rice, vegetables, sweet potatoes, sorghum, maize, wheat, peanuts, sugarcane, potatoes, pigs, sheep, cattle, soybeans, cotton
Natural resources	Coal, antimony, lead, zinc, manganese
Land use	10.3% cropland, 42.9% permanent pasture, 14% forests and woodland, 32.8% other (mostly mountains and desert)
Climate	Subtropical in the far south, cold and rainy in the east, hot and arid in the northwest

Sources: ABC-CLIO World Geography database; CIA World Factbook (https://www.cia.gov/library/publications/the-world-factbook); U.S. Department of State—China: Background Note (http://www.state.gov/r/pa/ei/bgn/18902.htm)

ECONOMY

This table offers basic economic information on China, including financial, labor, trade, and industrial statistics.

TABLE A.4. Basic Facts and Figures

	Economy
GDP	$4.2 trillion (2008 est.)
GDP per capita	$6,100 (2008 est.)
GDP by sector	Agriculture, forestry, hunting, and fishing—11.1%; mining, manufacturing, and utilities—40.9%; construction—5.4%; wholesale and retail trade, hotels, and restaurants—8.3%; transportation and communication—6.0%; finance, insurance, real estate, and business services (Hong Kong and Macau only)—1.9%; government services, education, and health care (Hong Kong and Macau only)—1.2%; other services (including finance, insurance, real estate, business services, government services, education, and health care for all areas except Hong Kong and Macau)—25.0% (2006)
Exchange rate	6.8 yuan = $1 U.S. dollar (2009)
Labor force	Agriculture, 43%; industry, 25%; services, 32% (2006)
Unemployment	4.0% (2008)
Major industries	Machinery and other equipment manufacturing, petroleum and petroleum products, telecommunications, chemical production, steel production
Leading companies	Agricultural Bank of China, China Mobile, Bank of China, China National Offshore Oil, Xinjiang Chalkis Corp., Tongwei Group, Meng Niu Dairy Group
Exports	$1.465 trillion (2008 est.)
Export goods	Clothing, footwear, fabric, machinery and transportation equipment, chemicals, petroleum and petroleum products, fertilizer, minerals, toys, textiles
Imports	$1.156 trillion (2008 est.)
Import goods	Machinery and transportation equipment, petroleum and petroleum products, telecommunications equipment, plastics, chemicals, fertilizer, steel, iron, foodstuffs
Current account balance	$368.2 billion (2008 est.)

Sources: ABC-CLIO World Geography database; CIA World Factbook (https://www.cia.gov/library/publications/the-world-factbook); U.S. Department of State—China: Background Note (http://www.state.gov/r/pa/ei/bgn/18902.htm)

COMMUNICATIONS AND TRANSPORTATION

The following table features facts and figures on China's communications networks and transportation.

TABLE A.5.　Basic Facts and Figures

	Communications and Transportation
Electricity production	3.256 trillion kWh (2007)
Electricity consumption	3.271 trillion kWh (2007)
Telephone lines	365.4 million (2007)
Mobile phones	547.3 million (2007)
Internet users	253 million (2008)
Roads	1,199,584 miles (2005)
Railroads	46,875 miles (2005).
Airports	467 (2007)

Sources: ABC-CLIO World Geography database; CIA World Factbook (https://www.cia.gov/library/publications/the-world-factbook); U.S. Department of State—China: Background Note (http://www.state.gov/r/pa/ei/bgn/18902.htm)

MILITARY

China has the world's largest military and is second only to the United States in military expenditures. The following table outlines some basic military statistics.

TABLE A.6.　Basic Facts and Figures

	Military
Defense spending (% of GDP)	4.3% (2007)
Active armed forces	2,255,000 (800,000 reservists) (2007)
Manpower fit for military service	313,321,639 males; 295,951,438 females (2008 est.)

Sources: ABC-CLIO World Geography database; CIA World Factbook (https://www.cia.gov/library/publications/the-world-factbook); U.S. Department of State—China: Background Note (http://www.state.gov/r/pa/ei/bgn/18902.htm)

EDUCATION

China has long faced difficulties educating its large population, but the educational system has advanced significantly and found ways to accommodate the country's many young people. The following table presents some basic statistics about education in China.

TABLE A.7.　Basic Facts and Figures

	Education
Literacy	90.9% (2000 census)
Mandatory education	Ages 6 to 15
Average years spent in school for current students	11 years (male: 11 years; female: 11 years) (2006 estimate)
Male enrollment in postsecondary education	22% (2006)
Female enrollment in postsecondary education	21% (2006)
Pupil/teacher ratio	Primary: 18 students/teacher; secondary: 18 students/teacher (2006 estimate)

Tables and Graphs

POPULATION

For much of recorded history, China's vast population has proved to be a source of both strength and difficulty. Today, the population provides troops for the country's army and workers for its factories, but it is difficult to properly feed and educate so many people. The nation that was the first on the planet to surpass 1 billion people has today become synonymous with overpopulation, and in recent years China has imposed a one-child-per-family rule in an attempt to slow its population growth. The following tables and charts show the growth of China's population from 1949 to 2007, and the variation in regional population as of 2007.

Population, 1949–2007

TABLE B.   Population, 1949–2007
Units:10,000 people

Year	Population
1949	54,157
1950	55,196
1951	56,300
1952	57,482
1953	58,796
1954	60,266
1955	61,456
1956	62,828
1957	64,653
1958	65,994
1959	67,207
1960	66,207
1961	65,859
1962	67,295
1963	69,172
1964	70,499
1965	72,538
1966	74,542
1967	76,368
1968	78,534
1969	80,671
1970	82,992
1971	85,229
1972	87,177
1973	89,211

(continued)

TABLE B. Population, 1949–2007 *(continued)*

Year	Population
1974	90,859
1975	92,420
1976	93,717
1977	94,974
1978	96,259
1979	97,542
1980	98,705
1981	100,072
1982	101,654
1983	103,008
1984	104,357
1985	105,851
1990	114,333
1991	115,823
1992	117,171
1993	118,517
1994	119,850
1995	121,121
1996	122,389
1997	123,626
1998	124,761
1999	125,786
2000	126,743
2001	127,627
2002	128,453
2003	129,227
2004	129,988
2005	130,756
2006	131,448
2007	132,129

Source: China Statistical Yearbook, China Statistical Information Network.

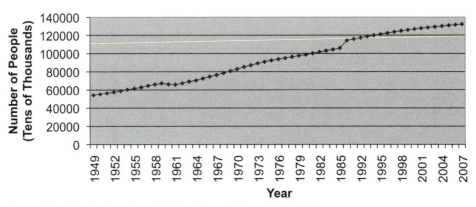

CHART B. *Population, People's Republic of China, 1949–2007*

Population by Region, 2007

TABLE C.   Population by Region, 2007
(Does not include Hong Kong SAR, Macao SAR, or Taiwan)

Region	Total Population (year-end) (10,000 persons)
National total	132,129
Beijing	1,633
Tianjin	1,115
Hebei	6,943
Shanxi	3,393
Inner Mongolia	2,405
Liaoning	4,298
Jilin	2,730
Heilongjiang	3,824
Shanghai	1,858
Jiangsu	7,625
Zhejiang	5,060
Anhui	6,118
Fujian	3,581
Jiangxi	4,368
Shandong	9,367
Henan	9,360
Hubei	5,699
Hunan	6,355
Guangdong	9,449
Guangxi	4,768
Hainan	845
Chongqing	2,816
Sichuan	8,127
Guizhou	3,762
Yunnan	4,514
Tibet	284
Shaanxi	3,748
Gansu	2,617
Qinghai	552
Ningxia	610
Xinjiang	2,095

Source: China Statistical Yearbook, China Statistical Information Network.
a) Data in the table are estimates from the 2007 National Sample Survey on Population Changes.
b) Military personnel were included in the national total population, but were not included in the population by region.

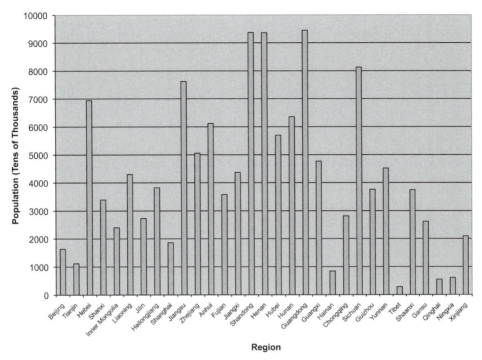

CHART C. *Population by Region, People's Republic of China, 2007*

AGRICULTURE

Although China has become a strong economic power in recent years, it has historically had difficulty feeding its population. Much of the country's soil has become polluted by the country's industrial growth, and today only about 10 percent of China's land is suitable for agriculture and crop cultivation. Still, because of its sheer size, the country is a global leader in the production of rice, wheat, potatoes, corn, peanuts, millet, rapeseed, cotton, soybeans, and tea. The following tables and chart detail China's recent agricultural output.

OUTPUT OF MAJOR AGRICULTURAL PRODUCTS BY REGION, 2007

TABLE D. Output of Major Agricultural Products by Region, 2007 (10,000 tons)

Region	Total Grain	Cereal	Rice	Wheat	Corn	Beans	Tubers	Cotton	Oil-Bearing Crops	Peanuts	Rapeseeds	Sesame	Fiber Crops
Beijing	102.1	97.6	0.3	20.4	76.5	1.6	2.9	0.2	2.2	2.2			
Tianjin	147.2	145.7	10.0	50.6	85.1	1.2	0.3	9.3	0.5	0.3			
Hebei	2,841.6	2,716.0	57.6	1,193.7	1,421.8	42.8	82.8	72.5	138.1	130.7	1.6	1.1	0.4
Shanxi	1,007.1	916.5	0.6	220.2	640.4	39.7	50.8	11.5	13.5	2.5	0.6	0.4	
Inner Mongolia	1,810.7	1,500.6	60.2	175.6	1,155.3	156.2	153.9	0.4	79.4	2.3	20.7	0.6	1.4
Liaoning	1,835.0	1,748.1	505.0	5.3	1,167.8	36.2	50.8	0.2	26.4	25.0	0.1	0.2	
Jilin	2,453.8	2,337.1	500.0	1.6	1,800.0	92.1	24.5	0.1	28.7	22.0		0.7	0.1
Heilongjiang	3,462.9	2,971.5	1,417.9	68.8	1,442.0	442.7	48.8		21.3	5.5	0.1	0.6	18.0
Shanghai	109.2	106.8	86.0	14.6	2.5	2.1	0.3	0.3	3.6	0.3	3.3		
Jiangsu	3,132.2	3,008.5	1,761.1	973.8	197.3	81.6	42.2	34.8	145.1	33.8	109.5	1.8	0.4
Zhejiang	728.6	678.5	636.9	18.4	10.0	28.2	21.9	2.6	33.0	3.6	27.2	0.6	0.1
Anhui	2,901.4	2,731.7	1,356.4	1,111.3	250.0	121.5	48.2	37.4	199.2	61.8	129.9	7.3	4.5
Fujian	635.1	515.6	501.0	1.5	11.8	15.4	104.1	0.1	23.3	21.9	1.2	0.1	
Jiangxi	1,904.0	1,815.7	1,806.4	2.0	6.4	27.1	61.2	12.8	82.7	38.3	41.7	2.7	1.2
Shandong	4,148.8	3,929.8	110.2	1,995.6	1,816.5	42.5	176.5	100.1	328.6	325.6	2.5	0.2	0.1
Henan	5,245.2	5,023.4	436.5	2980.2	1,582.5	91.8	130.0	75.0	484.0	373.6	85.9	22.3	4.8
Hubei	2,185.4	2,060.0	1,485.9	353.2	205.1	45.3	80.1	55.7	254.8	48.6	193.3	12.1	5.3
Hunan	2,692.2	2,551.3	2,425.7	3.2	116.3	34.6	106.3	24.4	110.1	17.1	91.0	1.1	14.4
Guangdong	1,284.7	1,109.8	1,046.1	0.3	59.2	17.6	157.4		77.7	76.7	0.9	0.2	0.1
Guangxi	1,396.6	1,319.2	1,112.5	0.6	204.1	22.5	54.9	0.2	33.8	32.0	1.3	0.5	1.2
Hainan	177.5	144.5	136.4		7.0	0.4	32.6		6.8	6.6		0.3	0.1
Chongqing	1,088.0	790.7	491.6	61.1	234.2	35.1	262.2		30.7	6.4	23.2	0.7	1.5
Sichuan	3,027.0	2,523.5	1,419.7	451.7	602.8	105.8	397.7	1.7	204.3	51.0	152.5	0.5	6.9
Guizhou	1,100.9	865.8	449.8	47.9	357.1	36.0	199.0	0.1	69.7	4.9	64.4		0.1
Yunnan	1,460.7	1,218.4	589.7	91.2	498.6	80.1	162.2		22.1	2.2	15.7		2.4
Tibet	93.9	90.2	0.6	26.5	1.7	3.2	0.5		5.2		5.2		
Shaanxi	1,067.9	947.6	73.0	359.1	493.9	47.1	73.2	9.0	39.1	7.1	27.4	1.6	0.1
Gansu	824.0	582.2	3.4	237.4	242.7	35.2	206.6	12.9	42.4	0.1	23.3		0.9
Qinghai	106.2	79.8		61.4	1.3	12.0	14.4		28.0		27.7		
Ningxia	323.5	280.2	60.5	61.6	146.6	1.9	41.4		7.7				
Xinjiang	867.0	826.1	62.5	341.3	393.7	20.7	20.3	301.3	26.9	0.8	7.0	0.1	8.9

Region	Jute and Ambary Hemp	Sugarcane	Beetroots	Tobacco	Flue-cured Tobacco	Silkworm Cocoons	Mulberry Silkworm Cocoons	Tea	Fruits	Apples	Citrus	Pears	Grapes	Bananas
Beijing									124.9	11.9		15.4	4.7	
Tianjin									61.9	6.0		2.9	11.0	
Hebei	0.1		53.1	0.4	0.2	0.1	0.1		1,491.5	247.9		346.0	94.7	
Shanxi			21.1	0.8	0.7	0.5	0.5		342.2	187.3		32.7	10.4	
Inner Mongolia			118.2	1.6	1.0	0.6			208.1	6.2		8.5	4.1	
Liaoning			5.0	2.9	2.3	4.8			532.7	151.5		76.2	49.4	
Jilin			5.0	3.0	1.0	0.2			232.8	13.3		13.0	13.9	
Heilongjiang			207.2	6.2	5.5	0.3			373.3	15.1		4.7	2.2	
Shanghai		1.0							112.4		24.0	3.2	4.6	
Jiangsu		6.6				11.2	11.2	1.5	642.7	61.8	4.7	62.8	20.2	
Zhejiang	0.1	57.4		0.3		9.6	9.6	16.0	701.5		198.7	36.1	26.9	
Anhui	3.0	23.9		2.6	2.4	3.9	3.9	7.1	749.5	40.4	1.9	93.0	17.8	
Fujian		56.4		12.5	12.4			22.4	594.2		238.6	16.4	8.7	88.4
Jiangxi	0.1	48.1		3.4	3.3	1.0	1.0	2.1	381.2		195.8	8.9	1.0	
Shandong	0.1			8.8	8.6	6.9	6.8	1.0	2,541.2	724.9	3.8	117.2	91.7	
Henan	4.7	16.6		23.9	23.5	2.4	1.8	2.6	2,088.6	352.3		80.0	41.9	
Hubei	0.2	14.9		5.9	3.9	1.2	1.2	10.5	654.7	1.0	211.6	49.3	8.6	
Hunan	0.1	70.0		16.8	15.9			8.8	630.6		277.9	13.3	7.3	
Guangdong	0.1	1,180.7		4.2	3.4	8.4	8.4	4.9	1,057.2		256.8	5.1		351.2
Guangxi	1.1	7,737.5		2.4	2.2	23.3	23.3	3.4	861.5		234.7	15.6	15.9	140.5
Hainan	0.1	405.8						0.1	306.8		3.0			142.2
Chongqing		11.3		7.2	4.9	2.9	2.9	1.9	175.9	0.7	104.4	20.6	2.3	0.2
Sichuan	0.3	102.0	0.2	16.9	12.1	10.9	10.9	13.0	592.0	29.7	232.5	82.0	18.0	2.3
Guizhou		67.0		33.5	31.2	0.2	0.2	2.8	112.9	1.1	19.1	14.8	3.3	0.9
Yunnan		1,491.1	0.1	79.1	76.7	3.0	3.0	17.0	252.0	23.5	28.1	24.1	9.4	54.0
Tibet									1.1	0.4	0.1			
Shaanxi		5.0		5.7	5.6	3.0	3.0	1.4	1,125.0	701.6	22.4	61.9	18.5	
Gansu			27.8	1.0	0.8			0.1	358.4	142.4	0.3	29.4	10.6	
Qinghai			0.7	0.1					3.3	0.6		0.5		
Ningxia			0.3	0.2	0.2				153.8	27.6		1.7	7.1	
Xinjiang			453.9	0.2	0.1				672.5	38.9		54.1	165.5	

Source: China Statistical Yearbook, China Statistical Information Network.

Output of Major Agricultural Products, 1978–2007

TABLE E. Output of Major Agricultural Products, 1978–2007
Units:10,000 tons

Year	Grain	Cereal	Rice	Wheat	Corn	Beans	Tubers	Cotton	Oil-bearing Crops	Peanuts	Rapeseeds	Sesame	Fiber crops
1978	30,476.5		13,693.0	5,384.0	5,594.5		3,174.0	216.7	521.8	237.7	186.8	32.2	135.1
1980	32,055.5		13,990.5	5,520.5	6,260.0		2,872.5	270.7	769.1	360.0	238.4	25.9	143.6
1985	37,910.8		16,856.9	8,580.5	6,382.6		2,603.6	414.7	1,578.4	666.4	560.7	69.1	444.8
1990	44,624.3		18,933.1	9,822.9	9,681.9		2,743.3	450.8	1,613.2	636.8	695.8	46.9	109.7
1991	43,529.3	39,566.3	18,381.3	9,595.3	9,877.3	1247.1	2,715.9	567.5	1,638.3	630.3	743.6	43.5	88.4
1992	44,265.8	40,169.6	18,622.2	10,158.7	9,538.3	1252.0	2,844.2	450.8	1,641.2	595.3	765.3	51.6	93.8
1993	45,648.8	40,517.4	17,751.4	10,639.0	10,270.4	1950.4	3,181.1	373.9	1,803.9	842.1	693.9	56.3	96.0
1994	44,510.1	39,389.1	17,593.3	9,929.7	9,927.5	2095.6	3,025.4	434.1	1,989.6	968.2	749.2	54.8	74.7
1995	46,661.8	41,611.6	18,522.6	10,220.7	11,198.6	1787.5	3,262.6	476.8	2,250.3	1,023.5	977.7	58.3	89.7
1996	50,453.5	45,127.1	19,510.3	11,056.9	12,747.1	1790.3	3,536.0	420.3	2,210.6	1,013.8	920.1	57.5	79.5
1997	49,417.1	44,349.3	20,073.5	12,328.9	10,430.9	1875.5	3,192.3	460.3	2,157.4	964.8	957.8	56.6	74.9
1998	51,229.5	45,624.7	19,871.3	10,972.6	13,295.4	2000.6	3,604.2	450.1	2,313.9	1,188.6	830.1	65.6	49.5
1999	50,838.6	45,304.1	19,848.7	11,388.0	12,808.6	1894.0	3,640.6	382.9	2,601.2	1,263.9	1,013.2	74.3	47.2
2000	46,217.5	40,522.4	18,790.8	9,963.6	10,600.0	2010.0	3,685.2	441.7	2,954.8	1,443.7	1,138.1	81.1	52.9
2001	45,263.7	39,648.2	17,758.0	9,387.3	11,408.8	2052.8	3,563.1	532.4	2,864.9	1,441.6	1,133.1	80.4	68.1
2002	45,705.8	39,798.7	17,453.9	9,029.0	12,130.8	2241.2	3,665.9	491.6	2,897.2	1,481.8	1,055.2	89.5	96.4
2003	43,069.5	37,428.7	16,065.6	8,648.8	11,583.0	2127.5	3,513.3	486.0	2,811.0	1,342.0	1,142.0	59.3	85.3
2004	46,946.9	41,157.2	17,908.8	9,195.2	13,028.7	2232.1	3,557.7	632.4	3,065.9	1,434.2	1,318.2	70.4	107.4
2005	48,402.2	42,776.0	18,058.8	9,744.5	13,936.5	2157.7	3,468.5	571.4	3,077.1	1,434.2	1,305.2	62.5	110.5
2006	49,804.2	45,099.2	18,171.8	10,846.6	15,160.3	2003.7	2,701.3	753.3	2,640.3	1,288.7	1,096.6	66.2	89.1
2007	50,160.3	45,632.4	18,603.4	10,929.8	15,230.0	1720.1	2,807.8	762.4	2,568.7	1,302.7	1,057.3	55.7	72.8

Year	Jute and Ambary Hemp	Sugarcane	Beetroots	Tobacco	Flue-Cured Tobacco	Silkworm Cocoons	Mulberry Silkworm Cocoons	Tea	Fruits	Apples	Citrus	Pears	Grapes	Bananas
1978	108.8	2,111.6	270.2	124.2	105.2	22.8	17.3	26.8	657.0	227.5	38.3	151.7	10.4	8.5
1980	109.8	2,280.7	630.5	84.5	71.7	32.6	25.0	30.4	679.3	236.3	71.3	146.6	11.0	6.1
1985	411.9	5,154.9	891.9	242.5	207.5	37.1	33.6	43.2	1,163.9	361.4	180.8	213.7	36.1	63.1
1990	72.6	5,762.0	1,452.5	262.7	225.9	53.4	48.0	54.0	1,874.4	431.9	485.5	235.3	85.9	145.6
1991	51.3	6,789.8	1,628.9	303.1	267.0	58.4	55.1	54.2	2,176.1	454.0	633.3	249.8	91.6	198.1
1992	61.9	7,301.1	1,506.9	349.9	311.9	69.2	66.0	56.0	2,440.1	655.6	516.0	284.6	112.5	245.1
1993	67.2	6,419.4	1,204.8	345.1	303.6	75.7	71.2	60.0	3,011.2	907.0	656.1	321.7	135.5	270.1
1994	35.5	6,092.7	1,252.6	223.8	194.0	81.3	77.7	58.8	3,499.8	1,112.9	680.5	404.3	152.2	289.8
1995	37.1	6,541.7	1,398.4	231.4	207.2	80.0	76.0	58.9	4,214.6	1,400.8	822.5	494.2	174.2	312.5
1996	36.5	6,818.7	1,541.5	323.4	294.6	50.8	47.1	59.3	4,652.8	1,704.7	845.7	580.7	188.3	253.6
1997	43.0	7,889.7	1,496.8	425.1	390.8	46.9	42.3	61.3	5,089.3	1,721.9	1,010.2	641.5	203.3	289.2
1998	24.8	8,343.8	1,446.6	236.4	208.8	52.6	47.5	66.5	5,452.9	1,948.1	859.0	727.5	235.8	351.8
1999	16.4	7,470.3	863.9	246.9	218.5	48.5	44.7	67.6	6,237.6	2,080.2	1,078.7	774.2	270.8	419.4
2000	12.6	6,828.0	807.3	255.2	223.8	54.8	50.1	68.3	6,225.1	2,043.1	878.3	841.2	328.2	494.1
2001	10.6	7,566.3	1,088.9	235.0	204.5	65.5	60.2	70.2	6,658.0	2,001.5	1,160.7	879.6	368.0	527.2
2002	15.9	9,010.7	1,282.0	244.7	213.5	69.8	64.5	74.5	6,952.0	1,924.1	1,199.0	930.9	447.9	555.7
2003	10.0	9,023.5	618.2	225.7	201.5	66.7	61.1	76.8	14,517.4	2,110.2	1,345.4	979.8	517.6	590.3
2004	8.7	8,984.9	585.7	240.6	216.3	73.1	67.7	83.5	15,340.9	2,367.5	1,495.8	1,064.2	567.5	605.6
2005	8.3	8,663.8	788.1	268.3	243.5	78.0	71.3	93.5	16,120.1	2,401.1	1,591.9	1,132.4	579.4	651.8
2006	8.7	9,709.2	750.8	245.6	225.5	88.2	82.0	102.8	17,102.0	2,605.9	1,789.8	1,198.6	627.1	690.1
2007	9.9	11,295.1	893.1	239.5	217.8	94.7	87.9	116.5	18,136.3	2,786.0	2,058.3	1,289.5	669.7	779.7

Source: China Statistical Yearbook, China Statistical Information Network.

Output of Cereal Crops, 1990–2007

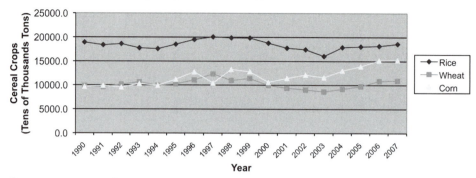

CHART E. *Output of Cereal Crops, People's Republic of China, 1990–2007*

Per Capita Output of Major Agricultural Products by Region, 2007

TABLE F. Per Capita Output of Major Agricultural Products by Region, 2007
Units:kilograms

Region	Grain	Cotton	Oil-Bearing Crops	Pork, Beef, and Mutton	Total Aquatic Products	Milk
Beijing	64	0.1	1.4	16.9	3.4	38.7
Tianjin	134	8.5	0.4	23.5	28.5	61.4
Hebei	411	10.5	20.0	44.4	13.1	70.7
Shanxi	298	3.4	4.0	15.7	0.9	24.0
Inner Mongolia	754	0.2	33.1	75.2	3.9	378.9
Liaoning	428		6.2	55.1	84.3	24.5
Jilin	900		10.5	54.4	5.6	17.4
Heilongjiang	906		5.6	35.5	9.0	133.0
Shanghai	59	0.1	2.0	8.4	17.4	12.0
Jiangsu	413	4.6	19.1	25.5	53.9	7.9
Zhejiang	145	0.5	6.6	22.8	82.7	4.7
Anhui	475	6.1	32.6	38.1	27.2	3.0
Fujian	178		6.5	35.1	149.0	4.6
Jiangxi	437	2.9	19.0	45.0	41.5	2.6
Shandong	444	10.7	35.2	43.1	76.4	23.5
Henan	559	8.0	51.6	47.6	4.9	23.0
Hubei	384	9.8	44.7	45.4	52.3	2.7
Hunan	424	3.8	17.3	58.8	26.8	1.2
Guangdong	137		8.3	25.7	70.9	1.3
Guangxi	294		7.1	46.5	51.9	1.5
Hainan	211		8.1	42.3	157.4	0.2
Chongqing	387		10.9	48.4	6.6	3.1
Sichuan	372	0.2	25.1	56.6	11.2	8.0
Guizhou	293		18.5	36.7	2.0	1.1
Yunnan	325		4.9	53.0	5.3	9.4
Tibet	332		18.5	83.5	0.2	81.4
Shaanxi	285	2.4	10.5	22.6	1.3	39.8
Gansu	316	5.0	16.2	27.1	0.4	13.3
Qinghai	193		50.9	56.0	0.3	45.4
Ningxia	533		12.8	33.8	11.6	127.6
Xinjiang	418	145.4	13.0	52.9	4.2	94.7

Source: China Statistical Yearbook, China Statistical Information Network.

ECONOMY

China's gross domestic product (GDP), and the gross regional products (GRP) of its various regions, have skyrocketed since the 1970s, a pattern that can be traced to the nation's rapid expansion of industrial production and its groundbreaking shift to a market economy. Readers can observe this steady upward trend in the following tables and charts. The GDP table and chart focus on the years extending from 1978 (the first year of China's Four Modernizations program) to 2007, while the GRP table and chart break down the 2007 data by region.

Gross Domestic Product (GDP) and GDP per Capita, 1978–2007

TABLE G. Gross Domestic Product (GDP) and GDP per Capita, 1978–2007
Units:100 million yuan, 2008 prices

Year	Gross Domestic Product (GDP)	GDP per Capita
1978	3,645.2	381
1979	4,062.6	419
1980	4,545.6	463
1981	4,891.6	492
1982	5,323.4	528
1983	5,962.7	583
1984	7,208.1	695
1985	9,016.0	858
1986	10,275.2	963
1987	12,058.6	1,112
1988	15,042.8	1,366
1989	16,992.3	1,519
1990	18,667.8	1,644
1991	21,781.5	1,893
1992	26,923.5	2,311
1993	35,333.9	2,998
1994	48,197.9	4,044
1995	60,793.7	5,046
1996	71,176.6	5,846
1997	78,973.0	6,420
1998	84,402.3	6,796
1999	89,677.1	7,159
2000	99,214.6	7,858
2001	109,655.2	8,622
2002	120,332.7	9,398
2003	135,822.8	10,542
2004	159,878.3	12,336
2005	183,217.4	14,053
2006	211,923.5	16,165
2007	249,529.9	18,934

Source: China Statistical Yearbook, China Statistical Information Network.

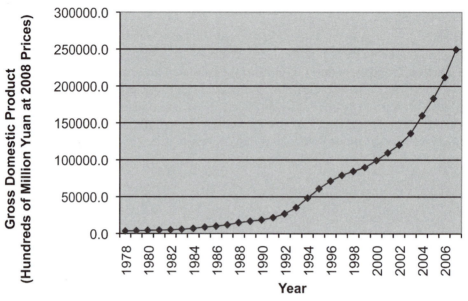

CHART G. *Gross Domestic Product (GDP), People's Republic of China, 1978–2007*

Gross Regional Product (GRP) and GRP per Capita, 2007

TABLE H. Gross Regional Product (GRP) and GRP per Capita, 2007
Units:100 million yuan, 2008 prices

Region	Gross Regional Product (GRP)	GRP per Capita
Beijing	9,353	58,204
Tianjin	5,050	46,122
Hebei	13,710	19,877
Shanxi	5,733	16,945
Inner Mongolia	6,091	25,393
Liaoning	11,023	25,729
Jilin	5,285	19,383
Heilongjiang	7,065	18,478
Shanghai	12,189	66,367
Jiangsu	25,741	33,928
Zhejiang	18,780	37,411
Anhui	7,364	12,045
Fujian	9,249	25,908
Jiangxi	5,500	12,633
Shandong	25,966	27,807
Henan	15,012	16,012
Hubei	9,231	16,206
Hunan	9,200	14,492
Guangdong	31,084	33,151

(continued)

TABLE H. Gross Regional Product (GRP) and GRP per Capita, 2007 *(continued)*

Region	Gross Regional Product (GRP)	GRP per Capita
Guangxi	5,956	12,555
Hainan	1,223	14,555
Chongqing	4,123	14,660
Sichuan	10,505	12,893
Guizhou	2,742	6,915
Yunnan	4,741	10,540
Tibet	342	12,109
Shaanxi	5,466	14,607
Gansu	2,702	10,346
Qinghai	784	14,257
Ningxia	889	14,649
Xinjiang	3,523	16,999

Source: China Statistical Yearbook, China Statistical Information Network.

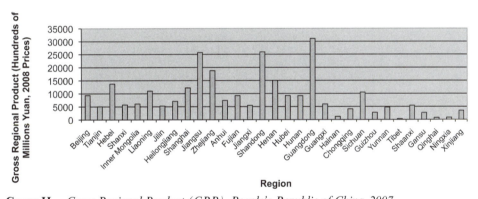

CHART H. *Gross Regional Product (GRP), People's Republic of China, 2007*

Economically Active Population, 1990–2007

As China has grown into one of the world's economic powerhouses, its people—mainly those who live in cities—have reaped some of the benefits. Many Chinese urban dwellers have formed a new middle class, which earns a living wage that provides some disposable income—and the leisure time to spend it. The upward trend of China's economically active population from 1990 to 2007 is illustrated in the following table and graph.

TABLE I. Economically active population, 1990–2007
Units:tens of thousands

Year	Number
1990	64,749
1991	65,491
1992	66,152
1993	66,808
1994	67,455
1995	68,065
1996	68,950
1997	69,820
1998	70,637
1999	71,394
2000	72,085
2001	73,025
2002	73,740
2003	74,432
2004	75,200
2005	75,825
2006	76,400
2007	76,990

Source: China Statistical Yearbook, China Statistical Information Network.

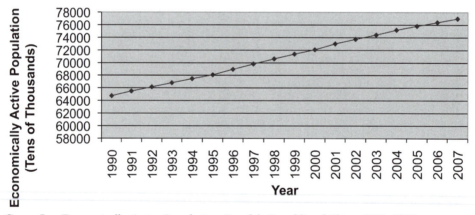

CHART I. *Economically Active Population, People's Republic of China, 1990–2007*

Employment by Enterprise Type, 1990–2007

Between 1990 and 2007, employment opportunities for Chinese workers expanded significantly. As China distances itself from the collective farms and factories of the past, employment opportunities now include non-state options like privately owned Chinese firms, foreign companies, self-employment, or casino-resorts in Macao. The following table and series of pie charts provide a clear breakdown of these new enterprises and how workers have shifted to them over the years.

TABLE J. Employment by Enterprise Type, 1978–2007
Units: Tens of thousands

Year	Government Enterprises[1]	Collectives and Cooperatives	Joint-Owned Companies	Private Enterprises[2]	Hong Kong, Macao, Taiwan Enterprises	Foreign-Owned Companies	Self-Employed
1990	19,611	3,549	96	170	4	62	2105
1995	24,123	3,147	53	1273	272	241	4,614
2000	20,922	1,654	42	3,550	310	332	5,070
2005	20,760	998	45	8,273	557	688	4,901
2007	21,514	888	43	10,116	680	903	5,497

1. Includes state-owned, rural township, and village enterprises.

2. Includes limited liability corporations, publicly traded corporations, and privately owned companies.

Source: China Statistical Yearbook, China Statistical Information Network.

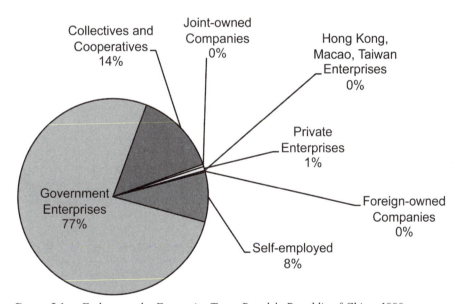

CHART J.1. *Emloyment by Enterprise Type, People's Republic of China, 1990*

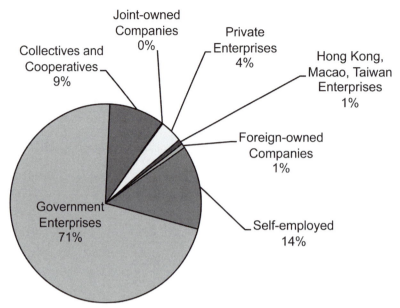

CHART J.2. *Emloyment by Enterprise Type, People's Republic of China, 1995*

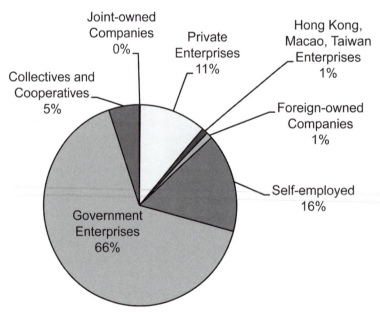

CHART J.3. *Emloyment by Enterprise Type, People's Republic of China, 2000*

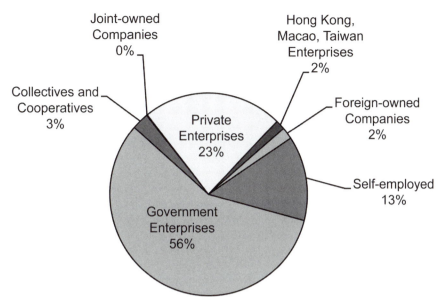

CHART J.4.   *Emloyment by Enterprise Type, People's Republic of China, 2005*

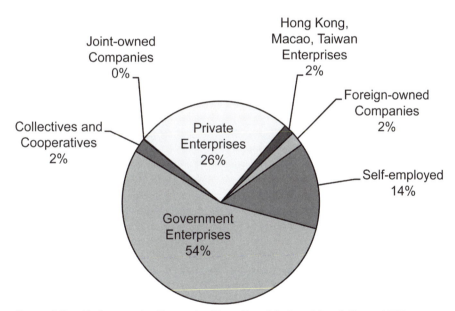

CHART J.5.   *Emloyment by Enterprise Type, People's Republic of China, 2007*

Employment by Sector, 1978–2002

Since China's Four Modernizations program was launched in 1978, the country's economic priorities have changed. This change is reflected by China's expanded economy, which today employs a huge workforce. The following table allows readers to follow the numbers for each sector between 1978 and 2002, with some sectors remaining fairly stable through this period, and others, such as construction, exhibiting huge increases in workers.

TABLE K. Employment by Sector, 1978–2002
Units: Tens of thousands

Year	Total	Agriculture, Forestry, Animal Husbandry, and Fishing	Mining and Quarrying	Manufacturing	Electricity, Gas, and Water	Construction	Geological Prospecting and Water Conservancy	Transport, Storage, Postal, and Telecommuni- Cation Services
1978	40,152	28,318	652	5,332	107	854	178	750
1980	42,361	29,122	697	5,899	118	993	188	805
1985	49,873	31,130	795	7,412	142	2,035	197	1,279
1990	64,749	34,117	882	8,624	192	2,424	197	1,566
1991	65,491	34,956	905	8,839	203	2,482	199	1,617
1992	66,152	34,795	898	9,106	215	2,660	202	1,674
1993	66,808	33,966	932	9,295	240	3,050	144	1,688
1994	67,455	33,386	915	9,613	246	3,188	139	1,864
1995	68,065	33,018	932	9,803	258	3,322	135	1,942
1996	68,950	32,910	902	9,763	273	3,408	129	2,013
1997	69,820	33,095	868	9,612	283	3,449	129	2,062
1998	70,637	33,232	721	8,319	283	3,327	116	2,000
1999	71,394	33,493	667	8,109	285	3,412	111	2,022
2000	72,085	33,355	597	8,043	284	3,552	110	2,029
2001	73,025	32,974	561	8,083	288	3,669	105	2,037
2002	73,740	32,487	558	8,307	290	3,893	98	2,084

Year	Wholesale and Retail Trade and Catering	Finance and Insurance	Real Estate	Social Services	Health Care, Sports, and Social Welfare Services	Education, Culture, Arts, Radio, Film, and Television	Scientific Research and Polytechnic Services	Government and Party Agencies and Social Organizations	Other
1978	1,140	76	31	179	363	1,093	92	467	521
1980	1,363	99	37	276	389	1,147	113	527	588
1985	2,306	138	36	401	467	1,273	144	799	1,319
1990	2,839	218	44	594	536	1,457	173	1,079	1,798
1991	2,998	234	48	604	553	1,497	179	1,136	1,910
1992	3,209	248	54	643	565	1,520	183	1,148	2,313
1993	3,459	270	66	543	416	1,210	173	1,030	3,740
1994	3,921	264	74	626	434	1,436	178	1,033	4,155
1995	4,292	276	80	703	444	1,476	182	1,042	4,484
1996	4,511	292	84	747	458	1,513	183	1,093	4,563
1997	4,795	308	87	810	471	1,557	186	1,093	4,862
1998	4,645	314	94	868	478	1,573	178	1,097	5,118
1999	4,751	328	96	923	482	1,568	173	1,102	4,969
2000	4,686	327	100	921	488	1,565	174	1,104	5,643
2001	4,737	336	107	976	493	1,568	165	1,101	5,852
2002	4,969	340	118	1094	493	1,565	163	1,075	6,245

Source: China Statistical Yearbook, China Statistical Information Network.

Average Wage by Enterprise Type, 1978–2007

Before the 1976 death of Mao Zedong, the founder of communist China, all of the nation's enterprises were state-owned and operated; private and foreign enterprises were banned. It was not until Mao's successor, Deng Xiaoping, launched the Four Modernizations program to improve China's industry, technology, agriculture, and military in 1978 that the country entered the modern economic world. The following table and graphs depict that sea change in China's economy by illustrating the extent to which Chinese wages have increased over recent decades.

TABLE L. Average Wage by Enterprise Type, 1978–2007
Units: Yuan

Year	Overall Average	State-Owned Enterprises	Urban Collective Enterprises	Private, Foreign, and Other Enterprises
1978	615	644	506	
1980	762	803	623	
1985	1,148	1,213	967	1,436
1990	2,140	2,284	1,681	2,987
1991	2,340	2,477	1,866	3,468
1992	2,711	2,878	2,109	3,966
1993	3,371	3,532	2,592	4,966
1994	4,538	4,797	3,245	6,303
1995	5,500	5,625	3,931	7,463
1996	6,210	6,280	4,302	8,261
1997	6,470	6,747	4,512	8,789
1998	7,479	7,668	5,331	8,972
1999	8,346	8,543	5,774	9,829
2000	9,371	9,552	6,262	10,984
2001	10,870	11,178	6,867	12,140
2002	12,422	12,869	7,667	13,212
2003	14,040	14,577	8,678	14,574
2004	16,024	16,729	9,814	16,259
2005	18,364	19,313	11,283	18,244
2006	21,001	22,112	13,014	20,755
2007	24,932	26,620	15,595	24,058

Source: China Statistical Yearbook, China Statistical Information Network.

Average Wage by Enterprise Type, 1990–2007

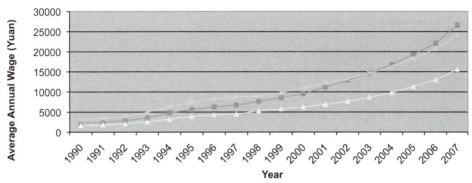

CHART L.   *Average Wage by Enterprise Type, People's Republic of China, 1990–2007*

Foreign Investment

During the early years of China's communist government, foreign capitalist investment was prohibited, as such ventures were in direct opposition to Mao Zedong's revolutionary policies. However, that changed with Deng Xiaoping's rise to power in 1977; he grafted a market economy onto the communist nation in an attempt to modernize China. Today, foreign investment is widespread in China, as shown in the following table and bar graph focusing on the year 2007.

Foreign Investment by Sector, 2007

TABLE M.   Foreign Investment by Sector, 2007
Units: 100 million yuan

Sector	Foreign Investment
National total	4,549.0
Agriculture, forestry, animal husbandry, and fishing	25.3
Mining	103.0
Manufacturing	3,098.1
Foods	140.3
Beverages	45.8
Tobacco	0.5
Textiles, apparel, footwear, and hats	212.2
Leather, fur, feather, and related products	50.8
Wood and straw products	18.3
Furniture	30.2

(continued)

TABLE M. Foreign Investment by Sector, 2007 *(continued)*

Sector	Foreign Investment
Paper and paper products	125.0
Printing and reproduction of recording media	16.1
Articles for cultural, educational, and sport activities	37.9
Petroleum, coal, and nuclear fuel	22.6
Chemicals	266.6
Medicine	39.0
Chemical fibers	37.0
Rubber	55.3
Plastics	68.2
Non-Metallic mineral products	134.1
Ferrous metals	57.8
Non-Ferrous metals	69.7
Metal products	120.6
General purpose machinery	126.4
Special purpose machinery	116.3
Transport equipment	179.5
Electrical machinery and equipment	159.4
Communication equipment, computers, and other electronic equipment	888.7
Measuring instruments and machinery for cultural activity and office work	31.7
Artwork and other manufacturing	45.1
Recycling and disposal of waste	3.0
Electricity, gas, and water production and supply	128.3
Construction	6.0
Transport, storage, and postal services	213.7
Information transmission, computer services, and software	19.7
Wholesale and retail trades	54.6
Hotels and catering services	63.6
Financial intermediation	0.3
Real estate	672.2
Leasing and business services	21.2
Scientific research, technical service, and geologic prospecting	8.8
Management of water conservancy, environment, and public facilities	87.1
Services to households and other services	1.2
Education	12.5
Health and social welfare	4.6
Culture, sports, and entertainment	21.5
Public management and social organization	7.3

Source: China Statistical Yearbook, China Statistical Information Network.

Breakdown of Foreign Investment in Manufacturing, 2007

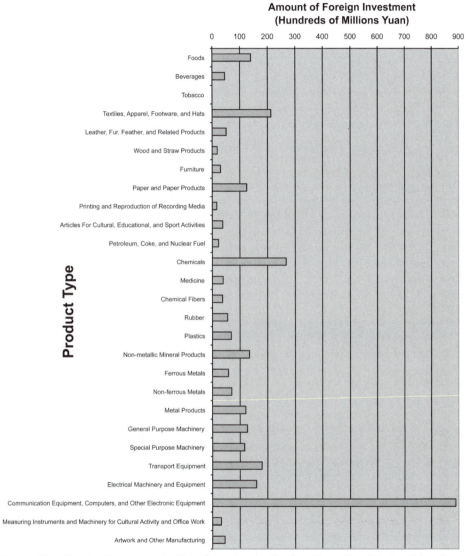

CHART M. *Foreign Investment in Manufacturing, by Product Type, People's Republic of China, 2007*

Energy Production and Consumption

China's increasing need for energy—and its capacity to produce it—has paralleled its explosive industrial growth, which began in the 1980s. By following the nation's energy production and consumption, readers can also follow this unmistakable trend. The first table and chart show the upward growth in both production and consumption between 1980 and 2005, and the second table compares China's energy resource production and consumption with that of the United States in 2007.

Energy Production and Consumption, 1980–2005

TABLE N.   Energy Production and Consumption, 1978–2007
Units:10,000 kilowatts

Year	Total Energy Production	Total Energy Consumption
1980	518,592	490,439
1985	696,062	623,938
1990	845,582	803,116
1995	1,049,910	1,067,339
2000	1,049,454	1,127,360
2005	1,675,151	1,828,169

Source: China Statistical Yearbook, China Statistical Information Network.

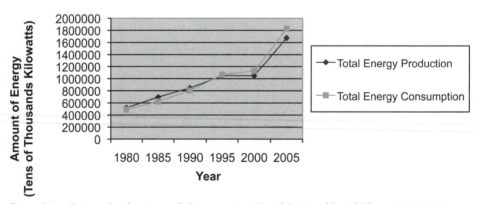

CHART N.   *Energy Production and Consumption, People's Republic of China, 1980–2005*

Energy Resources, Production, and Consumption of China and the United States, 2007

TABLE O. Energy Resources, Production, and Consumption of China and the United States, 2007

	China		United States	
	Total	**Per Capita**	**Total**	**Per Capita**
Coal				
Coal reserves	114,500 million metric tons	88 metric tons	242,721 million metric tons	809 metric tons
Coal production	8,822.2 barrels of oil equivalent	6.8 barrels of oil equivalent	4,017.0 barrels of oil equivalent	13.3 barrels of oil equivalent
Coal consumption	8,971.3 barrels of oil equivalent	6.9 barrels of oil equivalent	3,924.7 barrels of oil equivalent	13.0 barrels of oil equivalent
Natural gas				
Natural gas reserves	1.8 trillion cubic meters	1,384 cubic meters	5.98 trillion cubic meters	19,933 cubic meters
Natural gas production	69.3 billion cubic meters	53.3 cubic meters	545.9 billion cubic meters	1,820 cubic meters
Natural gas consumption	67.3 billion cubic meters	51.8 cubic meters	652.9 billion cubic meters	2,176 cubic meters
Oil				
Oil reserves	2.1 billion metric tons	1.6 metric tons	3.6 billion metric tons	12 metric tons
Oil production	186.7 million metric tons	0.14 metric tons	311.5 million metric tons	1.04 metric tons
Oil consumption	368 million metric tons	0.28 metric tons	943.1 million metric tons	3.14 metric tons
Hydroelectricity				
Hydroelectric potential	1,920 TWh	1476 kWh	701 TWh	2300 kWh
Hydroelectric production	482.9 TWh	371 kWh	250.8 TWh	840 kWh

Source: BP Statistical Review of World Energy June 2008; Hydro Potential Palmer 1992:34.

Urban Construction Projects Over 500,000 Yuan ($71, 291), 1995–2007

As China's industry and economy have expanded over the years, so has the nation's construction sector. Such business-oriented cities as Shanghai are said to be endlessly under construction, and large numbers of factories are being built in many urban areas. Yearly totals of major construction projects from 1995 to 2007 are noted in the following table and displayed on the accompanying graph.

TABLE P.   Urban Construction Projects Over 500,000 Yuan ($71,291), 1995–2007

Year	Construction Projects Started	Construction Projects Completed
1995	103,305	102,115
1996	111,211	108,256
1997	98,003	95,560
1998	116,513	102,572
1999	111,690	109,355
2000	113,225	103,749
2001	118,725	106,021
2002	128,224	104,087
2003	148,042	109,155
2004	152,363	113,145
2005	190,755	148,753
2006	203,963	162,383
2007	231,531	187,525

Source: China Statistical Yearbook, China Statistical Information Network.

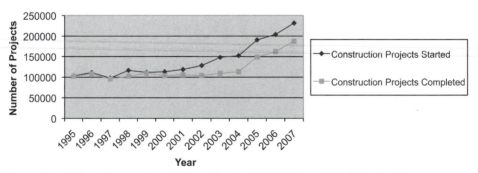

CHART P.   *Urban Construction Projects Costing 500,000 Yuan ($71,291) Or More, People's Republic of China, 1995–2007*

Construction Investment by Region, 2007

The following table and graphs show construction investment for 2007 in particular regions across the country.

TABLE Q. Construction Investment by Region, 2007
Units:100 million yuan

Year	Investment in Construction
Beijing	18,739
Tianjin	8,459
Hebei	14,902
Shanxi	8,401
Inner Mongolia	9,938
Liaoning	19,062
Jilin	6,839
Heilongjiang	5,814
Shanghai	19,581
Jiangsu	30,577
Zhejiang	28,363
Anhui	12,795
Fujian	14,632
Jiangxi	7,917
Shandong	25,037
Henan	15,544
Hubei	13,246
Hunan	11,587
Guangdong	33,738
Guangxi	9,491
Hainan	2,177
Chongqing	12,160
Sichuan	17,530
Guizhou	5,853
Yunnan	10,027
Tibet	622
Shaanxi	8,654
Gansu	4,043
Qinghai	1,557
Ningxia	2,498
Xinjiang	4,085

Source: China Statistical Yearbook, China Statistical Information Network.

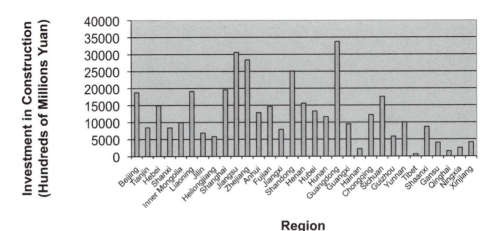

CHART Q. *Investment in Construction by Region, People's Republic of China, 2007*

OTHER

China's Ethnic Groups

Contrary to common belief, China is not made up exclusively of Han Chinese. The government now recognizes more than 50 ethnic minorities, and China is also home to many unrecognized ethnic groups. The following table provides the name, home region, language, and dominant religion of all of China's recognized ethnic groups—separate cultures that form a vast mosaic of humanity in the world's most populous country.

TABLE R. China's Ethnic Groups

Group Name	Population (2000)	Province/ Autonomous Region	Language	Religion
Achang	33,936	Yunnan	Achang	Buddhism
Bai	1,858,063	Yunnan and Guizhou	Bai	Buddhism
Blang	91,882	Yunnan	Blang	Buddhism
Bonan	16,505	Gansu	Bonan	Islam
Bouyei	2,971,460	Guizhou	Bouyei	Polytheism
Dai	1,158,989	Yunnan	Dai	Buddhism
Daur	132,394	Inner Mongolia, Heilongjiang, and Xinjiang	Daur and Han (Mandarin)	Shamanism
De'ang	17,935	Yunnan	De'ang	Buddhism
Dong	2,960,293	Guizhou, Hunan, and Guangxi	Dong	Polytheism

(continued)

Group Name	Population (2000)	Province/ Autonomous Region	Language	Religion
Dongxiang	513,805	Gansu and Xinjiang	Dongxiang and Han (Mandarin)	Islam
Drung	7,426	Yunnan	Drung	Polytheism
Ewenki	30,505	Inner Mongolia and Heilongjiang	Ewenki and Han (Mandarin)	Animism, Tibetan Buddhism, and Eastern Orthodox Christianity
Gaoshan	415,000	Fujian and Taiwan	13 languages; Malay/Poly-nesian family	Polytheism
Gelo	579,357	Guizhou and Guangxi	Gelo	Polytheism
Han	1,200,000,000	Majority in all provinces/regions except for Xinjiang and Tibet	Han (Mandarin)	Buddhism, Confucian-ism, and Daoism
Hani	1,439,673	Yunnan	Hani	Buddhism
Hezhe	4,640	Heilongjiang	Hezhe and Han (Mandarin)	Originally shamanism
Hui	9,816,802	Ningxia, Gansu, Henan, Hebei, Qinghai, Shandong, Yunnan, Xinjiang, Anhui, Liaoning, Heilongjiang, Jilin, Shanxi, Beijing, Tianjin	Han (Mandarin)	Islam
Jing	22,517	Guangxi	Jing	Buddhism and Daoism
Jingpo	132,143	Yunnan	Jingpo	Buddhism
Jino	20,899	Yunnan	Jino	Polytheism
Kazak	1,250,458	Xinjiang, Gansu, and Qinghai	Kazak	Islam
Kirgiz	160,823	Xinjiang and Heilongjiang	Kirgiz	Islam
Korean	1,923,842	Jilin, Liaoning, and Heilongjiang	Korean and Han (Mandarin)	Buddhism
Lahu	453,705	Yunnan	Lahu	Buddhism
Lhoba	2,965	Tibet	Lhoba	Tibetan Buddhism

(continued)

Group Name	Population (2000)	Province/ Autonomous Region	Language	Religion
Li	1,247,814	Hainan	Li	Polytheism
Lisu	634,912	Yunnan and Sichuan	Lisu	Polytheism
Manchu	10,682,263	Most in Liaoning; also in many other regions	Manchu and Han (Mandarin)	Shamanism
Maonan	107,166	Guangxi	Maonan	Taoism and Polytheism
Miao	8,940,116	Guizhou, Hunan, Yunnan, Guangxi, Sichuan, Hainan, and Hubei	Miao	Polytheism
Moinba	8,923	Tibet	Moinba	Tibetan Buddhism
Mongolian	5,813,947	Most in Inner Mongolia; also in many other regions	Mongolian and Han (Mandarin)	Tibetan Buddhism
Mulam	207,352	Guangxi	Mulam	Daoism and Buddhism
Naxi	308,839	Yunnan and Sichuan	Naxi	Doba and Tibetan Buddhism
Nu	28,759	Yunnan	Nu	Polytheism
Oroqen	8,196	Inner Mongolia and Heilongjiang	Oroqen and Han (Mandarin)	Shamanism
Ozbek	12,370	Xinjiang	Ozbek	Islam
Pumi	33,600	Yunnan	Pumi	Tibetan Buddhism and Taoism
Qiang	306,072	Sichuan	Qiang	Animism
Russian	15,609	Xinjiang and Inner Mongolia	Russian	Eastern Orthodox Christianity
Salar	104,503	Qinghai, Gansu, and Xinjiang	Salar	Islam
She	709,592	Fujian, Zhejiang, Jiangxi, and Guangdong	She	Polytheism
Shui	406,902	Guizhou and Guangxi	Shui	Polytheism
Tajik	41,028	Xinjiang	Tajik	Islam
Tatar	4,890	Xinjiang	Tatar	Islam
Tibetan	5,416,021	Tibet, Qinghai, Sichuan, Gansu, and Yunnan	Tibetan	Tibetan Buddhism
Tu	241,198	Gansu and Qinghai	Tu and Han (Mandarin)	Tibetan Buddhism

(continued)

TABLE R. China's Ethnic Groups *(continued)*

Group Name	Population (2000)	Province/ Autonomous Region	Language	Religion
Tujia	8,028,133	Hubei and Hunan	Tujia	Polytheism
Uygur	8,399,393	Xinjiang	Uygur	Islam
Va	396,610	Yunnan	Va	Buddhism
Xibe	188,824	Xinjiang, Jilin, and Liaoning	Xibe	Polytheism, Shaman- ism, and Buddhism
Yao	2,637,421	Guangxi, Hunan, Yunnan, Guangdong, and Guizhou	Yao and Miao	Polytheism
Yi	7,762,286	Sichuan, Yun- nan, Guizhou, and Guangxi	Yi	Polytheism
Yugur	13,719	Gansu	Yugur and Han (Mandarin)	Tibetan Buddhism
Zhuang	16,178,811	Guangxi	Zhuang	Polytheism

Source: "Ethnic Minorities in China." China Government site (china.org.cn).

Breakdown of Students and Graduates, 2007

China's evolution from an almost exclusively agrarian society to an industrial power has been fueled in part by education. Young people who might have worked on a collective farm from morning until night in decades past today attend school begin-ning at an early age. Thus, they are better equipped to understand the economic and technological needs of a modern society. This table provides a breakdown of China's student population from preschool to postgraduate education in 2007.

TABLE S. Breakdown of Students and Graduates, 2007

Level of Education	Students	Graduates
Postgraduate	1,541,115	311,839
Undergraduate and specialized college	27,195,304	7,070,532
Students taking exam leading to diploma	19,677	60,844
Other higher education	6,695	6,882
Secondary education	103,216,047	34,060,580
Primary education	107,898,711	20,994,369
Schools for juvenile delinquents	9,090	3,422
Special education	419,316	50,283
Pre-School education	23,488,300	10,491,152

Source: China Statistical Yearbook, China Statistical Information Network.

Air Pollution

Since the 1980s, countless factories and power plants have been built in China, and many more are under construction. This growth of heavy industry is almost exclusively powered by coal—possibly the dirtiest power source in modern use—and more and more automobiles are discharging higher levels of exhaust fumes into the air. The following table specifies air pollution levels in China's major cities, while its accompanying graphs show the relative levels of particulate matter, sulfur dioxide, and nitrogen dioxide for these cities.

TABLE T.   Air Pollution in Major Chinese Cities, 2007
Units: micrograms per cubic meter ($\mu g/m^3$)

City	Particulate Matter	Sulfur Dioxide	Nitrogen Dioxide
Beijing	148.348	46.622	65.942
Tianjin	94.326	62.003	43.008
Shijiazhuang	127.638	43.186	34.759
Taiyuan	124.490	76.277	26.718
Hohhot	84.258	65.715	47.693
Shenyang	119.351	54.332	35.964
Changchun	99.340	29.556	37.548
Harbin	102.140	47.904	60.019
Shanghai	87.751	55.134	54.260
Nanjing	106.879	58.296	51.392
Hangzhou	107.030	59.803	57.244
Hefei	116.134	23.186	25.814
Fuzhou	65.148	26.866	55.033
Nanchang	83.386	53.742	34.041
Jinan	118.427	55.844	22.696
Zhengzhou	105.186	68.608	45.452
Wuhan	123.255	61.384	54.674
Changsha	104.252	64.764	41.077
Guangzhou	77.085	51.430	65.000
Nanning	64.014	58.942	48.274
Haikou	43.499	8.562	11.942
Chongqing	108.195	65.260	43.975
Chengdu	111.304	62.112	49.164
Guiyang	85.030	55.184	23.386
Kunming	74.773	68.203	41.510
Lhasa	57.025	7.047	25.249
Xi'an	134.992	52.556	42.622
Lanzhou	128.638	59.616	41.647
Xining	115.290	28.047	35.181
Yinchuan	91.863	48.742	24.901
Urumqi	135.816	87.526	66.740

Source: China Statistical Yearbook, China Statistical Information Network.

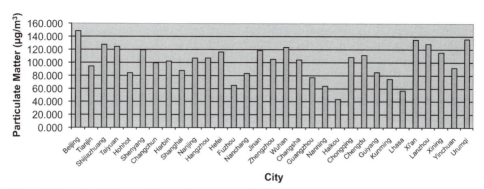

CHART T.1. *Air Pollution (Particulate Matter) of Major Cities, People's Republic of China, 2007*

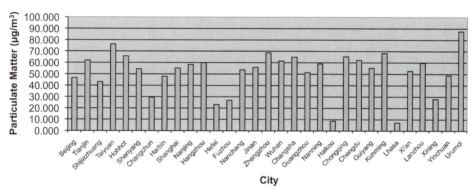

CHART T.2. *Air Pollution (Sulfur Dioxide) of Major Cities, People's Republic of China, 2007*

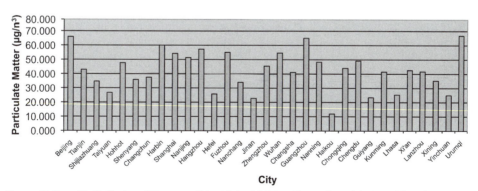

CHART T.3. *Air Pollution (Nitrogen Dioxide) of Major Cities, People's Republic of China, 2007*

Ownership of Passenger Vehicles, 1990–2007

China's economic growth has allowed more citizens than ever to own passenger cars, but the effect of this rise in the number of cars on China's roads is not entirely positive. It is not only coal-fired factories and power plants that have led to China's status as one of the world's most polluted countries, but also the huge increase in passenger vehicles, which spew exhaust into China's already polluted air. The following table and graph follow the steady, dramatic growth of China's total number of passenger cars from 1990 to 2007.

TABLE U. Ownership of Passenger Vehicles, 1990–2007

Year	Number of Passenger Vehicles
1990	240,700
1991	303,600
1992	417,800
1993	598,500
1994	786,200
1995	1,141,500
1996	1,430,400
1997	1,912,700
1998	2,306,500
1999	3,040,900
2000	3,650,900
2001	4,698,539
2002	6,237,600
2003	8,458,739
2004	10,696,913
2005	13,839,250
2006	18,235,657
2007	23,169,084

Source: China Statistical Yearbook, China Statistical Information Network.

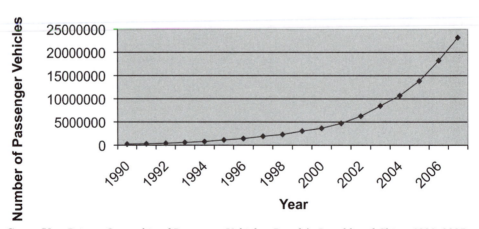

CHART U. *Private Ownership of Passenger Vehicles, People's Republic of China, 1990–2007*

Total Rural and Urban Household Expenditures, 2004–2007

China's longstanding gap between urban and rural income has never been wider than it is today. Modern Chinese cities offer employment and business opportunities unheard of during earlier communist periods, while such opportunities for rural workers have always lagged far behind. This pattern is clearly visible in the following table and pie charts. Though the expenditure breakdowns for rural and urban households are similar, the total income that both types of households have to spend is very different.

TABLE V. Total Rural and Urban Household Expenditures, 2004–2007
Units:100 Million yuan, 2008 Prices

Item	2004	2005	2006	2007
Rural household	17,550.6	19,228.2	21,106.7	23,913.7
Food	7,871.3	8,119.5	8,572.0	9,766.8
Clothing	916.6	1,038.0	1,183.6	1,360.3
Residence	2,839.6	3,363.8	3,834.9	4,368.1
Household facilities, articles, and services	680.6	778.6	891.4	1,048.6
Healthcare and personal articles	1,010.3	1,195.1	1,379.9	1,536.5
Transportation and communications	1,469.3	1,711.6	2,033.9	2,309.2
Recreation, education, and culture articles	1,888.9	2,064.4	2,149.2	2,149.3
Financial service	319.2	368.5	437.4	607.5
Insurance service	114.8	135.0	156.8	224.0
Others	440.0	453.7	467.6	543.4
Urban household	46,282.9	51,989.3	59,370.2	69,403.5
Food	15,265.8	16,615.9	18,277.2	21,287.1
Clothing	3,741.9	4,400.4	5,092.9	5,962.8
Residence	6,749.4	7,765.3	9,101.3	10,432.8
Household facilities, articles, and services	2,247.9	2,471.4	2,834.9	3,453.2
Healthcare and personal articles	4,139.9	4,788.2	5,300.7	6,172.1
Transportation and communications	4,586.0	5,456.1	6,470.4	7,754.4
Recreation, education, and culture articles	5,650.4	6,058.4	6,850.9	7,674.8
Financial service	1,530.7	1,744.1	2,016.3	2,563.8
Insurance service	1,041.1	1,214.7	1,493.5	1,921.9
Others	1,329.8	1,474.8	1,932.1	2,180.6

Source: China Statistical Yearbook, China Statistical Information Network.

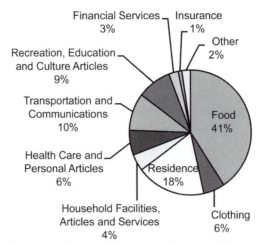

CHART V.1. *Expenditure Breakdown, Average Rural Household, People's Republic of China, 2007*

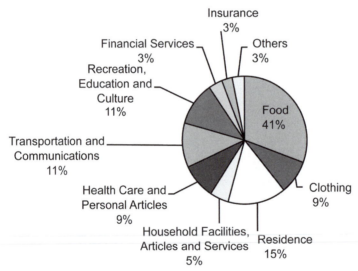

CHART V.2. *Expenditure Breakdown, Average Urban Household, People's Republic of China, 2007*

Internet Users, 1996–2008

The rise of the Internet during the 1990s left no part of the planet untouched, China included. Though the government has attempted to repress its citizens' free access to the Web, the number of Internet users among China's 1.3 billion people has climbed steeply and steadily through the years. The following table and chart track that increase for the years 1996–2008.

TABLE W. Internet Users, 1996–2008

Year	Number of Internet users
1996	620,000
1997	1,175,000
1998	2,100,000
1999	8,900,000
2000	22,500,000
2001	33,700,000
2002	59,100,000
2003	79,500,000
2004	94,000,000
2005	111,000,000
2006	137,000,000
2007	210,000,000
2008	298,000,000

Source: CNNIC (China Internet Network Information Center).

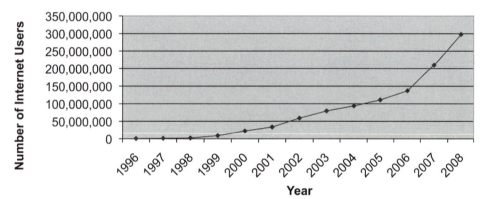

CHART W. *Internet Users, People's Republic of China, 1996–2008*

Number of Books, Magazines, and Newspapers Published in China, 1978–2007

China was once a mostly illiterate country whose subsistence farmers had little access to information from outside their immediate area. That has changed through the years, and today only about 9 percent of Chinese citizens are illiterate. This rise in literacy and education is paralleled by the growth in reading materials now available to the Chinese public. Though many Chinese publications are strictly censored by the government, the increase in the number of books, magazines, and newspapers available to Chinese readers may be viewed as a positive trend. The following table tracks the increase in such publications from 1978 to 2007.

TABLE X. Number of Books, Magazines, and Newspapers Published in China, 1978–2007

Year	Books	Magazines	Newspapers
1978	14,987	930	186
1980	21,621	2,191	188
1985	45,603	4,705	1,445
1990	80,224	5,751	1,444
1995	101,381	7,583	2,089
1996	112,813	7,916	2,163
1997	120,106	7,918	2,149
1998	130,613	7,999	2,053
1999	141,831	8,187	2,038
2000	143,376	8,725	2,007
2001	154,526	8,889	2,111
2002	170,962	9,029	2,137
2003	190,391	9,074	2,119
2004	208,294	9,490	1,922
2005	222,473	9,468	1,931
2006	233,971	9,468	1,938
2007	248,283	9,468	1,938

Source: China Statistical Yearbook, China Statistical Information Network.

Chinese Festivals
and National Holidays

Robert André LaFleur

China's modern festivals are closely tied to the agricultural rhythms of social life that date back at least as far as the Zhou [c. 1050–221 B.C.E.] period. The spring planting and autumn harvest dominate agricultural life, and the festivals connected to these vital periods remain the most significant in the Chinese calendar. The year begins with the Spring Festival (popularly referred to in the West as Chinese New Year), and festive gatherings punctuate the spring and summer months, finally reaching their climax in the Chinese harvest celebration known as the mid-Autumn Festival. The observances continue through the autumn and winter months at a somewhat slower pace, finally concluding with preparations for another New Year's celebration.

STRUCTURE OF THE YEAR—LUNAR AND SOLAR

The Chinese agricultural (and festival) year is traditionally divided between six yang months—as cold turns slowly to the warmth of spring and the heat of summer—and six yin months, as summer heat gives way to cooler weather. To this day, Chinese almanacs subdivide these units into 24 seasonal nodes of approximately 15 days each. The year begins with periods named "Beginning of Spring," "Rainwater," and "Waking of Insects." The spring equinox is followed by "Pure Brightness," "Corn Rain," and "Beginning of Summer." The year concludes with "Slight Snow," "Great Snow," "Winter Solstice," "Slight Cold," and "Great Cold." These periods have been celebrated in Chinese music and verse for many centuries, much as the agricultural and meteorological imagination in the West has been inspired by images of April, from Chaucer to T. S. Eliot. Representing more than a way to organize the calendar, the 24 "joints and breaths" lie at the heart of Chinese festival observances.

The lunar and solar calendar rhythms overlap to create a rich combination of Chinese festivals. The 15-day punctuations of the joints and breaths are overlain, as it were, by the 15-day divisions of lunar months—from the new moon to the full moon and back again—each with its own set of observances. Here, too, there are celebrations throughout the month, including the birthdays of major figures such as Laozi (2nd lunar month, 15th day), the Daoist immortal Lu Dongbin (4th month, 14th day), and the Buddha (4th month, 8th day). It is not unusual on such days—especially in Hong Kong and Taiwan—to see tables laid out with elaborate offerings of food, wine, and incense. Temples are often busy on such days, as well, offering a mini-festival atmosphere even on what might be a workday for many.

SOLAR CALENDAR HOLIDAYS

Of the solar holidays, only one can claim a long heritage that stretches back to agricultural origins in early China. The Qingming (Pure & Bright) Festival marks the fifth seasonal node, and was originally a celebration of spring in which communities came together to offer wishes for a successful farming season. The early-20th-century sinologist Marcel Granet has written memorably of these spring festivals, which took place in locations—holy places—that were imbued with the power of earth and departed ancestors. Over the course of centuries, the celebration tended to focus more on the extended family network and dedication to the departed. Today, the holiday is also known as Tomb Sweeping Day, and it is an opportunity for families to come together to tidy the ancestral graves, pay respects, and share meals together.

The solar New Year on January 1st is not nearly as widely observed in China as it is in other parts of the world, but some people in urban centers who do international business have begun to take notice. Other prominent solar calendar holidays in the Chinese-speaking world include Women's Day on March 8th, International Labor Day on May 1st, and Children's Day on June 1st. There are a cluster of holidays (some offering time off from work and school) in the spring and summer commemorating important events in modern Chinese history or significant institutions in Chinese society. Youth Day on May 4th honors students and workers who demonstrated in 1919 against Japan's colonization attempts in Shandong Province. The Chinese Communist Party's birthday is observed with editorials and government pronouncements on July 1st, and Army Day on August 1st has traditionally been a time for fostering ties between the army and the civilian population. Teacher's Day is observed in the People's Republic on September 10th, and celebrated in Taiwan on September 28th, commemorating Confucius's birthday.

China's National Day commemorates the founding on October 1, 1949, when Mao Zedong stood in Tiananmen Square and proclaimed the birth of the People's Republic after a four-year battle with Nationalist forces. The defeated Nationalists retreated to Taiwan, where the Republic of China continues to celebrate the Double Tenth holiday that hearkens back to the end of imperial rule in China and the founding of the Republic in October 1911. Rounding out the solar year, the Winter Solstice

Festival ushers in a transitional period between the end of one year and the beginning of another. In recent years, this period has also seen a growing interest in the Christmas holiday that is celebrated throughout the world.

LUNAR FESTIVALS

The lunar festivals have always been by far the most important in the Chinese tradition. The year begins with the Spring Festival, marking the new moon that falls between mid-January and mid-February. Most years have 12 lunar months, but since the lunar year averages approximately 354 days (a revolution of the moon around the earth takes approximately 29.5 days), an intercalary (or leap) month is inserted into the calendar approximately every 3 years. This accounts for the changing date of the Spring Festival, which often confuses observers outside of China. As Derk Bodde has pointed out, the Spring Festival is a complex and ever-changing outgrowth of practices dating back to folk religion in early China, such as the solar beginning of spring, the winter solstice, and even early exorcisms.

Spring Festival (Chinese New Year)

Throughout China, regardless of region, the festival remains the most important Chinese holiday, and it is difficult to understand life in China without having a sense of the greetings, family gatherings, and activities (both prescribed and proscribed) associated with the days of the festival. Public and commercial life in China—particularly in earlier eras, and extending into the 20th century—shut down for more than 2 weeks of feasting, visiting, and relaxation. In the late 20th and early 21st century, the celebrations have been significantly shortened, but most people still expect that they will have the opportunity to travel home during the festival. Public transportation is usually jammed to capacity, and people make travel plans months in advance.

The New Year celebrations begin with preparations that have traditionally included the settling of accounts from the previous year, the writing of couplets, and the cleaning of the household—activities that would be considered unlucky should they occur early in the New Year. New Year's Eve has always been a time for family observances, and the noise of fireworks has been prominent for many centuries. New Year's Day is a time for greeting family members and wishing them a prosperous year, as well as for giving children red envelopes (*hongbao*) with small amounts of money. The streets are quiet on the first day of the New Year since celebrations tend to focus on family gatherings. Beginning on the second day, people visit friends and more distant kin. They also send greetings to a wide array of friends, relatives, and colleagues.

Lantern Festival

The New Year's celebration ends with the Lantern Festival, which traditionally marked a time for whole families to leave the household to admire exquisitely decorated lanterns and show off their best spring clothing. Chinese literature over the centuries is filled with descriptions of teeming crowds, brimming markets, and public celebrations during the Lantern Festival, which, in earlier times, lasted four or five days. Today, it remains one of the highlights of the Chinese year, and is marked by lion and dragon dances, and the enjoyment of special sweet rice dumplings. The Lantern Festival is especially important in China's rural areas, but the urban celebrations have offered spectacles on a monumental scale for much of the last millennium.

Dragon Boat Festival

Other significant lunar festivals dot the calendar, the most significant of which take place during the fifth, seventh, and ninth moons of the year. The Dragon Boat Festival (the fifth day of the fifth month) commemorates Qu Yuan (c. 340–278 B.C.E.), a minister of the state of Chu who drowned himself in the Miluo River to protest the actions of his ruler. Tradition has it that people flocked to the river to try to save him. Unsuccessful, they threw silk-wrapped dumplings into the river to feed the fish, keeping them away from Qu Yuan's body. Today, the Dragon Boat Festival is marked by the consumption of *zongzi*, a bamboo-wrapped rice dumpling that is very popular in southern China. Dragon boat races are held all over the world, from Shanghai to London. In the Ming and Qing dynasties, in particular (and continuing to the present), the dragon boat races were a source of competition between villages and localities within urban areas, drawing large crowds of sightseers and supporters.

Herdboy and Weaving Maiden

Two months later, many Chinese celebrate the most significant holiday of what is commonly known as Ghost Month. The seventh day of the seventh month marks the reuniting of the herdboy and the weaving maiden, who, in stories dating back to at least the Zhou dynasty, were separated from each other and were only able to reunite once a year. Sometimes called "Chinese Valentine's Day," the traditional holiday has diminished in significance in China today, where the Western Valentine's Day has assumed enormous importance as a marriage date and time for exchange of gifts. The story behind the original festival, however, is familiar to everyone through tales, poems, and plays.

Double Yang Festival

Two months later, the last of the lunar double festivals takes place. Celebrated on the ninth day of the ninth moon, the Double Yang festival is a time to gather with friends and family, recite poetry, and distribute foodstuffs. The number nine is significant in Chinese thought since odd numbers are said to be yang and even numbers yin. Doubling any number gives it added prestige, and double nine is perhaps the most auspicious of all. It has traditionally been thought that the Double Yang Festival was a good time to climb to a high spot and look upon the countryside. Pilgrimages to China's sacred mountains—especially Mount Tai in Shandong province—were especially crowded during this period, and remain so to this day.

Mid-Autumn Festival

Although it actually takes place three weeks before Double Yang, the year that began with the Spring Festival is brought to its agricultural conclusion with the celebration of the mid-Autumn Festival on the 15th day of the 8th month, which marks the harvest moon. It is often said that the moon is completely round at this time, and the festival is a time for families to enjoy the short period between what was, in most parts of China, the end of the summer harvest and the beginning of the autumn harvest. Although the roots of the festival can be found in the agricultural rhythms and marriage alliances of early China, the festival quickly came to be associated with a range of moon legends, the most prominent of which tells the story of Chang E and her husband, the archer Hou Yi. Tasting the elixir of immortality that Hou Yi had gotten from the Queen Mother of the West, Chang E began drifting into the sky. Hou Yi pursued her and, in richly evocative mythological imagery, she became associated with the moon, even as he became one with the sun. Today, families sit together and view the full moon, enjoy a snack known as moon cakes, and tell variations of the Chang E story.

As we have seen, the final months of the year are marked by the October National Days and several minor festivals. As the yin months turn colder, the calendar notes days for the sending off of winter clothes, the Winter Solstice, and the exit of the kitchen god as he (so the story goes) makes his way to heaven to report on the family's conduct over the past year. The circle of the year is such that the winter lull in gatherings will give way, in time, to another New Year's celebration, and another cycle of festivals.

SIGNIFICANT LUNAR CALENDAR FESTIVALS

Spring Festival (Lunar New Year; Chinese New Year)
First Day of the First Lunar Month (mid-January to mid-February)

Lantern Festival
First full moon (15th day) of the first lunar month (February or early March)

Dragon Boat Festival
Fifth Day of the Fifth Lunar Month (usually mid-May to mid-June)

Reuniting of Herdboy and Weaving Maiden
Seventh Day of the Seventh Lunar Month (usually late July to late August)

Mid-Autumn Festival
Full moon (15th day) of the 8th lunar month

Double Yang Festival
Ninth day of the ninth lunar month

SIGNIFICANT SOLAR CALENDAR
HOLIDAYS AND FESTIVALS

1 January	New Year's Day
5 March	Qingming (Pure Brightness) Festival
8 March	Women's Day
1 May	International Labor Day
4 May	Youth Day
1 July	Communist Party Founding Anniversary
1 August	Army Day
10 September	Teacher's Day (28 September in Republic of China/Taiwan)
1 October	National Day (10 October in Republic of China/Taiwan)
21 December	Winter Solstice Festival

China-Related Organizations

BUSINESS AND ECONOMIC RESOURCES

The United States-China Business Council

The U.S.-China Business Council is the principal organization of U.S. companies engaged in trade and investment in the People's Republic of China. Founded in 1973, the council serves more than 250 corporate members through offices in Beijing, Shanghai, and Washington, DC.

Washington

1818 N Street, NW, Suite 200
Washington, DC 20036
Tel: 202-429-0340
Fax: 202-775-2476
Web site: http://www.uschina.org

Beijing

CITIC Building, Suite 10-01
19 Jianguomenwai Dajie
Beijing 100004, China
Tel: 86-10-6592-0727
Fax: 86-10-6512-5854

Shanghai

1701 Beijing West Road, Room 1301
Shanghai 200040, China
Tel: 86-21-6288-3840
Fax: 86-21-6288-3841

World Trade Organization (WTO)

The WTO is the only international organization that deals with the global rules of trade between nations. It encourages free trade throughout the member nations, including—since December 11, 2001—China.

rue de Lausanne 154, CH-1211

Geneva 21, Switzerland
Phone: (41-22) 739-51-11
Fax: (41-22) 731-42-06
Web site: http://www.wto.org
Email: enquiries@wto.org

CULTURAL EXCHANGE
AND EDUCATIONAL RESOURCES

American Field Services-U.S.A (AFS-USA)
Web site: http://usa.afs.org
American Field Services-U.S.A Regional AFS-USA Centers

For more than 50 years, the American Field Services-U.S.A has provided individuals, families, schools, and communities with international and intercultural learning experiences through a global volunteer partnership. With an impressive international exchange program, AFS sponsors more than 10,000 students internationally. Each year, AFS-USA makes it possible for more than 1,700 American students to live, study, and volunteer in 1 of 44 countries, including China.

AFS Central States

2356 University Avenue West, Suite # 424
St. Paul, MN 55114
Phone: (651) 647-6337
Fax: (651) 647-6628

AFS Northeastern States

32 Hampden Street
Springfield, MA 01103-1263
Phone: (413) 733-4242
Fax: (413) 732-3317

AFS Southeastern States

1610 West Street, Suite 202
Annapolis, MD 21401-4054
Phone: (410) 280-3000
Fax: (410) 280-3001

AFS Western States

310 SW 4th Avenue, Suite 630
Portland, OR 97204-2608
Phone: (503) 241-1578
Fax: (503) 241-1653

ASIANetwork

A consortium of over 170 North American colleges, ASIANetwork strives to strengthen the role of Asian Studies within the framework of liberal arts education to help prepare succeeding generations of undergraduates for a world in which Asian societies play prominent roles. The special focus of this organization is the liberal arts college and a large number of member institutions sponsor China-related programs, including study-abroad opportunities for students and faculty at member institutions. The organization hosts an annual conference with China-related sessions and publishes a newsletter.

Teddy O. Amoloza, Executive Director: ASIANetwork

Illinois Wesleyan University
205 Beecher Street
Bloomington, IL 61701
Telephone: 309-556-3405
Fax: 309-556-3719
Email: tamoloza@iwu.edu
Web site: www.asianetwork.org/

Association for Asian Studies (AAS)

AAS, the largest society of its kind, with approximately 7,000 members worldwide, is a scholarly, non-political, non-profit professional association that is open to all persons interested in Asia. Through publications, meetings, and seminars, it seeks to facilitate contact and an exchange of information among scholars to increase their understanding of East, South, and Southeast Asia. It counts scholars, educators, business people, diplomats, journalists, and interested lay persons among its members. AAS disseminates China content through its publications *Education About Asia*, *Journal of Asian Studies*, and *Key Issues in Asian Studies*.

Association for Asian Studies, Inc.

1021 East Huron Street
Ann Arbor, MI 48104 USA
Telephone: (734) 665-2490
Fax: (734) 665-3801
Web site: http://www.aasianst.org/

The Council for International Exchange of Scholars (CIES) is a division of the Institute of International Education (IIE) based in New York City. IIE is a private nonprofit organization that assists the Department of State in administering Fulbright grants for graduate study. College graduates, graduate students, and Ph.D. candidates in Chinese Studies may apply for Fulbright grants.

Council for International Exchange of Scholars

3007 Tilden Street NW, Suite 5L
Washington, DC 20008-3009
Telephone: (202) 686-4000
Fax: (202) 362-3442
Email: cieswebmaster@cies.iie.org
Internet: http://www.cies.org

Asia Society

The Asia Society is a national, nonprofit, nonpartisan educational organization that is dedicated to fostering an understanding of Asia and communication between Americans and the peoples of Asia and the Pacific. The society sponsors art exhibitions, performances, films, lectures, seminars and conferences, publications and assistance for the media, and materials and programs for students and teachers to build awareness of the countries and peoples of Asia.

725 Park Avenue
New York, NY 10021
Telephone: (212) 288-6400
Fax: (212) 517-8315
Web site: www.asiasociety.org

Fulbright Memorial Fund Teacher Program

Institute of International Education
1400 K Street NW, Suite 650
Washington, DC 20005-2403
Phone: 1-888-CHINA-FMF
Fax: (202) 326-7698
Email: fmf@iie.org
Web site: http://www.iie.org/pgms/fmf

The Fulbright Memorial Fund Teacher Program is designed to provide American primary and secondary teachers and administrators with opportunities to participate in fully funded, short-term study programs abroad, including China. Its goal is to increase Americans' understanding of other cultures through its educators, who will help shape the next generation of leaders.

Asia Foundation

Founded in 1954, the Asia Foundation is a nongovernmental organization that works with public and private partners around the world to promote development in the Asia-Pacific region. Among the organization's primary focuses are good governance and economic reform. The Asia Foundation is headquartered in San Francisco and has numerous Asian branch offices, including a Korean office based in Seoul.

The Asia Foundation

465 California Street #9
San Francisco, CA 94104
Telephone: (415) 982-4640
Fax: (415) 392-8863
Email: info@asiafound.org
Internet: http://www.asiafoundation.org

The Asia Foundation—China

Suite 1905, Building No. 1
Henderson Center
18 Jianguomennei Avenue
Beijing 100005
China
Tel: + 86 (10) 6518-3868
Fax: + 86 (10) 6518-3869
Email: beijing@asiafound.org.cn
Jonathan R. Stromseth, Country Representative, China

The Asia Foundation—Hong Kong SAR

c/o Hong Kong-America Center
Room 503, Esther Lee Building
Chung Chi College
Chinese University of Hong Kong
Shatin, N.T. Hong Kong
Tel: + 852 2971-0889
Fax: + 852 2971- 0773
Email: tafhongkong@asiafound.org
Laura Lau, Director, Hong Kong

Pacific Century Institute

8944 Mason Avenue
Chatsworth, CA 91311-6107
Telephone: (818) 227-6620
Fax: (818) 704-4336
Email: pci@pacificcenturyinst.org
Internet: http://www.pacificcenturyinst.org

The Pacific Century Institute (PCI) is dedicated to providing greater communication between the nations of the Pacific Rim. Headquartered in the greater Los Angeles area, PCI has overseas offices in Korea and Japan, and has offered a number of outreach efforts dealing with China since the late 1990s.

GOVERNMENT RESOURCES

Embassy of the People's Republic of China in the United States of America

2300 Connecticut Ave NW
Washington, DC 20008
Phone:(202) 328-2500
Fax:(202) 588-0032
Email: chinaembassy_us@fmprc.gov.cn
Web site: http://www.china-embassy.org

The Chinese Embassy's Web site is a good place to learn the official Chinese government's view on events in China and around the world. It also is helpful when planning a trip to China; see "Visas and Passports" at the Web site. The site also links to the five Chinese consulates in the United States.

Embassy of the People's Republic of China in the United States of America

Visa Office
2201 Wisconsin Avenue NW, Room 110
Washington, DC 20007
Phone: (202) 338-6688
Fax: (202) 588-9760
Email: chnvisa@bellatlantic.net

A visa application for visiting China can be obtained online or by writing to the embassy or to the consulate assigned to process visa requests from your state. You probably should heed the following warning from the Chinese embassy, however: "Please be advised that sending your visa application or document(s) to the incorrect office may result in complication or delay in processing or even denial of application."

All visa requests from the following states are handled by the Chinese embassy in Washington: Delaware, Idaho, Kentucky, Maryland, Montana, Nebraska, North Carolina, North Dakota, South Carolina, South Dakota, Tennessee, Utah, Virginia, West Virginia, and Wyoming. Residents of other states should contact the appropriate consulate office listed below.

Chinese Consulate General in Chicago

100 West Erie Street
Chicago, IL 60610
Phone: (312) 803-0095
Fax: (312) 803-0110
Web site: http://www.chinaconsulatechicago.org
Consular District: Colorado, Illinois, Indiana, Iowa, Kansas, Michigan, Minnesota, Missouri, Wisconsin

Chinese Consulate General in Houston

3417 Montrose Boulevard
Houston, TX 77006
Phone: (713) 524-0780
Fax: (713) 524-7656
Email: info@chinahouston.org
Email for Visa and Passport: visa@chinahouston.org
Web site: http://www.chinahouston.org
Consular District: Arkansas, Alabama, Florida, Georgia, Louisiana, Mississippi, Oklahoma, Texas

Chinese Consulate General in Los Angeles

443 Shatto Place
Los Angeles, CA 90020
Phone: (213) 807-8088
Fax: (213) 265-9809
Web site: http://www.chinaconsulatela.org
Consular District: Arizona, Hawaii, New Mexico, and Southern California

Chinese Consulate General in New York

520 12th Avenue
New York, NY 10036
Phone: (212) 736-9301 (24 hours); (212) 502-0271 (Monday–Friday 2:00–4:30 p.m.)
Fax: (212) 736-9084
Web site: http://www.nyconsulate.prchina.org
Consular District: Connecticut, Maine, Massachusetts, New Hampshire, New Jersey, New York, Ohio, Pennsylvania, Rhode Island, Vermont

Chinese Consulate General in San Francisco

1450 Laguna Street
San Francisco, CA 94115
Phone: (415) 674-2900
Fax: (415) 563-0494
Web site: http://www.chinaconsulatesf.org
Consular District: Alaska, Nevada, Northern California, Washington, Oregon

United States Embassy in China

3 Xiu Shui Bei Jie
Beijing, PRC 100600
Phone: (86-10) 6532-3431 (embassy switchboard)
Web site: http://www.usembassy-china.org.cn

American Consulate General, Chengdu

No. 4 Lingshiguan Road
Chengdu, Sichuan PRC 610041
Phone: (86-28) 558-3992
Fax: (86-28) 558-9221
Web site: http://www.usembassy-china.org.cn

American Consulate General, Guangzhou

1 Shamian Nanjie
Shamian Island, Guangzhou, PRC 510133
Phone: (86-20) 8188-8911
Fax: (86-20) 8186-4001
Web site: http://www.usembassy-china.org.cn

American Consulate General, Hong Kong and Macau

26 Garden Road
Hong Kong
Phone: (852) 2523-9011
Fax: (852) 2845-1598
Web site: http://www.usconsulate.org.hk

American Consulate General, Shanghai

1469 Huaihai Road (M).
Shanghai, PRC 200031
Phone: (86-21) 6433-1681 (direct); (86-21) 6433-6880 (consulate switchboard)
Fax: (86-21) 6433-1576
Web site: http://www.usembassy-china.org.cn

American Consulate General, Shenyang

52 Shi Si Wei Lu, Heping District
Shenyang, PRC 110003
Phone: (86-24) 2322-1198
Fax: (86-24) 2322-2374
Web site: http://www.usembassy-china.org.cn

The United States Embassy in China represents the United States government in China, provides services to Americans traveling and doing business in China, and processes visa applications for Chinese traveling to the United States. In addition to handling passports and birth registrations, the embassy provides information and assistance about notaries and tax and voting information. The United States also maintains five consulates in China: in Chengdu, Guangzhou, Hong Kong, Shanghai, and Shenyang.

NEWS RESOURCES

China Business World includes information on Asian markets, as well as educational and internship opportunities. The tourism link is also very useful. Available at http://www.cbw.com.

China Daily on the Web gives access to the *China Daily*, China's official English-language newspaper. Includes a searchable archive of past issues. Available at http://www.chinadaily.com.

China World Factbook from the CIA provides current economic and political facts about China, along with maps. Available at http://www.odci.gov.

South China Morning Post is Hong Kong's largest English-language newspaper in terms of circulation. Available at http://www.scmp.com.

Virtual China offers financial information, as well as general news and features dealing with contemporary China. Available at http://www.virtualchina.com.

TOURISM RESOURCES

Fodor's Web site: http://www.fodors.com.

Fodor's Web site provides mini-guides for several major cities in China. Each mini-guide gives travel tips, provides an overview of the city and a map, and recommends sights, activities, restaurants, hotels, shopping, nightlife, and more. A resource section includes more maps, Web links, and information on purchasing Fodor's extensive and well-respected guidebooks.

Lonely Planet

150 Linden Street
Oakland, CA 94607
Phone: 1-800-275-8555 or (510) 893-8555
Fax: (510) 893-8563
Email: info@lonelyplanet.com
Web site: http://www.lonelyplanet.com

Lonely Planet's Web site provides a thorough guide to travel in China, including when to visit, how to get there and how to get around, money and costs, events and attractions, and activities (including some off-the-beaten-track ones). Overviews of the history, culture, and environment of the region are available, as is a resource section with Web links, information on purchasing Lonely Planet guidebooks, and access to traveler's postcards with tips and useful current information.

Frommer's Web site: http://www.frommers.com/destinations/china/

Frommer's provides up-to-date information about travel to and from, as well as within, China.

A good resource for travel in China is the Travel China Guide, available at http://www.travelchinaguide.com. There is a very useful link to train schedules on this site at http://www.travelchinaguide.com/china-trains. It should be noted that train tickets cannot generally be purchased online, but the schedules can help a good deal in planning train travel.

LANGUAGE LEARNING RESOURCES

All major U.S. colleges and universities teach Chinese, and resources abound for those who are enrolled in a course of study or have the opportunity to take classes. The United States also has a number of very successful intensive language programs that are open (by application) to the public.

Middlebury College

Sunderland Language Center
356 College Street
Middlebury, VT 05753
802.443.5510
802.443.2075 fax
http://www.middlebury.edu/academics/ls/
http://www.middlebury.edu/academics/ls/chinese/

Monterey Institute of International Studies

Intensive Foreign Language Programs
460 Pierce Street, Monterey, CA 93940
831-647-4115
831-647-3534
silp@miis.com
http://language.miis.edu/ifl/
http://language.miis.edu/ifl/silp_pd_chinese

Beloit College Center for Language Studies

Summer Intensive Language Program
Patricia L. Zody, Ph.D., Director

Center for Language Studies

Beloit College
700 College Street
Beloit, WI 53511
Toll-free: 800.356.0751 (ask for the Center for Language Studies)
Telephone: 608.363.2277
Fax: 608.363.7129
Email: cls@beloit.edu
http://www.summerlanguages.com
http://www.summerlanguages.com/chinese/

SOCIAL AND CULTURAL RESOURCES

UNICEF is devoted to guaranteeing the rights of all children to survival, development, protection, and participation.

Address: 12, Sanlitun Lu, Beijing, 100600

Tel: (86-10) 6532 3131
Fax: (86-10) 6532 3107
Email: beijing@unicef.org
Website: www.unicef.org/china

Families with Children from China (FCC), the main organization for families with adopted children from China, can be found at http://www.fwcc.org, where one can access links to state and local FCC chapters, as well as other useful links.

Annotated Bibliography

The books and, where applicable, CD-ROMs, periodicals, and Web sites below are organized based on the chapters in this book, as well as the section on language, food, and etiquette. Every effort has been made to include accurate and readable sources that should assist readers who want to know more about China. The resources included in this section are, for the most part, general works on China. The contributors to this volume are happy to say that we have tested the vast majority of these books in our own classrooms, and have a good sense from our students that they are effective. For more specialized titles, please check either the References section at the end of each chapter or the bibliographies in the works listed here. Readers are encouraged to check the Beloit College Asian Studies Web site (see below) for recommendation updates, as well as those from our colleagues in other departments.

GENERAL WORKS

Of all of the subjects of this book, the award-winning interactive CD-ROM *Contemporary Chinese Societies* (2007), produced by the University of Pittsburgh's Asian Studies Program with grants from the Chiang Ching-kuo Foundation and the Henry Luce Foundation, is indispensable. It includes maps, charts, graphs, and a great deal of basic information on Chinese history, society, culture, economics, language, and politics.

Beloit College Asian Studies Web Site, www.beloit.edu/~asianstudies.

The contributors to this volume and our colleagues in areas of Asian Studies that could not be covered in the structure of the present volume have created an expansion and series of updates to the list below. The site also contains illustrations, translations, expanded references, and informative charts.

Ellington, Lucien, ed. *Education about Asia.* Ann Arbor: Association for Asian Studies, 2003.

This 80-page illustrated magazine, published three times a year, includes articles on China that are relevant for both teachers and general readers.

Spence, Jonathan D. *The Search for Modern China.* New York: W. W. Norton, 1990.

This is an excellent, lively history of China since 1600, written by a top historian. Although the book is long, it is a wonderful introduction to China's social, political, and economic development over the past 400 years.

GEOGRAPHY AND HISTORY

Ebrey, Patricia. *The Cambridge Illustrated History of China.* Cambridge: Cambridge University Press, 1999.

A well-written and beautifully illustrated history of China that balances political history nicely with social, cultural, intellectual, literary, and artistic approaches.

Ebrey, Patricia. *Chinese Civilization: A Sourcebook.* New York: Free Press, 1993.

This is the book that our students rarely sell back after our courses are over. In 100 nicely chosen and well-translated texts, Ebrey gives a wonderful overview of Chinese civilization that has the kind of depth that beginning or even experienced readers will find satisfying. Ebrey has also now produced a Web-based version entitled *A Visual Sourcebook of Chinese Civilization* (http://www.depts.washington.edu/chinaciv/) under a grant from the NEH, the Freeman Foundation, and the Chiang Ching-kuo Foundation of Taiwan.

Hansen, Valerie. *The Open Empire: A History of China to 1600.* New York: W. W. Norton, 2000.

This is the best general book on Chinese history before the modern period. Some previous background study is helpful before reading this work because Hansen has provided a tremendous sense of historical sources, ranging from archaeology to literature. It is the rare overview that includes as profound a sense of both primary and secondary sources of Chinese history.

Shaughnessy, Edward, ed. *China: Empire and Civilization.* New York: Oxford University Press, 2000.

This edited volume is a useful introduction to Chinese history and culture. Nicely illustrated, the book provides well-written, two-page layouts dealing with more than 100 key themes. No other book we know of introduces as many important cultural themes.

Smith, Richard J. *China's Cultural Heritage: The Qing Dynasty, 1644–1912.* 2d ed. Boulder, CO: Westview Press, 1994.

This book goes far beyond its subtitle in terms of its range. It should not be the first book in this list that you read, but it is a fine companion for Valerie Hansen's history of China to 1600. Richard Smith provides one of the best portrayals of a total world of Chinese history, politics, society, and thought that we have seen, and in a text that is accessible to most readers.

Wills, John. *Mountain of Fame: Portraits in Chinese History.* Princeton, NJ: Princeton University Press, 1992.

This book might have been a mere collection of takes on Chinese history and its major figures were it not for an author as skilled as Wills, who gives a historical narrative at the same time that he is creating a picture of individual lives. It is both accessible to generalists and appreciated by specialists, who enjoy the subtle, but not intimidating, depth.

GOVERNMENT AND POLITICS

Dreyer, June Teufel. *China's Political System: Modernization and Tradition.* New York: Addison Wesley Longman, 2000.

The best short introductory text on Chinese politics and foreign policy.

Ogden, Suzanne. *Global Studies: China.* 9th ed. Guilford, CT: McGraw-Hill/Dushkin, 2001.

The first half of this book contains a nice overview of recent Chinese history and its political system; the second half presents a good selection of longer recent magazine articles on all aspects of Chinese culture and society. A new edition is published every two years or so.

White, Tyrene, ed. *China Briefing 2000: The Continuing Transformation.* New York: M. E. Sharpe, 2001.

Published in cooperation with the Asia Society and updated every few years, this edited volume includes articles by leading experts on China's history, politics, economics, foreign policy, and related subjects.

In addition, those with an interest in current affairs related to China should consult the excellent Asia section of the weekly British news magazine *The Economist*, plus the Asia-based *Far Eastern Economic Review,* as well as the *Asian Wall Street Journal Weekly* and the web-based news journal *China News Digest* (at www.cnd.org). In addition, the magazine *Current History* has an annual issue devoted to China, usually published in September.

THE ECONOMY

Bergsten, C. Fred, Charles Freeman, Nicholas R. Lardy, and Derek J. Mitchell. *China's Rise: Challenges and Opportunities.* Washington, DC: Peterson Institute for International Economics and Center for Strategic and International Studies, 2008.

This book is one of the products of The China Balance Sheet Project, a multidisciplinary analysis of the "dynamics underpinning China's domestic transformation and emergence as an international power," with a particular focus on the U.S.–China relationship.

Eastman, Lloyd E. *Family, Fields, and Ancestors: Constancy and Change in China's Social and Economic History, 1550–1949.* Oxford: Oxford University Press, 1988.

This book's subtitle precisely describes the contents of the book. Eastman's account is an excellent, readable classic that is accessible to a general audience.

Huang, Yasheng. *Capitalism with Chinese Characteristics: Entrepreneurship and the State.* Cambridge: Cambridge University Press, 2008.

Huang's thesis is that Chinese reform policies facilitated rural entrepreneurship in the 1980s, but Chinese economic development since the 1990s has favored state-controlled urban China over private rural entrepreneurs.

Lardy, Nicholas R. *Agriculture in China's Modern Economic Development*. Cambridge: Cambridge University Press, 1983.

To gain a deeper understanding of the Chinese economy, one cannot go wrong by reading anything written by Nicholas Lardy. This volume is an excellent study of agriculture in the People's Republic of China during the Mao years and in the first years of economic reform.

Lin, Justin Yifu, Fang Cai, and Zhou Li. *The China Miracle Development Strategy and Economic Reform*. Hong Kong: The Chinese University Press, 2003.

Written by three Chinese economists, this volume is an excellent discussion of why China's economic reforms have been so successful. Lin is now the chief economist for the World Bank.

McGregor, James. *One Billion Customers: Lessons from the Front Lines of Doing Business in China*. New York: Free Press, 2005.

McGregor has more than twenty years experience in China as *The Wall Street Journal's* China bureau chief (1987–1993), as chief executive of Dow Jones & Co. in China (1993–2000), and then as head of a China venture capital firm and as a consultant. His book, as readable as his credentials are impressive, takes the reader inside the complexities of China's business world.

Naughton, Barry. *Growing out of the Plan: Chinese Economic Reform, 1978–1993*. Cambridge: Cambridge University Press, 1996.

This is the single best discussion of economic reforms in China between 1978 and 1993.

Naughton, Barry. *The Chinese Economy: Transitions and Growth*. Cambridge: MIT Press, 2007.

For a thorough, authoritative discussion of the modern Chinese economy, this is the book with which to begin.

Rawski, Thomas G. *Economic Growth in Pre-War China*. Berkeley: University of California Press, 1989.

In this innovative look at China's economic history prior to World War II, Rawski argues that China experienced more modern economic growth than had been previously described, and that the growth resulted in a growth in the average output per person.

World Bank. *China Quarterly Review*. Washington, DC.

Available on the World Bank's Web site, this report is an excellent source for up-to-date analysis of the Chinese economy.

Online Journals

Asian Wall Street Journal, http://www.online.wsj.com/asian.

This is a valuable resource for Asian markets as well as changing political and economic news.

China Business Review, www.chinabusinessreview.com.

Published by the U.S. China Business Council, this outstanding journal focuses on U.S. firms doing business in China. Although not intended as a scholarly publication, top scholars contribute articles to it. Other articles are written by a staff of resident expert journalists.

China News Digest, www.cnd.org.

Provides timely and balanced news coverage on China and China-related affairs, as well as information services to Chinese communities around the world.

Far Eastern Economic Review, www.feer.com.

Published weekly in Hong Kong (and owned by Dow Jones & Company), this journal calls itself "Asia's premier business magazine." It contains articles on politics, business, economics, technology, and social and cultural issues throughout Asia, with a particular emphasis on both Southeast Asia and China.

See also the newspapers listed in the "News Resources" heading in the China-Related Organizations section of this volume.

SOCIETY

A book that provides a truly comprehensive overview of Chinese culture and society has not yet been written, a testimony to the complexity of this topic. Listed below are books and films that provide insights into contemporary cultural and social issues from a variety of perspectives—literature, linguistics, ethnography. Depending on the reader's interests, each can serve as the starting point for a more in-depth understanding of present-day Chinese society and culture.

Barme, Geremie, and Linda Jarvin. *New Ghosts, Old Dreams.* New York: Times Books, 1992.

An excellent collection of short stories, poems, and personal essays by contemporary Chinese artists and intellectuals. Compared with much of what is translated and published by the state, the pieces in this book provide keen insights into the frustrations, and freedoms, of Chinese politics and culture at the end of the 20th century.

Croll, Elisabeth. *Changing Identities of Chinese Women.* London: Zed Books, 1995.

Some of the most interesting research on Chinese cultural and social issues in recent years has been research on women. Croll's book helps readers realize the importance of women's issues throughout the political changes of the past century and to understand the impact of political change on women's daily lives.

Davis, Deborah, and Stevan Harrell, eds. *Chinese Families in the Post-Mao Era.* Berkeley: University of California Press, 1993.

A collection of essays that looks at family life in contemporary China. The essays cover household structure, marriage, childbearing, and modern hardships.

DeFrancis, John. *The Chinese Language.* Honolulu: University of Hawaii Press, 1986.

An introduction to Chinese language that is both entertaining and thorough. DeFrancis debunks many of the myths about both spoken and written Chinese, as well as giving readers a solid understanding of how the language works.

Gao, Minglu, ed. *Inside Out: New Chinese Art.* San Francisco: Museum of Modern Art and the Asia Society Galleries, 1998.

This is an exhibition catalog for one of the first major exhibits of contemporary Chinese art in the United States. It includes essays from specialists in Chinese art, as well as full-color plates of the vivid images that are being produced by Chinese artists today.

Yang, Mayfair Mei-hui. *Gifts, Favors, and Banquets: The Art of Social Relationships in China.* Ithaca, NY: Cornell University Press, 1994.

An excellent ethnography that describes the art of social relationships in China. Yang describes the importance of *guanxi*, offering a detailed discussion of how it works and accounts of her experiences over the course of 10 years of research in China.

CULTURE

Bodde, Derk, and M.L.C. Bogan. *Annual Customs and Festivals in Peking with Manchu Customs and Superstitions.* Taipei: SMC Publishing, 1986.

Although this book can make for dense reading, it is one of the two most detailed works that allow readers a nonspecialist's access to the rhythms of daily life in urban China early in the 20th century (with hints about the cultural practices that have persisted for centuries).

Chang, Raymond, and Margaret Scrogin Chang. *Speaking of Chinese.* New York: W. W. Norton, updated edition, 2001.

This is a pleasant book for a general audience who, as stated on the book's back cover, "wants to know more about Chinese [language] without learning to speak or write it." It offers a breezy overview of the basic characteristics of the Chinese language, its history, and Chinese culture.

Eberhard, Wolfram. *A Dictionary of Chinese Symbols.* London: Routledge, 1986.

This book is just plain fun. Eberhard has created a list of important concepts in Chinese art, literature, and popular culture, many of which have persisted into the present. The many layers of meaning will surprise those who aren't used to multiple readings of symbols, but the book is sure to make readers think about symbols in Western societies in new ways.

Feng Menglong. *Stories Old and New: A Ming Dynasty Collection.* Seattle: University of Washington Press, 2000.

We recommend these stories as a balance to the texts that describe festivals and customs in isolation. Although those books are of tremendous value for the reader eager to master details, Feng's stories give rich (and often ironic) perspectives on life in 17th-century China that provide both slight parallels and stark contrasts with contemporary Chinese life.

Go, Ping-gam. *Understanding Chinese Characters by Their Ancestral Forms.* 3d ed. San Francisco: Simplex Publications, 1995.

Equipped with color photographs by the author, this delightful little book takes the reader on a walking tour through San Francisco's Chinatown, observing the Chinese characters on store signs. It explains the formative principles of the characters discovered and their evolution. The book also provides flash cards for learning the characters.

Li, Leyi. *Tracing the Roots of Chinese Characters: 500 Cases.* Beijing: Language and Culture University Press, 1993.

For both intermediate and advanced readers, this informative and carefully structured study traces the evolution and calligraphic styles of Chinese characters. Detailed illustrations by the author complement the intent of the text to posit the original idea of each character. Seven calligraphic styles, which also represent the stages in the evolution of each character—oracle bone inscription, bronze inscription, small seal script, clerical script, regular script, cursive writing, and freehand cursive—historically ground each explanation.

Lindqvist, Cecilia. *China: Empire of Living Symbols.* 1991. Repr. ed. New York: Addison-Wesley, 2008.

This book explains the origins of the characters and explores aspects of Chinese civilization through both art history and archaeology. Numerous photos, illustrations, and sketches enrich a thoughtful and challenging text.

Lowe, H. Y. *The Adventures of Wu: The Life Cycle of a Peking Man.* Princeton, NJ: Princeton University Press, 1983.

This is the other excellent book for learning details of traditional Chinese culture. Readers who are overwhelmed by detail will have a hard time with it, and might be encouraged to read just a few pages at a time. Those who love learning about cultural practices in great detail find this to be one of the most satisfying accounts they have read. The text is organized as the fictional, but culturally realistic, life of a little boy who grows into a young man in China in the early 20th century. It was originally written by a Chinese author in the 1930s for Westerners in Beijing.

Mair, Victor. *The Columbia Anthology of Traditional Chinese Literature.* New York: Columbia University Press, 1994.

Owen, Stephen. *An Anthology of Chinese Literature: Beginnings to 1911.* New York: W. W. Norton, 1996.

These two anthologies are superb collections of traditional Chinese literature—among the world's most diverse, and a foundation for much of modern Chinese literature (even when it was being attacked as reactionary or embraced as forward-looking during the tumultuous events of the 20th century). Mair's work is organized by genre, with all of the major genres represented. We recommend mulling over the poetry, which contains wonderfully effective images, before proceeding to longer pieces. It is also worth reading the jokes at the end of the volume, just to see how different cultural categories of humor can be. Owen's anthology is organized chronologically, which makes it a wonderful companion to historical studies. This anthology makes it easier to see the development of literary ideas during important periods of Chinese history. The translations (like Mair's) are fresh and memorable.

Moore, Oliver. *Chinese.* Berkeley: University of California Press, 2000.

For those interested in the history and the evolution of Chinese writing, this is a brief and easily understood introductory book. Well written, with more than 50 illustrations, it describes the major Chinese scripts, the formation of Chinese characters, and how these shapes developed, as well as the art of Chinese calligraphy.

Ramsey, S. Robert. *The Languages of China.* Princeton, NJ: Princeton University Press, 1989.

A book for linguistic students that concentrates on spoken Chinese. It provides a comprehensive linguistic history of all Chinese dialects, including the languages of the ethnic minorities. Both scholarly and comprehensive, the book benefits from the author's ability to analyze sophisticated structures in comparative terms.

Schneiter, Fred. *Getting Along with the Chinese.* Hong Kong: Asia 2000 Limited, 1998.

Pure fun: a charming book full of wit, humor, and insights about how to understand subtle details of Chinese culture. Accompanied by clever cartoons, the book offers many helpful anecdotes that illustrate both the bridges and the chasms that link and separate East and West.

Sullivan, Michael. *The Arts of China.* Berkeley: University of California Press, 2000.

Sullivan's history of Chinese art is arranged chronologically and is nicely illustrated. Like the literary materials mentioned above, this work is useful even to readers who are most interested in contemporary society. The book nicely balances historical and contemporary art traditions and is a highly readable account.

Yin, Binyong, and John S. Rohsenow. *Modern Chinese Characters.* Beijing: Sinolingua, 1997.

Coauthored by two linguists, this thorough exploration of Chinese characters addresses itself to readers who write Chinese at an introductory or intermediate level and seek a richer grasp of its printed forms. In a readily comprehensible manner, the book covers every aspect of Chinese characters, such as their origin, evolution, shapes, formations, total numbers, pronunciation, and calligraphy styles, as well as dictionary ordering.

Contemporary Issues

The Asian Opium Trade

Brook, Timothy, and Bob Tadashi Wakabayashi, eds. *Opium Regimes: China, Britain, and Japan, 1839-1952.* Berkeley and Los Angeles: University of California Press, 2000.

A collection of scholarly essays on the history of the opium trade in Asia. This source will be very useful to students to put the opium trade into the context of world history. Recommended for advanced students.

Pomeranz, Kenneth, and Steven Topik. *The World That Trade Created: Society, Culture, and the World Economy, 1400 to the Present*, 2nd ed.. Sources and Studies in World History Armonk, NY: M. E. Sharpe, 2005.

A lively treatment of many aspects of trade in world history. The most relevant chapter on the opium trade in Asia is Chapter 3, "The Economic Culture of Drugs." Recommended for all students.

China's Environmental Problems

Dai Qing, et al. *Yangtze! Yangtze!* Earthscan Canada, 1994.

This book by noted Chinese journalist and environmental activist Dai Qing presents the comprehensive case against the controversial Three Gorges Dam project. The Chinese government banned the book when it was first published in 1989. Recommended for students who are interested in modern Chinese politics and environmental studies.

Intercountry Adoption from China

Johnson, Kay Ann. *Wanting a Daughter, Needing A Son—Abandonment, Adoption, and Orphanage Care in China.* St. Paul, MN: Yeong & Yeong Book Company, 2004.

An informative collection of essays by China specialist Kay Ann Johnson, linking China's reproduction policies, infant abandonment, and adoption. Recommended for students who are interested in adoption history, gender issues in modern China, and Chinese politics.

The Beijing Olympics

Brownell, Susan. *Beijing's Games: What the Olympics Mean to China.* Lanham, MD: Rowman & Littlefield Publishers, 2008.

A very useful study for anyone wanting to understand why the Beijing Olympics were so important to China. Recommended for all levels.

Xu Guoqi. *Olympic Dreams: China and Sports, 1895–2008.* Cambridge, MA: Harvard University Press, 2008.

A detailed scholarly study of how sports and politics have intertwined in modern Chinese history. This book is especially important for understanding how the Chinese Communist Party viewed both domestic and international sports competitions. Recommended for advanced students.

Thematic Index

S__
E__
L__

Education

__S
__E
__L

S__
E__
L__

_S
_E
_L

S__
E__
L__

__S
__E
__L

S__
E__
L__

S__
E__
L__

__S
__E
__L

Social relationships and etiquette

Index

__S
__E
__L

S__
E__
L__

__S
__E
__L

S
E
L

S__
E__
L__

_S
_E
_L

S__
E__
L__

__S
__E
__L

_S
_E
_L

S__
E__
L__